*The Church and Social Change in Latin America.* Henry A. Landsberger, ed.

*Revolution and Church: The Early History of Christian Democracy, 1789-1901.* Hans Maier.

*The Overall Development of Chile.* Mario Zañartu, S.J., and John J. Kennedy, eds.

*The Catholic Church Today: Western Europe.* M. A. Fitzsimons, ed.

*Contemporary Catholicism in the United States.* Philip Gleason, ed.

*The Major Works of Peter Chaadaev.* Raymond T. McNally.

*A Russian European: Paul Miliukov in Russian Politics.* Thomas Riha.

*A Search for Stability: U.S. Diplomacy Toward Nicaragua, 1925-1933.* William Kamman.

*Freedom and Authority in the West.* George N. Shuster, ed.

*Theory and Practice: History of a Concept from Aristotle to Marx.* Nicholas Lobkowicz.

*Coexistence: Communism and Its Practice in Bologna, 1945-1965.* Robert H. Evans.

*Marx and the Western World.* Nicholas Lobkowicz, ed.

*Argentina's Foreign Policy 1930-1962.* Alberto A. Conil Paz and Gustavo E. Ferrari.

*Italy after Fascism, A Political History, 1943-1965.* Giuseppe Mammarella.

*The Volunteer Army and Allied Intervention in South Russia, 1917-1921.* George A. Brinkley.

*Peru and the United States, 1900-1962.* James C. Carey.

*Empire by Treaty: Britain and the Middle East in the Twentieth Century.* M. A. Fitzsimons.

INTERNATIONAL STUDIES OF THE

COMMITTEE ON INTERNATIONAL RELATIONS

UNIVERSITY OF NOTRE DAME

*The USSR and the UN's Economic and Social Activities.* Harold Karan Jacobson.

*Chile and the United States: 1880-1962.* Fredrick B. Pike.

*East Central Europe and the World: Developments in the Post-Stalin Era.* Stephen D. Kertesz, ed.

*Soviet Policy Toward International Control of Atomic Energy.* Joseph L. Nogee.

*The Russian Revolution and Religion, 1917-1925.* Edited and translated by Bolesław Szcześniak.

*Soviet Policy Toward the Baltic States, 1918-1940.* Albert N. Tarulis.

*Introduction to Modern Politics.* Ferdinand Hermens.

*Freedom and Reform in Latin America.* Fredrick B. Pike, ed.

*What America Stands For.* Stephen D. Kertesz and M. A. Fitzsimons, eds.

*Theoretical Aspects of International Relations.* William T. R. Fox, ed.

*Catholicism, Nationalism and Democracy in Argentina.* John J. Kennedy.

*The Fate of East Central Europe.* Stephen D. Kertesz, ed.

*German Protestants Face the Social Question.* William O. Shanahan.

*Soviet Imperialism: Its Origins and Tactics.* Waldemar Gurian, ed.

*The Foreign Policy of the British Labour Government, 1945-1951.* M. A. Fitzsimons.

*Bolshevism: An Introduction to Soviet Communism.* Waldemar Gurian.

# THE TASK OF UNIVERSITIES
# IN A CHANGING WORLD

# CONTRIBUTORS

RAMÓN BELA
GEORGE Z. F. BEREDAY
THOMAS P. BERGIN
LORD BOWDEN
JOHN BRADEMAS
ROBERT F. BYRNES
OLIVER J. CALDWELL
MATTEI DOGAN
F. G. DREYFUS
M. A. FITZSIMONS
LAWRENCE H. FUCHS
WILLIAM HABER
JOHN P. HARRISON
THEODORE M. HESBURGH, C.S.C.
PATRICK HORSBRUGH
HERBERT JACOB

BERNARD J. KOHLBRENNER
IVAN M. MAKSIMOVIC
FEDERICO MANCINI
M. V. MATHUR
PHILIP E. MOSELY
MICHIO NAGAI
DAVIDSON S.H.W. NICOL
NAI SUKICH NIMMANHEMINDA
TORGNY T. SEGERSTEDT
GEORGE N. SHUSTER
FRANCIS X. SUTTON
KENNETH W. THOMPSON
BERT M. TOLLEFSON, JR.
DOUGLAS V. VERNEY
HERMAN B WELLS
RUDOLPH WILDENMANN

# THE
# TASK
# OF
# UNIVERSITIES
# IN A
# CHANGING
# WORLD

STEPHEN D. KERTESZ

Editor

UNIVERSITY OF NOTRE DAME PRESS

NOTRE DAME          LONDON

# CONTENTS

38963     ix

# Contents

## Part Five

## Part Six

# PREFACE

In recent years universities on all continents have become centers of violent conflict involving important social and political forces and raising the most basic questions about university life. In view of the confusion about the role of institutions of higher learning, the Committee on International Relations of the University of Notre Dame sponsored three international conferences on "The Task of Universities in a Changing World." Almost all of the essays published in the present volume were delivered and discussed at these conferences, held in the Notre Dame Center for Continuing Education on April 16-19, 1969, and on February 25-28, 1970, and at the Rockefeller Foundation's Villa Serbelloni, Bellagio, Italy, on June 24-27, 1969. A Ford Foundation grant the University of Notre Dame received in 1965 and the hospitality of the Rockefeller Foundation in the Villa Serbelloni greatly helped to make these conferences possible.

One might well ask what connection exists between the problems of the university and the Notre Dame Committee on International Relations. The principal concern of the Committee is with political problems, and its research and publications for the last 20 years have examined ideological and social forces affecting the international politics of the contemporary world. Since we believe that in the present bewildering state of world affairs the universities should have a more profound sense of direction than that given by the archaic political bodies and obsolete societies of many countries, the Committee decided to examine problems of higher education.

The results are presented here. Even if the expected contributions were not forthcoming from a few important countries, the essays which the Committee did receive present a kaleidoscope of university problems in North and South America, Europe, Asia and Africa.

I take this opportunity to express to all contributors my sincere thanks for their co-operative spirit. During the planning and editing I greatly benefited from the wise counsel of George N. Shuster and M. A. Fitzsimons of the University of Notre Dame. In the last stage of the volume Charles McCollester served with expert knowledge as copy editor. His resourceful mind greatly expedited the process of publication.

S.D.K.

# FOREWORD
## The Universities and the Universal

### Stephen D. Kertesz

Institutions of higher learning fulfill important functions and are, in a sense, symbols of universalism. The future of mankind may depend on the orientation and effectiveness of their work.

The forces of universalism confront many problems today. The universal, regional and technical international organizations have many uses, but are handicapped by and reflect the shortcomings of a political system based on so-called sovereign states. This system has become unrealistic in the age of radio, television, rapid air transportation, nuclear power, missiles, communication satellites and space ships, and in an age of world-wide problems such as hunger, unemployment and enormous population growth. Other circumstances impede the development of a co-operative world society. Besides political and ideological rifts, there is the North-South chasm caused by important differences and conflicts of interest between the developed and developing nations. Instead of concentrating on farsighted policies and meaningful co-operation, the developed nations have produced dangerous weapons systems and are, in addition, polluting the air, water and soil as if driven to self-destruction by an evil spirit. They may also—often with the purest motives—run the risk of simply exporting these problems to the Third World under the guise of development aid, in the mistaken belief that industrial and technological 'growth' and educational systems as we know them in Western countries constitute a panacea for the ills of developing societies.

Historical precedents are of little help in our present era. The universities function in a world substantially different from bygone times during which the pace of change was slow and university education was restricted to a small elite. Since universities developed in Europe in the twelfth and thirteenth centuries, they have been the center of intellectual internationalism, although usually they have functioned under much less complicated conditions than today.

Until the dawn of the twentieth century both the medieval and modern state systems and the universities changed slowly and gradually and possessed a measure of intellectual unity. They developed in the homogeneous European world. For many centuries, European diplomacy and most European universities used the same language, Latin, also the language of the educated classes. Even later, when the universities began to use the vernacular, and the French language replaced Latin in diplomatic usage, ideological cleavages and the problem of semantics did not cause fundamental difficulties. The major philosophical and political ideas and value systems were comparable. Students could move from one university to another and feel at home everywhere. Dialogue in more than a technical sense was possible between scholars.

In the expanded world community of our time the universities function in much more heterogeneous societies. University education is no longer restricted to a small elite. Distances have little meaning, and large groups of students study in foreign countries. Despite greater mobility and instantaneous communication facilities, the different world views and value systems create enormous difficulties for international understanding. The natural sciences are the least affected by ideological cleavages. Even at the same university, dialogue is often not easy among the branches of the social sciences, let alone between the humanities and the social sciences. University departments have the tendency to become self-sufficient compartments.

The roots of the present predicament are mainly in the conditions of the twentieth century. The contemporary turmoil was foreshadowed around the year 1900—and in some countries, such as India, even earlier—when the Third World began to learn the ways of the West. Two world wars destroyed not only the European political system, but weakened Europe's leadership in other fields as well. The existence of ideologically-oriented totalitarian states caused additional difficulties. It is distressing that at least one-third of mankind lives today in closed societies where the university communities as well as the citizens do not enjoy freedom of expression and free communication with the rest of the world, although the interaction of ideas is a preliminary condition for voluntary co-operation and progress. Without freedom of thought and a free give-and-take, human curiosity has no outlet, and the universities cannot fulfill their task in the common venture of mankind.

In many countries important parts of the political system and the social structure are obsolete and no longer in harmony with a scientific and technological age. A historical relic, the national state, has remained the unit of international life. The existing international organizations are important particularly in functional and technical fields, but in the realm of politics they, like the national states, reflect the conditions and thinking of a bygone period of history.

The supreme task of the universities is to work, with all the conscious, committed decision the thought implies, for a genuine world society. Ideally, universities should not serve only the academic or professional interests of the scholarly community. They do have obligations to their own members; they have obligations to their own nations, but they have even greater obligations to the welfare of mankind—to all members of the family of men wherever they may be found—and it is in this last direction that their work must increasingly be oriented. The institutions of higher learning are navigating on uncharted, perilous waters, but their major consideration clearly should be tomorrow's world. Such an orientation does not mean abandonment of the traditional values of Western civilization but a broadening of scholarly interests in all major cultures.

Although in their work universities are handicapped by clashing values and the squeaking brakes of antiquated structures and practices, they continue to represent universal elements in the human spirit and experience; they are symbols of the unity of the human race. Knowledge is universal. Scientific methods are universal. Teaching about the atom, chemistry, radiation, astrophysics is similar in countries belonging to a variety of political and social persuasions. Unfortunately, while science, technology and organizational ability can be used for both good and evil ends, they have until now made the problems of mankind more awesome without contributing much to their solution. A generally accepted moral standard is of primary importance for human survival. As universities should be the homes of internationalism and freedom, their task is to clarify some of the basic purposes of human existence and agree on the ways and means to achieve them.

In our apocalyptic age the universities thus are expected to assume new functions. Although the primary objective of institutions of higher learning is, as always, to transmit knowledge and prepare the forthcoming generations for tomorrow's task, their involvement in the world's acute social and political problems has become nearly unavoidable. If the by-products of this involvement may defeat some of the purposes of higher education, the universities cannot sweep under the rug the unpleasant realities of our time. There is a tradition in the humanities recognizing that all human affairs are man's concern. As Terence put it more than two thousand years ago: *Homo sum; humani nil a me alienum puto* (I am a man; nothing that is human is alien to me).

Some important activities of modern universities are closely related to the problems of local communities, national societies and the whole political and social process of mankind. In the context of this substantial involvement in the affairs of a rapidly changing world society, one of the tasks of the contemporary university is to eliminate gaps and promote understanding among generations, social classes, races, and the rich and poor.

The university is no longer an ivory tower. The intellectuals of the academic profession willy-nilly are involved in the tremendous social changes of our time. These changes mean acknowledgment of the fact that the advanced countries are already in the post-industrial age, and their society must be transformed accordingly. In less advanced countries they mean at least new departures in agriculture and in industry—in some backward areas, transition from the stone age to agriculture and industrialization. Such changes involve more than simply recreating Western democratic society in the Third World; they involve tensions, upheavals, revolts, deeply affecting the task of universities. In the United

States this challenge is not an entirely new aspect of higher education. Success of the land grant colleges has demonstrated what institutions of higher learning can do for the solution of the urgent problems of the society.

The unrest of students is world-wide. If the causes and motives are different in various countries, there are common denominators. In most countries many students are dissatisfied with social and political conditions and alienated from the institutions of the "establishment." They have become active agents of change, sometimes through violent means. Despite abuses, one of the most encouraging signs of our time is the interest of youth in university problems and in public affairs.

Dissatisfaction at the universities takes many forms. These range from a few groups of almost nihilistic agitators in Western countries and Japan to student groups in Poland, Hungary and Czechoslovakia who have protested for elementary human rights, freedom of speech, freedom of inquiry, national freedom. Students in the East European countries have expressed aspirations for conditions taken for granted in the West.

There are, of course, serious causes for the dissatisfaction and alienation of youth everywhere. In addition to the accumulation of gigantic unsolved problems of the human condition, governments even of some highly developed democratic states have been unable or unwilling to create adequate physical facilities and a modern academic framework and environment for a rapidly growing student body. While flourishing industries and business enterprises have produced economic "miracles" in a few countries such as Japan, Italy and Germany, the governments and society have used only a small proportion of the G.N.P. for the development of higher education. And there are other difficulties. Students rightly complain that many of their courses do not illuminate the fundamental problems of our age. Pontification by academic mandarins in huge lecture courses likewise does not improve the morale of students who have little personal contact with their teachers.

The structure of the university needs reform in a changing world, but politicization of the universities is not a remedy. It should be avoided. The reasons are obvious. Is it possible to study seriously and teach effectively in an atmosphere of continuous agitation and excitement? There will always be worthy causes to fight for, and student leaders might be inclined to include such issues in their programs in addition to demands for more and more student power, especially for increasing student participation in university administration. This last is part of the present trend in student movements in many countries and the consequences might be far-reaching indeed. Consider the situation in Japan where numerous universities have virtually collapsed as centers of learning. It is not surprising that Japanese business enterprises have, on their own, established a network of special schools for their employees. Many distinguished professors in Japan have left the universities and some are now assisting those business enterprises. The latter are spending more money for special courses and research than the Japanese government contributes to the yearly operating expenses of higher education.

While it is gratifying to see that student interest in public affairs and in the general problems of the university has increased, surely violence and strikes are wholly out of place in a university community. Arson, bombing, sniping and other acts of terror and vandalism should be met with all the rigor of the law. The universities do not enjoy extraterritoriality and are not equipped to handle criminal cases. Terrorism can destroy the university as a citadel of free inquiry. Terrorist groups do not advocate or accept rational discussion but use violence to establish a minority dictatorship, presumably for the sake of goals that are never clearly articulated. Reasonable arguments vis-à-vis the members of such groups are exercises in futility. It is not unfair to say that these extremists and their "intellectual" supporters, whether members of the faculty or not, have excluded themselves from the university community—which must remain a center of scholarship and learning, civility and rational discourse, general questioning and toleration of opposing views.

It is difficult to overstate the danger of force and violence as presently exercised by student groups in some universities. If the student organizations demand and obtain more power for power's sake, the trend will be reminiscent of fourteenth-century Bologna where students hired the professors. It is not an accident that a book dealing with medieval Bologna has become a best seller in Japan. Nor are workers' strikes proper models for student strikes. In an industrial society the workers strike against a different interest group to increase their incomes and security, and to obtain other benefits. At universities, strikes mean the wasting of precious time which the students need for preparation for their futures. In a very real sense students strike against themselves.

One may hope that student movements today will help to bring about reasonable reforms of university structures and archaic societies. In an optimistic mood we may even believe that the present widespread dissatisfaction among students may be a sign of transition to a new era in which humanistic disciplines and considerations will prevail for all mankind. Humanistic values should influence political and social trends in modern as well as in developing societies. A large acceptance of humanistic ideas should prepare for a world-wide agreement on some fundamental moral principles and on means available to mankind for the creation of a new humanistic era in a more co-operative world society.

We may have a clear vision of these goals, but whenever the leadership of universities is in the hands of individuals who have little regard for broad humanistic values, it is almost impossible to adapt academic structures to modern conditions. In an age when the whole world is going through an accelerated modernization—or at least desires to go through it—people tend to forget that modernization is impossible without proper education. Modernization needs literacy in the highest sense, and that means thorough study of the humanities, the social and the natural sciences, as well as specialization, research and training for the immediate needs of a developing society.

Universities in the United States admittedly have special problems, some of which are discussed here. Two striking factors stand out. One is the large number of students: more than 40 per cent of young Americans enroll in colleges and universities. The other is the war in Vietnam which has acted as a catalyst of dissatisfaction. The end of the war, however, will not terminate campus unrest. The crisis we are currently living through may indeed prove to be just another phase in the breakdown of the liberal tradition which was undermined decades ago by the rise and success of extremist ideologies. The Left and the Right have both used such ideologies, and in many instances leftist and rightist totalitarian political currents have displayed peculiar similarities. In the East European countries some former Nazis had no difficulty becoming Communists after the Soviet occupation; they were welcomed into the fold. Extremists at universities display today the same unscrupulous relativist attitudes; they can easily be used by external forces.

Even without such outer-directed agitators and confused extremist groups, many social and political problems will remain parts of the human predicament and cause unrest on campuses. Although the solution of the urgent problems of society are not within the domain of universities, significant clarification through intelligent dialogue and debate can and should take place in a scholarly community. The faculty and students are rightly concerned with fundamental problems of social justice and the quality of life in our society. Resentment because of deterioration of ecological conditions is understandable and hopefully will give impetus to constructive discourse. Intellectual ferment in a university is not invariably fruitful, but it is the surest sign of the vitality of a scholarly community. Besides general problems of the society, the task and proper functions of higher education will be debated for many years on campuses.

The great advantages of the North American university system, we trust, remain its broad basis, its unity in diversity, its flexibility, and the understanding by public authorities, foundations and private persons of the requirements of an expanding higher education, including its financial needs. The past gives some grounds for confidence that universities in the United States will adapt to the exigencies of an evolving world society. Recognition of new ideas and values in the process of modernization and in the culture of other nations will continue to be of great importance.

The universities may have only a short time for laying the foundations of a world civilization. Along this road they must remain dedicated to the pursuit of knowledge and truth, as must any university worth its salt. At the same time they cannot avoid problems connected with social, technological and other rapid transformations. In this process they must re-examine some of the cherished assumptions of the traditional role and methods of higher education.

One of the reasons for our difficulties in higher education today is that many universities are either looking backward or trying to respond to immediate pressures. They seldom chart the path to the future. The discussions at our conferences have made some modest progress in the latter direction. The Notre Dame and Bellagio meetings have explored not only the causes of trouble at universities, but have envisaged new trends, alternatives, innovative approaches and desirable institutional reforms.

If the universities are to survive the present crisis, the combination of opportunity and orderly process must characterize their endeavors, even as opportunity and order are parts of the democratic system in any community. In a university the opportunity and orderly process must include the law of change, the creation of a transnational order suitable to the technological and social conditions of our time. Universities should examine desirable changes and initiate those which are imperative for the better future of mankind. We are confident that most universities will do the spadework and adapt within a reasonable time to the changing needs of a developing world society.

The aim of the present volume is to contribute to the clarification of the major issues we face, and of the choices societies and universities will have to make, the sooner the better.

# PART ONE

PART ONE

# THE NATURE OF THE CHALLENGE
## Traditional Organization and Attitudes of
## Universities Toward Contemporary Realities

### Theodore M. Hesburgh, C.S.C.

The university is among the most traditional of all the institutions of our society and, at the same time, it is the institution most responsible for the changes that make our society the most changing in the history of man. Perhaps the most central challenge facing universities in a changing world is: Can universities adapt themselves rapidly enough to survive amid all the changes they have stimulated?

It seems curious to suggest that an institution is contributing by its activity to its own downfall, or that, in other words, the university has caused so much change, so quickly, that it cannot change itself quickly enough to survive the conditions it has created.

What are the challenges of change for the university today? One might suggest several:

1) Its new and enlarged role in society: everyone and every institution today seem to be undergoing an identity crisis. Why not the university?

2) Its program to fulfill its role: curriculum, research, service, and the proportion among these.

3) Its governance: how it has been governed in the past and how its governance is likely to evolve in the future.

These seem to be the principal challenges of change facing the universities in the face of contemporary realities. One could likewise pose the problems in a much more cursive and less analytic and categorical manner. This would give us a list of questions and propositions such as the following:

1) Rapidity of change makes much, if not all, of the past seem irrelevant. This may be called illusory, but it is widely reflected in the ahistorical attitudes of today's students, caught up as they are with today's realities, problems, demands, and in the face of the dichotomy between what our society professes to be and what, in fact, it is. How can one hope to salvage what is good in the university's past? Must we jettison everything today in the name of contemporaneity and relevance?

2) Granting that the university should concern itself with contemporary problems and solutions, how can it do so while still remaining apolitical, au-

tonomous, free, and detached from the world as well, as it must, to exercise objective critique and evaluation? This is no easy task as we are learning to our sorrow.

3) How can the university in America double in size since 1950, expect the same magnitude of growth in the next decade, under much more difficult financial and social conditions, and still pretend to be somewhat of an elite institution, totally dedicated to excellence and high standards of performance? Or, more fundamentally, should it try to be dedicated to quality and equality at the same time? Will society allow it to do so even if it were possible? No easy answer here, but it does remain a fundamental challenge to the university in the immediate future.

4) Is there any other way for the university to defend itself against all the seeds of dissolution that burgeon within it today, except by somehow re-creating a vital university *community,* united by some common university goals and values, a community willing to articulate, profess, and defend these values, concerned enough to contribute to the life style, the responsible university freedom and autonomy that are best defended by being rightly and intelligently exercised by the community? What other force is there with which to confront the free wheeling of faculties, the occasional violence of students, the capriciousness of administrators? What other reality, than true university community of dedication, concern, and effort, can fend off the efforts from all sides to intrude into the affairs of the university, to abridge its autonomy, to dry up or condition its support? I can imagine no other solution.

5) Lastly, there is the challenge, greater than ever in times of rapid change, to keep the university from undergoing arteriosclerosis of the total educational process. With all knowledge doubling every fifteen years, with little healthy balance between specialization and wholeness of knowledge, with technology threatening to engulf humanity, with confusion of values manifested daily by horrendously twisted priorities, both public and private, with a whole long litany of similar problems left unmentioned, is this any time to resist change, or at least more profound and meaningful consideration of changes spelling improvement of education within the university?

Of course, if point 4 meant anything, the whole university and all of its constituent parts should be party to this fundamental study of the educational process on the university level. Otherwise, there will be no total commitment or conviction—only more fragmentation of purpose and dissolution of university integrity—by faculties more committed to disciplines than to the institution, by student activists who save by destroying, and by administrative mandarins who lose all in bureaucratic obscurantism.

Whether one poses the problem in nice clean categories or by cursive and impressionistic propositions and questions, it should be evident to all that we do have a serious problem that requires much wisdom and for which there are no obvious or easy solutions.

All things considered, it seems more promising to address myself to the cursive and somewhat impressionistic list of propositions and questions, rather than to hew strictly to the three categories that, in a way, may seem a more direct and cleaner approach to the problem, but which, on examination, prove less productive of real solutions. Our exposition then will follow the five questions and propositions outlined above.

I

The first point fundamentally has to do with change and its residue of confusion and consternation. No one could deny that the world has changed more since World War II than in any other quarter century in man's history. We have entered the Atomic Age, the Space Age, the Thermonuclear Age, the Age of Human Development, the end of colonization and the beginning of new nationalisms, the advent of the population explosion, the new Communications Age with the picture joined to the word and the whole world open to both types of educational communication from three synchronous satellites strategically placed in outer space.

Then there has been an increase of speed from 500 miles an hour to 25,000 m.p.h., a fiftyfold increase shrinking the world. This speed, when applied to computers seeking, correlating, or compiling knowledge, must be rated at from zero in the pre-1950's to multimillions of new speed capacity in all of these processes today.

Most of what has been mentioned heretofore has been in the category of physical change and progress. What of the spiritual and ideological? Here again, the change staggers the imagination. After more than a thousand years of enmity between Catholics and Orthodox, 400 years between Catholics and Protestants, today all movement is ecumenical, leading to the unity of Christianity. After centuries of human exploitation in slavery, actual, political, or economic, today all the talk is of human development, which Pope Paul VI says is the new name for peace.

Educationally, the third of the world that today cannot read or write may have a new answer through satellite broadcasts.

Even new moves towards peace are possible when we realize that today's armaments, mainly in the United States and the U.S.S.R., provide for 15 tons of TNT in nuclear form for every human being on earth. How much greater can the threat of global destruction become? By some reverse psychology, this may become the strongest argument for peace in our times.

This is the world of change in which the university today must find itself, its mission, and its ultimate meaning. In the face of so much galloping change, it is not really remarkable that students tend to think that what did not happen before 9 o'clock this morning is not really very important or significant. Never before have we had such an ahistorical group of students. But as Santayana has noted, those who ignore history commit themselves to repeat all of its errors. Somehow, when all is changing, there must be some constants, some anchors, some unfailing faith in God, or man, or truth, or the good, or all of these in some workable combination.

The university is the place where this combination has unfailingly been found in the past, and there is no place to expect anything better intellectually for the future. Here tradition leads to hope, not despair.

The only answer I can give to this dilemma is the answer of humanism to changes that are mainly technological. Man, no matter how much he changes, is still man, and his problems are still profoundly human. This means that the university, while coming to grips with change and the very real improvements to mankind that change makes possible, will not forget that its educational mission is always and everywhere profoundly human, concerned with the spiritual and moral constants that make man's history something quite different from animal history. What are these constants that profoundly concern the university? They are human realities like love and hatred, peace and violence, order and disorder, law and lawlessness, justice and injustice, beauty and ugliness, virtue and sin, and all the rest of the dichotomies that have characterized the human scene since Adam and Eve, Cain and Abel.

Whatever the claim of modern students to the importance of relevance, the university must insist that the ultimate relevance is man, human life, the vision and perspectives, the successes and failures of human history, so well dramatized in our literature, art, and cultural heritage. In educating students to live today and tomorrow, universities cannot forget to educate them for the long future that is theirs on this planet or elsewhere, for human is what human does, here or elsewhere in the universe.

II

The university has always been society's most persistent and tenacious critic. Today, university professors and students, and some administrators, are profoundly concerned about the quality of life, or the lack of it, in America and in the world at large. One thing is required for the honest critic: he must somehow be detached from the world he criticizes; he must be independent, autonomous, and free. One might, at this juncture, legitimately ask: How free are the universities today? They depend on the state largely for their support. Can they then freely criticize the state and its policies?

In the United States, 50 per cent of the cost of higher education comes from private sources. Can the university be free to criticize this sector as well?

I personally believe that the university can be a real critic of both the public and private sectors if it is honest, if it maintains within its university community a real commitment to openness, to rationality, to civility, to all the virtues that make the university, in the words of the poet laureate Masefield of England, "a splendid place."

Once the university ceases to be an open place of civility and rationality, its capacity to be the conscience of the public and private sector is severely restricted, if not destroyed. All of this is a question of noblesse oblige, if the university is true to itself and its traditions. It can do superbly what it alone can do in the most objective and apolitical manner. Once the confidence of the public is lost, it can do nothing; in fact, without public understanding and support, it will be starved to death financially, and will become unacceptable in word and deed to the great publics that it needs for survival as a very special kind of institution. Public support is, then, essential to the university.

### III

Most institutions would accept rapid growth as a sign of vitality and general acceptance; but it is a fact of institutional life that very rapid and uncontrolled growth is a danger to institutional integrity. Biologically, it is a popular description of cancer.

If there is one characteristic that might be taken as standard for all universities up until World War II, it is quality or excellence of performance. Willy-nilly universities tended to become elitist institutions, catering to a small, highly selective and highly talented and intelligent proportion of the total population. This was true world-wide, especially in Europe, Latin America, and Asia, and true after World War II in the new universities in Africa.

In America, and to a lesser extent in Europe, a populist ideal became evident after World War II, when increasingly larger proportions of all classes of the population flocked to the universities with the firm conviction that this was the one infallible path to greater personal success and greater promise in life. In Europe, this has become the underlying cause for the great present unrest of student populations, for the growth in numbers of students was not matched by an over-all growth in educational facilities or a modernization of university administration or curricular reform.

In America, the picture is more ambiguous. Here, there was an enormous expansion of educational facilities, mainly in the area of public higher education, but much in the private sector as well. The total capacity for higher education doubled, in less than twenty years, all the higher educational facilities provided since the beginning of the Republic.

As one private example I know best, this University (Notre Dame) built over $60 million in new facilities during those years, against a total of $10 million in the century previous, while the operating budget increased more than tenfold. Even granting considerable inflation in the value of the dollar, this was, in the private sector, an enormous growth in a very short period.

It might be added that in most cases, public and private, American higher education has had a comparable qualitative growth during the same period, due mainly to better secondary education following Sputnik, many internal curricular and administrative reforms, and a general upgrading of library, laboratory and faculty.

On the negative side, there was a general impersonalization of the total educational process due to the growth from 3 million to 6.5 million students, and to a general emphasis, on the part of faculties, to stress research over teaching in terms of their personal and professional advancement. Counterbalancing this, to some extent, was the idea that students themselves should take a greater personal interest and responsibility for their own education. Even so, these factors of impersonalization do account for much of the student discontent with their university education today, and this relates increasingly to what is taught, as well as how and by whom.

Looking ahead, the problems and the strains inherent in this rapid and often inorganic growth are greater still. The initially apparent problems are social, rather than educational. The recent report of the Kerr Commission on The Future of Higher Education outlines the problem clearly. While the report is entitled "Quality and Equality," I think I should have to admit, as a member of the Commission, that the thrust is on equality more than on quality of education, which will probably be treated more explicitly in a later report. Part of the problem is sheer numbers, but it runs deeper. On the numbers side, only 2 per cent of young Americans entered higher education a century ago, as against over 40 per cent today—50 thousand to 6.5 million students. Normal growth along present curves of development would indicate an increase to 8 million students by 1976. But the Kerr report tries to envision 9 million by 1976 by making it possible for an additional million students to come from the lower socio-economic class during this short interval of six years. Total costs would rise from $17.2 to $41 billion during this period.

The reason for the projected growth is seen from the present distribution of students by socio-economic class: 1st quartile—48%; 2nd quartile—28%; 3rd quartile—17%, and 4th quartile—7%.

Put in other terms by the Kerr Commission, in the highest socio-economic class, 19 out of 20 students ranking in the top ability group (highest 20 per cent) enter higher education, while only 10 out of 20 comparable students from the lowest socio-economic quartile do. The figures are probably much worse for lower-ranking students and for graduate students.

Americans are quick to see the inequity of this situation, and in correcting it by larger federal funding, there will undoubtedly be new problems created by repeating in the span of less than a decade a growth equal to most of the long history of higher education in America. Add to this an additional problem of poor educational preparation for the great majority of those in the lower socio-economic groups—because of poor neighborhood schools in poor neighborhoods with a shrinking tax base of support—and the problems are compounded. Finally, add to all of this the ultimate challenge of the knowledge taught by universities doubling every 15 years, mainly due to their research.

It has been said that never has there been so much expected and demanded of universities, despite a current lowering of their prestige in the public eye because of student unrest, occasional riots, and a consequent drying up, or conditioning by restrictive legislation, or inadequate funding of their private (50 per cent) and public sources of support.

Whether universities can grow as thus indicated and still maintain their traditional quality while expanding equality of access, is a question of enormous educational, social, and economic importance. One can speak of it with hope, but not without trepidation as well. There is no easy answer.

### IV

The fourth challenge is the most felicitous since it leads to what may be the best solution to all the others. If there is to be any hope for the modern university, it is in the re-creation of a sense of community within it, comprising a strong and organic unity of all its component parts, particularly faculty, administration, and students, and, hopefully, trustees and alumni as well, who are external to the university, but internal to its ultimate success.

The university today needs great inner strength, a strength that has been sapped by inner disunity: faculties that have forgotten that the most important function of a professor is to teach, to profess; students who have on occasion pressed dissent to a point of violence and boorishness that militates against those great central values of the university, reason and civility; administrators who have forgotten that their greatest function is to unite all the component parts of the university in an effort to define its basic goals and values, and to maintain them against all internal and external forces that would pervert or denature them.

The creation of such a community is no easy task. It will require a more realistic involvement of all the component parts of the university in the total task of the university to a new extent and, at times, in a totally new dimension. This has been happening to an ever greater degree in American universities where many councils, committees, and senates are now organized on a tripartite basis of faculty, students, and administration.

I should warn against a sense of panacea here, or a confusion of capabilities or functions, for students are not faculty, and faculty are not administration, and administration is neither faculty nor students, although they are in the service of both. What is needed is respect for each essential function, and a recognition of the necessity of various roles requiring various talents and capabilities.

Latin-American universities have equated all roles with much less than success. France over-centralized university control and administration since Napoleon's time, and now seems to be swinging in the opposite direction. The Anglo-Saxon world of universities has tried to realize university governance on a system of layers of influence: trustees, faculty, administration, with perhaps all too little student involvement. This latter deficiency is now being corrected, but it is difficult to change without over-reacting. Hopefully, the world experience will lead to world balance in university governance, although the present experience in change is ambiguous and ambivalent at best.

My only plea at the moment is for community, for total involvement of the total community to the full extent that each component part has something valid to offer, backed by real knowledge, real competence, and real commitment to the total reality of the university.

I have spoken of the internal strains from faculty, students, and administration, each of whom needs to reassess its best role and best contribution to the health and vitality of the total educational enterprise. I believe that trustees and alumni also have something of value to contribute, for the university is in the public domain whatever its sponsorship, public or private, and the trustees and alumni best represent the public of each university.

Community is, however, the central reality to be achieved. Only the total community can assure the unique reality and contribution of the university. Only community can vindicate the claim to freedom and autonomy, which are the essential climate of the university, by a responsible community exercise of freedom and autonomy. If the community is irresponsible or deficient, or worse, disinterested and uncommitted, the whole enterprise becomes suspect and any element of the community can jeopardize the whole endeavor by its failure to respond to the challenge at hand.

The great reality or lack of community reality says one thing: either the university rules itself or others will rule it to its ultimate demise as an open society that is characterized by rationality and civility, freedom and autonomy, the one institution that can validly criticize church and state, society at large, values, priorities, and the quality of life that surrounds it. There is really no middle ground here—the university is or is not, and university community spells the difference.

## V

We can conclude by insisting that in a time of total change, no institution, particularly no university, can survive without change. Wisdom is, of course, required for fruitful change, which means that change for the sake of change is not what we are suggesting. Where is wisdom? Again, we must have recourse to community for total wisdom must somehow reside within the total community.

There are some general guidelines, most of which have already been mentioned. The university should not be overwhelmed by technocracy; humanism is the university's best heritage. Values loom high in any assessment of university wisdom, and values are best manifested by the priorities that characterize the university enterprise. I would hope that universities might look to the ultimate realities that humanize all human concerns, and these are basically philosophical and theological concerns.

Perhaps this is too much to require of universities which are today, in large measure, secular institutions. But, I must insist that salvation for universities in a time of great change cannot be otherwise envisioned, for in no other way are there available those effective and immutable anchors that make for stability and progress in the face of change. If all is changing, the game is lost. What is needed is the vision of a great institution, ever new, ever old, with great traditions and great openness to face an ever new future.

# THE GROWTH AND TRANSFORMATION OF STATE UNIVERSITIES IN THE UNITED STATES SINCE WORLD WAR II

## The Magnitude and Complexities of the Challenge

### Herman B Wells

No one doubts that state universities have enlarged and changed since World War II. While the man on the street may have only a dim notion of what the university was like in the early 1940's, he knows that it has been replaced by something complex and strange. He no longer understands what a university is and does; and he is apt to be fearful of its enlarging influence and rapid growth. Yet he senses that the university is somehow necessary in this complicated world of science fiction-become-real.

As American society has moved from a strongly agrarian base to one in which industry and technology dominate, universities have been responsive to and even somewhat responsible for the change. But the swiftness of this transformation has prevented an orderly academic transition and a determination of what the state university's role should be. Private universities, of course, have also undergone change. However, both the tradition and the control of public institutions place them more readily at the service of society and make them more sensitive to change. There are, of course, various kinds of state universities. In what I say, I shall be referring in general to the kind with which I am most familiar: the Midwest state university.

It may be useful to note that out of World War II and the war years came many of the developments which stimulated the growth and transformation of the state universities. Possibly no event in this century led to such profound, even revolutionary changes in higher education. Among these developments were the beginning dependence of government and industry on the universities for research, training and skilled manpower; federal subsidizing of students' education through the G.I. Bill; new social concepts of who should and could be educated, resulting from experience with that G.I. education; a baby boom which would in due course send waves of students to colleges and universities, straining their facilities and resources and creating a need for vastly increased public and private support; new interest in other nations and cultures as

United States troops were deployed throughout the world; and the revelation of the effectiveness of massive concentration of talents and resources in hastening scientific discovery. Public universities, with their inherent flexibility, absorbed much of the impact from these developments.

While less tangible and traceable, social and cultural currents that were fanned during that period have also profoundly influenced the climate of our campuses today: the volatile issue of real opportunity for blacks; the questioning of values in a world threatened by nuclear weapons; the measuring of humane against inhumane uses of scientific knowledge; and the challenge by minorities of majority power. In recent years, manifestations of these currents on the campuses have been accompanied, probably quite coincidentally, by a reluctance among some state legislators to continue to have the state pay in the same proportions the mounting cost of higher education. May I interject the comment that, even though higher education expenditures are increasing, they are still not beyond the ability of society to meet them. One has simply to look at the rapidly increasing gross national product.

I will refrain from miring you in statistics, but since they are a shorthand of growth, a few may be helpful. Between 1945 and 1965, total enrollments in public higher educational institutions enlarged from 897,000 to almost 3.6 million, of which 2.9 million were in four-year institutions. During the same 20-year period, the total current expenditures for all public institutions of higher education, measured in 1965 dollars, went from $742.1 million to $6.9 billion. Much of this increase has paid for enormous increases in basic and applied research to meet critical national needs. The United States Office of Education estimates that enrollments in four-year public institutions will be approaching 5 million by 1975 and the corresponding total expenditures in 1965-1966 dollars will have reached $13.1 billion. Two trends should be noted: the shift in the ratio of enrollments between public and private institutions of higher education; and the shift in the proportion of operating costs carried by state taxpayers. Between 1955 and 1965, the number of students enrolled in public colleges and universities grew from 51.8 per cent of all enrollments to 61.6 per cent. By 1975, at least seven out of every 10 students will be attending public rather than private colleges and universities, if the projections prove accurate. While this shift was occurring, state appropriations for higher education have covered an increasingly smaller percentage of the total bill for public higher education. Between 1945 and the present, the average proportion of the expenses of state institutions paid by the state has decreased from 65 to 37 per cent. Defined in baldest numerical terms, this series of figures represents the magnitude of the challenge to state universities.

Since 1945 administrators have done a commendable, yes, a remarkable, job of providing physical facilities and services for the new numbers. Legislatures, while not granting all of the support requested and thereby creating future problems, nevertheless were sufficiently liberal to make this accommodation possible.

It was in the area of providing instruction that a compromise had to be made because of the shortage of available faculty. The expansion of teaching by graduate students shall be discussed in a later section.

These direct effects of growth were accompanied by indirect ones too numerous to be more than suggested. Some we have heard quite a bit about: the alienated student, the breakdown of communications, the new pyramid of bureaucracy, and that perpetual source of annoyance to a faculty—parking. There is much less awareness of a problem like the logistics involved in getting students from classroom to classroom quickly on a more extensive campus. Where time and foresight and imagination permitted, many of these secondary problems have yielded to planning. Some will simply become an accepted feature of the state university.

On the positive and lasting side, growth has meant a far richer curricular fare from which students may choose their courses. I am reminded of David Starr Jordan, president of Indiana University from 1885 to 1891, admiring Ezra Cornell's determination to found "an institution in which any person can find instruction in any subject," and commenting, "such a school does not yet exist among us, but it will come, and when it comes it will work a revolution in college education. I do not know where it may be or when, but in my dreams day and night I can see it, the college of the masters, the college of the twentieth century, standing as the rightful head of the school system of Indiana."

Growth has meant opportunity for diversification and specialization, both in instruction and in learning resources. Growth has brought heterogeneity to student bodies that formerly were homogeneous. And—not unimportantly— growth has made the acceptance of change easier in institutions proverbially harder to move than cemeteries.

Too, the problems of growth have stimulated inventive responses which may substantially benefit higher education. Conspicuous examples are the beginnings of institutional analysis, centers of higher education, and learning research. Until pushed to it by the dynamics of change, universities hadn't examined the assumptions upon which they had operated and hadn't questioned the guidelines of accepted educational practice. Through the aid of institutional research at both the local and national levels, administrators can know more about the alternatives they have in making decisions. The gap in knowledge about higher education has begun to be closed by centers devoted to that study and by a prodigiously growing literature on the subject—often based, I might add, on surveys which load administrative offices with questionnaires. In line with this trend has developed the practice of forming state and national commissions of experts to evaluate various aspects of higher education and to make recommendations for action. Basic information for administrative decisions has been further aided by the results of research into the processes of learning and of teaching. For example, we now know that a large class taught by a good teacher learns more than several smaller classes taught by mediocre teachers. Information of this sort will be increasingly important as the rising cost of higher education forces us into consideration of how we can best distribute our resources.

Another problem, student alienation, has also stimulated inventive responses. Thus we have had experimentation with residential colleges to provide students the advantages of the smaller unit along with those of the large university. Counseling services have been extended to cover everything from budgeting to academic first-aid stations. And regional or branch campus systems have become the geographical counterpart of cluster colleges, providing access to the resources of the large university but in a small-college setting.

So much for growth and the responses to its effects, which I have elaborated to provide historical perspective on the origins of the challenges state universities must face and their ability to respond to them.

As can be recognized, there are two kinds of challenges, external and internal. From outside the university comes a variety of pressures for university services. Industry and commerce seek research, manpower development and stimulation of economic growth. Labor wants strong programs of vocational and adult education. Government needs a wide range of academic assistance to carry out its programs. Foundations, too, are largely dependent upon faculty expertise for the execution of their projects. Churches, hospitals, public schools, cultural societies, the professions and many, many others look to the universities for consultations, conferences and institutes. Solutions to the problems of pollution, urbanization, water resources, transportation—to most of society's major problems—are expected from the universities.

The state university, of course, has always regarded public service as one of its primary responsibilities, along with teaching and research. These universities were usually founded to meet a vocational and practical need, with the result that application of knowledge has held equal importance with its creation. For state universities in particular, therefore, present needs and pressures present a complex dilemma. In a broad sense, the goals of the university coincide with those of the state and society. The university has a heavy concentration of the talents and resources which might generate solutions to some of the problems that stand in the way of progress toward regional and national goals. Support, forthcoming from the federal government and foundations for furthering these goals, broadens the possibilities of what universities can do and helps underwrite their operations, thus furthering *their* goals.

On the other hand, the relationship is unstable. Foundations and the national government merely employ universities as agents to perform services needed to accomplish certain objectives. And the priorities of those objectives can and do shift, with very disturbing effects on the agents.

Let me illustrate. The support of international education is a case in point. During the early part of the 1960's, college and university international programs, which had been struggling along with limited external funding, suddenly began to receive heartening grants from private foundations. There were grants not only for specific projects but occasionally for institution-wide development of diversified international programs. Indiana University, for example, received two of these larger awards which enabled us to build strong new area studies programs and strengthen established ones, to underwrite group and individual projects, and to add a needed international dimension in various areas of the university's work.

However, large foundations are now turning their attention more and more to the problems of urbanization and the ghetto. Having provided the impetus for a demonstration of what colleges and universities could do to develop their international programs and activities, the foundations feel that institutions should begin to shoulder the support or convince the government to do it, since it is clearly in the national interest.

Unfortunately for our hopes of maintaining and extending international educational programs, the government is moving away from rather than toward support. When President Lyndon B. Johnson spoke at the Smithsonian Institution in September 1965 of a new federal commitment to international education, and then signed the International Education Act into law 13 months later, it seemed that the backing of international programs was assured. But funds to implement the act have not been appropriated. Congress put a freeze on new programs, not already funded by fiscal 1967, until such time as war expenditures could be sharply curtailed. Moreover, a new isolationism is developing in America, associated with the unpopularity of the Vietnam War, foreign derogation of American endeavors abroad, and a grave concern about our growing internal problems.

I should like to interject a personal note here. Many of us are deeply troubled by this understandable but dangerous turning-inward. If the resources and, more particularly, the national attention of the United States are to be devoted to the problems of racial strife, air and water pollution, the plight of our cities, the spoilage of our national resources and similar pressing concerns, to the exclusion of those which affect us, though indirectly, from beyond our shores, then the dangers are very urgent and very real. To state the situation quite simply, we believe that the United States, in terms of national security, social and economic stability, and—above all—of its national conscience, must not turn away from the rest of the world. International education offers the most promising possibility of maintaining an intelligent, informed U.S. interest and concern about the needs and developments of the world outside. It is essential that we carry this message to the nation.

I have used the example of international education to illustrate one kind of complexity—the phenomenon of collapsing support—that may arise when universities avail themselves of opportunities to circumvent the financial limitations upon what they can do. An additional complication results from the fact that agencies seek services from only a segment of the spectrum of university disciplines, and often from only an applied branch within a discipline. If the university were free to balance the external support of favored areas with internal budgeting design, this complication might be minimized. However, both the uncertainty and dynamics of external support make such a compensatory procedure unworkable.

In practice, state universities rarely fall into the trap of serious disalignment. But the society of scholars has ever been sensitive to any rating of their perceptions, and selective support from outside inevitably offends that sensitivity.

We have also seen that a particular source of support may give offense. On the surface, the movement led by the New Left against university research and training contracted by the Department of Defense is simply an extension of its protest against the Vietnam War. Basically, however, it is an attack upon the partnership of universities and government—an ironic twist in view of the liberals' embrace of that partnership during New Deal days (or their advocacy of the "Wisconsin Idea" during the La Follette era).

The availability of external support has been a key factor in the development of another complex situation for state universities: the lessening of a sense of responsibility for institutional concerns on the part of the faculties. It is true that the shortage of academic manpower and the competition for academic talent, both among universities and from outside, have contributed to this trend. However, the faculty member with a contract or two as evidence of his grantsmanship need not feel tied to any particular university. His ties are with the granting agency. As Dr. Clark Kerr put it, "The agency becomes the new alma mater."

Thus at a crucial time in the life of the university, when pressures from within and without are severe and decisions for tomorrow must be made, the traditional source of a university's strength, its faculty, is somewhat aloof from its need for aid.

The problem connected with certain forms of external support are only one facet of the mounting problem of financing higher education. For state universities, this has been compounded in the last year or so by public reaction to campus incidents, the demand for student power, strident criticism of our national involvement in Vietnam, and student insistence on the right to control their own lives. Legislators, already harassed by calls for economy on the one hand and the manifold needs of state agencies on the other, have come under some pressure to restrict university budgets as a form of chastisement and to "make the student pay." Apart from the fact that it is generally parents, a large percentage of them state taxpayers, who "pay," any sober thought about such a means to handle an annoyance puts it in its true light: a case of cutting off the nose to spite the face.

Hopefully, the era of student disruptive demonstrations will be short-lived. Of more lasting concern to us are the developing philosophy and practice of bringing student fees up to the level of student costs. How far we have traveled from the principle of free education enunciated by our founding fathers! To give you an idea of what is happening, let me cite the example of Indiana University. Between 1963 and 1968, the ratio of student fees to state appropriations went from 35.2 per cent to 37.0 per cent, and on the main campus the change was from 29.0 per cent to 35.2 per cent. Without compensatory scholarship support, the university may foreseeably become again an opportunity open only to a privileged class.

Equally compelling our concern is the evidence of parochialism in the widening gap between in-state and out-of-state fees. This unfortunate national trend toward state educational tariff walls threatens to balkanize the cultural life of the nation, not to mention the threat to national unity. These tariff walls are in effect retrogressive because, as we long ago learned, a geographic mix is essential to the quality of education given on a campus. Carried to its logical extreme, the concept of state dollars for state students would require the end of migration in and out of the state! In the long run, the taxpayers of a given state cannot benefit any more from cultural barriers than they could from state industrial tariffs. In fact a lower efficiency and a higher cost would result from both.

The difficulties of administrative and faculty staffing in state universities are various and in some respects related to the problems of financing. At the top, heavy and multiple pressures are causing resignations from the presidential post in unprecedented numbers. By the fall of 1969, half of the presidents in Big Ten universities will have been in office three years or less. The movement in and out of other top positions in central administration and the creation of coordinate posts have tended to multiply problems of informational background and flow and to unsettle established patterns of relationship. Faculty members, knowing neither the new line of recourse nor the susceptibilities of their newly-appointed administrative colleagues, are apt to be thrown back upon their own resources.

Too, vigorous competition for faculty members, combined with their numerical shortage and with the economics of supplying instructional staff for students swelling every level from freshman to post-doctoral, has resulted in certain modifications and accompanying problems. The rank of instructor has almost disappeared and the teaching associate or assistant now fulfilling the responsibilities once performed by the instructor has neither gained the status and privileges of that rank nor determined whether his role should be teaching apprentice or advanced student leader. Politically, the "voice" of the teaching associates has seemed to ally itself with the student-power movement rather than with the goals and attitudes of the faculty at large.

A growing tendency to establish chairs and name professorships has re-ordered the professorial ranks: they run from assistant to special professorships where once they ran from instructors to professors. Along with this reordering are new pressures for research and productivity which leave a teaching gap filled more and more frequently by the teaching associate.

We need to acknowledge that the change from instructor to teaching associate is not just nominal; that a heavy load of teaching has passed from beginners to apprentices. The distinction is not inherently qualitative; it does require a realistic faculty accommodation and special efforts to educate the student body and public concerning the role.

So much has been written about student unrest and dissent, I shall touch upon it only lightly. In part, its origin lies in the great pressure upon students at the secondary level to achieve academically. Even if Sputnik had not startled American education into increased seriousness at every level of schooling, the pressures would have arisen, for high school students have realized that they must have a college education to qualify for job opportunities in the developing technical-industrial world of work and that their high school records would determine their admissibility to that education at a time when an abundance of applications had led to more selective admission policies.

Once admitted to this privileged and expensive world, students had great expectations of the training they would receive, the understanding they would gain about the puzzling world around them, and the opportunity they would have to continue maturing. For many students, these expectations in one way or another have not been met and the resulting disillusionment has provided fuel for demands to share in their own governance. These demands have been effective whether they have been peremptory or simply a threat. Not only regulations concerning student life have undergone change but curricula, grading, degree requirements, the approach to learning—all have come under scrutiny and in many instances have been modified.

One of the significant effects of student criticism has been the addition of relevancy as a criterion of curricular and course content. It challenges parochialism, traditional approaches and old conclusions, the neglect of the present for the past, the failure to relate subject matter to current situations, and the inadequate preparation of individuals for a very complex world. In some cases, "free universities" answering the need for relevancy have had a beginning alongside established universities, but more often the response has been examination and modification of curricula and courses.

The extraordinary seriousness of present-day students and their belief that the world can be bettered are reflected in the intensity with which the great social issues of our time command their attention.

I have indicated some of the sources and characteristics of growth and change in state universities since World War II. Let me turn now briefly to various determinants of their future before I present the major challenge ahead.

It is a matter of importance to state universities that the man on the street gain a better understanding of what the university is and does, how it affects the life he lives; for his willingness to support public higher education sufficiently to meet its growing needs will be a determining factor in such crucial matters as the costs students must bear, the new programs required by new social developments, and the quality of faculty members a state university can attract. What we know to be true, the centrality of the university in the life of the state and nation, must be effectively translated for the public at large.

A second determinant will be the ability of state universities to anticipate and manage growth and transformation. Data projections have been very useful for the planning function, but no similar apparatus has been created to measure the likely effects of social trends: black militancy, reaction to the war in Vietnam, the alienation of youth, etc. Until and unless such factors can be fed into planning, universities may continue to be subjected to pressures in a crisis atmosphere.

A third and decisive determinant will be the direction of faculty commitment. As universities have become integrated into the life of the state and nation, certain faculty members in many of the disciplines have been called upon to play quite a different role from that of the traditional scholar-teacher. The effects on undergraduate teaching and on institutional loyalty, I have already noted. Yet these new academic services are needed and valuable—are, in fact, responsible for giving universities a relevancy they lacked as "ivory-towers." Whether these two poles of faculty attraction—the campus and the public arena for applying knowledge and research—can be centered again in the institution, recovering institutional loyalty, is a challenge for the future. Perhaps they will come together in the "university cities" predicted for the year 2000, or a differentiation of faculty function may become the workable mode. In any event, faculties are certain to influence strongly and often shape the kinds of responses state universities can make to the challenge of change.

Students, too, will be a determinant, although to what extent actively depends upon the continuing exertion of student influence. Certainly, the modifications they have induced in such areas as grading practices, increased opportunities for independent study, revised curricula and requirements for degrees, and new disciplines are likely to be durable. It is also reasonable to suppose that the student movement may be subject to the law of diminishing returns. In many ways, however, it has been salutary both in questioning educational patterns and in serving notice that students cannot be neglected.

By and large, all of what I have been describing fits into a larger whole. I shall conclude my remarks by sketching this dimension.

The state university, in particular, has been oriented to an agrarian economy and to direct public service to an agrarian economy. The most dramatic illustrations of this service, of course, are the agricultural experiment stations. There are hundreds of other illustrations which, though less widespread and dramatic, were nonetheless a regular feature of the state university. All of these services were directed to local rather than massive concerns, in keeping with an agrarian society. For example, I might mention the Geological Services and Survey, and the practical services to many types of locally-focused organizations, such as the Home Demonstration Clubs.

Furthermore, the reason-for-being of state universities has been to provide higher education for young people who did not have the means to attend private colleges and universities. The ideal of an education of the highest quality for all who were qualified to enroll has been consistently upheld by the state universities. Moves to raise admission standards and fees ever higher conflict with that goal. As society has developed, there are new and different types of disadvantaged; where once it was the boy and girl from the marginal farm who were disadvantaged, it is now our ghetto youth. The struggle of the black American, in particular, calls for renewed initiative on the part of the state universities. In this respect, the student conscience has reminded us of our original goals. How the needs of black and other minority youth for improved education and better preparation for college can be remedied most effectively and quickly is a complex question. It constitutes one of the major challenges to state universities.

In great part, the university itself, along with the onrush of science, has been responsible for rapidly transmuting this country to an urban society. If the state university is to be anything distinctive to society rather than just another university, it has to develop in time an urban rather than an agrarian point of view in its teaching, research, and public service. Its service to business must recognize that modern day economic life is national and international rather than merely state-wide in scope. Its concern for the social and political welfare of the nation must be expanded to include the city in all of its complexity. Its supporting constituency has to learn to think of the state university in these terms and support it in these terms.

This fundamental reorientation of attitude, point of view, and mission has to be effected at the same time that we are engaged in meeting the profound problems of numbers, finances, instructional staffing and the like. The principal question, the principal challenge is this: while we are solving the other big problems, how are we to go about reshaping the service function, and the teaching and research to support it, in order to deal with the problems and opportunities of an urban society, from ghetto to stock exchange?

New areas of research are unfolding which offer a range of stimulating possibilities. Just as an example, there is probably a need for specialists in law and sociology to be probing into the causes of urban crime and methods for its control. Perhaps new theories and procedures need to be developed for solving the problems of poverty and its associated evils. We could promote contests on model blocks or sections of city living, similar to the competition for productivity in five-acre corn plots or for model farm systems.

In an urban, affluent society, the range of vocational opportunities is certain to widen. The demand for museum curators and symphony conductors may exceed the demand for corn geneticists. That which once was thought to be peripheral and frivolous has become a necessity, since acquiring a satisfactory life in the age of the machine involves much more than gaining economic sufficiency. The research and service enterprises of the state universities must be prepared to give community centers assistance in everything from city planning to the organization of art exhibits. Hence, the role of the state university as consultant and problem-solver for the urban society, and as patron and stimulator of those professions and arts that contribute to the good life, now has a vastly increased importance.

This is a dramatic shift, a compelling shift, giving to our type of university its greatest challenge and its best opportunity.

# EDUCATION FOR WHAT?
## The Debate Over Goals*

### Kenneth W. Thompson

My text, theologically and politically one of the wisest ever written, comes from Ecclesiastes:

> To every thing there is a season, and a time
> to every purpose under the heaven.
> . . .
> A time to be born and a time to die; a time
> to plant and a time to pluck up . . .
>
> A time to kill and a time to heal; a time to
> break down and a time to build up.
>
> A time to cast away stones and a time to
> gather stones together . . .
>
> A time to rend and a time to sew; a time to
> keep silence and a time to speak.
>
> A time to love and a time to hate; a time of
> war and a time of peace.
> . . .
>
> God hath made everything beautiful in his
> time: also he hath set the world in [man's]
> heart; so that no man can find out the work
> that God maketh from the beginning to the
> end.
>
> (3: 1-8, 11)

God's beautiful creation . . . and man with "the world in his heart." God's plan for the universe but no man able to perceive it from "the beginning to the end." A parable in two dimensions of indescribable beauty, truth and

---

* This contribution was delivered as a commencement address at Wittenberg University, Springfield, Ohio, June 14, 1970.

goodness, *and* inescapable contradictions, contrast and change. This in briefest compass is the story of mankind, the framework for petty strivings and great debates, the answer to our perplexity about good and evil, and a poetic reminder that men in every age must live with joy and sorrow, love and hate, birth and death, war and peace.

Modern man, for the most part filled with illusions, has had little time for this story. He has preferred other viewpoints; three modern philosophies illustrate this. In the nineteenth and early twentieth centuries, men embraced the idea of progress; mankind was on an escalator with destiny infinity, with man becoming better and better every day in every way. Hitler shattered this illusion and so did Hiroshima. A second world view that prophesied a new man was Marxism. For Marx, the economic system and means of production had corrupted man. Socialize the system and man would be transformed. Stalinism destroyed this illusion. Finally, in our day, there are new trends of thought prophesying the coming of a new man, and failing his acceptance, civilization doomed by the apocalypse. For many of us this hope is real. For some, it can be a source of strength. For all, it can be a spur to change. However, if 2,000 years of experience offer us lessons, it is that idealism bereft of the social realism of Ecclesiastes leads to disillusionment. To avoid despair, I would urge, therefore, that we approach our great debates in the spirit not of unending progress, Marxism or the latest version of a new man—but of Ecclesiastes. If, however, we approach our problems believing that the easy harmonizing of differences is possible or that perfect happiness is just around the corner, or that raising income or changing the growth rate will transform mankind, or that everything that is new and untried is good and anything tested in experience is bad, we shall invite disaster.

You have a right to know my credo or that of anyone who comes before you so you can adjust and make allowances. It behoves us all to face the question early, not late: What is man? Our eternal problem in seeking an answer is the contradiction inherent in man. My answer—and perhaps yours—would be that man essentially, and not for a passing moment in history, is a blend of the human and the divine. He matches his every strength (unselfishness, righteousness, faith, kindness, concern for the oppressed) with its opposite (selfishness, self-righteousness, idolatry, cruelty, oppression of others). Anything categorical we say about man is immediately open to contradiction. Since we approach our problems and predicaments not as devils or gods but as men, we are each of us bound in this human condition. If we could bring to the day's problems and predicaments this awareness and guiding spirit, we might be more forgiving, understanding and wise. For whether we are young or old, liberal or conservative, American or non-American, we need each other. Yet we do not understand one another. We are dangerous to each other. We fail to realize that we need others and others need us. So we hurt one another. Hence every community today, from the family to the nation to the world community, is a broken community. I ask you to be mindful of this—young and old—as we review some of society's most recent debates.

## THREE GREAT DEBATES

Americans have been locked in three great debates since World War II. The first looked outward to the rest of the world and sought to resolve the extent and character of our international responsibilities. It culminated in the 1940's in the Truman Doctrine, the Marshall Plan, and the North Atlantic Treaty Organization. We resolved as a nation to defend the independence of the nations of Europe whether threatened by old-fashioned or new style aggression. In the 1960's, this consensus broke down in Southeast Asia and the great debate continues in the protracted controversy over United States policy in Indochina.

The second great debate was joined over the issue of equal opportunity for all our citizens and culminated in the most extensive body of social legislation ever passed to further opportunities for minorities long denied the full blessing of life, liberty and the pursuit of happiness. In recent months and years, we have moved into a period of re-examination and consolidation, the full outcome of which remains in doubt.

The third great debate, interlinked with the first two, has been joined on the educational front as all of us have struggled to answer the questions: Education for what? For whom? How and where? No college campus has been immune; few have been denied freedom to participate. It is a sign of the times and a test of the health of our society that to the present we have preserved free discussion and open debate in a period of profound differences and deep emotions. While all three debates continue, it is the educational debate that remains most unresolved, for we are finding our way in a new era, exploring new goals and purposes, and seeking to create or rebuild institutions that have served us well over past decades and even centuries.

We are entering the stage where action replaces rhetoric. There is a time to speak and a time to listen, a time to criticize and a time to build, a time for war and a time for peace, a time to confront and a time to construct. Perhaps for this reason, a body like the American Academy of Arts and Sciences has recently launched a study of the role and governance of universities. So have scores of enterprising colleges and universities across the land. Men old and young have been sensitized and alerted. The unfinished business of educational reform, as I see it, is to invent and apply the bits and pieces of an emerging educational philosophy to the manifold demands of a new day. We need architects as well as activists, programs no less than protests, and practical demonstrations even more than demands. The call for help ought to read: Wanted—more workable doctrines for education.

The story is told, and I have no doubt it could be multiplied, that John F.

Kennedy, following his election, called on tried and tested administrators like Dean Acheson and Robert Lovett to ask their help. He confessed to a feeling of helplessness as he moved from politicking to governing. He was frank to say that few if any of those who helped elect him were equipped to help him to govern the nation. Is it not possible that the need in education today is remarkably similar? Are we not entering a new phase? Do those of us who have brought about change know those to whom we would entrust the powers of governance? Where can we turn for guidance and help?

## THE PRESENT CRISIS

Let me turn to the present crisis in its broader context. Change is the first law of the universe. No one disputes this; we accept it in the abstract. The rub comes when change confronts us in our homes, in the universities and on the streets. Change as an idea is comprehensible; as fact and reality it shatters our picture of the world and the sense of identity we carry into the world. Change, if it comes too abruptly, destroys personal security, social stability and the effectiveness of institutions. We are in trouble, grave trouble, because for many change has left us bereft of workable values, acceptable policies and accustomed life styles. The old world that had become manageable has passed; the new world has not yet been born. And no one can be certain that the new is the better world. This is the underlying cause of the debates and controversies that rage all around us.

The beginning of wisdom, I believe, is to determine where we are if we are to judge and evaluate whither we are going. Ours is an age of crisis—a crisis so profound that it requires comparison with the deepest crises through which we have passed in earlier epochs: the American Revolution, the Civil War, and the social revolution of the 1930's. Conservatives, liberals and radicals will enter into dialogue when they accept this fact. It will not do merely to herald a brave new world nor bewail its manifold expressions. Early in this century, William James called for an unusually stubborn attempt to think clearly. Painful and taxing as this challenge is, it alone holds promise for bringing us through to a brighter, more hopeful day. Hundreds and thousands must make a commitment not to praise or condemn change but to understand it. I ask you to embark on this journey this day, however far you have already travelled.

What is the nature of the present crisis? What are its causes and conditions? What are the tides of history that sweep men along and how do we measure and assess them? Three forces and conditions deserve emphasis.

The first is the *crisis of ideas;* we face new problems that demand new imperatives. Our problems are interrelated. They arise from the sheer size of the nation. They overwhelm us and render us powerless. Nations are in fact vast, sprawling collections of lesser nations or groups, each striving to be heard.

26

We live each day with new and rising expectations. Men have rejected the wheel of fate. They know now it is not foreordained that some be educated and others ignorant; that some are rich and others poor; some housed and others destitute; some fed and others hungry, some free men and others slaves. The new imperatives arising from the claims of men everywhere to get the nation moving again are grounded in residual values. But somehow we have failed to reaffirm or reinterpret these values. They appear as dogmas of a dead past. They seem fixed, frozen and ossified. We forget that the Constitution has endured because it has been a living, unfolding constitution. So too, religion historically has flowered with progressive revelation. Yet today's failures are not simply explained. We have fewer political theorists and fewer philosophers, yet there is a more basic cause for the poverty of contemporary ideas. It is the link between leaders and crises. For it is response to crises that gives us new imperatives. It is the chemistry of the man and the event that elevates and raises up great truths from the context of experience. This was true of Lincoln and the Emancipation Proclamation, Jefferson and the Declaration of Independence, Roosevelt and the Four Freedoms.

Second, *the context and tempo of change,* or the shape of today's crises. There are more people and less reflection; we struggle to take our bearings in the midst of a surfeit of problems and responses. We set time limits to the resolution of crises and demands, many of them non-negotiable. Compare this to an earlier, less hurried time; for example, Secretary of State Jefferson, who complained he had not heard from his envoy to Madrid for over a year and warned if this continued in the new year he would take action. Today we have cables and instantaneous communications, yet it required 534 meetings of numerous diplomats to bring about the Austrian Peace Treaty, and we are in the second year of the Vietnam negotiations in Paris. Thousands of citizens devote millions of man-hours of dedicated service every day of every year in preparing school budgets, negotiating teachers' salaries, countless other tasks seeking the common good. But this is not the stuff that headlines are made of.

Third, *the crisis of purposes and policies* or the confusion of ends and means. This is a great historic problem. Values and vitalities are not the same. Nor are thinkers and actors. We confuse utopias and programs. We cannot legislate the kingdom of heaven, yet as problems are packaged to sell, solutions have to have entertainment appeal. Drama and violence prevail; time and space are narrowed, if not obliterated. There is simultaneity of demand and response. No one can deny the genuine urgency of our problems, but are not present crises heightened by modes of presentation? We frame as two polar opposites the manifestation of outspoken moral courage and hard, quiet work on problems. But most international issues on which headway has been made have yielded as a result of "quiet diplomacy." And this is equally true of the domestic issues that divide us.

May I set forth an "unpopular thought"? Goals and values exist in one world; realizing them, in another. Skill and concentration in both worlds are essential. We suffer from a poverty of both. We need philosophers and doers. They can't be divorced from one another, but neither should they be confused. Nations suffer shipwreck if ends and means are too simply equated. The requirements differ: *thought* on goals calls for clarity, imagination, vision, idealism and prophecy; *implementing* or legislating them requires steadiness, patience and working together. Intolerance and alienation follow if we ask one to do the work of the other. Few men can double in brass; most live and realize themselves best in one or the other world. It is wrong to condemn the thinker for goals that remain unrealized or the doer for his compromises and the practical ideals he carves out of principles and ideals, which, though pale reflections of thought, are capable of realization.

For me, there are lessons closer to home, more intimately bound up with my workaday world.

The fundamental purpose stated in the Charter of the Rockefeller Foundation is "to serve the well-being of mankind." We have flown this same banner for over six decades; it is our "great generality" and organizing principle, and it prompts trustees and officers to dream impossible dreams, reach out for distant goals, experiment and take risks. The founders knew what they meant in terms of ultimate purposes. Their wise mandate has been a blessing and benefit for every age, but gave ready-made solutions or program statements for none. The breadth and sweep of the mandate lent dignity and nobility to the effort. It freed each new board member and officer group from the "dead hand" of the past. Because the ultimate concern was clear from the start, we have enjoyed a magnificent flexibility of programs and means.

The task of those who shape foundation programs is to give direction and content to a noble purpose. This requires continuous inquiry, review and, yes, strenuous debate. Controversies are joined, not over good and evil, but over balancing and weighing alternative goods. Charity (gifts to churches and hospitals) which was good at the birth of the foundation was not bad when public health interests took priority. Medical education was no less vital when the urgencies of feeding hungry people led to the establishment in 1943 of the agricultural program. Help to scientific research is necessary today; yet new approaches to improving the quality of life have supplanted the earlier emphasis on the life sciences.

The point is that once men enter into programming and policy making, they leave the realm of abstract truth and enter the far more ambiguous and uncertain realm of sorting out competing values and "goods." They face the task of viewing what is good in the context of time and place. They must examine what is both good and realizable, and what is good but yet beyond reach. Here they depart the calm and the detachment of the philosopher's library (or scientist's laboratory). Their preferences and choices are always a mixture of reason and emotion, virtue and the earth. Pride, profession and prejudice enter in; great decisions and blueprints partake both of the human and the divine.

*The Star and the Rudder.* Yet anything substantial and lasting in philanthropy, as in life, needs both a star and a rudder. There must be a vision, a North Star. We lost momentarily our awareness of this when we talked about "the end of ideology." There is no society which survives free of dreams and myths, a message the young seem to be telling us today. Moreover, the dreams must be credible to some sort of working majority and not totally offensive to existing minorities. Above all, those who are minorities today must believe in the "myth" of becoming a majority tomorrow, and if this seems impossible, at least of seeing the majority espouse their dreams and visions (Norman Thomas). One reason we never had a proletariat or bourgeoisie in the European sense was because no one felt permanently locked in or fixed in status, position or wealth. Today the problem for some is their feeling of frustration about personal worth and continued movement (where do workers go who are economically as prosperous as the bourgeoisie and culturally no more deprived, yet whose monuments in wood, glass and brick are despoiled and who feel continuous pressures to hold on to what seems only precariously theirs). They fear change because no one has given them credible visions of the better life that change might bring. In part, this is because today's social needs concern aggregates and groups more than individuals, while at the same time our ideals are increasingly individualistic. In part, it is because we are weakest in the 1970's in constructing a utopia of the common good. We (and for many of us this is autobiographical) have studied self-interest so frantically that we have neglected the general welfare, and are passing through an era when in the pursuit of what is good for the self all of us may betray our devotion to the broader good.

The rudder we need is skill in negotiating rough waters and rocky shores. Day-to-day life is full of contradictions and conflicts. Sometimes to preserve the sanctity of a principle we have to vote against it (we can applaud and support the purposes of a reform movement privately and publicly, but feel present measures called for are impractical and unworkable—*e.g.,* the General Motors campaign). We can espouse a group's aims but question temporarily their methods. We are forced to measure social gains against the cost of social disintegration. The only permanent minority in society consists of leaders who, flying the flag of idealists, try to steer a realistic course, building new coalitions and consensuses for changing ideals, compromising where necessary, clarifying and legislating where possible, always "keeping their cool."

This is the context in which we must view today's criticism, whether on the Right or on the Left. Those who condemn their leaders for compromising are right. Those who say we are short-sighted and sometimes wrong-headed are also right. When we declare that leaders have failed, we are right. Those who predict the apocalypse may be proven right (one would hope only that they would not gather to celebrate the confirming of their prophecy like the group of German social scientists who, meeting in Frankfurt in 1938, congratulated one another that they had foreseen the rise of Hitler).

Yet beyond all human success and failure there is a tragic element in life and politics. With all the criticisms from young and old, Right and Left, we may not see this profoundly enough. The elements of disharmony, whether in personal or national life, seem always to outweigh those of harmony. We fail more often than we succeed. We are all guilty of not doing enough or thinking imaginatively enough. We are selfish and myopic. We gain security at the expense of the insecurity of others. We abuse the gains we make as again and again, in life and history, the exploited become the exploiters and the victims the new tyrants. And those of you who perceive our failures all too vividly will fail in your turn. If anything is foreordained, it is this. Yet whenever there is hope, there is an endless struggle to create new equilibria on which to base social advancement. This is the grubby side of imagination. There is no higher task for living leaders, young or old, whatever the odds of failure, than to undertake this noble task. It is the practical side of idealism so often ignored by those who stand on the sidelines and cheer or condemn.

### EDUCATION FOR WHAT?

A great philosopher in another age proclaimed that survival was a race between education and destruction. Yet to restate this leaves unanswered the question, "education for what"? The Germans under Hitler were a highly cultured people, yet wreaked destruction on the world; our own consciences are uneasy after Hiroshima and Nagasaki. More recently, the nation's battlefields have been our centers of learning. In light of this fact, the philosopher's distinction between education and destruction calls for another look.

In part the issue turns on the meaning and purposes of education. From the standpoint of a democracy, we have linked education to the open society and to open minds on whom it depends. The educated man, we say, is someone not locked in by passions. He is sensitive to alternatives and aware of consequences. He is an agent of change and an instrument of progress. "We have to live by what truth we can get today and be ready tomorrow to call it falsehood." Men need to have their eyes on the stars, for the problems are stratospheric. But their feet must be on the ground. "We must walk in the right direction, but we must walk step by step." This notion of education for responsibility presupposes both process and purpose, for openness is based on some form of commitment, whether to science, progress, or truth. We can afford to be open because there are moorings and benchmarks. With William James, we can say: "It is not thinking with its primitive ingenuity of childhood that is most difficult but to think with tradition, with all its acquired force..."

This answer to the timeless question "Education for what" has been "sufficient to the day." It has accorded more or less with the trends of the time and the spirit of the people. Now we find ourselves in a world that is unmistakably new. It is a world rent by social and biological revolutions, sweeping alternations in interpersonal relations and national moods. Not only is there a population explosion, but more young people, more poor people, more impatient people, more non-white people, more new nations. We have less time to ponder and less willingness to forgive or forget or to practice restraint. Life styles for many have visibly changed and for many more there are far-reaching questionings and doubts about who we are and where we are going. This growing movement presents us with questions that outnumber answers. We cannot be clear which aspects are transient and which will persist. Having witnessed the demise of the nineteenth-century idea of unending progress, we may be misled if we assume that world forces today are driving mankind, though not without risk, toward a higher moral and political plane. Yet men live by faith.

I would answer the question, "education for what" in four necessarily over-simple propositions: first, education while fostering individualism and equal opportunity—cornerstones in the national creed—must likewise help give us a sense of identity of who we are as a people and as part of mankind. Circumstances sometimes serve to make us more virtuous than we are or have been; they can also make us more evil. When we were less knit together by technology and communications, we could afford many nations in one and different levels of opportunity and citizenship. Today a house divided cannot stand. But this must be done in the context of equality. We have to recognize belatedly Woodrow Wilson's warning: "A nation is as great and only as great, as her rank and file." Achieving equal opportunity is almost always socially disrupting. It feeds on its inner dynamics and momentum. We jostle one another as we seek to be equal. The stridency of voices across the land call to mind Caliban in *The Tempest:* "We taught them to speak but what is the profit of it if they curse us." If the pain and offense is too great, it may arise from the poverty and narrowness of our views for "One is not rich but poor, when one can always seem so right" (Marianne Moore). This surely touches both those who provoke and those who are provoked. The stages of growth of every society include periods of deep contradictions and schisms. Every action and counter-action must be viewed in this light. The end of the story in periods like ours is seldom in the event. In times like these "the deepest feel-

31

ing shows itself in silence, not in silence but restraint." Miss Moore's wise words may appear as counsels of perfection. If we could follow them, though, we might find that whatever our differences, there were deep-running tides of unity which strident debate had temporarily obscured.

Secondly, I would implore you that in education we avoid the apocalyptic view. Martin Luther's great phrase, quaint as it may sound, still has relevance: "Even if I were told that the world was going to pieces tomorrow, I would still plant my apple tree today and pay my debts." For modern man, it may be asking too much to cling to this faith. In personal and national life, we are driven over the precipice of tolerance, so continuous and all-consuming are the crises we face. As with the man who is grievously ill, we cannot always accept the "learn to live with . . ." admonition. Instead of bearing our burdens, we are told there are only two choices: either the apocalypse or the new man, and with him a new world. Yet as late as the present, the new man does not walk among us nor are there discernible, comprehensive or total solutions in sight. Those who question what is, offer mini-solutions to our great national problems. For the despair and immorality of the American family, the best we are given is the commune, which no one sees as a solution for the nation nor a means of much hope or joy. If those who see themselves as new men are to guide society, they must do better than this. But failing that, they would do well to practice restraint in announcing the apocalypse.

Third, education must help us return to the market place and the conference table. It must help fashion capacities for public and private decision making. The trouble with silent majorities and marching minorities is that while they are silent and marching, someone else makes the great decisions. Pericles warned of this: "Each fancies that no harm will come of his neglect, and by the same notion being entertained by all separately the common cause imperceptibly declines." We need to add that it is not participation as some kind of aimless and noisy activity we seek. Nor is it self-righteous factionalism seeking only to divide and destroy. It is participation at the point of leverage on policy. The guideline is still to act responsibly. With Bonhoeffer we need to say: "It is easier to act on abstract principle than from concrete responsibility." And to be concrete we must immerse ourselves not in problems in general, attacked fitfully and dropped, but in matters, however limited, where we have earned the right to be heard.

Finally, the greatest need of all, whatever one's temper, is for precise and definable targets following patiently discovered and determined routes. We need to adapt and build social institutions, cope with population, grow more food, improve the environment, foster world co-operation on specifics, limit and circumscribe conflict, improve television, and on and on. None of these steps may bring a new world, but they may contribute. And *Gulliver's Travels,* which often comes at our problems more directly than current writings, has observed: "And he gave it as his opinion that whoever made two ears of corn, or two blades of grass to grow upon a spot of ground where only one grew before would deserve better of mankind and do more essential service to his country than the whole race of politicians put together."

You will say I have tried to tie the Gordian knot, to link processes of continuity and change. And I plead guilty. But so did Alfred North Whitehead who wrote: "It is the first step of wisdom to recognize that the major advances in civilization are processes which all but wreck . . . society. . . . The art of free society consists, first, in the maintenance of the symbolic code; and, secondly, in fearlessness of revision. . . . Those societies which cannot combine reverence to their symbols with freedom of revision, must ultimately decay. . . ."

# THE UNIVERSITIES AND
# PUBLIC POLICY
## Challenges and Limits

### Philip E. Mosely

Under the impact of the industrial age the nature and the extent of the involvement of university scholars and thereby, inescapably, of universities as major centers of liberal education, of professional training and of research, in the investigation of problems, both national and international, have changed greatly with each new generation. And each generation must, inevitably, re-examine and redefine the nature and the limits of that involvement, particularly with respect to those issues that in the end are subject to being decided, or at least shaped, by public authorities, by public funds and ultimately by public opinion.

The purposes and the needs of education and research are themselves a subject of public policy. Their functions are defined and financed either directly, through decisions made by public authorities, or indirectly, through decisions made by private donors, both individual and corporate, or by foundations for the basic purpose of serving the public interest as the donors interpret it. Both as recipients of support by society and as instruments supported by society for developing systematic knowledge and new research on problems of public policy, our universities, as centers of education and research, are intimately involved with the definition of the public interest and with decisions made in the name of public policy, by whomever it may be defined. The wide dispersal of these functions of definition and decision is a special, almost a unique, feature of American life in comparison with the highly concentrated systems that regulate these matters in many other countries.

In the present period of discontent with many of our situations, unrest and confrontation, and rethinking of national purposes, the evolving relationship between universities and public policy, which has been shaped piecemeal over several generations, is again being challenged, this time from several different viewpoints. A good many scholars and substantial numbers of students express a sincere concern over, and sometimes a deep hostility to, the participation of some university scholars in the investigation of problems of public policy. Vocal groups assert that the universities have become handmaidens and even prisoners of special interests. Sometimes these critics seem to regard any involvement of universities with public policy as "unclean." In effect they urge scholars to retreat from the problems of the "real world" that lies just beyond the campus gates and to build a new ivory tower of "pure" learning remote from the practical concerns of the society, the nation, or the outer world.

Other critics, on the contrary, are deeply offended by the persistence of many problems—violence in national and international life, poverty, unequal opportunity, racial discrimination. They then go on to place responsibility for these continuing problems on scholars and universities, rather than on the slow pace of social and political change, or on the failure of active and concerned groups to mobilize public opinion in support of new solutions. They seem thereby to attribute to scholars and universities an omnipotence that they certainly do not possess. Extreme representatives of this view sometimes maintain that all work of teaching and learning is "irrelevant," serves to justify and perpetuate ingrained social injustices, and should be suspended while the universities devote their resources to solving the problems of the ghettoes, bad housing, pollution, discrimination, the arms race, wars, inequalities among nations and so forth. In contrast to the first body of critics, this second tendency demands that the universities must be completely and solely engaged in direct social and political action, rather than in their traditional functions of helping each new generation become better educated and, hopefully, more effective citizens and in trying to build a systematic body of knowledge about urgent problems.

## THE LIBERAL ARTS TRADITION

To place in perspective this unrest and uncertainty about the relation between universities and public policy it may be helpful to call to mind the two main traditions which, in uneasy co-existence and often in competition, have shaped the purposes of American universities. One of these is the tradition of liberal education, derived from Athens through the Renaissance, based on the idea of developing "the whole man"—intellectually, aesthetically, spiritually, physically —to make of him an exemplar of "virtue," in the classical sense of a person whose abilities are highly developed, harmonious and ready to be put to the service of society.

The beneficiaries of the liberal tradition may, as in the Athenian and English experience, take an active and effective role in public life, or they may not. In any case, on the basis of this tradition the British did quite well, in the nineteenth century and part way into the twentieth, in preparing a small elite to manage the affairs of a rather large part of the world. A "First" in Classics, preferably combined with a "Blue" in rowing, gave preferential access to the Indian Civil Service and to other administrative and intellectual elites. A man of vigorous mind and body and of mature character could, it was assumed, master the specific bodies of knowledge he would require for the execution and, with longer experience, the making of policy for a vast nation or continent. "Area studies" of India played no part in his preparation for public and administrative service.

Viewed in retrospect, classical studies did offer great intellectual advantages. The Classics led able students into a profound understanding of a complete civilization. It opened to full appreciation the political, social and legal institutions of the ancient world; it developed an appreciation of the interrelations of all its aspects—its philosophies and religions, its arts and literatures and its rise and decay. In a basic sense the Classics were and are a variety of "area studies," turned to a past and seminal civilization, one that has vastly enriched and shaped the later history of the Western world. The "area studies" that have enriched many university curricula since World War II constitute, from this vantage-point, an effort to develop a similarly systematic and comprehensive understanding of major world regions and cultures and to make the fruits of this understanding available to educated people in our own society and, increasingly, in other societies. Since we must all live in a small world, in which no area is any longer remote or inconsequential, it is all the more urgent for all peoples to know their "world neighbors."

A liberal education is therefore central to our concept of a healthy and self-directing society, and I believe that its role is going to be even stronger and certainly more indispensable in coming decades. One factor pointing in this direction is the widely held assumption that the Western world is on the verge of becoming the first generally affluent and post-industrial society mankind has known. One consequence of this far-reaching "sea-change" is that vast numbers of people will spend less and less time in working, in producing goods and services, and more and more time in educating themselves to perform the complex services of managing the affairs of society and in innovating, that is, in exercising powers of imagination and foresight. In addition, as larger and larger numbers of people come to participate in cultural, social and political activities, they will have to spend more and more time in equipping themselves to do so. Finally, with the extension of the average span of life and the shortening of the period of intensive labor, people will need to find challenging and satisfying uses for the time thus liberated from the mere struggle to gain a livelihood. This reshaping of demands on the individual may lead to apathy, drugs and greed for sensation, or it may lead to a heightened participation in active arts and sports rather than to "spectator" roles, to devoting years of mature vigor to improving life at home and abroad, and to more active participation in public life at many levels. To achieve these heightened possibilities, people will need to engage in continuing self-education of a liberal type throughout much of their lives.

A parallel trend is visible today in the many specialized professions on which the functioning of a complex society depends. In many professions people have discovered that the purpose of education at the liberal arts and professional levels is not to acquire a body of knowledge that can be relied upon for the next 40 years, but to learn how to learn throughout a lifetime. More and more frequently, engineers say they must "re-tool" their skills every 10 years or become obsolete. For physicists and biologists, the span may be only five years. Business executives are more and more "sent back to school" at regular intervals, especially as they must learn at each higher level to relate specific business decisions to the changing political, social, cultural and international environment. If a person relies today upon professional knowledge acquired 20 years ago, he is less and less likely to operate effectively; if he relies today upon a knowledge of his society and of the world that he gained 20 or 40 years ago, he is in danger of forming simplistic opinions and making unrealistic or inappropriate decisions.

These examples make it clear that universities have a rapidly expanding responsibility, not only for educating each current generation of young people, but also for promoting and guiding a lifelong effort of continuing self-education. An understanding of this expanding role of universities will help us understand why universities have a special and growing responsibility for the study of public policy, as a part of their responsibility, not only for transmitting accumulated knowledge, but for developing new knowledge appropriate to new needs. Since rapid change is now the norm and not the exception, and since change is more and more shaped by public policy, the question is, not whether it will occur, but whether it will help mankind fulfill its unlimited potentialities.

### THE UTILITARIAN TRADITION

We can now turn, more briefly, from the role of liberal education to the other great mainstay of American education, the utilitarian tradition. Of course, ever since the founding of the medieval universities under the aegis of the Church, two professions—theology and law—flourished in the seed-bed of the liberal arts, and to them medicine was added at an early stage. In the nineteenth century, teaching, dentistry, architecture, engineering, the physical sciences, agriculture, history and the social sciences ceased to be solely the domain of "cultivated amateurs" and became central parts of the university, in both purpose and structure. In the twentieth century business administration, journalism, social work, library science and international affairs have been added to this roster of university-transmitted professions. In the history of American education, the Morrill Act of 1863 was a turning-point in directing specific support to the needs of agriculture and "the mechanical arts."

The "multiversity" of today is often a federation of professional schools or faculties, each with its own objectives and its own constituency. For a time, it seemed as if the central purpose of a liberal education was being eroded and forgotten in the pressure to provide a wide range of skills and to professionalize both training and standards. In part it was the demand, from the second decade of this century on, for a higher level of training in the professions that led to a new emphasis upon a liberal arts education and to many experiments in adapting it to serve its twin purposes, not always compatible, of preparing enlightened men and also preparing them for more demanding levels of professional performance and of research.

The utilitarian tradition has deep roots in American life. A continent had to be developed, and new technologies in every field had to be developed and applied. The drive for broadened social mobility meant that higher education had to equip more and more people to achieve their own potentials for useful and profitable roles in a rapidly changing society. Although universities devoted much attention to professional needs for the material development of the continent, through education in agriculture and engineering, and in law—the profession that has traditionally conducted a wide range of relations within a polity—they were slow to become aware of the broader and less visible needs for training in public policy. And within that broad field they were even slower in mobilizing resources for the study of world affairs, perhaps because there was and still is no natural or well-defined "constituency" that demands and supports the study of public policy in its international aspects.

THE RESEARCH FUNCTION

Finally, a third function which society delegates in part, though not exclusively, to universities is the development of new bodies of knowledge through research. Here again, research on foreign affairs and foreign areas has been a late starter. The great needs for and the potential benefits of new knowledge were clear from the beginning in agriculture. They spread rapidly in the field of technology, with the creation of great institutes, and after the Flexner Report of 1910, research rapidly won a central place in medicine. The balance between transmitting accumulated knowledge and the creation of new knowledge through research has shifted dramatically during this century, until research is now described as America's biggest and fastest-growing "industry" and a source of emulation and envy for other advanced societies. Today no university is regarded as strong and progressive unless it has developed powerful drives toward the advancement of research, to a point where many students, faculty and administrators raise vehement questions as to the proper division and allocation of roles between general education, professional education and research. Again, while the universities are playing a modest and laggard role in research on public policy, compared with research in many other fields, many people are questioning today the nature, purpose and justification of university research on public policy, including international affairs.

Perhaps the root of this present unrest lies in a rather widespread failure to distinguish between the instrumental and the teleological functions of research. "Instrumental research" is obviously a "good thing." It is obviously a "good thing" to build more durable and safer highways, to produce six grains of rice instead of one, to discover penicillin, or to extract petroleum more efficiently. But the more basic questions are teleological and relate to conflicting purposes and values of society as a whole. What highway capacity is needed in relation to other land uses? How do factors of highway construction and the psychology of drivers interact to promote greater or less safety? How can increased rice production be related to the problems of bringing about a more satisfactory relation between food supply and population? Will improved methods of petroleum extraction increase or diminish the risks of pollution?

Research on public policy is bound to be more controversial than most types of technological research. In research on matters of public interest it is much more difficult to separate the instrumental from the teleological aspects; conflicts among differing and competing values are easily perceived and strongly felt; interests, both material and psychological, are felt directly and expressed vigorously; and every concerned person, whether a leader or a man-in-the-street, feels entitled and is entitled to have a view of that interest and to defend it. The issues are too important for the power of decision to be delegated to experts. The study of public policy, whether national or international, is clearly less well defined than many older and highly respected fields of research, and it is less understood and more vulnerable to criticisms, whether justified or not, by powerful leaders or by student demonstrators.

## RESEARCH IN PUBLIC POLICY

Despite or because of the present turbulence, the effort to define the range, limits and quality controls of public policy research, including the study of world affairs, will go forward, sometimes through exciting achievements, sometimes through egregious failures, always through trial-and-error, following the pattern set by older, more established fields of research. For this, the guarantee lies in the vast scope and crucial importance of the problems themselves, including the problem of survival in an age of nuclear power and rapid population growth. The problems themselves evoke the response, sooner or later. What is more uncertain is whether we are equipped to identify the real problems quickly and accurately enough and to state the terms of the problem correctly; about our possession of that ability there is great uncertainty.

It is traditional, and probably inevitable, that research in public policy should respond to felt and already urgent needs. For example, the first systematic efforts to examine the causes of poverty within an increasingly productive economy were made in England, in the 1850's and again in the 1890's. In the early decades of this century, the spoliation of the environment led to research as well as to legislation. By the 1920's more and more people, including some scholars, were aware that the increasing complexities of modern societies were creating "big government" with a need for a wide variety of experts and with facilities for systematic research; thus the science of public administration took form in the 1920's and 1930's. The devastating impact of the Great Depression led to intensive and institutionalized efforts to examine the nature and causes of fluctuations in the economy and the structure of national income, to input-output studies and econometrics. A massive refocussing of research talents and research resources is presently being brought to bear on problems of the natural and social environment, especially on the impact of public policy.

By comparison with most other fields of public policy, the study of international relations has lagged far behind the needs. Despite the brilliant individual work of talented historians, jurists, economists and other scholars in several decades prior to 1941, it must be said that the focusing of remotely equivalent bodies of talent and resources upon problems of world affairs dates basically from World War II and its aftermath of conflicts and forebodings of even greater conflicts. If the study of public policy has traditionally lagged behind the objective needs of the society, that is even more true of research on foreign policy and on major foreign areas except Western Europe. And now, after a short spurt in little more than a single generation, the inability of research to answer all questions and to provide universally approved "solutions" is subjecting the field of international studies to new attacks from all sides and to a severe and conceivably disastrous curtailment of support from public and private sources.

This tendency is both illogical and paradoxical. The problems of world affairs are only now being defined in more comprehensive and more realistic terms, and the difficulties of providing systematic knowledge, checked against realities, are now perceived more clearly. Second, the provision of "solutions," if any, depends on political leaders, on interested groups of all kinds, and on a common understanding among many nations. Research is not witchcraft; it can provide more and more systematic knowledge, but it cannot provide instantaneous solutions for deepset problems. Adequate research can provide better but always incomplete information and analyses, but it contributes only a small though not negligible element to the making of decisions. It can hope to define the range of choices; it does not make those choices.

There is, in the third place, a potential factor of finality that is present in some decisions about international policies, to a far more serious degree than in domestic affairs. If tax relief on new industrial investment is set too high or too low, the results may be serious in some lines of production and for some producers. However, there is time to review previous decisions or to make new ones. If, however, a failure to interpret correctly the fears or the intentions of an adversary should lead any nuclear-armed power to use this arsenal of weapons, there would be large elements of "finality" in the consequences, so much so that most people are unwilling even to think about the kind of a world in which the survivors would have to grope their way.

### RESEARCH IN FOREIGN POLICY AND FOREIGN AREAS

Thus the level of risks is higher in international and strategic policy than in domestic policy. There is a lower level of knowledge about the problems and about the many other peoples involved in problems of foreign policy. And there is an alarming degree of finality in some of the decisions that have to be made from time to time.

The level of expert knowledge is often dangerously low. At one time in the early 1950's the United States had three experts on Indonesia, which had just emerged to independence. Within a few days one was reported killed in ambush on a jungle road, and one was killed by a car on the streets of New Haven. In 1954, a year in which far-reaching commitments were being made by the U.S. government with respect to the future of Vietnam, Laos and Cambodia, there was, so far as I can ascertain, not a single American who knew Vietnamese, Laotian, or Cambodian culture at first hand. It would seem, offhand, that American foreign policy research was critically absent in the early years of the American role in Vietnam, and that it is, to say the least, illogical or premature to place on nonexistent research scholars the responsibility for decisions made at that time by political and military leaders who were perforce judging the situation by analogy to quite different situations in countries far removed from Indochina.

Finally, we should recognize that foreign policy decisions—or indecision— by definition involve foreign peoples and cultures, and that we perhaps need more and not less knowledge about them—about their values and institutions and their past and probable behavior—than we do about our people at home. Otherwise, the all-too-prevalent ethnocentric fallacy too often leads political leaders and public opinion to attribute to others the values, hopes and potential reactions that we assign, often mistakenly, to our fellow countrymen. And then we may use force, too much and too long, to force events to conform to our own expectations.

It has been painful for Americans to discover, in dealing with some of the many problems in the outside world, that they are not omniscient. While it is true that no decision maker, and no individual, knows all that he needs to know in order to make decisions, and that all decisions are therefore based on relative degrees of ignorance, still, common sense suggests that on balance it is important to raise the level of carefully scrutinized information and projective analysis and to reduce the degree of reliance on ethnocentric complacency, hunches and wishful thinking. Since Americans are often confident of their own good intentions, as defined in terms of their own values and traditions, they need to be on their guard more systematically against a tendency to self-righteousness. A decent respect for the values and traditions, and even for the inexplicable psychological quirks, of other peoples is helpful in avoiding that pitfall, which, if fallen into too often, may, as a response to disillusionment, bring on reactions of self-denigration and feelings of impotence.

We need to know the limits as well as the range of American power. Some of those limits are set by the American character, for there are means of action available to which we would not resort except in a state of panic or despair. That is why we as a people cannot conceive of nuclear warfare even though both major nuclear powers base their ultimate assumptions about policy on the conviction that either one or both of them would, under certain circumstances, resort to it. There are other means of influence, such as economic, cultural and educational aid, that we use halfheartedly because influential policy makers and taxpayers cannot "see" immediate and "hard" results.

Other limits to American power are set by the traditions and views, the hopes and fears, of other peoples. Here is it doubly important for decision makers, and for informed public opinion, which grants options or withholds them from the policy makers, to have available more abundant and more systematic information and analyses, and this resource depends to a considerable extent on the availability of research and its products. The availability of research knowledge depends on the long-range accumulation of intellectual and research resources, and this, in turn, rests primarily on the ability of universities to nurture these resources and to foster their application.

Finally, in all study of public policy, both domestic and international, there is the problem of change. It is not easy or simple to explain in retrospect why certain events took place. It is a far more chancy occupation, and one highly vulnerable to criticism, to attempt to analyze and present a range of possible alternatives to current policies. On the other hand, decision makers are constantly making judgments, often anguishing judgments, about the future course of events and about the ways in which American action or inaction is likely to influence them. People who bear these great burdens deserve whatever assistance they can secure from scholars who have devoted many years to analyzing the conditions and policies of other nations. And for this, more and better research is needed, not less.

## UNIVERSITIES AND INTERNATIONAL STUDIES

How do universities attempt to cope with the responsibilities they have so recently shouldered in the field of international studies? Some of their functions are not very much in dispute, for example, the teaching of international relations and area studies. The universities and colleges have responded vigorously, especially since World War II, to the rapid increase in demand for knowledge about the outside world. Courses in international relations or world politics were a great rarity in 1940; today they attract a large constituency within the rapidly growing discipline of political science. Equally striking has been the proliferation of sub-specialties, such as the study of international organizations (the study of international law antedates that of international politics by several centuries), international social forces, strategic thinking, the making of foreign policy, regional integration and so forth.

Some people believe that teaching should emphasize the expression and advocacy of certain lofty goals, such as world order, or an atom-free international society, or a conflictless relationship among all nations; the expounding of strongly felt hortatory purposes is both necessary and inevitable, just as the study of law assumes that human conflicts can be managed, for the benefit of all, by the constant adjustment of interests and rules to the overriding need of the polity for both order and justice. On the other hand, more progress has been made over the past three decades in the empirical examination of events and problems. As a result of very great efforts, scholars in the field of international relations and area studies have broadened and deepened the available fund of systematic information. Today teachers and students begin their labors from a far more solid and comprehensive base than was true 20 or even 10 years ago.

One factor in this rapid if uneven advancement of knowledge has been the effort of many scholars to come to grips with problems as they arise and must be dealt with in the "real world," the world of human affairs, the world of incomplete knowledge, risks and contingency judgments. Experience in public policy has greatly stimulated research on foreign policy and has helped many scholars define the forces at work and stretch their imaginations to encompass wider and more realistic definitions of alternatives and their potential consequences. The marriage of research with policy experience has enriched and matured the entire field of international affairs; a divorce between scholarship and public policy, which some critics are demanding today, would impoverish both teaching and the resources needed by an informed citizenry.

A second function of universities in the field of international and area studies is to equip Americans and others for various types of service. The public agencies of the United States have enrolled growing numbers of young Americans for a wide range of service in international affairs, both at home and abroad. Other governments, recognizing their own needs in this field, have sent substantial numbers of present and prospective foreign affairs officers and analysts for advanced training in American centers and have also, to a limited extent, begun establishing similar training centers of their own. International organizations of many types, in addition, provide limited but interesting opportunities. Finally, some two million Americans, apart from the armed services, are working abroad in a wide range of business, banking, engineering, legal, cultural and educational activities. For most of them, specialized professional training and experiences have been the prime qualifications, but a small minority have received their training in programs of international and area studies. For a young engineer, businessman or lawyer, for example, to go into a Latin American country without some understanding of the role of trade unions or the military, or of ideologies and political leadership patterns, is to be exposed to making all manner of ethnocentric mistakes in judgment and action.

Specific training for careers in international and area studies is almost completely a function of a few major institutions; even for them it has been made possible financially only through large-scale support, first, by the major foundations and, more recently, by public funds. Unfortunately, and most shortsightedly, both these channels of support have been dwindling rapidly just at a time when the value of trained people and the need for systematic research have come to be recognized more fully than in the initial stages of development.

A third function of universities has been to work toward the emergence of an international scholarly community in the field of international studies. Area studies, it is true, had developed earlier in Europe than in the United States, but their strengths were primarily in history and the humanities. To these disciplines postwar area studies in the United States have added several fields of contemporary analysis, such as political science, international relations, economics, sociology and so forth. Similarly, American scholars have recently led the way in the development of international policy studies. This "leap forward" has aroused the emulation of a fair number of scholars and educators in other countries and has stimulated a modest but growing interchange of training and experience in the field of policy studies.

In the medium run it is essential to promote the international spread and acceptance of international and area studies, so that each nation or each region can rely on its own contingents of experts to help it analyze its own needs and potential contributions to both understanding and action in an increasingly interdependent world community. Many American universities, supported by foundation and government grants, have been making valuable contributions to the emergence of an international scholarly community of world affairs studies. Yet support for this effort, barely begun in the past 20 years, has declined markedly in the past two or three years.

## THE UNIVERSITIES AND POLICY RESEARCH

No one would maintain that university scholars should refrain from the study of past policy; such a self-limitation would reduce the science or art of history to a variety of antiquarianism. The issue, then, is whether scholars should investigate current and prospective problems of public policy. Since past, present and future constitute a seamless web, scholars generally begin their attempts to probe evolving problems by examining relevant past and present experience; in fact, one of the main obstacles to an imaginative investigation of political futures is the natural tendency to project continuity rather than change. The process of attempting to define the possible future is going on constantly, and political leaders and commentators make it their principal preoccupation.

It is difficult to see why scholars, who share the same concern for the future and who may possess valuable bodies of knowledge and experience, should refrain from devoting some of their energies to the same crucial purpose. Of course, in dealing with future problems, scholars enter the competitive marketplace of policy and controversy and can claim no special exemption from the risks of its rough-and-tumble. They become subject to the same hazards of backward-looking, blind spots and wishful thinking as anyone else. Like the analyses and predictions of politicians and commentators, the scholar's projections of problems and recommendations of policy should be subjected to rigorous and periodic review, as a means to promote more systematic and objective processes of analysis in the future.

### UNIVERSITIES AND CLASSIFIED RESEARCH

More widespread doubt and controversy arises over the issue of whether classified research on public policy has any place in universities. In principle, it is undesirable for universities to engage in classified research in the social and policy sciences. It is undesirable for some university scholars to have available bodies of data that are denied to their colleagues and students. It is undesirable for the results of their analyses to be withheld from the scholarly community and the broader public. However, the size and the impact of the issue of secrecy have sometimes been exaggerated. To appraise this problem realistically, it may be helpful to examine briefly the reasons for such secrecy and also its consequences.

Many types of research make use of materials that remain closed to outside scrutiny. This applies, for example, to investigations based on questionnaires and interviews. The Bureau of the Census asks a broad sample of the citizenry to provide a wide range of data and promises to assure the confidential character of the individual responses. Investigations of a wide range of social issues are similarly safeguarded against disclosure of information relating to individuals. In the field of social psychology, specific bodies of data are used mainly for statistical purposes; it is the custom, when any one person's replies to questions are presented as a case study, to avoid actual identification of the source of the data. Similarly, when business executives respond to monthly and quarterly pollings about their expectations for the level of activity of their firms or their intentions with respect to capital investment, they know that these data will be treated as confidential. When a historian or political scientist elicits concrete information or background interpretations from an active politician or diplomat, he can attribute these data to the sources only with their permission.

By extension of the same rules of privacy and discretion, a government agency may make available to a scholar certain bodies of classified data; the agency thereby retains both the responsibility and the right to determine whether that information may or may not be made publicly available. The individual scholar is therefore responsible, in advance of knowing what the classified data may or may not reveal, for deciding whether or not to accept the restrictions that go with accepting or seeking access to such restricted data. Stated in this way, there would appear to be a definite and serious incompatibility between the government's requirement for treating some bodies of information as classified and the scholar's duty to be frank and open with his colleagues, his students, and whatever broader public he may reach through unimpeded writing, teaching and speaking. In practice, the incompatibility is usually slight, but it exists at all times and is a natural source of distrust and concern.

Information is classified by government agencies for two main reasons. One is that the given data may be of value to a potential adversary. By withholding it from him, the national security may be enhanced, at least for some period of time. It may also be useful to keep an adversary in the dark regarding what is or is not known to a U.S. government agency. For this reason there is a continual tug-of-war between the executive and the legislative branches; what the legislators feel they need to know in order to fulfill their responsibilities may be defined by the executive as valuable to an adversary.

A second reason for classification of data relates to the policy-making process. A government agency should be able, in confidence, to review and criticize existing policies and to explore and debate a wide range of alternatives to them. Such studies become government policy only after the new policy has been announced by the President or by an executive officer to whom he has delegated that authority. The very process of thinking about policy can be inhibited by premature disclosure, and in that case the governmental leviathan could be denied even its small present capacity for thinking about alternative policies. Of course, "government through leaks" is widely practiced, through "trial balloons" launched by government officials to pre-test public and group reactions to new policy proposals, or through "unauthorized" leaks designed to rally support for or against a policy. These widespread practices, however, merely modify and do not abrogate the government's need to treat the policy-making process as confidential and privileged.

Granted the legitimate role of classified data in the operations of government, what are or should be the relations of the independent scholar to them? In most scholarly research, classified data generally play a very minor role. Most of the time, the same data are available in unclassified versions, through congressional hearings, the press and numerous other sources. The same issues arise and are normally discussed almost simultaneously in a classified and an unclassified setting. For some types of studies, the scholar may find important advantages in checking the publicly available data against that available to the government. He may still give stronger credence to his unclassified sources, or in the process of comparing the two bodies of data, he may actually help government analysts interpret them more rigorously. In any case, after comparing his unclassified data with government-held data, the scholar may, at some times and on some subjects, be in a better position to appraise the varying reliability of the public data and to shape his own interpretations with greater confidence in his data base.

In principle, such a process of "osmosis" between classified and unclassified data need not and should not inhibit the independent scholar. Nearly, though not quite all, of the useful data exist in both forms, and it is usually a question of judgment and patience in sifting the more reliable from the less reliable data. The scholar who on certain days examines and discusses data on a classified basis will shortly be presenting his own analyses, as a teacher, author or commentator, in an unclassified setting. Any independent scholar will presumably arrive at a single set of analyses and policy recommendations, and his findings and his policy projections, presented in a classified setting, will be fully compatible with his public assertions and predictions.

A scholar who participates in the policy-thinking process within government is bound, both by his own conscience and by his oath of office, to safeguard the secrecy of these deliberations. He cannot say, "I gave such-and-such advice" to a government agency, or "So-and-so advocated this or that policy." So long as he observes the rules of discretion as to what is discussed "in another place," the scholar is entirely free to present his own policy ideas as widely and as vigorously as he can. In other words, so long as the scholar resists the temptation to "run and tell," or to inflate his own role by self-important hints, he can be useful in the crucial function of policy thinking and still remain completely free in the public expression of his own views. Thus, the problem, a real one, of access to classified data and participation in classified deliberations on policy, can in practice be reduced to minimal proportions and rendered fully manageable within the limits set by both governmental requirements and the duty of the scholar to safeguard his own and others' freedom of thought. And, as a final safeguard of scholarly independence, each scholar is entirely free to refrain from seeking access to classified data and from accepting an invitation to participate in policy deliberations within government.

## UNIVERSITIES AND GOVERNMENT-SPONSORED RESEARCH

A separate but related issue is that of government contracts in support of university research on problems of international policy. In practice, such programs are few and small, especially in comparison with the far larger volume of government support for research in the fields of medicine, education, social welfare, the natural sciences and technology, but since they exist their advantages and disadvantages should be examined.

For the government to gain access to systematic bodies of knowledge and policy analysis through research contracts is a valuable asset in policy making, and to deny this access would be to impoverish the resources available to that process. But, it is objected, a government agency may allocate research contracts in the expectation that the results of the research will support its own predetermined conclusions and, to put the matter bluntly, may be "buying brains" to buttress its own preconceptions. Such risks can conceivably arise, and it is the duty of the independent scholar and the independent university to search their consciences with care before embarking on a government research contract. In practice there are serious safeguards against these risks, though no safeguards will operate with complete efficacy and at all times.

One safeguard lies in the fact that government support for policy research in the field of foreign affairs is relatively small in volume and has declined in recent years. In addition, a university is entirely free to reject any contract which carries with it any implication of predetermined conclusions. A second safeguard rests in the desire of scholars to protect both the reputation and actuality of objectivity. Scholars dealing with policy problems, whether by their individual efforts or under government contract, may, like politicians and commentators, arrive at very different conclusions, but they all have one thing in common, their need to preserve a reputation for objective research. Scholars have only one capital, that of talent backed by integrity, and that capital can be dissipated almost overnight if they abandon that standard. In this respect, research in the policy sciences is certainly more vulnerable to criticism and suspicion than in medicine, natural sciences and technology. Therefore, scholars in public policy fields are and should be even more sensitive than in the "hard" sciences to upholding a high level of individual and professional integrity.

A third safeguard for the relative objectivity of scholarly research under government contract lies in the fact that, fortunately for scholarship and the country, government contracts are only one among various sources of support. Generally, government backing of new and difficult areas of international research has lagged far behind that provided by those unique institutions, the American private foundations. Typically, the foundations have, over the past 35 years, provided the risk capital for the development of interdisciplinary area studies of all major world regions, for the growth of research on problems of strategy, economic and political development, international organizations, decision making, the impact of science and technology on world affairs, and a host of other sub-fields within the study of international relations. These pioneering efforts have usually been engineered by university scholars, with both intellectual and financial contributions by the foundations; government support has become available a good deal later, once the need and the merit of the new field have been proven. This "double harness" support has been a great source of scholarly development, the envy of other major countries. The simultaneous shrinking of both foundation and government support, therefore, presents grave risks to the continued health of the entire field of international relations.

### PUBLIC POLICY AND UNIVERSITY RESEARCH

What would be the probable consequences if universities and university scholars were, as some more extreme critics urge, to withdraw from research on public policy, particularly on international affairs? One consequence would doubtless be to concentrate research and informed thinking about situations and policies behind the closed doors of government agencies and under the seals of secrecy. With that would go by the board the present interplay between governmental and independent research. True, not all independence of analysis and policy recommendation would disappear, for some government agencies encourage a great deal of independence of thought and conduct strenuous debates over future policies while others are more conformist in the atmosphere they generate. Nevertheless, the use of well-informed and independent contractors and consultants tends to strengthen the spirit of responsible independence within the government apparatus, and this support from the scholarly community for independent thought would, of course, disappear if a high fence were built between them.

Many men and women in government service are reinforced in a spirit of independence because they feel themselves both a part of a government service and an acknowledged member of a scholarly community; that second sense of belonging to a broader body with its own academic and professional standards would be eroded. Finally, there is the question of the "in-and-outers," those scholars and experts who may move one, two, or three times in their lives between academic and government service. This pattern, which is almost unique to American ways of studying and making policy, would soon be disrupted. The tendency to build a high wall between scholarly work and government service would make government research and thinking more and more self-isolated and would gradually deprive the scholarly community of its present rather broad access to the actual problems and concrete circumstances of events and choices in the real world.

Another advantage of the present role of the American academic community is that it greatly broadens the flow of information and debate to an informed public. By their articles and lectures, by television and radio programs, hundreds of scholars are constantly informing a small but attentive public—often those who make opinion—about issues, prospects and policy choices as they see them. A similar role is now being played by scholars in some West European countries, but even there a gap often exists between the more philosophical approach of the scholar and the professional silence of the civil servant. In addition, the quality of analyses by journalists is often improved through their easy access to a wide range of scholarly analysis, instead of relying almost entirely on the day-to-day flow of the news and the fluctuating definitions by editors of what constitutes publishable "news" on any given day.

This interplay between the scholarly community and public policy has developed over the past 30 years, to become an important, though not decisive, factor in research, in policy making and in informing public opinion. Through the dignity and security a university provides its scholars, it strengthens their spirit of both innovation and responsibility. One result is the wide range, improved quality and massive volume of systematic knowledge thus made available. The fund of research knowledge produced in the United States is several times more voluminous and more comprehensive than all the equivalent information generated in all other parts of the world!

Another result is that the informed segments of American citizenry are better informed than similar segments in other societies. This is important, for American decisions, made or not made, often have far-reaching and even drastic effects on other nations. Since citizens of India do not vote in U.S. elections, it is all the more important for many Americans to be well informed about the possible consequences of continuing, increasing or ceasing U.S. aid to India's economic development.

Policy making in the American setting rests upon the interplay of many components. One of these is political leadership. Relatively diffused and dispersed in matters of domestic policy, political leadership is highly concentrated when it comes to dealing with international and strategic problems and with other nations. A second component is the professional bureaucracy, which has grown tremendously in numbers and responsibilities, in specialized knowledge and skills, since 1940. A third component is the vast flow of information and commentary through the greatly expanded channels of communication, together with the flow of popular reactions back to the policy makers in the executive and the legislature. A fourth is found in the sphere of pressure groups of all types and purposes, mobilizing information and supporters, twisting the arms and bending the ears of the policy makers.

A fifth component is that offered actually or potentially by scholarly research. Its work is perhaps more immediately useful to the political leadership, both executive and legislative, and access to its work passes primarily, though not exclusively, through the labyrinth of bureaucratic structures. Its product is often utilized and popularized by the communications media, and pressure groups like, as often as possible, to clothe their ideas in scholarly garb.

The policy of a powerful country is a fearsome responsibility, and foresight in policy thinking is a scarce commodity. If the universities and, through them, the scholarly community can strengthen, even modestly, the quality of research into world problems, if scholars can help, however slightly, to raise the quality and range of foresight, it is their duty to do so. In descending from the ivory tower into the arena of policy debate, scholars must, of course, expect to be buffeted from many sides. They cannot be participants in the policy process and remain immune to criticism and challenge. On the other hand, they can, if they make the effort, bring to bear an increasingly systematic approach to the study of policy problems and an unusual degree of intellectual independence.

In this sense the scholarly community has begun to serve as a "fifth estate" in the complex and painful task of helping define problems that are crucial to the welfare and even the survival of mankind. It has taken up, almost unwittingly, an important part of the task of thinking about public policy in a turbulent world. Neither it, nor the universities which nurture and sustain it, can turn back from shouldering one share of that new burden.

# AUTHORITY AND THE USE
# OF POWER

### William Haber

## I

The topic assigned to me, "Authority and the Use of Power" has more current relevance in the universities than ever before. One has but to read this morning's newspapers and refer to the reports of Dr. Hayakawa on the situation at San Francisco State, or to review the troublesome developments on the campus at Harvard University, or to scan the statement representing a sort of "manifesto" of the American Council on Education to recognize that this topic is of more than theoretical or academic significance. The three items referred to above suggest quite clearly that the universities are in some sort of trouble.

I was a bit startled yesterday when Dr. Charles Malik referred to the fact that developments at the University of California in Berkeley, and on the American campuses in general, have damaged the world image of our country and of higher education in our universities. It was clearly inferred that if our country and our universities cannot manage their own affairs, we are hardly in a position to set the world aright. While Dr. Malik's statement startled me, there is much truth in it and it is a sobering observation for all of us. Turmoil and disruption on the American campus may be symptomatic of something more significant in the life of a nation.

## II

The campus is a microcosm of the world. The world is not stable. These have not been years of peace and calm. It is, perhaps, not an exaggeration to say that we are going through a series of multiple revolutions in the United States, and perhaps in some other countries, especially in the Western World, as well. One has but to identify seven or eight significant developments to indicate the nature and the magnitude of the transformations which are taking place.

I refer first to the research revolution. We are spending some $20 to $25 billion per year in research and development. The result is that today's methods, processes, materials and markets become obsolete tomorrow. While a substantial portion of such research is related to missile development and space, a considerable amount, and increasing in size, is not so classified. The universities have become centers of research. At the University of Michigan, for example, on whose faculty I have served for more than 30 years, the research outlays are almost as large as the total operating and maintenance budget of the University—about $65 million per year. Little or none of this comes from the state government. It is provided by foundations, federal agencies and private corporations.

Inevitably, such a vast outlay of funds for new methods and materials has created a new technological revolution. Two of its major characteristics are the computer and automation. The explosion of knowledge in recent decades required the computer to store it, retrieve it, and process it. Most experts observe that we are only at the beginning of the revolutionary changes in our technology. Quite naturally, such vast changes in technology have also created a skills revolution. It has been observed that by 1985, about half of our labor force will be working on skills and on jobs which have not yet been invented. The jobs which are growing, the so-called "bright future" jobs of tomorrow, are related to thinking. They are less concerned with making "things"; rather, with providing services. Their common ingredient is more education. Millions in our labor force hold "dead-end" jobs which are disappearing.

The civil rights revolution is another illustration of a vast social, political and economic upheaval. Accommodation to these changes is difficult for the white community as it is for the black. Once having started, it cannot be turned back, and it should not be. Education and training, jobs, housing, status—opportunities in all of these areas are being expanded. This is taking place, not quietly, nor always peacefully.

Nor should one omit the affluence revolution, for this is a truly affluent society, richer in goods and services than any in our history or anyone else's history. We have fashioned an economic institution that is capable of doubling the standard of living in less than 25 years. The average family income in the United States in 1968 was over $8,000. It will not be very long before it could be $15,000 at 1968 prices. The war on poverty is directly related to the fact of affluence. The paradox of over 20 million people with incomes less than a third of the average is hard to justify in a democratic society.

The population explosion represents another revolutionary development. Its consequences have had and are having an overwhelming effect. Since the days when I was a graduate student at the University of Wisconsin, less than 45 years ago, the American population has doubled from about 100 million to over 200 million. The effect of this "crowding" upon pure air, dirty water, highway safety, urban blight, rapid transit, to mention only five items which come to one's mind immediately, is quite devastating.

## III

Inevitably, this kind of a society, the product of vast social, political and economic transformations, affects the behavior of people and what is required of them. For one thing, it has created an overwhelming demand for college-trained people, and this is going to continue. As of 1969 over 7 million American young men and women were on a college campus. This represents over 40 per cent of the college age group. A fantastic figure indeed! How large this is can be gauged by observing that the comparable figure is probably no more than 12 per cent in England; less than 10 per cent in France and only 7 per cent in Italy. By 1975 nearly 9.5 million young people will be on some college or university campus, representing perhaps more than 50 per cent of the college-age group. No other nation makes this sort of an investment and has this kind of a commitment to education beyond the secondary level. This is in itself a revolutionary development. The number of institutions, their size and the complexity of their administration have increased. Large classes and much new "educational technology" have resulted. We should not assume that this is just happening because this is what the young people want. Quite contrary, the social and technological forces referred to demand this expansion in training and education beyond the secondary school level.

In addition to size and growth, there is another facet of education which has been labeled by Riesman and Jenks as "The Academic Revolution." Many books have been written on this theme and that of the multiversity since Clark Kerr's book, *The Uses of the University,* came out in 1963. Universities have ceased to be merely places where one does teaching, where one transmits the acquired knowledge of the ages. The good universities have always been, and most universities are getting to be, places which contribute richly to the acquisition of new knowledge. In fact, the "publish or perish" syndrome may in part be responsible for the neglect of undergraduate students. One does not easily advance in a distinguished university merely by teaching 6 or 8 hours a week. It is what one does in the laboratory or in the library that influences status and advancement. I am told that even at Notre Dame "publish or back to the parish" is not an uncommon way of judging faculty.

A third facet is the universities' role in public service. It is not the secluded cloister any more. It is not the place where one leaves the active life in order to reflect, to write, to think and to teach. The professors and scholars are "involved" in the turmoil of economic, political and social life. The first few persons named by President Nixon to public office were professors; one from California Tech to be science advisor; another from Harvard to be foreign affairs advisor; a third from Chicago to be secretary of labor; and a fourth from the University of Michigan to be chairman of the council of economic affairs. The students may have a good case in thinking of themselves as neglected. At my own university at Ann Arbor over 800 "teaching fellows," all graduate students, do an overwhelming proportion of all the teaching of freshmen and sophomores.

Still another change in the university is the increasing proportion of graduate students. At the University of Michigan for example, 40 per cent of the student body of over 33,000 in Ann Arbor are graduate students. Many of them are married. Their average age is over 26. Sometimes universities are charged with preoccupation with graduate education and training to the neglect of the undergraduate. This may or may not be true; there is no question, however, about the fact that an increasing proportion of college students anticipate continuing beyond the B.A. degree. This is true at Michigan; it is equally true at most distinguished universities and will, in the next decade, be true for most universities.

IV

These developments—size, preoccupation with service, the increasing emphasis on graduate education and research—taken together do lead to student grievances. They have many. Since young people are congregated on the campus, it is natural that their grievances against society and against the university come to a boil there. All the tensions and frictions of our society, many of our frustrations, are expressed on the college campus.

They do have an impressive list of grievances against society. They can be passed over quickly, perhaps merely by mentioning them, but their significance should not be underestimated. They are rather overwhelming and they color the attitudes and behavior of the young generation. To begin with, they are opposed to the war in Vietnam. Those who are most vocal consider it an immoral involvement by the United States. Consequently, they are also opposed to the draft, which affects their educational plans and their lives. These, too, lead them to oppose, or at least to question, the propriety and the equity of some university requirements. For example, since the Selective Service system drafts young men whose academic performance is below acceptable standards, the students question the propriety of grading and class ranking. There may be many reasons why the system of grading students ought to be changed. The young critics of this generation are primarily opposed to the traditional grading procedure since it facilitates the draft and thus sustains the war. They are also opposed to what they call "the military industrial complex." The phrase is not theirs. It was, in fact, originally used by President Eisenhower upon leaving the presidency. To the students it has special significance.

It indicates that there is undue corporate and military influence upon our society and upon the university.

These five grievances stand out. The conclusion of the war, "any conclusion," would remove one of the overriding factors which has influenced student unrest. While the war continues, these items are on the student agenda for protest and resentment. There are other grievances against society. For a time the students were actively involved in the "civil rights movement"; they were hardly neutral when it came to the so-called "war on poverty."

The university is hardly in a position to do very much about many of these grievances. It cannot stop the war, it cannot abolish the draft; through education and training it can make a modest contribution toward the elimination of poverty—for the next generation. Through admissions and employment policies it could, over time, make a considerable contribution to raising the level of training and education of black people. By and large, however, universities in the United States are not "action societies" and could become such only at the risk of compromising their role as institutions for learning and research. In fact, a radical change in the role of the universities could very well endanger their public support, whether from the legislature or private philanthropy.

Students also have grievances against the university. Some of them, as we have seen, are related to the war, like grading and ranking. The opposition to the R.O.T.C. is in the same category. Others are related to what one might call "the revolution of these times." Thus students are interested in the investment of university funds, whether they help to sustain antidemocratic institutions like apartheid in South Africa. Their opposition to "classified research" which involves many universities is also an outgrowth of opposition to the war or to the military industrial complex. They complain also of neglect, which grows out of the fact that the university is preoccupied with public service, with graduate training, with classified research—all these are often conducted at the expense of undergraduate education. They are also concerned with what they call "relevance." They claim that much of what we teach has little relation to their lives and to what is likely to happen to them tomorrow. This is particularly emphasized by the black students who insist that they are being exposed to a "white, middle-class philosophy"; that the economics and sociology we teach will not help them in the ghetto; that not enough universities have a program of black studies. White students often also say that much of what is offered in the humanities is little related to the revolution of these times.

There is, no doubt, some truth in this. A university is not designed to be entirely "relevant" in an occupational sense. It would, in fact, be a great tragedy if every subject would be relevant. There would be very little place for Plato or Socrates or Thomas Aquinas or St. Augustine. To be sure, there are many who believe that what these men of ideas had to say is quite definitely as relevant to today's problems as it was to the problems of earlier societies.

The issue of relevance is related to another facet of student activity. I refer to "student power." It is a strong word, but it really means some involvement in "decision-making." Universities have traditionally been run by the faculty and the administration, mostly the former. The role of students was passive, "take it or leave it." In a different frame of reference than the present age of social protest, it would have been presumptuous for students to suggest that they should have something to say about the curriculum, about language requirements, about the quality of teaching, about the involvement of universities in the "urban crises," about black studies, about matters of tenure and about students being solely responsible for discipline for improper student conduct. On all of these matters they now insist that they have much to say; that they wish to be involved; that the decision should not be made without student participation and often in more than an "advisory capacity."

Much of this is healthy. Universities are, after all, conservative institutions and students, being less conservative and deeply troubled about the ethics and the social crises of our time, are compelling the faculty and the administration to re-examine both the structure and the program of higher education in America. Universities have probably not been adequately involved in the urban problems often existing next door to them. Our universities, located in large cities, have often been quite disinterested in the urban crises on their front door. John Gardner said once that if these institutions left the communities where they have existed for more than a century, they would hardly be missed, since they have been uninvolved in the communities' crises.

The interest and pressure from students is compelling a rethinking by the college and the university of its relation to the bright young men and women who now compose its student body. This is, without doubt, one of the brightest generations of college students in American history. The error which they make, and it is a serious error, is that they often confuse being bright and being sharp with being wise. The latter requires more experience than the undergraduate possesses.

Nevertheless, their dissent and their objections cannot be wished away. Some of their grievances the universities cannot do much about; others ought to be seriously considered. There is, in fact, already a substantial revision on many a campus of the role of students in academic decision-making on crucial matters.

V

How much "authority" the university official—the dean or the president —has, is, of course, a serious question. A major transformation in the very idea of authority has taken place. Power and authority have been seriously diluted. Only a short time ago one would have thought that there was no question at all about the authority of the Vatican. Now one should not be too certain in view of the serious questions being raised by priests and bishops about this or that pronouncement of the Pope. In the political area the absolute monarch hardly exists. The monarchies in Ethiopia, Saudi Arabia, in other places in the Middle East and here and there in Asia and Africa are likely to be short-lived. In most nations, the queen or king is a symbol. The prime minister rules by the consent of Parliament and when consent isn't there, he resigns.

What is true in political life is no less true in industry. One would have assumed that the president of General Motors had a fantastic degree of autocratic authority. One learns, however, that he is somewhat like a university president. He has a host of committees—one for changing models, another for pricing policy, a third for philanthropic gifts to education, and so on without end. We used to call him "the boss." That is much less true. A collective bargaining contract has much to say about hiring and even more about "firing," and very much more about wage rates. It is all worked out in what has come to be called "industrial jurisprudence."

Even when one turns his attention to the "labor union baron," one brings to mind John L. Lewis, "Jimmy" Hoffa, James Beck and others of their era. George Meany is hardly of that type and Walter Reuther* heads a rather democratic union. His union members and those of other unions often reject collective bargaining agreements negotiated by the leadership. Moreover, automation is likely to dilute even the power of the strike. It is already true that a strike against a telephone company or an electric power company does not necessarily affect the flow of electric power or the availability of telephone service.

Perhaps the greatest symbol of authority in the history of the world is the hydrogen bomb. But no nation has the freedom to use it. In brief, authority is a highly circumscribed idea. It is authority without freedom.

This is especially true in the academic community. The university has for over 500 years been an institution without a power symbol. It is a "rickety organization." It is one of the few places where it is still possible to have a job with considerable status at a relatively fair salary and an amazing amount of freedom from organizational or institutional interference. The traditional concept of "management" really does not apply to a college or university. It is rather nihilistic. It does apply, to be sure, to the building and grounds department where employees "punch in and punch out" and where they are told what to do next and what to do later. It applies also to a great degree to nonacademic personnel, but it hardly applies to the professor. To suggest that

---

* This address was delivered before Reuther's death in 1970.

he should punch in in the morning and check out when he leaves or have some supervision over his "work load" "so that the Legislature will know how many hours he worked"—all this would be outrageous. Nevertheless, some changes toward better management, cost benefit analysis, are taking place. It would be unfortunate if it went too far, for teaching and research hardly lend themselves to the sort of time controls which may be indispensable in other lines of work.

VI

This is the age in which students are testing and challenging every constraint. Nothing is sacred. Clothes, razors, refined language, compulsory requirements, drugs, "the establishment"—all are being challenged. Frankly, I am not really worried about whether the universities will survive. I believe they will. There is too much at stake. When the chips are down, the faculties will recognize the issues and begin to isolate that element among the student body which is bent, not upon reform, but upon destruction. My fear is what is going on will do a lot of damage to the students involved. At this stage of our development their "revolution" is not going to succeed. There is far greater danger from the backlash; namely, the revolution of the Right. Public disenchantment with the college and the university will harm, not only the students, but the institutions. The experiences at the universities of Wisconsin, Berkeley, Harvard, Brandeis, Chicago, and Illinois and a dozen or more other places one might mention hardly justify public complacency. Legislators are asking critical questions. Legislative proposals (both national and state) represent a threat to the institutions. No institution is really secure. Archibald Cox, the distinguished former Solicitor-General now on the faculty at Harvard, in commenting on the Columbia University uprising is said to have remarked that what happened in Columbia could never happen at Harvard. It did so a year later.

A part of the problem is the faculty. As conservative bodies, faculties have much to conserve. They accommodate too slowly to change. My own personal experience confirms this generalization. The president of our University some years ago asked if I would chair a Commission to develop a new university calendar. University calendars are sacred things; they cannot be changed easily. Most college and university calendars fit the agricultural society of a hundred years ago. We were asked to convert the calendar so that the University could operate on a year-round basis. We hit a buzz saw—the faculty. While there were many good reasons for opposing the particular type of proposal we suggested—the trimester—I fear that opposition would have come to any proposal for change. Dropping the compulsory language requirement for a bachelor's degree is another illustration where strong resistance prevails and change takes place only after much struggle. I am reminded of a friend in Columbus, Ohio, a much older man whom I see periodically and who always greets me with the statement that "he has seen many changes in his lifetime and has been against every damn one of them."

Students have much to contribute and, in my view, ought to be involved on curriculum committees, in discipline problems; they ought to be consulted on policies involving major university direction. I want to emphasize that they should be consulted even on problems involving promotion and the quality of teaching. Advice and consultation is quite different from "student power, the right to make decisions."

VII

University officials are being tested as never before. Deans, vice presidents and presidents have never had to be more resourceful. "Power" and "authority" are not quite adequate, even if they were possessed in the fullest measure. A personal experience of some years ago may be worthwhile to relate. About seven years ago, the radio reported that "University of Michigan faculty voted to strike on Vietnam." It appeared that some 50 to 60 University faculty members signed a petition to the effect that they would not meet classes and thus protest U.S. policy in Vietnam.

What position does a dean take on this sort of a challenge? Certainly a faculty member has a right to express his views as a citizen on United States foreign policies. This dean thought that not meeting one's classes was not a proper way to express these views. The proposed strike was building up support and the dean could not avoid being involved.

At the University of Michigan, we have a Center for Research on Conflict Resolution, then headed by a distinguished economist with an executive committee of nationally known scholars from sociology, psychology and other social sciences. I assembled its executive committee. They were startled to be brought together. I merely indicated that there was a conflict and that while they were working on major world conflicts, like the Cold War or the admission of China to the United Nations, I had one right on the campus at the University, and since they were supposedly experts on conflict resolutions, I needed their counsel. My question may have startled them. It is much easier to solve conflicts in the abstract than real ones on your doorstep. One of the most distinguished members of the committee, a vigorous opponent of the war in Vietnam, did not agree with the idea that a faculty strike on that issue was appropriate. He felt that public attention would be diverted to the issue of the right to strike and the Vietnam issue would be lost. Nevertheless, he thought that some face-saving retreat for those involved was essential. He suggested a "teach-in."

I confess that I had not heard that phrase, which has in the past few years become part of our vocabulary. In any event, the strike was called off and a teach-in was arranged. Classrooms, auditoriums, amplifying equipment, speakers, all were provided. And from 7 p.m. until 7 a.m., the issue of Vietnam was debated with as many as 3,000 students participating.

### VIII

This is but one issue. Many others have been on the agenda, among them, black studies, classified research, language requirements, R.O.T.C., a relevant curriculum and others. These are vital questions, and I am reasonably certain that this is not a phase which will disappear; it represents the beginning of an age where persistent questions will be asked and universities and faculties must find answers. When I went to school, I went to study; when my son went to school, he went to run the university. I went to take the curriculum; he went to remake the curriculum. This is the age when administrators must be prepared to accommodate to change, often unexpected change.

### IX

What kind of conclusions does all this lead to? I am prepared to suggest that dialogue and protest and dissent are part of our culture. With equal emphasis, I would urge that the rights of those who do not wish to be disturbed are equally sacred. Persuasion, yes; disruption, no. The dividing line between one and the other is often not clear. It is easy to say as the president of your distinguished University of Notre Dame has said, that the protesting student will have a few moments to decide whether he wishes to remain a member of the university community. If so, he will desist. If not, he will be arrested. I doubt whether the first sit-in which takes place at Notre Dame will be resolved that quickly. It is important to state one's position. There is also something to be said for tolerating a certain degree of ambiguity. There are too many areas in which victories are not possible. University-student relations, like marriage relations, call for a process of accommodation, of adjustment and compromise.

The university is a precarious community. Someone has characterized it as a fragile institution. It is indeed delicate. The experience at Berkeley and Columbia confirms this conclusion. Democracy does not have great authority, only dictatorships do; and universities are democracies. In the midst of crises they must develop the forms and procedures which will make it possible to deal continuously with the issues which face them. We ought to make a line clear—the right to protest and to dissent but not to disrupt. It does not follow, in my view, however, that every instance where the line is crossed requires the presence of police force.

The universities have always been the seedbeds of dissent. In these times it is against a world created by new science and technology. Every accepted ideology is subject to question, not excluding patriotism, religion and the value system. It is natural that the questioning will be done by young people and not by obsolete folks over 30 like me. Finally, it would be tragic if, in a period when accommodation to change is so important, universities were weakened. It would be equally tragic if the universities took a position which, in effect, gave power to those who do not really believe in the institution. This is what often troubles us about S.D.S. and the young radicals. They know what they are against. I am not yet persuaded that they know exactly what they are for.

# THE UNIVERSITY IN THE '70's

## John Brademas

The decade of the 1970's will present the American higher education community with the most formidable challenge it has ever faced.

In sheer size and numbers, our colleges and universities will have to expand enormously in order to meet the demand for broader educational opportunities for all segments of society.

At the same time our university community is being subjected to intense pressures from both extremes of the political spectrum which threaten to compromise the traditional principle of academic freedom.

In spite of these pressures, American higher education will be called upon to play a major role in the solution of the grave social problems we will face in the 70's. Historically, our colleges and universities have made important contributions to the general welfare, whether through agricultural extension, scientific research, or the training of manpower for industry and government. Today there is an even greater need for the universities to help in the task of improving the quality of life in America.

I would like to address myself to some of the major issues with which American higher education will be concerned in the coming decade.

I shall not even pretend to be exhaustive, but I shall touch on some of the problems in that relationship which I think all of us can agree are important.

First, there is the question of money.

Over the past decade the federal government has assumed an increasingly larger burden of the cost of education generally and of higher education in particular.

Federal investment in higher education has mushroomed from a little over $1.1 billion in fiscal year 1958 to an estimated $4.6 billion in fiscal year 1970.

I shall not here rehearse all the reasons for this extraordinary growth.

But I observe only what David Riesman said recently: "When one considers the plight of our mental hospitals, of our prisons, of our inadequate welfare and our other starved public services, it is clear that higher education has been in many states the secular cathedral of our times."

But there are some storm clouds on the horizon of federal involvement in our colleges and universities. I shall cite only a few.

In the summer of 1969 the National Science Foundation published a report on federal support of science between 1963 and 1967 which showed that although there has been an annual increase in NSF support of science, the yearly rise had slipped from 42 per cent in 1965 and 32 per cent in 1966 to 9 per cent in 1967—a very steep drop in the rate of increase.

*The New York Times* on October 5, 1969, carried a story headed, "Inflation and Budget Cuts Cause Alarm Among Scientists Seeking Research Funds." That the federal government for this year has less money for medical research and research training than the year before, had, says the article, induced "alarm that sometimes approaches panic among scientists and medical educators."

In *Science* magazine on September 26, 1969, its editor, Dr. Philip H. Abelson, urged scientists to develop, in his words, "the political clout" to stop what he called "the mindless dismantling of American science."

And I note here that some programs authorized for higher education, such as the International Education Act, Public Service Education, and Networks for Knowledge, remain completely unfunded.

In his budget message in 1969, to cite another instance of the darkening skies for our colleges and universities, President Nixon cut his request for funds for education (administered through the Office of Education) for fiscal 1970, $370 million below President Johnson's request for the same year— nearly half the funds for higher education. The budget for fiscal 1970 barely restores federal education money to the 1969 level.

There are, of course, reasons for the bleak outlook for federal financial support for higher education: (1) the continuing drain on our resources caused by Vietnam; (2) the genuine concern in both Congress and the Administration about inflation; (3) President Nixon's sense of priorities— education does not seem to be among them; and, finally (4) the attack on the university as an institution from both Left and Right.

You will not therefore be surprised to learn that there has been a sharp reaction to this situation both inside and outside Congress among those for whom education does have a high priority.

The most striking evidence of this reaction was the recent Congressional attempt to increase appropriations for education, in spite of intense opposition from the Administration. Although the Administration gained its immediate goal when the President's veto was upheld by the House of Representatives, this victory might well turn out to be a Pyrrhic one. The education funding fight cost the Administration a tremendous amount in terms of the prestige and influence it had to invest in order to insure victory. The pro-education forces, on the other hand, were goaded into action by the Administration's opposition. The political influence of an organized education lobby cannot be discounted in the future.

In spite of the short-run defeat of those advocating increased funds for education, over the long run it is generally admitted that the federal investment in education at all levels must increase in the years ahead.

With this rise, there will come profound problems for our colleges and universities; without it, the problems will be greater still.

Why are we going to have an increase in federal support for higher education?

Reason number one has to do with the number of students.

In the academic year 1955-1956, there were some 2.5 million students enrolled in degree programs in our colleges and universities. Today there are 6.5 million—and by 1975 there will be 10 million.

Beyond mounting enrollments, other demands on colleges and universities contribute to steep increases in expenditures.

The expanding volume of research and a widening commitment to public service operations are just two. Black studies, urban studies, training of Peace Corps volunteers—all of these mean increased costs.

A broadening of the curriculum, a need for sophisticated new equipment, more library resources—these developments all cost money, too.

A sharp rise in graduate and professional education also hurts because the cost of educating graduate students is several times that of educating undergraduates.

Moreover, tuition fees for next year are up an average of 10 per cent for non-resident students at state universities—with some, especially in the Big Ten, going as high as 50 per cent for out-of-state students.

This trend has developed at a time when tight money has caused banks to restrict their loans to students and the federal government has decided against adequate expansion of the other federal student aid programs.

All of these pressures then have meant sharp increases in costs. In 1955-1956, the over-all capital and current expenditures of all higher education institutions in the United States was $4.1 billion; a decade later, the figure was $11.4 billion, and Office of Education projections tell us we must invest $34 billion annually in higher education by 1975. Others estimate the figure will be even higher.

Where is the money to come from? Alan Pifer, president of the Carnegie Commission, stated the case succinctly: "We are forced to a very simple conclusion. If the nation's needs for higher education are to be met in the years to come, the Federal government will have to accept the principal part of the financial burden."[1]

Mr. Pifer predicted that the federal share could come to as much as 50 per

---

[1] Speech delivered at the annual meeting of the Association of American Colleges, Jan. 16, 1968.

cent of all support of higher education by 1975, compared to the current figure of a little over 20 per cent.

He warned that incomes from endowment, gifts, tuition and fees will represent a declining share of the total support for higher education. He forecast the same proportional decrease in support from state and local governments.

That gap, Mr. Pifer concluded, must be filled by the federal government.

This viewpoint has been echoed by a number of voices in recent weeks. More than two years ago the Carnegie Commission on Higher Education, headed by Dr. Clark Kerr, recommended a doubling of federal support for higher education in the immediate future—not the long run—from a figure of little more than $4 billion to $8 billion annually.

Last February I joined my Republican colleague, Congressman Ogden Reid of New York, in introducing the Higher Education Bill of Rights, to implement the recommendations of the Carnegie Report.

Our bill would make the financial assistance available to some 3.6 million students in the first year, about six times the present number. This coverage would expand to include about 5.8 million by 1977, the last year of authorization of the bill. Senators Edward M. Kennedy (D-Mass.), Jacob K. Javits (R-N.Y.) and Winston L. Prouty (R-Vt.) have introduced a similar bill in the Senate.

But providing more federal funds for higher education, difficult as it will be to do so, won't resolve all the problems inherent in the relationship between Washington and the campus.

Let me touch upon a few of these issues.

First, there is the lack of coordination of federal higher education programs. Federal support for higher education has evolved on an ad hoc basis. More and more federal agencies have become involved in administering education programs. We have not really developed any intelligible set of national policies to guide future government assistance to our colleges and universities.

I do not for a moment want to suggest there is some easy mechanism by which order and rationality can be introduced into the area of federal support for higher education any more than for any other area of federal involvement.

Moreover, the values of diversity and pluralism are essential to the nature of American higher education and obviously I am not proposing federal control of our colleges and universities.

What I do want to suggest, however, is this: If, as Mr. Pifer predicts, the federal government is shortly to become the largest single financial supporter of our colleges and universities, then all of us both in and out of higher education have a responsibility to give closer consideration to the question of how major policy decisions affecting it are to be made in the years ahead. I should think that colleges and universities in particular would want to be sure that their views are effectively felt in the making of government decisions that affect their destiny.

Beyond the issue of developing some kind of mechanisms and processes for shaping federal higher education policies, there is another issue in the relationship I must mention.

I refer to the problem represented by the phrase, campus disorder and student unrest.

Some years ago, after I was first elected to Congress, I spent a good deal of time on college campuses, urging students to take a more active interest in politics. I don't make that speech any more!

No longer do we think of a university as Woodrow Wilson did. According to Wilson's definition, a university was "a place removed, calm science seated there, recluse, ascetic, like a nun, not knowing that the world passes, not caring, if the truth would come in answer to her prayer."[2]

Recent developments have made the Wilsonian university a thing of the past. Our universities have become, over the past decade, a focal point for the conflicts which characterize our society as a whole. The days of academic seclusion and calm meditation are gone forever.

It is, in my view, a great mistake to assign but one cause for unrest on American college campuses.

For convenience, I would divide the causes into three general categories:

First, I believe there is a small, but nonetheless significant group of revolutionary extremists on our campuses who wish to destroy the university, not to elevate it and improve its quality. With this group and the violent tactics that some of them are willing to employ, I have no sympathy.

It would, however, be a great mistake to assert that the existence of such groups is the only or the principal reason for disorders on our campuses.

The second cause involves criticism of the way in which our colleges and universities are run. The students cite such issues as the curriculum, military-related research, impersonal faculty-student relations, the role of students, faculty and administration in governing the institution, and the relationships between the university and the community of which it is a part.

All of these are among the reasons the students are critical of the university. I do not say one must agree completely with the criticisms: rather that these are among the criticisms that motivate some of the unrest.

The third major cause of student disorders is the entire spectrum of problems within the wider American society: most obviously, the war in Vietnam, the draft, racial discrimination, poverty, and the feeling on the part of many students that our country is so concerned about material gains that we are not

---

[2] Address delivered at Princeton University Sesquicentennial Celebration, October 21, 1896.

really interested in making real the ideals that went into the shaping of the American democracy.

Now, if there is any truth in what I have just said, it follows that there is no single, sure-shot answer to the problem of campus disorder. If the causes are several and complex, the answers are likely to be several and complex as well.

It is certainly most unwise for Congress to pass laws cutting off federal assistance either to students involved in disorders or to universities where they occur.

Yet we came perilously close in early 1969—by an 18 to 17 vote on the House Committee on Education and Labor—to passing highly restrictive legislation. I must warn you, moreover, that the effort in Congress to write such repressive legislation into the statute books is still very much alive. In October, 1969 the military procurement bill passed by the House contained a provision that, in the language of the committee report, "ties together the attitudes of colleges and universities and their record of cooperation with the Department of Defense and the Armed Forces in the areas of Reserve Officers Training Corps and military recruiting on the campuses with contracts for research and development to the school and to individuals on the faculty and staff of that school."

I will conclude by saying that with respect to the amount of federal funds for higher education, with respect to the planning process for distributing those funds, and with respect to maintaining the independence of our universities from unwarranted federal intervention, I believe that the American university community must play a far more vigorous role than it has so far played.

And when I say university community, I mean administrators, faculty, students and governing board.

I would like to conclude my remarks with some brief observations on two related subjects.

How should universities be governed?

How do students see their role both in the university and in society?

First, on the question of the governing of the universities and the appropriate place of the students therein, let me observe that I don't think we yet have a very clear answer, and that there ought probably to be different answers for different institutions anyway.

I believe that there is a compelling case for an enhanced student role, but I also believe that we must take care not to romanticize what Kingman Brewster of Yale, in a most perceptive address before the Yale Political Union on September 24, 1969, called "the political symbolism of participatory democracy."

That symbolism, President Brewster warned, "is an illusion when applied to many of the academic and financial decisions which direct an academic institution."

"The answer," he said, "to the legitimate student demand to have protection against incompetent and unresponsive administration is not formal *representation* in all matters. It is administrative *accountability.*"

So I conclude that we must not be too quick to leap on any particular bandwagon with respect to how we should change the governing of our colleges and universities to meet changing times.

But neither should we assume that all is well with the system, for manifestly that is not the case. We must therefore seek to make changes that will not necessarily be the same for all institutions.

In conclusion, I would like to make one further point about students.

I was in Japan in September, 1969, participating in the Second Japanese-American Assembly in Shimoda, and talked with some professors, students and university administrators about the causes of student disorders that have so plagued Japanese universities in recent months and years.

I came away with this general impression, with which most of my Japanese friends did not argue, that the motivation for Japanese students to attack their universities is essentially destructive and anarchic. That is to say that they have no particular reform which they seek to champion either of Japanese society or of the university.

On the other hand, I believe that much of the motivation behind the student protest in the United States is essentially constructive and idealistic, and with specific goals with regard to changes they seek both in the university and in society.

As Archibald MacLeish said recently of American students, "It is an angry generation, yes, but its resentment is not a resentment *of* our human life, but a resentment *on behalf of* human life; not an indignation that we exist on the Earth, but that we *permit* ourselves to exist in a selfishness and wretchedness and squalor which we have the means to abolish. Resentment of this kind is founded, can only be founded, on belief in man. And belief in Man—a return to a belief in man—is the reality on which a new age can be built. . . ."[3]

Yet the results of a survey published in the October, 1969 issue of *Psychology Today* shows that the idealism of the majority of the university students today is generalized and abstract in nature, and that a principal characteristic of today's student generation is "privatism."

"The critical question," concludes the survey, "is whether their (the students) social idealism, though abstractly stated and daintily enforced in pri-

---

[3] Charter Day Address, University of California at Berkeley, April, 1969.

vate life, will be moulded into a commitment to transform society toward their goals. Or will it be the hypocrisy of the present generation, raised to a higher level of rhetoric?"

So who today's university student is, what he wants and the nature of his values—all these are questions that still require analysis and answers—as do the other issues which I have tried to discuss: How shall we govern our universities? How much federal money shall they be given? How shall this money be spent?

# PART TWO

PART TWO

# THE HUMANITIES AND
# EDUCATION FOR HUMANITY

## M. A. Fitzsimons

The humanities are central in today's academic turbulence and in the cultural crisis of which it is a manifestation. The crisis, with its long genealogy and manifold issue in society and the academy, is real enough. The heritage of an age of individualism in which many traditional forms of authority had survived is passing through the ordeal of irrelevance. In exaggerated reaction to the communitarian requirements of society, not to mention industrial society, this heritage is not simply found wanting but is pronounced to be corrupting, misleading or irrelevant. The disparity between institutions, values and received ideas and the needs of society is so great that past experience may also be dismissed as irrelevant for what some will ponderously call "the end of the neolithic age." Ill-equipped and confused, we face the problem of adaptation and innovation required by the encounter of civilizations in our world.

Behind the rituals of protest is an identity crisis: modern man simply does not adequately know who he is and what he is. A venerable historical interpretation sees in the Renaissance the time of the discovery of man and the world. The discovery, now dulled and confused, must be made anew for ourselves. All the more, if institutions and values are to be reshaped to the measure of man, it would be well to know what the measure is.

The academic response to direct challenge has been a flurry of curricular and disciplinary changes. And reform is so evidently desirable that change may for a time serve as ersatz improvement. Some of this change, however, is a form of blind man's buff in which the improvisation, though not entirely aimless, reveals that the experiment is seeking both method and goal. The humanities, the traditional liberal area for human self-discovery, experience the same flighty treatment and are sustained by a wavering faith.

For many reasons American college teachers have been vague or lacking in candor about the role of values in humanistic education. Today the university is criticized for failures in the realm of ends and values, issues within the sphere of the humanities. The criticism urgently calls for stock-taking, an examination of academic conscience, and what academic people have called self-study. Here, then, I propose to present some of the difficulties, misgivings and vision of one teacher of the humanities today.

As credentials I adduce thirty years of teaching history, a subject within the humanities but closely linked to the social sciences; fifteen years of editing a journal, *The Review of Politics,* that professes special interest in the historical and philosophical approach to political realities; and some breadth of interests, partly serious and partly wayward. I hasten to authenticate these credentials with the contemporary note of ambivalence: like many teachers I have read very little on educational philosophy and practice and have managed somehow to mistrust or ignore those who would regularize or ideologize my "mystery."

There have been moments when I was tempted to think of the stores of discourse about humanism and humanity as a ridiculous form of species chauvinism. To one kind of unlordly hyena was given laughter: modern man, the destroyer and cosmic polluter, reserves for himself a species idolatry. Man also gives himself a bad image: he is the naked ape and the cretinous lord of creation. Much of this bad press for man is, at most, only selective bookkeeping; it is not so much untrue as incomplete.

Man may be very many things. The absence of an inevitable course brings us to the very beginnings of education and humanism. The human young are plastic at the cost of long dependence: they must learn to be men. Though there are bounds to this plasticity, it is immeasurable enough so that no single person can pass for a universally valid model of a man. Nor can a single generation or civilization exhaust the potentialities of humanity.

Beyond that, man has strained flesh and bones in aspiration to realms beyond the senses; he has worked out ideas of transcendence and some of his religions have proclaimed that he is in the image of God and that his life's goal is to imitate the loving self-sacrifice of the Son of God. The understanding of man and his nature, then, must take account of man's relation to God or, at any rate, man's conception of God. Historically, the humanities have usually taken some bearings in divinity and, even in an age of theothanasia, come ultimately to the answerless questions to which religions respond. Nevertheless, Christianity and humanism have not lived as loving partners in the peaceable kingdom.

From the beginning, as myths attest, it was the fate of man's unbalanced nature to strive to become as a god and to forget who he was. Tragedy in Greece was intended to remind him of the human condition. Since the eighteenth century, it was widely believed, the human condition as fate had changed. For man was claimed autonomy and self-determination. Many found that human achievements provided the strongest warrant for man's autonomy that was often interpreted to mean repudiation of God. Now in the twentieth century the world man made threatens to wither his humanity.

In American universities the humanities have included the study of literature, language, philosophy and history, which is a relative latecomer in the academic study of humanities, and more recently the fine and performing arts. These humanities formed the core of a program of liberal education. The latter was originally intended to inspire the beginnings of a quest for knowledge of self, other men, and the institutions in which they live, so that a man may fulfill himself with some freedom in his own life, in living with family and friends, and in the various societies of which he is a part. Such a training prepares a man gradually to discover himself and his potentialities in considering the ranges of human achievement—always with the sense that no old map is definitive: there is always an undiscovered country with new heights and stretches to be charted. Such self-discovery is exhilarating and yet, cautioning, for great achievement is possible only when man recognizes his limitations: mankind is finite and the individual more so. To aspire unlimitedly is a definition of frustration and self-defeating arrogance. Yet man's restlessness and unquiet heart manifest in some way the image of his kinship with the maker of the world and man.

Such self-education enables man to balance the unstable forces of passions and to coexist with the excesses of his own temperament; to recognize that love is not easy and cannot be passed out like a lordly drunk distributing coins —that it may be more authentic in silences than in protestations; that if man is to go down one street, he cannot at the same time go down another—and just possibly may never go down the other. In the course of it he may be expected to practice the art of thinking, to analyze and be critical, to learn and experience the force of discipline and habit, to cultivate the imagination and the will, and to entertain questions of ends and values so that he neither loses direction nor is paralyzed by persisting problems.

The humanities have been excessively affected by limitations deriving from their origin in the Graeco-Roman world. The Greeks despised labor: they saw in one man's slavery the basis of another man's freedom. Over the centuries, then, the humanities have been indifferent to economics and pretty largely to politics and society—the social sciences. The humanities have had an individualist bias, which has been enormously strengthened by the social individualism that American society has anachronistically prolonged into two centuries of industrialism. The reaction to this may be very adverse to the humanities.

The humanities have been based on a conception of man that saw him as more than an animal and less than a god; he was tempted both to bestiality and to high-flying hubris. Within these extremes man, if free of servile toil, can find fulfillment in the arts that made for the distinctive but uneasy mode of being human. Fulfillment, however, like happiness, is not a goal to be sought directly. Where that is done, the goal, so selfishly formulated, becomes elusive and frustrating. The religious person may see in this a kind of empirical warranty that man must go beyond himself. As Matthew Arnold put it in "The Sirens":

> Can men worship the wan features
> The sunk eyes, the wailing tone,
>
> Of unsphered, discrowned creatures,
> Souls as little godlike as their own?

Or does the poet's rhetoric err in making one answer inevitable?

Christianity, as I have suggested, had a vision of man that heightened human instability. But Jerusalem and Athens reached an accord in the medieval university where philosophy and theology were the major liberal studies. That cultural order prevailed into the fourteenth century and long beyond. From the fourteenth century, however, it was also challenged by the stirrings that became the Renaissance—with Europe reaching out to the ancient world for models of wisdom and refinement. Then classical education was born, partly as the issue of a revolt against prevailing university curricula. This classical education has meant the study by one civilization of the major works of an earlier and related civilization. In this case Greek and Roman literature and thought is the source from which the human arts were to be learned.

This classical education involved learning the Latin and Greek languages. Often enough pedants and tyrants turned the classics into endless basic training over the hurdles of ancient grammar. These suicidal devotees completed their work shortly before our own time. But even today classical education can elicit a response only less than the Renaissance passion. Classical education has been the great basis for general education and for the formation of generalists. Today it is unacceptable but only as the exclusive basis for general education. The breadth achievable in classical education may partially be accounted for. Rome established the humanities as an object of study after a remarkable work of borrowing and adaptation. The wonder of this openness is rarely allowed for. We are inclined to assume that the borrowing was inevitable and to reproach Rome for its unoriginality.

The religious divisions inaugurated by the Reformation give an additional importance to the study of the Greek and Roman classics: the study was common to Catholic and Protestant and so provided a basis for communication.

At times, classical humanism constricted the prospect of humanity, as is strikingly evident in the Battle of the Ancients and Moderns. Broadly speaking, the Moderns gradually prevailed in essentials in the field of culture, whereas education was long dominated by the Classicists. For the Ancients the Golden Age was the past; among some of the Moderns was a belief in progress and, for a smaller number, a millennial hope. If indeed there is progress, man cannot entirely be prepared for the future: and at the very least man must turn from past humanity to the way he is changing or being changed. Where there is substantial progress, man must take account of the new man.

Science and industrialism changed the world and offered men novel experiences. Labor took new forms and sought new significance. Society entered upon a process of steady modification. Discredited ancient creeds like democracy attracted new and regenerative fervor.

In the face of such tremors of the social landscape classical humanist education was slowly transformed. To demands for rapid change it was inanely argued that the special value of a classical education was its lack of immediate usefulness. Only a complacent society could accept this argument but it is even more difficult to characterize the asininity of those who advanced it. As early as the sixteenth century there began a tradition of criticizing university classical education for being buried in language and the arts and for failing to prepare people for a world of many states, rivalries and public service. By the eighteenth and nineteenth centuries, this European world had accumulated bodies of knowledge that went far beyond the achievements of the Greek and Roman world. To the curriculum were added natural sciences and historical inquiry into the kingdoms and nations of Europe.

The European universities, of course, had never been citadels of humanistic studies in the modern guise of general education. On the continent the universities had a strong professional bias and, otherwise, were devoted to critical scholarship and scientific research. The curricula of Oxford and Cambridge, assuming that general education had already begun and would be carried on in society later, offered degrees for reading in single subjects or a program of more humane letters. European university education was for a limited group, for an elite or for those with elitist ambitions.

The American experience has been notably different. By the twentieth century increasingly larger proportions of American youth were attending universities. Even 20 years ago Michigan State University could make the sobering boast that its enrollment had doubled in every decade of the century. Growth of such magnitude, on occasion, compelled educators to reassess what they were doing. In the first place, it had to be recognized that in the new circumstances a college education was not a special mark of the would-be elite. If Everyman was Bachelor of Arts, then what distinction could be made between all the rest and Everyman? In such circumstances would there be a bottom of the barrel to scrape? Were we all cream of the cream, a land, so to speak, of cream and honey? Clearly, however, we were not nearing the Golden Age, although it could be hoped that American democracy and universal education made for a high level of moral living.

This advantage was substantially nullified by some of the values and institutions of American society. Furthermore, and secondly, American state and other universities had accepted the goal of serving society—but service could impair the detached critique that the universities as trustees of humanistic studies might also be expected to direct against the perversions and dislocations fostered by society. This relationship involves a delicate balance, for in the West a university cannot but be in part an expression of the culture of its society. It should not be an aloof refuge but it should have ivory towers. If the ivory tower university may symbolize irrelevance, individualism and sterility, the university scholars who cannot withdraw to loneliness, perspective and possible creativity are likely to perish in the thin air of expediency and in the enervating cycle of short-term views.

The opponents of the democratic venture of near universalism in higher education argue that in effect it goes against the very nature of things. Leo Strauss has reiterated the position that liberal education is inevitably the preparation of an elite to rule, for only a few will become truly free and therefore able to rule.

The weight of experience is on the elitist side. But the weight of past experience does not invariably hold for the future. If the elitists are right, the American educational effort is certainly wasteful. Nevertheless, our enterprise is remarkably flexible and has, as the jargon goes, many tracks. We have devised a remarkable structure of courses with numbers and credits so that the credits become currency for a degree. Courses are to a considerable extent as interchangeable as the currency. Many of the courses are rigidly compartmented or better departmented and their educational results are measured by an implausible and ingenious levying of papers, quizzes and examinations. Surprisingly, this improbable arrangement has worked, unevenly, but it has worked. It provides variety of personal and subject-matter stimulation, a varied offering of courses based on a conventional pattern with a number of apparent novelties that may in varying measure be attributed to educational statesmanship, copying of status schools, ingenious salesmanship or, generally, the "who gets what" interplay of faculty interest groups. Inevitable superficiality may make for tedium but not for harrowing boredom. And the arrangement does not readily foster the more insidious forms of pedagogical tyranny.

The arrangement, for it is not a system, suffers from a lack of focus and from two educational imperialisms. The lack of focus is synonymous with plural approaches that separately present and sometimes fragment the divisions of inquiry and knowledge. As every teacher, to paraphrase Paul Valery, must suggest or imply an idea of man, the student may hourly move from the image of classical or religious man to man as controller and programmer of man. The effect is confusing and may be stunning. The imperialisms that threaten the liberal arts college and its provinces, the humanities, have been identified by Jacques Barzun as those of the high school and of the professional graduate school. The former, especially some prep schools, may offer the equivalent of college courses and their students upon coming to college may be exempted from courses in the humanities. If the high schools should genuinely pre-empt part of the work of general education, this should be matter for rejoicing to all but the professorial trade unionists, the electricians and carpenters on college faculties. If colleges can devise more advanced courses that will serve the cause of education, well and good. If not, the reduction of the four-year college span is in order, no matter what difficulties the reduction may create for subordinate activities. Above all, spirited resistance should greet proposals to make the college a mental leaf-raking project or a disguised detention home, that is, to extend the four years of college to five years so that colleges can keep the young from flooding the labor market. If American society with its horrendous problems cannot find tasks for its young (and to speak in my own interest, its older) people, it deserves a fate worse than the most fervent anti-American can wish for it.

The second imperialism, which looms formidably from its base in the university, involves specialized departmental interests undermining general education. The department, staffed as it is by its devotees, is founded on specialization, which it may wish to promote as early as possible in a student's career. Where this outlook prevails, a department's introductory course, even when it is a college requirement and, therefore, a part of the general education curriculum, may be taught as initial specialization without concern for the larger questions that should inspire general education.

Compared to the European system, American practice has allowed great flexibility. But the pace of social change, the rapid proliferation of problems and, in the absence of rigorous and painful discrimination, the awesome accumulation of information and items to be learned (knowledge explosion is the pompous and, for the humanities, the incredibly illusory name used to describe this) intensify the process whereby the teaching of any one time becomes an anachronism and the sere fruit of a tree other than the golden tree of life.

This present situation is remarkable for many things: surely among them is student flattery of the teachers they attack. The late Joe College did not find education immediately relevant and he sought a life away from the labors, aridities and tyrannies of what he equated, pedantry and learning. Joe College had his eye on a heavenly city, the American way of life, and believed that college helped his passage there. He did not rebel against the pedagogues who stood as obstacle-witches to the hero in his quest. These were figures to be outwitted, suffered, or endured much as chic Catholics once offered up their more difficult acquaintances. Today, radical students, who attract enough mimetic support to mistake themselves for a Toynbee creative minority, attack the irrelevance of their teachers, apparently because they had hoped for more, inasmuch as they know that American society is not a heavenly city. Indeed with vehemence and exaggeration, characteristic of youth movements, some of the radical Left describe our society as utterly corrupt, a judgment, that, if mine, would end all my hope for an improved future. I have been touchingly invited by those who knew nothing about me to abandon the irrelevancies I "profess" and to join them as an equal in building a just society. Where this thinking has some consistency, we even learn that the effective restructuring of the university must await the beginnings of revolutionary social construction. There can be no mistaking the totalitarian temper of such talk. At any rate, it is entirely suicidal, which may pass as a strong synonym for irrelevant.

The more practical criticisms on my own campus echo issues raised throughout the nation: the courses themselves are too fixed in the lines of subject matter and its divisions, in adherence to specified meetings and lectures, and in adaptation to a competitive society. One point is a criticism of past and present practice: the desire expressed on behalf of students for association on informal basis with faculty members.

The proposal to have one or more pass-fail courses in a semester is at best a minor reform and not at all the basis for comprehensive reform. Grading or rating achievement is inescapable and, in the main, may be expected to be helpful. But how is work graded? And what do examinations examine? Examinations cannot be the *raison d'être* of a humanities course designed for general education; on occasion they have been made so. Grades, possibly even more than money, have been foolishly overprized and used for misguided purposes. Cannot reform be attempted where the fault actually lies? The question, asking for directness, has in America a noncontemporary resonance. The proposal to abolish grades all around is almost entirely deleterious. It yields to the guilt feelings of the well-endowed and good performers and to the pretense of the ill-motivated, and perhaps the ill-equipped that they can truly love the subject for itself when grade considerations are removed. The whole point of excellence is that it excludes the equality of everything and is reached by marking and seeking to exceed the good and the better.

The rejection of a competitive society takes many forms. First of all, the competitiveness of the collegiate world is presented in exaggerated terms and as something nigh unprecedented. Then the attack on competition leads to an attack on grades. It is not recognized that competition may provide a stimulus in dull days and a provocation to work that in time may become more highly motivated.

Testimony cited in favor of abolishing grades usually fails to note that successful classes without grades are responding to a special challenge. But all of us cannot burn always with a gemlike flame; there are good and bad days and on the bad ones routine may be salvation. There are humdrum days and anguished days in the academy and in the concentration camp.

John Gerassi, one witness, is at war with competitiveness. So to a class at San Francisco State[1] he announced that everybody would get an A and urged students to do "whatever the course inspired them to really want to say." Some did nothing but "never before have I received such solid, thoughtful, meaningful work from not only registered students, but also auditors." The most illuminating work, Gerassi judged, was "the product of a collective —including a 20-page poem about Nicaraguan rebel 'General of the People' Sandino, written by six students working together. Does it matter whether or not it was good? .... To the future of mankind, what will matter will be the attitude of such students who can relate and correlate their egos to try to create together."

For Gerassi, then, no grading and no authority, "except the authority willingly delegated because of respect earned not through knowledge and 'objective' competitive accomplishment, but through the use of that knowledge in warmth and human consideration."

Gerassi is the herald of an age of heartwarming conmanship. His radicalism here seems to be an obvious preliminary to raising the cry: "All power to Dale Carnegie and Madison Avenue."

If I have cited Gerassi at length, it is because he is frank about his objectives. Generally a very low level pervades the discussions of grade reformers.

Mervin Freedman has written in favor of altering and "liberalizing grading programs so that students in their early college years will not be dismissed for academic failure. The goal, he has proclaimed, is joyous life fulfillment and for such a goal presumably everyone will be seriously motivated—a solution to the problem of quality that is not likely to become an educational classic. His vision of the future he has compared to the "arrangements at Oxford and Cambridge" .... where "acceptance of the student by a college will mean a commitment to educate him."[2] Here, the word "educate" is entirely misleading and the author has not mentioned that the apparently easygoing atmosphere and liberty of Oxbridge is grounded in a competitive system far more formidable and taxing than the American system which troubles Professor Freedman. What he has done here is as imprecise as suggesting that the permissiveness of the "Abbey of Theleme" was for just anybody.

The student desire for closer personal association with teachers has something to do with the contemporary quest for community as well as the desire for physical togetherness that I lost as a high-school commuter in the New

---

1 Gerassi, "Trouble at San Francisco State," *New York Review of Books,* X, Number 7 (April 11, 1968), 45.

2 Freedman, *The College Experience* (San Francisco, 1967), pp. 177-178.

York subways. There are, I believe, some people who loved Beethoven's Ninth Symphony and mankind until they experienced the Living Theatre. The admirable Robert A. Nisbet has quoted a Columbia student to argue the elevating conclusion that the purport of this demand is that teachers be conscientious teachers and competent scholars. That is not the meaning of the Notre Dame students' wishes and for that matter Nisbet's point is in a venerable polemic tradition: hortatory idealism smuggling in a conclusion. As I understand it, the demand is not that the teacher be more effective but that he be affecting.

This quest for feeling togetherness, in tribe, gang, or community, must be taken into account in any teaching. As reaction to mechanical and bureaucratic society, the search makes a valid criticism in behalf of humanity. But it is an instinctive reaction that immediately goes beyond the limits of humanity. Man in tribal groups feels in group fashion and ignores the discrimination and decencies that must weigh on the individual mind and conscience in civilization. Humanity involves social ties and joys but man's conscience may also require an inescapable loneliness, which man may avoid only at the cost of impairing his humanity.

Under prevailing circumstances the other criticisms can only be met by expedients. Among the prevailing circumstances is the widespread unwillingness of faculty purposefully to discuss educational objectives and philosophy. This antipathy to generalizing and theorizing is grounded in American culture; it is supported by a recognition of the diversity of faculty views and the consequent difficulty of such discussion; and it also serves to protect existing educational interests including departmental autonomy. General educational discussions often confirm this antipathy. First of all, the discussions are frequently thin—there are great possibilities in a musical comedy about the academic world that might be called "Jejune Moon." Secondly, because discussions of general education are too often ideologies to serve existing interests. New combinations and approaches that will override existing arrangements require not a compromise bargained by competing interests but a response to serve agreed objectives.

The objective of the humanities, man's growth in understanding himself, is largely achieved through the interplay of opinion, provocative questioning, and the recognition of persisting dilemmas. Opinions and insights, however, are not random and equal; they present varied measures of comprehension and penetration of life. Properly the first task of the humanities is to awaken and broaden the intellectual awareness of the student and to direct his enlivened concern to the major issues and questions of human living.

Ideally, but definitely not in practice, the humanities and the demands of specialized studies are in no irrepressible conflict. The study of the former may precede the latter and presumably the humanities-trained professional is humanly and socially superior to the single-minded professional or scholar. But even if the prep and high schools and the professional ambitions of students and faculties remove from the curriculum the general education courses in humanities, it is still likely that many professional teachers will teach their courses with an eye to relationship, relative values and the range of human purpose.

It may be argued that for a humanities course to be profitable, it is necessary to have a good teacher. A professional course, on the other hand, has a subject matter that remains important and demanding no matter what the teacher's quality is. And the very intangibility of humanities education makes it suspect to some scientists and professional educators—and makes quality control of it very difficult for administrators. The role of personality, the inevitable diversity in some humanistic studies, and the absence of rigorous and unvarying methods, predispose some to look on humanistic education as an affair of dilettantes disguising themselves in the masks of the geniuses of the past.

In the twentieth century classical education has given place to liberal and general education. The latter properly extended the corpus of its teaching texts to the masterworks of Western civilization. The selection and approach have presented many variations. A major advantage of the Great Books approach is that it encompassed both theology and the history of science. The approach, also, has fostered its own major disputes, especially between those who would add to the program a strong concern with writing, history, and social science and those including Mortimer Adler who find in the canon of the Great Books all that is needful for general education.

It may be granted to Adler that his textbooks, the products of great minds or creative spirits, do not date. Additionally, the Great Books Seminars foster a direct response that lectures cannot easily inspire and have the advantage of the group discussion, a kind of love-feast sacrament for some of today's students.

The combined courses formally entitled humanities may involve briefer selections from a wider area than the great books and may be organized under headings that proclaim contemporary concerns. The contemporary *jihad* against irrelevance was anticipated by a long vogue of the modern: there was a preoccupation with the literary and intellectual works of the most recent phase of Western civilization. Such exclusive concentration on modern authors in general education and even in scholarship is decidedly questionable in terms of scholarship but above all for its educational value. Students may properly expect that a collegiate curriculum will put them in touch with some vital inquiries of contemporary society and prevent them from being a stranger (alienation, of course, is more "in" than was mononucleosis for a time) in their own world. But exclusive concentration on the modern is about as relevant as self-imprisonment, for it confines us to man agonizing in the cultural crisis in which we live. In the face of man's modern impairment and laceration the student may never acquire any sense of the range of human powers and creativity and he may mistake the spiritual nihilism or desperation of much of the prophetic tradition in modern art for social documentation.

I can see no grounds for sharply separating the fine arts and music from the humanities. But I also insist that the university and the arts do not happily coexist as though they were soul-mates. Notre Dame's College of Arts and Letters distinguishes among the following areas: humanities, creative and fine arts, social sciences, and natural sciences and mathematics. This separation of the creative and fine arts from the humanities is imposed by a number of practical considerations as much as it is by principle. But what is the principle? Does it involve the ancient prejudice against manual labor and the act of making? Does it involve the rare academic restraint of recognizing that for creativity in the individual arts, unlike the team arts of theatre, orchestra, and film, the academy is more coach, cheering section and Monday-morning quarterback than alma mater. In the vocal music field we can perhaps accept operatic folklore and allow college credit for all except tenor singing courses.

The arts tell us much of what we are and may be. Cultivated taste and the love of beauty and form may help to shape a style of living and thinking. But to use art as a religion and as the *magister vitae* of the individual and society is wholly questionable, for it is to rule personal relations, the transitions of our temporal state, by images and by what then becomes pedantry of style. In the complex relationship of literature and politics note should be made that literature illuminates society and bears upon politics. But literature has its own purpose and no more than the cinema does it offer political guidance.

This is to say that the humanities today involve some inevitable dangers and have special weaknesses of this particular moment.

First of all, the task of the humanities is to be urgently concerned with the quality of human living and with raising questions of value. The absence of a firm sense of human values, that is, of the necessities of humane living, has made for the inadequacy of social criticism and reform in the last two centuries. Our reforms have sometimes been as ill-conceived or limited as the conditions they were designed to amend.

Accordingly, today the university should essay a constructive role where it once followed a course that had destructive effects, at least, in part. As popular attendance at universities began its twentieth-century rise, university teachers often proved to be enlightened solvents of the religious, family and social beliefs of their students. Some sociological studies dispute the statement that university teachers have had such an effect; they argue, in the vein of Thomas Love Peacock, that education gives a permanent bent to one's stupidity and merely serves as confirmer of values already acquired. This view does not accord with my experience. Frequently the dissolving was done and only the most fragmentary faiths or values replaced the lost faith.

The constructive work is all the more necessary today because the pace of change challenges our values and opinions in Chinese firecracker fashion, which is what William James said, or should I say, in chain reaction? For the time being the injunctions of authority are little regarded and it is insisted that value judgments must be made by the individual conscience. Curiously enough, however, very little attention is paid to the formation and enlightenment of conscience. Today, clichés, emotionally charged words and protest charades may still be the source of values adopted without reflection, not to mention searching thought. Some young people are bearers of the "counter culture" and many of them are its prisoners. A first task of the humanities is to help save the individual and society by prodding the individual to cultivate his conscience and to learn the implications of making value judgments. The vogue of language analysis in philosophy may be a clarifying influence but in the living forms in which I have encountered it the influence has not been helpful to moral education. Most of the traditional humanities may serve to this end, if the teacher is concerned for human education rather than his own advancement in administration or even in his discipline. Admittedly the teacher will have to be a Socrates—and he will have to recognize that value judgments are matters of opinion and that opinions may vary in incisiveness, sublety and refinement.

In view of our problems it must be sorrowfully recognized that the level of our public discussion is often deplorably low. Individualism, legalism, public relations trickery, political vulgarization and demagoguery contribute to this low condition. What social conclusion of any kind can be ruled out by a proponent of enforced family limitation, who can argue that just as the law limits a man to one wife, so it can limit a family to one child? Or what evidence of thought is in Dr. Kingsley Davis' program for population restriction including the abolition of dependency allowances and the offering of tax incentives to unmarried people? Dr. Davis waves aside fears of military weakness from a reduced population by citing the example of Israel which "has shown that manpower is of very little importance militarily, that modern wars are pushing buttons and paper work."[3] Such extravagant and reckless statements almost guarantee that an issue will not be seriously discussed.

On the one hand man should study ideas and achievements historically so that he learns how he is limited by time, circumstances and necessity. But the humanities should also be studied aesthetically, ethically and philosophically —not bound by time. The former approach by itself may inhibit the imagi-

---

[3] *New York Times,* October 5, 1969.

nation and even the will. But the latter needs the former so that we remember who we are—and do not imagine that all things are possible and at once.

The present task of humanistic studies in general education is to foster the development of the individual's resources and being and in enriching his awareness to enable him to relate awareness and conscience to his democratic fellows of a technological society and to the people of the world's cultures who have in a limited way become his neighbors. Almost no system of education, at the present moment, pretends that it can render man a kind of ventriloquist dummy who will somehow echo set answers—or that it can enable him to run through a life-course for which he has been programmed. But since my childhood, at any rate, there have always been academic voices concerned to remove the burdens of freedom and frustration from man by making destiny efficient and a science.

Today these machinophile Platonists talk about programming men. They would reduce mankind to a ventriloquist dummy. The product is repulsive but it is all the more ridiculous that the ventriloquist has nothing to say, apart from his doubtful belief that the dummy will no longer be a source of trouble.

Man, if he is to remain relatively free and human, will constantly be called to choose and to establish priorities. And it is this task of choosing for which he requires preparation. Even if standards and principles were abundant, universal and radiantly clear, the problem of moral decision making, involving the assessment of realities and the weighing of possible courses and consequences, remains very complex. Some of this sense is acquired by living, that is, by on-the-job training. We know, moreover, that the young are not subject to initiation rites and there is ample evidence that the older generation has not informed them or served as models. So—the problem of responsible moral decision making in ascertaining values, and in moral questions, presents unusual difficulties. It is highly doubtful whether the human resources available, that is, those who will volunteer for this work are sufficient for the general establishment of the program. Practical men may understandably grow impatient with a problem that may be almost insoluble. The problem, nevertheless, does not go away.

If the humanities must deal directly with the good life and moral questions, they must also go beyond the trammels of the past. If they remain closed to the achievements and visions of science, they may more properly be regarded as genteel anachronisms.

The humanities must begin with biology; man in his pride must come to terms with himself as animal and as partly in nature. Throughout his life he is likely to have to learn and relearn that in some measure he can transform his nature and even transcend it—but he cannot deny it without self-destruction or rousing avenging furies. Nor is he the creator of himself and of society. This was once obvious enough but it is not today, when high-flying notions that might be proper guidelines for the creation of a new world are praised as sincere idealism. If under one aspect nature means limits and boundaries, it also means possibilities to man, who may acquire some control even of his genetic code. Such power may make life more desirable: it could as well make it more hideous.

Literature and the arts have been a principal source of education of the emotions and sensibilities. Today we can add psychology. For purposes of general education something more than an introduction to the strict science of psychology is needed, for the achievements of the strict science are too limited to the subject of perception and learning. For general education purposes not enough can be learned from the study of rats. An introductory course should then range from the control-inspired areas of science to some account of psychological theories in relation to the life problems of the individual.

But the humanities must also take account of man's social nature. There is no good reason for classifying government only with the social sciences.

I would submit that most political theorists as well as macrotheorists in sociology and even in economics are dealing with issues of large concern to the humanities. And the humanities teacher may concentrate on what is basically a concern of the study of government. As an example, the admirable Notre Dame freshman humanities seminar, given experimentally since 1967, has been defended primarily as a course to awaken the student as a developing human being who will presumably respond to the personal setting and the relevance of the questions raised, as well as to rigorous training in reading and writing. Here, I suspect, we are back at the old measures and men problem. The apologists of the humanities course argue that introductory courses given by particular departments within the humanities are professionally oriented and emphasize content and methodology to the possible neglect of the student's needs. But, barring a protracted Maoist "cultural revolution," even the humanities seminar is likely to have its apparatchiks, bureaucrats, mandarins, pedants and drill sergeants. And a learned and imaginative teacher of government should be able to raise more incisive questions about man's civic life than are to be found in the sustained shrillness of the political writings of Noam Chomsky. The teacher of government may be expected to be superior in revealing the inadequacies of some readily given answers concerning the students' relation to the world.

The academic teaching of the humanities has not grown with the expanding world of modern times. Eric Ashby, in fact, has defined a university as a "mechanism for the inheritance of the Western style of civilization." Now Western scholars and humanists, as individuals and as Orientalists, have illuminated the history and features of Asian and African cultures. But the curriculum has not been widened to enrich our notions of humanity by African and Asian humanity, to consider their vision of man and to provide their cautionary tales about human behavior and excess. Until 1945 Europeans studied largely European history and in the United States Western History courses were called world history into the 1960's. In curious fashion the extension of the range of humanistic studies to include Oriental readings and Oriental and African art has been urged for minor practical reasons of national interest rather than on the unimpeachable grounds that the masterpieces of Oriental civilization enrich our conceptions of man and his possibilities, of the world, and of God.

Some colleges have instituted courses in non-Western areas, an unimaginative title clearly of self-regarding origin. Others have been sufficiently well-endowed and generally resourceful so that they have established elective courses in Oriental Humanities. The widening of the curriculum is not easily done—you cannot simply append Confucius, *The Tale of Genji,* and the *Koran* to an already existing course-list of readings. The works and art of other civilizations must be approached through a study of their culture. And it is well for man to see himself and his culture from another cultural perspective. It is above all well for him to recognize that his culture, which makes so much available to him, also limits him almost in the fashion of a Kantian category. The escape from the harsher limitations of the category requires as a first step the recognition of the category.

If the humanities, then, turn to questions of value and decision making and open themselves to the vision of science; if they broaden their scope to meet with subjects that are classed with the social sciences and their realm is extended to embrace Asian and African man, then the humanities may help to make modern man human.

They may recall to us that men and women have a nature, plastic though it is. Today the possibilities in front of us may induce forgetfulness of the limits. Margot Henthoff, for example, has written in physical rebellion against her womanhood. Her objective is that women should have a full and equal part in the world's public life (a man's world and rotten). She is summarizing another author when she notes that for woman to be more than the eternal footman it will be necessary to destroy the family system and reproduction within the female. But she approves and adds:

> This future is made at least faintly plausible by projected advances in biology which deal with the artificial production of life. Add to this the increasing need to limit population and you have the possibility of eliminating women *qua* women altogether.[4]

---

[4] *New York Review of Books,* January 16, 1969, p. 3.

This sketchy utopia of Mrs. Henthoff goes beyond the nightmares of George Orwell and Aldous Huxley.

To yield to my own point of view I should hope that students would learn that though group action is frequently clumsy, men must learn to respect or be patient with limits that inhere in the nature of many people moving together. The clumsiness inheres in the fact that men are persons. Mass action may be speedier but it is primitive. Violations of rights and public order, to vindicate a claim to a new right or for high-minded or pecksniffian causes, may cause damage out of proportion even to the good sought. Those who would extend the sphere of liberties will be more effective, and less counter-productive, if they recall how slowly liberties have been won and how precariously they have been maintained.

This is a view that is contested and disregarded. The attack is oblivious to the lesson drawn by many in the 1940's that the individual conscience encounters ambiguities and recalcitrant dilemmas in relating morality and political action. Against this is hurled the lie direct followed by the flooding play of an indignation that finds the presence of some evil evidence of thoroughgoing corruption. The attack is grounded in the magnitude of the problems and discontents in our society. It then proceeds to the stupefying conclusion that these problems are open to fairly quick solution or that a new society in replacing the old—how? by revolution, right on!—will provide satisfactory institutions. The further jump is made that students and teachers will be the avant-garde in evolving the solutions or in spelling out revolution. This is to suggest that the university will leave behind its more limited work and bourgeois integrity in order to undertake the task of brain-trusting and agitpropping for the revolution. The humanities, here, would be ruled out—as Lenin ruled them out, for, in inculcating moderation even in hope, the humanities are thought to be touts of the ruling class.

Louis Kampf, author of a book *On Modernism,* concluded that the study of the humanities today, far from making young people aware of their capacities, "forces them to ignore themselves." Reality is a world desperately in need of change but liberal education either pretends that the need does not exist or that academic routine will take care of it. The humanities, disguising the dislocations of industrial society behind the mask of a traditional culture, have become "the educational system's unwilling collaborators in destroying our experience—that is, our humanity."[5]

The above criticism conveys an attack on genteel remnants in the humanities but extends it to their modern substance. The aspiration that enables a

---

[5] Louis Kampf, "The Humanities and Inhumanities," *The Nation,* September 30, 1968, p. 310.

man to feel the love that moves the stars may readily turn into a hatred of man the trouble-maker. The very brilliance of the future man may envisage can also drive him to hate the bald or hairy human mess that stands in the way of millennium. Very recently in browsing through journals I came across a revealing sample of the millennialist's hatred for man. The author argued that "the experience-oriented, mystical, internationalist, tribal hippie is the only working . . . example of a feasible future man." The hippie's "whole philosophy of being encompasses and adjusts to the three primary facts of truly modern man: (1) overkill, (2) psychedelic modification of man's nature, and (3) electronic permeability." The hippie is separated from "the political *is* but lives in the political *must*." Man must evolve genetically from the egocentric, territory-protecting carnivore to "a passive, 'charitable,' altruistic" herbivore. "In the near future controlled evolution will be commonplace, but in order to guarantee that future, biochemical modification (that is, the use of psychedelic drugs) is imperative now." So to guarantee that we shall survive into a warless world, we must in the interval tame ourselves with LSD. Finally, with underground television comes an age of electronic humanism as psychedelic electronics break down "the barriers between the me and not-me," and "allow the total permeability (interpenetration) of self and environment."[6]

This is a characteristic piece of modern utopianism. Its striking quality is its belief in progress and its fear of man. By playing on man's nervous system with drugs man may be brought to the point where you can breed out, so to speak, the genes for original sin.

Utopianism may be a form of ironic criticism but otherwise it is quackery. It goes from the present with its evil and problems to the glorious future by ideological patent medicines, short cuts and other trickery.

A venerable American tradition is prepared to call even the most difficult demands and impossible aspirations of the young and reformers—idealism. Let the word stand and, if we do, we cannot pretend that railings and tantrums against the nature of things are creative or anything other than suicidal. Dr. Timothy Leary has voiced this extraordinary subjectivism in his statement that if man can control his nervous system, he can manipulate and control the world (or to use an old-fashioned word, reality). On another level young people emphasize interpersonal relations somehow without being much concerned with the persons being related.

Man cannot create the world anew, but with mighty prayer he may renew his soul.

The humanities are concerned with awakening man's capacities and help-

---

[6] Hugh Fox, "American Mystique," *The Colorado Quarterly,* Summer, 1968, pp. 38-39. Arthur Koestler has also made much of drugs as tamers of man.

ing to fulfill them. I have suggested that to be human is to live in an uneasy balance. Today, the humanities may need support for research and publication but that is not a first priority either for the sake of the humanities or for the civilized living they must foster. Funds are needed to encourage experiments in general education and teaching and generally to encourage venturesomeness in teaching.

Venturesomeness is a must for devising the courses in decision making, value judgments and morals. Beyond that the humanities must slough off their past exclusivism to enter into rapport with the study of group man and to broaden the concept of humanity with the views and insights of Africa and Asia.

The balanced human being is finally a work of moral art. Balance requires the participation of all human constituents. If the sleep of reason produces monsters, it must also be said that the dictatorship of reason is a self-betrayal. Some of our radical students make it a reproach to their teachers that we are excessively rationalist. The French sociologist, Michael Crozier, agreed with them and found in our country "an arrogance of rationality" to match the "arrogance of power" of which Senator Fulbright has spoken. "It is a kind of folly" to assume that "a rational view of the world based on the inevitability of scientific progress can cope with a fragmented, culturally diverse society full of complex emotional problems."[7]

Some glimpses of the humanist art of balance are afforded in lines from Richard Eberhart's Harvard Phi Beta Kappa poem, "Sanders Theatre."

> A ritual exists in which existence
> Measures itself against its limitations.

---

[7] *The New York Times,* December 15, 1968.

# SOME CONSEQUENCES OF THE
# DEVELOPMENT OF SCIENTIFIC
# SOCIAL SCIENCES

Herbert Jacob*

It currently seems fashionable alternately to disparage or extol the accomplishments of social science. On the one hand, the accomplishments of social science seem dwarfed by the social problems that confront us. We are threatened by international conflict, by population explosion, by irretrievable pollution of our environment, and by deeply imbedded internal conflicts, to name only a few of our problems. Experts give us little assurance that we can solve those problems in a rational manner. On the other hand, the social sciences have come a long way in a very short time, and despite their shortcomings have made considerable contributions to social welfare and to social understanding. The seven years of economic growth and stability that this country has experienced since 1960 was not entirely an accident of circumstances but was a product of controlled development. Our manipulation of childhood environments in Head Start and regular school programs is the consequence of considerable research in child development and learning behavior. Our understanding (if not avoidance) of racial conflict has been increased by sociological and psychological inquiry.

I shall not endeavor to defend one position or the other; there is some measure of truth in both hope and disparagement. Rather, I shall attempt to clarify what is encompassed in the scientific study of human behavior and what some of the consequences of such a study are. Although I shall concentrate my attention on the latter topic, the first needs careful specification if my comments are to be taken seriously.

I

I am constantly amazed at what some elements of the general public and academic community take to be social science. Included are studies in history, biography, social comment, legal analyses of institutions, and manhole-cover

---

* I approach the subject as a practitioner and not as a philosopher of science; I regard this as an opportunity to reflect on my trade rather than to engage in it. This paper is not the product of scientific research into the subject matter. It is the result of my decade of experience as a political scientist and of my conversations with colleagues

counting, as well as survey research, mathematical modeling, laboratory experimentation, and computer analysis. Although there are many texts on the scientific method,[1] the extension of their definitions to the social sciences has not penetrated deeply enough to make clear what is to be excluded from a discussion of social science. My understanding of the scientific examination of social behavior includes at least the following three elements: (1) the subject matter selected for study must be selected on theoretical grounds; (2) the analysis must be conducted in such a fashion that inferences can be made within known limits of confidence; (3) the analysis must be amenable to replication by others. Let me clarify each of these requirements.

There are many grounds upon which to study a phenomenon. It may be popular to study one thing rather than another. The data may be more readily available for one subject than for another. Granting agencies may be more interested in one subject. The subject may strike the scholar's fancy. None of these are appropriate criteria for scientific inquiry. The only appropriate ground is that the selected phenomena raise (or promise to answer) questions which are significant to the theory, model or perspective which is currently used to describe a portion of social behavior.

Theory or models contribute to the agenda of scientific inquiry in many ways. Deductions from theory produce predictions (not forecasts) which can be tested. The theory will specify the conditions under which certain phenomena may be expected. We then look for that set of conditions and the associated predicted phenomena. Such a search is a scientific study. On the other hand, a theory or model may not be adequately accounting for behavior which has been observed. The attempt to square theory with observed data may also be scientific inquiry. Simple description—no matter how precise, quantitative, or elegant—is not part of a scientific enterprise unless that description is explicitly associated with a theoretical model.

The fact that research topics are chosen for theoretical reasons does not mean that scientific research is value-free. The choice of theoretical perspective and the choice of a subject for study do involve preferences. Moreover, the outcome of scientific studies may have policy implications by showing the consequences of past or future actions. Nevertheless, value preferences do not *control* the agenda for scientific research. Whatever the by-product of such research, its purpose is the furthering of knowledge and understanding and not the directing of social action. Hence my emphasis on theoretical criteria for choosing the subject of inquiry.

---

who are far more experienced than I am and who work in other disciplines. These comments should be treated as first estimations rather than the last word.

[1] For a much more detailed discussion of scientific methods in social research, see Ernest Nagel, *The Structure of Science* (New York, 1961) and Abraham Kaplan, *The Conduct of Inquiry* (San Francisco, 1964).

Secondly, the analysis must be conducted in such a fashion that inferences can be made within known confidence limits. If that is not done, we have no way of knowing what we really know—to what population the inferences can be made and how likely it is that they are wrong. This requirement has many implications for the collection of data and their analysis. It means that data must be collected in a systematic fashion which controls known sources of error and randomizes unknown sources. We must know the consequences of the data-collection procedure we use, so that we may identify possible sources of error. The universe from which data are drawn must be fully specified so that inferences can be limited to that universe. Ideally, we should be able to specify with precision the confidence limits of our inferences; that requires that we use statistical measures whose distributions are known. Much of the literature of methodology centers about these problems: how to collect data so that error variances are known, how to make inferences, how to minimize known error variance, and how to capitalize on random error variance.

Third, to be scientific a study must be made in such a manner that others may replicate it and test its conclusions. That means that the data-collection and analysis procedures must be fully specified. It also means that some credit must be given to those who replicate studies. Replication is essential so that the procedural and theoretical assumptions of researchers can be tested continuously. Through replication, research findings become the property of the entire research community rather than of an individual researcher. Confidence in results need not depend solely on the reputation of the individual researcher but can be buttressed by the continuing research output of a professional discipline.

Note that I have not included experimentation as a requirement for scientific study. It is only one of the several data-collection techniques which meet the prerequisites I have outlined. Experimentation permits the observer to control the variables more directly than in other modes of data collection; it permits swifter assignment of causality. However, I would not call all experiments scientific. For instance, much work has been with student populations where inferences to the adult universe cannot be made within known confidence limits. Moreover, if the experiments cannot be replicated or are not designed to test hypotheses derived from theory, I would not term them scientific even though they took place in a laboratory.

My understanding of social science leads to many other exclusions. Subject matter does not define social science. There is no element of social behavior which may not be studied using scientific methods. But simply because social behavior is being examined does not mean that the study is social science. The journals in almost every discipline are full of articles which are not scientific. Some of the most popular commentaries on social behavior do not meet scientific standards. One may admit, for instance, that much of what Erving Goffman says is insightful, but it is not the result of scientific analysis. Likewise, the myriad of articles on legal and social problems which fill our nation's law journals are not scientific analyses. Not everything that is said about social behavior is social science.

Secondly, not everything bearing numbers is social science. Counting is scarcely a new art for social commentators. Even Moses conducted a census, but he was scarcely a social scientist. It is fashionable to adorn social commentary with numbers ranging from proportions of people interviewed who favor something to economic statistics on market behavior. But neither the stock exchange pages of *The New York Times* nor the crude data reported numerically constitute science.

Third, while the computer is an enormous aid to scientific analysis, it is not part of a definition of social science. Computer print-out impresses only the uninitiated. It easily provides mountains of nonsense which must be carefully winnowed by the analyst. It makes complex statistical techniques available to many people who have only a slight knowledge of what these techniques entail with the result that misinterpretations of data abound. Indeed, social science journals currently publish numerous articles wherein arguments are adorned with meaningless significance estimates or with correlation coefficients which explain little of the variance. Such statistics are used because the computer routinely calculates them. While the computer may be a significant aid to social science, it can also be a hindrance when misused in these ways.

Fourth, social science need not be the product of large grants or teams of researchers. Much of the work in social science is now done on grants and in teams for reasons that we shall explore in a few moments. But some significant work is still being done by the individual researcher working with small funds that are the functional equivalent of research support provided by libraries and graduate assistants. The measure of science is not the size of the grant, its source, or the number of senior men on the project. Conversely, the fact that a project is funded by an unpopular agency or involves many men from several disciplines does not exclude it from the scientific category.

In short, social science is not designated by the external symbols which so often are thought to be associated with science. The scientific study of social phenomena is theoretically oriented, grounded in inferential logic and replicable. It is also often quantitative, statistical, and experimental, but these latter characteristics are the incidental rather than the necessary concomitants of social science.

II

The kind of enterprise I mean by social science is often a complex, costly undertaking because it requires the careful collection of data on social behavior. Ethical constraints raise the costs of observing people beyond those of collecting data on mice. The fact that people interact with their environment (even when it happens to be a research environment) also raises costs. Most important, systematic observation which controls or randomizes error is far more expensive than casual observation. The social scientist does not see anything beyond the ken of the journalist, but casual, journalistic observation does not permit inference within known confidence limits or replication. Systematic observation requires a much greater investment of financial and organizational resources.

Many of the consequences of the scientific endeavor to which I want to call attention are caused by the high investment of money, people and skills. High costs have organizational consequences and implications for the independence of the scientist. They also affect his role as social critic.

The high cost of much social science can be illustrated by the costs of collecting data through a sample survey. A survey which uses a form of random sampling and is carried out by trained interviewers costs at least $30 per respondent, plus another $10 per respondent for processing the data so that they can be utilized by the analyst. Thus, the minimal cost for a survey conducted in a concentrated area is $40,000 for 1,000 respondents, the minimum usually required for sampling adequacy and the statistical control of a large number of variables. The cost is higher when respondents are scattered over a large geographical area as in a national survey. The costs for observing behavior in a laboratory or for observing them on a street corner are not less; indeed, they may be much higher because such observation must be conducted by more highly trained and more expensive personnel.

The high cost of data collection has several implications. The first is that social scientists have become dependent on outside support. Very few can finance their own research. They must seek funds from government agencies or private foundations. This situation is not unlike that in the physical and biological sciences, but it is a new one for social scientists.[2] Students of society had been accustomed to working independently, drawing either on their own

---

[2] A gross indicator of the trend is indicated by the following data on research support reported by authors of articles in the principal journals in economics, political science and sociology.

Proportion of articles for which research support was
received from foundations or government agencies

| | 1930 | 1940 | 1950 | 1960 | 1968 |
|---|---|---|---|---|---|
| *American Economic Review* | 5%(22)* | 0(36) | 11%(27) | 39%(23) | 68%(28) |
| *American Political Science Review* | 0 (12) | 0 (9) | 8 (26) | 22 (32) | 57 (51) |
| *American Sociological Review* | —— | 8(52) | 14 (59) | 43 (47) | 72 (46) |

* Number in parentheses indicates total number of articles in each year.

wealth or from their salaries. The social scientist now finds constraints imposed by his need to obtain funding for his research. Those constraints operate in a number of ways. They induce social scientists to speak in terms of scientific orthodoxy because fellow scientists judge their applications. A new approach is somewhat less likely to be funded because it lacks spokesmen on the reviewing committee. The need to obtain funds induces scientists to construct their research designs to appeal to the whims of agencies which happen to be momentarily richly funded rather than in ways which are strictly appropriate for the analysis which is planned. It makes scientists inordinately sensitive to shifts in the interests of funding agencies. When the Ford Foundation or the federal government shifts its interests, it means disaster for one group of scientists and a bonanza for another. Political scientists have seen foundation whims in the last decade veer from metropolitan politics to Latin-American politics to African politics to the politics of development and to urban problems. Then Ford withdrew almost entirely from research support in favor of "action" programs. Each shift reflected a response to a perceived social or political crisis rather than a substantive discovery which altered the scientific agenda. Social scientists adjust by juggling their priorities and by finding ways to examine their theoretically fundamental problems within the constraints of current foundation and government fads. Thus the scientific enterprise as I described it in my opening remarks has been corrupted by extraneous considerations—extraneous in terms of the theory which is being examined but essential in terms of the resources which make scientific work possible.

I have seen no evidence that scientifically sound proposals have not been funded because they were politically unpopular with the authorities, that is, because they might have led to conclusions which the authorities did not like. Such claims are sometimes made, but often by proponents of projects which should not be funded on scientific grounds alone. On the other hand, it seems true that projects of dubious scientific value are funded because of their popular appeal or because they do advance the value preferences of the funding agency.

I do not think influence from nonscientific quarters is entirely inappropriate. If a considerable expenditure is to be made from public or private funds that can be used for other purposes, it ought to compete in terms of ultimate pay-off. Scientists do not have the right to expect unlimited largesse. The question is not whether some control should be exerted over such expenditures, but how much and what kind. As long as the criteria are those of scientific pay-off and the reviewing committee remains open to novel approaches and theories, I do not object to outside review of project applications. But political, social, and scientific orthodoxies are objectionable. One means of protecting against the imposition of such orthodoxies is to maintain a multiplicity of sources for funding research. These need to be both private and public. They need to be under the control of different groups within the scientific establishment and responsive to different elements of the general population. Such diversity probably provides the best guarantee of vigorous growth in the social sciences.

Even under these conditions it cannot be denied that the social scientist's role of social critic has been curbed. But dependence on outside funding is only one of several causes for his decline as a social critic. Equally—perhaps more—important is his reliance on scientific theory to guide research and analysis. The net result is that many social scientists now feel disinclined to be social critics. I would prefer that even more social scientists explicitly disavowed their critical function. I know some of my colleagues will disagree vigorously with me on this point, but it seems to me that social scientists are not in the best position to be critics of society. They depend on some portion of an establishment for funding. Their knowledge is specialized; they are locked into a status quo of one sort or another by the existence of the phenomena that they examine. They are obliged to set aside their value biases when analyzing their data. Others may certainly use their studies as the bases for a critique of society, but critic and scientist may be incompatible roles. The social scientist as teacher may contribute to social criticism by training a cadre of social commentators, men and women who understand the results of social research but do not engage in it. The scientist himself, with his commitment to social theory rather than social action, is an ineffective agitator.

Organizational change is another consequence of the high cost of data gathering and the high degree of specialized knowledge that data collection and analysis requires. This change has occurred in several dimensions: social science is less frequently an individual enterprise, it has spilled over institutional boundaries, and it has broken disciplinary confines.

Social science has increasingly become a group enterprise, but no single pattern of institutionalization exists. For many scientists, collaboration is an informal, ad hoc arrangement with a number of colleagues and technicians recruited for a single project. The group disperses at the end of the project. Alternatively, the single researcher contracts portions of his project to a service bureau like the Survey Research Center at the University of Michigan. He is also likely to use the services of a computer programming group at his institution's computer center. Such service agencies exist to provide ad hoc services to researchers in many disciplines. For other researchers, affiliation with a research group is more permanent and the group is institutionalized as a "Center," "Institute," or "Bureau." Even in the former case, a good deal of administrative work is associated with the research project and often requires the full-time services of administrative assistants to submit payrolls, write reports, and handle negotiations with other administrative bodies and the fund-granting agency. The personnel in research groups typically include clerical assistants, administrative assistants, technicians, and apprentices who are completing their graduate training. All these are in addition to the senior social scientists to whom the grant has been made and who are responsible for the project.

Such complex organizations have many consequences. The social scientist finds that he needs to acquire a new skill: to co-ordinate the work of many subordinates. He needs to learn to delegate work while retaining quality controls. For many social scientists who were trained in a more individualistic era and had little apprenticeship experience in a large shop, this produces considerable difficulties. The problems are reflected not only in unrealistic research budgets but also in disappointing research results which come as a consequence of inappropriate or inadequate organizational control. Other consequences are directed at the university where most social science research is done. The researcher's time is divided between two organized groups, the department in which he teaches and has administrative obligations, and the research group which finances his research and also plays a considerable role in training his graduate students. If research and graduate training are the first preferences of the social scientist in the university, he is likely to become more closely attached to his research group than to the university department. Since research funding comes from outside sources, university officials (including the department chairman) are able to exercise little control over such scientists. Administrators find themselves forced to agree to leaves of absence whenever the researcher requests them and is able to finance them. The researcher's teaching load and the courses he gives reflect his research interests and needs more than the department's teaching program. As long as research brings prestige and funds to the university, the researcher will occupy a favored position in his department. When an academic department is almost completely staffed by such researchers, undergraduate training becomes a residual activity.

Organizational and financial ties generated by data-collection problems also undermine departmental structure in other ways. Most social science departments provide few services for the researcher. Unlike a chemistry or physics department which encompasses some laboratories, social science departments have few or no research facilities attached to them. Many do not even have adequate office facilities for typing research reports and administering research funds. Little or no space is provided for laboratory facilities, conference rooms, computer facilities, data-storage facilities, or offices for the technical staff associated with research projects. Moreover, university budgets often do not allow research to be carried out without establishing separate funds and organizations. The most obvious example is the difference in the way in which library and computer facilities are handled. Every professor has free use of the library and may even request the addition of a specialized collection for his research. But only those professors with special funds may use computer facilities. It is true that a limited amount of money is available to most professors who show a need for it, but computer facilities are rarely available on the same free basis as the library is. Yet for much social science research, the computer is more important than the library.

Indeed, we may go further in our comparison of computers and libraries. No administrator would think of building a library and filling it with books without providing a card catalog and a system for withdrawing books. Certainly, no librarian expects each user to devise his own catalog system. Yet many universities build large computer centers and equip them with the latest machines without making adequate provision for developing the software programs that make the computer useful to researchers. Consequently, almost every research budget must provide funds for custom programming, and each research organization must develop its own program library, usually duplicating those of other researchers elsewhere in the university. New computers are bought and old ones retired with little concern for the costs of translating existing programs into the language of the new computer, in part because the purchasing organization, the computer center and the university, have no great investment in software.

The failure of universities to provide research facilities within existing organizational structures has resulted in the growth of new organizational units for social science on the university campuses. Groups of researchers obtain funds to build and staff structures which are explicitly excluded from instructional uses. They stand on university campuses, are staffed by researchers with nominal appointments in university departments, and are serviced by the administrative functionaries of the university. But they are organizational islands in the university and resist integration into university life and function.

Social science research also has spilled over institutional boundaries. Increasingly it is carried out in institutions that are affiliated with many universities or which contract their services to them. The most prominent example is the Inter-University Consortium for Political Research which began in 1962 with 15 members and now has 120. It serves a number of functions. It provides research training for graduate students at a level which is beyond the reach of most of its members. It also provides a data repository which permits researchers at one university to use the data collected at another institution. Such multiple use of data is a relatively new phenomenon and one which has advanced more rapidly in political science and economics than in the other social science disciplines. It represents an attempt to recover the original costs of data collection by more extensive use of data sets. Once the collector has finished his analysis, he deposits them with a data archive and permits others to use them for their own analyses. Such secondary analysis of data has long been the practice with census data, which is originally collected for government use but has always served as the data base for many scholarly projects. Now, not only census data but data on behavior in legislative, executive and judicial institutions, public opinion data, and economic data are stored in data archives for secondary analysis by scholars who were not associated with its collection. Such inter-university co-operative ventures also affect the role of traditional departments in the university. They require faculty time which the university or individual professors donate to manage their affairs. They help bring the research-oriented faculty member to institutions which do not have sufficient local resources to sustain him. They enable researchers in institutions with few resources to compete with better endowed institutions. They spread the potential for social science research far beyond the confines of the major universities and research centers. On the other hand, they also spread the research-oriented distortions of curricula and faculty time to institutions which have greater demands for traditional instruction and which possess even fewer resources to compensate for such distortions.

Another organizational consequence of the new social science has been a crumbling of disciplinary boundaries in social science fields. To an increasing degree, the individual social sciences are no longer distinguished by techniques of data collection or analysis. Their distinctiveness now rests exclusively on theoretical perspectives which are peculiar to each discipline. They share data-collection and analysis techniques and thus have much in common with one another.

The sharing of techniques is widespread. For instance, although experimentation was first developed in the social sciences by psychologists, it is now widely used by sociologists, political scientists, and even economists. Survey research was first used most widely by sociologists but is now a principal tool of political scientists as well as economists. Aggregate data were the principal source of data for economists but now are shared with political sociologists, demographers, and political scientists. Participant observation and field research was the principal tool of anthropologists but is also used by sociologists and political scientists. Content analysis is beginning to be used by political scientists although the technique also is applied by other disciplines interested in human communications.

The same is true of analytic techniques. Economists pioneered in social science applications of regression analysis and curve-fitting but sociologists and political scientists are now adapting these techniques to their own uses. Concern over the measurement of attitudes is reflected in the development of a sub-field in psychology called social psychology. Its equivalent does not yet exist in political science but its methods have been widely adopted. Mathematical modeling has been long practiced by econometricians, but a whole new breed of mathematical sociologists, psychologists and political scientists is being trained in similar arts. And though the theory of games was developed by mathematicians, one of the uses of this theory in the social sciences has been by political scientists interested in the formation and maintenance of coalitions.

The sharing of data-collection and analytic techniques has had widespread consequences for social science practice. Researchers can no longer depend on training in their discipline alone. They must also read the journals and follow the development of two or three related disciplines. In designing their research, collecting their data, analyzing it, and reporting their results, they often use the services of colleagues in related fields. Research teams now consist of men trained in several fields. Moreover, reports by social scientists appear in journals of disciplines other than their own and they appear at each other's professional meetings to read papers. A number of hybrid disciplines have begun to appear, like political sociology, administrative sciences, socio-legal studies, urbanology—to name only the most prominent and best established ones. These hybrid disciplines are often served by separate journals. They are also beginning to organize their own disciplinary associations.

These developments have also had their impact on the universities. Again, they weaken ties to traditional departments because researchers often have closer ties to colleagues in other disciplines than to their own departmental colleagues. They collaborate across departmental lines in offering courses to graduate and undergraduate students. They also offer courses within their respective departments which have a considerable degree of overlap. This is true in methodology courses; almost every social science department now has its statistics program and its data-collection training program. Many cover the same material although with varied degrees of sophistication, with different levels of prerequisites, and with different examples in the exercises. It is also true in some substantive areas. For instance, courses in urban politics exist in many sociology as well as political science departments; courses on public opinion often are listed in psychology as well as sociology and political science departments.

The new hybrid disciplines clamor for recognition within the academic structure. They do so in the form of special programs, institutes, and eventually departments. Several universities already have departments in urban studies, social psychology, and administrative science; the first socio-legal studies department is in the process of being formed although a number of universities already have interdisciplinary programs in that field. Such developments are not novel; they duplicate a trend that has existed for a long time in the physical and life sciences. They mirror the fragmentation of knowledge as it expands. They reflect the need for greater specialization as the content of each discipline expands so much that no individual can comprehend all of it. For universities, however, these developments represent new demands for staff, space and overhead facilities. While new departments in a few pioneering (and usually already strong) universities may be financed by grants, the continuing costs must eventually be incorporated into the university's budget. These developments both reflect the vigor of growing disciplines and portend new pressures on already overburdened budgets.

III

These manifestations of social science research have a far-reaching impact on students and teachers. It is not easy to speak about teaching and research without touching many raw nerves. I want to suggest that so many nerves are raw because of unfulfilled and perhaps unfulfillable expectations about the social sciences.

The present generation of undergraduates comes to a university with a broad spectrum of demands and expectations. Many come simply because that is what their parents, relatives, friends and teachers expect them to do after finishing high school. Just as they unwittingly transferred from grade school to junior high school and then to high school, so they proceed to a university when they have attended high school for the requisite number of years. They come with few goals, though they believe that a college degree will help them earn a better living. Eventually, most of them will decide what occupation they want to enter and search for training (not an education) that may teach them useful skills. They also come to college hoping to have a good time; they look forward (with some anxieties) to a life free from parental control, although not free from all control since they often eagerly accept the control of peer groups and become savagely conformist in dress, hair style and activity.

Others come to college and university with quite different goals. They have already picked out an occupation or are already incipient intellectuals with the desire to acquire wide-ranging knowledge. Some want freedom to study what they want as they want it; others want to work as the apprentice of a famous professor. Some come to college seriously engaged in social protest and reform while others are completely withdrawn from social engagement and seek only to gain better knowledge of themselves.

No single program can satisfy all of these demands. The large university is not a small town, homogeneous in its values and conformist in its behavior. Instead it is a myriad of sub-cultures.

It is safe to say, however, that most students in the large university are not incipient intellectuals and have no desire to become egg-heads. They come from families which rarely read books, listen to classical music or enjoy art. Their homes are filled with the din of television and the roar of the power mower. Their mothers can engage in little else than small talk and their fathers in little else than shop talk and sports talk. If they come from working-class backgrounds, they are unlikely to have learned the art of conversational disputation; if they come from middle-class backgrounds, the principal social activity of their parents is likely to be the asocial cocktail party.

Coming from such backgrounds, it is little wonder that reading, thinking, writing and creating are foreign experiences, seen as irrelevant to everyday life. These are school activities, to be endured when they are required but not to be engaged in during one's spare time or to be considered preparation for life outside the university. Consequently, much of the teaching in the social sciences appears quite irrelevant to many students. This is not a consequence of large classes, impersonal lectures, or the use of closed-circuit television. It is the result of having students at universities who are not interested in learning what the social sciences can teach them. Many students intensely prefer a large lecture class which requires little personal involvement to a small seminar which imputes to them an interest they do not have.

In addition, the curriculum of the social sciences has become increasingly irrelevant to those exceptional students who do wish to learn what they can about the society in which they live but who are not interested in becoming social scientists themselves. They want to learn about economics like they learn in some places about physics; they wish to know what this body of knowledge can tell them about their environment. They want to be told about the research of famous scientists rather than be taught to replicate it. But curricula are not developing in that direction.

As the staff of social science departments becomes more enmeshed in specialized research, it becomes less interested and in some cases less able to teach the generalist about the findings of their discipline. Curricula increasingly reflect the growing degree of specialization in research. In political science, for instance, three courses in comparative politics used to suffice: one on western Europe, one on the U.S.S.R. and totalitarian systems, and one on developing nations. Today, the specialist on the Soviet Union does not feel qualified to teach about politics in satellite countries; the specialist in Western Europe has become a specialist in European integration but has little knowledge about the domestic politics of separate nations or the legislative, party, judicial or electoral processes on the Continent. And most tellingly, there are no specialists on developing nations, but only specialists about particular aspects of development or particular nations. The expert on Ghana cannot speak about Ecuador or Thailand.

The methodological and scientific elaboration of the social sciences has created another gulf between the professor and his students. The professor is interested in teaching his students about the methods of research and experimentation. For the researcher the results of current research are more interesting for the task of defining the next project than for describing life as it really is. But the undergraduate social science student is not interested in the next research project.

Thus in economics, sociology, psychology, anthropology, and sometimes in political science, curricula are developed for the budding social scientist. Such curricula emphasize the theory of the discipline, research methods and research practice. This is still not the only major that can be taken in these fields, but it is the major that is of increasing interest to the faculty. However, it is of little interest to the student who concentrates in one of the social sciences because of a general interest in human behavior but who has no intention of becoming a social scientist himself. The student is more likely interested in social causes than in social analysis.

Consequently, social scientists are in the ironic situation of learning more and more about society but being less able to communicate it to their undergraduate students because those students come to them with incorrect expectations about what social science is. The students would like to think big thoughts about the big questions. They would like to emulate Plato without possessing Plato's talent or experience. What they hear instead are theories about minute elements of social systems together with the evidence that has been amassed about them. They may be made to suffer through statistics and methodology courses even though they have no intention of ever using such skills. Little wonder that some students are disenchanted by such an experience.

The professor's research interest may also leave him inaccessible. This is not necessarily because he is so engrossed in research that his research activities take up all his time. It is worth noting that students in the physical sciences and biological sciences seem less concerned about the inaccessibility of their professors although those men are as involved in research as their social science colleagues. It is not true that social science research isolates the professor in distant laboratories. Rather, I would suggest their inaccessibility is the product of students' lack of interest in their research. Those who major in the physical sciences are likely to become scientists of one sort or another; they are concerned with the work their professors do and often are keenly interested in learning how to do it. The laboratory sections attached to their courses are an essential part of their training and bring them a step closer to the work of their professors. By contrast, most social science students are not interested in their professors' research; they have no laboratory experience themselves and are not interested in obtaining it. The students' social-issue concerns are remote from the research interests of their professors. Although professors may have open office hours, no long lines form in front of them because students and professors lack common ground on which to communicate. Students are impatient with the isolated work done in research; professors are disappointed by the 'non-professional' attitudes of their students. The gap between them is not the result of the amount of work professors do or their physical inaccessibility; it is the result of different interests.

## IV

The trends I have been describing also affect graduate training. It is becoming more highly specialized and is bringing student and professor into closer collaboration. But it also often produces skills which are not marketable.

Specialization has followed closely upon the heels of expansion of the disciplines. That specialization has occurred on several levels. First, as research has become more and more detailed, it has led to the examination of ever smaller segments of the social, political, economic and psychological elements of human behavior. In political science, for instance, 15 years ago it was perfectly normal to ask a student to offer American political institutions and behavior as one of his fields. Now that is practically impossible, with very large bodies of literature in the sub-fields of voting behavior, political parties, legislative behavior, administrative process, judicial behavior and policy analysis. It is a substantial task to concentrate in any of these sub-fields. Where there was once one field, there are now six. The same has occurred in the other social sciences. Consequently, students are studying narrower portions of their disciplines. Where the program of study is still relatively broad, students are vigorously agitating for narrower divisions of their discipline and narrower requirements for their studies.

Broad language training is another casualty of the growing specialization. An increasing number of universities have abandoned language requirements for advanced degrees. Sometimes intense training in one particularly relevant language is substituted; elsewhere a methodological requirement has been adopted. Often, no new requirement has been substituted in recognition of the fact that specialization by itself is overburdening many graduate students.

Moreover, graduate work increasingly involves the kind of research that the professors are doing. In many cases, the student is assigned a part of his professor's research project as his own dissertation work. A large part of graduate work is research training on the assumption that graduate students will become researchers like their professors. That may be true of a growing number of social science graduate students as fewer of them leave school for general administrative work in the government or in private organizations. But on the other hand, many of the students go to teaching positions where little research is expected and few resources exist to promote it. They are thus trained for a task they cannot and will not perform. Their training, however, has not suited them particularly well for teaching non-research-oriented undergraduates although that will be their principal task. Many graduate students do not realize this discrepancy between the training they receive and their expected work until they are in the middle of writing their dissertations and on the job market. Then, at the height of their research involvement, they learn that little research will be expected of them and that they will have few opportunities to engage in it.

The involvement of graduate students in research projects also has the effect of lessening the control of departments over their training and their careers. Their major professor employs them on grant funds, thus by-passing fellowship competition. He controls their training, although he generally has to accommodate the student's program to the minimum requirements imposed by the department. He supervises the dissertation, selects the committee before which it is defended, and finds a job for his protégé. In some institutions, he even controls the admission of students because he controls the funds by which students may be attracted to the campus. All of this may result in excellent training for the student. But it disperses control and lessens the collegial involvement of a department in graduate training.

## V

So far I have discussed only some of the organizational consequences of a scientific social science. But there are other consequences as well. One that is particularly troublesome is its impact on the belief systems of those who are exposed to it. I would like to suggest that its impact may be as troubling to traditional modes of social and political thought as the advent of scientific study of natural phenomena was to modes of religious thought in the sixteenth century.

Like religious belief systems, much political thought is based on the unsystematic observation of shrewd men who nonetheless had limited experience and restricted social perspective. Political philosophers articulated value preferences and goals in eloquent language or tightly reasoned logic. But their empirical reference points were usually observations of people within their own limited circle or the unsystematic observations of others. For people in the United States, they did not produce a rigorous ideology, but rather a loosely connected body of beliefs that has been uncritically accepted by the mass media and by those who attempt to inculcate civic virtues through schools, political platforms, or church pulpits. This body of beliefs includes a conviction in the efficacy of education in producing a Civic Man, a faith in the efficacy of the vote, a skepticism about the moral code of politicians, but a faith that the electoral and legislative process produces legitimate obligations. Even-handed justice is believed to be the product of a centuries-old adversary process in the courts. 'Politics' is often evil, and many decision-making processes are supposed to be insulated from it, like the judicial process, school boards, regulatory commissions, and the governance of middle-class suburbs.

But citizens are urged to vote on election day and participate in the political process.

There are many obvious contradictions among these beliefs. They reflect the ambivalent feelings of the mass public. It is no great accomplishment for the social sciences to poke holes through this belief system and destroy its credibility by careful studies into the reality of political and social life. For instance, it is easy (and has been done often) to show that the removal of partisan politics from a city's government leads to middle-class, group politics under city-manager or nonpartisan ballot.[3] Replacing popular election of judges with a bar-selection scheme (as advocated by many lawyers) replaces the influence of the public and publicly elected officials with the influence of private-interest group members.[4]

Perhaps more significant—because they lie closer to the core of the American political belief system—are the results of voting studies.[5] They show that most voters inherit their political associations from their parents; that education does not produce more rational decision making; that the independent voter is often the least (rather than the most) informed voter. Moreover, some recent studies of rioters show that people who are relatively well established in their community and feel relatively efficacious about the electoral system are more likely to be among the rioters than more marginal inhabitants.[6] These findings must be linked to those which show that legislative and administrative decision making is marked by a tortuous process in which the public plays only a minor role. The result is that students in the social sciences leave the classroom a good deal more cynical than when they entered it. The effect of their studies is to deepen (what for many seems to have been a predisposition) their distrust of 'the system.'

Moreover, much of the analysis of social scientists emphasizes the symbolic role of overt political behavior. The rituals in the courtroom are described as symbols to appeal to the emotional dimension of man. Voting is described as participation in a mass ritual which has the effect of identifying the voter with the regime; it is described in terms of its effects on the voter, not on the offi-

---

[3] Edward C. Banfield and James Q. Wilson, *City Politics* (New York, 1966), pp. 150-167.

[4] Richard A. Watson and Rondal G. Downing, *The Politics of the Bench and the Bar* (New York, 1969).

[5] *See* especially, Angus Campbell, Philip E. Converse, Warren E. Miller and Donald E. Stokes, *The American Voter* (New York, 1960).

[6] Robert M. Fogelson and Robert B. Hill, *Who Riots: A Study of Participation in the 1967 Riots,* Supplemental Studies for the National Advisory Commission on Civil Disorders (Washington, 1968); Karl H. Flemming, *Who Riots and Why: Black and White Perspectives in Milwaukee* (Milwaukee, 1968), pp. 36-37.

cials who are elected. The Constitution, the flag, the national anthem, and the Presidency are described in similar terms—as symbols as well as instruments of social control.

I do not have the hard evidence to support my conclusion about the consequences of teaching these facts to contemporary American college students. My personal observations, however, are that we are stripping away the foundations of their political beliefs without offering a replacement or even seeing it as our obligation to do so. Social science findings emphasize the contrast between value positions which students have uncritically accepted from their elders and social reality as they are taught to view it in the classroom. The contrast leads some students to accept the equally unrealistic—but appropriately cynical—view of such commentators as Herbert Marcuse. Having been taught that our society does not attain its norms even when its leaders proclaim them, having been trained to look at the reality lurking behind appearances, some students are willing to leap to opposite value conclusions. Convinced that the ordinary individual is powerless in our political system, they assert that we need to radically alter our society to give him power or that we ought to abandon our concern for the individual and subsume him to society in value preferences as well as in fact.

Thus the social sciences contribute to the disarray of the world around us. This is demonstrated by the way in which social science jargon has penetrated common parlance. It is common to hear talk about alienation, social disintegration, dissonance, rising expectations and so on. The technical meanings of these terms are often not understood by those who use them, but their use of them reflects the eagerness with which a portion of the public and its leaders seize upon social science research to confirm their uneasiness with social realities as they perceive them. The breakdown of social taboos of long standing are reassuringly described in social science terms of conformity and deviance without a full understanding of the social functions of taboos and the consequences of replacing one set with another. Deviance, disarray, disintegration are justified by reference to social science terms, although social science research only describes and analyzes such phenomena and does not attempt to justify them or plead for their acceptance or rejection.

The disarray we see around us is, of course, the result of other social forces as well. We cannot deny that our society is under great tension with the threat of nuclear destruction ever upon us. We also cannot deny that our rapid urbanization, the transformation of labor by computers, the growth of leisure, and the high degree of affluence accented by considerable poverty add to social unrest. But it is no accident that among the vanguard of the restless are precisely those who are the most exposed to social findings, the students in our universities.

## VI

The scientific social sciences pose many problems to the universities of the present and the future. They mount challenges to the structure of universities and their organization of teaching and research. I have no doubt that we will see some considerable changes in that structure in the next two decades with a sharper division between graduate and undergraduate teaching and with a spin-off of many research functions to non-university institutions which are now in the process of being established. More important perhaps, the changes which are now taking place in the social sciences will eventually be reflected in new curricula which will provide a layman's training in human behavior and will educate social critics and cognizant citizens in programs separate from those for nascent social scientists. Such curricula in social criticism may come closer to meeting the expectations of the average university student who comes to college with some vague ideals and with no desire to emulate his professors. It may also better fill the need for experts who can plan social reforms.

The most important challenge of the social sciences lies in their undermining of the social myths which bind contemporary society and whose erosion threatens to contribute to the disintegration of that society. I do not know where the new myths will come from nor what they will be. I doubt, however, that they will come from the work of social scientists. But come they must, for societies need the bonds which common myths supply and which provide some of the foundations upon which consensus can be built. Perhaps developing such myths will be the work of the new social critics whom I believe we must train.

# COLLEGE AND NON-COLLEGE
## The Changing Social Values of Education

### George Z. F. Bereday

Professor Mosely has ably related the role of the universities to the questions of policy and political and international relations. It is my task to relate the question of universities, or rather more broadly the question of the world of education at large to society, to social structure, to social class and to the role that education plays in these matters.

Harold Nicolson in a charming book, *Good Behaviour—A Study of Certain Types of Civility,*[1] recalls an obscure nineteenth-century work by a German sociologist named Schelderup on the habits of the household hen. It was noticed in that rather forgotten study that whenever a random group of hens is introduced into a chickenhouse, an invisible order of ranking soon arises among them. Soon, by force of personal integrity or perseverance, one hen works its way to the top of the group and that hen—we shall call her No. 1— has the first right of the trough when the feed is distributed; she pecks all of the other hens away when they get in her way; she continues as undisputed queen of the roost. And so from hen No. 1, down the line; hens 2, 3, 4, and 5, *ad infinitum,* establish themselves in an invisible but nonetheless very real order; the order involves priority. Hen No. 1, when offended by any other members of the group, pecks indiscriminately. She is never pecked back by other members of the group. Moreover, when hen No. 1 pecks hen No. 2, hen No. 2 discharges her fury by pecking hen No. 3, and so on down the line until it comes to the last hen in the society of hens which is pecked by everyone and has no one to peck. It is that hen that is probably a suitable subject for research in hen psychiatry.

This established order is a very human and social characteristic. Wherever human societies have existed, systems of ranking supported by status symbols, supported by visible honors and recognition of position and rank, have arisen. Whenever egalitarian societies have been attempted, from early Christian community to the Paris Commune, this kind of ranking order very soon seems to have become the rule. One might geometrically speak of this kind of order as a process of elongation of whatever geometric structure we imagine society to be. If it be a triangle—the few at the top, the many at the bottom—it is al-

---

[1] New York, 1955.

ways a process of elongation, from the base of the triangle to the apex that affects human societies. As this process of elongation occurs, so does the revolt against the increase in inequality, and history is as full of egalitarian revolts and protests as it is of emerging stratifications. Egalitarian discontent perennially burrows at the foundation of established social systems. We ought perhaps to look at societies realistically, not as static but as dynamic. At a given time some individuals are engaged in the social class elongation process, while others, in protest, are engaged in the "flattening" process, and the tensions thus generated continue all the time.

It is not my purpose here to evaluate from an ethical point of view the merits of the perennial stratification struggle, except perhaps to say that both the process of expansion of inequality and the process of reduction of inequality have their merits and their uses; otherwise they would not have persisted. It is very clear to Americans, who are by nature egalitarians (and to myself personally, who, as a new American, rather enthusiastically leans in that direction), that systems of inequality bring in their wake patterns of snobbery and social insecurity that scar visibly and sometimes permanently all persons subject to their operation. This is particularly true of the more cruel patterns, such as race discrimination, or exploitation of working people or of women or of young persons.

It is equally clear, however, that the persistence of the institution of inequality is proof of some functional utility; else the ritualistic expressions of it would simply not survive. What, for instance, are we to make of the fact that stratification heightens social conflict? In this day and age, when a great many serious and thinking people devote so much attention and so much lamentation to the violence that occurs in various phenomena of our lives, it is perhaps not irrelevant to ask whether conflict is in itself undesirable—as it seems in the opinion of so many—or, rather, whether it is a desirable social characteristic. Studies of war and conflict have always indicated that a great economic and social spurt forward occurred during these periods of unrest and unhappiness. Indeed, this republic, the benefits of which we all share, originated in violence and in armed conflict and has persisted in displaying these features in many ways, from the assassination of political figures to football games, to television serials, as well as to campus disruptions. Conflict is perhaps very legitimate, though in a democracy a last-resort type of activity by which men attempt to adjust themselves to existing power and to their own deprivation of such power. Conflict induced by upward social striving at least partly vindicates a measure of inequality.

In societies which have reached a certain degree of quietude through opulence as well as democratization, there comes into existence what might be referred to as a very serious motivation vacuum. It is common knowledge —which should not be interpreted as cynicism—that hunger and social ambition are excellent motivational factors for mankind, provided they are not at the level at which total poverty or social subjugation deprives the affected people of any kind of initiative. The latent fear of hunger or of revolutionary rage are fantastically strong motivating factors for eliciting the activity of society in all fields, including education.

With regard to stratification, it is clear that in a democratic society the motivation vacuum is quite serious. Established ritualistic ranks and titles are absent, and rank cannot be inherited either in the form of hereditary titles or coats of arms—nor indeed in this day of joint stock companies in the form of substantial use of an extraordinary amount of money, by which I mean a lavish display of luxury of an Oriental-nabob type. Democratic society tends to de-emphasize existing ranks; in fact, there is odium attached to the display of privileges and snobbish distinctions. In comparison with other societies at least, not much is left for the socially ambitious to strive for and dream of. Hence, whatever else it may gain by equality, society loses that part of human exertion that derives from dreams to ascend the social ladder in a hierarchical system.

The question of what could be brought into our society to replace the incentives stemming from these natural conditions is a very valid question for consideration. Such considerations have ranged in practice from the sublime to the ridiculous. The present advisor to the President of the United States, Professor Daniel Moynihan, took perhaps the first step in his career by suggesting to the State of New York that there is revenue to be gained from charging an additional five dollars to applicants for motor vehicle registration who would like to have their initials in the front and back of their automobile instead of a numbered license plate. Apparently, one can exploit, to the advantage of the state taxing authority, this very natural though somewhat less than spectacular human craving for difference and distinction. Efforts to stimulate motivation range from providing labels of this type, to offering positions of real power and prestige, to devising some system of honorific titles within a democratic society, be they political titles or, last but not least, educational titles. It is the contention between the plus and the minus in a mathematical rather than a value sense, between the egalitarian and the elitist, which has in this present day affected most powerfully the institution of education.

Stratification increases incentives so necessary in education but it also "contaminates" the essence of learning. Normally speaking (by "normally" I would refer to a historical, natural-law type of approach), the world of education was and should be a world apart from society. It is a place where a small minority of people gather and know that they can converse in peace; hence, the founding of a university as a community of scholars in the old traditional sense. It is a place where a certain percentage of the members of society needs to be trained for accomplishing the professional tasks required by society, but on the whole men meet there in order to engage in general rather than professional preparation, perhaps to seek "ornamental rather than useful knowledge," to use Benjamin Franklin's celebrated but often forgotten distinction. It is a place, above all, where men of creativity assemble in order to expand man's essential vision of the vast, surrounding universe, the fringes of which we only inadequately probe and before which we stand in total terror.

By historical tradition the world of education handed down to us by our ancestors ought to be a classless society, a nonsocietal institution. We are very aware of the fact that this is not so. It has not been so, at least since the days when society's industrialization and technologization sufficiently broadened the demand for various professional skills. Freeing various groups of people from the necessity of scratching the soil to elicit a meager existence has been the means whereby the world of education began to burgeon. It began by enticing persons who were not primarily interested in education, as it was historically conceived, but who became interested in education because of the economic and social gifts it now offered.

These people brought into play professionalization and mass attendance, neither of which had in older days been thought of as having a place within the world of education. Training professional soldiers became the business of formal educational institutions. Apothecaries began to be as formally trained as doctors. Preceptors and tutors became teachers who were trained differently than clerks and theologians. Clerks of law and theologians were the earliest to find their way into institutions of higher education. Their professionalization began the process of expansion which in our times has grown to the point where one of every three young Americans takes at least 14, if not 16, years of education and where the second takes at least 12 years. This process has begun to be adopted throughout the world. At the present time, only five societies educate more than one of 10 students for 14 or more years of education. A small group of "have" nations is separated by a widening gap from other nations. But as this process of mass education begins to affect our society and related ones, something significant is happening to the world of education. It becomes a monopoly through which alone social status and distinction can be conferred.

In other societies—and to an extent in our own—there exist safety valves outside the educational system for those ambitious persons, who neither by inclination nor perhaps by capacity are academically gifted. By means of such safety valves, it is possible to make money without schooling and there are rich men who pride themselves today that they can hire any number of Ph.D.'s though they themselves never went to college. It is possible to make one's way in the world of sports. It is also possible, at a totally unwarranted level of rewards, to make one's way in the field of entertainment and popular arts. Still built into society, there are and always have been, safety valves whereby men of ambition, men of thrust, men who wish to establish dynasties and aristocratic lines, men who wish for a larger share of the power and goods of the world than seemed to have been allotted them by fate, could proceed to realize their legitimate or illegitimate ambitions. The world of education remained relatively untouched—might I say safe?—from the operations of these men.

These margins of safety have been decreasing in our time. This is most clearly visible in the Soviet Union where if one wishes to make a career in production, which is the Communist equivalent to amassing wealth, one must graduate from the appropriate economics or engineering faculty of the universities. If one wishes to make one's way in the field of sports, one must graduate from appropriate academies of sports. If one wishes to make a career in the field of public entertainment or art, he must graduate from the appropriate academies of public entertainment or art.

Here, in the U.S.S.R. and related societies, we see carried to a final and logical conclusion the proposition that in a society such as ours, that is, in an industrial, technological society, all jobs are reached through formal education. In a technological society managers are extremely scarce; all new societies underproduce natural managers. While the available talent has to be brought to the position of optimum use, all such societies suffer, not from overproduction but from underproduction of talent, and have to make do with second best because they cannot always secure the best leaders. It is very clear that these societies push education into a position of monopoly. It becomes a giant sieve of talent, not only a source of intellectual excitement, not only a source for probing the mysteries of the universe, not only a place where men polish themselves by contact with ideas of other men, but also a place where careers are made, where ambitions are realized, where social tensions are deployed, where relative positions of other groups in the educational community and other peers in one's own community are watched carefully from the corner of one's eye, where relative achievements and standards are important, where educational tracks become hurdle races for social ambitions, and educational degrees become badges of status and substitutes for the titles of nobility. Perhaps some of the problems our educational system is coping with at the present time stem from this development, the growing pains of this kind of system.

To illustrate the nub of what I wish to highlight, unless the young American male is tattooed or marked in some visible way, in bathing trunks he looks indistinguishable from any other young American male in bathing trunks. And yet on the beaches of Waikiki, two distinct groups of American males compete for the bikinied coeds: the young students from the University of Hawaii and the so-called "service" boys from the Pearl Harbor bases. As a matter of record, when the young man in bathing trunks appears from behind the palms and zeroes in on the coed, she can tell from 500 yards whether he is a University of Hawaii student or a Pearl Harbor serviceman and she treats him accordingly.

Education is becoming the sole road to high position in a society in which other marks of distinction are not increasing but decreasing. How many of us can appear in public with white poodles to give ourselves a vicarious feeling of excellence? In our society the distinction between college and non-college becomes imbued with social meanings as well as educational meanings. We have been pushing educational stratification to replace or supplement other types of stratification. As late as 10 or 15 years ago, David Riesman called our society "the network of veto groups." John Kenneth Galbraith spoke of "countervailing powers." In such a balanced concept of society education could be visualized as only one competing skyscraper on the Manhattan skyline. Men of education were "countervailed" by men of arms and by men of government and by men of wealth and by men of cloth. All these groups were competing and balancing out each other in a general universe of democratic relationships. If it still can be said that this pattern exists, it is passing away to be replaced by an educational monopoly. In a private conversation David Riesman has described the society of today as one of indeterminate chaos from which anything or nothing might arise. More extreme men, such as the late C. Wright Mills or those others hostile to the establishment, see a visible functional structure, a technotronic structure, but nonetheless a structure of ranking, arising directly out of the system of education. With it and perhaps because of it, there comes a change in the nature of the American feeling about such matters and about American traditions.

Professor Philip Jacobs from the University of Pennsylvania is currently engaged in a comparative study of the values held by political leaders at the local level in four societies, an oddly assorted group of societies to be sure—the United States, India, Yugoslavia and Poland. Nonetheless, in 30 local communities in these societies, all available leaders have been polled on matters such as the desirability of economic growth, the desirability of equality, etc. Of the most startling conclusions reached by Professor Jacobs to date here are two:

One, among the nations compared, Americans score highest on commitment to economic growth. The American leaders are committed to change, to expansion, to increasing sales charts. But at the same time, Americans score lowest, significantly lower than any other of the examined societies, on the egalitarian values, particularly on the belief that it is the business of a society to attempt to neutralize rather than enhance social distinctions. In the United States a feeling has taken hold that a growing democratic society is based on a *total* upward rise of the citizenship, not in terms of relative rank and social distance between the lower and the higher groups. We are now talking about the system of elongation, or at least about maintaining the distances between groups. The image of social structure in the United States is a diamond with the most numerous middle class dominant, but we are talking about elongation upwards of the entire structure, not of diminishing and flattening it. If one places the struggle for civil rights or the fight against poverty within this framework, it is small wonder that so much disenchantment surrounds the issue.

Second, an equally interesting finding by Jacobs is that in the business of development and change, education is the only clearly inhibiting factor, that is to say, the higher the education of the leaders polled, the less willing they are to commit themselves to change, the more they are for the status quo, the more intensely concentrated they are on preserving the position of inequality which they have already—probably meritoriously—achieved. These changing patterns of values revealed in this study are one item that can be added to the general picture as it emerges, a picture which might very well be described in terms of Benjamin Disraeli's "Two Nations," and a picture which by rule of thumb we might call the "College—Non-College Watershed in the Nation."

I use the words, "the rule of thumb," advisedly. There can be no talk about unity within the non-college group or within the college group and, therefore, no class struggle in the sense that the Marxists have envisioned it. Within the college group there exists a veritable pecking order of institutions, specializations, ascriptive additions to educational status legitimized by education or which legitimized education received. We have a scale from genteel, rural college for the gentlemen, to a multi-university of a heterogeneous metropolitan type to a poor man's junior college or a teachers' college type. We have the welter of distinctions and maneuverings for positions within a group that really prohibits our viewing the college group as a united group. Perhaps only one thing could, or would, or does, unite such a group, and that is an attack by the members of the "out" group.

Within the non-college group, it is also very difficult to talk about unity of purpose again, except perhaps when such a group is attacked from above. John Gardner in his book, *Excellence*,[2] has pointed rather tellingly the way in which any attempt to distinguish oneself, to shine, to move ahead, to make a career, is being reacted to by others, by one's peers, who attempt to tear down the thrust and to maintain the integration of the mover within the lower world. That is how the non-college relates to the college world. Until and unless there is a really cohesive social coalition of college men, we are not likely to see a really cohesive coalition of non-college men. Rather, non-college men are divided into such broad but alien categories to each other, as self-employed and employees, regionally conscious patriots of various types

---

[2] *Excellence, Can We Be Equal and Excellent Too?* (New York, 1961).

and descriptions, ethnic and racial units, religious sects and what have you.

We can only, therefore, talk of the two worlds and the two nations in American education in a very limited rule-of-thumb sense. More appropriate would be to view society as a continuum of different groups spread along the ranks of educational attainment and only imperfectly divided by the watershed of college and non-college. That we must do, without even entering into the purely technical considerations as to what should be considered college and what should be considered non-college. About such distinctions, of course, there rages an extremely lively discussion everywhere in the world including the United States. To quote just one instance, American higher education statistics, which are so high in terms of percentages of the age group served, are disputed almost universally because they include the freshmen and sophomores who in other societies, so it is claimed, are more comparable with the senior high school age groups than with the early university age groups. This is a technical difficulty which I cannot go into nor, indeed, solve, for there is no established comparative standard of equivalence between educational attainments of different countries at different levels of education.

With these general characteristics in mind, we may now proceed to speculate briefly upon the social and educational effects upon the nation of the emerging social order made up of the two layers, college and non-college, or to borrow a Soviet simile, of managers and the managed. To take the managed group first, it is not very clear what is going to happen to them. On the surface, this group was affected in the 1930's and 1940's—and continues to be affected—by what appear to be contradictory principles concerning attitudes towards education. On one side, education is considered a positive value. It is desired both intrinsically and extrinsically by everyone. Mothers, particularly working mothers, worry about the performance of their children. The deviance of our young persons, the long-haired philosophers who in earlier biblical days would have been considered holy proponents of catholicism, is decried because they reject the educational path of progress. The commitment to education as a value is displayed in the countless hagglings for bond issues, continuous attempts to build adequate schools, the fantastic and beautiful expansion of school buildings, the continuing renovative process of the curriculum, the care exercised to produce more and more good teachers, and so on and so forth. On one side, the mass of Americans is education-prone, if not "hung up" on education.

On the other side, as Merle Curti and countless others have long indicated, Americans have always accompanied their thrust for education with a curious anti-intellectualism, a suspicion of the "brain" and of his thirst for power, a resentment of the expert and his snobbism. Americans, while in some ways educational, also are exceedingly anti-educational with respect to educational institutions.

This can be related to the level of education received. The lower the level of education, the stronger the mixture of latent admiration for school and overt hostility towards school and the products of school. How will this mix develop in the future? Nobody can tell, for there are all kinds of variables involved. For instance, how will those educated in college exercise their influence? Are they going to be gentle and humble guides, platonic guardians in the best sense of the word, elder brothers who lead the community to a juster and more equivalent distribution of all the privileges of society, or are they going to be maldoers, like Michael Young's meritocrats, who attempt to pervert the privileges which they have achieved by monopolizing them for their own children? It is by now almost an iron law of education that there are always going to be people who will attempt to change the system of educational selection for leadership into an aristocratic selection system of leadership. This is not as difficult as it may sound since it is a matter of common knowledge that even in a plural educational selection, the children of the better-off persons are likely to score better on all the tests that are presented. The actual outcome of intellectual selection, as Jacques Barzun has pointed out in *The House of Intellect*,[3] is not going to be significantly different whether you recruit your elite on the basis of parental income or on the basis of the achievement of the children in schools.

On the sorting out of that mix, on how educated men will behave in relation to less educated depends the attitude of the noneducated. It depends upon the viability retained by careers that still exist outside education, in theater and sports, in business and politics, and on the field of battle; and on how open the society outside education will remain so that those who become educational "drop-outs" can be described as "drop-ins" in some other pattern of achievement. If such avenues continue to exist, they will serve as safety valves to prevent society from reaching a position of tension. If the safety valves disappear, as the indications are that they may, the tension and the pressure points will become more significant.

It depends also upon how lenient or how strict are the regulations at the top of the educational system, for whenever the entrance into and the exit out of the highest reaches of education is exceedingly strict, the net effect is the regular production of "rejects" and rejects are never friends of the system which rejected them. Any stringent examination system for selecting those who will participate in the highest educational training and, therefore, in the highest emoluments after graduation, produces every year fresh ranks of "also rans," of "almost made its" who, by virtue of having been rejected, become enemies of the system and eventually ruin and destroy it, if history is any guide.

---

[3] New York, 1959.

On these various inputs will depend the outputs, the relationship of the non-college man to society at large and to the college group that manages the society and, indeed, as some might say, sustains it. It is easier to predict in a final analysis what will happen to the college group in the educational society of the future. Within the universities, the consequences of the pressure of numbers are already being felt and are, therefore, easy to forecast. The larger the student body in the universities of this or any other country, the more the university will be forced to become a school and the less will it be able to perform the function of a research institute. In older days, the function of the university was simply recruitment of the next generation of scholars, and the degree granted was that of "licencia docendi," the license to teach.* In such a university the emphasis was on adding to knowledge, on broadening the vision of men. When the ranks of the university population expand, the disseminating or perpetuating function of knowledge gains very clear ascendance over the additive function that is traditional to the university.

Consequently, it can be predicted that as numbers increase, pressure will be so exercised on the university that it becomes more of a school. The faculty will be asked to behave more like a resident teaching body than as a research body whose defined function is, as Professor Mosely has indicated, "to serve outside the walls of the university as it is to serve inside the walls of the university." University administrators will be forced to behave more like school principals, whose duty it is to walk the corridors and sample the feeling and atmosphere of the school, rather than administering. Administration is a dirty word in education. But what seems legitimate in business today presumably should be legitimate in the university as well. When a man administers $10 million this seems a specialization in its own right; it is rewarded by a salary which is either too high in business or too low in the university, but it is a function which is clearly a fulltime job and should be legitimately regarded as such.

More students will be asking that the product of their curriculum, of the educational fare that they receive, have some kind of relevance, of meaning other than the historical-traditional meaning of learning things because they are good for their own intrinsic value. This last point, the point of relevance, is not only the function of numbers but the consequence of that lowering of the general intellectual level that comes with the increase in numbers. The word "lowering" is a loaded word because quality is lowered in terms historically and traditionally derived, and it may be there is some other quality that needs to be added or superimposed in order to offset the loss of the traditional standards of quality. But, the historical standard of quality is all we have at the present time, and we should not too light-heartedly sell short the no-

---

* Variations of this system still exist in numerous countries (Editor).

tions by which it is defined: the ability to handle abstract concepts and a sixth sense which permits the relating of seemingly unrelated things, the Newtonian sense that when the apple falls on your head you suddenly realize that it is gravity law that is operating.

Be it as it may, when we get larger numbers in the university, we get other shades of ability than the abstract. And the question of relevance (as John Dewey pointed out in his plea for "interest as the center of instruction") of what is taught to what is to be expected of the person in later life will be raised more and more insistently. The university, therefore, will be more and more subject to the impact of the mass of its new consumers, and its research function will gradually be blunted, just as it has already been largely blunted in the Soviet Union, where it now largely exists in outside research institutes. In the United States, too, the research function is slowly seeping out of the universities. Professor Mosely's involvement in RAND Corporation is in itself an example of what is happening.

Faculties, however, are conservative by definition. All teachers are conservative. Even when teachers are liberal, their liberalism is conservative. One of the most conservative societies today, both politically and emotionally, is the Communist society. Yet it is a society where educated men hold the reins most closely. Faculties are conservative by definition, in the sense that the university is one of the few agents of stability in society, and like the church, therefore, operates as a center of attraction to which gravitate conservative men, men who abhor violence, men who like to play with ideas rather than with acts and deeds, men who prefer voice and words to construction. The university, being so constructed, is likely to find change less easy to cope with than almost any other person or institution. Student pressure is only the first element of change and in a sense, the weakest, because as offshoots of academic life, students are and will more and more come to be regarded as faculty apprentices. And that is really all they seem to want at the present time.

But along with the avant-garde pressure by students for the reform of the university, I predict that other pressures will arise. And the historical university may have to give way to some more democratic kind of institution. The old university was a republic of princes, a network of independent fiefdoms. How did President Nathan Pusey put it in describing Harvard, "A system of independent departments loosely united by plumbing"? The new university would be a place in which not only the faculty, who are sovereign by right, not only the administration, who must handle the formidable task of administration since nobody else will, not only the students who come willy-nilly, sometimes more nilly than willy, but also the innumerable special service officers, the research assistants, the many but totally unrecognized visiting faculty, the innumerable clerical groups and the unsung superintendents of the school buildings who are also a pressure group to be reckoned

121

with in the future, will claim to have some right to participate in the decision making or at least in the process of communication about the future of their institution.

Therefore, if the portents are what they seem to be, I envision for the university some kind of revolution towards a syndical organization from the corporate organization which it is at the present time. The universities, nonetheless, must continue to be—and, I hope, will continue to be—the safeguards of the stability of the country. If this is the case, they will remain the first and the prime target of assault by the rapidly changing society surrounding them. This type of ongoing assault they must simply be prepared to take on the chin, and what will emerge, if the solidity and strength of the university (which, after all, has been tested by time) is to be preserved, will be a modified and still more modified stability—perhaps not as a rapidly changing film, for that is not in the nature of the university structure, but as a series of slides revealing the partial success and partial failure of the attacks on the alma mater fortress.

If this is not the case, if the university's stability and its function of safeguarding stability does not survive, then the transition from university to school will become complete in the future. We will no longer be justified in talking about college and non-college categories, but rather we will have to change our terminology to talk about people with secondary as opposed to people with tertiary education, this distinction meaning no more in the future than the present distinction between primary and secondary education means.

# CONTINUING EDUCATION IN THE UNITED STATES

## The Challenge and Responsibility

Thomas P. Bergin

There exists in America today a new and determined revolution in the whole concept of education, a revolution which has been brought on for the most part by the vast and sweeping changes taking place within our society which so quickly render yesterday's knowledge obsolete. The fundamental change in the rate of knowledge accumulation has made it imperative that the concepts and structures of our educational systems be completely rethought and radically restructed.

There was a time when a person could anticipate living his life in the world into which he was born. This is no longer true. The world today has changed and the propensity for change continues at a frenzied pace. We are constantly being called upon to act and react with almost staccato frequency. As a result, it is imperative that all of us, at all educational levels, young and old, continually seek opportunities for self-renewal, opportunities which permit us to update our knowledge, extend our understanding and clarify our concepts. Particularly, those concepts which permit us to know and thus better understand the great human problems of our time and their relevance to our society.

The current revolution in education taking place in America is not to be confused with the ordinary modifications and changes which have traditionally occurred in educational methods and curricula in response to the normal pace of social change. Rather, the revolutionary adjustment currently taking place is to that of a society in perpetual flux.

For the most part, our educational system in the U.S., until recently, operated on the assumption that learning was a formalized activity for the individual which was restricted to the first 18 to 25 years of life. The current educational revolution, now well underway and indeed essential, conceives the situation as a process of lifelong learning from early childhood to old age. It assumes that this concept will become a normal part of everyday living simply because there is no other way to deal directly with the problems emerging from the galloping new rate of knowledge accumulation in all fields.

This new revolution in education is dramatically different from the earlier and familiar image of adult education and extension work, which has customarily been regarded as a way to provide learning opportunities for people who never completed their schooling; or an opportunity to give school dropouts the equivalent of a high school diploma; or a method for Americanizing immigrants; or a means of providing recreation and use of leisure time for the elderly. As important and valuable as many of these activities are, they are now in sharp contrast to the all-important and urgent need for an involved and informed citizenry, a citizenry which is continually being apprised of the changes taking place and the pressing responsibilities of freedom which require its attention in improving the quality of life for all.

To meet this challenge we have developed in the United States well-ordered programs in continuing education. These are programs which permit our citizens to discover new paths which enrich life and hopefully free men from hatred, narrowness of mind and frustrating anxieties.

The great and primary objective of continuing education, as I believe it is conceived in the United States, is to bring education and educational experiences closer to life; a life which continually takes into account the real demands of the actual nature of modern individuals and societies; individuals and societies whose development and progress is enriched and guided by persistent exposure to the new knowledge as it is developed in the sciences and humanities; knowledge which may assist in meeting the ever pressing requirements of economic and social development.

It is no longer true that the university can adequately serve at a distance. The professional man today cannot escape premature professional obsolescence unless he is willing and able to continue his education throughout his lifetime. Unless medical doctors continually avail themselves of new knowledge, countless lives are needlessly wasted or lost. Unless lawyers continually avail themselves of new knowledge in the law, our communities and nations are deprived of this new measure of justice. Neither the individual nor the society in which he works can afford to postpone the introduction of new knowledge for a generation. Now as never before, we are all responsible for the prompt introduction of new knowledge and its early, fair and effective application in the service of man. Thus, the universities must seek out and serve professional people and mature citizens throughout their lives wherever they may be. In continuing their high purpose in the search for truth in such a critical and challenging moment in history, the universities in the United States are no longer solely dedicated to their youthful elite, even though youth might represent the most talented in the country. Society's problems must be solved today, by the generation in command, by intelligent adults. The successful application of new knowledge to the human affairs of man has required community after community to seek the services of the university in solving these problems.

It is for this reason that many American universities are currently reaching out and going beyond the ordinary campus limits, and accepting greater responsibility in the whole area of continuing education, particularly as it relates to the ever greater recognition of the human problems of the world community.

This new knowledge dilemma poses particularly serious problems for the university because at any given time we can teach only that which we know or that which is being developed. And yet that which we now know may in the future, through additional knowledge, be proven untrue or be considerably altered. Corrections of this type of knowledge and further interpretations of it must come through continuing education.

By way of example, it is estimated that the intellectual half-life of the science and engineering students we are educating at the present time is less than eight years. That is, more than half of what the student has learned while pursuing the undergraduate degree will be obsolete within a decade. And half of what he or she will need to know eight years from now is not currently available.

It is significant, I think, that 80 per cent of those who take part in our continuing education programs do so for reasons of self-improvement. They are interested in keeping abreast of public affairs and knowing more about their particular responsibilities within the community as well as updating their technical knowledge. Less than 20 per cent of all those taking part in continuing education programs do so for college credit, that is, preparation for specific degree programs.

In facing up to these unprecedented challenges, which must ultimately affect the world society, Americans in recent years have set in motion a host of programs designed to work toward a high quality education for all. The projected goals of excellence and equality of opportunity in education are being pursued more vigorously and with greater determination than ever before in the history of our country. Our commitment of financial and human resources to education has reached unprecedented proportions.

Over the past five years the Congress of the United States has passed over 40 major bills supporting education. Education has become a major growth industry. Total public and private expenditures for education during the past school year reached something like $50 billion, or about 6 per cent of our gross national product. Compare this with the $4 billion we spent on education at the end of World War II. Over 100 million Americans are currently involved in education, as students, teachers, members of school boards or trustees of colleges and universities.

At the present time more than 30 million American adults annually take part in some form of structured continuing education activity. The participants include all income levels and practically all ages. Ordinarily, the great majority of those seeking continuing education are under 40 years of age;

nearly four out of five are under 50 years of age. Aside from age, there seems to be no other personal characteristic or life pattern which sets the adult student apart from the general population. There are ordinarily an equal number of men and women participating, with only slight discrepancies in religious background. There is no discrepancy in race when Negroes are compared with whites of similar educational background.

Perhaps one of the most distressing aspects of our continuing education program in the United States at the present time is the fact that those who need it the most are securing the least. On the average, only 4 or 5 per cent of those with little formal schooling seek opportunities in continuing education as compared with 47 to 50 per cent among those who have had more than 16 years of educational training.

It is projected over the next two decades that the population in the United States will increase by some 35 to 40 per cent, while the increase in the number of people under 35 will probably represent 75 per cent of the total population. Within this same period, it is estimated that there will be 70 per cent more adults who have been to college and some 65 per cent more who have attended high school. There will be 20 per cent fewer individuals with only a grade school education. In such an environment, it is obvious the potential audience for continuing education programs is increasing at a much faster rate than the population as a whole.

There seems to be no limit to the variety and forms which continuing education assumes in the United States. Currently it embraces the tremendously expanding university extension programs, manpower training, public school extension, basic adult education, independent study and correspondence courses, formal on-the-job training, religious education, professional seminars, and a vast array of federal and state employee seminar programs.

There are, of course, many and varied programs of continuing education conducted by the federal government. A great number are contained in the Manpower Development and Training Act of 1962 and the Adult Basic Education Act of 1966. The United States armed services conduct the largest and one of the finest independent study programs in the world. Recently, some 44 federal programs, many involving universities, called for expenditures of more than $1.4 billion for federally assisted adult education studies to meet the nation's health manpower needs. In fiscal 1968, $763 million was approved to train some 224,000 health workers. There are some 88 additional programs supported to improve the training of federal employees while on the job.

At an early age, American industry learned that investment in training and occupational education was every bit as important as physical plant investment. As a result, the nation's greatest occupational training ground is within the industrial and business establishments. It is estimated that well in excess of two million workers are engaged in formal programs of continuing education within industry. Between 80 and 90 per cent of all vocational and technical training in the United States is supported by business and industry. There are some 32,000 private trade and technical schools that provide occupational and technical training supported by the private sector. Private industry has been increasingly dependent upon these programs to insure a better educated work force and ultimately a market for its know-how.

In addition to what we traditionally think of as the continuing educational activities of the major universities, that is, the extension division and the adult education programs, we have in the United States at the present time some 85 centers for continuing education in operation. There are an additional 20 to 25 either under construction, or scheduled to be built. The number of these centers has grown from 12 in 1953 to 85 in 1969 and the number of conferences conducted has increased from roughly 4,000 in 1953 to some 60,000 in 1969.

By and large, these centers represent on-campus residential study for adults over short periods of time. Ordinarily, the conference and seminar programs are highly concentrated upon the updating of knowledge in a particular profession, or they may represent an interdisciplinary approach in the extension of new concepts. They are designed to provide further understanding on a broad spectrum of the interrelationships of change and their effects upon man and his environment.

Perhaps the growth, significance and impact of continuing education centers in the United States are appropriately represented in a brief review of our own experiences at the Center for Continuing Education at Notre Dame.

After many years of serious concern and careful planning, the University in the spring of 1966 embarked upon a bold new program and long-range commitment to continuing education. In the words of the president, Father Hesburgh, the Center was to become "a crossroads, a beacon, a bridge . . . encouraging traffic from all directions, providing a welcome for good ideas from whatever source . . . a place for pilgrims: where all could listen, speak, argue, discuss, dialogue and hopefully learn."

Within three short years, the Center has provided vast new educational opportunities for thousands of individuals who would not ordinarily have had the opportunity to come to the university. The Center is, indeed, in the mainstream of the total intellectual life of the University and our society. The dedication of the Center in March, 1966 provided the setting for the now famous international conference on the theological issues of Vatican II to which we invited some 60 distinguished philosophers, theologians, historians and educators from all over the world, many of them the architects of the council itself. It was attended by some 1,600 in all at the University, and was televised through closed circuit to 10 major cities in the United States. The Center is

127

uniquely equipped with exceptionally fine simultaneous language translation facilities similar to those used at the United Nations. We were able to carry as many as five different languages for this conference.

In the course of the first three years of operation, the Center has held over 900 symposia, seminar and conference activities. In the first year alone, we held 342 such conferences. I estimate that the total attendance, that is, those registered, over the past three-year period, is in excess of 120,000. We are running about 50,000 registrants a year at the present time.

These programs and conferences range from problems of poverty, literature, mental health, birth control, criticism in the arts, world demography and civil liberties; cancer research, diplomacy, urban renewal, poetry; to problems of literacy, clerical celibacy, pornography, juvenile delinquency, welfare administration and responsibility in city government. A great number of these conferences were initiated by the Center. Some were initiated by the various academic disciplines at Notre Dame. Some came as proposals from outside the university and we then structured the programs, provided the academic input and scheduled the event.

Very quickly, to name but a few, here are some of the most significant and important conferences we have held over just the past few months:

1. a journalism workshop for high school students and the news media;
2. the Midwestern Symposium on Current Trends in Antibiotic Therapy;
3. an international conference on freedom of residence;
4. a community response to crime, with Mayor Lindsay of New York City and U. S. Congressman John Brademas of Indiana;
5. major Tensions in American Education, with Congressman John Brademas; Mr. McGeorge Bundy, former special assistant to John F. Kennedy; Harold Howe, at that time commissioner of education in the United States, and Francis Keppel, a distinguished professor and educator.

The university learns as it teaches. The rewards of the continuing education programs flow to the university as well as from the university. The conference activities within these centers provide fresh, new experiences for the faculty as they come in contact with those who come to the campus to participate. This, in turn, generates new vitality for the university.

The continuing explosion of new knowledge, the sweeping rate of discovery through research and technology, the flood of daily events which present new concepts, changing values and shifting social and political philosophies are not easy to live with. Only the most determined can keep their balance and remain relevant. Yet this is precisely what our present society and environment demand. The tempo of our times will no longer permit us the luxury of a citizenry that is unaware and uninformed. We cannot now afford to have our citizens withdraw and dismiss the unfamiliar, cling to the old, fight the new and remain indifferent to the many human problems and social changes going on about them.

I think John Gardner, the former secretary of Health, Education and Welfare in the U.S., in his book entitled *Self-Renewal* (New York, 1964), has captured this in a very special way. In his section on "The Individual and the Innovative Society," he has said, ". . . One of the clearest dangers of modern society is that men and women will lose the experience of participating in meaningful decisions concerning their own life and work . . . that they will become cogs in the machine simply because they feel like cogs in the machine. All too often today they are inert components of the group, not participating in any significant way but simply being carried along like grains of sand in a bucket."

It would be inaccurate and unrealistic for me to imply that the programs in continuing education in the United States are going to emerge as the single most important area of concern. Surely our academic programs and teaching responsibilities for the undergraduate student and the challenge of university research and graduate work must continue to have their priorities. It is not so much a question of how each of these would rank, but rather how effectively our existing resources can now appropriately be applied to this new area of responsibility.

It is perhaps a phenomenon of our time that the great distinction between youth and maturity tends to be sharply diminished within the context of continuing education. Both young people and adults are a part of the same changing environment, in the sense that they must live intensely and react swiftly within the time of their existence and the environment in which they find themselves. The adult is able to render service only if, like the youth, he is prepared to learn and by his performance succeeds in accepting and implementing change. He has in common with the youth the fact that both are continually developing and preparing for the future within the realities of the moment. Perhaps another very important factor is the fact that adults are obliged to learn from the young at least as much as they are able to offer.

The unprecedented rate of change and the magnitude of people being affected by change in the world is such that the public service aspect of the university takes on an entirely new dimension. This public service aspect is perhaps embraced more fully within the concept of continuing education than any other single aspect of university activity.

The role of the university in social change is now, and must be, quite different from what it has been in the past. It is perhaps the single most important organization of professionals, able to see the principles of life, the problems of society and how that society may, or may not be directed towards greater fulfillment. The university is perhaps the only remaining institution

129

which has the possibility of seeing our society and seeing it whole, yet with all of its parts and all of its problems.

The great number of diverse tasks which the university has been called upon to perform in the world has given it far greater breadth of insight and penetration into the great human problems of man. As a result, it has made the university responsible for a new mission it never had before.

As we view most universities in the United States today, we recognize that they are not only educational institutions, but that they also play a tremendously important role in the social and economic life of people. As our knowledge changes so do our people, and people ultimately change the world. It is through universities and the opportunities that they provide for lifelong learning that people find inspiration and new courage, courage to promote the welfare of others and advance the course of civilization.

This, I believe, is the focus and ultimate objectives to which our continuing education programs in the United States are committed.

# ENVIRONMENTAL CRISIS AND THE UNIVERSITY

Patrick Horsbrugh

## THE GLOBAL CONTEXT

The prevalence of crisis in environmental conditions of every kind, in every place where human habitation exists in organized form, is now beyond dispute and the university has become the focus of expectation for measures that may relieve the distress.

The 1960's will be seen as the period in which the environic crisis was recognized as overwhelming and inescapable. Heavy is the hand of natural retribution that springs from man's ceaseless aggravation of the ecological orders in his thrusting desires to dominate all that he surveys.

There is ironic justice in the timing of such retribution in the sense that we can now see the essential unity of the earth as our flight from it is achieved, and can realize that the human befoulment of any part inevitably involves the whole.

While the issues of pollution may be considered as scientific, social, ecological or economic, they are primarily political, for any change of mood and motivation must be made by deliberate decision. International anarchy, stimulated by environic devastation, is now so real a possibility that reputable scientists are repeating the alarm that it may already be too late to redeem the existing environic damage because of the increasing pressures of populations and their demands.

As the decade of the 1960's terminates, the global ramifications of such conditions have been recognized by the Swedes whose domestic record in scenic seemliness and civil order has long been praised and envied. The permanent Swedish representative at the United Nations has raised the subject and gained the agreement of the General Assembly to hold an international conference on "The Problems of Human Environment" in 1972.[1]

In brief, the condition of the physical environment is in peril and the survival of all species upon which human continuity depends is threatened. As the ecological orders are challenged by the consequences of our inadvertence,

---

[1] Statement by Sverker Åström, Swedish Representative, Ambassador, December 3, 1968, in the General Assembly, United Nations.

the natural forces retaliate with ever increasing severity. The spiritual inspiration of the landscape declines, moral justifications and standards lose their relevance and the intellectual confidence of society withers away.

It is appropriate, therefore, that amid these conflicting human pressures—political, social and economic—the university should emerge as the principal forum from which to explore the possibilities of resolution and create an ethic of behavior that may yet divert the approaching environic catastrophe which will bring the demise of organized society, for environic condition is the primary insurance of domestic well-being and international peace.

The university, being the most intellectually advanced yet tender of all human institutions, is the natural storm center in the ultimate vortex of this environic crisis, after political ineptitude, scientific ignorance, economic greed and social misadventures have wrought havoc on our most delicate biosphere.

It is for these reasons that I plead for a new concept of university life and vitality which may demonstrate an earnest harmony between man and plant, material and purpose, structure and place, behavior and consequence that can, even yet, be achieved within the existing dimensions of any university.

THE UNIVERSITY

Since the university is endowed with form no less than with function, and since it is a place no less than a program, it is subject to all the influences, natural and man-made, which constitute environmental quality and crisis of condition. By 'its very nature the institution is much affected by physical characteristics of location and of social standards, but the hazards of environic vitality have only recently been recognized.

Any review of the task of universities in a changing world would be deficient if the urgent subject of environics were ignored, and it is my privilege to suggest that it is this issue of crisis in environmental condition that takes precedence over all other topics listed or implied on the program of this symposium.

I shall begin and conclude with student responses within this context of crisis, the former disruptive, the latter purposeful, and I hope to demonstrate that upon the health of the environment all else depends and suggest that the university represents the logical, and indeed the only instrument whereby this priority may be proved and where a revised pattern of behavior may emerge from the social bewilderment that prevails.

May I draw your attention to a report for the United Nations Commission for Social Development—prepared by three sociologists, one American and two British—which provides evidence of the impending forces of disruptive change with which we must now contend.

This "Preliminary Report on Long Term Policies and Programs for Youth in National Development"[2] furnishes estimates which are especially disturbing to those of us who are directly concerned with the physical condition of the environment in general and with the social concepts that determine the design of university enviria in particular. The report declares that the influence of youth "will begin to predominate in world affairs," that "world opinion is going to become increasingly the opinion of the world's youth and the generation conflict will assume proportions not previously imagined."

The report continues with the warning that young people "are prepared to march, to demonstrate, and to riot if necessary in support of views which may not be those of the electorate, nor of the majority, nor yet of those in government."

The document concludes with the suggestion that "young people need to know where they stand, what is intended for them, and when," and I shall take these three issues of 'standing,' of 'intention' and of 'timing' as the trilogy of factors within which to mold the arguments for the primacy of my subject, environmental crisis, the university opportunities which such crises afford, and the ferment of student initiative which such crises create. These factors represent the influences which surround the topic of this symposium on the "Task of the Universities in a Changing World."

The extraordinarily confident and commanding phraseology used in the U.N. report seems calculated to emphasize the existing hostility between generations. While it may be true that "young people need to know where they stand" the declaration implies the perpetuation of their subordinate position in relation to a continuing authority. The dogmatic statement, "what is intended for them," implies a superior decision that is tantamount to fate, while the coda, "and when," determines indisputable control. Indeed, all the causes of student disruption would seem to be confirmed by this curiously insensitively-worded recommendation, notwithstanding the earlier interpretations of the reasons for revolt, so carefully explored by the authors.

The connections between these conditions of 'standing,' of 'intention' and of 'timing' and my topic, the Environmental Crisis and the University, are immediate and indivisible from the surrounding physical conditions that prevail, because these conditions reflect our standards, cultural and ethical, and especially our comprehension of things natural.

We are known not only by our works, but by our enviria also, and I propose to develop this theme of environic condition as the ultimate measure of social stability, of which campus self-confidence is the instinctive sensor.

---

[2] Prepared by the Social Development Division of the United Nations in co-operation with other U.N. organizations. January 7, 1969.

I would ask you to recognize that the general environic crisis which surrounds all universities is part of the crisis of condition that prevails within the boundaries of individual institutions themselves. The administrative separateness of city and campus should not conceal the state of influence that each exerts upon the other, for environment, like time, is indivisible. It can be assessed, it can be measured, but it is continuous and cannot be divided, anymore than it is possible to separate city from country and urban from nonurban conditions in our search for social self-sufficiencies.

It is within this context of physical restraint that I wish to concentrate upon the particularity of the university, and to consider the environic conditions within and around the institution that we have inherited, and for whose progress we are so concerned.

### DEFINITIONS—REVISIONS OF CONCEPT—SCALE

Having emphasized the concept of the indivisible physical unity of the environment, I wish to define, also, the term 'crisis' in the original Greek sense, meaning a 'point of decision,' and to remind you that the Chinese equivalent of crisis has two meanings, that of danger, and that of opportunity. When I associate the term with environic conditions, I intend that it shall convey the combined sense of social aspiration tinged with the ethical uneasiness which presently assails us when confronted with the visual and aesthetic evidence of material misuses of every kind.

These factors of physical condition, emotion and intellectual rectitude are inseparable elements of the nervous tensions which we now recognize as the signals of crisis, that critical moment implying sudden change, surprise, unpredictability, the instant of decision. Each condition militates against the other, but all originate with the erosion of the natural amenities caused by increasing population pressures.

As a result of wide-ranging personal advantages in travel and observation, I am convinced that the supreme dilemma which confronts humanity at this moment in history is simply that of environic condition. As the populations of the world increase, as their social expectations expand and the life-supporting resources are consumed, the healthful state of the biosphere emerges as the most vital single all-embracing factor in determining human survival.

There can be no doubt whatever about the priority of the 'environic imperative.' Our reluctance to appreciate the many warnings provided by the behavior of the natural forces can only be described as extraordinary to the point of genocide, on a global scale. Meanwhile, the U.N. report declares "young people need to know where they stand." They stand, it seems to me, with the rest of humanity, confronted by environic disaster, to which their intuition has awakened them.

THREE-POINT APPEAL—PRIORITY OF ENVIRONIC CONDITION

In associating the general environmental crisis of physical condition with the university, I am speaking as a designer, concerned with three interrelated issues which I submit for your consideration.

First, there is the urgency of determining conditions; second, the inspiration of student initiative; and third, the identification of university opportunities.

The university appears to represent the only available instrument with which to contend with the diminishing chances of social survival, to grapple with governmental processes and decision, to harness the potent facilities of organized communications, wherewith to develop a crash program of environic education and revised behavioral standards towards the biospheric elements. As a nation, these United States possess each of these components— universities, communication systems and human resources—in fair measure, within which it should not be difficult to galvanize academic forces to meet the challenge by the use of existing broadcast media of every kind, and by revising personal behavioral standards in accordance with new ethical valuations based upon ecological tolerances. The university is at the emotional hub of the environmental crisis, since there is no other social facility that can review (with detachment and yet with compassion), digest and resolve the contradictory social values and desires which now beset organized societies at every cultural level.

The environic predicament transcends political ideologies. It is common to all forms of economy, primitive and sophisticated, and is undermining the social self-confidence at every age. In response to the demands of the U.N. report that young people need to know "what is intended for them," I can imagine no better intention in such an emergency than the better use of the university community and system for the testing of ideas to sustain a quality of life that is indeed 'cultural.'

*Student Initiative.* In the secondary matter of student initiative we may depend, I believe, upon the phenomenon of instinct which forewarns the rising generation of inherent dangers in continuing social habit, and repels them from repeating the actions of their progenitors. This basic impulse determines the differences of opinion and causes reaction between one generation and another. The present world-wide student resurgence may be seen as an example of youthful suspicion that the established mores are somehow deficient. If this instinct is indeed an emotional force, it would seem appropriate to seek and harness such reactions to positive purpose within the structure of the university so that a forward direction can be given to such dissident factions.

Were an environic "crusade" to be called in the face of our impending ecological catastrophe—a crusade that relied on the purposefulness of mankind and on the promotion of concepts of relative value attuned to biospheric limitations—the responses might surpass anything ever experienced in military recruitment, social fervor or religious devotion. Can there be any greater opportunity for the expression of genuine, thrusting student initiative than the security of mankind through improved understanding of environmental conditions? Can there be any greater cause for which to strive, or which could better stimulate student energies, imagination, and sensitivities than that of environic redemption? The U.N. report demands that young people need to know "what is intended for them and when"; the 'when' is now.

Other opinions may be quoted in confirming the need for fresh recognition of the university as the crucible in which to test and promote revised concepts of envirial value. Rene Dubos, of Rockefeller University, believes that "the most important aspect of human ecology is that all environmental factors exert a direct effect on the development of human characteristics, in health as well as in disease," and that "human ecology involves not only the immediate and direct effects of environmental forces, but also their indirect and long-range consequences."[3] He then passes from this priority to emphasize that "Such knowledge cannot be obtained from the study of oversimplified biological systems. It requires the analysis of actual human situations and the use of experimental models reproducing some selected aspects of these situations." I suggest that the university itself is the only immediate instrument, organized, self-sensitive and simmering for the chance to respond as an "experimental model" for the study of environic conditions—human imposition thereon and reactions thereto—in the general search for a quality of life which is becoming evermore difficult to sustain.

Professor Dubos believes "that human ecology could be readily developed into a flourishing experimental science," but he warns that the universities cannot respond effectively because they are too frozen in well-defined disciplines. "When a problem of the society presents itself, the university cannot re-create itself fast enough to do the job."

While this observation may seem to be true, it should be challenged on the basis of rising student conviction that students can, indeed, revise their own attitudes towards social improvement of every kind. The topic of human ecology, recommended by Professor Dubos, should provide effective crusading appeal. The challenge to youthful aspirations was re-emphasized by Dr. Margaret Mead in the American Museum of Natural History's annual lecture, "Man and Nature," delivered in March 1969. She declared that "for the first time in human history there are no elders anywhere who know what the young people

---

[3] Consumer Protection and Environmental Health Service Conference on Human Ecology, *Scientific Research*, March 3, 1969, p. 23.

know." She implies, I think, that the older generations will be obliged to respond to issues as they may be seen by the young, even as the disparity in the distribution of ages shifts inexorably in favor of youth, and in spite of the fact that there are no youths anywhere who know what their elders now know.[4]

There is no task, I suggest, that is more relevant, or which offers greater opportunities for the union of the experience of age and the vigor of youth than that of environic studies, embracing the subject of human ecology and absorbing the instinctive energies of those who inherit our conditions with such suspicion.

Environic condition, I submit, is the social priority of our time, the principal academic program deficiency and the foremost political aggravation with which we must contend, and I can offer some evidence of sound and forethoughtful student response in support of revised academic programming regarding the physical design of the university, the determination of students to involve themselves in pressing social issues beyond the campus, even the ability to reach out and influence international policy-making at the level of the United Nations itself.

*University Obligations.* In the tertiary matter of identifying university obligations, I use the Chinese interpretation of "crisis" as meaning opportunity, and emphasize that once the priority of environic condition has been established, the university is the logical instrument wherein to re-create a form of life and livelihood that is more harmonious with the ecological factors whose order we have disrupted with such dire consequences.

A substantial lead has already been taken by the University of Southern Illinois in the matter of ecological evaluation where Buckminster Fuller has established his unique international reference, The Inventory of World Resources. Without some system of biospheric assessment there can be no realistic evaluation of relative territorial resources or development of priorities and policies, and this leadership needs support, for the obligations are so widespread that no single political or industrial enterprise can ever be sufficient. With improved means of information retrieval and interpretation, this repository can sustain other centers of subscribing zeal. There must be no restraint in the matter of resource-planning out of fear of duplicating effort, for the urgencies are too detailed and too widespread.

The smallest practical social entity of disciplined, self-exploratory significance is, I suggest, the university itself, where its location, its form and its collective personality combine to provide a vehicle for "the proper study of

---

[4] Critical comment by Dr. Charles Malik after the delivery of this paper, April 18, 1969.

mankind . . . ," a place where the subject "is man"[5] in the context of environic condition where "human ecology could be readily developed into a flourishing experimental science," as Dubos has suggested.

*Campus Planning.* While I am emphasizing the need for horizon-wide comprehension in our appreciation of context in physical planning, I plead also, for detailed reconsideration of the practical enframement of the processes of education, the university campus itself. For some undefined reason, the campus remains largely ignored as a particular design specialty in spite of all the new universities under construction, and despite all the scramble for educational expansion and improvement of accommodation.

I would like to hear your response to my plea for the creation of a recognized graduate-level design program devoted especially to the function and form of the university as a fundamental social facility no less than an academic precinct, with a design program consisting of three parts:

(a) that will analyze the historic development of the university as exemplified in Western countries and their equivalent in Islamic, Hindu, Buddhist, Shinto and other cultures;

(b) that will consider the psychological microclimate of learning, amid a socially distracted atmosphere; the changing impulses of contemporary youth; the relationships between ages; the relevance of experience; the transmission of information; and the stimulation and momentum of excellence (in the sense that is described by former Secretary of Health, Education and Welfare, John Gardner, in his books *Excellence* and *Self-Renewal*)[6] with reference to the hope of wisdom;

(c) that will treat with planning dispositions, design and materials; their significance in educational facilities of all types, universities, technical schools, grade schools and kindergartens, accommodation for the disabled, the retarded, and for the captive of every kind, man and beast, in the enforced seclusion of penitentiaries and of zoos.

## THE SILENT SYMBOLISM

When considering the environmental crisis and the university, it is prudent to recall the evidence of changes in physical planning—as distinct from cur-

---

[5] "Know then thyself, pressure not God to scan; the proper study of mankind is man." Alexander Pope, *Essay on Man,* Epistle 2, 1. 2.

[6] *Excellence—Can We Be Equal and Excellent Too?* (New York, 1961) and *Self-Renewal—The Individual and the Innovative* (New York, 1964), in association with the Educational Facilities Laboratories, Inc., New York City.

ricula—that have occurred throughout the history of European college development, from its acknowledged beginnings in the twelfth century.

Campus planning varies from the extremes of the ordered informality of incomparable medieval Oxford and Cambridge to the regal formality of Jefferson's University of Virginia and the axial authority of the University of Notre Dame. Between these extremes of clarity lie variations such as the disunity of Pennsylvania State University, the co-ordination of Aarhus University, the casual precinctal composition of the new rural and urban campuses of the University of Sussex, and the University of Illinois in Chicago.

From these widely differing examples of planning it is possible to perceive a silent symbolism that proclaims the changing concepts of form and purpose, from rigid quadrangles and incidental accumulations of quadrangles (within the competitive irregularities of the urban fabric) to the axial anatomies suggesting law unlimited and order omnipotent, forethoughtfully laid out in expectations of continuous expansion. There is a constant interaction in layout where emphasis shifts from subtly designed juxtapositions where the identity of any building is obscure, where the location of control is concealed, to the obvious domination by the administration center.

*Diversity Within Unity—The Enclosed Plan.* While recognizing the antiquity of the universities of Paris and Bologna as "studia generalia respectu regni," the incidental college-urban association is best seen at Oxford (c. 1190) and Cambridge (c. 1209), since their original patterns of self-enclosed collegiate form are more easily recognized within the urban context than is the case with other institutions of comparable age.

These coagulations of colleges form the epitome of the concept of "universitas," the equivalent of the Roman collegium and are expressive of an association of persons organized for some common purpose, encompassing teachers, students, craftsmen and professionals. They represent, most eloquently, diversity of plan without loss of purpose, and possess particular architectural individuality, notwithstanding the similarity of materials and of constructional system.

The intermingling of university buildings with the city should be especially appreciated for its significance in social exchange and economy of site, together with the fact that the urban structure does not focus upon any special space or building whereby to establish the position of administrative power. No palace, no city hall, no university senate, no forum, no market dominates the plans of Oxford or Cambridge, yet the sense of order prevails. While the colleges of the "universitas" may vary in size and in grandeur, their dispositions remain unspecified, and no attempt is made to draw attention to the seat of college authority. (Indeed, the autonomy of each college is fiercely safe-

139

guarded and general assent is difficult to achieve, as those who are familiar with C. P. Snow's *The Affair* will remember).[7]

*The Open Plan.* The dispositions of the original North American colleges are very different in that the enclosed continuity of the European planning was abandoned in favor of open discontinuity in the placing of buildings whose individual isolation was seldom compromised.

Although Harvard (1636) was rigidly contained within its railed "yard," each building is separate from its neighbor and the sense of unity is achieved only by the quality of the spaces between the structures. The planning of the universities of Laval (1663) and Yale (1701) followed a similar formula and, as at Harvard, care was taken to insure remoteness from the community— urban and rural—and no recognition was accorded political influences. Again, no design emphasis was given to the location of control within the university itself.

In contrast, William and Mary College (1693) differs from these institutions in that it was built in court-like form at the colonial capital of Williamsburg and deliberately placed on axis with the Capitol itself, as one of the three principal features of the city plan. For the first time, it seems, higher education was thereby visibly symbolized as an integral part of the intended social development of the state, governing authority, legislative body and popular enlightenment.

A hundred and twenty-five years separate the Williamsburg college from that tour de force in formal academic planning created by Thomas Jefferson which was to influence the design of American college-building for the next century.

Jefferson's design for the University of Virginia (1819) is unique in that he accepted the classical authority of the axis and placed the domed library upon rising ground as the focal point of the layout, arranging the subsidiary buildings along the avenue, in strict order, and confirmed the structural regimentation with generous plantations of trees. The visual effect is simple yet grand, while the symbolism of position and purpose is obvious.[8]

---

[7] C. P. Snow, *The Affair* (New York, 1960).

[8] Frederick Doveton Nichols, in *Thomas Jefferson's Architectural Drawings* (Portland, Me., 1961), describes Jefferson's work thus: "Jefferson not only designed the buildings and supervised their construction, with all the attendant difficulties of securing proper materials and competent workmen: he also had to coax money from a reluctant government and keep frugal legislators from changing his designs. They were continually pressing for a single large building, but as Jefferson wrote to Thornton, 'instead of building a magnificent house which would exhaust all our funds, we propose to lay off a square . . . the outside of which we shall arrange (with) separate pavilions.' Clearly he set forth his high goals: 'the great object of our aim from the beginning has

## EDUCATION FOR WOMEN

After this monumental gesture in academic design—which emerged slowly at the persistence of the former president—was dampened by the responses of a reluctant state legislature, there was a pause in such sponsorship. Private initiative responded in favor of women and colleges of university rank were established: Wesleyan College (Georgia, 1836); Mount Holyoke (1837); Vassar (1861); and Smith (1871). Each institution consisted of one bold structure (of the kind preferred by officialdom for the University of Virginia, instead of the court-like plan determined by Jefferson) which contained all the accommodation, administrative, academic and domestic, and stood isolated from the community within a planted park of elegance and arboricultural significance, in which additional buildings eventually would be arranged.

## THE MORRILL ACT

With the passing of the Morrill Land Grant Act (1862) and the subsequent construction of campuses in every state of the Union, this new symbolic and noble formula of central dominant structure and subsidiary elements was repeated with little planning variation across the nation. The designs are formal, authoritative, and obvious in the relationship of their various parts; they are dependent for aesthetic effect upon the visual appeal of the perspective of central axis, with counter axes as expansions may warrant. Each campus was laid out at a distance from the city as an insurance against mutual encroachment. Only in a few instances were sites chosen adjacent to cities containing the state capitol, but the formal association between Capitol and College as expressed at Williamsburg was never repeated.

## THE AMERICAN CAMPUS

I consider that this insistence upon axial symmetry for the design of higher educational institutions throughout the nation is, in essence, an American planning concept, and encompasses landscaped areas no less than buildings, as one consistent and interdependent system of open spacial composition—a campus, in fact, where the emphasis is laid naturally upon rural rather than

---

been to make the establishment the most eminent in the United States. . . . We have proposed therefore to call to it characters of the first order of science from Europe . . . but by the distinguished scale of its structure and preparation . . . to induce them to commit their reputations to it. . . . To stop where we are is to abandon our high hopes, and become suitors to Yale and Harvard for their secondary characters.' "

urban associations, as might be expected under the influence of land-grant inspiration.

Even as the skyscraper stands as the foremost American contribution to the development of architecture, so the campus represents, I contend, the outstanding American contribution to planning, even though the park, avenues and mansion-like compositions are strongly reminiscent of the European landscape formula of aristocratic significance. While the suggestion of an educated elite may have been deliberately intended, these silent symbols of good order are challenged, inevitably, and the contemporary campus plans show that the formalities and hierarchial implications are most subtly concealed by means of irregular dispositions returning once again to the precinctal qualities of somewhat mediaeval guild-like exclusiveness. The current planning trends appear to suggest by their form a subconscious preference for an enclosed and introvertial private college character in place of the once confident declaration of open education facilities, accessible to all.

### NOTRE DAME DICHOTOMY

Here at Notre Dame we have a clear and comparative example of these developments in the thrusting formality of axial design, the quiet Harvard-like enclosures and the exclusive Oxford-like courts, that deserve special attention. The original grand axis of the avenue leading to the presiding Dome (with the subsidiary buildings placed along the way, and with the spacious grass cross-axis which endows the campus with nominal meaning) is now in competition with a parallel axis, adjacent but invisible from the original alignment, on which are threaded the stadium, the library, the dormitory's towers and Stepan Center (slightly off-axis). In this design dichotomy the authoritarian symmetry still lingers, but it is more diagramatic than actual. The new axis is repeatedly interrupted so that the potential visual impact of perspective and vista is lost, and the civic design opportunities of grandeur are ignored.

The two axes have no mutual design association whatever in that they represent different concepts of spacial appreciation, of kinetic quality, while the unifying effect which an open axis affords has been carefully nullified by the placing of each feature upon the line of emphasis, thereby denying each building's symbolic significance. The size and form alone of the structures must inform the visitor of the purposes they are intended to serve.

### ARCHITECTURAL DILEMMA

Architectural expression must also be considered as part of the environmental crisis, for concepts, materials and structure have undergone greater changes throughout the past century than in the entire course of architectural history. No longer is it possible for one generation to transmit intellectual consistency to its successor through unassailable confidence in its own architectural achievements. Where the emphasis is on novelty, there can be little regard for maturity.

The prevailing design emphasis upon anonymity can be as easily appreciated in physical planning as in the slackening of social formalities, and is achieved readily enough in architectural terms by use of the mass-produced building elements which the stringent economic limitations require.

While structural dimensions have become enormous and the general appearance of the campus may now resemble that of the city (the University of Texas at Austin), that special "sense of place" which has been, hitherto, the distinction of an academic resort is drastically reduced.

The original simplicity of the American block-by-block campus composition begun at Harvard and formalized with the Morrill Act, cannot be repeated indefinitely in response to the increasing demands for accommodation. Monotony results from repetition of structures and the fear of uniformity in building design results in a tendency towards wayward self-consciousness in shape and disposition, as exemplified in the recent buildings at Michigan State University.

In the desire to create new universities, as well as to expand existing institutions, new forms are being evolved which may respond to the yen for identity amid the growing environic uniformity, and for personal purpose in surroundings that are tranquil and conducive to the educational processes.

It is not surprising, then, to perceive a return to the introvertial college forms of medieval Europe, and there are many examples of new North American and European universities, whose plans demonstrate this current trend in environic design which favors the ancient precinctal form. I suggest that this shift in concept is very much part of the general crisis of condition, and is symptomatic of the subconscious desires to which campus designers should respond. I stress, also, the paradox between expansive programs and introspective planning.

In a changing world, identity of place, as well as of purpose, is of great psychological importance; and identification with place is, I believe, one of the major design issues in assessing the causes of social hysteria. It seems that the easy recognition of an individual college as an immediate personal envirium has given Oxford and Cambridge a relatively lasting cultural significance, and that this person-place association is the principal reason for their academic continuity and renown throughout the centuries.

I recognize, of course, the introvertial character of court-enclosing designs, as in Mediterranean and Islamic habitations, where external influences are deliberately excluded, but in the pursuit of learning and for the cultivation of independent opinions such an environment may be advantageous in these times when social and academic interaction is so vibrant.

Objections of "isolationism" and "ivory tower" detachment will be raised, but I would remind you that in times of social turmoil, seclusion is instinctively sought, for cultural continuity may be achieved only in such seclusion. It would seem from the evidence of the professional magazine that the court form of planning for domestic as well as academic use is returning to favor on both sides of the Atlantic. The desire for academic seclusion in college design in Britain continued after medieval times and received renewed architectural impetus during such differing periods as the eighteenth century's age of reason, the nineteenth century's age of endeavor, and remained in the scattered structural additions of the interwar periods of this century's age of revision.

In the case of the Winston Churchill College at Cambridge the design records a direct return to the medieval court-by-court enclosure, implying an exclusive assembly of 'the few.' The implication of favoring an elite would be denied with vehemence, of course, at this moment of determined effort towards egalitarianism; nevertheless, there is the subtle silent symbolism, which re-poses the question of whether it is really possible to provide ever higher academic standards for ever larger numbers who enforce their entry upon academia by the insistence upon some 'right.'

Quality, by its very nature, is not a quantitative commodity. Indeed, you may care to debate that the social concept of equal opportunities can be carried to academic heights only at the cost of that excellence which is the very foundation of academic justification, and personal endeavor. The environmental crisis is an intellectual crisis also, and all genetic record stands testimony to the relationship between quality of person and of place. In environic seemliness is recognized the nature of the people. In the matter of environic health, there can be no compromise.

### EMPHASIS ON INFORMALITY OF PLAN—SHIFTS IN RELEVANCE

There is a curious irony in such events, when the numbers of institutions increase, but where their influence on the social routine appears to decline. Since authority is currently at a discount, and administration prefers anonymity in boards of trustees, the open axial declaration of Thomas Jefferson's noble design, powerful enough to rally around it any growing metropolis, seems now to represent a waste of effort, and a misjudgment of the national scale and the possible development in social grandeur.

Indeed, it will be appreciated that we are overtaken by a shift in territorial and academic objectives. The irony continues in that real-estate values do not now depend upon convenience of location, quality of structure or cost of creation, but upon the encompassing condition. Only by attention to the condition of the environment can the crisis in human conflicts be reduced, for upon the state of the general depends the health of the particular.

*Political Influence on Site Location.* There is, also, a vital political factor which should be noted respecting the disposition of Oxford and Cambridge, in that neither of these august institutions was established in, or had much association with the recognized economic or governmental centers of London or Westminster. Indeed, unlike Paris, London did not possess a university until the founding of the University of London in 1836.

While the Morrill Act may have established the financial obligations between federal and state governments and the university, the designers were careful to avoid any political symbolism in the placement of the campuses. Even in the location of the University of Wisconsin (1849) at Madison, the University of Nebraska (1869) at Lincoln and the University of Texas (1881) at Austin, where the campuses are adjacent to capital-city sites as a result of private gifts of land, the exceptional opportunities for the creation of civic grandeur were consistently ignored. These deliberate planning disassociations of campus from capitol represent a curious quirk in the American official character, it seems, since they were taken at a time of mounting national self-confidence when axial planning, beaux-arts inspired, was in the ascendancy and in emotional accord with the spirit of the day.

*Implications of Expansion.* The success of the Morrill Act in providing the basis for regional agricultural and mechanical programs is beyond challenge. I consider that this has contributed more than any other single act of Congress to the social stability, and to the agricultural and industrial prowess of this nation. But, the expansions bred of success have introduced, inevitably, other factors which lead directly to a campus environmental crisis arising from size.

The crisis of campus magnitude is compounded by the time-distances between buildings, by the visual tedium of pathways in perspective, by maintenance difficulties and by the physical erosions which undermine the sense of environic quality. The uniformity of the new block-by-block design imposed by economic restraints has brought reaction in favor of the concentration of structures into intricate shapes and structural continuities. This constriction is in marked contrast with the spacious axial forms of the previous century and is strongly reminiscent of the monastic cohesion so necessary in any self-selective and highly motivated society.

The university can be the cultural crucible in which to mix the ingredients for a fresh quality of life and for renewed endeavor in the redemption of the physical surroundings which have become, so suddenly, so sour.

## STUDENT INITIATIVE

This, then, is the substance of environic crusade, and it leads me to the third and vital issue of my basic trilogy of priorities: campus symbolism and student initiative. May I remind you again of the phrase from the U.N. report— "young people need to know where they stand, what is intended for them and when"—and raise the urgency of 'when,' together with the unfathomed potentialities of students when challenged by a definite objective, clearly seen and well defined.

Since the environmental crisis and the university is not a subject which permits finalities or conclusions, I wish to leave with you three positive ideas on what might be done, here and now, to promote better comprehension of the environmental crisis: (1) in terms of academic and urban cohesion; (2) in terms of practical leadership of youth in general, and (3) in terms of direct national and international political leadership in the determination that, henceforward, all land is sacred to all species.

These three diverse but interrelated concepts have reached me almost simultaneously from three students of undergraduate level, and I hope that I can convey them to you with the sincerity with which they were initially presented to me.

## CAMPUS CONCEPTS

The first concept arises with a Texas student and concerns campus design and social enviria.[9] He proposes the concentration of campus facilities within pedestrian dimensions, which is obvious enough, but he includes a justifiable selection of urban services ranging from shops to apartments for a variety of persons who do not necessarily possess any campus affiliation. He was unaware of those mediaeval precepts already mentioned, but developed his own instinctive ideas from personal observation on the need to stimulate genuine, unpretentious social interaction between the self-selective student society and the townsfolk. He found encouragement in these ideas in the treatise on the "Functional Design for a University," prepared by Leslie A. Osborn, M.D., in 1965,[10] wherein the author bases his theme not on the teaching of subjects, but upon the education of persons.

Moreover, his work was expanded by a colleague who emphasized that the

---

[9] Richard Fletcher III, Texas.

[10] Leslie A. Osborn, M.D., Fellow, American Medical Association; Fellow, American Psychiatric Association; Diplomate, American Board of Psychiatry and Neurology, author.

policy of inclusiveness should be carried to the extent of involving all conditions of captive community such as the penitentiary and sanitoria for the mentally retarded and for the physically handicapped.[11] In the case of criminals, he pleaded that there was no chance of success in rehabilitation if institutional isolation were maintained. The facilities required by penologists are the same as those concentrated in universities and not available to prisoners, who, if they are to be returned to society, are in the greatest need of educational inspiration, vocational training and above all that sense of social participation which is the very essence of a vital university.

The proximity of wildlife habitat amid community activities is also essential, he argued, as a constant reminder of society's obligation to plan for the protection of all species rather than to design selfishly for human convenience alone. The physical planning concepts that were offered acknowledged the difficult security and mutually protective necessities, but showed extraordinary perception, sense of humanity and design imagination.

These themes reveal the sterility of social segregations of every kind, and illustrate the fresh vitality that could arise by increasing popular participation within the academic environment and from the association of different ages, aims and intellects.

So far as I am aware, there is no recognized center in these United States or abroad where such concepts of design and experimental behavior can be explored in theory, and in practice, notwithstanding the huge reinvestments to which governments of most political persuasions are presently committed.

An International Institute for the Study of Educational Enviria is required wherein those environic sensitivities may be developed which can foster that "style of life characterized by intellect and rationality" for which President Hesburgh has recently appealed.[12]

*Student-Managed Institutes.* The second concept concerns student social action, and arises from a Colorado student[13] who is a shrewd observer of the Kennedy mystique. In association with others, he has developed and drafted a potent proposal for the creation of The Robert F. Kennedy Student Institute for Social Action. While the suggested administrative form of the institute is conventional, the whole undertaking is to be student-wrought and run, and is devoted to "the prospects for building an American Community to which Senator Kennedy dedicated himself." It would concentrate upon social action projects such as "The Mexican-American circumstance," American-Indian resurgence, Appalachian redevelopment and Negro-urban enterprises where

---

11 Wayne N. Longfellow, Texas.

12 Rev. Theodore M. Hesburgh, C.S.C., TV interview, March 1969.

13 Ronald Passarelli, Colorado.

147

educational facilities shall form the basis of each program in response to Lincoln's admonition that "you cannot escape the responsibilities of tomorrow by evading them today."

If Dr. Mead's declaration is true that "there are no elders anywhere who know what the young people know," then there is no justification for delay in testing this earnest and self-developing concept of social need and student thrust. It is inevitable that somewhere soon, positive initiative will be implemented by substantial academic action, or by insubstantial vacuum, as in the case of the Real Great Society's "University of the Streets" in New York City.

*International Policy-Making.* The third student possesses a unique agricultural heritage in Indiana[14] and consequently is most keenly aware of the signs of territorial devastation which abound. He has responded to the Swedish ambassador's previously mentioned initiative with proposals of his own for the holding of an International Youth Consensus in 1971 upon the original agenda for the 1972 conference on "The Problems of Human Environment." While there are innumerable student U.N. procedural meetings, there is no precedent, it seems, for the holding of such a critical event in advance of a major U.N. conference where youthful opinion may identify priorities and stress urgencies on a subject of such vital significance to the generation about to inherit these problems.

After three days of briefing at the State Department, and at other relevant Washington offices, this youth had several meetings with Swedish and U.N. officials with such positive effect that drafts for a "precursor" consensus are now in preparation, whereby the fullest possible student initiative and participation may be achieved in the advocacy of international principles of conservation and human attitudes, ecological, ethical and economic, toward our shared biospheric conditions.

I hope that in citing these three examples of student perceptivity I have been able to demonstrate that the topic I have been assigned, "Environmental Crisis and the University," is indisputably the prime task confronting universities in a changing world; that healthful environic conditions are fundamental to sustained social well-being, and that by setting the example within its own boundaries the university can establish the necessary moral standard and harness student initiative for positive purpose.

From where can such leadership be expected if universities fail to respond, and focus the instinctive initiative that they momentarily possess?

Even as the times require a reputable university to declare a continuous program for the study of university life, form and purpose, so too, is it urgent for a renowned institution to proclaim a program of systematic conservation,

---

14 LeRoy Troyer, Indiana.

ecological, ethical and cultural. All that has been done towards this end is but a slow beginning and justifies Rene Dubos' doubts about the ability of academia to mount a study devoted to human ecology.

### ENVIRONIC CRISIS INEVITABLE

The 'environmental crisis and the university' emphasizes the conflict of numbers and of demands beyond that which can be sustained by the existing facilities, natural or man-made. It is not yet a crisis of political ideology, though this too may come to pass. The university still caters to a limited population and the ever-unanswerable question of "how many" is inescapable.

Since the university cultivates an intellectual elite, it attempts to perpetuate that exclusiveness which should be justifiable on the basis of excellence, as already suggested. Prince Philip restated this feature of academic life during a recent TV interview when he referred to the general student unrest and obviously enjoyed reminding his audience that the university is the "most established," self-perpetuating establishment in existence, since all its administrators are university graduates. An environic crisis of physical condition is inevitable, therefore, if the concept of the individual "right" to advancement in higher education becomes prevalent, and if the economic means, private and public, are not sufficient to permit this right to be fulfilled. Even though the university student enrollment has now reached admirable proportions, there is always the risk of general disenchantment with both physical conditions and academic standards, where by comparison a "University of the Streets," as developed by The Real Great Society, Inc., in New York City in 1967, may appear to be more relevant and more appealing.

In these terms, the plight of any university approximates that of a city that outgrows its strength, where its extremities become strangers to its heart, where the population has mentally and physically forsaken the fabric of its origin.

Meanwhile, the pressures to provide higher educational facilities for all continues, and the new physical forms that have resulted show, again, the silent symbolism of our collective state of mind: constriction rather than expansion, seclusion rather than involvement.

As the sense of belonging to place, to group, or devotion to purpose diminishes in the rising tide of anonymity so, too, does the pride of possession disappear.

*Cultural Crucible.*   A fresh esprit is required on campus to resist this crisis of self-befoulment. I believe that this very moment of intellectual turmoil and administrative tribulation provides us with the stimulant which will produce a resurgence in our sense of values ecological, ethical and social, whereby the

149

quality of place becomes a parallel academic aim together with that of personal improvement.

### SUMMARY

In summary, may I transpose the three issues, environic priority, university opportunities and student initiative upon the demands of the U.N. report on student restlessness, which suggests that "young people need to know where they stand, what is intended for them . . . and when," with which I began.

Upon the priority of environic health and condition, the argument is the same whether the scale be global or personally immediate. Humanity in general and cultivated societies in particular will perish if the natural conditions are unduly disrupted, and only by making quality of environment our foremost concern can we sustain conditions permitting an orderly society to continue and develop. This dictum establishes not only the social priority, but determines the political urgencies, the resource strategies and the economic balances. It also ensures that environics becomes the supreme academic subject, being both theological in spirit and practical in operation. This is where we "stand."

On the matter of university opportunity, can you suggest any organization, inherited or projected, which is better suited for leading a crusade in the defense of environic qualities; the redemption of territorial, aquatic and atmospheric abuses; and for the re-creation of the human and wildlife habitat that is so persistently sacrificed in pursuit of immediate gain without regard for the retribution which natural forces will demand from our successors, even as we now pay the interest upon transgressions wrought before our time? The universities are the vehicle for such a campaign. This is what is "intended."

The pool of student initiative is unfathomable, and with imaginative encouragement it should be possible for universities to persuade the students to mount a national environic health, education and welfare resurgence, comparable perhaps to the Peace Corps; global in scale, as urgent an issue as that of any military threat to national sovereignty; as penetrating in detail to touch every form of specialized artificial habitat from hospitals to zoos; embracing conditions as diverse as high-density city centers and wildernesses.

Unless the overwhelming urgency of the environmental crisis is seen for what it is, a threat to human survival, the university will have failed in its universal purpose to show generations "what is intended for them." The "when" is now.

# PART THREE

PART THREE

# UNIVERSITIES AND THE
# DEVELOPING WORLD

Kenneth W. Thompson

We have taken it for granted that universities stand at the center of enlightenment and progress in this country, and it would be surprising if this viewpoint had not been carried over in our relations with the rest of the world. A debate has raged between those who maintain university development is premature in the developing countries and those who give it primacy. The former argue that first priority should be given to the building of elementary and secondary schools and to the fashioning of relevant vocational programs. They would have Americans and Westerners generally turn their attention from higher education to primary and secondary education, which is the cornerstone of any emerging educational system.

For various reasons this viewpoint has not prevailed. First, universities exist in many areas of the developing world. They are a fact—however much they may be a fledgling fact—of life. Second, some national leaders argue that in their role as responsible political leaders, they cannot afford to turn over responsibility for educating the very young. It will not do, they say, to acknowledge any weakness in the ability to train and bring forward young men and women in those years where education is most formative to intellectual and moral development. The East African leader, Julius Nyerere, once said, "If I leave to others the building of our elementary school system, they will abandon me as their responsible national leader." Third, universities and colleges, for better or for worse, have become a primary requirement of a new nation. In the beginning they set great store on having an undergraduate institution. In recent years, even within such interdependent nation-states in a particular region as Kenya, Uganda and Tanzania, national leadership has felt obliged to call for the building of professional schools in essential fields like medicine and agriculture.

## THE BASIC ISSUES IN INTERNATIONAL EDUCATION

All of this means that higher education is going forward in the developing countries and that no force within or outside is likely to change or upset this fact. It is nevertheless relevant to ask with respect to these new universities, "Education for what?", "Education for whom?", "What are the priorities?"

153

Each country must inevitably apply its own criteria, and the answer to the question, "What kind of education?", will depend on which of various possible criteria they see fit to emphasize. Some nations looking at their universities may stress the relevance of education to urgent national problems. According to this approach, new universities cannot afford to give priority to anything but immediate national needs. Based on these criteria, health or food or engineering are likely to be primary fields of interest. The training of technicians takes priority over the training of humanists. The development of paramedical personnel is thus more important than the preparation of fully-trained medical personnel.

Another criterion sometimes stressed is that of excellence. According to this view, quality should take priority over every other concern. It must be the task of institutions to train national leaders in every field, of such quality that they may hold their own anywhere in the world. The universities must be a school for statesmen, whether in science, education or statecraft. And they must prepare the best managers of industry, not merely a few such leaders.

A third criterion is concerned with the three levels of education which might be given emphasis. A country can give primary stress to higher education, to elementary-secondary education, or to vocationalism. It can seek to bring about job training at the most practical possible level. It can build a scheme of apprenticeships for work in the fields of immediate importance. Whichever of these fields it singles out will affect the overall educational system. The choices made as to which level of education to give priority to are probably the most fundamental choices of all.

A fourth criterion which influences choice arises when the question is asked, "Education for whom?" In one form or another every country is confronted with a choice between mass education and the training of an elite. False as an either/or selection may be, the educational system chosen will reflect the stress that is placed on literacy as opposed to leadership, on training in the basic skills as opposed to training in fundamental knowledge.

Another point at which selection and choice become pertinent is in determining the purpose of education. Is the goal some specific form of educational competence or is it wisdom and judgment? Is it specialists that are sought or generalists? The famous axiom comes to mind, "Education is not making men clever today but wise forever." Is it sending men into society well-stocked with information and detailed knowledge as against providing them with the tools for deciding important questions?

Another criterion develops in response to the character of a society. It makes considerable difference whether training is designed for the public or the private sector. Where the public sector constitutes a major portion of economic and social life, education must somehow register this fact. Obviously, the choice in the end is not one or the other but some combination of both.

The real issue involves how the system is ordered and how its totality shapes the particular aspects of the educational organization.

*The Relationship to Educational Exchange.* The development of universities today is inescapably an international question. The transportation and communication revolutions have decreed a world drastically shrunken in size. Space has become relative. The key issue for any given country is its particular set of relationships with the outside world. Not every foreign country is relevant to a newly-developed nation. Paradoxically, in this respect the U.S. is both relevant and irrelevant to developing nations. In an interrelated world the United States now finds itself at the center. This has not always been so, and as we move into the twenty-first century, it may once again not hold true. In their day the Spaniards, French, British and Germans before us occupied an equally prominent place. Yet while we stand at the center, the relevance of American education is limited because we are inescapably an island of plenty in a sea of poverty. In a broad sense, the United States remains a developing nation. But in a narrower sense, the gulf between the United States and the newly independent states is great and becoming greater.

For better or for worse, the flow of students in international exchange has reached such proportions that thousands of foreign students now study here. Each year the United States Department of State grants passports to more than 100,000 American students going abroad, with about a fourth of them in quest of formal education. The two-way flow in education is further demonstrated by the movement overseas of hundreds of American professors for purposes of research and teaching. Indeed, international education in the last third of the twentieth century has increasingly come to mean participation in institution-building in the developing countries. Where once the relationship was entirely one of American professors in American universities teaching non-American students, now more and more Americans are going to Asian and African institutions to teach and work with Asians and Africans. Our era is one of experimentation. Over 200,000 people annually are studying outside their own countries. Education is a magic word throughout the world. It has a mystique of promise and hope. Too often, though, its content remains uncertain and unclear.

*Changing Patterns.* The questions of most immediate concern to Americans are "What is the American component?" "What is our part in the changing patterns and relationships with education and developing countries?" To assist in education in any country remains a delicate matter. Institutions and nations are continually in a state of flux, and while some yearn for a more static world, this course leads to stagnation. With all its difficulties, a revolutionary era provides new opportunities and challenges. The present era offers possibilities for good and evil; not all change is good. At one point in history the challenge for mankind was primarily physical. Survival was the only matter at stake. Survival is still an issue, but today it has moral and political overtones as well. Vast changes are occurring in those areas with which we are establishing new patterns and new relationships. Profound changes involving human emancipation mark our era. In a comparatively few years, a billion people, or one-third of mankind, have passed from colonial to independent status. From 1946 to the present, nearly 75 new names were entered on the roster of national states. Within nations, changes no less dramatic are taking place. More than a century after the Emancipation Proclamation we in this country are finally realizing its objectives. Human development is being stressed in the hope that it may keep pace with technological change.

In this context what should be the form of the American component in international education? As, in one generation, the measure of speed has changed from the gallop of horses to jets breaking through sound barriers, the relevant question has been reduced to how we are to bring modern education into line with the new technology. Where should the contribution of American educators be made? How ought it to be brought to bear? It is easier to raise the question in specific cases than to answer it in general. However, the beginning of an answer might include elements of the following:

1. At least at the level of undergraduate education, the American component should be overseas or in the field. This involves sending Americans abroad wherever possible and desired, rather than bringing 100,000 foreign undergraduates who are often untrained and rootless to the United States. A case can be made for operating programs, for field staff and for men who devote their careers to service abroad. In undergraduate education, a case can be made for taking the American component abroad and blending it with indigenous elements.

2. Americans seeking to help should come as partners, not as patrons, directors, or even substitutes. One risk some of the new universities must face is that the American presence may be used to excuse a Nigerian or an Indian absence. The good that can be done by an American working with a qualified counterpart, who will be prepared, as soon as possible, to take the American's place, cannot occur if the counterpart is absent.

3. An effective American component must constitute a certain critical mass, difficult to determine in advance but essential if impact is to be achieved. The number of Americans abroad seeking to serve must be large enough to exercise an influence. At the same time their number must not be so enormous as to create a problem of "over-presence."

4. To me, the case seems irrefutable for the establishment of a career service in international education. Americans who would work with non-Americans abroad must do so on the basis of continuity. Today, the success of the Rocke-

feller Foundation in agriculture is bound up with the competence of its agricultural operating staff. These men, taken together, bring to bear several hundred man-years of experience. In an earlier era, the International Health Division of the Rockefeller Foundation had a comparable history. It is suggestive to compare the experiences of these two groups of permanent career servants with those of the A.I.D. and its short-term personnel. In another sphere, a beginning, at least, has been made by the Rockefeller Foundation in the forming of a similar career service, this time in the broad area of university development. What strikes those who work with Americans in activities of this kind is that an American commitment to people making up a career service is an earnest of involvement that goes far beyond annual appropriations in a budget.

5. Americans must blend and merge in service abroad with the national staff of recipient countries. The Mexican Agriculture Program of the Foundation succeeded in part because it was assimilated from the start within the Ministry of Agriculture, losing its American character in favor of a Mexican one. This pattern, initiated with such skill by Dr. J. George Harrar, has been continued and extended to other areas.

6. Americans working abroad must be serviced if they are to do their job. This requires cars and houses, food and amenities, equipment and books, seeds and fertilizer. It hardly pays to ask someone to serve abroad and then forget about his needs once he leaves American shores.

*Changes in International Co-operation Among Old and New "Developers."* The change which is most fundamental in the interaction of developed and underdeveloped countries is the establishment of a network through which men and ideas flow back and forth rather than moving in only one direction. At the heart of the changes in co-operation is a shift in patterns of international education. The rock-bottom principle for undergraduate education for developing countries is to put the heaviest stress on building the system at home, at least in the more general fields. From the standpoint of the United States, this points to more rather than less need for participation in graduate studies. If the United States seeks to continue, on a massive basis, its concern both with undergraduate and graduate training, then American agencies and programs will compete with one another over the prostrate form of institutions in the recipient country. There are all too many cases of United States programs at cross-purposes, of competitive recruitment of young people, and of sowing seeds of alienation for young Africans or Asians drawn into appointments outside their own country much too soon. There are always advantages for young men in pursuing training in their own country, in its classrooms and on its playing fields. Human associations arise which can be vital in the governance of a country. The chances for a relevant curriculum are greater. The changes that have been brought about in international education stem from the need to strike a balance between Americans fervently seeking to be helpful and Americans being prudent and realistic.

The first rule, then, for a developing country, is to turn its mind to institution building. It must see education as its major concern. It must seek the development of fields of study, not necessarily at advanced levels, but at the level of basic core preparation in the fundamental disciplines.

The changes involve a trade-off, with the United States sending abroad hundreds of professors, while receiving thousands of foreign undergraduate students in already overcrowded institutions. American institutions must turn their minds to the building of cadres of educators willing and able to work abroad. In Britain today there are approximately 120 English-language teachers serving the British Council. Their laboratory is the world's educational systems. Their task is the teaching of English in non-English-speaking countries. This example could be carried further outside of Britain and in other fields. At least it offers a possible alternative to the patterns under which A.I.D. negotiated 129 separate contracts for 72 United States universities involved in international education efforts. It is always difficult to determine the proper limit to place on those who want to work abroad. There are problems in building a cadre of specialists: future commitments, long-term obligations, pensions and security. But these difficulties have not been insuperable in other areas and presumably need not be so in the field of education.

One aspect of the new form of international co-operation that carries over from the more than 50-year history of the old forms is illustrated by the fellowship programs which various agencies have evolved. In these programs selection is vital. It must never be forgotten that it is future leaders who are being chosen. There can be no substitute for professional evaluation of those to be trained abroad. It is urgent that anyone going abroad have a position to which he can return. Out of a sample of 1,000 fellows, the president of the Rockefeller Foundation in 1960 found that only one had failed to return to his post. An existing position can be as much an incentive to return to one's native country as any other factor. Where fellowship programs can be linked with efforts of visiting scholars, international co-operation is almost certain to have a lasting effect. A visiting professor may pick or train his successor. The goal is to leave behind a deposit of trained people. There is no way for this to occur except to decide, by means of a well-ordered plan, to match the visitor with a successor or a teacher with a group destined to play its future role whenever and however it can.

### PROBLEMS OF DEVELOPING UNIVERSITIES

There remains a series of urgent problems with which men must cope if international education is to succeed. These include:

1. The availability of relevant teaching materials. By and large, non-Western materials are lacking. A classic case of educational materials which were exported abroad with somewhat limited success is Columbia University's Contemporary Civilization course. The course was entirely Western-oriented and the examples seemed remote from the experience of many within the new universities. Somehow the gap must be closed between materials with relevance in one culture and those required by another.

2. There are problems which confront those who seek balanced educational development. When the stress is exclusively on relevance, what is often obscured is the crying need for many insights, disciplines and perspectives. Institution-building may begin with agriculture or medicine, but it ought never to end there. In Paul Appleby's words, "There is need to begin to make a mesh of things." Especially in primary societies there is a heavy overlay of interdependent factors. Merely to look at the technological side may be to miss an even more important factor.

3. University development in large nations calls for patience, resolution and continuity. For Americans who would serve abroad, this is a painful requirement. For an impatient people patience is often the most difficult virtue. For scholars anxious to achieve an early academic payoff, continuity of service abroad is a high price to pay. It is often forgotten that the very successful Rockefeller Foundation Mexican Agricultural Program has a 27-year history, although its latest phase has been the one in which the program has been internationalized. In the area of foreign assistance, it is easier to make an impassioned appeal to Congress and public leaders to take a stand than to persuade them to face the fact that their activities, to have any impact, must extend over a decade or more. It is popular today to speak out against all forms of international co-operation, to put stress on the cost, waste and inefficiency of such programs. However, if 50 per cent of our international programs were successful, this would represent a higher average than many of our domestic programs in disadvantaged areas. Moreover, the comparable scoresheet with programs grounded in military efficiency is one which still leaves room for foreign assistance. Much of what we do in the way of international co-operation in education is a form of technical aid wherein Americans tend to know what they are about. It would be tragic if this was lost sight of in the present climate of hypercritical talk.

4. Another unsolved problem is that of mobilizing the best talents of those who would work abroad and those who would co-operate with them. The lesson of most programs is that the honor roll in each individual effort centers around the few, those with an extra measure of ability and devotion. If these few are present, a development effort involving numbers of people can be constructed in concentric circles around them. Men of lesser talent and knowledge and limited service have a contribution to make, but their efforts require first-class talent at the center.

5. A further unsolved problem in international co-operation arises from the American penchant for criticism. There are many reasons for this. Failure, disappointment and violence make news. All too often they leave constructive accomplishments behind. Yet stress on failure obscures:

a. An international service impulse that motivates hundreds of Americans in the Peace Corps, in applied science faculties, in science training, and in humane and social sciences.

b. That those who have worked abroad have the right to call for "a fair hearing." All too often they are put to the test by those who view their efforts from airports on a worldwide reconnaissance junket. Elementary fairness would seem to require that assessment of what is being done abroad should be based on more than a quick reaction of the weary traveler stopping off between flights.

c. That a basic issue in international co-operation efforts stems from the anatomy of American politics. Those who criticize foreign assistance claim that they are saving hard-pressed American taxpayers. It is well to recall that foreign aid, including international co-operation, by and large has no constituency. The only constituency is made up of individual Americans of compassion and commitment. The compassion reaches out to the suffering, poor, deprived and needy. The commitment is to apply, expand, share and join together. But these acts of good will characteristically involve individuals, not a mass movement of people and interest groups.

These problems, which involve recipients no less than donors, which have their source in the sensitivity of those who are given help as much as in those who give it, are at the root of the building of universities in the developing world. At this stage it is impossible to offer more than a list of issues and problems. If progress is to be made in the new universities, however, these and many other questions must be studied and considered.

## THE FUTURE OF UNIVERSITIES IN THE DEVELOPING WORLD

Universities in developing countries are at best fragile and infant institutions. They have not yet been tested and tried as have developed institutions. Their success is thus not easy to measure. Almost everyone is caught in the severest kind of political and economic cross fire. Student enrollments have multiplied so dramatically that faculties which were designed for small-scale education have been thrown overnight into large-scale efforts. This trend is bound to continue. Institutions are unlikely to grow rapidly enough to fill the vacuum. It is expecting too much that universities which might have done their jobs with skill and distinction under optimum circumstances can be as effective under great financial and political pressure.

Moreover, there are, inevitably, hard times ahead. The developed countries which have had a primary role in international co-operation may at some future point in time reduce their commitments. And the future is to some extent already upon us. There are such straws in the wind as the reduction of Britain's overseas efforts. There are signs as well in the shift of emphasis from international to domestic programs in the United States. What the effect will be if withdrawal and termination of international educational co-operation occur prematurely is not easy to say, but it is almost certain that there will be problems.

The future of the new universities is also bound up with their ability to look realistically at their economies. Every nation and every university must provide for itself some forms of professional training. The status of international co-operation remains too unpredictable to entrust all advanced training to others, and yet few of the fledgling nation-states have the resources to undertake advanced training in all fields. At some point they must make a choice. They must choose to do some things and leave others undone. While medicine is essential, perhaps not all its branches are (such as open heart surgery). If agriculture is required, veterinary science may not be essential for each independent country within a region. The balance sheet will have to be struck between the desirable and the essential, and along the way painful choices will have to be made.

Yet these choices will inevitably reflect needs and requirements that lie at the heart of national development. It can hardly be said that the growth and development of a nation can take place in the absence of higher education. This being the case, developing universities can afford very little which smacks of luxury, while much will be exacted which involves harsh necessity. Faced with necessities, responsible leaders in difficult times have come forward with solutions. Perhaps it is not asking too much to hope that a new breed of leaders—emerging in the new countries, in part as a result of developing universities—will do the same.

# CO-OPERATION BETWEEN
# UNIVERSITIES OF DEVELOPED
# AND DEVELOPING COUNTRIES

Bert M. Tollefson, Jr.

It is a pleasure to be here once again at Notre Dame. I congratulate the University for its continued interest in international educational problems and for sponsoring this conference.

Whenever I am in an academic environment, I am reminded of the great educator, A. Lawrence Lowell, who once wrote in a jocular mood that "Universities are full of knowledge; the freshmen bring a little in and the seniors take none away, and knowledge accumulates."

There is nothing really new in the idea of co-operation between universities of developed and developing nations. Indeed, long before higher education began to assume its present shape at the medieval universities, there was co-operation in the transmission of learning between groups of scholars in the "developed" countries of the earliest times and those in the less developed ones. Knowledge passed from ancient Egypt and Mesopotamia to Greece, and from Greece at a later stage back to the Middle East and North Africa. Then the torch was passed to Rome and through Rome much of Greek thinking passed to medieval Europe.

Not all of it passed through this channel, however. The language of educated people everywhere in the Middle East and North Africa was Greek for many centuries, even under the Roman Empire. When Islam took over the area, the Greek classics were translated into Arabic and for several centuries the universities at Baghdad, Damascus, Cairo, Tunis and in Muslim Spain were in the vanguard of learning. Aristotle was studied for science and philosophy and great teachers in Arabic like Avicenna and Averroes, as well as Moses Maimonides (who was a Jew), in the eleventh and twelfth centuries advanced thinking in these fields as well as in mathematics and medicine.

James Michener, in his recent book *Iberia,* quotes Louis Bertrand, the French expert on Spain, as saying that "The concept of the university was Muslim, even though the teaching was 'terrible in its verbalism and almost entirely theological.'"

Despite the hostility between the Christian and the Muslim worlds, the teaching of these Arab thinkers reached the former and greatly influenced the budding universities in Western Europe, then an "underdeveloped" region. In fact, the thought of Aristotle returned to Europe via re-translations into Greek of the Arabic translations from Greek and formed the basis of the philosophy of St. Thomas Aquinas.

Although Christian Spain expelled the Moors (and the Jews) after the conquest of Granada in 1492, the year the New World was discovered, much of the best of Arabic thinking had already become embodied in Christian thought.

The Spanish conquistadores were shortly followed to the new world by missionaries, members of religious orders with close ties to universities in Spain and elsewhere in Europe. They quickly founded schools of all kinds.

The oldest university in the Western Hemiphere is the University of Lima, Peru, now known as the Universidad Nacional Mayor de San Marcos, founded in 1551. Spaniards founded seven other universities in Latin America before Harvard was started in 1636, as well as two in the Philippines.

Harvard, of course, was founded in 1636 by Protestant clergymen educated at the ancient universities of England, as were most of the other early universities in what is now the United States.

In a similar fashion, our host today, Notre Dame, was founded by a French religious order, the Congregation of the Holy Cross, in 1842. On its own, the American Notre Dame here in South Bend later played the major part in the founding of St. George College in Santiago, Chile in 1943 and another Notre Dame College in Dacca, East Pakistan in 1949.

Some of the European powers did not make so much of a point of education in the early years of the colonial effort as did Spain, but in time there were universities in most of the colonies—universities which tried and in many cases succeeded in maintaining the same standards as those in the metropole.

American educational specialists have had no reason to criticize the standards of those European-related universities in three of the traditional fields in which they have concentrated: law, the arts and letters and philosophy.

Our contribution to universities abroad in these fields has been modest, reflecting the relative growth of our society. Most American scholars defer to their colleagues in the countries concerned when it comes to teaching French, Spanish or the literature indigenous to the developing countries, and our contributions so far in the area of philosophy are not so great as those in science and technology. Where the country's legal system is based on the Anglo-Saxon common law, most of its legal advisors tend to come from England, and we Americans are hardly great experts on the civil law—although lawyers trained in Louisiana, where the civil law is basic, have helped developing countries adapt modern commercial law, fundamentally Anglo-Saxon in origin, to the civil law.

However, we have had a lot to contribute to the teaching and practice of medicine, the remaining traditional discipline.

Furthermore, we have questioned—to use the currently fashionable word —the "relevance" of many of these traditional concepts of education to the needs of the developing countries. And here we can bring to bear upon these problems America's own unique contribution to university-level education, the "land-grant" college.

As you all know, the Morrill Act of 1862 provided grants of federal land to the states to finance the establishment of colleges to emphasize the teaching of agriculture and what were called in the act the "mechanic arts." This provided a great impetus for developing research and teaching capacity in these hitherto neglected fields.

The *International Encyclopedia of the Social Sciences* says in its article on the university that "The view that higher education can legitimately be practical and diversified was not confined to the land-grant institutions but was also adopted by many of the older universities."

While the study of law, medicine and the liberal arts clearly must be fostered in developing countries if they are to achieve and maintain a high level of growth, the American-style "practical" type of university education is also necessary to enable these countries to develop their industry and agriculture as economic foundations.

American-style universities have been in operation abroad for many years —among them Robert College in Istanbul, the American University of Beirut and the American University of Cairo. But it was not until the Point Four program got started in 1950 that the United States government began to take an active interest in this process.

We could see that what the less-developed countries needed was precisely the type of education in which the United States was pre-eminent. They required the development of human resources on a broad scale in a way that the older, elitist universities could never accomplish. New techniques had to be introduced into these countries and new institutions had to be created which could both develop available resources and teach society as a whole to utilize them.

The present (1969) administrator of the Agency for International Development, Dr. John A. Hannah, pioneered in bringing the knowledge of the land-grant universities to bear upon the problem of development.

Just nine days after President Truman had proposed the establishment of what came to be called the Point Four program in his inaugural address of January 20, 1949, Dr. Hannah, as president of the National Association of State Universities and Land Grant Colleges, wrote to the President offering the "full co-operation" of the Association in carrying out the program.

The first director of the Technical Co-operation Administration, which initially administered Point Four, was a president of a land-grant college, Dr. Henry Bennet, of Oklahoma A&M, now Oklahoma State University.

It was this university which provided one of the earliest examples of American assistance to institution-building in the developing countries by helping to establish the Haile Selassie I University in Ethiopia in 1952. The University was to be an Ethiopian prototype of a land-grant college. Oklahoma State's first and basic assignment was to locate a site for the university, construct the physical plant, develop the curriculum, recruit staff and students and start it operating.

Another assignment under the same contract was to establish a secondary school for agriculture. Yet within the country O.S.U. was unable to find a single Ethiopian with a bachelor's degree in any phase of agriculture.

More recently, in 1959, while participating as a delegate in the Food and Agriculture Organization's annual conference in Rome, I was startled to hear from representatives of the Sudan that despite their extensive forests their country did not have one trained forester. Others in this audience have had similar experiences which dramatize the continuing need for training local personnel for later help in administration concurrently with the very beginning of the building of a new institution.

In this sort of situation, the U.S. faculty member acts as an innovator, or agent of change, concerned mainly with the transfer and translation of ideas from one culture to another. In the beginning, of necessity, he sometimes has to do almost everything himself. As trained citizens of the country join him —a very slow process—the American moves into an advisory role and becomes more involved with policies, procedures and practices. In this way, what has been merely a collection of people and activities is translated into a real, living institution.

Building such an institutional foundation and structure is always a very slow and sometimes a quite painful process. Administrative work such as this also tends to pull the U.S. team member away from the substance of his profession, and he can begin to lose something of his competence in his specialty.

Institution-building projects were begun in the early days of Point Four in all of the major A.I.D.-receiving countries. Over the past 18 years, they have produced a wide variety of colleges and universities, research institutes, vocational schools and even primary and secondary school systems. By now, most of these institutions are staffed with trained local personnel.

At this stage, there must be a change in the nature of the relationship between the local institution and those who are providing it with assistance from abroad. The institution has been built; it now becomes important to strengthen its links with the rest of the local society.

For example, an institute designed to teach public administration may be turning out a substantial number of graduates qualified for the civil service each year. But if the civil service is unwilling to accept them because of a failure to consult the civil service bureaucracy in the initial stage of institution building, it will have failed in its mission, even if it somehow manages to survive.

As the nature of the task thus shifts from the construction to the operational stage, the requirements and demands put upon resources from abroad also change. Where the U.S. faculty member played the role of the technical advisor in the earlier stage, he now must relate to his host counterpart as a professional colleague, on a basis of full equality.

However, all too frequently there has been a failure to recognize the transition point as the process of institutional development moves from one stage to the other. We may fail to see the importance of these required role changes on the part of the U.S. university team members. For example, almost by definition the advisor works at a distance, influencing policy levels without getting heavily involved at the working level. This method of operation almost automatically precludes the type of close relationship between equals required for effective, jointly-developed solutions to current operational problems.

I suspect that this problem of shifting gears is at the heart of the recurring difference of opinion between A.I.D. and some of our own universities concerning the timing of the termination of an institution-building project. The universities tend to believe that assistance to the process of institution building must continue clear through the development, or operational stage; A.I.D. has generally felt that external assistance must withdraw after the host institution is "built" to allow it to stand on its own feet. Both approaches are questionable since each denies the existence of different stages calling for different types of activities, resources and skills. Once the concept of two stages is accepted, it is possible to concentrate on the problem of transition from one to the other. However, a basic conceptual reorientation may be needed to grasp the total institutional growth pattern and to see that the A.I.D.-financed portion is only one part of the pattern—a part directly related to later stages in the institution's life. Procedures must be developed for the identification and co-ordination of all relevant collateral activities not funded by A.I.D. Faculty exchanges, for example, have provided an adequate basis in some cases for the needed "development" stage activities.

There are many other aspects of A.I.D.'s collaboration with the universities which I know would be of particular interest to this audience.

Given the present state of institutional development in the less-developed countries as a result of the work of the past two decades, I think we can say that technical and professional advisory services, based on individual expertise, should no longer be the basic thrust of university technical assistance. What we must now consider is the total capacity of the assisting institution. The problems arising from its development must be researched on a programmed basis; these results must be fed back into the curricula at the co-operating American university. As a result, later programs should produce U.S. nationals more competent in the field of international development as distinct from the more specialized fields, as well as foreign nationals trained more responsively to the development needs of their countries.

The American universities which have approached the technical assistance challenge in this manner, on an institutional commitment basis, have found that to bring in an international aspect across the whole range of their institutional life has actually increased their capacity to produce graduates who are not only interested in working on international problems but who are also more effective and productive in domestic work.

An increasing number of U.S. universities (indeed, of universities throughout the world) are becoming aware that the infusion of international interests with the total life of the institution is really essential to their basic educational mission. Many such universities have experimented over the years with a variety of largely unco-ordinated international activities such as junior-years-abroad, faculty and student exchanges, advisory and consulting services, etc. They are pleased with the opportunities such activities make available to their faculty members and students, but seem sometimes to fail in reaping the full benefits of these activities in terms of their own institutional growth.

It is at this point that the university begins to realize the importance of fostering an intensive interdependence between its various activities overseas and its on-campus activities concerned with teaching and research. Such interdependence is essential if the university is to realize maximum benefits from its overseas activities. At the minimum, it must offset the cost of overseas activities in terms of pulling faculty away from teaching responsibilities, straining the university's administrative capabilities, and disrupting personnel policies on recruitment, promotion and tenure.

This interdependence requires that the different overseas activities of the same American universities be co-ordinated with each other so as to be mutually reinforcing if at all possible. For example, an area studies center on South Asian culture provides little support for a program in Latin American agricultural productivity. The usual pattern of international activity in a university "just grows," like Topsy, from the interests of individual faculty members, resulting from the experiences which sabbaticals and consultancies have given them. It takes a fair amount of institutional self-discipline, as well as an awareness of the need for it, to try to channel the energies of disparate but dedicated faculty members to avoid a collection of diffused and, hence, diluted academic ventures.

The question of just how to channel these interests into a co-ordinated

167

program is much simpler to ask than to answer. Such a determination depends upon a rather complete knowledge of the nature of the interests and talents of the institution's faculty, a knowledge not easy to come by.

It may be interesting here to recount the experience of the Academy for Educational Development of Colorado, in its preparation of an A.I.D.-sponsored report on University Resources for International Development. The Academy approached a sample of 118 colleges and universities for information on their international activities. Since the information required was rather detailed, the initial response of many of the institutions' presidents was that money and resources required to make such an institutional inventory could not be spared. However, in the majority of cases, the institution eventually came to the conclusion that this was something which should have been done long ago, and which it was absolutely essential to do if the institution was to move ahead with any kind of a co-ordinated effort in the field.

There are obviously many ways in which a given institution might co-ordinate the international interests of its faculty. The pattern which emerges will ordinarily be a function of the way in which particular overseas activities relate to on-campus activities. For example, most faculty and student exchanges take place between departments covering the same disciplines. But if the overseas activity is concerned with institutional development, there should be intensive involvement in a multi-disciplinary situation. In turn, if this type of activity is integrated with the home campus, a healthy interaction is forced between the area-studies people, traditionally concerned with history, literature, anthropology, etc., and the professional schools. It is the rare campus where these two groups even speak to each other, let alone understand one another.

If such co-ordination is achieved, what results is not an imposition of some individual's particular interest in an institutional program, but a natural set of interdependent linkages by means of which overseas experience generates research programs, which in turn provide new material for course improvements, which then stimulate further interest and participation in international activities. Once this process begins, it is natural for the international dimension to find its way into every appropriate corner of the university's activity.

We at A.I.D. recognize fully that such an international dimension, in addition to providing a university with an institution-wide payoff for its overseas activity, provides for the feedback of accumulated development knowledge into the production of new knowledge in this field. Nor is the fact lost on us that the quality of personnel assigned to university contracts abroad seems to improve sharply when the overseas activity is no longer treated as secondary to the university's basic educational mission.

In recognition of the implications of having overseas development assistance activities integrated with the rest of the university's and of the fact that

168

some of the Agency's past policies have perhaps encouraged peripheral treatment on campus, the universities got together with A.I.D. and undertook to develop a new approach to their relationship. This step was taken at the initiative of the National Association of State Universities and Land Grant Colleges and with the support of the American Council on Education and other major college and university associations.

This new approach, designed for long-term institution-building projects, is called the Institutional Development Agreement and is described at length in a report by the same name, which has been widely distributed and is available at A.I.D.

Recognition in the agreement of the interrelatedness of the various programs of a university is made in what is called the "operational plan." One section is devoted to a description of corollary activities which are relevant to a particular development assistance project. The new agreement actually has provisions for providing some support for campus activities related to the project activity abroad. For example, funds may be made available, on a cost-sharing basis, to be administered by the university, to encourage a faculty member returning from an overseas tour, to take up to six months for the purpose of writing about his experience, defining research program requirements, developing new curriculum materials, etc. In addition, there is a provision for the joint financing of campus residencies for up to a year between two regular tours overseas. Under such an arrangement, a professor could tie in a project consultancy with his regular teaching and research functions. It also encourages the development of long-term career patterns in which a man could anticipate a six- or eight-year program of assignments moving back and forth between the U.S. campus and a developing institution overseas.

In order to encourage the American university to see the overseas project as part of its own program, the agreement has several new emphases: It places the responsibility for project implementation more squarely on the university's shoulders, operating on the basis of its own pre-approved policies on pay, leave, travel and transportation, training, etc.; it stipulates that the university make all team selections from a high-level, central administrative office and that procedures and criteria for promotion and personnel evaluation for the field team be integrated with on-campus policies and procedures; it allows greater variability in the length of individual tours, permitting improved dovetailing of domestic and overseas activities, and so forth. Of course, the decision of the university to undertake the project in the first instance should be an institution-wide decision involving both faculty and administration, as well as all departments and schools with any potential connection with the project.

These new arrangements and procedures should result in a better style of working relationships between A.I.D. and the universities—greater mutuality, greater awareness among all concerned of the university's responsibility and its stake in the results of the project, and greater acceptance of broader goals which transcend the individual project. To use the words of the Joint Report:

> The fact that the university applies its own purposes, policies and methods to A.I.D. activity is what makes its participation in the foreign assistance field so valuable. This, too, is the reason why relationships between A.I.D. and the universities should be designed to implement not a pact between buyers and sellers of standard services, but rather a partnership made in a common and highly sophisticated cause.

One element of this common cause is the emergence of a U.S.–Less-Developed Country educational network, consisting not merely of individual contacts and exchanges, but of institutional programs, courses of study and centers of specialized competence and scholarship. Such a network cannot emerge until our involvement in this field moves from the individual to the institutional level. And this will not happen until the individual interests, talents and experiences of faculty members are inventoried and analyzed in a joint faculty-administration exercise and then translated into a programmed set of emphases, directions and goals against which all proposed university programs can be assessed and planned.

An increasing number of colleges and universities in the United States are beginning to feel the need for international activity, even if they have not yet defined what it might mean for their particular institution. And while it is quite possible, as some have observed, that most academic institutions might have had difficulty in making effective use of International Education Act funds three years ago, had they been made available, more institutions every day are engaging in the exercise of determining just how they might introduce an international dimension into their educational programs.

Paradoxically, however, at this particular time in history, the opportunities for "internationalizing" higher education appear to be decreasing. The International Education Act is still unfunded. The private foundations have decided to reduce their international activities in the face of mounting domestic problems. Even for those universities which have already made significant international commitments, A.I.D. funding has been cut back because of decreased appropriation. And it is harder than ever for state legislatures to look beyond the borders of their states, let alone those of the nation, when planning their educational budgets.

The universities come to A.I.D. for support in developing this international dimension, pointing out that, after all, A.I.D. is a primary consumer of these international capabilities. But the decision has been made, and correctly so, that the responsibility for strengthening the U.S. academic community as a whole belongs to the Department of Health, Education and Welfare, H.E.W. (with minor exceptions such as Section 211[d] of the Foreign Assistance Act). But then someone is quick to observe that H.E.W. is having enough trouble with its "own" problems. So whose problem is it?

The cry is made that funds for international education cannot compete with the pressing needs of here-and-now domestic problems. But could it be possible that our sluggishness in understanding the plight of our nation's minority groups, for example, is somehow related to the ethnocentrism and cultural myopia of the American educational system? *This is* a here-and-now problem!

The fallacy in the "failure to compete" theory lies in the not-uncommon assumption that international affairs are peripheral to the basic objectives of U.S. education and, thus, competitive with it. There are even participants in international education who perpetuate the fallacy by seeing it as an add-on bonus. As long as it is conceived of in this fashion, it will indeed have difficulty in "competing" with other problems for support.

It matters not whether one studies educational psychology, plant breeding, public administration, law or whatever; one's education is simply incomplete without tying in to the world-wide network of knowledge. There are very few areas of knowledge that cannot benefit significantly from some kind of international dimension. Of course A.I.D. will benefit from an increased capability in the field of international development, as universities internationalize themselves, but the nation as a whole will realize much broader benefits. One can already see benefits accruing to the nation as a result of university participation in the A.I.D. program.

What are those benefits to the nation? The first and most obvious benefit —in terms of dollars and cents—is that the greater the area expertise in American universities the more sure-footed American business can be when it ventures into new areas. This same expertise, of course, assists the traditional diplomatic work of the State Department by increasing its competence in the area.

The enrichment of university programs also provides intangible benefits which cannot be measured in financial terms but which are nevertheless real and lasting.

Getting down to the specific, here are some examples of benefits accruing to America from overseas university programs financed by A.I.D.:

The medical faculty of the University of Illinois learned much in its work with the Chiengmai University of Thailand which turned out to be applicable to its efforts to improve public health and preventive medicine in the city of Chicago.

What the Illinois doctors learned in Thailand was how to use a very small professional staff to treat large numbers of people—by the intensive use of paramedical personnel, the so-called semi-skilled.

In Tunisia, the Harvard School of Public Health is using fortified cereals —vitamins, minerals and lysine—to improve the nutritional standard among the people in a remote area. The isolated location permits the measurement of results in a way which would be impossible in the developed world. The undernourished in the United States, those for whom cereals are a major part of the diet, may well benefit from Harvard's Tunisian experience.

A.I.D. has provided a series of grants for private industry and university research into high protein foods. It is believed that the food value of pork and chicken can be improved through better fortified feed. These A.I.D.-sponsored programs were primarily intended to improve nutrition in the less-developed countries but American food producers will also have access to the results—and American nutrition will improve.

The overseas experience has broadened literally hundreds of American scholars who have returned to take on more responsible posts in their home institutions. Of course, the nation benefits whenever any one of us realizes a fuller potential.

Sometimes a triangular relationship has been developed. One U.S. university entered into a partnership with a British university in connection with an A.I.D. contract for work with a West African university. Their joint work helped the personnel of the institutions to get acquainted. Since then, several of the English faculty have taught at the American university and students from the American one travel annually to the United Kingdom for special courses at the British university.

These arrangements do not necessarily end when a country reaches the point where it no longer needs U.S. economic assistance. An American university and a university on Taiwan which had been working together under an A.I.D. contract have continued doing so after the A.I.D. contract ended. Each year they exchange both faculty and students in both directions. And the American university, as a result, has greatly improved its capabilities in the field of Oriental philosophy!

When the international aspect of education is viewed in its relationship to domestic needs, one conclusion seems inescapable: the academic community will be remiss in its educational mission if it fails to develop this international dimension, defined in each institution's own terms, as an integral element of its educational program.

But we come back to the old "chicken-or-the-egg" problem; how do we get the process started? I don't believe it is a question of waiting till the mood of Congress changes, or till the problems of poverty, prejudice, prices and pollution decrease, even if we could afford the time. I do believe that when the international dimension of education is seen as essential to the American educational process, *in the eyes of the academic community itself,* and therefore, a domestic problem in its own right, support for it will be generated in legislatures, foundations and so forth.

However, a major conceptual reorientation will be required among all concerned before this international dimension is seen in its proper perspective. And the initiative for this redefinition of educational objectives is squarely in the hands of the academic community. It will not happen by itself.

# THE PEACE CORPS AND
# AMERICAN INSTITUTIONS
## The Not So Hidden Agenda

### Lawrence H. Fuchs

It was a point of pride with R. Sargent Shriver, first director of the Peace Corps, that he picked politically sophisticated and ambitious men for top positions. He intended that the Peace Corps should be a recruiting ground for young activists who wanted to improve the quality of life in their own country. In choosing country directors for the Peace Corps, he sought what he called "leaders of men" rather than experts in a particular country or some aspect of development. In staffing Peace Corps-Washington and Peace Corps-overseas, he recruited vigorously black men and women of ability for high-level appointments. When talking about the many faces of the Peace Corps, he sometimes spoke of the fledgling agency as the force which would push Americans in other overseas agencies out of their golden ghettoes and into more direct contact with the plain people of the host countries in which they lived. In doing these things, he was following the will of Congress, which in the Peace Corps Act twice stipulated ways in which the Peace Corps would serve to improve the quality of life in the United States.

The three purposes of the Peace Corps as outlined in the Declaration of Purpose, Section 2 of that legislation, are well known to followers of the agency. The Peace Corps, it states, "shall make available to interested countries and areas men and women of the United States qualified for service abroad and willing to serve, under conditions of hardship if necessary, to help the peoples of such countries and areas in meeting their needs for trained manpower, and to help promote a better understanding of the American people on the part of the peoples served and a better understanding of other peoples on the part of the American people." Much of the history of the Peace Corps is the story of the inner tension among those three objectives. The main conflict has been between the first objective on the one side and objectives two and three on the other. Usually, it is put in terms of the job versus intercultural understanding.

Less well advertised, although not quite hidden, in Section 5 (k), is a provision to implement the effective re-entry of volunteers to the United States. It reads:

In order to assure that the skills and experience that former Volunteers have derived from their training and their service abroad are best utilized in the national interest, the President may, in co-operation with agencies of the United States, private employers, educational institutions, and other entities of the United States, undertake programs under which Volunteers would be counseled with respect to opportunities for further education and employment.

Implicit in this provision is the assumption that volunteers will learn something overseas which will make them more effective in the United States. The Peace Corps, in short, as indicated by the legislation which created it and by the ideals and utterances of its first leader and most articulate spokesman, was intended to have an impact on American institutions.

In trying to assess the nature and extent of that impact, I am shocked by the realization that virtually no hard research has been authorized by the Peace Corps on the subject. There are surveys of returned Peace Corps Volunteers (P.C.V.)—their attitudes and their employment; there is an excellent report on the Peace Corps and the University by Paul Hanna; there is a fine task force report on returned volunteers initiated by Director Joseph Blatchford; there are wonderful essays and speeches by Harris Wofford and Phillips Roupp; there is even a newly created Office of Voluntary Action aimed at having ex-Peace Corps volunteers translate their experience overseas into action for social justice at home; and there are, of course, the impressions of thousands of ex-volunteers and Peace Corps staff members. But there is no hard research worthy of the name—a shocking and unforgivable fact.

How do the impressions add up? If one thinks in terms of those American institutions which have had the most direct contact with the Peace Corps as an agency—other segments of the American government and universities—the answer seems to be one of disappointment. Looking instead at those institutions that have been in the forefront of social change in the United States in the late 1960's, in the fields of education, race relations and poverty, the influence of the Peace Corps appears to be exciting, promising and perhaps even significant.

## THE PEACE CORPS AND THE FOREIGN SERVICE

Although the available statistics are so flabby that they are not worth using, it is clear that a remarkably small percentage of returned Peace Corps volunteers and ex-staff members have gone into the foreign service, U.S.I.A., A.I.D., or other governmental agencies in the field of foreign policy. The Louis Harris surveys show large-scale disenchantment by volunteers with American foreign policy and its agents. Shriver's dream of invigorating American foreign policy with the points of view, energy and experience of the volunteers has not materialized. As far as I know, only two ex-staff members were appointed as ambassadors following their Peace Corps work who had not previously served as regular foreign service officers.[1] Although Glen Ferguson and Franklin Williams served with distinction in Kenya and Ghana respectively, they are now out of the foreign service and have been fighting domestic urban battles from the vantage point of universities. Shriver, of course, served as ambassador to France, but he is expected to enter the domestic political wars and to commit his energies and talents to the great battles in the United States soon.

It seems thoroughly clear that the Peace Corps has not affected the life styles of other American personnel working overseas, a goal which many of its early founders had passionately, if silently, desired. The fleets of automobiles, the hosts of servants, the cost-of-living allowances, and segregated compound living inveighed against so stridently in *The Ugly American* have not been reduced. In fact, many of us now think we gave too much emphasis to the question of style. Sensitivity and competence does not necessarily come with a hair shirt; but many of us have been disappointed that the Peace Corps emphasis on living deeply in other cultures has not been followed by other agencies overseas.

I recall that in the fall of 1962 I drafted from Manila a short statement (sent either to McGeorge Bundy or Arthur Schlesinger, Jr.) to be used as the President's Christmas and New Year's message to American governmental employees overseas. I believe that the statement fared well at the hands of editors in the White House, but by the time it came back from the State Department for the President's signature, my emphasis on the traditional American regard for revolutionary nationalism and the need for Americans to live deeply in other cultures had been given shibbolethic treatment which rendered it ineffectual.

I suspect that if any change has taken place in life styles of Americans overseas, it has been that Peace Corps staff now live much more like other American foreign service officers than they used to. I saw the change even during Shriver's tenure. Our policy in the Philippines was for staff members to stay away from American compounds and American schools and to live—in housing appropriate to our positions—in Filipino neighborhoods far from each other. Some of our "living down" was unnecessary. Our top staff man in Mindanao had built a fine nipa-thatched house for his wife, himself and six children at a cost of only a few hundred dollars. It was in a central location and quite like a house which a relatively impecunious staff member at the Zamboanga Normal College might have. He and his family loved it and so did Filipinos, but no one would have begrudged him more spacious or sophis-

---

[1] Nathaniel Davis, who came to the Peace Corps from the foreign service, went to Bulgaria as ambassador after a tour in the Peace Corps as deputy director of programming.

ticated quarters. Some of our interpretation of the Peace Corps ethic was simply stupid. I drove an over-age jeep in Manila, for example, which broke down frequently. (It had last been used in parachute drop tests before we picked it up as surplus.) Later, many in the second and third generations of Peace Corps staff in the Philippines moved into American compounds and began to accept graciously the perquisites and benefits which went with overseas representation of the United States government.

The Peace Corps should, in my view, give up the fantasy of changing the life styles of other American agencies overseas, if it still holds to it. In the first place, what is appropriate for the Peace Corps may not be appropriate for others. More importantly, others are less likely to change if Peace Corps officials and volunteers *try* to change them. This is not to say that the Peace Corps should retreat one step from its own emphasis on unostentatious living and close, regular communication with our hosts in their languages with empathic respect for their values.

## THE PEACE CORPS AND THE UNIVERSITIES

Shriver's dream of changing the foreign service has not been realized, but neither has his hope of significantly affecting American universities. There is no question that Director Shriver and other key Peace Corps officials who came to Washington in January 1961 envisioned a much broader role for universities and private agencies in the Peace Corps than later materialized. The first organization chart showed not regional divisions as developed in the Office of Program and Development, but rather a three-way division of programs run by private agencies, universities and the Peace Corps itself. The report of Shriver's task force to the President on March 4, 1961 lists five ways that Peace Corps operations could be run abroad. Direct administration by the Peace Corps itself, now the rule, was listed fifth.

First were the private agencies (including unions) which were to be given the job of not just training, but of recruitment, selection and administration of P.C.V.'s overseas. "It is important," stated the task force report, "that the Peace Corps supplement and extend the early pioneering efforts of the private agencies rather than bypass them or swallow them up in a public program . . ."

Listed second were programs to be run by universities. Here the wording read: "It is time for American universities to become truly world universities. The Peace Corps will help with this transformation . . ." Anticipating some of the complaints that would be made against university requirements in contracting, it continued, "Although there is no reason to believe that the costs of carrying out Peace Corps projects through university contracts will be low, the advantages of this approach should weigh heavily against any inefficiency in any decentralization."

The first C.A.R.E. community development program in Colombia had that organization handling training and playing a role in selection, but, in almost every other case, the issue of direct versus delegated administration was resolved on the side of those who preferred Peace Corps control. Notre Dame and the Indiana Conference Organization were not allowed to play as large a role as they desired in recruiting and selection for the program in Chile. A major decision was not to give Pennsylvania State University the responsibility in the field for the program in the Philippines which was to be the largest by far during the first two years of the Peace Corps' existence. A decision was made very early not to deal with religious organizations operating abroad, thus ruling out some of the best qualified and experienced among potential administrators. Universities and agencies were given parts of country programs to administer with varying autonomy, but they were not given complete control over programs.

In making these decisions, the Peace Corps must have been at war with itself. Shriver spoke frequently and eloquently on the need to decentralize; yet he had to move quickly and massively with men he could trust as his own. For better or worse, Peace Corps chose not to become a grant-making institution, and kept in its possession the important responsibilities of selection, training, programming and field leadership, while occasionally delegating portions of these responsibilities by contract to universities and private institutions (in training, non-Peace Corps organizations have been responsible most of the time).

Still, Director Shriver set a target for 30 per cent of the Peace Corps volunteers to be under private contract and Peace Corps received its money from Congress—always sympathetic to the idea of decentralization—on that basis. Shriver, believing in the efficacy of decentralization, gave the directorship of the Office of University and Private Institutional Relationships to one of his most vigorous and persuasive men, Franklin Williams, who had framed on his wall a copy of Interim Policy Directive 2.1 REV which stated . . . "The policy of the Peace Corps is to give preference in the administration of projects to private agencies and universities . . ."

Through 1964, the Peace Corps contracted to universities and private institutions to administer a number of projects, including: C.A.R.E. in Colombia; Notre Dame in Chile; the Heifer Project on St. Lucia; the Experiment for International Living in Espirito Santo State in Brazil; Arizona State University in another Brazilian state; and the National Grange in Liberia. Until 1964, Director Shriver seemed to lean toward having contractors undertake full administrative support for volunteers for at least a portion of the in-country Peace Corps program. He tended to oppose the idea of having contractors' overseas representatives just for technical support added to an existing Peace Corps staff, probably thinking that such technical support contracts were too much in the fashion of A.I.D.

The policy was completely reversed in the first part of 1964. Many directors in the field, including myself, had asked for technical assistant Contractor Overseas Representatives (C.O.R.'s) to be added to their staffs. At the same time that Shriver became somewhat more sympathetic to technical assistance through C.O.R.'s, Peace Corps began to move away from its early commitment to decentralization of administration through universities and private organizations. A $3 million contract for U.C.L.A. to administer and provide technical assistance in the Peace Corps Nigeria Program was turned down. The policy was now clear. It was against full administration, but permitted the idea of C.O.R.'s strictly for technical support. With that policy came the end of the Office of University and Private Institutional Relations and university affairs were moved under training.

The preponderance of university experience has come through training, and, to a lesser extent, recruiting. Every one I know who has looked closely at the Peace Corps-university training relationship has come away with the conclusion that generally it has not been a satisfactory one. It is conceded that success has been achieved in one area—language training—where both universities and the Peace Corps have benefited as a result of the research and experimentation in developing quicker, more intense methods of teaching languages. As Paul Hanna put it in his 1969 report:

> As an impatient generation of reform-minded students has discovered, the university is an institution that is stable, slow-moving, even ponderous . . . uncommitted to social and political action, interested in research and publication, dedicated to long-term specialization rather than short-term training. In short, its style is in many ways the antithesis of the Peace Corps.[2]

While relationships in practice are not as horrendous as that conflict implies, they are rarely smooth and there are inevitable, unvarying complaints on both sides. Whatever type of training contract the Peace Corps makes with universities—single-program contract, a contract for a series of programs, or a core contract to cover a project director and a support staff—universities complain that the Peace Corps cannot provide the necessary lead time, thus limiting the quality of the program. The Peace Corps often complains that universities are too academic and/or do not commit their best people to train volunteers.

Success in the transfer of Peace Corps language-training techniques to the universities has been impressive. In the summer and fall of 1967, the Peace Corps experimented with eight programs in accelerated, super-intensive in-

---

[2] Paul Hanna, *The Peace Corps and the University: A Report of the Special Committee to Study Peace Corps-University Relations.*

struction: three in Spanish; one in French; and one in Afghan-Farsi; one in Swahili and Luganda; one in Hindi; and one in Sesotho. In these programs, language instruction was given eight hours a day, six days a week for approximately four months. The result exceeded all expectations. Fluency was achieved which often took 8-12 weeks to obtain in the old 4-6 hour/day program. The universities where these techniques were tried could not help but be impressed. As a result of training experiences at Dartmouth, that college has introduced into the regular curriculum intensive French courses which call for 14 hours of class work per week and now offers freshmen a one-month high-intensity French language course. Enthusiastically welcoming this large-scale involvement of the Peace Corps in language teaching are those scholars who have worked for years in the face of minuscule interest in their esoteric specialties. Today, because of the Peace Corps' impetus, hundreds instead of tens of students are studying what were thought of as exotic languages with the intention of actually using them.

In addition, the Peace Corps has invested approximately $1 million in new language texts for languages which were never taught formally in this country before. Nearly 50 universities have participated significantly in the development of these materials.[3] Since one of the purposes of the Peace Corps is to cosmopolitanize the United States, it is not insignificant that special competence has been developed at the University of Texas in teaching of Pashto, at the University of Utah in Amharic, at the University of Indiana in Moroccan and Tunisian Arabic, at the University of Washington in Quechua, and at Brigham Young University in Samoan.

Except in the area of language training noted above, the Peace Corps has not been notably successful in bringing the world to the universities. Nor has it had a substantial impact on curriculum or pedagogy. One recalls the consequences of the thinking and action of Arthur E. Morgan and the Antioch work-study approach to education or Malcolm X and the influence of his thinking on the emergence of Afro-American studies. Harris Wofford and others have consistently pressed for the Peace Corps to recognize itself as a new model of a university for the world but specific proposals that would help that model become visible and more effective rarely have been accepted.

The Peace Corps has also given some slight impetus to the Antioch education-abroad idea, organized at the college in 1956 and limited, at first, mainly to Western Europe. Later much of the rest of the world was opened to Antioch's students. Not surprisingly, few other universities or colleges followed the Antioch model until the Peace Corps. Now, according to a returned Volun-

---

[3] Peace Corps Faculty Paper #1, "To Speak As Equals: Language Training in the Peace Corps, 1961-68," Allan M. Kulakow.

teer Services Report,[4] 33 institutions give credit to returning Peace Corps volunteers as a matter of policy, the amount depending on pertinence of training and service to the academic program undertaken.[5] Twenty-seven other institutions have given credit in individual cases.[6] Of course, a great many colleges offer undergraduate study abroad in various countries, e.g., Pepperdine College in Germany; Tufts University in Italy, but rarely is the emphasis on work or service. The academic setting has been transferred, but it remains academic.

At the present time, the only program which incorporates preparation for Peace Corps service into the student's regular academic degree course is located at the State University of New York College, Brockport, where mathematics and science teachers are being trained for service in Latin America. The program, which began in 1967 with 25 students, and has tripled since then, is generally praised. Students at Brockport join the program at the end of their second or third year (they may transfer from other colleges or universities). Following a summer of special course work, they take a program to meet their needs as degree candidates and prospective volunteers. Before graduating and going overseas, they spend a final summer term practice-teaching with Spanish-speaking children. Following their two years of service as Peace Corps volunteers, they can return to Brockport for graduate study, having earned substantial credit for field studies.

In the past year, a number of institutions began actively planning degree-program options to include domestic or overseas volunteer service in addition

---

[4] "Undergraduate and Graduate Education," A Returned Volunteer's Services Report, Peace Corps, Washington, D.C. December 1969.

[5] Brooklyn College, University of California (all branches), Colorado State University, Columbia University, Columbia Teacher's College, Cornell University, Dartmouth College, Georgetown University, George Washington University, University of Hawaii, Lincoln University, Montana State College, University of New Mexico, New Mexico State, Northern Illinois University, Notre Dame, Occidental College, Ohio University, University of Oklahoma, University of Pittsburgh, Roosevelt University, Sacramento State College, San Francisco State, Southwest Texas State College, Stanford University, State University of New York (Brockport and New Paltz), Syracuse University, Utah State University, University of Utah, University of Wisconsin (Madison and Milwaukee) and Wilmington College.

[6] Antioch College, Arizona State, Brown University, Catholic University (Puerto Rico), University of Chicago, Claremont College, Denison University, Howard University, University of Illinois, Iowa State University, Kent State University, University of Kentucky, University of Massachusetts, University of Minnesota, University of Missouri (Kansas City), University of Nebraska, North Carolina State College, University of North Carolina, University of Pennsylvania, Pennsylvania State University, Portland State College, Princeton University, Purdue University, San Jose State College, Southern Illinois University, University of Washington, and Williams College.

to appropriate course work. In the plans being activated by Colorado State College, Merrill College of the University of California at Santa Cruz, Emory University, University of Massachusetts' College of Agriculture, State University College at Old Westbury, New York, Swarthmore College, and the University of Wisconsin at Green Bay, the off-campus periods will range in length from one summer to 14 months.

In the intern program, the trainee combines Peace Corps preparation with his regular course work at either a baccalaureate or master level, thereby earning university credit for some of his Peace Corps training. The program is open to students who are finishing their undergraduate or graduate degrees in the academic year in which training begins. The first phase combines credit and non-credit activities. The second phase, following graduation, emphasizes intensive language training. In the final phase, interns receive one or two months of training in the country where they will serve as volunteers.[7]

The first experimental program began at Radcliffe (open to Harvard and Radcliffe students in 1967) where President Mary Bunting had already encouraged students in the establishment of an Education for Action Program dedicated to "increasing the relevancy between the students' academic program and their involvement in social action." After a second year, Boston and Brandeis universities were invited to join a co-operative venture in which nearly 100 volunteers were trained in 1968-69 for service in African, Latin American, and Caribbean countries. In 1969 the program was limited to Harvard-Radcliffe, and 24 seniors from Boston-area colleges were accepted to begin academic year training for Senegal and Chad. On-the-job training overseas began at the end of June.

Powerful groups at most major universities simply have no interest in problem-oriented curricula in which service and field studies are an integral part of the student's experience. Clearly, if one strongly believes that the mission of the university, apart from research for knowledge, is to impart knowledge to the young in an academic setting, there is not much point in supporting a problem-centered approach to education based on field experience. Yet, the Peace Corps has done little to publicize the Brockport model, which appears to be quite successful, and there must be dozens of Brockports where that model could work.

Nearly all of the Peace Corps-University relationships in recent years center around training. The largest single training center at the University of Hawaii at Hilo has been studied most intensively. Since 1962, more than 85 Peace Corps projects have trained volunteers at the University of Hawaii's

---

[7] These experimental programs have been described well by Phillips Roupp in Peace Corps Faculty Paper #2, "The Educational Uses of the World: Experiential Learning and the Peace Corps." December 1968.

Peace Corps Training Center at Hilo on the big island of Hawaii. More than 4,800 volunteers have been trained for projects in Ceylon, Fiji, India, South Korea, Melanesia, Micronesia, Nepal, the Philippines, Western Samoa, Thailand, and Tonga.[8] In each project, a combination of language, cultural and technical experts was gathered in what must be one of the largest cross-cultural training centers ever developed. The pedagogy of the Center has been problem-solving and task-sharing. It has emphasized education to facilitate cross-cultural communication in the carrying out of a job and has actively involved trainees and staff in ongoing community activities such as health service, flood control surveys, practice teaching, and road and bridge building. It probably comes as close to a model for training for world citizenship as any educational institution. Yet, on the major campus of the University in Honolulu, most senior professors know virtually nothing of the activities at Hilo. Acknowledging the need for closer intellectual ties between the University and the Center, the task force report on the University of Hawaii's Hilo program called for the formation of a board of directors composed in part of Center staff and University faculty members whose research activities are consistent with the Center's development objectives. It also recommended the establishment of graduate internships with appropriate University departments which would eventually result in degree-granting programs with a developmental emphasis.

This last proposal (made so gingerly, almost tentatively) gets near to the power centers of any major university, its graduate programs. Generally speaking, the men who control grants, junior appointments and educational policy are primarily interested in the production of new knowledge and not in the application of knowledge or in the development of experiential learning programs for undergraduates. In a handful of universities—S.U.N.Y. at Buffalo which has a program in social intervention, Yale which is building a center for applied behavioral sciences, and now possibly at the University of Hawaii—there is a growing interest on the part of some senior social science professors in applied behavioral science programs for graduate students. But the progress remains terribly slow (and I call these programs "progress" in a world where the application of knowledge to social problems lags badly, even though I recognize the university's primary functions are the discovery of knowledge and teaching in more traditional ways).

Because universities are slow and ponderous as the Hanna report emphasizes, it is up to the Peace Corps to take the initiative and recognize the legitimacy of its domestic mission by prodding and helping those elements within universities which want to develop new models for experiential, problem-

---

[8] Task Force Report, University of Hawaii-Hilo Training Center. Revised, October 1969.

solving learning and by taking specific steps in Peace Corps programming to help volunteers make more of what is often a complex and rich learning experience. Harris Wofford's suggestion to provide at least one full-time educational assistant on every overseas Peace Corps staff seems worthy of a trial at least for a number of the larger programs. Typically, volunteers overseas or those who work in our urban ghettoes or mental hospitals come back to the academy enriched by a complexity of emotions and ideas but remain relatively undisciplined and inarticulate in sorting them out. The academy does very little to help, but neither does the Peace Corps.

Recognizing that the third goal of the Peace Corps is as important as, and not incompatible with, the first two goals, that point of view should be advocated honestly and persuasively with Congress and host governments (there is ample evidence to believe that honest presentation will be persuasive, in my view). In addition to Wofford's suggestion for continuing educational officers on large Peace Corps staffs, there are two major steps for the Peace Corps to take, beyond those already planned by the Office of Voluntary Action (discussed later), which recognize its educative function in co-operation with universities and colleges. The first is to put under each regional program director an officer in charge of promoting intern and service degree programs. The Peace Corps Director should expect each of his four regional directors to be responsible for the multiplication of such programs. The second should be for the establishment of a Peace Corps policy which required each regional director to contract on a C.O.R. basis for universities to administer completely —and I'll discuss some of the difficulties in a moment—at least one out of every five Peace Corps programs (the proportion might be increased in time). Some of these programs could be fairly large. Others could be mini-programs as explained below. The total number of volunteers in university-run programs would not add up to 20 per cent, but it would be substantial. For fiscal year 1971, a strong effort should be made to reach 15 per cent.

The Peace Corps, in my opinion, should once again return to its early intended policy of contracting to universities for total administration—recruiting, selection, field supervision, and technical support as well as training—of its programs. Today, there are certainly countries where private organizations, including universities, would be more welcome than an agency of the United States government. Here at home, there are radical, activist, potential volunteers who now eschew service with the government, but who might find it attractive to serve while learning under university auspices.

When a university takes on a Peace Corps program in an area where it is already strong—either through its traditional scholarship or A.I.D. contacts or previous work with the Peace Corps—it should be able to offer a service degree option as well as an intern program. Peace Corps contracting should allow for research of a substantial and long-range character which, rather than comprising the mission of service and development should, in the long run, make programming more rational and effective. But, it will be argued, Peace Corps cannot wait for the long run. That is a position I would have taken in 1961. My time perspective has changed somewhat as well as my respect for the significance of the third goal of the Peace Corps.

Admittedly, there are countries where a substantial research effort may compromise other aspects of the Peace Corps mission either because staff and volunteers may not work as hard on them and/or host countries may be suspicious of research. But surely there are countries which will recognize the legitimacy of research along with service, particularly under university auspices, as a way of helping to educate Americans further about their countries, particularly if the research tends either to strengthen an appreciation of them, v.g., history, literature, music and art, and anthropology, or to help their programs in agriculture, education, health, or urban planning. And surely there are programs where research by a continuing education officer with the help of some volunteers, which in addition to making them more thoughtful about their work, may make them more effective in it by improving their morale.

Can universities do the job of recruiting? Notre Dame did a superb job by all accounts in recruiting about one-half of Chile I. Can universities do the job of administration overseas? The Indiana Conference in Chile and Arizona State in Brazil did it. Others are capable if the Peace Corps wants them. Would training improve? No one knows for certain. But so much of the difficulty in university-Peace Corps relations in training comes because of the institutional separateness of those responsible for training from those responsible for the overall Peace Corps effort. Missed signals, contracting hassles, second guessing, and the resultant mutual suspicion should be reduced in programs where universities feel they have an integrated responsibility for recruitment, selection, training, continuing education and supervision in the field.

Universities which contract for total management of programs should organize a relatively permanent campus facility such as already exists at the University of Hawaii to accommodate the total functions of such contracts. It should be prepared to engage its top personnel in overseas planning and training. It should be organized to help the volunteers fit their experience into an integrated plan of study-work-service-study for which ample credit is given. It should facilitate their re-entry to graduate work or positions in social service in the United States where their newly acquired skills and experience can be put to work.

In addition to these larger programs, the Peace Corps can contract for a variety of projects which require more highly specialized and skilled personnel than is customary. A vast array of such requests is coming from host governments all over the world. Universities might take one or several of such requests. For example, Iran wants four B.S. graduates in agronomy, two volun-

185

teers who hold masters' in agronomy, and five with B.S. degrees in soil conservation. I don't know the best university to contract for this program, but several, including the University of Pennsylvania, the University of Texas, the University of Utah, Indiana University, the University of Michigan, and Portland State College, specialize in Persian, Iran (or the Near East) and have access to an agricultural college. It is a question of matching the requests with university strengths and resources. For example, Chile wants specialists in wildlife management, wood technology, national park administration, entomology, home economics, organic chemistry or biochemistry, microbiology, nutrition and chemical engineering. All of these specialties couldn't be filled by St. Louis University or Vanderbilt University, both of which have Chilean specialties, but either institution is capable of filling some. Turkey wants 13 volunteers who have B.S. degrees in psychology or social work. Johns Hopkins, which specializes in Turkey and teaches Turkish, could do the job. There are more than a dozen other examples from the list of recent requests made to the Peace Corps by other governments.

## THE PEACE CORPS AND PRIVATE ORGANIZATIONS

The Peace Corps should also re-evaluate its policies with respect to private organizations. In 1964, relations with private organizations were put under a small, separate division, reflecting the vast change in the intention of Peace Corps leadership with respect to the role of private organizations that had taken place since the first Task Force Report was written in 1961. It was a choice of being absorbed by an increasingly strong and hostile Program and Development Office or continuing to be ignored but at least surviving for a while. Today, private organizations have little to do with the Peace Corps. Yet, apparently over 300 such agencies contacted the Peace Corps in the first six weeks of its existence to express an interest in performing some aspects of Peace Corps work. The theory behind early Peace Corps receptivity to such interest is no less valid than it was in 1961.

First, there are some tasks in which a private organization has a special expertise which could help P.C.V.'s perform better; second, there are some countries in which private organizations have had long and successful experience; third, there are some countries not now open to an American governmental agency which are hospitable to private organizations; fourth, the pluralism in the administration of programs serves as a system of checks and balances on cost effectiveness and other goals by providing competition; fifth, and closely related, pluralism will lead to healthy experimentation and the development of new approaches to volunteer service; and finally, the Peace Corps will strengthen private organizations which have labored for decades in this and related fields, and the private organizations will advertise and promote the idea of volunteer service abroad.

If the theory is so good, why was it not followed?

In a few cases, private agencies did not do a good job. For example, one of the nation's most powerful farmer's organizations apparently failed three times in two countries. But, by and large, private agencies did as well or better than the Peace Corps itself. C.A.R.E. generally was credited with much of the early success the Peace Corps had in Colombia; in East Pakistan, the Experiment in International Living was recognized as having done a superb job.

Yet, there is widespread disenchantment by private organizations—including C.A.R.E., the Experiment in International Living, and the American Friends Service Committee—with what has often seemed to be hard-driving, insensitive, and roughshod tactics by the Peace Corps. Whatever the past, it is time to think and act anew. In retrospect, the mistakes of the past seem largely to have had to do with internal power struggles within the Peace Corps rather than the issues. Understandably enough, the men who were given primary responsibility for programming wanted the authority to go with that responsibility. They did not want competing programs in the field outside of their control. The Peace Corps representatives and their staff in the field were sometimes threatened by the problem of multiple identity for Peace Corps volunteers. Whatever the reasons—and there were others—it is time for a fresh look. I propose that a policy be established which obliges regional directors to contract for one of every five of their programs to be run by private organizations, including unions, businesses, and other profit development corporations as well as the nonprofits. Thus, 40 per cent of all Peace Corps programs would be under the control of C.O.R.'s, either universities or private organizations.

THE PEACE CORPS AND SOCIAL REFORM

While the impact of the Peace Corps as an organizational entity on American institutions—governmental, university, and other private—has not been as large as was once hoped, the influence of returned Peace Corps volunteers (now some 40,000) has been, however incalculable, extraordinarily impressive in my opinion.

It has long been my view, told most fully in a book called *Those Peculiar Americans*,[9] that for a majority of volunteers the Peace Corps is a powerful emotional and mind-expanding experience which is likely to have profound effects on our most basic institutions, the family and education.

---

[9] *'Those Peculiar Americans': The Peace Corps and the American National Character* (New York, 1967).

187

Now, the evidence seems overwhelming that the Peace Corps has also been a training ground for social reform in the United States, although not through the more traditional institutions—except in education below the college level —as much as in the invention and nurturing of new ones. Shriver led the way with his appointment as first director of the Office of Economic Opportunity. Even before that, former Peace Corps staff from the Philippines persuaded the Massachusetts legislature and Governor Endicott Peabody to establish an antipoverty organization for the Commonwealth which would feature volunteer service (the Commonwealth Service Corps).[10] Subsequently, the first director of VISTA and the first director of the Teacher Corps, Glen Ferguson and Dick Graham, were chosen from the ranks of former Peace Corps representatives. Three separate development firms, with an emphasis on the promotion of social justice at home, were formed and are led by former associate directors and powerful figures in Peace Corps-Washington: Warren Wiggins, William Haddad, and Sol Chafkin. Roger Landrum and other ex-Peace Corps volunteers, with the help of Harris Wofford, began a new organization called The Teachers, Incorporated, a nonprofit group aimed at recruiting, training, and placing teachers in projects where they might act as allies of communities in their struggle to achieve a more self-directed, community-based, realistic and humanistic education. Like many other returned Peace Corps volunteers, Landrum turned to education to explore alternative styles of teaching, classroom structure and curricula in order to develop effective nonviolent strategies for fundamental educational change.

While almost half of all returning volunteers either began or continued a program of higher education with apparently not much impact on the environment of universities, a substantial proportion of returning Peace Corps volunteers turned their energies to education below the college level with what appears to be disproportionate impact wherever they have gone.

The first program which co-ordinated the use of ex-volunteers was formed in 1963-64 in the Cardozo District of Washington, D.C. Because of the verve, cultural empathy, dedication and flexibility which they brought to a difficult teaching situation, other systems became interested in recruiting ex-volunteers. New York State appointed a Peace Corps co-ordinator to do the job. In 1967, Philadelphia asked its director of the School Systems' Office of Integration and Intergroup Education, Robert Blackburn, a former deputy Peace Corps director in Somalia, to sign up as many volunteers as he could.

Driven by a teacher deficit which fluctuated between 800 and 1,200 teachers a year, Blackburn consulted with Peace Corps volunteers then teaching in

---

[10] I became the first chairman of the Commonwealth Service Corps Commission and John Cort, who had served as associate representative in the Philippines, became the first staff director.

Philadelphia before issuing his invitation to volunteers in the field about to terminate their service. The response was much greater than anticipated and almost 200 volunteers finished out the school year with most of them teaching in inner-city ghetto schools despite the fact that only 10 per cent met the stringent certification requirements of Pennsylvania. The volunteers were irritants to conservative principals just as they were overseas. They wanted to cut through red tape. They identified with children and parents and progressive teachers. They caused conflict, were disruptive and often disliked, but everyone I have spoken to who has looked at the Philadelphia situation, while agreeing that 200 returned Peace Corps volunteers did not turn the system on, nevertheless saw them as a force for change (hopefully constructive) far out of proportion to their numbers. Did the Peace Corps experience mean much in Philadelphia? The answer undoubtedly varies from volunteer to volunteer. But one whom I know personally—Wayne Guise from Philippines 3, who lived with his wife in the ghetto and taught instrumental music in six schools—answered that if it hadn't been for the Peace Corps, he probably would not have been living or teaching in a ghetto area.

It is the field of education which offers returned Peace Corps volunteers the greatest opportunity for acting as agents of social change. Education remains the largest single volunteer activity overseas, and, among those volunteers who switched their careers as a result of Peace Corps service, a larger proportion moved to education than to any other field. Combined with an increasing commitment to social justice at home and the acquisition of strategies and skills for effecting social change, a large number welcome opportunities to teach in urban schools.

In recent months, the Peace Corps has received two exciting proposals which would combine its resources with those of universities, private, nonprofit organizations, and urban school systems. The first, initiated by the Southern Consortium for International Education and the Atlanta Service-Learning Conference, also involves the Teacher Corps. Under it, approximately 30 interns will begin in June 1970 to work for an M.A.T. or M.Ed degree, combining their academic work with teaching in the school system of Atlanta and in volunteer work in the community. Participants will have the opportunity to decide before the end of the first academic year whether to complete their degree solely through service with the Teacher Corps in the Atlanta school system or to include a two-year teaching assignment with the Peace Corps. Prior to beginning, simultaneously, his first year of internship in the Atlanta schools, and a program which includes cross-cultural studies, the trainee will enter a summer, community-based internship program with the Atlanta Service-Learning Conference. In January of 1971 he will choose either to complete the program under the Teacher Corps or to become a Peace Corps volunteer who will complete his M.A.T. degree during his service and upon his return to

Atlanta. If the intern chooses Teacher Corps continuation, his second year will be under the Teacher Corps program in the Atlanta school system and the work for the master's degree and all requirements for certification will be completed by the end of that year. If he chooses the Peace Corps, the volunteer will return to Atlanta to complete his degree and begin teaching in the school system with a wage scale commensurate with three years of teaching experience.

The second idea originated with Education Development Center, Inc. in Cambridge and Newton, Massachusetts. It calls for the placement of a combination of experienced urban school teachers (several cities are now being approached), graduate students from schools of education which normally feed those systems and graduating seniors from local universities, to meet the requests of certain host countries for more experienced teachers and certain combinations of skills in education. What is strikingly new about this proposal is not that the American volunteers will receive appropriate credit at their home institutions for their field work, but that they will also be engaged in a special mission of social studies curriculum development for their own school systems, based upon their experience overseas. The proposal has the exciting possibility of creating a new esprit among volunteers who are interested in social change through educational change at home as well as in performing service in developing nations. At the same time, with proper co-ordination, it may affect curriculum planning at the undergraduate and graduate levels as well as in the school system itself. These plans call for a systematic approach to educational change in the United States through the Peace Corps, while nearly all of the change to this point has been random and informal.

Volunteers have also been active in a variety of social and political action groups. Members of the Madison Committee of Returned Volunteers canvassed and campaigned for Eugene McCarthy prior to the Wisconsin primary and also campaigned for a "yes" vote on the referendum calling for a Vietnam cease-fire and withdrawal. The Washington, D.C. Committee of Returned Volunteers became one of the most active C.R.V. groups to support the Poor People's Campaign, with its members comprising teams of speakers who addressed interested civic and church groups on the goals of the campaign. They also assisted the campaigners in Resurrection City, and participated in the Solidarity Day March.

Opposition to the Vietnam War has probably been the major force in bringing together the R.P.C.V.'s. The New York Group of the Committee on Returned Peace Corps Volunteers was formed in 1966 and a year later published a position paper on Vietnam which brought forth a quick response from more than 2,000 returned volunteers who subscribed to its antiwar position. But the National Committee of Returned Volunteers which now calls for the abolition of the Peace Corps itself, branding it a tool of American foreign policy and cultural imperialism, probably has much less effect because of its stridency and occasional bad manners than the large number of returned volunteers who work in race relations, education, or in some form of social and political change activity outside of the committee.

That returned Peace Corps volunteers are ripe for such activities was made clear by results of the Louis Harris survey released in January 1970. Comparing returned volunteers with early terminees and young men and women who had declined an invitation to serve in the Peace Corps, Harris found consistently that the returned volunteers had more liberal—and even radical—political attitudes than the others. While the results did not prove that Peace Corps service influenced the volunteers in the direction of liberalism, they did reveal that returned volunteers come back with a determination to help solve present domestic problems. Volunteers showed strongest support for more federal government participation in solving domestic social problems than did the declines (83 per cent to 69 per cent stated that the government should have a larger role in raising the standard of living of the poor). They put more emphasis on the need for speeding up equality for blacks, and a substantially higher proportion supported the use of force by blacks than declines (40 per cent versus 28 per cent).

Social action was also emphasized by Warren Wiggins' Trans-Century Corporation survey, the results of which were released in October 1969. A very high proportion of volunteers, particularly the younger ones, felt that the Peace Corps should do more to introduce volunteers to the problems facing America. One way would be to establish regional information clearinghouses which would act as information and dissemination points where volunteers in local areas could find out the names, addresses and skills of other volunteers located within the same area and receive employment in counseling services with respect to social action. These would be housed in Transitional Centers which would enable returned Peace Corps volunteers to discuss various fields of social action with visiting professionals and to consider available alternatives.

Another approach found a large proportion of volunteers—once again led by the young—favoring the establishment of 1,000 social action fellowships for returned volunteers to work in governmental and private social action programs. At least the first of these proposals has a good chance of coming into being. It is now being actively supported by a newly created office in the Peace Corps, the Office of Voluntary Action, headed by C. Payne Lucas, former director of the African region for two years and a Peace Corps director in Africa for four. Lucas approaches the third goal of the Peace Corps with missionary fervor. It seems clear to him, as it has to so many of us, that whatever good the Peace Corps might do in countries overseas, its greatest impact is bound to be on the United States.

The Transitional Center idea was proposed in the Task Force Report on Returned Volunteers in the United States to Director Blatchford (May 27, 1969) and Lucas wanted one to be opened that summer for 300 volunteers. Fifty returnees at a time would come to the Center for a cycle of four to five weeks to find out what's going on in this country and to confront employers, including universities, who are active in some aspects of the quest for social justice.

Lucas also wants to solicit the co-operation of large employers, foundations and universities to accept returned volunteers as interns in social betterment programs they would sponsor. Another idea which he has encouraged has come into existence as the Independent Foundation, an organization of ex-volunteers, which hopes to find seed money from larger foundations to help young people, including returned volunteers, to write proposals to implement new social action programs. Finally, the Office of Voluntary Action is attempting to establish a model for the use of returned Peace Corps volunteers in Washington by channeling them into action in housing, education, welfare and various other kinds of community service. For the first time in its nine-year history, the Peace Corps is making a concerted organizational effort to aid and direct the social-action impulses of returned volunteers.

## CHANGING AMERICAN INSTITUTIONS BY CHANGING PERSONS: AN APPROACH TO HUMAN DEVELOPMENT

Whatever organizational efforts the Peace Corps and others make to utilize returned volunteers, it seems to me that the largest impact on American life will come mainly through their changed values, attitudes, and styles. Whatever new directions the Peace Corps takes in the 1970's—and I am for a decade of pluralism that would include experiments in binationalism, turning over management and training of the overseas volunteers to the host country, multilateralism, which may include combinations of two or three countries (perhaps even the Soviet Union) working together, exchange programs which include Volunteers to America (not yet funded by Congress but now under Peace Corps' jurisdiction), as well as university and private agency programs—the heart of the Peace Corps experience will be the travail and pain and growth which comes to young men and women who try to carry out a task to improve the quality of human life while living deeply in another culture. Such an experience for tens of thousands of young Americans cannot help but affect profoundly the society in which they now live.

The Peace Corps has a great deal to teach Americans, not so much through immediate impact on our institutional life, as by teaching us old ways of relating and loving in families and other close relationships. By putting volunteers into traditional cultures, the Peace Corps gives them a chance to gain new perspectives on the strengths and weaknesses of human relationships in their own society. In the Philippines, it became clear to me after reading hundreds of reports from volunteers and talking to almost as many, that they became not only more sensitive and caring in their own relationships, but that they also became much more aware of the loneliness and emptiness of many relationships in the United States.

A boy from South Carolina who spent two extra years in the Philippines wrote after returning home: "As I mentioned in my last letter . . . People are so alone, so lonely, so desiring to give themselves and yet holding themselves back at the same time . . . the urge to be separate, to not touch the other or open to the other, is very strong." He had experienced the loving warmth of close familial relationships in the Philippines and was made acutely aware of the impersonal and competitive character of American life.

Warmth, closeness, lovingness and dependability often appear to characterize the relationships in families of traditional cultures. This is not to say that depth in relationships is characteristic of those cultures (nor is it to say that other cultures are free from their own kinds of neuroses and psychoses). Anthropologists in the South Seas have often noticed what appears to them to be unwillingness to become deeply involved with others. But there is a quality of give and take, ebb and flow, and mutuality which volunteers experienced in the Philippines and elsewhere which seemed to many of them and to me to be strikingly lacking among Americans.

To learn this by living it is vastly different from learning it by reading about it. The volunteers, at least many of them, took the time to care. Living in a Filipino village for two years without any possibility of a raise or promotion, without any need to manipulate others, they could afford to show their caring. One boy wrote that Filipinos will remember "the little things that showed I cared for them, drinking *tuba* and dancing folk dances and singing folk songs, talking to them in their own language, the thousand and one things that go into meaningful relationships whether a word or not has ever been spoken." Dozens of other volunteers concluded that their capacity to give and receive love in relationships had been developed through their exposure to Filipinos in the villages. In this, the Peace Corps volunteers of the Philippines are not alone. Although Peace Corps programs and the attitudes of Peace Corps directors vary considerably from country to country, volunteers from every continent have told of becoming sensitive and caring in their relationships.

The change in volunteers is a corollary of their awareness of a certain kind of underdevelopment in the United States. It is an understanding that Americans have been so busy getting and doing that their capacity for being in relationships with others, particularly those closest to them in their own families, has been blunted. In the Philippines, the emphasis on harmonious interpersonal relationships did not make volunteers value honesty less, but it made them appreciate sensitivity and caring more.

The Peace Corps affects American life because it is primarily an instrument of human development, not just economic development. Filipinos and others unquestionably change in the direction of Western, and particularly American, values as a result of contact with volunteers, although the changes may be much slower than many people had thought they would be. But Americans change too. As one girl from Wisconsin said of her Filipino teacher friend, "I affected her life, because she affected mine . . . we wanted to experience each other." They affected each other because their experiencing of each other went beyond the ordinary qualities of friendship between persons from the same culture. By being involved in each other, they were involved in each other's cultures. It is possible to read about other cultures but it is highly unlikely that one can become involved in them through reading. Being involved, as one ex-Peace Corps volunteer put it, has "the power of giving pain or pleasure." This boy, who had served in Nigeria, understood as profoundly as any Peace Corps volunteer from the Philippines that it was the emotional experiencing of the other culture through relationships with individuals which changed him. He has written: "This to me is the meaning of the Peace Corps . . . it is the call to go, not where man has never been before, but where he has lived differently; the call to experience first-hand the intricacies of a different culture; to understand from the inside rather than the outside; and to test the limits of one's own way of life against another."[11]

It seems to me from watching the encounter of Peace Corps volunteers with Filipinos that the American cult of individualism has severely limited the human development of Americans in certain aspects even while advancing it in others. It also appears to me that where encounter between Filipinos and Americans was penetrating and sustained, changes took place on both sides, leading, in Teilhard de Chardin's conception, toward the convergence and complexification of man. By convergence, de Chardin meant the tendency of men to incorporate the results of differentiation into an organized unified pattern. Man is the only species that has succeeded in remaining a single, inter-breeding group; rather than diffusing biologically as do birds or other species, man converges through biological fusion and cultural diffusion toward a union of the whole human species. But while the family of man emerges, individuals become more complex and differentiated.

Filipinos and American Peace Corps volunteers became more alike in some ways, even as they became more aware of their differences, each side tending

---

[11] This is from a superb short pamphlet by David Shickele, called "When the Right Hand Washes the Left," A Peace Corps Discussion Paper, 1966.

to draw from the culture of the other those aspects of man's humanness which seemed lacking in themselves and yet attractive. The process of change of fundamental values and personality characteristics within great cultures is slow, but it is going on all the time and will now be speeded by the increasing number of human encounters that take place across cultures. Human behavior is a sum of beliefs, values, attitudes, feelings, words and other actions which constantly interact and affect each other. It seems, to me, impossible to say that feelings are always prior to beliefs or values, or vice versa. One feels something about women, nature, or God and what one feels is in part determined by beliefs which have been handed down for generations by men whose feelings in relationship to women, nature, or God helped shape those beliefs. One speaks or acts out of beliefs or values or attitudes or feelings, or a combination of them, but action itself affects beliefs, values, attitudes and feelings.

All human societies are underdeveloped, and there are probably no men in any culture who have not suffered from spiritual, emotional, physical, or aesthetic underdevelopment. Many Filipinos (and undoubtedly other Asians, too), even when they are critical of excessive individualism and activity in Americans, begin, after long contact with them, to value the individual freedom of Americans not only to make choices for themselves but to communicate more openly and directly with persons in authority. While they may recognize that excessive individualism can lead to loneliness and selfishness, they also feel the extent to which the emphasis in their own culture on family-centered group cohesion has inhibited certain aspects of their personal development. Americans, after becoming involved with individuals from the more traditional cultures—if they follow the experience of many Peace Corps volunteers—will feel that certain aspects of their own development have been hindered by the highly individualistic, planful, purposeful culture in which they have been reared. They may like political democracy and economic prosperity no less than before but they see something more. For surely, Americans are far behind others in their capacity to appreciate and understand mystery, or in expressing their bodies freely and rhythmically, or in absorbing and merging confidently and harmoniously with nature, or in feeling the joys of mutuality in relationships. In these ways, Peace Corps volunteers and other Americans will be changed through deep and lasting personal encounter with other cultures even as Africans, Latin Americans, Asians, Polynesians, and others are changed by Americans toward more rational, scientific ways of perception and cognition and toward more independent and achievement-centered behavior.

Cultures will converge but individuals will become more complex. We are now entering the age of multicultural personalities whose identities, being complex, are uncertain and who suffer pain because of that uncertainty. We inherit in our cradles our cultural values and our styles of thinking and acting, but they are subject to change as a result of personal encounter with others holding different values.

Studies show that thus far modifications of personality as a result of inter-cultural experience are infrequent, but that is because the experiences are rarely as penetrating or sustained as they were for many Peace Corps volunteers in the Philippines. If we are to judge by the experience of some of them, Americans may develop their abilities to give and receive love as a result of basic personal encounter with Asians, even if it means becoming involved in relationships which prescribe continuity of commitment and obligation. Americans may become less self-reliant as they feel the beauty of belonging in relationships, even when it means counting on others and being depended on by them. They may learn to reject Emerson's advice to "unhand me" and even see certain consequences of the cult of self-sufficiency as barbaric and unhuman. Whether this will be done in families or in other new, perhaps experimental, relationships, or both, seems to me more risky to predict than that it will be done.

If I understand many young Americans correctly, they are saying they no longer want independence geared toward either production or consumption. They no longer want to be either inner-directed (in the driven, Puritan sense) or other-directed (in the market-oriented sense) men and women. They value productivity less than their grandfathers and consumption less than their fathers, but they cling steadfastly to the ideology of independence. Now they speak of independence to fulfill or actualize intimate, caring relationships. It seems as if a growing number of Americans want what they call self-direction or autonomy plus a greater sense of belonging. In the past a sense of belonging has implied more than caring for and being cared about and even more than sharing with others. As Peace Corps volunteers from the Philippines know, it has meant being counted on by others, being responsible for others and being obligated to others. It is these three concepts—being counted on, responsible for, and obligated to others—that cause many Americans discomfort. They hope to get the caring and sharing aspects of belonging through an interpersonal commitment which grows out of the existential situation without being tied down or made dependent. It is an ambitious and possibly illusory goal.

Peace Corps volunteers in my view tend to, in philosopher Martin Buber's words, become less individuals and more persons. Individuals emphasize their separateness from others. Persons engage in a dynamic I-Thou relationship which is an encounter of interfering as well as accepting love. Individuals are preoccupied with protecting their separate selves apart from others. Persons are concerned with expressing themselves in society and in relationship to others. Are individuals or persons more autonomous? If words mean anything at all, there is no such thing as the autonomous human being. We are the creatures of our cultures, as the American celebration of autonomy and self-sufficiency shows. Development, if we are to judge from the experience of Peace Corps volunteers and Filipinos, cannot be measured on an autonomy or a dependency scale. It is something which transcends culturally biased over-simplifications.

The nature of human change in the process of human development remains largely a mystery, but surely it is something more grand and complex than what Americans have seen as direction toward self-sufficiency. That is unde-niably a part of our development as humans, but only a part. To care and be cared for, to have a sense of belonging, also has to do with our development as human beings. As one Peace Corps volunteer in the Philippines wrote, his relationships with Filipinos "gave me ties . . . and gave me sudden inexplica-ble intimations of brotherhood with all people." The emerging family of man will not be Americanized, Europeanized, Africanized, or shaped only by Asian values. It will be, if the Peace Corps gives us a clue, a family that increasingly appreciates the marvels of mystery as well as the symmetry of science, the peace of passivity as well as the power of productivity, and the balm of be-longing as well as the satisfaction of self-sufficiency.[12]

---

[12] These last several paragraphs were taken from my book, *'Those Peculiar Ameri-cans': The Peace Corps and the American National Character.*

# THE NEW HUMANISM
## International and Intercultural Programs
## in the State Universities of Illinois

Oliver J. Caldwell

Higher education in today's world is a comparatively conservative and in-elastic organism in an environment which is generally volatile and unpredict-able. Thus there is often a wide gap between the governance, the instruction, and the research and services performed by universities and the needs of the societies which support them.

American universities face special challenges growing out of deep national involvement in world affairs, the rebellion of blacks and other minorities, and the disenchantment of many white students with the white ethnocentric "es-tablishment." Scholars are being forced out of their ivory towers, and scholar-ship is increasingly involved in applying knowledge and wisdom to the improvement of the human condition.

I would like to make initially several points: First, as we look back over the last 25 years, the American university has changed greatly compared to its pre-World War II prototype. Higher education in this country has been blessed by gifted and imaginative leaders who have helped many universities to begin to adapt to the changing needs of our society.

Second, the innate conservatism of higher education which many of us de-plore is not entirely deplorable. The interaction between urgent demands for innovation, and reluctance to abandon the past, has enabled American higher education to keep its traditional roots while educating citizens of the twenty-first-century.

Third, many of the forces imposing change in our universities result from a growing imbalance between the emphasis given hard sciences on the one hand, and the social sciences and the humanities on the other. Military and industrial demands have stimulated since World War II a rapid mushroom-ing of research, teaching and services in the sciences, both pure and applied. A reason for student unrest is the conviction among many sensitive young people that the educational establishment is neglecting man, his ideas, his works and his problems.

Fourth, a principal area of concern to academic rebels is the lack of hu-manistic education designed to help people overcome the barriers of ignorance, prejudice and pride which separate the nations from each other, thus keeping alive the possibility that the gifts of science may be abused in a final war which could destroy humanity.

Finally, the barriers of race and class within our own nation are increasingly offensive to young people who have been taught in church and in school that all peoples were created equal. The establishment is being challenged to practice what it preaches.

In this paper, I will attempt to review some of the creative innovations in cross-cultural and international education which are being tested or have been proposed in the state universities of Illinois. The Midwest is often regarded as a center of isolationism and conservatism. As a relative newcomer to this area, I have been gratified by what is being done in the universities of the American heartland to prepare a new generation for living and leadership in a global world, and to bridge racial and cultural gaps separating our own people. What we are trying to do in Illinois is typical of what is being done in many states. I suggest the foundation of a new academic humanism is being built.

Americans and their universities existed in a condition of comparative isolation prior to the Japanese attack on Pearl Harbor. Suddenly our people found themselves fighting a massive war on many fronts, in Europe and Africa on the one hand and throughout the length and breadth of the Pacific Ocean on the other. It was necessary to train millions of men to live and to fight in many strange and alien places. The achievement of victory required that officers and men learn a great deal more about certain parts of the world than they had been taught in our schools and colleges. Tens of thousands of Americans had to learn certain exotic and difficult languages, such as Japanese, Chinese, Arabic, and Russian. There were not enough professors to teach these languages and traditional methods of instruction were too slow. Linguistic experts recruited informants, some of them prisoners of war, to force-feed young Americans and thus enable them in a few months to communicate in strange tongues. Out of these wartime academic expedients grew new and improved methods of teaching foreign languages.

Successful co-operation with our allies, as well as successful government of conquered territories, required that involved Americans know something of the cultures of both allies and enemies. Furthermore, individuals who learned to speak a new language frequently developed a curiosity concerning the customs and the aspirations of the people who spoke that language. Thus, area studies acquired a new popularity and importance. Area programs usually involved the study of at least four different fields in a particular area, such as history, language and literature, economics and government.

Before the war was over, more than 10 million Americans had gone overseas, many of them to remote places they had never heard of before Pearl

Harbor. Some of us hoped that when we returned, we would find deep changes in our Western-oriented universities. We hoped that the millions of veterans who fought in the Pacific and in Asia would demand that American education orient itself towards the whole of mankind rather than exclusively towards Greece, Rome and Western Europe. We hoped that the military achievements of our black comrades and of the Nisei, and of all other minority groups would permanently break the barriers of race in our nation.

These dreams, except in a limited way, did not materialize. Then and now, most of our military men carry Main Street with them wherever they go. It was and is an exception when an American soldier is able to relate effectively to a non-Western culture. Many find it almost as difficult to relate effectively to the French, the British, the Germans and other Europeans with whom they are associated. In spite of World War II, the Korean conflict, the Vietnamese war, NATO, SEATO, and all of the other international military, cultural and commercial involvements of the American people, we are still basically an ethnocentric white North American society.

It is against the historical background of isolationism and ethnocentrism that we have to weigh the importance of what American higher education has accomplished in the past 25 years. In spite of our national failures, including the refusal of Congress to approve appropriations for the International Education Act, and the reluctance of many leaders in and out of our government to give effective support to anti-poverty, and anti-discriminatory programs, during the period since World War II many American universities have made important progress towards joining the human race.

What is happening in Illinois is evidence of the evolution of a new educational philosophy in the United States. According to a report[1] published by the Board of Higher education in December, 1968, there were at that time 269,294 students enrolled in public institutions of higher learning. This figure was more than double the enrollment of 129,870 six years earlier in 1962. In 1968, there were 153,060 students enrolled in private colleges and universities. Altogether, 55.7 per cent of our youth in the 18-to-21 age group were in college, as compared to 41.5 per cent only six years before.

Quantitatively, this was a remarkable achievement. Equally impressive have been the gains in the quality and content of higher education in Illinois.

Because of limitations in time and space, we will consider here only certain humanistic innovations in the six senior public universities in Illinois. This brief account cannot do justice to recent creative innovations in higher education, both public and private, in this state.

These universities, in what is often described as the center of American iso-

---

[1] Growth in Illinois Higher Education 1962-68. A Report of the State of Illinois Board of Higher Education, December, 1968.

lationism, have developed a series of challenging cross-cultural and international programs which may not be appreciated in other states, and are virtually unknown abroad.

The University of Illinois is a major center for international service through the Agency for International Development and other public and private agencies. Programs at Champaign-Urbana and technical assistance overseas are carried on in many countries. Years ago, while on a trip through India for A.I.D., I was impressed by the quality of the personnel that had been contributed by the University of Illinois to programs in India.

The University of Illinois has published a booklet describing the international activities of the university during the current year. They involve nine colleges and the Institute of Labor and Industrial Relations, supported by substantial special library facilities. In addition, there are four major area studies program.[2] Functional units and technical assistance programs total 11;[3] these involve extensive overseas activities carried on by specialists contributed or recruited by the University. There are also 10 programs[4] which make it possible for students from this university to pursue their studies in other countries. Illinois is a member of the Midwest Universities Consortium for International Activities in which it co-operates with the universities of Wisconsin, Indiana and Michigan State in the promotion of international academic activities.

Another interesting program is called Extension in International Affairs. It sponsors conferences on world affairs for citizens of Illinois where they discuss such topics as "The Crisis in Southeast Asia," and "Responsibilities of a Super-Power in International Politics," and "The Middle East Crisis: Prospects for Peace." This university has become a potent force in the development of informed public opinion in Illinois regarding world affairs.

Eastern Illinois University provides a major in Latin American Studies, op-

---

[2] African Studies Committee, Center for Asian Studies, Center for Latin American Studies and Russian and East European Center.

[3] Business Education Project in Tunisia; Center for Comparative Psycholinguistics; Center for International Comparative Studies; Center for International Education & Research in Accounting; Council of United States Universities for Rural Development in India; Jawaharlal Nehru Agricultural University, India; Njala University College, Sierra Leone; Program for International Research, Improvement, and Development of Soybeans; Tehran Research Unit, Iran; Uttar Pradesh Agricultural University, India, and University Extension in International Affairs.

[4] Architecture Semester in France, CIC Summer Program in Mexico, Elementary Education Semester in England, Engineering Junior Year in Germany, Engineering-Science-Architecture Summer Work Experience Abroad, Illinois and Iowa Year Abroad Program in France, MATESL Internship in Puerto Rico, Russian Language Summer Study Abroad, Science Education Internship in Puerto Rico and Independent Study Abroad.

portunities for its students to study at Trinity College in Dublin in the summer, and a summer study project in Mexico. These are in addition to the special seminars and courses of study presented by the university which introduce its students to the world outside the 50 states.

Northern Illinois University has an important Center for Southeast Asian Studies for both undergraduate and graduate students. This involves teaching and research in the departments of political science, history, social anthropology, economics, geography, and foreign languages.

N.I.U. also offers interdisciplinary programs on international relations in Latin American studies, and an interdisciplinary approach to the teaching of international business.

Every summer students of this university have opportunities to study overseas in five to eight countries in a variety of disciplines including art in Europe and Japan, classical studies in Greece, social science and Spanish language studies in Mexico and English literature at Oxford. The College of Education has a training program for students interested in community services in Puerto Rico, and business students have opportunities for job traineeships in various business enterprises in Europe. Finally N.I.U. encourages independent study by its students overseas, usually in the residential programs of other American universities.

Western Illinois University has a substantial program of summer studies in a number of countries operated under the supervision of a Dean of International Education. The countries and overseas institutional affiliations change from year to year. The theory here is that students will learn more through personal experiences in other countries than in a classroom situation.

Illinois State University offers courses in Latin American studies and a number of specialized courses in the cultures of the non-Western world, in such departments as geography, history and English literature. In addition, I.S.U. offers its students a number of comparative courses in economics, world population, and resources and government.

The primary aim of the international programs at Illinois State is to internationalize the curriculum, to escape from the limitations of the traditional North American-Western European orientation which still permeates American higher education. This is being done in a number of ways, including the offering of substantial travel grants to enable members of the faculty to gain overseas experience by attending institutions in other countries and carrying on post-doctoral study abroad. Thus, a professor in any field may receive an opportunity to see his discipline in the perspective of another culture.

The needs of the black students at Illinois State are being met by courses in Afro-American literature, black history, black art, black music, the economics of the ghetto, and a number of other related fields.

Southern Illinois University seeks to introduce its students to mankind and to provide many services to peoples from other lands. It enrolls nearly 2,000 black students, and has provided special opportunities for students, both black and white, to study the traditions, achievements, aspirations and problems of the Afro-American. An interesting branch of the university in East St. Louis enrolls gifted young black students whose scholastic background is too limited to permit them to enroll as regular university students. These disadvantaged young people receive special tutoring to enable them to take their place in Southern Illinois University at Edwardsville.

A unique S.I.U. program involves the use of the dance, as taught by Katherine Dunham, to bring underprivileged black students into the world of educational opportunity.

S.I.U. in Carbondale currently has contracts with the Agency for International Development to carry on technical assistance programs in Vietnam, Nepal and Afghanistan. The Ford Foundation has enabled the university to work with the authorities of Nigeria to improve the quality of instruction in that country in English as a second language.

Recently, A.I.D. granted a million dollars to S.I.U. to set up the first Center for Vietnamese Studies and Programs in the United States. The most recent addition to S.I.U. overseas operations is a contract offered by the Food and Agricultural Organization to enable Southern Illinois University to strengthen agricultural education at the Federal University at Santa Maria in southern Brazil.

S.I.U. is broadening its curriculum to make it possible for its students to learn more about the world outside the United States and Europe. A survey of the curriculum indicated that about 300 courses are listed which include materials relating to human achievements, aspirations and problems outside the United States. These courses represent an investment of about $4 million dollars per annum for instruction.

S.I.U.-Carbondale has developed a unique interdisciplinary cross-cultural program known as Intercul. This is an attempt to give general studies an international and intercultural orientation. Many of the American students enrolled in the Intercul Program are living with foreign students, and academic credit has been given to students who participate in these arrangements.

Northern Illinois University, Illinois State University, Western Illinois University, and Southern Illinois University are all members of a consortium, The Associated Universities for International Education. They are co-operating in a variety of ways to promote the improvements of language and area studies on member campuses. They also plan a series of centers for study and research in other lands. The first such center is the Center for Tropical Studies at Belize, British Honduras.

At Southern Illinois, important work is being done by several departments, notably philosophy, in recruiting distinguished scholars from other lands who teach our students in the context of their own culture and tradition. A student who majors in philosophy at Carbondale is likely to acquire a considerable appreciation of the philosophical foundations of Japan, China and India.

One of the most important and dynamic developments in public higher education in Illinois is in black studies. Success in this area must be followed by incorporating in the curriculum more adequate materials relating to other American minorities, such as American Indians and Americans with a Spanish heritage.

An overview of state higher education in Illinois would indicate that there is a great deal of activity on some campuses in intercultural and international education, and there appears to be a trend towards the aspects of learning which emphasize the unity of humanity and contribute to the improvement of the human condition.

(a) There is a growing faculty and administrative acceptance of the need for creative innovation in cross-cultural and international education. Some of our universities are examining themselves with a view to broadening the traditional goals of higher education.

(b) There are many new innovative educational opportunities at both the graduate and undergraduate level. However, the average student is a cautious person who often appears to be dubious about academic innovation. Certain new programs are not adequately appreciated by the majority of our students. The imaginative Intercul Program in Carbondale has not received the student support that it deserves.

(c) There is continuing resistance to interdisciplinary co-operation. The result is a tendency to put new programs in existing departments, something like putting new wine in inadequate old bottles. Instruction and research across national and cultural frontiers often are hampered by traditional disciplinary restrictions. Both undergraduate and graduate students are increasingly interested in problem-orientated interdisciplinary studies. These studies are sometimes resisted by conservative professors with some support from conservative students.

(d) There is a real intellectual gap between serious and committed students, and professors who advocate change, and the opponents of innovation among faculty and students. An increasing number of military veterans, returned Peace Corpsmen, black students, students of Mexican-American, and Puerto Rican background, and other students from all classes of society, feel that they are being short-changed by the standard curriculum. They are supported by a substantial number of teachers, young and old.

(e) These people are the sources of the unrest, and the growing militancy of students and faculty members who demand changes in the curriculum, in methods of instruction, in governance, in the whole structure of the university, to make it a more effective organism for the improvement of the human condition. This unrest is intensified by the success of some creative and innovative departments in opening their windows to the world.

(f) Activism in national and international affairs is stimulated by the extension of intellectual frontiers across national and cultural barriers. This extension creates a new empathy, as young people begin to see man as one family on this planet. Thereafter, they are unwilling to condone traditional political and military policies dominated by ethnocentrism. The Vietnam protesters are at least partially motivated by their belief in the oneness of humanity.

(g) It is a traditional view that a principal role of the university is to perpetuate and expand the high culture of our Western society. For the past generation this high culture has been dominated by the hard sciences because of the enormous expansion in the body of scientific knowledge, and by the demands of defense and industry. Thus our high culture, which was basically literary at the turn of the century, has recently become scientific.

Now the pendulum seems to be swinging in the other direction. Many scientists are fearful of the uncontrolled use of what they have wrought. Many intellectuals, young and old, are rebelling at the domination of our universities by the military, by industry and by impersonal science. Our high culture may again develop a strong literary leadership, and a new humanistic orientation which will involve all major cultures and all major literatures of mankind.

(h) Characteristic of this new humanism is the growing concern with the solution of human problems. Scholars, young and old, are attacking an establishment which condones racial injustice and the existence of extensive hunger and poverty in the richest society that man has known. Many scholars of history, the languages, sociology, anthropology, philosophy and the sciences are disrupting the meditation of their colleagues at the meetings of their learned societies with insistent demands that their disciplines become involved in bettering the condition of the poor and the outcast of our world.

In summary, there seems to be a movement in most intellectual disciplines in many American universities, both inside and outside of Illinois, towards a new concern with the improvement of the human condition. There is also evidence of a growing recognition of the essential unity of humanity. These trends derive a major portion of their strength from the growing international and cross-cultural programs in our universities.

In the American heartland, we see the beginning of a strong, new humanism, a reorientation of state-supported higher education towards meeting the human needs of human beings. This trend was emphasized in the state of Illinois with the publication of Position Paper #79, submitted by Dr. James B.

Holderman, its new executive director, to the Illinois Board of Higher Education.[5]

Dr. Holderman's views are supported on a national level by a Report to the President's Environmental Quality Council on Commitment to Problem-focused Education, and also by the report by Gregory Anrig to James Allen, former U.S. commissioner of education, on the need for innovation in priority areas in American education for the purpose of relieving social tensions.

The Holderman Report summarizes the major problems faced by our universities in this way:

> We have . . . identified three indictments of our society which appear in nearly all critiques: (1) the environment, to which no single man, corporation or nation can lay claim, is being fouled almost beyond repair, whether by air and water pollution or by nuclear fall-out and devices of defoliation; (2) 'the establishment,' as the students define it, will not admit to the possibility that ideologies can be refashioned to begin the journey toward world peace; and (3) the disadvantaged are being exploited.

It goes on to establish its point of view as "The Human Needs and Quality of Life Thesis," and proposes that no new programs be approved in the Illinois State system of higher education unless they are designed to meet human needs and improve the quality of man's life.

Two major criticisms have been leveled at these recommendations: First, the pre-eminence of the traditional disciplines which now dominate our universities is being threatened (those of us who support Dr. Holderman's views

---

[5] The tenor of Dr. Holderman's remarks is one of inquiry. He questions the purposes of modern public colleges and universities: whether they are institutions for the pursuit of truth in detachment from the practical and political world, or whether they have responsibilities of relating to and serving that broader society of which they are a part.

In an attempt to explain the disintegrative elements of today's American society, Dr. Holderman examines what he calls (a) the "alienation of the disadvantaged," and (b) the "alienation of the advantaged." He sees the disadvantaged in America as being on "the brink of revolution *with cause*" (editor's italics). An end to all discrimination, better communications, and an increase in the capacity of public and private institutions to respond to the disadvantageds' "frustration of powerlessness" are suggested as the means for best coping with the just complaints of this group.

With respect to the perplexing problem of the "alienation of the advantaged," Dr. Holderman hypothesizes that much of this disaffection for the "system" stems from disappointment in and anger with the quality of life attributable to that system. He suggests that higher educational institutions should be more concerned than they are with the quality of life—both social and environmental. Specifically, he proposes that "The Human Needs and Quality of Life Thesis" become a governing principle in the planning of new programs in the State universities of Illinois.

believe it is high time that our universities give priority to the solution of social problems and the improvement of the human condition).

Another group of critics claims the Holderman Report is no more than a rediscovery of the Morrill Act; but perhaps it is time for our state and land-grant universities to rediscover it. Lord Bowden recently wrote: "I have always regarded the Morrill Act as the most important event in the history of Western education."[6]

What is happening today is that the principles incorporated in the Morrill Act are being extended in many directions to incorporate new disciplines, and to apply new knowledge and wisdom to healing the wounds in our social order, and to building better lives for all peoples.

Humanistic studies are a connective tissue between the past, the present, and the future of man. These are studies which enable man to understand himself and his neighbors. They help the student to apply the fruits of scientific scholarship to the improvement of the human condition.

Once the frontiers of humanism were the limits of a single culture. The frontiers of the new humanism encompass all of the people who live on this beautiful blue planet we call the earth.

In a halting and cumbersome way, the universities of the state of Illinois are moving towards a new awareness of the oneness, the interdependence of the people of Illinois with all people everywhere.

---

[6] See below p. 237.

# THE EXCHANGE OF PERSONS
# AND THE CULTURAL POLICY
# OF NATIONS

## George N. Shuster

I shall begin with something written by Robert Ulich in an essay entitled, "The Great Ambiguities of Thought,"[1] published a few years ago—that is at a time when one could see pretty clearly what the fate of the United Nations would be during the period that lay ahead. Ulich wrote:

> We no longer live in isolated dwellings. Our neighbor is no longer the farmer next door—or perhaps least of all the man next to us in a big apartment house. Certainly the 'next' should also be part of our knowledge and loyalty. Strangers at home cannot be at home in the world. Those who cannot lay a brick cannot build a house. And I even suspect that those who cannot love a dog cannot love mankind. Least of all should we see a contrast between our liberal individualistic tradition and a desire for the unity of mankind.
>
> The contrast appears only when individualism is but a better word for egotism and when unity mistakes itself for mechanical collectiveness. Everyone who works upon himself opens the door to humanity, and whoever cares for humanity enters deeper into self, and thus helps to balance the ambivalence that has been part of man through the centuries.

It seems evident that as we attempt to redefine the exchange of persons in academic society as well as in the wider society we should bear these observations very much in mind. But we must first ask ourselves about the framework in which such exchanges must be carried on. Why is it for instance that individuals can create societies, but very rarely can societies beget larger societies except through resort to force? One would have thought, for example, that after Europe had blundered and staggered through two world wars and agreed for a while on a concept of a United Europe, it would proceed to draw viable conclusions from the notion of solidarity. But De Gaulle seemed to think of a United Europe only in terms of the Carolingian empire; and instead of witnessing an abatement of linguistic nationalism, we have been forced to note its intensification in Belgium and elsewhere.

---

[1] Robert Ulich (ed.), *Education and the Idea of Mankind* (Chicago, 1964), p. 33.

I believe, indeed, that on balance the centrifugal forces have been more active on the scene of contemporary history than the unitive forces. That is, while the strength and importance even in diplomatic terms of the United Nations have declined, the tide of separatism has risen. If this were attributable only to the fade-out of colonialism, one might say, well, sooner or later there will be a process of settling down. But this is not our present situation. A paltry dispute about a bit of boundary can arouse more emotion in Latin America than the concept of economic union. The repudiation of the United States by Cuba is matched by the defection of Czechoslovakia inside the Soviet Empire. Most ominous of all is the gulf which seems to yawn between China and the Soviet Union.

The situation cannot but affect profoundly the policies governing the exchange of persons. I attempted some time ago to formulate a theory of cultural relations, among which exchanges form a very important part, and have written about one aspect of it as follows:

> What is the international dimension in cultural affairs? The answer is, free trade in cultural goods. And what are these goods? They may I think be defined as those accretions of information, inquiry and creative artistic achievement which are the concerns of the modern university. Intellectually considered, they can conveniently be summarized as the accumulation of knowledge and method which the human mind has built up round those fundamental, reality-revealing intuitions which in their totality form the present outlook of mankind.[2]

This conception is admirably illustrated in the informative and effectively phrased addresses which Glenn T. Seaborg devoted to scientific exchanges of persons and information. Dr. Seaborg tells us, for example, that such exchanges have taken place on a broad and friendly basis between our scientists and those of the Soviet Union in all areas other than those considered inviolable by reason of national interest. The natural sciences lend themselves particularly well to this kind of intercommunication. Their findings are couched in a language which by its very nature is not associated with politics or any other form of value exposition. It is a universal language—the first Esperanto that has ever proved viable. In view of the overriding importance of the natural sciences not merely in terms of human welfare but also in those of the apprehension of the relationship between man and nature, one must of necessity hope that conversations between scientists, regardless of

---

[2] Paul J. Braisted (ed.), *Cultural Affairs and Foreign Policy* (Washington, D.C., 1968), pp. 24-25.

209

ideological or other differences, will steadily increase both in number and diversity.[3]

Yet having said this one must come back to what was pointed out earlier, namely that the centrifugal forces in our society are extremely powerful. Until UNESCO was created in 1945 by men and women who believed that if the revival of Nazism could be prevented peace would be assured, the "national dimension" of cultural relations prevailed everywhere. UNESCO's was a naive view, no doubt, but we now know better than we ever did before that it had nobility and even what one might term meta-practicality. In other words, there must be a viable idea of peace before peace can be realized. Perhaps our current greatest difficulty is that we cannot imagine what the world would be like if there were no armed forces or conflicts in which they could engage.

Cultural relations, as Europe and the United States thought of them during the period which followed the imposition of colonial status on so much of the world, seem to have passed through three stages of development: first, that of Christian missionary effort; second, that of great philanthropic organizations, a notable instance being the Rockefeller Foundation, which blended religious considerations with more secular concepts of cultural relations; and third, that of almost completely secularist efforts to combine technical and other forms of cultural exchanges in order to provide assistance to peoples in need. It must be noted that not only did the three efforts indicated often work side by side, but also that very complex forms of bilateral and multilateral cultural interpenetration were created.

The missionary period fostered national interests while being supranational and religious in character. For example, anticlerical governments in France supported the efforts of Catholic missionary communities to convert the "pagans" because in so doing they often taught the French language and exemplified French culture. Other European countries did likewise. Less widely known is the fact that the United States also did so, at least to a certain extent. For instance, during many years the State Department relied for information about the Orient on a large group of missionaries. Remarkably enough, these missionaries became in time far less antagonistic towards one another and far more co-operative with their environments. What was done by them to foster education not merely in the countries they served but also

---

[3] This point of view was strongly reinforced in an address given at Notre Dame University on October 16, 1969. Cf. the Notre Dame *Observer* of the following day. Edward Teller was quoted as saying that the "question of secrecy is perhaps the most urgent question scientists should discuss." He suggested that the United States "open up all the way and stop imitating the Russians; we can do this, we may induce them to open up and imitate us."

through sending young people to the United States for higher education is as yet a largely unwritten chapter in our cultural history.[4]

Exchanges fostered by the foundations have increased greatly in number and in variety. But it is now far more difficult to disengage what they are doing from the mammoth enterprises of government, both national and international. A kind of romantic aura therefore surrounds the earlier history of the Rockefeller Foundation, but the attacks it sponsored on tropical diseases and on medical ignorance, to mention just two of its crusades, were realistic enough to satisfy anyone. The pattern established, that of unselfish service and of tactful professional leadership, has been ably followed by other foundations. Their efforts will never compare in scope with those of governments, but they are far less subject to political change and therewith to accusations of self-interest.

The mighty tidal wave of cultural exchange which rushed in with World War II and persisted during the Cold War was not wholly different in motivation from the modest trickle devoted, for example, to fostering the Good Neighbor program of President Roosevelt. But its value to the nation was stressed far more vigorously. The campaign to eradicate Nazism, at least during the five years immediately after the war, was fought with regiments of experts, propagandists and exemplars of our culture. But it was followed in both Germany and Japan by a tranquil bilateral program of exchanges, stressing university professors and students particularly. The rapidity with which the Federal Republic was altered from a seedbed for moral and political leprosy to a garden in which friendship was to blossom is indeed one of the remarkable changes in modern cultural and political history.

The Cold War, transforming as it did all agencies of the U.S. government into anticommunist task forces, ranging all the way from the Army, the Navy and the Air Force to the delegations to the U.N. and its subsidiary organizations, had, however, its nostalgic side. Large segments of our population continued to hope that an agreement could be reached with the Soviet Union. This hope was doubtless stronger in the hearts of scientists, but it ran the gamut all the way from devotees of *Pacem in terris* to admirers of the Bolshoi Theater. We should of course not disparage these things. The simple truth was that until we in the United States could reach an effective agreement with the Soviet Union the armament race simply had to go on.

It was the Cold War which first opened our eyes to the tremendous demand on the part of peoples released from colonial rule or from abject economic dependency for some kind of status on the scale of decency. We began to see with mingled clarity and disillusionment that the outcome of the ideological struggle would depend not only on the measure of security obtainable from

---

[4] Cf. Kenneth Latourette, *Christianity in a Revolutionary Age* (New York, 1958).

being ahead of the pack in terms of armament, but also upon whether the peoples of the world would keep in step with our conceptions of the good society. As C. W. de Kiewiet, one of the ablest students of these problems, has indicated,

> Misconceptions and complacency may turn that struggle of the new nations to fill the vacuum of power and satisfactions into radical channels. New experiments, new methods of organizing society, new imports of power and competence, altogether would constitute a grim alteration in the political and economic shape of the world. If there is a Communist challenge, this is it.[5]

Nevertheless, though this challenge has persisted during all the amazing changes to which the human scene has been subjected during the past four decades, it seems impossible not to conclude that nationalism has been the principal disruptive force. Certainly what is happening along the northern border of China is not an ideological conflict. Nor has suppression in Czechoslovakia been the result of diverse interpretations of Marx. But there are two events in particular which seem to me to throw light on the task which present makers of cultural policy confront. The first is the Nigerian-Biafran struggle, so costly in terms of human life and so horrible because of the sacrifice of children. But it would seem that the principal reason why the fighting dragged on is not Great Britain's treaty commitments, or Russian shipments of arms, but the extreme reluctance of other African states to become involved lest they in turn become obliged to face similar rebellions in their own territories.

The other event is the mistreatment of the Jewish minority in Russia and Poland. The service of a small number of Jewish Communists to their party in Poland has been notable. Still this has not prevented the government from proceeding against them with great ruthlessness. This action is as racist in character as was Hitler's. Nor perhaps is it as far-reaching in scope as anti-Semitism has been in the Ukraine. All three are expressions of nationalism, of folkishness, and not of any semblance of a desire for human solidarity.

At any rate, it seems to me quite clear that when we in the United States now think of the exchange of persons in the broadest sense of the term—that is, within the framework of the international interpenetration of knowledge and achievement—we must take into account the fact that a very radical change in our overall orientation is needed. We have thought pretty generally since the U.N. was established, and very specially since the Alliance for Progress was created to deal with economic and social improvement in Latin America, that our real task was to create forces which would promote tech-

---

[5] *Higher Education and Public International Service* (Washington, D.C., 1967), p. 26.

nological and scientific improvement at a rate sufficiently rapid to make the survival of democratic institutions possible. To be sure, we have not always waited for the improvement to work out automatically, but we have acted to prevent a given country from becoming "anti-democratic," which meant of course pro-Communist. The Dominican Republic and Vietnam are examples.

I shall discuss the situation in Vietnam in this context only. If one began to reason that technological and agricultural improvement must come about quickly enough to make the survival of free institutions possible in Southeast Asia, one necessarily had to think also of the development of the Mekong River area, which would be of immense—perhaps incalculable—benefit to the whole of that region. As a matter of fact, it was this to which our attention and that of the U.N. was directed for years. But of course such a vast engineering effort demanded some kind of political stability. Of this there was barely enough in that area to permit the U.N. to build one relatively small dam and to carry out an irrigation project. The sums expended on these are, however, less than 1 per cent of what the real job would require. Therefore we of the United States as the principal preservers of "democratic institutions" were more and more irrevocably drawn into thinking about political stability. Only so, we thought, could the fruits of our future heavy investment, not in terms of profit to ourselves but of benefit to the region, be justified. The first consequence was the assassination of Diem and the liquidation of his rule, which we very likely could have prevented if we had considered him and it sufficiently democratic. That left Hanoi, assuredly not democratic either, to be dealt with; and soon quicksand was under our feet everywhere and we have floundered in it these many bloody years. So of course, the development of the Mekong area is just as remote as it was when we first began to think about it.

There is no intention here of playing the game of history remaking or of trying to suggest easy solutions to difficult problems. Cynics have long since said that creating the human race was God's only blunder. One may not agree with them and still conclude that the price of human advancement comes high. But a couple of questions need to be asked. Is our long-standing assumption correct that whatever is done by the United States should have gratitude and compliance for its rewards? Or should we take seriously what is doubtless the neuralgic point in *Pacem in terris* and say that a free ideological market will bring about a viable solution? In this case we would not be seeking to keep Communists out of any place or situation. Rather we would say to any given people: We are here for your benefit; and if you think somebody else could do better, well and good. To me it would seem that the truth lies somewhere in the middle. I do not think we can exclude propagandizing completely, for the simple reason that our opponents will not do so. Still the simple fact of the matter is that at present we cannot refute the widespread notion that our benefactions are imperialistic. It has often enough been suggested that since the private foundations have been very effective and have achieved that effectiveness without being called imperialistic, all government expenditures for social and economic development should be turned over to the universities and other private organizations. Some have even suggested that if private industry took over the development enterprise it would succeed. I entertain some doubts as to whether the Congress would ever go along with such proposals, and unfortunately, both universities and business have boondoggled a good deal.

Still accusations of "imperialism" are part of everyday life now. We must meet them with probably diminished capability. Perhaps one is in for surprises, but the likelihood is that the personal endowments of our ambassadors and our representatives on international bodies will for a time grow steadily less impressive. Certainly one could already cite horrendous examples. But let us simply note the factor of abrasion—the kind which has worn distinguished university presidents to a frazzle and military commanders to a sense of their inferiority. For the first time in our history brilliant military leaders are nobodies, and college presidents are found guilty of having done too much too soon, or too little too late. I would feel better about some student uprisings, for example, if they did not seem to be mushy forms of Franciscanism without any of Francis' discipline and astuteness. What if some campus leaders were to say some day: we suggest that we acquire the skill, the knowledge and the dedication needed for guiding the project of human development to a worthy goal?

All I can add here is said with reluctance and reservations: the present mood of people in many countries is, not so much in terms of the natural sciences but certainly of the social sciences and the humanities, far more hostile to "North American interference," as they term it, than it has ever been before. The testimony of very able workers in Latin American vineyards is explicit. Few foreign students not now in this country any longer want to be taught by us. Neither do foreign teachers and professors, however much their teaching needs to be improved. All this leads me to believe that we may be obliged to welcome to our shores men and women who will tell us why they believe we could be doing better than we are, though they may be naive and unrealistic enough to turn our stomachs. We may be obliged—and here I find myself in complete agreement with Dr. de Kiewiet—not to stage our hopes on this, that or the other specialist, but on carefully recruited groups of able men who will represent a variety of disciplines and attempt valiantly to work together.

Still I do not wish to surmise that the almost omnipresent revival of nationalist emotion can be overcome, say, by efforts to proceed immediately to the unification of mankind. Realizing that satellite broadcasting will soon provide a powerful instrumentality for the education of both children and adults, I would nevertheless observe that broadcast blanketing of the United States

214

has not ushered in effective approaches to the solution of our own social and community problems. Indeed, it may have rubbed sentiment to the raw and created more tensions than it has helped to relieve. Why should we suppose that coming down from three global platforms broadcasting will do any better?

Let us go back to Robert Ulich. Every decent form of comradeship is precious. If I understand one Frenchman, perhaps he will understand me. Should I be able to listen to an Arab with Socratic attention, I may have a chance through him to make some Arabs take a more realistic attitude toward the Israeli. Therewith, of course, we come to that aspect of cultural exchange to which the academic community has been especially dedicated. The number of students, professors and other serious inquirers whom we have sent overseas, or whom we have accepted in our midst, is enough to remind one of that passage in the Book of Revelations which speaks of the thousands of representatives of the tribes of Israel coming into the presence of the Lord. Since this discourse is designed to deal with theory rather than practice, I am quoting no statistics. Some people think we have not done enough. This is what comparable persons in Europe, Great Britain and the Soviet Union also think. But if one sought to arrive at a sum total it would doubtless be highly impressive. During the State Department regime of John Foster Dulles, Robert Thayer was instructed to make a survey of the private sector insofar as the exchange of persons was concerned. We have had no sequel to that survey. I suggest that anyone who is interested in that kind of thing should consult Mr. Thayer's report, out of date though it be.

I believe that on this sector of the exchange front—the phrase is more militaristic than I should like it to be—we note that the revision of the Fulbright program, placing more of a burden on other nations, is a rather inept way of mapping out a new course. Certainly, however, we should do this planning in concert with our European friends and possibly even with the Soviet Union. Taking our stance from this moment in history, we have sent thousands of young people overseas in the Peace Corps and voluntary organizations. We have all kinds of "Years Abroad," some of them very good indeed, and others more questionable. We have the perennial itinerant professor, sometimes doing very useful work in terms of communication and research, and sometimes entering into a fraudulent relationship with a library. Meanwhile, of course, our hippies are reclining on the outskirts say, of Casablanca, and some of our soldiers are raising holy hell round about Bamberg.

But—and this is a suggestion and no more than that—we might seek so to manage the exchange of persons that it would be less one-sided. Student groups abroad might be matched by student groups over here. Fulbright and similar scholars should be less sedately but more carefully screened. Above all, I believe that we should look at the world realistically and decide where the centers of power will be situated 50 years hence. In Western Europe, certainly. In China obviously. I have an abiding obsession that in the not too far distant future the Soviet Union will be plagued by nationalistic cross-currents and may not be able to cope with them with too much success. Latin America, despite its obvious weakness, is growing stronger every day. Doubtless therefore the world picture will change and the relative stature of the United States will decrease. This means that the nation must make frugal and efficient use of its resources now and during the decades that lie ahead. The exchange of persons can, if properly assessed in the light of its history, remain the most notable and dependable of the channels through which those resources can move. We must think in big and little terms alike—of the Mekong River, to be sure, but also of the perennial boy silent on his peak in Darien.

# CULTURAL RELATIONS BETWEEN IDEOLOGICALLY DIVIDED COUNTRIES

Robert F. Byrnes

The direct role of the American university in cultural relations with institutions of higher learning in countries with political systems and values different from ours has increased enormously in the past two decades. It has taken place because of the rise of American power in a shrinking world, the revolutionary changes which have occurred in the character of world politics, growing American interest in other parts of the world, and the changing character of American education and the function of the university. Consequently, the universities, and all those engaged in scholarship and teaching, have been impelled into an important, new and difficult role in America's relations with other peoples and their governments.

This function is fascinating, stimulating, valuable, often unpleasant and even dangerous—and inevitable. It has helped universities to improve research, instruction, public information, and the understanding of other countries and cultures, of a changing world, and of ourselves. It has also helped our scholars to co-operate with other nations' scholars and students engaged in the same kinds of universal and eternal study as we, to our shared advantage. However, because of the financial costs which cultural relations involve, and because of the nature of international relations today, this growing activity has helped to blur the line between education and politics (or even political warfare), has threatened to make the university an instrument of foreign policy, and has therefore exposed it to domestic and foreign political pressures. Each Western country has created different kinds of organization and different systems for maintaining relations between the universities and the government. However, in every case the effort to ensure that control of university programs be of, by, and for the universities, and that research and instruction remain independent of international politics has proved complicated and frustrating.

This is a particularly appropriate time to discuss the university's role in cultural exchanges between ideologically divided countries, because American universities have just completed their first decade of cultural exchanges with the Soviet Union and some of the countries of Eastern Europe and because the uneasy situation in Czechoslovakia and Eastern Europe may raise questions in the near future about whether and how these relationships can and should be continued. Moreover, one day we will certainly face the same opportunities and challenges when exchanges of young and old scholars are begun with the universities of mainland China. Only a rash man would dare to estimate at what date we shall begin cultural exchanges with mainland China, but surely we should review our past experiences and identify both the problems faced and the advantages enjoyed from the relationships our universities have had with the Soviet Union so that our policies on exchanges with China will reap the benefit.

Some kinds of cultural exchanges, such as national exhibits or ballet troupes—which receive the most publicity and claim the greatest share of public attention—are not properly the responsibility of the university and should therefore be excluded from its area of interest. The kinds of cultural exchanges with which universities have been involved and in which they will no doubt remain most interested are exchanges of books and of publications of all kinds; of graduate students and scholars; of teachers, particularly of language teachers and of specialists in language instruction; and, ideally, exchanges of professors of history and chemistry, of biology and economics, indeed of every important field of instruction. Conferences of scholar-teachers constitute another important, traditional type of exchange, one which is arranged and administered with relative ease and which, of course, is always most valuable when truly international.

Universities participate in exchanges in other ways as well. They send and entertain cultural groups, such as university bands, concert orchestras and athletic teams. Indeed, the University of Minnesota band in 1969 was the first American artistic group ever to go to Siberia—and return. Universities have also played an important role in the exchange of groups of specialists in various scientific and technical fields. Moreover, they frequently serve as hosts and provide interested audiences for music and dance groups which come to the United States on a commercial basis.

Briefly, universities should engage in cultural exchange programs with Communist countries whenever our government has official relations with that Communist government and when relations are civilized and of mutual advantage, even though participation in such exchange programs has created serious problems for the universities and even though the universities' role in international exchanges raises fundamental questions concerning the ways in which our institutions of higher learning will function in the future. The main reason universities should become involved in exchange programs with ideologically different countries is the simple fact that, as Whitehead said, "The proper subject of study of the university ought to be the universe." One part of the universe is, of course, at the moment controlled by Communists.

218

Since the American university or college should study the universe—past, present, and future—it inevitably has the responsibility to study that part of the world now ruled by Communists. Moreover, in order best to understand another part of the world, another culture, another point of view, our scholar-teachers should study in that country and with the scholars and other citizens of that country, whether their special fields of interest are history, literature, economics, music, folklore, or indeed any other aspect of the country's history and culture.

Fundamentally, this point is at the center of the area studies concept, which Professor Philip Mosely and others developed in the 1930's: one should go to Eastern Europe if he wishes to know and understand that part of the world, just as we would hope and expect that a Hungarian interested in American literature or architecture or agricultural development would come to the United States to continue his study. Such opportunities not only enable the scholarly specialist to increase his knowledge and understanding, but also help him and his university to assist the ordinary citizen better to understand the world in which he lives. In other words, it is the responsibility of liberal education in the last third of the twentieth century to have Americans continue their study in the Soviet Union and in other Communist countries, and to have scholar-teachers from those countries work here as well.

A university should also become involved because we live in a shrinking international community in which no nation exercises a monopoly on knowledge or on the best means of finding it. We have the obligation, as chemists or physicists or historians or teachers of language, to acquaint ourselves with scholars and their work the world over, to share with them whatever discoveries and techniques we have mastered, and to learn from them whatever advances they have made. We do indeed live in one small world and are members of one family. This, of course, was well known in other eras, such as the Middle Ages, which saw the universe as a whole and were not so afflicted as we by nationalism and the dreadful consequences of a series of destructive wars. In the Middle Ages, when the foundations of the modern university were being laid, the traveling scholar was even more common than he is today. A citizen of Christendom and a responsible member of a universal scholarly community, he knew several languages well, was the product of a number of universities of the Western world, and considered himself at home throughout the area. Moreover, he recognized and acted upon the conviction that all share the same interests and have an obligation to work together. As St. Thomas, the greatest of the medieval scholars put it, "We are all the same distance from eternity."

In our age, one other element enters: We have a special responsibility to assist scholars in other countries who are living and working in less comfortable and less free circumstances than we. The history of the last 30 years, indeed of the past 150 years, provides a number of excellent illustrations of the kind of special obligations our blessings have bestowed upon us. In the nineteenth century, for example, French universities assisted Polish scholars, who came to Paris as refugees from Austrian, Prussian, or Russian rule, to continue their scholarly work and labors on behalf of their people. In the 1930's and 1940's, English and American institutions aided scholars from China and from European countries overrun by the Axis powers. In our efforts to work with the scholars of the Soviet Union and Eastern Europe, we are simply continuing a tradition with medieval roots, which we share with other cultures, and which is, in fact, a universal tradition.

In other words, American universities have their roots in universities such as Cracow and Charles University in Prague, as much as in the Sorbonne and in Oxford. Just as these institutions helped us by the work they did 600 years ago, so we have an obligation to help them as part of the eternal search for knowledge. We should, in short, distinguish between the temporary political condition and the eternal human condition. We should be firm towards Communist governments, but gentle and cooperative with scholars in countries ruled by Communists.

Universities should become active in cultural exchange programs for other reasons as well, including the need to defend the university from external influence or simply to prevent others from assuming the functions of the university and adversely affecting its development.

The main threat here, of course, comes from government, but there are other threats as well. Curiously, American foundations, benevolent institutions which have helped us all, constitute one of the hazards. Thus, a foundation can lure a university into activities abroad which are beyond the capacities and the interests of the university but close to the central goals of the foundation. Foundations sometimes compete with universities, as the Ford Foundation did through its program in Eastern Europe. Moreover, the administration of programs by foundations or other organizations which select scholars from other countries to work on American campuses (in a system in which the universities do not participate in the selection decisions but are nonetheless expected to serve as hosts) obviously raises basic problems for the universities which some foundations have never succeeded in understanding. Simply put, selecting and sending scholars and graduate students to institutions of higher learning in countries ruled by Communists—and accepting the same types of men and women from those countries—is so significant and delicate a task that the universities should retain authority, lest they imperil their independence and even existence.

Professional organizations constitute another potential threat. For example, when we have academic exchanges with mainland China, the medical sciences might serve as the first element. Medicine is perfectly neutral; it is even better than neutral because it is a most beneficent element. The Chinese are interested in American medicine, in part because so many Chinese doctors received their medical education in the United States, and because most American doctors are interested in helping peoples in all countries. Moreover, we could no doubt learn a good deal from the Chinese in a number of medical fields. In short, launching the exchange in the field of medicine would be a sensible step. If this should occur and if the American Medical Association should become the American administrative agent for such an exchange, this professional organization might so emphasize its own interests as to give less attention to the interests of the American people, the American universities, and the American government than they require. Historians might act in the same way, if they should administer a special program with mainland China. Indeed, one of the decisions most quickly reached in the early days of the exchange program administered by the Inter-University Committee was that responsibility should be given to the universities as a whole. Thus the exchange program would not engage only those Americans especially interested in Russian studies, but would give equal access to any scholar who might find it advantageous to study in the Soviet Union. In short, the universities must direct the programs—or at least control them—in order to ensure that the interests of all fields of knowledge are given proper weight.

In this country we have benefited from the absence of certain kinds of organizations existing in other Western countries. For example, in some West European countries, "friendship societies" administer exchanges with the Soviet Union and some of the countries of Eastern Europe. The Communist Party in the United States has a small program for sending Americans to the Soviet Union, but it does not have a program for bringing men and women from the Soviet Union into the United States, which would make it an exchange. We have been blessed in that no organizations of this kind have developed, if only because such programs would cause confusion among the general public.

Finally, universities should become active in cultural exchange programs with Communist countries because the immense political importance attached to such exchanges makes high intellectual quality of paramount importance. Exchange programs are essentially political. Even though the universities, their scholars and their students are basically interested in improving and expanding research and instruction, and even though the Inter-University Committee's programs with the Soviet Union were begun by the universities two years before there was a cultural exchange agreement between the United States and the Soviet Union, the nature of world politics and of the relationships between the United States and the Communist countries ineluctably bestowed extraordinary political significance upon these programs. The Russians are interested primarily for political reasons. It is also clear that the

221

American government and the American people likewise view the programs as one way, in this deeply divided world and these hazardous times, of maintaining ties, reducing tensions, educating each other and increasing mutual understanding. Moreover, the most important personal relationships which have developed between Americans and Russians, in fact almost the only relationships beyond those among diplomats, are those which have developed between scholars in this country and scholars in the Soviet Union. It is therefore essential that academic exchange programs be maintained and that they be maintained by those who are most competent and most interested.

One of the most obvious paradoxes over the years is that the program which has had the greatest impact within the Soviet Union has been the academic exchange program, which was established and administered by scholars whose goals have been academic, not political. It is clear also that the intellectual nature of these programs, which emphasize academic quality, is directly responsible for their political impact. If the universities should abandon their primary goal for a political effect, or if they should allow the government or another outside agency to control their program or alter its goals, the political influence of the academic exchange program would rapidly decline.

The reasons why universities should participate actively in cultural exchange programs are abundant; the problems which this engagement produces are almost as impressive. The most important difficulty stems from the conflict and tensions caused by the nature and function of the university. Ideally, the university is somewhat isolated from society, or, at least, so placed as to be able to maintain a calm atmosphere in which serene, unhindered and independent judgments can be made. Ideally, it is not affected or influenced by outside forces—particularly political ones—either domestic or foreign. In short, it should be an independent institution, in a society and of a society, but free. However, many universities in many countries are not independent, and some institutions which are called universities are not really universities, but simply training institutions.

Thus, an American university which participates in cultural exchanges with Communist countries to some degree becomes a ping-pong ball of domestic political discontents and international politics. Those involved in the work of the Inter-University Committee learned this lesson very early, because the Committee was established when Senator Joseph McCarthy had considerable influence in this country. The founders of the Committee turned to Pennsylvania State University as the most protected administrative instrument for its program, in part because the President of Pennsylvania State University was the brother of the President of the United States. However, Milton Eisenhower declined the opportunity to establish the program at Pennsylvania State University, because of the political hazards he thought it would raise, and he thereby quickly educated interested scholars concerning some of the basic domestic political problems involved.

At the very same time as our universities are being attacked from the Right on the grounds that they are aiding the Communists, they are also attacked from the Left, especially the student Left and the new isolationists, because they are serving "American imperialism." They are also attacked by some emigrés from the Soviet Union or from one of the countries of Eastern Europe on the grounds that exchange programs strengthen Communist regimes, as indeed, in a sense, they do. In other words, whenever a university engages in cultural relations with Communist countries, it becomes prey to domestic political pressures which threaten all its activities.

Another serious problem reflects those philosophical and moral issues which beset universities in the last third of the twentieth century because of the pressures foreign governments can impose on American institutions. Specifically, to what degree should universities surrender their influence upon our educational programs to foreign governments, as occurs to some degree in our program with the Soviet Union, and as may one day occur in an educational exchange program with mainland China? Thus, American universities nominate graduate students and scholars for study in countries like the Soviet Union or Hungary. The foreign government naturally has the authority to grant or deny visas and to place a scholar in university "X" rather than university "Y." The Soviet government has, in fact, denied admission to the majority of our nominees who wish to study the Soviet economy, and it will not allow an American political scientist to study anything of political importance in the Soviet Union. Thus, the Soviet Ministry of Higher and Specialized Education will not admit an American scholar who wishes to write a biography of Stalin, to study the Stalin-Trotsky controversy of the 1920's, to analyze the relationships between government and the Party at any level in the Soviet system, to describe relationships between the Party and the army, to determine how Soviet foreign policy is made, or indeed to investigate many other problems political scientists ordinarily study here and in other countries. Consequently, American political scientists who wish to go to the Soviet Union select subjects which are not sensitive and not politically important. In short, they and their sponsoring organizations surrender authority over their research program to a foreign state.

Organizational and operational problems create another difficulty for universities engaged in cultural exchange programs. Very few American universities have defined their priorities for the last third of this century. Few university officials have thought systematically or clearly about the position foreign exchange programs should occupy in a system of priorities. Are they more important, for example, than mastering the knowledge being created in all disciplines, both old and new? Are they more important than our responsibilities to eliminate the ghettoes, or to assist the disadvantaged in the United States? What kinds of priorities do we have?

Moreover, even when scholars and universities have defined their priorities with scrupulous care and even when they recognize that the cultural exchange programs should be of, by, and for the university, the universities are organized in so rickety a fashion, that they are not prepared to handle the problems which arise. Most faculty members and administrators would have great difficulty in describing just how their own university is organized and where the lines of authority and power centers are. In fact, as our students have discovered in recent years, American universities, in their glorious freedom and independence, have drifted into a Micawberish state of disorganization, splendid for the faculty and perhaps also for the students but not so competent for responding to today's needs.

Within this general and comfortable disarray, the universities' lack of sense, absence of coordination, and neglect of management of their work abroad and of their work in international studies is most depressing. Very few universities, perhaps none, have a coherent view of their work overseas, of their activities in Communist countries in particular, and of the correct relationship between their activities abroad and the instruction of undergraduate and graduate students and of enriching the faculty and curriculum at home. This incoherence not only exists within individual universities, but it is even more true of relations among universities. In fact, these relations resemble those among the German states in the seventeenth century, with the exception that the rulers of those states had relatives in other states who provided at least a family connection. In our case, approximately 2,200 different sovereign states (colleges and universities) almost deliberately conceal from each other their activities of mutual concern. In other words, we are not coordinated. One of the major needs in this country is the creation of a kind of American Council of Universities to administer or coordinate exchange programs.

This issue is brought into sharp focus through examination of the costs of cultural exchanges. It is difficult to define educational costs, particularly the true costs, when compared with dollars spent for tuition, board and room, books and supplies, and other necessities. Programs involving scholars in several countries with different educational systems are, of course, even more difficult to assess. Moreover, such programs also carry considerable hidden costs, in the form of time and energy contributed by administrators and scholars, by foreign student offices, and by others involved. Finally, the administration of an international exchange program is especially expensive because it includes not only the travel of the participants, but the careful detail work necessary for selecting and placing participants, improving language facility, moving families as well as scholars, and negotiating the agreements and the many disagreements which arise.

Thus, while it is difficult to define costs accurately, it requires approximately $10,500 to send an American graduate student or a young scholar to the Soviet Union for an academic year. This is the equivalent of four American graduate school fellowships. Thus, usually without realizing it, when American universities have sent a scholar to the Soviet Union, they have decided that sending that scholar, and accepting a Soviet scholar in return, is more important than giving four graduate fellowships for study in residence.

Moreover, academic exchange programs are expensive in total. It would cost about a million dollars to send 100 young American scholars to the Soviet Union for an academic year. No university, nor any group of universities, has the funds to finance such a program. The universities have therefore had to request assistance from private foundations and from the American government. When a university is dependent upon government for large funds over long periods of time, it puts its independence in some jeopardy, because an organization which advances large sums of money into a program over long periods of time ordinarily, perhaps inevitably, seeks influence over policy and direction. Thus far, we have kept this problem within proper limits in our exchanges, but exchanges with mainland China will raise even more serious issues, because the expenses will be so great and because the political problems will be so delicate and complex.

While the problems just discussed are significant, the most obvious difficulties universities face are their relations with various agencies of the American government. For example, the Federal Bureau of Investigation, which bears clearly defined and important responsibilities, in the first year of the exchange tended to assign agents to follow scholars and students from Communist countries. Some officers of the Central Intelligence Agency, for understandable reasons, in the early years thought that a group of young Americans who knew Russian well, who were well informed concerning the Soviet Union, and who were to spend a year in that country, might constitute excellent sources for intelligence information. Both of these problems were resolved quickly and amicably before, in fact, they arose, but they are fundamental, and they are issues which our sister universities in countries ruled by Communists have clearly not settled.

The main government instrument with which there is potential conflict is the Department of State, which not only has full responsibility for defining and executing American foreign policy and advancing American national interests abroad, but also possesses the necessary expertise and full knowledge. The officers of the Department naturally believe that outsiders, including professors, should not interfere in the Department's responsibilities, because, while they may radiate good will, they do not comprehend the large picture of the national interest and instead often insist upon dealing with Communist universities in ways which may threaten other more important programs in which the Department itself is involved. Consequently, a division concerning principles and procedures almost inevitably opens between the Department of State and universities, or indeed any private institution which becomes involved in relationships with the monolithic Communist state. In this conflict, the principal root of disagreement is the Department's responsibility for the national interest as a whole and for a large number of private interests as well, at a time when university scholars and administrators are concerned primarily with academic exchanges and consider these the most important element among all relationships with the Communist state. Disagreement almost inevitably arises: the universities consider that their interests are being sacrificed to other less significant ones, while the Department sees the universities as selfish and parochial in their concerns.

Disagreements over particular issues, such as the selection and nomination of Americans, placement of foreign scholars in American universities and opportunities for Communist scholars to travel within the United States, derive from this basic division in responsibility and authority. Thus, when we have an exchange program with mainland China, an American university will no doubt wish to send a professor to China who the Department of State, for one reason or another, believes should remain in this country. The Chinese will naturally seek to send scholars in scientific and technical fields in which we are more advanced than they, and some of these fields will be militarily or politically sensitive. The university will wish to accept the scholar; the Department of State and other agencies will prefer to deny him a visa. Chinese scholars will wish to travel throughout the United States to visit a number of research centers, but American government agencies, such as the Department of State, the Atomic Energy Commission, or the Department of Defense, will on occasion seek to restrict this travel for security reasons and because Americans will be so closely limited on travel in mainland China. The American universities will consider this an infringement on the free right to travel and study on the part of the foreign scholar, whom it will rightly insist be treated like any other scholar. In short, conflicts of a basic and bitter nature will arise.

Problems of a more serious type appear with other governments, especially Communist governments. Some are sure to arise whenever an American goes abroad. Americans teaching and studying in a country as close to us as Canada or England often encounter, and sometimes create, political and intellectual difficulties, because studying in a foreign culture in itself raises problems. These become especially sensitive when the governments are hostile or even suspicious. Moreover, a special sharpness arises because the United States is more advanced—especially economically and politically—than the Communist countries with which it deals. Interests and resources are not the same, and raise problems on both sides, because the sharing of resources and opportunities among unequals is always painful, even when both sides share a common culture.

Communist countries also have different organizations, principles, and values than the United States. Thus, American universities do not deal with Soviet universities; they deal first with the Ministry of Foreign Affairs, the Soviet government agency which negotiates and signs the cultural exchanges agreements. The second most important Ministry involved on the Soviet side is the KGB, the Committee on State Security, or the secret police. In the Communist system the KGB has special authority when Soviet citizens go abroad and when citizens from another country are admitted, particularly for a relatively long time to an institution as central as a university. The third Soviet organization involved is the Ministry of Higher and Specialized Education, which ostensibly controls higher education in the Soviet Union. Thus, American universities deal with powerful government agencies in a totalitarian system, while they speak only for themselves in this country. Moreover, the kinds of exchanges are carefully restricted by the Soviet government, a fact which some of us who are most enthusiastic tend often to forget. So far, exchanges have been restricted to the provision of opportunities for research on a carefully limited and controlled basis. The kinds of fundamental and ordinary relationships which occur without formal agreements and the work of special organizations simply are not permitted by Communist governments. Such relationships would include the teaching of English and of American history or of chemistry in Soviet universities by American instructors, and instruction in Russian and in Russian history and in physics in American colleges and universities by Soviet scholars. Soviet scholars and citizens in general do not have ready access to books, journals, and newspapers published in the United States, and cooperation on common research projects, such as water pollution, is still impossible.

In short, the nature of the Communist political system and the government's restrictive policies are at the core of our difficulties. American scholars are not allowed to visit most of the universities in the Soviet Union and, under the Inter-University Committee program, may work at certain universities but not in the research institutes of the Soviet Academy of Sciences. In the first 10 years of our exchange program, the Committee placed Soviet scholars in 62 different American universities throughout the United States, while 295 of the 300 American scholars who spent a full year in the Soviet Union studied in only two universities, Moscow State University and Leningrad State University. The Committee's administrators were not even allowed to visit most of the other Soviet universities. Americans admitted into the Soviet Union are restricted in access to archives, libraries and living sources of information. They are forced to pay discriminatory prices. The basic questions therefore arise: How long should American universities accept this kind of situation? What sense of dignity and propriety do we have? Just where is the dividing line? How should we respond?

The problem is far more complicated than it appears, because the powers of both our government and our universities are so limited in such situations.

We cannot force the Soviet government to treat our scholars as we treat theirs, or to allow our scholars the freedoms and opportunities necessary for their work. At the same time, we cannot, and will not, inflict similar restrictions on Soviet scholars working in this country, because this would be a violation of our own system and would in the long run harm us even more than it would the offending country. On the other hand, consenting to these inequitable arrangements in the hope of improvement may lead American universities to accept them on a permanent basis and to drift into a kind of moral demobilization, in which the will to defend the university's best interests simply withers away. Eternal vigilance and a willingness to be demanding in negotiations and resolute in insisting that agreements be honored are therefore especially vital.

In addition, Americans face other problems, such as the intervention of the police in the activities of scholars who are carrying on their studies in proper fashion. A goodly number of Americans who have studied in the Soviet Union have been harassed by the KGB; some have had to endure frightening "interviews," and others have been expelled. Many have been attacked in the Soviet press. While these charges and actions have been irresponsible and without foundation, they have naturally cast a shadow upon the reputation of those attacked. In short, an exchange program with a Communist country carries an element of hazard for the individuals as well as the institutions engaged.

Finally, everyone interested in cultural relations and in promoting a more peaceful world must recognize that our academic exchange programs with the Soviet Union and with the countries of Eastern Europe have provided significant benefits to those countries and their regimes. In fact, the Soviet government must clearly believe that the exchanges offer significant advantages—indeed, benefits greater than we derive—or it would not maintain them. Similarly, our government obviously believes that the agreement is more to our advantage than to that of the Soviet Union, or it would not continue it. In short, the cultural exchange agreements are considered mutually beneficial and must remain so.

The Soviet benefits are considerable and highly visible. Approximately 80 per cent of their participants study science and technology in the United States, and we must assume that they return after having acquired important scientific and technical knowledge and techniques. By means of the program, the regime has acquired increasing favor among Soviet intellectuals by allowing some Soviet scholars the opportunity to live and work abroad. This step has also helped persuade the Russian people that their government is indeed a peaceful one and a respectable member of the family of nations. Such programs also affect the foreign view of the Soviet Union and help to remove the discredit under which it labors because of its repressive and isolated system. The exchange programs also enable the Soviet Union to carry on a kind of dignified propaganda in the universities of the United States. Indeed, the program may also be used to train Soviet specialists for more effective propaganda work, and other political work in Soviet government institutions, an advantage to them which carries a hidden bonus for us, because the United States profits when even its most hostile critics are well informed and understand us.

Even so, we should continue these programs and expand them when possible, particularly if they remain under the control of the university and if the proper safeguards can be maintained. Indeed, the results of the programs we have had with the Soviet Union and Eastern Europe, which will presumably be reproduced when we have exchange programs with mainland China, demonstrate beyond question the great utility of these exchanges for the universities and for the national interest.

The principal benefit, and the primary justification, are the remarkable improvement and expansion in the quality and quantity of American scholarship on Russia and Eastern Europe, an improvement so striking that there is no comparison between what is now written and taught about Russia when compared with research and instruction in the 1930's. We now have a relatively large cadre of teachers and scholars (about a thousand) who have lived and studied in the Soviet Union for an appreciable period of time. In 1955, perhaps 10 American scholars had had that kind of experience. More important than quantity, of course, is quality, since our publications and our teaching reflect a degree of knowledge and understanding far beyond the level available as recently as 10 years ago.

Another great advantage is the confidence our scholar-teachers possess about their teaching and writing. In other words, American education has passed a demanding test. For example, our medievalists will never be certain that their knowledge and understanding of medieval Europe are correct, because they will never be able to visit medieval Europe. Those Americans who were teaching and writing about the Soviet Union before they studied there were in the same position. Now that they have lived in the Soviet Union and tested what they learned from reading, from listening, and from talking with emigres, with what they have learned from working in Soviet libraries and archives and talking with Soviet scholars, their work has passed a test which will never arise in medieval studies and which as of the moment has not yet arisen for Chinese studies.

In almost the same way, the cultural exchange programs have contributed to the revolution in foreign language instruction which has swept the United States in the past decade. Those who studied Russian in the days before they could continue their research within the Soviet Union usually learned only to read the language, since there would apparently be no opportunity to speak it. Now that hundreds of scholar-teachers have lived in the Soviet Union, they have enormously increased their competence in Russian, and have come to a better appreciation of the value of knowing the language well. As a result, they have helped to revise and vastly improve Russian language instruction within our colleges and universities.

Another consequence has been the geographical spread of research and instruction concerning Russia and Eastern Europe. In 1939, scarcely any American universities offered a seminar in Russian history. Indeed, at that time, Russian history was taught at the graduate level in only three or four institutions. It is now taught throughout the United States. This has helped to change the nature, the character and even the spirit of the American university. Thus, the university I know best is quite different from 1950, when its faculty included only one trained scholar or teacher on Russia. The university now has 40 specialists on Russia and Eastern Europe. When an institution sprinkles this number of scholars throughout its faculty, it obviously contributes significantly to changing its spirit. In fact, the specialists on Russia and Eastern Europe are among those who helped encourage Latin American studies, African studies, and Asian studies. Moreover, I am sure we also understand ourselves better than we did because of the exchange program, and that this understanding will be further expanded by programs with mainland China.

Finally, in spite of all of the shortcomings of our programs, they have brought scholars and universities together and have increased cooperation between the universities and the Department of State so that all have benefited from the enterprise and have acquired greater understanding of each other. Thus, there are many ways of learning about the activities within one's discipline, but service on a national selection committee, policy committee, or advisory committee informs one about men and women in his field of study from throughout the United States in a truly excellent way; and this has become an extraordinarily useful influence. Through the exchange program, American scholars and administrators have deepened their understanding of the problems with which the Department of State has to cope, so that the disagreements inevitable in an open society are based on solid fact and on understanding of the nature of the problems involved. This is a most significant bonus. It will help in particular in our dealings with China, because the field of Chinese studies has been much more deeply divided, and much more critical of our government's policy than the Russian and Eastern European field ever was.

The final consequence reflects the paradox mentioned earlier. Even though the universities have no political goals in mind and, in fact, have sought to keep their exchange programs isolated from politics, the political consequences of the academic exchange programs have been considerable. They have increased the understanding in this country of Russia; they have helped to reduce those tensions of the last 10 years which reflected sheer ignorance.

230

They have also had a very significant influence within the Soviet Union and Eastern Europe. Briefly, a first-rate American scholar at Leningrad State University, in organic chemistry or Chinese studies or Russian history of the nineteenth century, can profoundly affect the Soviet scholars and students with whom he works because he is that elite group's first window on the world, because they understand for the first time on a human basis what an American scholar is and, therefore, the qualities of the country from which he comes. Since Soviet society is a closed and hierarchical one, and since rumors and information of a personal kind flow in a different way than they do in this country, the impact of the American presence as it reverberates throughout the elite, is very significant indeed.

In summary, cultural relations between American universities and ideologically divided countries raise very serious problems. At the same time, they promise—and provide—magnificent benefits. American universities should become involved for many reasons. Similarly, our experience demonstrates that universities should be eternally vigilant if they wish to preserve their quality and their independence. Cultural exchange programs, even with suspicious and hostile countries, help our universities to perform their true functions effectively and in such a way as to contribute significantly towards reducing tensions among nations. After all, the exchange of scholars, of information, and of ideas places the conflict between ideologically divided countries on the field on which we are best able to compete and specifies the situation where peaceful competition or ideological coexistence can best be waged, to our advantage as well as to the advantage of those who live under Communist rule.

# PART FOUR

# ENGLISH UNIVERSITIES
## Problems and Prospects

### Lord Bowden

I should like to begin by making a few remarks about our English universities. Most of the difficulties which face them are similar to those which confront other universities all over the world, but I shall be especially concerned with those which seem to me to be peculiarly important to us in our small overcrowded island, and I shall discuss some of the problems in the new universities which were created in so many countries by expatriate Englishmen.

I shall speak of the interaction between universities all over the world, of the rise of a new clerisy, and of the extraordinary and apparently insoluble problems which have been posed to the civilized world, and to every university in it by that astonishing migration which has become known as the Brain Drain.

I shall show you, I hope, that many of our problems have their origins deep in the past, and I shall be unable to explain some of them without referring to the ancient universities which once dominated the intellectual life of Europe, whose medieval titles of Master, Doctor and Professor we are proud to bear today, whose structure, organization, examinations and administrative processes have been so jealously preserved throughout the centuries, but whose failures and follies and unsolved problems haunt us to this day.

### THE ENGLISH UNIVERSITIES—YESTERDAY, TODAY AND TOMORROW

Many of the problems of our English universities, like those of universities the world over, are due to unprecedentedly rapid changes in the whole of society and to the stresses caused by the rapid growth of the whole educational system. I shall speak only briefly of the growth of our universities, which, though it has seemed spectacular to us, has been much less dramatic than the growth of the universities of America. The student population of England may not have grown as fast as that of France, Germany and Italy, but I think that the buildings and all the other facilities of the expensive institutions have been developed at a most gratifying speed. This may explain why we have been so fortunate and had little serious trouble from our students. Many of them are uneasy and dissatisfied, but they have never rioted like the Germans, the French and the Dutch, the Japanese, the Italians, or the Americans. Both university staff and students are seeking a new role for themselves in our changing society.

Some English traditions have profoundly influenced university development in many other countries. John Harvard was once a member of my own Emmanuel College in Cambridge, but I shall discuss some of the less familiar problems of the new universities which have been established since the war in what used to be our Colonial Empire. Some of our traditions have been invaluable, others have been quite unimportant, but some, I have come to believe, have been disastrous. We see some of the results of our own mistakes more clearly under the harsh light of the tropics than ever we saw them at home in the gloom of the English Midlands. May I try to set the stage?

Oxford and Cambridge are both ancient universities whose traditions date back to the Middle Ages. They have much in common with the other ancient foundations of Europe and dominated our whole educational system for hundreds of years. They still enjoy enormous social and intellectual prestige, although they were intellectual backwaters, enclaves of the Church of England and playgrounds for the upper classes throughout the whole of the nineteenth century when England became the wealthiest and most influential country in the world.

The Industrial Revolution was probably the most important event in our history. It was made by self-taught men, most of whom never went near a university, and who owed nothing to academic tradition. University dons, steeped in port and prejudice, regarded manufacture and trade as unworthy and degrading. Oxford in particular prided itself in its isolation from the forces which were revolutionizing the world around it. Cardinal Newman eloquently urged the pre-eminent importance of a Christian Liberal Education, but he disliked original scholarship because Porson, who was the best classic of his generation, was never sober after lunch! When Gainsford was Dean of Christchurch he asserted in a university sermon: "The advantages of a classical education are two-fold. It allows us to look with contempt upon those who have not shared it, and it fits us for places of emolument, both in this world and in that which is to come."

One could laugh at such follies as the eccentricities of men long since forgotten, but they haunt us still. Many of the young men who went to Oxbridge became colonial administrators. They took these extraordinary ideas to the underdeveloped world, and all over the world today men seem to be trying to re-create an idealized version of Cardinal Newman's Oxford, and in the process they are, I think, doing great harm to the cause of education and to the progress of mankind.

The developing countries of Africa and India are changing more rapidly than ever before. Their leaders have unrivalled—unique—opportunities. The intellectual opportunities and the excitement which are to be found in a country which is transforming itself and becoming part of the modern world must challenge all the ablest men of their generation.

But do the universities of these countries accept their obligations and their opportunities to become involved and to help? I have the impression that they regard the whole world of industry and the machinery of government with detachment, suspicion and alarm—just as Oxford did a hundred years ago. I shall come back to this point later on.

Most of the men who created modern British industry were educated in ill-organized, deprived and poverty-stricken colleges which gave vocational training and a smattering of science to thousands of middle-class youths and poor boys.

The government's neglect of these institutions was one of the great tragedies of education in England. Colonial governments never understood them, so our ex-colonies are saddled with an idealized version of only half our educational system. No wonder some of them have been disappointed by the results.

Despite the indifference of Oxford and Cambridge, the other English universities which were founded in the nineteenth century were profoundly influenced by von Humboldt's reformed universities in Germany. The "civic universities," led by Manchester, introduced university research long before Curzon declared that "the amount of original work which has been done in Oxford is quite inconsiderable—it cannot possibly hope to emulate a university like Harvard." There was a time when Continental scholars said that Oxford could no longer claim to be a university at all. It was, so they said, "nothing more than an extravagant finishing school."

But England has never understood, or appreciated, or accepted, the ideals of the land grant colleges of America. I have always regarded the Morrill Act as the most important event in the history of Western education. It enunciated the idea that universities should study the problems of contemporary society and should teach all who cared to learn. Land grant colleges were derided by English academics—most of whom were devotees of the classics and totally ignorant of the world—and they described these new foundations as "places where men are taught to throw manure about and act as wet nurses to steam engines."

But the great American West was conquered in the laboratories of the land grant colleges and their graduates tamed a continent. And they did this when a few of our civic universities had begun with great trepidation to study engineering and chemistry, but when all the wealth, all the prestige and all the interest of Whitehall were devoted to the young gentlemen of Oxford and Cambridge who studied the classics before they went out to govern the Empire.

There were a few technical colleges in England which would have liked to follow the example of the land grant colleges—in fact, I believe that many of the ideas which inspired Morrill had originated in England. But the point I want to make is that no one can understand the difficulties of our own universities today unless he realizes how slowly, how reluctantly and how recently staff and students have accepted the enormous importance of universities, their ideas and their laboratories to the industry, the business and the administration of a great modern state.

I think it is tragic to watch over countries following our example. It is even more tragic to watch the devastation of the great American universities which has resulted, I think, from the perversion of Morrill's ideas. The interests of society have been identified with the interests of the Pentagon and university graduate schools have come to depend for their funds on the Army and the Navy, which, I believe, paid for more than three-quarters of the research budget of M.I.T. last year. It was bad enough 10 or 15 years ago, but the situation has been intolerable since the war began in Vietnam. Even the most splendid and impressive organisms have within themselves the seeds of their own decay.

But I must return to the academic scene in England. At the end of the last war, England had two ancient universities, still obsessed by the nineteenth-century traditions of liberal education; we had the University of London and we had some two dozen civic universities of various sizes.

Many dons had been profoundly impressed by their experience as administrators and applied scientists during the war and were in a mood for change and reform. There is no doubt at all that if Hitler had used German university scientists as effectively as we used ours during the war, his armies would have won in 1939 or 1940 and that this meeting—for one—could never have been staged, but that is another story.

It was clear that the demand for colonial officers was not going to last, and that Oxbridge would seek other careers for its graduates. The man in the street wanted his children to be educated better than he had been; most important of all it was clear that our industrial pre-eminence was gone forever. The parlous state of our industry and the clamant demand for more and better industrial scientists and engineers stung the government into action. Our universities had to expand and at the same time we had to develop the whole of what some humorist called our educational system.

This idea was accepted in about 1948 and 20 years later we are still trying to understand it and to cope with its implications.

The Butler Act of 1944 reformed the schools and made it easier for our bright children to be properly educated. It led to a rapid increase in the size of the sixth forms from which the universities recruit their undergraduates. In a very fundamental sense it was the Butler Act which made university expansion inevitable. Since the act was passed, the number of schoolchildren under 15 has increased by 29 per cent and the number over 15 has increased *by 250 per cent.* The act recognized two types of school—the old-fashioned grammar school for academically gifted children and the so-called technical or secondary modern schools for children whose talents led them to more practical and less theoretical studies. Butler hoped that these schools would all have parity of esteem, but they never achieved it and pupils from public (boarding) schools and grammar schools have almost monopolized the universities. The grammar schools reserved all their places for children who could pass the so-called "11-plus" examination. Children who failed to go to grammar school went to secondary modern schools and the middle classes found to their dismay that they could no longer buy places in the best local schools as they had done in the past. They sent more and more of their children to boarding schools and began to agitate against an examination which made it possible for the clever son of a plumber to go to a good school, whereas a rather dimmer middle-class boy had to go to the despised secondary modern school from which he could not hope to go to college.

It has always been possible for poor English boys to get scholarships to school and subsequently to university. My father was a poor man and my own education at grammar school and in Cambridge cost him nothing.

Middle-class parents have never accepted restraints on the careers of their children. They are well aware of the importance of university education and they urge their children to go to university if they can.

It has been most interesting to watch the campaign against the 11-plus exam which was led by frustrated middle-class parents. The exam was much more fair and equitable than the system which preceded it as a method of selecting able children, but it has been condemned for its unfairness—no single test can possibly select children with complete certainty. The test may work more often than not, but ostensibly it has been abolished because of its occasional failures and the whole idea of the selection of able children for special treatment seems to have gone forever.

In the future we are to have universal comprehensive education for all our children. The middle class, who have always been the principal and traditional beneficiaries of the state system of education, will be able to influence their young and drive them along, whereas many clever boys from working-class homes get very little encouragement from their parents, and they often fall behind in school by the time they are 16 or 17. They may be under pressure to earn a living because schoolboys get no maintenance allowance while they are in school.

Ever since 1959, children who go into the sixth form at school, pass their examinations and can get a place in a university are assured of one of the most generous grants in the world—which covers both tuition fees and the cost of maintenance. The rush to universities began. We were more fortunate than we realized when the state left universities to choose their own students and accept no more than they had room for.

Today the son of a middle-class parent has five times as good a chance of going to university as a boy of comparable ability from the working class, but because the working class is so big and includes so many bright boys, our universities have almost as many working-class boys as middle-class boys. In this respect at least, ours are the most democratic universities in Europe. But the system which sent bright poor children to college at the "expense" of worthy middle-class boys who were not very bright at the age of 11 may not last forever.

The British public can always deceive itself; the 11-plus exam was abolished in the name of equality of opportunity. The change may do a great deal to preserve the status of the middle classes!

I need not describe the reports from Barlow to Robbins which have discussed the problems of higher education. They have chronicled our failures and inspired our achievements. Barlow demanded that our universities produce more technologists—and the universities themselves insisted that, if schools of engineering are to grow, so must all the other faculties if the mysterious "balance" of the faculties was to be preserved. Robbins suggested that university places should be provided for all qualified students to read the subjects they like most, regardless of the prospects of newly fledged graduates in society.

For a generation we have been expanding our universities as never before. Nearly half of them have come into existence in the last 10 years—when I was born we had fewer universities in proportion to our population than any country in Europe except Turkey. We now have 45. Our university population doubled in 10 years and it is still growing. Our university buildings and equipment must be worth £800M or more.

But we never forgot that the American university system had doubled in size more quickly than ours did; that every year the Americans spend about as much on new buildings as all of ours are worth put together, and that every year the university population in America increases by the equivalent of the whole of our own student body.

The proportion of Negroes who go to college in America is higher than the proportion of Englishmen who go in England.

But it is not as simple or as bad as you might think from a bare recital of these statistics. We have only 45 universities—there are more than 2,000 in America which give degrees. They vary enormously in quality among themselves. In any list of the 20 best universities in the world, half would undoubtedly be American—and it is my belief that in a list of the 20 worst universities on the planet there would be several from the United States.

The universities of Great Britain are much more homogeneous in quality. The government gives grants for buildings and for staff which are designed to make it possible for each of them to compete with all the rest, and all examinations are moderated by external examiners whose task it is to make sure that the standard of a degree of one university is, as nearly as possible, the same as that of a degree from any other.

The spectrum of institutions in America is continuous from good to bad. In England the title of "University" and the privilege of granting degrees are granted by royal charter. We pretend that our universities are all equal, but we have a whole series of other institutions; some of them may be as good as universities, there are scores of small commercial colleges and technical schools, and of course we have thousands of wretched little night schools.

This extraordinary collection of institutions which educate our young people after they have left school has been given an apparent cohesion which it demonstrably lacks by describing it as the "binary system." All the institutions which are not chartered universities form the "public sector" of the system. They were expected to be "more responsive to the needs of the State," to quote a rather unfortunate phrase which the Secretary of State afterwards much regretted. He seems to have thought that university education was too expensive and that institutions in the public sector would be very much cheaper.

If they are cheaper it is because the facilities they offer to their students are much less attractive than those in the universities. They may have to be improved, but, be this as it may, we already have a flourishing public sector in our binary system. Many countries would describe some of these "inferior" institutions as universities, so I must talk about them. A few figures will help.

In 1957 three-quarters of our young people left school at the age of 16, but there were 103,000 students in our universities, 33,000 in colleges of education—all of whom expected to teach—and 13,000 taking advanced courses in other colleges of further education.

Last year there were: 200,000 students in universities—nearly twice as many after a decade of unprecedented growth; but there were 106,000 in colleges of education—considerably more than three times as many; and 71,000 in advanced F.E.—and this is an increase of $5\frac{1}{2}$ to 1.

To put the matter in another way, in 1957, 7 per cent of their age group were undergoing higher education, of whom 60 per cent were in universities. Last year, 14.3 per cent were undergoing higher education, but only 44 per cent of them were in universities.

No one foresaw this explosively rapid development of higher education outside the universities and we are still uncertain what will happen next. Five years ago it was decided that no new universities would be founded until 1975, but the pressure of demand has obliged the government to announce the establishment of a couple of dozen polytechnics which will rationalize and co-ordinate the work of existing colleges and establish some new ones. They teach such subjects as art, music, commerce and some branches of technology which are unfamiliar to universities. They will not be permitted to give degrees of their own but they will prepare students for degrees to be awarded by the newly established "Council for National Academic Awards." Three years after it was founded, the C.N.A.A. gave more degrees than any university in England except London.

It is going to become harder and harder to distinguish between new polytechnics and old universities and it is my own belief that we might as well admit that having established 20 universities in the last decade, we are in process of founding as many more in the next five years. I may remark that this interpretation of events would be passionately rejected by most universities, and by the Department of Education and Science, and equally passionately welcomed by most of the new polytechnics. I shall be fascinated to watch the unfolding drama.

## THE COST OF EDUCATION

And now I must refer to the mounting cost of education which so worries the Chancellor of the Exchequer in London. He has the same problem, poor man, as all the finance ministers in the world!

The total cost of British schools and universities of all kinds rose from £686M in 1957 (when for the first time in our history it exceeded our national expenditure on beer) to more than £2,000M last year (when for the first time it exceeded the total cost of all types of liquor and approximated to the cost of defense).

In 1957 education cost 3.5 per cent of the gross national product. It is nearly 6 per cent of a much bigger gross national product today. Our economic growth has fluctuated between 3 per cent and 6 per cent per annum, whereas the cost of education has risen at an average of 10 per cent throughout the decade.

Ten years ago our universities cost less than £40M—or about 6 per cent of the total bill for education. (This was less than the egg subsidy.) This year they cost more than £200M—which is 10 per cent of the much bigger education budget. The cost of university education in Great Britain has risen at an average 17 per cent per annum. The cost of primary and secondary education is about nine times as great as the cost of the universities, and it is increasing much faster in absolute terms.

Every government in the world would like to know for how much longer the cost of education can increase so much faster than the value of the G.N.P. which pays for it. If the world stopped spending quite so much on education, would the wealth of the world cease to grow?

We all seem to believe that education is a prerequisite to economic growth and most of the plans of underdeveloped countries have been based on that assumption, which we in the West encourage them to make. Some of them spend 15 per cent or even 20 per cent of the G.N.P. on education, and they do so in the hope that it will help them to become wealthy. In fact, it has become disconcertingly clear that there is very little correlation between the cost of education and the rate of industrial growth. There is certainly no correlation between the class of the degrees my contemporaries got in Cambridge and the size of the car they drive today!

Lancashire was the workshop of the world at a time when most of its workmen signed their marriage lines with a cross, and England was the wealthiest country in the world when it was the most illiterate in Europe. Perhaps, after all, we are mistaking cause and effect. Perhaps the wealthy countries expand their educational systems when they can afford them and because of public demand. I wish we could identify the real motives which drive countries to expand their universities.

How much expansion came from an overoptimistic estimate of the economic return on education, how much from a desire for social progress, and the opportunity that education offers to smash the barriers of class and caste? How many universities were built as prestige symbols? How much of the craving for education (and I shall refer to this again) is due to a desire for mobility, and the pressure to join the modern equivalent of the medieval Church?

Predictions about future changes and the future growth of universities—and of the rest of the educational system—are notoriously unreliable. We can be sure that the whole machine will continue to grow, but how far, how fast and for how long? If the G.N.P. obstinately refuses to grow more than a third as fast as the growth of educational expenditure, we shall have to decide —and before very long—what fraction of our G.N.P. we can really afford to devote to education in all its forms. If the present trends which have been established for several decades continue until 1980, which will soon be here —education in England will be costing more than the present budget of education and defense put together, and between 8 per cent and 10 per cent of our estimated G.N.P. Could we afford it? Should we afford it? If we do will it be to validate that gloomy view that "more will mean worse"?

## THE PROBLEMS OF UNCONTROLLED AND CONTINUOUS GROWTH

I believe that many of the strains under which our economy labors are due to the phenomena of long continued exponential growth and I would like to mention some other examples of this phenomenon. Some may be familiar to you—others may surprise you.

The number of scientists in the world seems to have grown very steadily ever since the time of Newton. It has doubled every 10 years or so for more than 200 years. Of all the scientists who ever lived, three-quarters are alive today; and of all the science known to the world, three-quarters has been discovered in the last 30 years. But—and this is my point, until very recently the total number of scientists was quite small—we have more scientists in England today than we have clergy and Army officers combined. If this steady progress to which we have become accustomed for so long were to continue for another 60 years, every human being would be a scientist.

The number of scientific journals has grown faster than the number of scientists and the number of books in our libraries has increased exponentially for a couple of hundred years or more. In another couple of hundred years at this rate all our university buildings will be completely full of books!

The number of men in the electrical engineering industry has doubled every eight years since about 1860. If the process continues until the end of this century, every employed Englishman will be an electrical engineer and one can prove equally clearly that he will be a chemist, and I suspect he will be stuck in a traffic jam.

The cost of science has grown even faster than the number of scientists. It has been doubling every six or seven years since the beginning of this century. The budget for R. and D. in the U.S.A. today is more than the whole federal budget that Roosevelt had at the time of Pearl Harbor. If it were to go on increasing at 16 per cent compound interest until the end of the century, then the whole G.N.P. would be spent in this way! And yet, only last month I read that a cut in the rate at which their budget is increasing had been bitterly opposed by several American scientists.

My point is that many trades and professions and industries which have grown independently and exponentially for decades and even for centuries will come inevitably and fatally into competition and conflict with each other within the next few years, unless they change their habits very soon.

Exponential growth in nature—among for example the aphids on a rose bush, is only the first part of that familiar zigmoid curve of growth.

Many of our troubles both nationally and internationally come from our failure to realize that very many of our institutions (and our industries) are reaching a point on the growth curve where growth slows down and begins to flatten off.

It is ironical and tragic that our generation was the first to have analyzed these growth patterns, and the first to realize just how much the modern world owes to education and the sciences, yet we shall have to slow down and stop the growth of the very institutions which have developed regularly for several generations—and made us what we are.

Our rising expectations—which are based on the experience of many years of steady exponential growth—are already in conflict with more slowly rising possibilities, and very soon we have to expect a disparity between expectation and achievement which may destroy us.

We see these trends in America, we see them in Africa and India and we see them at home in England.

All exponential growth must stop sooner or later and it has begun to be clear that in England, at any rate, the scientific world will stop growing much sooner than most people realize. The expansion of our universities after the war began because of the demand for qualified scientists and engineers for industry. For many years the universities created two places for science-based students for every one place for the arts. For 15 years students came from the schools to fill the new places in our universities, but three years ago it began to be obvious that there was a swing away from science throughout the whole educational system.

The proportion of sixth-form pupils in English schools who study science has fallen from 42 per cent (in 1962) to 31 per cent in 1967. Despite the growth in our sixth forms the numbers in our science sixths has begun to decline and it shows signs of falling dramatically before 1972.

I think that our educational system, like most others, is fundamentally unstable. As soon as a subject becomes really important in the outside world, and industry bids for the qualified men who are teaching it, they leave both schools and universities to earn more money. The subject is no longer taught properly in the schools and the quality of university staff declines. Students are no longer willing to learn and the situation gets rapidly worse. There has been a shortage of good science masters in English schools for years. As soon as computers became important and industry needed mathematicians to use them, potential teachers of mathematics left the schools. Today more than half of all maths teaching in English secondary schools is in the hands of teachers who have no formal qualifications as mathematicians. The National Association of Teachers of Mathematics thinks that the decline may have got out of control and passed the point of no return. They say that it is quite possible that effective teaching of mathematics may stop in most English schools within a generation. And this at a time when the importance of numeracy is greater than it has ever been.

A cynic might assert that no really useful subject will be properly taught, and that only those subjects which are known to be absolutely useless will be sure of a place in our schools in years to come! If this is so, and the idea does contain a grain of truth, it may explain why so many students are so restless and complain that their university courses lack relevance.

They feel, as a scholar remarked a hundred years ago, that "intelligent persons could not fail to observe that the subjects to which their attention was directed (in Cambridge) had no relation to any profession or employment whatever, and that the discussions connected with them had no analogy to those trains of thinking that prevailed in the ordinary intercourse of society."

There are still dons who accept this very remarkable tradition with equanimity, if not with enthusiasm. I still remember mathematicians who toasted "The Higher Mathematics—and may it never be of any use to anyone!"

## THE ODDITIES OF ENGLISH UNIVERSITIES

Some of the problems of English universities are unfamiliar in other countries. Our students take their first degree after three years in university. Our student/staff ratio which is about 9:1 is probably the best in the world. Our students get lavish grants which cover the whole cost of their education including both fees and living expenses. Our failure rates are relatively small and average between 10 or 20 per cent in different faculties. Nevertheless our students have had to specialize much more than those of other countries and the specialization begins in the schools. Pupils in the sixth forms of English schools have already learned a great deal of what in any other country in the world is regarded as first or second year university work. But they are able to do this only because they have abandoned so many subjects forever at the age of about 14. At this age, or thereabouts, they decide to specialize, let us say in classics or science or the arts, and they do so with no idea at all of the implications of their choice. Not enough of them want to read science and engineering. It is true to say that in England we allow the future of our schools and the future of our universities, the future of industry and the future of society itself to be determined by 14-year-old schoolboys, each of whom commits himself at this absurdly early age to an irrevocable decision which cuts him off forever from about half the careers he might prefer when he is 22. No other country in the world seems to be so foolish.

I believe that science and engineering have recently become unpopular in several other countries. For example, the number of postgraduate students of physics who want to do research in American universities dropped from 55 per cent of the total in 1967 to less than 44 per cent in 1968. Before long there may be a surplus of academic physicists in America and the growth of American science may have halted. What will this world-wide change in the ambitions of our students do to the industry of the world?

There is in fact no reason to believe that we are educating people who will be really suitable for society in future. University appointment boards help us to decide what to do, but they are as baffled as we are if they have to predict future needs. Students come to university for many reasons. They may be sent by their parents, their schoolmasters may influence them, they may like the idea of another three years of academic life at the taxpayers' expense. Nowadays some may come because they would like to take part in a riot while they are still young enough to enjoy it—or because they are in search of material for a definitive paper on "The Behavior of the University President Under Strain." The subjects they study have been determined for the very oddest reasons. But at the end of their course they expect that society will accept them and find something for them to do and allow them to make use of whatever it is they have learned.

If the number of vacancies matches the number of applicants, it can only be a coincidence—because at no stage in the entire operation did anyone plan it that way.

Already some arts graduates and social scientists find it hard to find jobs and they resent the failure of society to provide them with work which matches their training, their talents and their expectations, but although the supply of scientists may be drying up, the demand for them is growing as fast as ever.

Our students are worried about their future careers; but their problems are as nothing to those of students in some other countries and I believe that this is one of the most important causes of student unrest. Two years ago there were more than 900 graduates in archaeology in the Sorbonne. What are they doing now? Unemployed graduates are vocal and potentially dangerous and they can destroy a university or even a government!

I can no longer ignore another phenomenon which is due in part to the failure of life to match the hopes of the young, a phenomenon which is quite dramatically and disastrously affecting the universities of every country in the world—that enormous and unprecedented migration of scholars which has become known as the "brain drain."

### THE BRAIN DRAIN

Scholars and engineers have always wandered about the world in search of a better life. The development of Canada, Australia and the United States produced the most remarkable migration of which history has record. Millions of people crossed the ocean and their departure made it possible for Europe to maintain and improve the living standards of those who stayed behind. If the New World had never been discovered, the Old World would have faced catastrophe from overpopulation and starvation. This migration was both important and beneficial to everyone.

But the nature of migration and of migrants has changed dramatically in the last decade. At one time any able-bodied man could go wherever he could find a home. Today most countries will accept skilled, educated men, but very few want any more unskilled laborers. University graduates have become mobile, they move freely about the world, leaving their illiterate countrymen behind them. Since most of them seem to leave poor, underdeveloped countries in the hope of settling in wealthy, more highly developed societies, this very specialized migration has become known as the brain drain and its consequences are felt in every country in the world. It is not going too far to say that it is distorting the pattern of education all over the world and it may well be destroying forever the bright hopes of some of the underdeveloped countries.

There have been brain drains before and governments have attempted to stop them. Seven hundred years ago the city of Bologna and its university decided to make sure that their professors did not leave and set up rival schools in other cities. The rules were quite explicit. A younger teacher of no great reputation who left would be fined 200 ducats. A famous man more than 50 years old would be hanged if they caught him!

One of Arkwright's apprentices, named Samuel Slater, fled to America after memorizing the details of his master's inventions. He established the American textile industry in Rhode Island in 1790. Our people would have hanged him, for we guarded our industrial monopoly as jealously, as ferociously and as unsuccessfully as the Americans guarded the secrets of the atom bomb nearly 200 years later!

The migration of skilled men from East Germany to the Western world left the East in poverty and made the West wealthy. West German firms offered all kinds of inducements to the graduates of East Germany, until the Communists built that wall and shot everyone who tried to cross it. Since the migration stopped, East Germany has become prosperous—the wall has done what it was built to do.

The brain drain has been with us for centuries, but no one has ever been able to stop it by administrative policies which we can accept today. We do not want any more Berlin walls for example, but we do face a most serious problem.

In 1967 we lost nearly half our graduating class of engineers. We sent 198 Ph.D.'s to America in 1961 and over 400 in 1965 and the number has been rising ever since. Englishmen used to be able to rely on getting visas to admit them to the United States, but in 1968 America changed its immigration laws. The country will admit well-qualified men wherever they come from regardless of race, but they must all take their place in the queue. The new law may slow down the migration of Englishmen, but a bill is already before Congress to admit them freely again.

The Swiss have lost so many of their best engineers that they fear for the future of their universities. But the Frenchmen stay at home, for three very good reasons—*la langue, la cuisine et les femmes.*

It costs £20,000 to educate a Ph.D. and he may produce a quarter of a million pounds worth of ideas during his professional lifetime. Great Britain has probably been contributing as much to the development of American industry by sending too many of our skilled and highly educated men there, as our Ministry of Overseas Development is giving to all the backward countries put together.

But the brain drain is not a simple translation of our people to America, it is in fact an enormous migration of educated men from the poorer countries towards the wealthy countries. Europe and Canada are staging posts. For example, Canada received 7,800 qualified migrants in 13 years and lost 4,800 to America, leaving a net influx of 3,000, half of whom came from England. The new medical school in Dahomey has produced 70 doctors of whom 54 are practicing in metropolitan France—about 80 per cent have left. Ghana sends her medical men to Western Germany. More than 11,000 of the 41,000 doctors in American hospitals were foreign born—many came from Britain and others from South America and India. Two-thirds of all the interns in hospitals in the northwest of England came from India. There is a terrible shortage of qualified medical men in all developing countries, but we need them and make it worth their while to stay here. I was able to follow a class of 49 students who began to study electrical engineering in Buenos Aires. Forty failed, one was killed in a riot, four went home to their native countries, three emigrated to America and one came to Manchester and told me the story. That leaves an output of zero. How can any country afford to establish and maintain a university system if it produces no graduates to build up the new industries whose profits have already been mortgaged to pay for the universities?

No country can relate its needs for manpower to the number of its own graduates. Not any more. The rich countries get richer and poor countries poorer. Industrial demand is still growing exponentially in America, but the supply of native American graduates does not keep pace.

In an attempt to keep their mobile educated men at home, the poor countries have to pay them salaries which are similar to equivalent scales in America. But the average income of ordinary men depends on the gross national product. For example, a doctor in England earns three or four times as much as a skilled craftsman. In Ghana he will earn less than he would in England (and so he will be tempted to come here), but he earns 20 or 30 times as much as a Ghanian farmer who makes less than £100 a year by working on his little clearing in a steaming jungle.

The education which makes a graduate Ghanian doctor or an engineer so valuable was paid for by his government—that is to say by taxes collected from workingmen—and a week of a university course costs as much as the average taxpayer earns in a year.

But if the brain drain can cause such havoc in the poor countries from which the migrants come, what does it do to America, where they all hope to go? The migrants themselves may become wealthy, but what do they do for the betterment of mankind?

Three-quarters of the American research and development program is now in defense and space industries. These enormous giants are growing rapidly and inexorably. Whole cities and states depend upon them and would go bankrupt without them, but does Washington control them anymore? Was Eisenhower right to warn his countrymen about their potential for harm? They had, he said, a momentum of their own which is wholly independent of the needs of the community—and of the world. The defense and space budget this year is about $80,000M, which is more than the gross national product of Great Britain. The program depends entirely on scientists and engineers. That is why research and education in the United States have been distorted. Our universities and the Swiss universities and the Canadian universities and the universities of poor countries in Africa and Asia find themselves chained to the chariot wheels of the American juggernaut which put a man on the moon, and this machine, let us remind ourselves, was created after the Americans had already produced the nuclear equivalent of about 100 tons of dynamite for every living human being and had established a method of delivering it to any point on the face of the earth. If they build that ABM system, they may need half the engineers in England, but "that," as one of them said to me, "will be your problem."

The economy of the United States is in an extraordinary condition. The real needs of the population, by which I mean their food, their houses, their clothes, their motor cars and so on, can be met by the efforts of about half the working population, so the government must find work for the rest. It seems to me that in her defense and space programs America has created the biggest pork barrel of all time and the most extravagant, most sophisticated and most dangerous system of outdoor relief ever devised by a great nation in peacetime.

Has there been anything like it since the government of imperial Rome ruined itself—and the world around it—by spending 40 per cent of its revenue on the circus?

It is time for an observer to protest when he finds that fields in Africa, India and all over the world may remain uncultivated because of an attempt to put a dozen men on the moon and a few more on Mars.

The development of the world is being checked by the toll that America is levying on countries less wealthy than herself. How much longer can the rest of us allow our graduates to move about the world as they have for thousands of years? Will their migration justify that perplexing Biblical adage: "To him that hath shall be given and from him that hath not shall be taken even that which he hath," upon which Karl Marx based his whole political creed? He predicted that the rich must become richer while the poor become poorer in a capitalist society.

In every industrialized country the enormous increase in productivity, the pressure of organized labor and the social conscience of the electors have invalidated this theorem. Wealth in an industrial country does not depend on poverty in the same country; machines do the work which once was given to the laboring poor.

But the rich countries are becoming richer at the expense of the poor countries and they do so because educated men go to America, because America is spending so lavishly to combat the menace of the Communism which Marx inspired in Russia and China. This seems to me to be the supreme irony of history.

The only great countries whose graduates do not flock to America are China and Russia. Will they be the only countries which are safe from the thraldom of Marxism as it was originally expounded by the maestro himself?

It is an interesting possibility.

## PROBLEMS OF UNIVERSITIES IN UNDERDEVELOPED COUNTRIES

Some underdeveloped countries in Africa spend as much as 20 per cent of their G.N.P. on education because they want to become rich like us. Their universities have been among the most expensive in the world to build, although they are educating some of the poorest people in the world. But it has become disconcertingly clear that there is no correlation between the amount of money a country spends on education and the rate of its economic growth.

Despite their astonishing achievements and their many successes there is no doubt that some universities, especially those in India and Africa, produce graduates for whom there is no prospect of employment and whose expensive education will be almost useless once they have left the university. But the graduates believe that they have a right to a career which protects them from the more sordid details of life. They want to work in the civil service or they want to work in the university. They expect to be rich. They loathe the idea of teaching if it takes them away from the capital and a dozen of them told me last month that they think it is intolerable that men like themselves who had been so expensively educated at public expense should be expected to live in a village and help poor people to read or to improve their agricultural productivity. They know that most of the elders became cabinet ministers or permanent secretaries as soon as they graduated. There are no more jobs like these to be had, but if they cannot do as well they will be dissatisfied for the rest of their lives—and emigrate if they have half a chance.

How much should a poor country spend on education because it is a good thing which everyone expects? How fast can the system develop in a country in which most people still live in poverty and despair?

No Western government knows what to do with dissatisfied students, but both Russia and Maoist China insist that graduates must go into the villages and work among the poor. The followers of Mao in India would like to do the same and they are beginning to attract a great deal of support for the idea. The state of Kerala has the best schools in India; it has a higher proportion of graduates than any other state; it has more graduate unemployed and it was the first state to vote the Communists into office. Will other countries do the same?

I have come to believe that there is something fundamentally wrong with much African and Indian education. Some of its practices are startlingly like those which made medieval schoolmen so ineffective and so notorious. For example, the Professor of Building in Kumasi told me that when he took some of his students onto a building site and picked up some sand to rub it between his fingers and decide if it was free from clay, his students were profoundly shocked that an educated man like him should touch the ground; they seemed to think it would defile him! How can students who have graduated as builders be effective in such circumstances? How can students of agriculture help the villagers if they never go in the fields themselves?

Far too many Africans still suffer from diseases which are due primarily to the difficulty of separating men from their own excrement. Pure water and better sewers would probably do more to improve the health of Africa than all the hospitals in the world.

These poor people need better drains; too many of their university students have been taught Euripides in the original Greek by devoted expatriate Englishmen.

The educational machine has created a caste system which is based on education. A very few fortunate men are educated at enormous expense and become wealthy; the majority remain ignorant and poor. It is only too obvious that the process which selects the men who will become rich is arbitrary and essentially unfair. The poor must have noticed that neither dons nor graduates seem to care much for the rest of the population. We created these extraordinary universities and we did so, let us remember, in the hope and belief that we were giving to the poor, undeveloped countries the key that would unlock the spiritual and material treasures of the West. Our universities, we believed, were the best in the world. Africa must have some like them.

The Africans themselves wanted the same liberal education which produced the men who used to govern them. No one seems to have remembered Justin Smith Morrill and his "cow colleges," whose graduates tamed a continent. No one remembered that even in England when we were educating men to govern half the world, we were trying at the same time to educate others who could run our industry and make the country wealthy.

The universities of Africa and India will probably prove to be the most important and lasting of all the legacies which were bequeathed to these countries by Great Britain.

I think that we can be very proud of them, up to a point, but I think the ideas which they have taken from us may go far to destroy them if they are not very fortunate. We might have done very much better, but in fact we gave these people the universities which we ourselves had taught them to admire, and which they in turn demanded.

Our own universities have helped to preserve our own class structure. Why should we be surprised that the new universities are creating a similar class structure in Africa and India? Our universities neglected technology for centuries. Why should we expect the new foundations to do better, while they are still so young? British industry has never been helped very much by university dons, or by their research schools. Why should we expect new and impecunious universities to make a dramatic impact on the industry and agriculture of primitive societies?

Many politicians are beginning to have doubts, and to wonder how they can exploit the enormous investment they have made in buildings, in staff, and in grants, donations and scholarships. The masses are getting impatient; they want to improve their standard of living, and they want to do so soon. They want the universities to help and if need be they may insist that they do something practical to justify their enormous privileges and the apparently unlimited funds that have been entrusted to them, both by local taxpayers and by the world at large.

The situation may change quickly and dramatically and I do not think that the universities will be able to protect themselves indefinitely from the scrutiny of their fellow men merely by reminding them of academic freedom and university autonomy, for these most admirable principles are very abstract and very hard to understand. They perplex us sometimes even in England, despite our age-old traditions; I am afraid that they can mean very little to some African politicians.

### REFLECTIONS ON THE HISTORICAL BACKGROUND

And now, if I may, I would like to talk about the notorious problems of university unrest. Why have students become so dissatisfied? There must be scores of reasons, but I hope to convince you that some of the events of last year can only be understood by studying the universities of medieval Europe.

I am glad that we are meeting in Italy. The University of Bologna is the oldest in Europe and it is not far from here. The universities of Paris and Oxford, which are nearly as old, were always controlled by the masters, much as they are today, but for several hundred years Bologna, like the other ancient Italian universities, was organized and run by students who were wealthy enough to pay their professors and who used the power of the purse to discipline all the men whom they engaged to teach them. The universities which were run by students who dominated both their universities and the cities within which they lived, have been forgotten for hundreds of years; very few people realize that such extraordinary institutions can have ever existed. The students of ancient Bologna used to elect one of their number as rector. The whole university, students and professors alike, swore an oath of allegiance to him, much as barons and knights swore fealty to their new-crowned king. This young man took precedence over everyone in Bologna, except the bishop, and after feasting with his friends, he rode forth to preside over the colorful tumultuous pageantry of a great medieval city—and become its chief magistrate. Those must have been the days! And Bologna was the place!

The system disappeared from Italy 400 years ago, but not before it had gone from Italy to Spain, and from Spain to the University of Lima in Peru, which is 100 years older than Harvard. University students have always had power in South America and they have always played an important part in the administration of their universities. When I was a young man, everyone thought that the masters had won and defeated the students forever, but in the last few years the traditional system of ancient Bologna has risen like a phoenix all over the world.

The really serious trouble began in California after exiles from the Argentine brought these forgotten ideas to North America. Two very different systems of government which existed in the two oldest universities in Europe and which caused endless conflict all over Europe in the Middle Ages are causing the same old rows all over again!

The London School of Economics was disrupted last year by students who wanted to run the school, just as the students had always done in medieval Italy. They were arguing about the very same subjects, and behaving in the same way as the students who almost wrecked the University of Avignon 600 years ago when Italians who went there with the schismatic Popes wanted to introduce the Italian system of student government into a French institution which was being run by the masters. The Popes fulminated against students who wanted to elect their own rector for a hundred years or more.

The more I think of it, the more I come to realize that it is the traditions of the medieval universities and the problems which they left unsolved which are making life unendurable for so many students and dons today. Some educational traditions have been marvelously tenacious. Universities were as much a medieval creation as representative government or trial by jury. Their curricula have long since been forgotten, but their academic titles, their organization and some of their problems live on.

The ancient universities and their scholars completely dominated the intellectual life of society. No other academic institutions of which we have record have been so influential. The three pillars upon which medieval society rested were the empire, the Catholic church and the universities. Ours will never do any better than that. Universities were very important, but they had their faults, and they have never lacked critics.

The schoolmen were fascinated by words, by their meanings and by their ambiguities. The controversy between nominalism and realism went on for years. What is the meaning of reality? Is a table real, or is it merely an idea in the mind of God? What do we mean by the Real Presence at the Eucharist? Arguments such as these were taken over by noblemen and princes and caused some of the longest and bloodiest wars in history. In fact, they almost ruined the civilization of half the countries of Europe and destroyed the hegemony of the Catholic Church.

The labor of the medieval schoolmen, those acutely intelligent, dedicated men, who dominated the universities for centuries, produced what Mr. Wells once described as the biggest intellectual dunghill in history. They discredited themselves and their universities. In the end the world was *bored* with them, and impatient with their arrogance.

Ordinary men began to study the world in which we live and the skills of the craftsmen whose labor made it habitable. The schoolmen despised them, but it was the craftsmen and scientists who created our modern world—the world in which the universities are growing so fast.

I sometimes wonder anxiously if history may be repeating itself and some universities in America, in Europe or even in Africa, may be reviving some of the more unsavory features of medieval scholasticism. Some of the signs are there to read.

The medieval schoolmen wandered all over their world. They owed their primary allegiance to the church and to their scholarly disciplines; the fortunes of individual universities were much less important to them. They were indifferent to facts—the facts of nature, the facts of history and the facts of life. They put their books in the place of things. They tried to decide how many angels could dance on the point of a needle by purely abstract reasoning. They trained pure intellect and encouraged habits of heroic industry, but they left uncultivated both imagination and the sense of beauty. They taught men to think rather than to enjoy their lives. Was it in Madrid, or in Berkeley, or in Manchester, that the students were complaining of the very same things last month?

Throughout the Middle Ages students were much more anxious to learn than teachers were to teach. Students complained about the incompetence of their teachers. The doctors and professors tried to avoid teaching; they drew their salaries, but they left the teaching to half-trained bachelors of arts. I am afraid that some professors today are just as bad.

A hundred years ago the classical education which dominated all the universities of the world at the time had become as arid and as remote from fruitful contact with realities as the education of the Middle Ages. The whole history of education is a melancholy record of misdirected energy, stupid routine and narrow one-sidedness. It seems to be only at rare moments in the history of the human mind that an enthusiasm for knowledge stirs the dull waters of the intellectual commonplace. What was a revelation to one generation becomes an unintelligible routine to the next. But the case for a university education, even of the worst and most stultifying kind, has always rested on the bland assertion, so frequently made and so hard to verify, that an educated man usually shows his superiority even in the most severely practical affairs of life.

For hundreds of years kings and princes found their statesmen and men of business in the universities. The rapid growth of the universities throughout the Middle Ages was due to the demand for educated lawyers and administrators. Their schools were as professional as any of ours and their students demanded that they should be. It was Talleyrand who asserted that theologians had always made the best diplomats. There never has been a time when a majority of young men were prepared to go to university unless they expected to better themselves. No wonder so many are dissatisfied today.

Rashdall has told us that it was in the student universities of Italy that professors were most competent and their duties were most effectively discharged. Their students would not pay for bad teaching and they fined a professor who was late for his lecture, or whose class dropped below four pupils because of his inadequate teaching. Students in ancient Bologna gave a professor a day off to get married, but he had to be in front of his class next day—he could not take time off for a honeymoon! The most hard-pressed professor today has never been quite so harshly treated as they all were in ancient Bologna, when it was the most famous law school in Europe.

I think it is worth reminding ourselves even today that throughout the whole of the Middle Ages students wore the tonsure; they were in minor clerical orders, they claimed to be immune to the due processes of the civil law and they demanded to be judged and sentenced by ecclesiastical courts.

Saint Thomas à Becket was murdered because he refused to allow the meanest clerics to be sentenced by the civil courts, even after they had been found guilty by ecclesiastics. The most famous of all English martyrs died to affirm the right of all the clergy to be immune to civil law.

Students rioted and they murdered one another as well as the unfortunate laymen in whose cities they lived, and they did so with impunity. There is record, for example, of a student in Oxford who raped a local girl and murdered her father when he tried to defend her. He was heard before the magistrates, found guilty and sentenced to be hanged, but because he wore the tonsure the Chancellor of the University removed him from jail and tried him in his own court. There was no doubt of his guilt, but because he was a cleric he was sentenced to say half a dozen penitential psalms and as a final and ultimate punishment he was sent down from Oxford to Cambridge. No wonder the townsfolk hated the students!

Furthermore, throughout the whole of the Middle Ages the campus of a university had the same privileges as those of many ecclesiastical buildings. They were places of sanctuary into which the civil authorities could not go and in which a felon could be free from his pursuers.

These traditions have been unknown to the law for many a long year, but students all over the world today wear their hair long to distinguish themselves from their contemporaries. They claim to be immune to the law and they insist that the university is still a place of sanctuary. The riots in Paris in 1968 only got out of hand after the police had invaded the courtyard of the Sorbonne. Students and professors stood side by side on the barricades to repel them just as their predecessors had done on the very same spot hundreds of years ago.

My own students, all of whom are scientists and technologists, are convinced that they are allowed privileges which are unknown to the law and denied to ordinary men. They are certain that their university campus is a place apart and that the police have no place there. They are sure of these things, but they are nonplussed if I suggest that such rights were abolished by King Henry VIII when he dissolved the monasteries and destroyed the dominant church.

## CONCLUSION

Universities have always been in trouble. They have had to withstand the attacks of emperors and kings, popes, bishops, knights, mayors, magistrates and outraged citizens, and they have done so successfully for hundreds of years. They have been able to adapt themselves to the changing world, and they have shown themselves to be the toughest and most durable of all the institutions which have come down to us from the Middle Ages and upon which our society depends so much.

Their intellectual achievements have shaped our civilization, and some controversies which they initiated have provoked men to fight the most devastating wars in history. There were times when the universities exercised enormous power, and there have been times when the world was content to ignore them.

Some universities were dominated by their students for hundreds of years, but most of them have always been ruled by their staff. I think it is true to say that the students ill-used and maltreated the staff—when they had the power, much worse than staff have ever treated their students, but this may be a matter of opinion.

Universities have been centers of pure scholarship, they have been centers of political unrest. Staff and students have fomented dissent, they have rioted and pillaged; they have sunk into apathy and sloth, and sometimes the universities themselves have degenerated into exclusive and expensive clubs for the scions of the aristocracy. It is astonishing that throughout all their history they have tenaciously preserved their traditional organization and their formal structure of staff and students, of matriculation and graduation.

They have usually closed their ranks and united to withstand the attacks of the outside world, but today they are riven by internal dissensions, and perplexed by their own successes and by their unprecedented growth.

Some campuses look like battlefields, or like a street in London after a blitz; some of them may soon be closed forever, but I think that the universities will surmount their troubles and survive. They have survived before, when one might have thought that they would be destroyed. Some universities have collapsed, and been eclipsed for a hundred years or more. The University of Prague incurred the wrath of the emperor who burned the rector, John Huss, at the stake to placate the Catholic Church. Prague did not recover for years and students who fled from it founded such famous universities as Heidelberg.

Students and police have been fighting and killing each other during the past few years, and we have been horror-struck to read of it, but we should remember that hundreds, and even thousands of students and laymen killed each other during the Middle Ages within a mile of St. Mary's Church in Oxford. More, so Rashdall tells us, than perished on many an English battlefield. The situation in Tokyo is nothing like that—yet.

The fact is that the civilized world cannot survive without the universities and come what may, it will preserve them. I feel a certain sober optimism, in spite of everything.

# THE GOVERNMENT AND POLITICS
# OF A DEVELOPING UNIVERSITY
## A Canadian Experience

Douglas V. Verney

In Canada, more\* perhaps than in any other country, the 1960's have seen such a quantitative change in higher education that it must be judged a qualitative change as well.[1] A significant number of new universities, including my own York University, Toronto, have come into being, and most recently a system of community colleges has been created to cope with the large number of students who wish to proceed beyond high school but who are unable to obtain university places.[2] In my own province of Ontario the number of stu-

---

\* I am indebted to Mrs. Iris Mason, Librarian, Department of University Affairs, Province of Ontario for her help in preparing the footnote material.

[1] The Dominion Bureau of Statistics, Ottawa (DBS) produces statistics on Canadian universities in *Canada Yearbook* (annual). Its Education Division publishes *Survey of Libraries* (annual) and *University Student Expenditure and Income in Canada* (occasional). Its Higher Education Section publishes *Canadian Universities, Income and Expenditure* (annual), *Fall Enrollment in Universities and Colleges* (annual), and *Salaries and Qualifications of Teachers in Universities and Colleges* (annual).

The Department of External Affairs, Ottawa, publishes *Survey of Higher Education;* notes for the guidance of students considering university study in Canada (annual).

The Association of Universities and Colleges of Canada (A.U.C.C.) publishes *University Affairs* six times a year and the *Proceedings* of its annual meetings. The A.U.C.C. was established by act of parliament in 1965. It succeeded the National Conference of Canadian Universities (N.C.C.U.), the executive agency of which had been the Canadian Universities Foundation (C.U.F.).

The Canadian Association of University Teachers (C.A.U.T.) publishes the *C.A.U.T. Bulletin* quarterly.

Two recent commercial ventures are *Canadian University* (Toronto: Maclean-Hunter, 1966-), monthly, and *Canadian News Facts* (Toronto: Marprep, 1967-), twice monthly.

[2] See for example the reports of the Committee of Presidents of Universities of Ontario (Toronto: University of Toronto Press) : *Post-Secondary Education in Ontario, 1962-1970* (1962), *The Structure of Post-Secondary Education in Ontario, Supplementary Report No. 1* (1963), *The City College* (1965), *From the Sixties to the Seventies: An Appraisal of Higher Education in Ontario* (1966), *System Emerging, First Annual Review, 1966-67* (1967), *Collective Autonomy, Second Annual Review, 1967-68* (1968).

dents attending university has doubled in the past four years. Five years from now it will have doubled again.

I am at a developing university. In political science a distinction is often drawn between Western democracies, Communist systems, and developing areas, and it is assumed that the developing areas are different in kind. Books are written about the government and politics of these countries.[3] But at the time when many of my American colleagues were studying developing areas, I decided to have firsthand experience of such a situation by becoming part of a developing university, or as we call ourselves in Canada, "emerging universities."

My conclusion has been that there is no fundamental difference between an old and a new university. We are all legatees of the experience of older institutions.[4] I am even inclined to doubt whether from a strictly scholarly point of view the developing countries are different from developed countries in any significant *political* sense.

Of course in our propaganda those of us in new universities like to stress our unique position. In this way we obtain extra government grants because of our special emerging status.[5] Perhaps the term "developing area" has been accepted by countries because they too want to be in a position to accept largesse. But it still puzzles me that scholars should be prepared to adopt classifications in their discipline which may not be based primarily on scholarly considerations. Is this an example of the corruption of the university about which students complain?

In a sense the experience of a new university is the reverse of Plato's investigation into the nature of man.[6] If in the *Republic* Plato sees the state as man writ large, a new university enables us to see the university writ small. One gains an insight into the workings of an institution, and though in time the organism grows (it is an organism not a machine), and though the locus of decision making may be harder to discern, one remains vividly aware of how a university works and more important of how it should work.

I want to make four main points. First, I must say something about Canada's extraordinary university expansion. In many ways it resembles your own

---

[3] The standard work is Gabriel A. Almond and James S. Coleman, *The Politics of Developing Areas* (Princeton, 1960).

[4] All professors at new universities are graduates of older institutions. Presumably all politicians and civil servants in new countries have been educated under colonial regimes.

[5] For Ontario see *Report of the Minister of University Affairs 1967* and *Report of the Committee on University Affairs 1967*. These are the first reports. They list no publisher or date.

[6] For York University see Murray G. Ross, *The New University* (Toronto, 1961) and *New Universities in the Modern World* (London, 1966). Dr. Ross was president of York University.

earlier developments, but the present rate of growth may be even higher than anything you have experienced, because it started so much later—around 1960.[7] Secondly, I wish to discuss the problems of a new university and to suggest that new universities as such seem to follow no common pattern. If we take the two most spectacular Canadian developments—Simon Fraser University atop a mountain outside Vancouver, British Columbia, and York University on the northern fringes of metropolitan Toronto, a rapidly expanding city of between two and three million—we find they have followed different paths.

Thirdly, although Canada has no Vietnam and no ghettoes, and though its universities have no ROTC, Canadian universities new and old are meeting many of the problems faced by American universities. We are heirs of the great universities of Europe and the United States. And increasingly we find ourselves heirs of Cromwell, Jefferson, Robespierre, Lenin, Mao, Castro, and above all of Mario Savio and his friends at Berkeley in 1964.[8] Today, political ideologies are important not only as the embodiment of ideas which a university should impart as part of mankind's intellectual tradition but as a challenge to the very nature of the university as we have known it for a hundred years.[9] As early as 1966 my university president held a conference to discuss ways in which York could avoid becoming another Berkeley and also in

---

[7] See Edward F. Sheffield, *University Development: The Past Five Years and the Next Ten* (Ottawa, 1961). Also George F. G. Stanley and Guy Sylvestre (eds.), *Canadian Universities Today* (Toronto, 1961) and *Enrollment in Schools and Universities, 1951-52 to 1975-76* (Ottawa, 1967). The rate of Canadian university growth is evident from the following approximate estimates compiled by George Michie, formerly Research Officer, Department of University Affairs, Province of Ontario:

| Year | Graduate Students | Total Regular University Students |
|---|---|---|
| 1955 | 5,000 | 74,000 |
| 1965 | 18,400 | 195,000 |
| 1975 | 43,000 | 460,000 |

[8] John R. Seeley, "Quo Warranto: The 'Berkeley Issue' " and "The Berkeley Issue in Time and Place," in Howard Adelman and Dennis Lee, *The University Game* (Toronto, 1968).

See also Richard W. Burkhart: "Mario Savio's call to action and the founding of the U.G.E.Q. [Quebec Union of Students] were independent events but less than two months apart. The Twenty-ninth Canadian Union of Students (1965) Congress adopted an activist semisyndicalist stance." "The Emerging Students' Society," Tripartite Commission on the Nature of the University [McGill] Vol. 1, April 1968. Position paper No. 9.

[9] D. C. Williams, "The Nature of the Contemporary University," *Proceedings,* A.U.C.C. 1968, p. 104.

order to discuss a report entitled *University Government in Canada*.[10] Yet oddly enough, despite our open-mindedness and inclusion of students on every body except the board of governors, and of faculty even on the board, we seem in some ways to be following in the same direction as Berkeley. We do, of course, have certain distinctive Canadian characteristics such as a Scottish respect for learning and a latent anti-Americanism, though the latter is much milder than any found elsewhere.[11] But some Canadians see a threat to national cultural survival in the appointment of so many Americans to our faculties in the last two or three years. They fear that the United States may lose Vietnam, but gain Canada.[12]

Fourthly, having described our expansion, compared two new universities, and suggested that universities everywhere are the legatees of the American Revolution started at Berkeley, I would like to meditate on some of the tasks we face. I think that while we may feel powerless to control the current of events we must think in terms of ourselves as responsible individuals: It is we as individuals who make decisions, not faceless institutions. And I think we should regard the challenge less in terms of crises than as what the Chinese call "interesting times."

It seems in Canada that just as university professors and administrators came to believe that power and prestige had at last passed to them as *the* factor in promoting economic growth, power was about to slip away—to governments and taxpayers on the one hand and to students on the other.[13] Are we perhaps at the start of a secular Reformation, with professors going the way of the

---

[10] Sir James Duff and Robert O. Berdahl, *University Government in Canada*. Report of a Commission sponsored by the Canadian Association of University Teachers and the Association of Universities and Colleges of Canada (Toronto, 1966). See also *Governments and the University*, the Frank Gerstein Lectures, York University, 1966 (Toronto, 1966). A study of the relations between universities and governments has been sponsored by the Canadian Association of University Teachers, the Association of Universities and Colleges of Canada, the Canadian Union of Students and L'Union Générale des Etudiants du Québec and financed by the Ford Foundation. A.U.C.C., *Proceedings*, 1968, p. 65.

[11] "Living next to you is in some ways like sleeping with an elephant. No matter how friendly or even-tempered is the beast, if I can call it that, one is affected by every twitch and grunt." Prime Minister Pierre Trudeau, National Press Club, Washington, D.C. March 25, 1969.

[12] Among the critiques note Al Purdy (ed.), *The New Romans: Candid Canadian Opinions of the U.S.* (Edmonton, Alberta), and The University League for Social Reform's *The Americanization of Canada* (forthcoming).

[13] "This Report has been sponsored by *the entire university community* in Canada" (my italics), Claude Bissell, President of the University of Toronto in *University Government in Canada*, Foreword, p. v. The sponsors of the study (commissioned in 1962) did not include the federal or provincial governments, board of governors, or students.

monks? Who would have predicted in the reign of Henry VII when England was settling down as a nation that so many beautiful English abbeys would soon be destroyed? Who knows or cares what happened to the monks? Or are we at the start of a new form of world-wide revolution, different from anything previous, whether 1917, 1789, 1776 or 1642? Or should we even consider the possibility that this is the end of a particular civilization? (Is it any wonder that so many good students in Canada are studying history these days?) Again I have to remember that the English people not only allowed the monasteries to be destroyed in the sixteenth century but from about 400 A.D. to the late nineteenth century allowed themselves to be deprived of the hot baths and central heating introduced by the Romans.[14] Who is to say that our civilization, any more than Hitler's *Reich,* is to last for a thousand years? May not a new and uncivilized generation simply be uninterested in the technological revolution, in the computers which so many people have allowed themselves to think symbolize our advanced civilization?[15]

I

In our country the university population explosion is due not only to a high birth rate after 1945 but also to the large-scale immigration of skilled and professional people—only a third of my colleagues in my department were born in Canada—and above all to the transformation of the universities from European-style elite institutions to American-style instruments of mass higher education. York University is an indication of what I mean by qualitative change. Founded in 1960 the university moved in 1961 from its original temporary quarters on the campus of the University of Toronto. It transferred to a pleasant suburb in northeast Toronto in a setting of 30 acres of beautiful parkland surrounding Glendon Hall. Another 70 acres in the valley below provided plenty of space for sports activities. Until 1965 Glendon College, as it is now called, *was* York University. In 1965, 500 acres of steppe, or what seemed like steppe in the winter, on the northern boundaries of metropolitan Toronto was ploughed up to form the main campus of the *real* York University, a university which is expected to have 9,000 full-time students by 1970 and 20,000 by 1980. Glendon College remains an integral part of the university with its 1,200 bilingual (French and English) students; but it bears very little resemblance to its huge offspring.

---

14 Winston S. Churchill, *A History of the English-Speaking Peoples,* Vol. 1 (London, 1956), p. 35.
15 Note the connection between culture and technology assumed by Lucien Pye in *Aspects of Political Development* (Boston, 1966) and *Communications and Political Development* (Princeton, 1963).

I should like to give you an introductory glimpse of Canadian higher education by a sketch of the Canadian scene. The Canada that most people abroad know is the Canada of comparatively old and distinguished universities; of Dalhousie in Halifax, Nova Scotia, and several small colleges in the Maritime provinces; of Laval in Quebec City, the oldest French Canadian university and the oldest foundation in Canada, dating from the seventeenth century; of McGill in Montreal, that contemporary symbol of anglophone predominance in the economic life of the province of Quebec; of Queen's in Kingston, Ontario, with a tradition of public service that befits a Presbyterian foundation only 100 miles from Ottawa; and what is probably the largest and most distinguished university in Canada, the University of Toronto.[16] There are in Ontario other important institutions such as McMaster and the University of Western Ontario. West of Ontario there are the newer provincial universities of the three prairie provinces, Manitoba, Saskatchewan, and Alberta. Finally beyond the Rockies there is the University of British Columbia. In some ways the westward pattern of development has followed the American. By contrast with the small denominational colleges found in the East there are the large provincial universities of the West. But only a third of Canada's people live in the eight provinces east and west of Quebec and Ontario. Nearly a third live in Quebec where an educational revolution has taken place.[17] Higher education used to be Catholic and rural. Today it is increasingly secular and urban. The University of Montreal is one of the largest in Canada and there is now to be a University of Quebec.

But over a third of all Canadians live in the central province of Ontario, the heart of Canada and the richest of all the provinces. It is here that some of the most interesting changes are taking place. The pattern has not been either small colleges or large provincial universities with branches in smaller centers. Instead there are 14 separate institutions (though the Spinks Commission in 1966 recommended a University of Ontario, at least for graduate work.)[18] Since the 1950's Ontario's universities have expanded enormously. Not surprisingly many an enterprising American publisher regards this market for his

---

[16] For Canadian development see Robin S. Harris (ed.), *Changing Patterns of Higher Education in Canada* (Toronto, 1966), and Edward F. Sheffield, "Post-Secondary Education in Canada" in *Universities and Colleges of Canada 1969* (Ottawa, 1969), pp. 15-17. There is a critical review of reports on Canadian research resources in Robert B. Downs, *Resources of Canadian Academic and Research Libraries* (Ottawa, 1967), pp. 11-20. For Ontario developments see *The Structure of Post-Secondary Education in Ontario.*

[17] For Quebec see *Royal Commission of Inquiry on Education:* Report of the Commission (Quebec, Queen's Printer, 1963-1966), 5 vols. (The Parent Commission).

[18] *Report of the Commission to Study the Development of Graduate Programmes in Ontario Universities* (Toronto, 1966). (The Spinks Report.)

wares much as he used to regard California. Today our province supports not only the University of Toronto, Queen's and Western but Brock, Carleton, Guelph, Laurentian, Lakehead, McMaster, Ottawa, Trent, Waterloo, Windsor, and York. Four years ago there were about 40,000 students enrolled in these fourteen universities compared with 11,000 in five universities in 1939. This year there have been 80,000 in attendance (compared to 90,000 in California and the State University of New York, SUNY). Six years from now there will be nearly 150,000. In other words we are doubling enrollment every five or six years. Four years ago in Canada there were 195,000 students: six years from now there will be nearly 45,000 *graduate* students alone.[19]

Some new universities absorb old institutions. One of the more interesting developments has been the physical transfer of Osgoode Hall, the law society of Upper Canada with a distinguished old building in the heart of Toronto, to the York Campus where it will form the law faculty with 600 students. Some, like McMaster and Guelph, are old colleges that extend themselves to become provincially assisted universities. But several are brand new and are designed in part to bring university education within reach of all Ontario residents in this vast province. Some of these institutions will for a considerable time remain comparatively small, for example Trent, modelled after Oxford and sometimes called Balliol on Trent. Here the students wear their long green gowns in the streets of the city of Peterborough. Many of the new institutions are anxious to move into graduate work as befits a status-conscious university. It is doubtful whether all of them can offer graduate work in all fields, but the province has been reluctant to be too categorical since no one knows what new trends may emerge. After all it is not long since many people at the University of Toronto thought of York as a useful place for three-year general B.A. degree students, leaving four-year honors students for Toronto to handle.

By 1980 then, the downtown University of Toronto, already internationally distinguished in a number of fields besides English, in which Northrop Frye rubs shoulders with Marshall McLuhan, will have 20-30,000 students, up to a third of them in the graduate school. York in the north of the metropolis will have a similar total, probably one-sixth of them graduate. To the east and west of the city there will be two large colleges of the University of Toronto, Scarborough and Erindale each with 5,000, and in the northeast, more central than York or Scarborough or Erindale, there will, if all goes well, be Glendon College, York's bilingual liberal arts college with 1,200 students. An experi-

---

[19] See *Financing Higher Education in Canada,* being the Report of a Commission to the Association of Universities and Colleges of Canada (Toronto, 1965). (The Bladen Report); also *Graduate Studies in the University of Toronto,* Report of the President's Committee on the School of Graduate Studies, 1964-1965 (Toronto, 1965). (The Laskin Report.)

mental cooperative called Rochdale College, which seems to be run by the students themselves, has been set up with the blessing of the universities. They invite professors to join their seminars as resource persons.[20]

II

Now I turn to my second point, the problems of a new university. By comparing two new Canadian universities I intend to suggest that there has been no common pattern of development—so far at any rate.

Many people in the United States think of York University when they reflect on university expansion in Canada, and indeed we think they should. For our expansion is of such a magnitude that even Americans are occasionally surprised. When I was chairman, an expansion rate of 50 per cent (occasionally 100 per cent) of everything—staff, students and dollars—was the rule. But I think it is probably more illuminating to draw comparisons between York and the other new Canadian university which has aroused attention—Simon Fraser University outside Vancouver. What accounts for the extraordinary difference between two institutions which were expected to be so similar in development and have proved to be so different?

Simon Fraser is distinctive on at least five counts. First, it is said to be architecturally superb, set high up on a hilltop between the sea and the mountains and with a magnificent central plaza. Secondly, its chancellor was the redoubtable Gordon Shrum, academically able enough to be a professor of physics at the University of British Columbia and dean of its graduate school; with sufficient administrative expertise to be nominated chairman of B. C. Hydro by the premier of British Columbia; and with enough political pull to be able to determine the site of the university and the direction it was to take. Thirdly, Simon Fraser aimed high from the start, admitting 2,500 to its first class in 1965 compared with York's 76 in 1960. Fourthly, to demonstrate its freedom from hidebound tradition, the university tried to do without the usual academic departmental structure in the social sciences. Finally, such being the speed of its development, the suspicion with which people in western Canada have viewed the eastern universities, and its desire to do things new, Simon Fraser University appointed a high proportion of non-Canadians, especially Americans, to its staff. In 1968 it was reported that only 32 per cent of the faculty were Canadian.

York is different. Architecturally it has not, so far at least, achieved distinction. I say "so far" because the architects have worked inwards from the com-

[20] Dennis Lee, "Getting to Rochdale" in *The University Game*, pp. 69-94, and Alan Edmonds, "Today it's chaos, tomorrow . . . freedom?" *Maclean's*, Vol. 82, No. 5, May 1969, 68 ff.

paratively drab grey and red brick outskirts of the campus and are only now at the white central core. Here the Humanities and Social Science Building will be joined by a large plaza to the main library: the effect we are assured will be outstanding. Some people, however, think that the existence of a large plaza may, as at Simon Fraser, encourage demonstrations.

Our original plan called for four clusters of four colleges each. These sixteen colleges were intended to be the home of 16,000 students and to provide faculty offices and lecture halls. Up to a quarter of the students were expected to be in residence, but all students would dine in the college dining hall, meet the college master and the fellows, play on college teams and, if possible, find the college unit with its thousand members a congenial place amid the multiversity environment, especially in the first and second years before the specialization within departments which is a characteristic of many Canadian universities. (York undergraduates may not join fraternities.) But now the pressure is upon us to take more graduate students. With limited resources shall we construct another professional faculty building or another college? It is not certain what our response will be, but at least we shall not slavishly follow the plans of the early 1960's when the undergraduates seemed of primary importance because these were all that we had. As a result of formula financing the government gives us more money for graduates than for undergraduates. As a metropolitan university we may be better equipped for graduate work than some of the smaller new universities. Yet to opt for graduate students is not necessarily wise. Many of the most lively students are, of course, undergraduates. And one day someone in Canada is going to ask why an American-style graduate program, inspired by Germany and adapted for a nineteenth-century American undergraduate body of considerable heterogeneity, should be adopted uncritically in Canada's rather different environment. (For example, do Canadian specialized honors students who have performed creditably in eight courses or more, each of them a year long in duration in their chosen field, really require graduate course work in the same discipline?) York, I have suggested, lacks the architectural appeal of Simon Fraser, but it has enjoyed a rational but open-minded approach to problems such as graduate studies which bedevil an expanding institution.

In the second place York has not had an autocratic Chancellor Shrum. Unlike Simon Fraser, York has not been censured by the Canadian Association of University Teachers[21]—a grave and unusual event in Canada.

Thirdly, the expansion at York, though now in top gear, started with a handful of students. A great deal of thought went into the acclimatization of freshmen through the college system and until recently all members of the

---

[21] "Development at Simon Fraser University" and "Removal of Censure of Simon Fraser University," *C.A.U.T. Bulletin,* Vol. 17, Nos. 1, October, and 2, December, 1968.

university, including the president and director of libraries, did their stint of freshman advising. I am not sure that the system flourishes so well today but certainly the original hope of closer staff-student relations was for a while fulfilled.

It is the fourth difference which in my experience is crucial in the government of an institution: the absence of a departmental structure in the social sciences at Simon Fraser and its presence, at least since 1962, at York. It seems that new institutions attract idealists who insist that there must be none of the hidebound structure which characterized the old university from which they were anxious to escape. What they fail to realize is that the students and newly appointed young members of the faculty have had no such experience and soon feel lost in a strange and unstructured environment. People find it hard to believe that things really are in an unstructured state and they soon form the opinion that there *is* a structure and a policy but that it is hidden from them. Next they imagine that they are being manipulated. Rumors take the place of information and a tense situation develops. I would conclude that the most important feature of any new institution is that there has to be a clearly understood structure and decision-making framework, and that a massive dose of confident paternalism is necessary to compensate for the insecurity which so rapidly develops in a strange environment.

Not that we escaped problems at York. The departmental structure set up in 1962 came too late to prevent a faculty explosion in 1963, but it did enable the Faculty of Arts and Science to settle down from then on. Nothing like the turmoil which engulfed Simon Fraser in 1968 and led to the resignation of two presidents in one year took place. One thing that has puzzled me has been the failure of university authorities to act when trouble is brewing. I now think I can see why. Senior men are attracted to new institutions because they see a challenge and an opportunity. Once they have accepted the challenge they are inclined through the rest of the president's interview and the lunch which follows to acquiesce readily with the ideas expressed by the president. He, too, of course has seen a challenge and an opportunity. But he may subconsciously regard his professors as bricklayers of the building he hopes to construct, rather than as fellow architects. But to attract them he emphasizes their role as architects. After an initial honeymoon period it becomes apparent that not everyone shares the president's philosophy, and indeed this may have changed as a result of pressures by the government to create a large institution rather than a small one which produces new and exciting ideas. And administrators are soon too busy to be able to explain everything.

Our explosion occurred partly because the president had to agree to set up a large university, whereas some professors felt they had been attracted by the prospect of a new college with an experimental curriculum. I survived in part because my motivation was not so much an experimental curriculum as a desire to test out Kingsley Amis' famous dictum regarding university expansion: "More means worse." I was fortunate also in that I had been through something like this earlier. In the Egyptian desert in 1945 I treated the troops under my command as though they were veterans, glad that the shooting had stopped. Within a short while I had trouble. For these men were new recruits flown out from England, and what they needed was structure, leadership, and activity. It was a lesson that was to prove of great value. My American colleagues who have studied the government and politics of developing areas while I have been with a developing university have been surprised at the role of the military in times of crisis. My experience has been that those of us with wartime military experience do have a built-in advantage with a university in crisis, thanks to our training.[22]

I think we also had an advantage at York in that unlike Simon Fraser we were never a "young university." If in some ways the appointment of older professors caused difficulties, it certainly provided ballast when the going was rough. Now we have people of all ages and this problem does not arise.

Instead we have a new problem. Recognizing the demands that a new institution makes on its leaders we have adopted a policy of rotating our administrators. We have also felt that it might be unwise to have deans and chairmen appointed indefinitely on the old Anglo-Canadian pattern. But this policy means that many of our administrators are at present being rotated, just at a time when administration has become less attractive than ever. We have also begun to think it wise to make special provision for eminent scholars who do no administration and little teaching, without sensing the full implications of this policy.

The weakness of York, like so many universities today is due, I suspect, to a failure to recognize priorities. We know there is a shortage of good middle-aged professors. We need them to run our universities. But we are telling them not to get involved in administration and we are even encouraging them to be irresponsible scholarly prima donnas flitting from university to university to the highest bidder. Are we perhaps looking for an image instead of reality? I must say that when I read the comments of the student activists and note the reward system of university administrators who rate the consultant with little time for students above the good teacher who refuses commercial temptation, I find myself sympathetic with the students. I suspect that York's new policy of appointing research-oriented professors without, apparently, emphasizing their responsibilities for teaching and library-building, to the university and to Canada, may yet cause trouble comparable to that at Simon Fraser.

---

[22] This does not mean that the military as such should be allowed to penetrate the academy.

This leads to the fifth comparison: the appointment of non-Canadians to the faculty. Unlike Simon Fraser, York did not until recently (except in sociology) appoint many Americans. Last year, however, eight of the ten new senior appointments in my faculty were of Americans and my own department, which had been largely Canadian under my chairmanship, became predominantly American under my American successor. I have indicated that Americanization has become a controversial issue in Canadian universities. In defense of the policy of appointing Americans it is pointed out that there are not enough Canadians qualified to fill the vacant positions; that the traditional sources of recruits in Europe are unable to meet the demand; that Canada has only now been able to attract good American talent and to reverse the brain drain; and that if Canada is to compete with the United States it needs to import the best American know-how.

On the other hand it is argued that younger Canadians would be qualified if there had been foresight after the 1956 conference on Canada's crisis in higher education,[23] and if something had been done to prepare for the expansion of the 1960's; that Americans are demanding and getting salaries in excess of those which senior Canadians have obtained and that some Canadians —John Kenneth Galbraith, David Easton, Harry Johnson—have been better qualified than some of the recently acquired American scholars and have gone abroad; and that it is one thing to import talent in such fields as science and technology and quite another to appoint foreigners in key administrative positions in the social sciences and humanities where they can appoint fellow nationals who share their particular ideology.

Let me give one example of what I mean. Americans, perhaps more than most scholars, are reluctant to pontificate outside their own specialty. The professor who teaches, say, the mass media therefore uses American illustrations and American books. Until he has lived abroad some years, he takes little cognizance of the fact that in Europe and Canada the notion of the media, particularly radio and television, being solely in private hands is unthinkable. American textbooks and professors take CBS, NBC, and ABC as the norm. They are accustomed to private ownership, not to the CBC or BBC or the publicly owned facilities common in many other countries. Paradoxically, although many Canadian students are caught up in the recent American revolution against the system of private capitalism, this system has never been fully accepted in a country like Canada, where, for example, the CBC, Air Canada, and Canadian National Railways, are all publicly owned enterprises.

I myself have never fully accepted the argument of free trade since as a young adult in the United States I learned, contrary to my British liberal free-

---

[23] C. T. Bissell (ed.), *Canada's Crisis in Higher Education,* Proceedings of the National Conference of Canadian Universities, November 12-14, 1956 (Ottawa, 1957).

trade childhood, that the United States grew rich behind tariffs against British-manufactured goods. I can see no reason to assume that Canada can afford to ignore the implications of American imports, whether of goods or services. For one consequence of importing American professors is that they attract to themselves American graduate students who in open competition are often as good as Canadian applicants. This is partly because many of the best Canadian graduate students apply to universities that are staffed by Canadians, or prefer to study under American professors in the United States. Half of the graduate students in my department are Americans and they naturally act as teaching assistants. Increasingly we find Canadian professors and graduate students are being used to teach Canadian government and politics, leaving political science as such to be taught by Americans.

To compete with Americans, the Canadian not only has to know about Canada and possibly Britain, but he has to be acquainted with American political science and to be respected by "the profession," and so he is at a disadvantage. Some Canadians reject the "American science of politics"; some distinguish between the "American profession" and the international community of political science scholars. The American professor often sees America (not the United States but *America,* North and South) through different eyes. To him English Canadians, French Canadians, Southerners, West Indians and Latin Americans all have something in common; they are deviants, deviants from the American norm. (I must admit that when I lived in England I had a similar feeling about the Irish, the Scots, and the Welsh, to say nothing of the Europeans.) This assumption raises problems in Canada involving the preservation of our own culture, problems which have been rarely understood by American students of comparative political culture. Indeed Canadian students are beginning to complain that American scholars use the behavioral approach because it underplays the unique qualities of the American political system. I suspect that you will hear more about "American cultural imperialism."

It is evident from this survey of two developing Canadian universities that only in Americanization is there a common pattern of development. Nevertheless we may all have some problems in common, and perhaps American universities have experienced some of these too. But one thing you do not have, and that is a powerful, though well-intentioned, next-door neighbor.

## III

My third point is that of student power and the legacy of Berkeley. Many people have pointed out that Canada has few of the elements which we are told have helped to create unrest on American campuses. The very reluctance of our universities to become research institutions and to allow themselves to be identified with the existing power structure instead of being critical of all power structures is perhaps a source of strength. But in fact we also have student unrest and American student agitators are as welcome on Canadian campuses as on their own. On February 11, 1969, there was destruction at Sir George Williams University in Montreal far exceeding in value that at any American institution.[24] On March 27, fearing that a demonstration outside McGill University might get out of hand, the government of Quebec notified the federal government that federal troops might be required there. At my comparatively docile institution parking signs have been torn down, not by a mob but by members of the student council.

Canadian universities have their own built-in weaknesses. Although dependent on public funds they are governed by private boards of governors. The power of these philanthropic businessmen (they are philanthropic not only in their willingness to help the university financially but in giving freely of their time and energy) has in fact diminished as that of the government has grown. To my old-fashioned mind they have provided a buffer between the university community and the government which no other group could rival. But to many people they represent big business and a certain way of life. It can even be argued that some are associated with *American* business. Might they put the profit of American corporations before the Canadian national interest? So far this question has hardly been raised, but one may expect to see it raised again.[25] The foundations which have so nobly supported many university inquiries, when no one else would listen, have usually been American foundations. Has their support been totally disinterested? As for the political parties, some people think that both major parties in Canada may be dependent on American goodwill because among their contributors there may be American corporations. The chief minor party, the New Democratic Party, is dependent on unions which are affiliated to American unions. Occasionally in the past Canadian nationalism has won out, but generally there are too many interests involved, and too many Canadians have close ties with the United States for this mood to become dominant. Are the students perhaps the only independent group? If French-Canadian students have been the source of Quebec nationalism, might English-Canadian students in due course be the source of a new English-Canadian nationalism?

Like most people I am ambivalent over student power. I cannot believe that senior undergraduates, still less graduates of 25 or more are unable to act as full-grown men and women but must be treated as apprentices. After all, when in January, 1946, I returned to Oxford as an undergraduate, having re-

---

[24] Neil Compton, "Sir George Williams loses its innocence," *Canadian Forum*, XLIX, 579, April 1969, 2-4.

[25] John R. Seeley mentions it in *The University Game*, p. 142.

linquished my own command, I was still only 21. And nobody in my previous regiment had been over thirty.

But I do hold the medieval view that a student has a different *status* which he must accept. In the same way, when a man becomes a husband he has to behave differently from the way he did as a bachelor. This has nothing to do with age or maturity, simply with a change in status. The university is not *in loco parentis.*

But if we expect our young people, who are mature adults, to accept the medieval notion of *in statu pupillari,* the notion of their status as pupils, we have to behave with equal propriety as masters. If we as professors seem primarily concerned with advising government or industry, with sitting on committees, with writing for fellow professionals who share our passion for *minutiae* and distrust of general issues, if indeed we seem to despise those who fulfill their duty as masters, that is to say the teachers who hand on the tradition of scholarship personally to the next generation—then clearly the pupils are going to reject that relative difference in status because they believe it has no genuine foundation. For if there are no genuine masters there can be no real pupils. The students can argue that a revolution must occur in order that a new and proper relationship can be re-established.[26] I am reminded of the traditional contrast between the nobility in England and France in the eighteenth century. In England the nobles are said to have been active on their estates, encouraging agriculture and developing industry; in France the nobility associated with the king at Versailles so that when the revolution came they had no roots among their people. Many professors in great universities seem to be as rootless as the French nobility, and to be the cause of the very revolution they deplore.

Some people think that the problem results from a generation gap. It has been my good fortune in these last few years to have my wife attend my university as a full-time undergraduate. Although a good student, well-known to everyone in the faculty and administration, she discovered she shared the students' criticism of the system. I therefore doubt whether the "generation gap" is an adequate explanation; hence my concern about status and our use and misuse of our position.

I have said that in Canada, as elsewhere, we are introducing the American graduate school, for want of a better alternative. What some of us outside

---

[26] Compare the difficulty which some professors and administrators have had in comprehending student unrest in *Student Participation in University Government,* a study paper prepared for the Committee of Presidents by its subcommittee on research and planning (Toronto, 1968) with the papers on "The Nature of the University" by Professor C. B. Macpherson, president of the C.A.U.T., Peter Warrian, president of the C.U.S., and most surprisingly, Gerard Pelletier, the Secretary of State for Canada at the annual meeting of the A.U.C.C. (*Proceedings, 1968*).

the United States detect is a curious reversal of roles between graduates and undergraduates in the American academic mind, with the adoption of paternalism towards graduates at the expense of the undergraduates. This may be the cause of some of our problems. When I was a pupil the dons were responsible for my general welfare. The provost and Lady Ross were at home to tea every Sunday during term; the dean provided beer on occasional Wednesday evenings. But the graduate students were considered to be mature scholars able to work on their own. Certainly at a later date when my own research took me to Sweden I had no one to supervise me. I had to teach myself the language and find my way about Swedish libraries and archives and government agencies where I had to interview people in Swedish. I was without any guide other than an elderly Swedish professor who took an avuncular interest in me from time to time. But I had to satisfy knowledgeable scholars in both Britain and Sweden before the material was published.

I am puzzled by a system where the climax is the comprehensive examination which leads to congratulations and celebrations. Oddly enough, the dissertation at this point has not been started and the topic may even be undecided. I can understand a graduate program where, to ensure that a dissertation is not begun by unqualified persons from other institutions, certain qualifying courses must be taken. I can see the advantages of going to a leading graduate school and through course work meeting a variety of interesting professors. But to regard the dissertation as of lesser significance than the comprehensive examination seems to me a failure to grasp scholarly priorities. Yet it is this system which is being adopted widely in Canada just as, I suspect, you are mending your ways and reforming the graduate school. Unfortunately for us, the so-called cultural lag which means that we do tomorrow what Americans do today is fast disappearing, at the student level. Through some mysterious extrasensory perception students everywhere seem to be seizing on the same issues at the same time. Life may be difficult enough for professors in the United States; it is even more difficult for elderly professors in Canada who have thought of themselves as senior scholars and who are now assumed by the students to be obsolescent. There may be a greater gulf between students and faculty and students and administration in some of the *older* Canadian universities than anywhere else. For whereas the new institutions are finding their latest American ideas challenged, some professors in the older institutions have not yet caught up with the American era and are still oriented towards Europe, and England in particular.[27]

---

[27] For further materials on Canadian universities consult *Canadian Books in Print* (1967); *Canadian Periodical Index* (1947); *Canadian Education Index* (Canadian Council for Research in Education, 1966-); *A Bibliography of Higher Education in Canada*, R. S. Harris and A. Tremblay (Toronto, 1960; Supplement, 1965).

## IV

Finally, having said something about Canadian universities generally; having compared two new universities in particular; and having discussed some of our more pressing problems, I must fulfill my promise to say something about my own reaction to recent events.

It is a sign of the pace of change that my earlier conclusion, drafted at Christmas, 1968, is already out of date. You are not, I am sure, particularly interested in the lessons I have learned in a new institution—to do the job in hand and to try not to worry too much about the way other people do theirs; to resist the temptation to take on too many tasks; and to bear in mind that there are always plenty of good people available if you look for them and are not afraid of youth. ( I sometimes think good people rise to the top not because they are pushful and ambitious but because they are not wanted lower down and there is nowhere else for them to go.)

Rather you are concerned about the university as an institution. Is it under attack because it has neglected one of its primary tasks, the transmission of scholarship to the students? If so, then a reform of universities that increases the power of the teaching faculty and students may help to solve the problem. Or is it that we are living in a revolutionary age in which universities, including their professors, are identified with the forces of reaction?[28] Increasingly one is assured by the young that liberal detachment and objectivity are impossible, that we all have our prejudices whether we recognize them or not. And we are informed that rational discussion can only take place when there is agreement on basic assumptions—which today is also denied.

I do not myself see how the middle-aged, however well-intentioned, can stop the extraordinary tidal wave of deep feeling that is sweeping through the universities. Moreover, I would hesitate to set myself up as being in the right and to describe the new generation as wrong. But it is by no means certain that the student radicals for their part are always right and that calmer

---

[28] Students in new institutions with pretensions regarding research are hardly likely to accept such bland statements as Robert Down's remarks on "The Role of Faculty and Library Staff" in *Resources of Canadian Academic and Research Libraries,* pp. 60-61: "In the future, librarians will be able to rely less on faculty members for aid in book selection, because academic careers are being built increasingly not on teaching but upon research and publication and foreign assignments, with little time left over for the ordering of books." Such assumptions may explain why J. C. McClelland has said: "One part of the student protest movement thinks it knows the name of the game: confrontation politics. It believes that university government reflects the general social norm, a power struggle in which pressure groups operate from positions of strength," in "The New McGill—A Place for Liberty?" Position Paper No. 11, Tripartite Commission, McGill University, 1968.

counsels will not ultimately prevail.[29] Although I look to the future with some trepidation, I have to admit that so far the experience has been as exhilarating as it has been humiliating. It has been humiliating to discover that 20 years of teaching, research, and administration have not made me as useful a member of academic society as I had hoped. I too face the prospect of being considered obsolescent by the young. But it has been exhilarating in that never have I met such lively students, eager for me to read and to enjoy the books that have stimulated them, interested in knowing my gut reaction to arguments and events, and willing patiently to explain to me how we can learn together.

Perhaps at Catholic Notre Dame I should not say this, but if we are facing a new, secular Reformation, of the universities rather than of the church, then we may perhaps hope for some purification of our souls. And even if the situation is more serious and if the turmoil presages the end of a European civilization comparable to the age of Greece and Rome, we can console ourselves by remembering that in the long history of political theory even the centuries lose significance. For all the glory of Rome, and this I *can* say at Notre Dame, the student of the history of political ideas passes rapidly from Plato and Aristotle to the writings of St. Augustine.

I have suggested that developing areas and developing universities are not necessarily different in kind from those that are developed. But just as St. Augustine came not from Rome but from North Africa, so it is possible that intellectual and spiritual guidance may come, not as we suppose from the great universities of the Western world, but from some genius in a poor country. As we debate the task of the universities in a changing world, let us see ourselves in perspective. God may not be expecting quite as much from universities as we think He does.

---

[29] At such a time, attention may be drawn to Alexander Israel Wittenberg, *The Prime Imperative: Priorities in Education* (Toronto, 1968).

# THE SITUATION OF
# SWEDISH UNIVERSITIES

Torgny T. Segerstedt

I have been asked to speak about the present situation of the Swedish universities. Of course, we have our special or national problems, but on the whole I think that our problems are similar to problems all around the world. It is no exaggeration to say that university problems, and especially student unrest, constitute truly international phenomena today. You can confront such problems in Addis Ababa and Nairobi, as well as in San Francisco, London, Paris, Prague, Berlin and Uppsala. Although the university situation in developing countries differs substantially from that in highly industrialized ones, I believe that we can find a common denominator: the rapid change of society. The change, obviously, influences university life and the function of universities in society. And this fact must be of consequence for the life of university teachers and students.

For that reason, one may group the problems of university life today under three main headings: (1) the change in society; (2) the change in university structure; and (3) the change in the students' situation. Perhaps those headings are valid in all countries, but I am restricting my use of them to describe the prevailing situation in the Swedish universities. I am, however, aware that they are not mutually exclusive.

## THE CHANGE IN SOCIETY

Sweden is rapidly becoming industrialized and urbanized. The process has been proceeding throughout this century, but it has been accelerated during the 1950's and 1960's. In the middle 1950's about 18 per cent of the population was still engaged in rural professions; now it is less than 8 per cent. This development is due mainly to our increasing knowledge, that is, to international cooperation among scholars. The consequence has been that society is becoming more and more dependent on all kinds of science. We talk about the "electronic revolution" and the "biological time bomb," and these are slogans for grim realities. But we must not forget that an absolute prerequisite for this development is international cooperation between universities and scientists.

The influence and power of research has had an enormous impact on the panorama of professions. Some professions are disappearing (for example, farmers and craftsmen) and others are being born, such as service men for computers, mass media experts and technical specialists in education and medicine. It is difficult to predict what will be the most common profession in the year 2000, even as we acknowledge that the majority of present students will be active in society at the time. It has, however, often been pointed out that the directly productive occupation, as well as office jobs, will probably decrease in number because of mechanization and rationalization of industrial work. Most people will be occupied in service jobs at different levels. By *service job* I mean professions in *social services,* such as education, medical care, child and old-age care, as well as positions in *commercial services,* like hotels, restaurants and gasoline stations.

Most of the social service professions will require university education. Not only do such tasks presuppose an extensive training; they also presuppose expensive investments. The consequence is a growing competition for financial support among the different sectors of social life. In the early 1960's the majority of us did not clearly realize how the applications of science would exact such heavy demands on our resources; nor did we grasp that we would be forced to assign priorities to our reasonable demands. Now we must ask the question: Which do we prefer—heart transplantation or better old-age care, better education and more research or improved child care, desalinization of seawater or space research? I am sure that problems of priorities will be characteristic of university life in the 1970's.

### CHANGE IN UNIVERSITY STRUCTURE

The growing importance of research and education has changed the role of universities and transformed their structure. With regard to research, I think it is correct to say that the volume of university research has markedly increased since World War II, and that the trend has further developed through the 1960's. The table on the facing page will illustrate my point.

I think I am correct in saying that at least 90 per cent of the grants shown are used for university research, and it must be noted that the research councils are dominated by professors.

The most spectacular fact, however, is the enormous increase of students. When I was a freshman in 1927, the total number of students in Sweden was 7,200 or 1.2 per cent of the potential student population at that time. In 1967 the student body had increased to 74,000, which means 9 per cent of the present population. The figures are still higher now, probably about 110,000 or over 10 per cent. This very fact of mass education can probably explain a lot about what is going on in the universities all round the world. The universities have changed from "university" to "multiversity" and from "multiversity" to

TABLE 1. Grants to Swedish Research Councils (in thousands of Swedish Crowns) *

| Councils | 1966-67 | % | 1967-68 | % | 1968-69 | % | 1969-70 | % |
|---|---|---|---|---|---|---|---|---|
| Medical research | 18.308 | 22.9 | 22.321 | 24.5 | 26.718 | 23.7 | 35.300 | 23.5 |
| Research in humanities | 4.098 | 5.1 | 4.517 | 5.0 | 5.163 | 4.6 | 6.300 | 4.2 |
| Social science | 3.305 | 4.1 | 3.618 | 4.0 | 4.136 | 3.7 | 6.400 | 4.3 |
| Science research | 21.348 | 26.8 | 24.409 | 26.8 | 28.044 | 24.9 | 36.400 | 24.3 |
| Atomic research | 9.418 | 11.8 | 10.159 | 11.1 | 11.775 | 10.5 | 14.400 | 9.6 |
| Agricultural research | 5.100 | 6.4 | 4.834 | 5.3 | 5.774 | 5.1 | 7.825 | 5.2 |
| Technical research | 18.200 | 22.8 | 21.325 | 23.4 | 31.000 | 27.5 | 43.435 | 28.9 |
| Totals | 79.777 | 100.0 | 91.183 | 100.0 | 112.610 | 100.0 | 150.060 | 100.0 |

* To this may be added the funds from the Bank of Sweden Foundation for social research, which in 1967-68 had 15.000.000 Swedish Crowns at its disposal. In 1968-69 and 1969-70 about 18 million Swedish Crowns were available.

279

"megaversity." Some Swedish statistics may illustrate that point. In Table 2 we may see the number of students leaving high school, formally qualified to enter the university, as well as the rate of passage from school to university.

TABLE 2. Number of Students Leaving High School, Formally Qualified to Enter the University, and the Actual Rate of Entrance into the University

| Year | Number | % of Total Pool for Year | Rate of Entrance into the University |
|------|--------|--------------------------|--------------------------------------|
| 1950 | 5,776  | 6.5  | —   |
| 1960 | 11,377 | 12.0 | 66% |
| 1968 | 38,700 | 29.9 | 77% |

Table 3 shows the number of university students enrolled in universities by branch of study. In the academic year 1960-61 the social sciences still belonged to the faculty of Letters but commercial colleges were independent.

TABLE 3. Number of Students Enrolled in Universities by Branch of Study (1960-61 Social Science belonged to the Faculty of Letters)

|  | 1960-61 | 1964-65 | 1967-68 | Fall 1968 |
|--|---------|---------|---------|-----------|
| Letters | 15,200 | 13,800 | 22,100 | 26,900 |
| Social Science | 1,300 | 18,000 | 32,600 | 37,900 |
| Science | 5,200 | 9,600 | 15,100 | 17,600 |
| Law | 2,100 | 2,700 | 5,500 | 6,900 |
| Medicine | 3,300 | 4,200 | 5,600 | 6,400 |
| Pharmacy | 300 | 400 | 400 | 400 |
| University Technology | 5,000 | 7,500 | 10,000 | 11,000 |
| Odontology | 1,100 | 1,200 | 1,400 | 1,500 |
| Theology | 800 | 1,000 | 1,200 | 1,300 |
| Total | 34,715 | 56,241 | 91,307 | 109,900 |

The tables indicate that the universities are no longer educating a social elite, but a rather important part of an entire year's group. This mass education is, of course, very expensive and for that reason planning and assigning of priorities is, as I have already pointed out, a matter of growing concern for all authorities. In Table 4 we can see the costs of university education and research:

TABLE 4. Estimated Costs of Higher Education in Sweden
(in 1000 Swedish Crowns)

| Costs | 1950-51 | 1960-61 | 1966-67 |
|---|---|---|---|
| Working costs | 48.627 | 267.379 | 509.640 |
| Investments | 15.850 | 79.727 | 311.006 |
| Grants to research councils | 7.902 | 36.745 | 119.875 |
| Number of students | 16.600 | 36.320 | 77.500 |
| Running costs per student | 2.930 | 7.400 | 6.655 |
| Investments costs per student | .955 | 2.195 | 4.012 |

As a consequence of these high costs, we can notice an increasing interest on the part of the government with regard to university activities. This also, of course, means centralization and control.

I suppose that this is an international phenomenon as well. But since Swedish universities are all state universities, we tend to feel the concern and power of the state rather heavily. (You must not misunderstand me: the government or state is reforming our structure, while we are dependent, for our budget, on the money allocated by parliament. But there is no ideological pressure on us. We may be conservative, liberal or Communist; nobody is interfering with that part of our lives.) I must admit, however, that the autonomy of Swedish universities is nonexistent. I doubt that there is much autonomy left in any country, with scientific research getting more and more expensive.

I think that we can look upon the much discussed new organization of studies at the philosophical faculties in Swedish universities, as an expression of governmental interest in university education because of its economic importance. The reform implies that teaching is to be organized in a number of "lines of study," following a principle of successive options. The student will decide the main direction of his studies, his "line of study," by choosing a particular area at the beginning of his university life. Normally, after one year of study he will be faced with a second choice among a number of alternative study courses based upon the same introductory study course. During his third year the student will usually be able to choose freely among the study courses provided. Teaching in different subject fields will be given in "study-courses" which will be divided into "course units." Study courses and course units will be assigned points corresponding to the input of work required to complete the course and take the relevant test. Full-time work during one academic year is assessed at 40 points.

This reform is also an expression of the democratization of our universities. Up to the end of World War II we could say that the majority of students came from the upper classes, and mostly from families with some kind of academic tradition. Nowadays most of the students are "first-generation" students. They bring, consequently, no traditions or ideas from home about the ideal university life. The reform means that university education is becoming more similar to high school education. The students have less freedom, since they have to start with a choice among 17 introductory subjects and their second subject must be chosen from among a limited number of courses. The third subject is, as I pointed out, quite free. The intent is that there will be less drop-outs, better planned studies, and ultimately a higher production of graduates. The same arguments are used to defend or explain the pending reform of graduate studies. Up to now we have had a licentiate examination given between the first degree and the doctor's degree. According to the new bill, the licentiate examination will disappear and one will normally obtain his doctor's degree after four years of graduate studies (seven years overall after leaving school). The minister of education has pointed out, however, that the doctor's degree must not be regarded as the final station or end for scholars who are going to be research workers. After the doctorate, there is first a position called *forskar-assistent* (research-assistant), to which a person may be appointed for two periods of three years each. After that, he may become a *docent* (assistant professor) over a period of nine years.

It is difficult to evaluate this reform. It depends on the number of chairs as assistants and docents that exists, and on how many new professorships will be founded to train young researchers. If we look upon the changing structure of our universities from a very broad point of view, it may be said that it reflects a general rise in our educational standard, since the first three years of university education may be considered a continuation of our "gymnasium" and the four years spent in obtaining a doctor's degree represents, at completion, an extremely well qualified elementary university degree. From the universities' point of view, however, it means that we will have to provide more elementary education, more mass education, and that for that very reason there is an obvious risk that we are lowering our standards. If that will be the case or not depends on the resources provided for our postgraduate work. All these reforms mean that students to a certain extent lose their privileges, a loss that is, of course, mostly felt among students with academic family traditions. That may be one reason why many revolutionary student leaders belong to the upper classes rather than to the lower ones.

I have already pointed out that many students are first-generation university students. Consequently, they possess better educations than their parents and sometimes their elder brothers and sisters. We can thus talk readily about an educational generation gap. That is one reason why the necessity of adult education and continuing education has been much discussed in Sweden during the last two or three years. The Riksdag has declared that in the name of equality adult education must be given priority. It is felt that men and women, forty years of age or more, must enjoy the same opportunity to adjust themselves to the new demands of the labor market and at the same time it is felt that continuing studies of a general nature may enrich the personalities of such people. But I think that the strongest motive is the rising demand of vocational life.

In planning university reform, there has been considerable talk about the necessity of giving university education more orientation toward vocational training. The problem is to determine which occupations are going to survive into the next century. The only thing we know for certain is that many of today's jobs will be obsolete and that many new ones will emerge. It is difficult to prophesy the kind of profession for which we ought to train young people. It may for that reason be better to furnish a general education than a specialized one, since general education gives the student a chance to adjust himself to a changing society. A general, all-around education may be more useful in the future than a specialized, narrow, vocational one.

A small brochure has been published recently by the new Royal Committee for Higher Education (called U-68), about the goals and objectives of higher education. It is rather unusual for a committee to invite the general public to discuss its problems, and the brochure may be seen as a sign of the general public concern with educational questions. The committee makes the common division among (a) vocational training, (b) general education and (c) personality formation. On the whole, the trend is to put the stress on vocational training, a reasonable enough emphasis considering the enormous mass of students. On the other hand, we have the uncertainty of what future professions will be. As far as I can gather, most university-trained people will have research-dependent jobs of one kind or other. They will have to adjust themselves to the new situation created by progress in research. For that reason, I believe that a general training in scientific theory and research methods must be the best preparation for continuing life-long education. All of which probably means at least five years of basic university training.

We know that we need more doctors and dentists; we are not quite sure with regard to engineers. But those faculties are the most expensive ones, as is shown in Table 5.

The most crowded faculties are those in liberal arts and the social sciences. It is not easy to predict the kinds of occupation that will be waiting for students graduating from those faculties—some will find jobs in mass media, some will work in developing countries, but quite a few will have to create

TABLE 5. Working Costs Per Student (in Sweden) by Branch of Study, 1967-68

| Faculty | Costs per student (in Swedish Crowns) |
|---|---|
| Art | 1.800 |
| Theology | 2.600 |
| Law | 1.300 |
| Social science | 1.400 |
| Medical | 14.900 |
| Odontological | 18.300 |
| Pharmacy | 5.800 |
| Science | 5.400 |
| Technology | 10.250 |

their own jobs and careers. Personally, I feel optimistic: A good supply of well-trained men or women will be the cause of new demands. And there are many fields left to conquer in the social sciences.

### THE STUDENT SITUATION

The fact that some faculties are overcrowded means a poor student-teacher ratio. If we look upon our universities from the student point of view, I think this will be one of the most obvious and perhaps shocking things. As a student, there will be little chance to talk to a professor—students will be anonymous and education will be impersonal. I regard this situation as one of the main causes of student unrest and revolt and of the demand for more influence and participation by the students in university affairs. In Table 6 we can see the professor-student ratio at the graduate level. Naturally, the ratio is much worse at the undergraduate level.

As a result of the overcrowded faculties and the uncertainty with regard to the future labor market for university-trained students, there have emerged new university functions such as vocational counseling, counseling regarding study techniques and remedial activities for human-relation problems. Mere overcrowdedness seems to create mental health problems.

I think there are three main factors which must be noted when discussing the student situation. First, the housing problem. Traditionally the students rented quarters in town. That is impossible today. It was possible when Uppsala, for example, housed 3,000 or 4,000 students. But it cannot be done with 24,000 students. We have built so-called student towns (dormitories), in which the students rent their rooms. It implies that thousands and thousands of students are living in the same blocks and I think this is important

TABLE 6. Ratio between Post-Graduate Students and Professors or Assistant Professors, 1966. Distributed according to faculty and/or subjects

| Subject or faculty | Students to teacher |
|---|---|
| History-philosophy | 15.6 to 1 |
| Language | 10.3 to 1 |
| Psychology-education | 36.9 to 1 |
| Other social sciences | 11.5 to 1 |
| Math-physics | 11.1 to 1 |
| Chemistry | 19.4 to 1 |
| Biology | 12.5 to 1 |
| Theology | 5.5 to 1 |
| Law | 1.0 to 1 |
| Medicine | 2.7 to 1 |
| Odontology | 12.0 to 1 |
| Pharmacy | 3.5 to 1 |
| Technology | 3.9 to 1 |

for the formation of attitudes. It is quite easy to communicate ideas, transmit values and make propaganda when you have people of the same age and same activities living so close to each other.

Second, the increase of female students. When I was a student, there was only a very small minority of girls at the university; now they are in the majority in some faculties. It means a change in alcohol consumption and in sex life. I suspect our students do not quite live up to their reputation with regard to sexual freedom. In any case we have an increasing number of married students, a fact which may be regarded as a sign that there is a certain social pressure to conform to more conservative social codes. The trend to marry complicates the housing problem. We cannot only build single rooms, but must have small family flats as well in our student towns. Married life naturally interferes with university studies. The delay affects mostly the girls. It is rather difficult to be an effective student if you have a wife and children around you, but it is still more complicated if you have children and a husband to take care of.

In a way social problems have come closer to the student of today than to former generations. Mostly because of mass media, the same is true with regard to international affairs. Students feel their responsibility for the future of mankind and are impatient at the way the older generation is handling the problems, and they want, for that very reason, to participate in political, edu-

285

cational and administrative decisions. Swedish students have always had rather strong organizations and through those organizations have had the opportunity to influence their own situation. During the last year the government has passed laws giving the students the right to elect members to the academic council, the educational committees of the faculties and the boards to institutions (departments). These reforms will guarantee the students a certain influence on university affairs. How it really will work we do not yet know.

As in many other countries, we have a group of students who have a very negative attitude towards our universities, education and research. They do not believe in objective theories or truth but maintain that scientific research is just one instrument in the struggle for power. Those groups will certainly not be satisfied by the contemplated reforms. They represent a small but active minority. Their future role in university life depends on the effects of the reforms I have described.

# PROBLEMS OF THE
# FRENCH UNIVERSITY

## F. G. Dreyfus

The past few years have seen French higher education undergo profound change, first at the impetus of the government, in particular the two ministers of national education, Christian Fouchet and Edgar Faure, and then under the influence of research movements, in particular the *Mouvement national pour le developpement et l'expansion scientifique,* directed by Professor Lichnerowicz. There were conferences at Caen and Amiens, and the texts reforming the organization of education published by Mr. Fouchet.

In May 1968, the student crisis resulted in large part from the lack of adaptation of French education, the insufficiency of governmental action as regards the number of students in classrooms and the refusal of counseling, to which the services of the ministry were committed. As a result, certain opposition ministers caused the reforms of President Edgar Faure dealing with the structure of the universities and the participation of students in their administration to be superimposed on the university's plan.

What is the sociological background of these reforms and what reactions have they engendered?

### SOCIAL ASPECTS OF UNIVERSITY EDUCATION

For ten years we have witnessed in France a rapid democratization of university instruction.

In 1954-55 there were 150,000 students in France; in 1958-59, 184,000, in 1964-65, 367,000, and in 1967-68, 497,000. They were distributed as follows (in thousands):

| Faculties | 1954-55 | 1958-59 | 1964-65 | 1967-68 |
|---|---|---|---|---|
| Letters (Liberal arts) | 40 | 53 | 122 | 167 |
| Science | 35 | 60 | 113 | 136 |
| Law | 38 | 32 | 74 | 109 |
| Medicine | 29 | 31 | 44 | 65 |
| Pharmacy | 8 | 8 | 12 | 17 |
| IUT (University Institutes of Technology) | — | — | — | 5 |
| | 150 | 184 | 365 | 499 |

287

To the current 500,000 university students may be added the number of students from the various institutions of higher learning not attached to the universities: *grandes écoles,* 55,000; preparatory classes for the *grandes écoles,* 28,000; higher technicians, 34,000. Altogether these total 117,000. In 1967-68 there were 606,000 students in France as opposed to 190,000 in 1954-55. The number has more than tripled.

As a result, there has been a change in the distribution of the students from the various social backgrounds, as the following table demonstrates, by percentages:

| Father's Occupation | 1960-61 | 1966-67 |
|---|---|---|
| Farmers | 6.0 | 6.6 |
| Owners in industry and commerce | 17.8 | 14.9 |
| Liberal professions | 28.8 | 29.3 |
| Intermediate professions | 18.4 | 15.8 |
| Employees | 8.2 | 8.5 |
| Workers | 5.3 | 9.9 |
| Miscellaneous | 15.5 | 15.0 |

We are thus witnessing an appreciable increase in the proportion of students of modest origins. The percentage of sons of employees and of workers has increased from 13.5 per cent in 1960-61 to 18.4 per cent in 1966-67.

In comparison to other countries in Western Europe the French situation is relatively favorable. But the growth of higher education poses a number of great difficulties.

To what is this growth due?

It is due first to an important development in secondary education. From 1955 to 1965 the number of students in secondary education more than doubled.

| 1955-56 | 616,000 |
|---|---|
| 1959-60 | 951,000 |
| 1964-65 | 1,503,000 |

In 1968-69 the number will have tripled—1,900,000. Also, since 1966, more than 200,000 young people, 25 per cent of a generation, have decided to take the *baccalauréat.* A large proportion of them—about 60 per cent in normal years—have been admitted to this examination; in 1966 there were 106,000 *bacheliers;* in 1967, 133,000; and in 1968, 170,000. But one must recognize that 1968 was an exceptional year.

Ninety-five per cent of these *bacheliers* are presently entering the university. No system of selection of students entering the faculties exists, and every student who has passed the *baccalauréat* may enroll in a faculty. It would be helpful to emphasize that France has one of the highest rates of passage of students from the level of secondary education to that of higher education as the table below shows.

Percentage of Secondary School Graduates Entering Higher Education

|  | 1955 | 1965 |
|---|---|---|
| Austria | 62% | 54% |
| Finland | 64 | 70 |
| France | 76 | 92 |
| Italy | 59 | 79 |
| Low countries | 43 | 40 |
| Romania | 43 | 41 |
| Sweden | 46 | 60 |
| Yugoslavia | 60 | 70 |

Source: UNESCO

The lack of any selection principle contributes, as extraordinary as it may seem, to aggravating the social structure of the French university. Among students from the working classes there is a process of self-selection, while all the young people from well-to-do families enter higher education.

This situation contributes to an overloading of the faculties and explains in particular the insufficiency of instructors for the first-year students. In 1967-68 there were 109,672 students in their first year in a faculty, distributed as follows:

| Law and economics | 24,500 |
|---|---|
| Science | 24,000 |
| Premedical studies | 18,000 |
| Letters | 38,000 |
| Pharmacy | 4,500 |
| Total | 109,000 |

In certain faculties a normal ratio (15 students per instructor) would absorb all instructors in that faculty. This is particularly the case in the non-scientific faculties.

First-year students are also very badly counseled; this explains why a considerable number of them fail at the end of their first year of study.

Faculty Members in Various Faculties (1967-68)

|  | Law | Letters | Science | Medicine | Pharmacy |
|---|---|---|---|---|---|
| Professors and *Maîtres de Conferences* (lecturers) | 825 | 1,318 | 2,062 | 2,207 | 364 |
| *Maîtres Assistants* and *Assistants* | 1,318 | 3,424 | 8,002 | 4,692 | 985 |
|  | 2,143 | 4,742 | 10,064 | 6,899 | 1,349 |

At the end of this year about 53 per cent of the pre-university medical students are admitted, but only 42 per cent succeed in letters and only 36 per cent in law.

The absence of a selection system aggravates the students' insecurity during their first year of study, and results in their being very badly oriented.

The *Commissariat general au Plan,* in his preparatory work for the Fifth Plan, calculated the recruitment needs for graduates of higher education. The data can be found in the table below:

|  | Candidates in 1967 | Recruitment needs in 1967 | Enrolled first year in 1966-67 | Estimated number of graduates in 1971 |
|---|---|---|---|---|
| Licence in science and Engineers | 18,500 | 27,000 | 46,000 (including the students in preparatory classes at the Grandes écoles) | 15,000 *licencies* 11,000 engineers |
| Medical science | 4,500 | 8,000 | 25,000 | 10,000 |
| Law | 4,500 | 10,000 | 25,000 | 10,000 |
| Letters | 1,200 | 11,000 | 38,000 | 15,000 |

In 1967 the needs were not met in the scientific, medical and juridical disciplines. They were fulfilled, however, in the literary disciplines. In 1971 a balance will almost be attained in the sciences and in medicine, but there will be an overabundance in the two fields to which the largest number of students have been attracted in the last few years—letters and law.

Thus the absence of careful selection and orientation and the nonexistence of short university curricula (the university institutes of technology in 1968-69 had only 5,000 students, less than one per cent of the total number of students) have led higher education to an impasse which certain instructors and political figures have recognized. But the opposition of teacher and student unions has led the present minister to reject all serious orientation and counseling policies.

CONNECTIONS BETWEEN HIGHER EDUCATION AND RESEARCH

If one is to believe the official texts and the innumerable professions of faith of French instructors, there can be no instruction without research. Unfortunately, matters are not so simple.

Doubtless, the instructors (professors or *assistants*) have, in theory, a relatively light schedule of instruction (25 weeks of three hours teaching per week for the professors, five to eight hours for assistants and lecturers) in order that they may assume research tasks. But under present conditions the large number of students as well as the time-consuming activities of administration, have forced instructors to occupy themselves with nothing other than teaching. Moreover, in numerous universities, despite the will of the legislature, research and instruction have been separated through the establishment of *Unités d'Enseignement et de Recherche,* with the emphasis on research. This has been particularly the case at the universities where research activity has been most intense: Grenoble, Montpellier, Nancy, Paris, Strasbourg, and Toulouse.

Moreover, the part played by private research is relatively small and with rare exceptions the ties between private research and university research are very weak.

The French university, for ideological reasons, has for many years not sought collaboration with industry. Only in the last couple of years has a stirring been felt in at least some universities, such as Grenoble (nuclear, electronic, and hydraulic studies), Strasbourg (nuclear studies, chemical study of macromolecules), Toulouse, and Paris.

Public centers of research not affiliated with the universities have also been established. The oldest was established in 1869—*l'Ecole Pratique des Hautes Etudes*—and comprises six sections: three scientific, one religious, one literary, and one in the social sciences. In 1936, the *Centre National de la Recherche Scientifique* (C.N.R.S.) was founded, and as of 1968 it contained 5,664 researchers divided among 11 literary sections and 24 scientific sections, in the following manner:

| | C.N.R.S. research workers | No. of young research workers | Instructors in faculties Professors and Maîtres de Conference | Maîtres Assistants and Assistants |
|---|---|---|---|---|
| Physical sciences | 4,768 | 538 | 4,633 | 14,025 |
| Social sciences | 896 | 28 | 2,043 | 8,842 |
| | 5,664 | 566 | 6,676 | 22,867 |

The demands of modern research have led the C.N.R.S. to create its own laboratories. The C.N.R.S. currently possesses over 100 laboratories whose work encompasses all scientific fields—mathematics, astronomy, physics, chemistry, geology, oceanography, biology, social sciences. There are occasional associations between the C.N.R.S. laboratories and university laboratories. The C.N.R.S. laboratories are often directed by professors from a faculty or from an engineering school. Such people comprise 21 per cent of the C.N.R.S. researchers. The remaining 79 per cent are distributed among laboratories of the various faculties (59 per cent), the large scientific establishments, and establishments little related to national education (8 per cent).

Furthermore, centers of research, more or less independent from the university, also exist. The best known of these are:

The *Commissariat à l'Energie Atomique* (C.E.A.), whose responsibility is to take any useful measures for the development of atomic energy with a view to its utilization in various scientific fields, in industry, and for defense (energy, arms, radioisotopes, but also mining, nuclear engineering, electronics, etc.).

The *Centre National d'Etudes Spatiales* (C.N.E.S.), which directs the programs of study and research related to astronomy, astrophysics, cosmic physics, telecommunications, etc., and is working for the perfection and realization of space vehicles (launching devices and satellites).

The *Direction des Recherches et des Moyens d'Essais* (D.R.M.E.), which occupies itself with military research. In particular it handles the *Office National d'Etudes et de Recherches Aérospatiales* (O.N.E.R.A.).

The *Institut National de la Recherche Agronomique* (I.N.R.A.), whose mission is to facilitate the development and improvement of agricultural production, is also in charge of veterinary research, rural socioeconomic research, forest research, and hydrobiology. It supervises 200 laboratories and its work is more closely associated with the professional spheres than with the university, the latter being not as a rule concerned with agricultural problems.

Six other large centers of research have leading roles to play:

The *Centre National d'Etudes des Télécommunications* (C.N.E.T.), which devotes its activities to research in the fields of telecommunications and electronics.

The *Institut National de la Sante et de la Recherche Médicale* (I.N.S.E.R.M.), created in 1964, whose role is to coordinate medical research in France and which works in constant liaison with the *Centres Hospitaliers Universitaires* (C.H.U.).

The *Institut National d'Etudes Demographiques,* which has extended its research to a large number of human problems.

The *Institut National de la Statistique et des Etudes Economiques* (I.N.S.E.E.).

The *Office de la Recherche Scientifique et Technique d'Outre-Mer* (O.R.S.T.O.M.), which covers all the fields connected with the study of physical, biological and human spheres in arid and tropical areas.

The *Fondation Nationale des Sciences Politiques,* which coordinates political science research, and, often, social science research.

All these institutes, even though they may use some of the facilities offered by the universities, do not always work with them as closely as might be advisable. To mention only the social sciences field, one cannot dispute that the activities of such research centers as the *Centre d'Etudes Sociologiques* of the C.N.R.S., the Sixth Section (economics and social) of the *Ecole Pratique des Hautes Etudes,* the *Fondation Nationale des Sciences Politiques,* or the I.N.E.D., are much more effective than those carried on by the university centers proper. Weight of tradition, partitioning of faculties, heavy duties of instruction and burdensome work loads of students—all result in hampering the efficiency demanded of university research. It explains the wish of some researchers for forming *Unités d'Enseignement et de Recherche,* essentially oriented towards research.

It must be pointed out that research has not, by and large, been assigned the proper degree of importance by the French population. Undoubtedly, efforts have been made in the past few years on the government's side, but the average "big business" firm is still not interested.

One immediately sees the mediocrity of the expenditures on research in France when compared to Great Britain or the United States, and the deficiency of research financed by private enterprise.

Thus, the isolation of university research becomes more clearly apparent.

This isolation is due to a large extent to the university's fear of becoming "colonized" by private industries and capitalism. The university also refuses to collaborate on applied research. Thus, an enormous effort toward developing mutual understanding must be made in the forthcoming years; the *Orientation Law* of November 7, 1968, which anticipates the participation of outside individuals in the administration of the university, can be of help.

National Expenditure for Research and Development, 1963-64

| | Amounts of Expenditures | | | Sources of Expended Funds (%) | | | |
|---|---|---|---|---|---|---|---|
| | *Absolute value in million $* | *Per capita in $* | *% of Gross National Product* | *Private business* | *State* | *Private institutions* | *Universities* |
| France | 1,299 | 27.1 | 1.6 | 51% | 36% | — | 11% |
| United States | 21,075 | 110.5 | 3.4 | 67 | 18 | 3 | 12 |
| United Kingdom | 2,160 | 39.8 | 2.3 | 67 | 25 | 1 | 7 |
| West Germany | 1,436 | 24.6 | 1.4 | 66 | 3 | 11 | 20 |

Source: OECD

This same law also implies the effective financial participation of the economic sectors in both university life and research.

New areas can be developed at various levels of both fundamental and applied research. The greatest effort ought to be made, particularly in the latter area. Regardless of who is at fault, the risk is that the university may devote itself to pure research and allow specialized public and private centers to monopolize research in general. The French university would then be nothing more than an organization disseminating a culture and a science to be developed by others.

The establishment of *Unités* of university research isolated from *Unités* of education risks the same inconveniences. Thus, we must find structures which are sufficiently flexible to permit the intimate association of research and education. In this respect, it may perhaps be possible to form for each university a fund, maintained by the regional authorities and economic interests, which would be administered by a joint committee of university people and heads of companies and which would permit the financing of research on new modes of instruction.

If the French university fails to make a considerable effort, both financially and intellectually, it risks the possibility of being cut off in coming years from both research and economic life.

### YOUTH AND THE UNIVERSITY SYSTEM

The May 1968 crisis increased the confusion of students. It violently questioned the entire university system, which had been submitted in the past to a repeated and vigorous censure by instructors. Reference can be made here to the issue of the magazine *Esprit* for May-June 1964, which was entitled

"Faire l'Université." In line with some of the students, the instructors vigorously criticized the traditional division among letters, law, science, medicine and pharmacy, and expressed their wish for a true revolution. Likewise, they protested against the methods of instruction, in particular the examinations and the magisterial courses. But it could be noted, as the newspaper *Combat,* in fact, did, that "what is striking in this issue (of the paper) is that the spirit of censure prevails over the spirit of reform, or rather, that reflecting upon what is not working properly does not bring out a clear vision of the future."

What young people think of the university was the theme of innumerable publications; we will consider only two works here: *La Remise en question de l'Université* (University at issue)—July 1968 special issue of *Sciences de l'Education* magazine; and *Quelle université? Quelle société?* (Which university? Which society?)—Collection *Combats, Le Seuil.*

What was actually questioned was the university itself: "The university is a diploma factory. This implies that the professor, as a productive element, is assigned a place in the hierarchical structure. The student is but a product on his way to becoming merchandise."

The university appears to be tied to the society of consumption and, consequently, is attacked as such. Moreover, its organization follows a hierarchical pattern, according to which the teacher strictly conforms to prescribed instructions and programs, while the student's role is limited to receiving instruction.

The French system allows for nothing but the transmission of predigested knowledge; this permits the selection of the necessary elite for the management of bourgeois society. A crisis definitely exists since it is not possible to educate 600,000 students with a system designed for the molding of an elite. A system of education based on everyone's participation in the dynamic process of learning must be found..

To be rejected: an instruction which is intensive and abstract, an instruction founded on monologue, an instruction which is restricted to certain social classes.

And to be anticipated: a human and concrete instruction, an instruction founded on thinking and dialogue, an open-to-all instruction.

What a minority of students rejects is a school policy which is not based primarily on the questioning of society itself.

What the majority of the students criticize is a policy founded on a selection system which creates a feeling of insecurity among the students, at least during the first cycle.

The students criticize the "secondarization of the first cycle."[1] It must be

---

[1] The French phrase, *"secondarisation du 1er Cycle,"* refers to a teaching process that is common at the undergraduate level in the United States. Students are sometimes required to drill, memorize, etc. Many in France object to this process.

noted that a large number of instructors would be of an opposing viewpoint, like Mr. Grégoire, who in the magazine *Esprit,* quoted earlier, writes: "We must clearly distinguish between undergraduates and graduates, as is the rule in the Anglo-Saxon countries. For the former, education should be secondarized and a series of processes should be applied which still seem to us unworthy of the university: lessons learned in manuals and exercises which are directed and corrected. A multifarious framework will be necessary . . ."[2]

Thus, there is a sharp disagreement between instructors and students: the masters want a system of teaching which is strict and organized, the pupils wish for the greatest freedom. It is true, of course, that in student eyes education has not so much the goal of developing understanding as of developing a critical attitude with regard to society.

This is what many students claim: "The student movement is questioning the foundations of society, which in its eyes is a society of classes and of consumption, which involves the growing need of production and therefore of work, and which is thus alienating all strata of society."

What some students hope for "is the power of teaching, a community of professors and students, a group of persons of good will searching together to define their responsibilities to themselves and to others, a community where a totally shared knowledge would be reinvented."

All this leads students to demand again that the role of the university must be: an effective social service of education open to all, and a permanent place for contestation and dialogue.

In order to realize these objectives, the autonomy of the university with regard to all external powers must be assured. It is a preliminary for the establishment of a free and effective student power in institutions of learning, and for both political and syndical freedom of expression in the faculties.

Autonomy can be budgetary, in order to avoid all financial interferences; administrative, in order to fight bureaucracy, and pedagogic.

*Cogestion* (sharing of responsibility and authority by teachers and students) is autonomy in practice; it introduces participation, that is, the decentralization of internal power in the university; it permits the institutionalization of dialogue and the introduction of responsibility in the administration of establishments. The power of *cogestion* belongs to a combined assembly.

Thus one sees what are the major demands and attitudes of the student movement in France today:

Protest against society, in particular the alienating society of consumption.

Rejection of a strict pedagogy, alienating and bound to a concept of educa-

---

[2] Roger Grégoire, "Faire l'Université, Dossier pour la réforme de l'enseignement supérieur," *Esprit* (May-June, 1964), p. 744.

tion which is selective, and founded on a fear of the future because orientation is lacking.

On the positive side, the goal is, participation and responsibility through *cogestion* in a regained autonomy. This amounts to six principles:

1. Restructuring the university can only be accomplished by the university itself.

2. Every university must become a permanent forum for questioning of the political and social structures.

3. Every university must assume the functions of research, education, and culture.

4. Every university system must permit access to the university by all.

5. The university must be based on a new teacher-student relationship at every level.

6. The university year must be questioned.

Most of these principles were accepted and put in operation by the Orientation Law of November 7, 1968, which anticipates councils composed equally of students and instructors in every department. The university councils and the regional and national councils of education and research include instructors, students, and persons exterior to the university.

THE FINANCING OF THE UNIVERSITY

The university in France is financed almost exclusively by the state budget. Only the state gives the funds necessary for the operation of the university. Since 1958 the budget has grown in the following manner (in millions of francs):

|  | 1959 | 1961 | 1963 | 1965 | 1969 |
|---|---|---|---|---|---|
| Operation of the universities and faculties | 23 | 54 | 120 | 156 | 264 |
| Equipment | 60 | 115 | 80 | 135 | 180 |

The above does not count expenditures for personnel. For personnel the figures have evolved as follows:

|  | 1960–61 | 1964–65 | 1968–69 |
|---|---|---|---|
| Professors and lecturers | 3,585 | 5,218 | 6,676 |
| Assistants | 4,316 | 11,524 | 22,867 |
|  | 7,901 | 18,739 | 29,543 |

Expenditures for instructors have been considerable in that they have increased 350 per cent in eight years; as for the budget, that for operations increased ten times while the equipment budget tripled in ten years.

Participation of regional and local authorities in the financing of higher education is, with rare exceptions, nonexistent. The same is true for the participation of the various industrial and commercial enterprises. Expenditures for secondary and primary education are the responsibility of the state and the departments, and the university is not concerned. The budget for national education presently represents nearly 20 per cent of the state budget and about 5 per cent of the national revenue.

In conclusion, it can be said that the French university has undergone a severe crisis but that its effort at adaptation, both in structure and in budget, must eventually enable it to overcome its difficulties, even though the persisting resistance to change from numerous instructors does not facilitate such evolution.

# COMMENTS BY PHILIP E. MOSELY*

Professor Dreyfus' paper quite properly emphasizes one of the central factors in the critical situation of French higher education: its very rapid growth, especially since about 1954. By that time France had completed its recovery from the effects of the war and was already launched on a process of economic expansion more rapid than at any time since the 1850's and 1860's. As shown on page 287, the number of students increased from 150,000 in 1954-55 to almost 500,000 in 1967-68, and of course there has been a further increase in 1968-69. These figures refer to the numbers of students enrolled in the universities and do not include some of the most important institutions, the so-called "great schools," such as the Polytechnic and the famous School of Public Administration, which train an élite of students. Professor Dreyfus next discusses the social origins of the student body. His data point to the slow but substantial increase in the numbers of sons and daughters of workers and the continuing predominance of the middle and the upper middle class.

* Professor Dreyfus was unable to participate in our second conference on universities in the Villa Serbelloni, Bellagio, Italy, June 23-27, 1969. His paper was distributed to the participants and Professor Mosely made the above comments on it. The transcript of his comments was sent to Professor Dreyfus, who, in turn, made the observations published in footnotes 1 to 5 (Editor's note).

Professor Dreyfus goes on to a problem that stands in the forefront of attention as a consequence of the new French law on higher education, that of the system of admission to the university. In France, as in Spain, completion of the examinations at the end of the secondary school entitles a student to admission to a university. Yet, since admission to some of the faculties, especially in science and technology, is necessarily limited by the size of laboratories and other physical facilities, the overall pressure of numbers has resulted in a large increase in those faculties that rely primarily on lectures and libraries, such as the humanities and social sciences. On the other hand, except for teaching, these latter faculties do not prepare their students for any very definite or stable careers. Thus, for a growing proportion of the student body there is a high degree of uncertainty regarding the purpose and future usefulness of their higher education. One consequence has been to stimulate discussion of whether and how to limit enrollment in the universities. This reform, if adopted, would establish a special examination for admission to the universities, and the completion of the baccalaureate would no longer guarantee admission to a university.

One problem, a long-standing one under the French system, is the great psychological and social strain that falls on students when they sit for the baccalaureate examination. There is enormous pressure on the individual student to surmount that hurdle; failure in the baccalaureate is assumed to set for life a low level of expectations and achievement. There is enormous pressure on the lycées to push the maximum number of candidates through, and there is a very great counter-pressure to hold down the number that pass because completion of the baccalaureate entitles a student to admission to a university. Thus, large numbers of competent students are afflicted with a "Fail" in the baccalaureate simply because the numbers admitted to the university must be held down. French secondary education is on a high intellectual level, and yet many people who in other countries would have their certificate of completed secondary education are denied that certificate in France, simply because in effect the two requirements—completion of secondary studies and admission to the universities—are combined into a single and rather terrifying set of examinations. Professor Dreyfus hardly touches on this very important problem of the various proposals for changing the methods of admission to higher education.

Other problems, characteristic both of France and of many other countries, arise from the growth in the numbers of students. For example, the increase in the number of qualified professors, lecturers and other instructional staff has been much too slow, and this has led to a serious decline in contact between students and professors. Coupled with the overcrowding of lecture courses and the general failure to provide professors with office space in which to confer with students, the expansion in numbers has intensified this important source of student discontent. The traditional system worked so long as each professor had a reasonable number of students and could eventually come to know the abler ones well. Today most French students feel they are anonymous faces to their professors, and that their professors have very little interest in them. This in turn leads to a solidarity of students against professors and to a surrogate "class war" of students against those who should be their mentors and friends. Professor Dreyfus' essay hints at this problem without probing into it.

Another problem arises from a disproportion between the needs of French society for educated people and the provisions for meeting those needs. In some fields far too few people are being trained, as in the sciences and technology; in others, too many are being trained, as in the case of sociology. In the "events" of June 1968, the students of sociology were often the most volatile among student groups. Unlike the situation in the United States, where sociologists have a wide range of interesting careers open to them both in teaching and outside, in France and more generally in Europe, this is not yet the case.

A further problem arises from the separation that has grown up between teaching and research. Many potentially able teachers hardly teach at all; many teachers, swamped by the large numbers of students, must either forego the opportunity for research or teach in a perfunctory manner. Professor Dreyfus has presented a very interesting description of the rapid postwar expansion of research but he has not brought into the picture the various strains that emerge from the growing estrangement between research and teaching. One by-product of this development has been an important change in the method of preparing and recruiting professors in higher education. The previous system—the *aggrégation*—is rapidly fading away. The newly appointed professors achieve distinction—and university chairs—through an almost exclusive devotion of their time and effort to research, often with little or no experience in effective teaching. The result is, almost inevitably, high rewards for research and low rewards for effective teaching. The additional strain that this imbalance places on the professor-student relationship is a notable factor in the present and continuing problems of universities in France and elsewhere. Professor Dreyfus' essay does not touch on these developments or their consequences.[1]

The most important single instrument of the remarkable postwar develop-

---

[1] Since it is in the research-teaching dichotomy that Mr. Mosely sees reason for the profound unrest of our university, it is necessary that I supply an item of additional information.

In France the best science students are drawn towards the "great schools" or towards private industry. Teaching and research, while retaining brilliant elements, also offer outlets to students of varied potential. And in these two fields only those who attain the grade of titular professor by means of a thesis, benefit from brilliant and well-remuner-

ment of research in France has been the *Centre National de Recherches Scientifiques,* which was established in 1936. The C.N.R.S. has a large number of research workers organized in six principal sections and some 35 subsections, covering all fields of learning and offering great opportunities and rewards to research talents. In addition, there are, outside the university and C.N.R.S. systems, numerous important research institutes, for example, in atomic research, agronomy, telecommunications, medical research, and so forth. This wide-ranging network of research institutions offers conditions of work vastly superior to those of the universities in terms of research facilities provided, time available for research, remuneration and prestige. The results for the advancement of research have been truly remarkable, but an unforeseen consequence has been, as in the Soviet system, a rather sharp separation between the interdependent functions of research and teaching. In addition, the difficulties since 1968 in the universities have led some of the best scholars to abandon their teaching posts and seek refuge in research institutes, which are less exposed to turbulence. Some of the best scholars believe that this is the only way in which they can accomplish original work of research and at the same time continue the training of a small number of talented younger scholars. Thus, the deep-seated problem, and its consequences, are being worsened by the failure to tackle the basic needs of both expanding and improving higher education systematically.

Within the universities the problems of inadequate facilities, too few libraries and laboratories, too few teachers, have led to serious disruptions. Yet, even a very large effort, backed by great resources, cannot quickly remedy these unfavorable conditions. The legitimate and long-standing grievances of the student body are compounded, not resolved, by the methods to which a large and active minority has resorted in order, not merely to express its discontent, but to capture the universities and transform them into an instrument of "revolutionary reconstruction" of the society and the polity.

Perhaps Professor Dreyfus has interpreted rather too strictly the request to provide a description of the organization of French higher education and has

---

ated careers. Except in certain specific cases (the Center of Nuclear or Spatial Research, the Center of Research of Rare Enterprises), pure research does not offer vast vocational opportunities. This is one of the principal reasons for the crisis in research in France. To be the holder of a chair in a university or to direct an institute are much more desirable than to devote a whole life to research, which is honored very little.

It seems that there is a misunderstanding concerning the definition of what we call research. For us, conforming to the definition of the C.N.R.S., real research does not begin until after the master's degree and the *Diplôme d'Etudes Approfondies.* The work which is done for the master's thesis cannot be considered, we feel, as true research. It is an initiation into research, and many students seem to content themselves with this type of work. One cannot say of an *agrégé,* the simple author of a thesis, that he is a researcher. *Comment by Professor Dreyfus.*

therefore devoted too little attention to the problems of growth and adaptation. However, his essay has given a proper emphasis, I feel, to the question of the isolation of research from teaching at the advanced level and to the tendency for the new generation of scholars to be trained largely outside the universities, through the national research centers, to whose role he refers briefly.

Professor Dreyfus discusses some of the causes of the crisis in the French university system. He is quite right, I feel, in stressing the severe tensions that develop within the student body over the examination system and the award of diplomas. Since students must invest several years of hard work in securing their degrees, the question whether the system and conditions of instruction will enable them to receive their diplomas is a source of great strain. Related to this feeling of uncertainty is the problem of adequate guidance. Despite a threefold increase in the number of students over a period of some 14 years, the problem of guidance has been overlooked until recently; it will, hopefully, receive more attention in the course of implementing the new law of November 1968, the "Edgar Faure" law.

I sometimes have the impression that our restless American graduate students want to move toward a French system under which there would be relatively few formal courses or specific requirements, and their performance would be measured in comprehensive examinations to be taken at a late stage in their instruction. Many French students, on the other hand, want to move toward the American system of well-organized departments, a definite sequence of courses within the curriculum, and a steady progression of examinations to be taken at frequent intervals, so that they will have better assurance that they are mastering the subjects and methodologies in the course of their training, rather than studying for two or three years without much guidance, only to be confronted, at the end, with a wide-ranging and demanding set of examinations. The decisive effect of the examinations, coupled with the lack of individual guidance, leads to an unnecessarily high proportion of failures and thus to great social and financial waste both for the individual and for the educational system. Perhaps many students who eventually fail could have been guided into other careers at an earlier stage and the scarce resources of the educational system would be used less wastefully.

Professor Dreyfus discusses briefly some of the main criticisms advanced by the students. One of these is the emphasis upon the lecture system. In France and elsewhere the impersonality of the large lecture is often compounded by the absence of adequate auditoriums and classrooms. Too often the students are unable to find seats in the lecture halls; often they listen to the lectures over a loudspeaker or simply buy and study the notes. Indeed, they might be better off if they spent that time reading and studying and made no attempt to attend the lectures; this is difficult because of inadequate libraries. Customarily, students have no opportunity for discussion and individual consultation with their professors until they reach the seminar stage. Yet overcrowding is very frequent at that crucial stage. If a seminar has 40 to 100 students, it becomes another name for a lecture course.

One further factor, which Professor Dreyfus does not stress, is the tendency for the full professor to be in complete charge of his field, and thus to exercise potentially autocratic power over students and junior teaching faculty.[2] The sometimes arbitrary use of authority often results in mistrust and antagonism between the professor, on the one hand, and the assistants, over whose careers and prospects he exercises so much power on the other. One strong argument for moving from the system of individual and separate chairs to a system of departments is that the single-handed authority of the professor is diluted and perhaps corrected by the judgments of a body of peers. Great scholars have risen to eminence under the chair or cathedra system, and have trained other able scholars to follow them. Yet, the prolonged dependence of assistants on a single professor has often been both humiliating and debilitating.

An important factor, to which Professor Dreyfus refers briefly, is that, in France as elsewhere, the students are demanding much more individual discussion and participation. In addition to small seminars, with 15 members or less, the students want more extensive direction of their research and they want to begin their individual research at an earlier stage and not first spend four or five years simply passing various set examinations.

Professor Dreyfus emphasizes the desire of many of the students, now that the social basis of recruitment has been widened, to broaden the inflow of students even further. Many students feel conscience-stricken at their special opportunities, and they denounce the universities and "the system" for not making the same facilities available to all. With this feeling goes another tradition, one that is far from new, of the role of the university as a critic and innovator within the society as a whole. Where many students go astray, in France and elsewhere, is in assuming that the university can be captured and forced to serve as an instrument for directly changing the policies of government or for revolutionizing society.

Professor Dreyfus has emphasized primarily the internal factors that have led to many problems, to unrest, and to efforts, before and since the unrest, to modernize the educational system. Probably for lack of time, he has not discussed a number of other questions, for example, the creation of new universities, their purposes, and the implications of this new development. In this connection it is interesting to note that the disturbances of May 1968 in France began at the new University of Nanterre, located on the northern outskirts of Paris, which was being created in part on an American pattern. One problem

---

[2] The full power of the titular professor, which the law of 1968 remedied, was a real power only with respect to the students and the assistants. For some time, the assistant professors, as titular heads, enjoyed a very real independence. *Comment by Professor Dreyfus.*

at Nanterre was that of scheduling construction. A special feature, contrary to older French tradition, is that a large part of the student body is housed in dormitories, and that the dormitories thus bring together a large number of young people with a common status and many common grievances. On the other hand, the construction of the library had not yet been completed, so there was no place for the students to work. Thus, conditions at Nanterre were very favorable for the "spontaneous combustion" of student discontent, to which a small but intelligent minority of militants could then supply the element of "revolutionary" leadership.[3]

Professor Dreyfus' report summarizes clearly the problem of structure and organization within the French university. One question which needs fuller examination is how far the universities will be enabled to develop as centers of advanced research or whether there will be a continuing and perhaps even more rigid separation, as outlined above, between the two interdependent functions, teaching and research.

Ideally, the developing scholar should have open to him a direct and orderly progression from the early stages of his advanced training to the most advanced opportunities for research. For a young French scholar, the question of being invited, or not being invited, immediately after completing his professional training, to continue his research in one or another of the institutes or centers within the network of the *Centre National de Recherches Scientifiques* is crucial to his scholarly and personal future. The scholar who receives this invitation may well go on to a highly fruitful career in research. Those who are passed over may find themselves confined to teaching in secondary schools and in the provinces. It is little wonder that, partly as a consequence of this rigid dichotomy, the teachers' unions are one of the principal centers of social unrest and militant ideology.

Probably through lack of space, Professor Dreyfus' report says little about the problems of university administration and planning, the lack of foresight in planning the expansion of teaching staff and physical facilities, the lack of personal contact with students, and the militant discontent felt by a substan-

---

[3] If Nanterre was an explosive faculty, one can say that the organization was a mediocre one because of a lack of financial means. Indeed, for 40 years the situation was allowed to deteriorate at the University of Paris; the professors at the Sorbonne opposed everything which might menace their monopoly (see on this, the analysis of G. Gusdorf, *The University in Question*). Also, since 1964, everything had to be done too quickly and with too few means. On the other hand, France, a relatively poor nation, can offer only a limited number of quality universities; local political reasons brought about the proliferation of numerous small universities (ten in a few years), greedy for funds. These new creations can only be imperfect structures, especially since the uniformity of the French system forbids their specialization or differentiation. *Comment by Professor Dreyfus.*

tial part of the student body. His report does not discuss the demands or proposals for participation by the students, including for example, their participation in the appointment and promotion of professors.[4] It is not clear on what basis students who are beginning their specialized training can participate in deciding who is or is not qualified to provide that training. This demand, if pursued to a logical conclusion, could lead to the extreme situation, which is now well established in many Latin American universities, in which the students, organized in political parties and acting through a separate elected body, exercise a direct veto over the appointment of all professors. Several of my colleagues at Columbia University, who had agreed to co-operate in a joint program with a university in Argentina, were dismayed to find, on arriving at their posts, that they had not yet been officially appointed since the students had not yet interviewed them and therefore had not decided whether they would be allowed to teach.

The question of financing is, of course, basic to the development of advanced teaching and research. The rapid growth of industry, science and technology in France since around 1954 has led to a relative starving of the universities, with the serious consequences which Professor Dreyfus has outlined. On this and other topics it would be helpful, in a comparative study of universities and their problems, to have a somewhat fuller treatment. However, within the purpose which Professor Dreyfus has set himself, he has given an enlightening and concise account of the problems of French education.[5]

---

[4] The law of 1968 made the participation of the students in the appointment and promotion of professors formally impossible. This rule has been applied in all French universities with the exception, perhaps, of Vincennes. *Comment by Professor Dreyfus.*

[5] With respect to the guiding of the students, the French system rejected the tutor system for a long time and founded higher education on the notion of masterly courses and noncontrolled personal work. If, in the faculties of medicine and science, the proportion of work sessions and small seminars increased each day, it was not the same for the nonscientific faculties.

| 1968-69 | Law | Letters | Sciences | Medicine | Pharmacy |
|---|---|---|---|---|---|
| Teachers | 2,143 | 4,742 | 10,064 | 7,289 | 1,349 |
| Students | 141,490 | 189,900 | 135,700 | 101,830 | 21,500 |
| Ratio-Teacher Student | 1/70 | 1/40 | 1/13 | 1/13 | 1/16 |

One can thus demonstrate an enormous deficit of teachers in the nonscientific disciplines, and another noticeable deficit in the scientific disciplines; however, the situation has noticeably improved overall. In 1938-39, there was one teacher for 34 students, in 1952-53, four for 67. *Comment by Professor Dreyfus. All Professor Dreyfus' comments were translated into English by A. J. Lambrinu di, Director, Hood College Foreign Study Program.*

# CAUSES OF THE FRENCH STUDENT
# REVOLT IN MAY 1968

Mattei Dogan

It will be recalled that in May 1968, France was shaken by a violent up-heaval generated by the fusion of a student revolt and a general strike. Born within the university, the agitation rapidly spread to the working class, so that at the end of May, 10 million workers were idle.

If, in attempting to explain why the university erupted, one limited his analysis to the daily press and to the plethora of mimeographed tracts handed out during the "revolutionary days," he would emphasize the agitation by small, well-organized groups. The fact remains, however, that on several occasions tens of thousands of students took to the streets to demonstrate their discontent. It would be difficult to explain their participation or the response of the student mass to the alarums of organized groups if the idea of general, student dissatisfaction were not retained.

We do not intend to analyze here either the ideology of the militant student groups or the chronology of the events of May 1968. We will attempt to uncover some of the major factors which led to the upheaval of the French university. They are diverse; some are demographic, historical, political and economic, while others concern more specifically the organization and content of French education. Still others involve the whole of French society, particularly the place of the university in an industrialized society. Obviously, these factors cannot be isolated one from another; they must be taken together because they had a cumulative effect. Nevertheless, out of a concern for clarity, we will consider them separately.

## THE DEMOGRAPHIC EXPLOSION

From the beginning of the nineteenth century until the eve of World War II, France was characterized by a low birth rate. During those generations, French society and its institutions accommodated themselves more or less willingly to the situation. Immediately after the war, however, the birth rate revived and rose sharply. Amidst the enormous political, economic and social problems engendered by the war, the unaccustomed phenomenon of a sudden growth in population began to exert pressure on the society.

The educational system was one of the first institutions to feel the push of the new generations—first in the kindergartens, next in the primary schools, then in the lycées, and finally in the university. Partly because it was occupied with equally pressing matters, the government waited until late before beginning to build new schools and train new teachers that were needed to cope with the sudden cohorts of school children, lycée students, and ultimately university students. The government, which prided itself on its rational planning policy, failed to allow for the needs of the new generations of students. When the young born between 1945 and 1947 entered university some 20 years later —to simplify matters, let us say just prior to the May events—neither the university structure nor its facilities were prepared for such an influx. In the period from 1949 to 1957, enrollment in the French university rose from approximately 150,000 to 220,000, but over the eight-year period from 1959 to 1967, it jumped from approximately 230,000 to over 500,000. The buildings at the Sorbonne, erected in 1900 to accommodate 15,000 students, had to make room for three times as many in 1967. Hence, the drama of lecture halls bursting at the seams.

## ACCESS OF NEW SOCIAL STRATA TO UNIVERSITY EDUCATION

In France as in other countries, the modernization of the economy, the development of technology, and the rise in the standard of living have resulted in the continuation of studies beyond adolescence for a greater percentage of the young population. Consequently, the flow of students through the French university has slowed, adding still another dimension to the problem of overcrowding. Whereas, before World War II only a small percentage of French youth (2 per cent) between the ages of 20 and 25 entered college, today a quarter of the same age group go on to higher education. This marked rise in the number of students has been accompanied by a profound change in the students' social backgrounds. Formerly the great majority of students came from the urban and rural middle classes. If today the proportion of students from working-class families is still much lower than the percentage of workers in the active population, the number of students from modest social backgrounds is, nonetheless, considerably more important than it was 30 years ago.

Therefore, the French university system has experienced a double crisis of growth since World War II: an increase in the number of students due to the demographic explosion and the democratization of education brought about by social pressure from the rising classes.

## NAPOLEONIC CENTRALIZATION OF THE FRENCH UNIVERSITY

All French higher education is administered by the state through the Ministry of National Education in Paris. Antiquated for years, this centralized system is a Napoleonic legacy. What might have seemed a modern creation at that time is little now, according to many observers, but an arthritic institution. Given the increase in the student population and the higher percentage of lycée graduates who wish to continue their studies at the university, bureaucratic centralization constitutes an obstacle to the evolution of the various schools and thus to their adaptation to the modern world.

With approximately 50 per cent of the French civil service in its employ (760,000 persons including administrators, office staff, and teachers from primary school through the university) and 20 per cent of the national budget in 1968, making it the largest ministry in the French state, national education constitutes a gigantic centralized public service. It is easy to imagine the weight of such an administration in the hands of department heads and assistant department heads, who seem to use their genius to envelop the administrative process in mystery in order to reinforce their own positions in the bureaucratic labyrinth. Enigmatic and ungainly, such administrative tutelage does not facilitate rational progress. Reforms in the university, as in some other administrations, are often possible only through crises, as Michel Crozier has noted.

Just as with the P.T.T. (Postal, Telephone, and Telegraph Administration), the various branches of the university were subjected to direct administration from the Center, thus leaving them virtually no power of decision. Once the annual education budget had been passed by the national legislature, the Ministry controlled expenditures in almost every aspect of the national educational system including the university. Until the May revolt, it also had the final say in matters of university administration, general policy, codes of discipline, study programs at all levels and regulations concerning the granting of diplomas. All decisions came from the Ministry, all petitions for further decisions went to the Ministry, and until the Ministry spoke, there was little to do but continue petitioning and wait.

Naturally, since the Ministry of Education had to handle virtually all the problems raised by the entire French educational system, as well as to cope with the problems endemic to its own bureaucracy, the situation was often confused and decisions were frequently delayed. For example, in July 1967, the schools of letters did not know how many students to expect at the beginning of the academic year in October. They had even less idea of how many hours had been allotted for formal instruction. Since May 1968, the Faure educational reform law (named for the Minister of Education, Edgar Faure) has granted the schools some control over their educational policy; however, they do not possess financial autonomy, so much of the problem remains. In September 1969, many of the professors and assistants at the experimental university center at Vincennes, near Paris, had not been paid for the previous semester, and the students struck in sympathy. As in the past, the funds granted to the schools by the Ministry of National Education often depend more on financial bargaining and on decisions far removed from the university than they do on rational calculation. By the mid-1960's, such administrative tutelage no longer responded to the needs of the university.

The excessive centralization and laborious bureaucracy of the Ministry of Education could no longer live up to the enormity and complexity of the task assigned to it. As Alain Touraine has remarked, "The University is a rigid system controlled directly by a centralizing administration, enamored of order and principles, overwhelmed by routine, incapable of defining objectives or adapting its methods to changes." It could not handle the growing student population to its satisfaction, nor could it cope with its numerous ramifications: the need for orientation and counseling, the problem of housing, the requests for scholarships, and the lack of suitable jobs for the students who were graduating. Its inability added considerably to the tension.

The centralization of decision-making power in the hands of the Ministry had another serious flaw. Not only did the various schools not have the power to decide; they also lacked the power to negotiate. Consequently, when signs of trouble began to appear in 1967, negotiations between school administrations and radical students and any resulting agreements or decisions had to have the approval of the Ministry. Thus the centralization of the system encouraged the students and the faculty to focus their dissatisfaction on the government. Touraine has also emphasized this aspect: "Wherever the institutional system is rigid and incapable of negotiating, the rebellious movement has more of a chance of going beyond the university and of calling the power of the government itself into question. . . ." In fact, that is precisely what happened.

### AN INEFFECTIVE SYSTEM OF SELECTION

Any student who has passed his baccalaureat and who wishes to enter the university, has the right to do so. Moreover, tuition fees are virtually nonexistent when compared with those American students must pay: in 1968, the equivalent of 18.00 dollars per year. Selection of students in France occurs at the end of their university studies and not at the beginning. Many students, after having spent several years in university classrooms, are compelled to give up their studies without having been able to acquire the degree they were hoping for.

On the subject of student achievement, we have a detailed study by Alain Girard. University studies produce a low yield in terms of numbers of degrees. This situation stems from the absence of a selection process prior to the students' admission to the university. As one example among others to indicate the meagerness of student advancement, Girard cites a study by Gaudemar and Kayser, "Dix années d'une génération d'étudiants dans la Faculté des Lettres de Toulouse (1956-1967)." Out of a sample of 835 first-year students (*propedeutes*) in the school, 228 did not take the final examination. Such a massive abstention raises the question of "false" students. Who are they? Some of them are individuals who lack the determination to continue their studies and who enroll in the university in search of a pleasant atmosphere. They come for the easy life. Such young people were able to play their roles in the explosion of May 1968. "False" students may also be those persons who enroll in the university in order to take advantage of the social benefits offered by student status. Among this 26 per cent group, others are salaried workers, who did not have time to prepare for their exams. Still others are also enrolled in another school, whose courses they follow assiduously. It is more a question of phantom students than of "false" students. Thus, 228 students did not take the exam, leaving 607 who did. Of these 607 students, 187 did not pass, 420 received the first-year certificate, but only 205 passed with marks high enough to go on and be granted the *licence,* the French equivalent of the Bachelor of Arts degree: only 25 per cent of the total 835. Of those, only 9 per cent ultimately received a higher diploma.

Noelle Bisseret's research complements Girard's study. Out of 6,919 first-year students enrolled in the School of Letters in Paris in 1962-63, 21 per cent did not sign up for the final examination, 3 per cent did not show up, and 8 per cent failed and did not receive the first-year certificate. Thus 32 per cent of the students gave up their university studies. For the second year, Bisseret gives statistics that show that of the 21 per cent who tried to pass the exam the second time around, only 36 per cent obtained the first-year certificate (that is, ⅓ of those retaking the year's program). Of the 42 per cent enrolled for the licence, only 14 per cent received two certificates, 28 per cent received one, 52 per cent none, and 5 per cent refused to answer the question.

The importance of this loss becomes even more serious when one considers the number of years required for the licence. According to certain studies, again cited by Girard, a third of the students complete their programs in three years, another third take four years, and the final third need from five to seven years.

Is such a system rational? Logically, one cannot help but raise the question of selection prior to admission to the university, given the percentage of students lost during the first years of university and the increasing length of time required to complete a degree. The number of students cannot be permitted to go on increasing indefinitely if they are not all capable of reaching the same level; a selection system has thus certainly become a necessity. However, whatever system is chosen, it will demand the creation of services, numerous and diversified enough to permit each student to find a place and a field of concentration which conform to his needs and aspirations. The system of enrollment in the university cannot be modified at the highest level of university life without having already established means of orientation and selection throughout the university.

Even before the war, students from bourgeois backgrounds, who failed their baccalaureats or the national examinations for admission to one of the great professional schools (*"les grandes écoles"*), were frustrated by their failure. The adult world placed so much importance on the exams that if a student failed, he felt rejected and isolated from his social circle. (The total number of students was smaller at the time.) During that period, university failure often favored extreme rightist tendencies. Today a failure on an exam pushes the student toward the Left. How can this shift be accounted for? With the democratization of education, the students who are unlucky on exams are more and more numerous. They constitute a considerable force and they know it. Hence, a certain "proletarization" of the students who are "stuck" in their "university factories." Their refusal to accept the conditions prescribed by their studies brings them closer to the workers. In spite of their bourgeois background, under certain specific circumstances which seem to prevail in the schools of letters, the students lean toward the extreme Left.

In the autumn of 1968, the students succeeded, by intimidation, in gaining the right to pass their exams in much larger numbers than in previous years. As a result, 1968 witnessed a devaluation of university diplomas.

## THE ABSTRACT STYLE OF FRENCH UNIVERSITY EDUCATION

French university education places more stress on the form of self-expression of knowledge than on its content. It attaches great importance to verbal prowess, stylistic beauty and graceful expression. But it concerns itself very little with whether or not the ideas shaped by the articulate student are in any way connected with a practical activity. Especially the schools of letters have not in the past prepared their students for practical work after graduation. This theoretical character of French education is institutionalized in the very organization of university studies. Until recently, professors lectured "ex cathedra" on their subjects, and the students listened passively. Since the May crisis, seminars and small study groups have developed within the university.

Two consequences seem to us particularly important. First, the lack of specific, tested skills means that at 25, without a profession, without money, and sometimes without even a place to live, many graduates can count only on chance to find their position in society.

Moreover, as many observers have remarked (among them Raymond Aron, Stanley Hoffmann, Laurence Wylie, René Remond and Michel Crozier), verbal prowess, dexterity in manipulating abstract subjects, and lack of practical experience in testing ideas or theories in concrete situations often has the effect of divorcing French students from a sense of responsibility. Without getting too involved in semantics and philosophy, one might say that frequently the untested idea, once expressed, becomes the reality. If an opportunity presents itself to put certain ideas into practice, as was often the case during the May revolt, and if the idea succeeds in fact, then the experiment proves the correctness of the idea. If, however, the idea fails in application, then it is often viewed not as the fault of the idea but as the responsibility of enemy forces. While this is obviously a caricature, it contains many traits faithful to intellectuals in many countries. But in France (and in Italy) it is perhaps more visible and more frequent.

### THE SATURATION OF TEACHING POSITIONS IN SECONDARY EDUCATION

Traditionally there has existed a division of labor between the university and its schools of sciences and letters on the one hand, and the high professional schools (*grandes écoles*) of engineering, science, business and public administration on the other. While both categories would come under the general rubric of the university in the United States, they are completely autonomous in France. Some times administered by a ministry other than the Ministry of National Education, the high professional schools are more difficult to enter and are considered the pinnacle of the French system of higher education. Only the finest students get in, and their graduates have no trouble finding a job. They are courted by both private enterprise and public administration, both of which are run primarily by graduates of the *grandes écoles*. The number of students in the *grandes écoles* represents approximately one tenth of the total student population in higher education (the percentage varies according to which schools are included.)

The schools of sciences and letters in the university system have always concentrated on preparing future secondary school teachers. Their courses are oriented toward the national recruitment examination for secondary school teachers. During the first decade following World War II, many students could look forward to teaching in lycées because of the growth of the secondary school population. But the period of growth led to one of stabilization. In fact, indications that the number of students and thus the number of teachers needed would level off were apparent for several years before it actually occurred. Nevertheless, the percentage of students entering the schools of letters has continued to increase. Hence the imbalance, which has resulted in unemployment for many university graduates. In order to avoid misrepresenting reality, we must distinguish between the "literary" schools and the "scientific" schools.

It would be judicious to include in the "literary" category not only the schools of letters but also those of law and economics. While the former concerns itself essentially with preparing future teachers, the latter two have little interest in openings that might occur in secondary education because of the slight attention paid to law and economics in lycée programs. The schools of law and economics train students for administrative, judicial, or economic careers. Nevertheless, jobs in such fields also pose problems for the students. In effect, the education is often very general and abstract and does not truly prepare the student for a career in which experience in business is essential. Still, those schools offer more opportunities than the schools of letters when it comes to finding a job.

The "scientific" category includes the schools of medicine, the natural sciences, pharmacy and the exact sciences. They prepare students for a specialized, practical activity. Their education is more oriented toward the acquisition of a practical profession than toward abstract, cultural knowledge. They are also more open to the possibilities of research and contemporary discoveries in other parts of the world. Armed with workable knowledge and a practical experience, the graduates of these schools have no difficulty finding employment.

Before the general revolt in May, the most open agitation by militant students was led and encouraged by radicals at Nanterre, a suburb of Paris. Many of the militant students, later "revolutionaries," were enrolled in "literary" schools, particularly in departments such as sociology and psychology. In fact, Daniel Cohn-Bendit, one of the students who emerged as a leader of the May revolt, was in the department of sociology at Nanterre. The fact that many of the most active radicals during the May events were "litteraires," suggests that a student's discipline—the material taught and the future offered him—in some way shaped his response to the revolt.

UNEMPLOYMENT AMONG YOUNG GRADUATES

Except in rare instances, unemployment in France since the beginning of this century has stood at 3-4 per cent of the active population. Such a rate of unemployment is technological; to that extent it may be considered normal. Thus it cannot be counted as one of the causes of the crisis France passed through in May 1968. However, for young people looking for a job the first time, this rate of unemployment is very important. In fact, according to the first results of the March 1968 national census on the active population, the number of unemployed persons under 25 was found to have increased three-fold between 1962 and 1968, while their share of the population seeking work had increased from 29 per cent to 39 per cent. The essential reason for this situation was the lack of adaptability of the French university to the needs and demands of the modern society.

While the most pressing needs of the society demand a faster increase in the number of scientists and doctors graduated by the university, it is the schools of letters that are growing most rapidly. Even today France is witnessing a serious decline in the number of lycée students planning to take the baccalaureat leading to scientific studies. This push into literary fields had become excessive even before May, at least to the extent that many students were taking a dead-end street. The failure of the university to prepare students for a marketable skill can only favor the rise of unemployment among the young.

The failure of certain schools in the university to adapt to the evolving economic needs of the country is such that many departments are overcrowded while others, which are essential to the national economy, are undersubscribed. Students desert certain disciplines either because of a lack of information on employment after graduation or because of a fear of the subject's possible difficulty. Consequently, there is a considerable imbalance among various disciplines. Many students choose at random. How could it be otherwise when there exists no serious organizations even within the university capable of counseling students on fields of concentration that will assure them of employment in the future. This is another example of the mythical nature of the famous French planning system.

## THE PRIVILEGES OF FULL PROFESSORS AND THE STATUS OF TEACHING ASSISTANTS

The professor's role is to transmit the knowledge of his special field. This knowledge confers on him a certain academic prestige. In the past the professor was an "authority," who enjoyed addressing an audience conscious of his intellectual value. Even before May, the audience had changed; the increasing number of students undermined the existing relations between master and disciples. In the schools of letters the professor delivered a formal lecture on his personal research, which was often brilliant, but by the middle of the 1960's, it was no longer adapted to either the level, the needs, or the number of his students. They were obliged to listen passively to what was often incidental to their particular academic programs; the professor's detailed research did not necessarily provide them with a basic education. The assistants were responsible for seeing that the students' instruction was completed on a more fundamental level. Their work became routine and was often carried out under deplorable conditions.

The assistants and master assistants of the French university are not the counterparts of American assistant professors and associate professors. While master assistants have some status, assistants have no professional status; they are named to their posts for a limited period of time and are responsible to a full professor, in a sense more as his collaborators than as teachers in their own right. Moreover, the master assistants are usually not very young. The majority of them are between 30 and 35. Sometimes, especially in the natural and experimental sciences, the assistants are as knowledgeable as the "mandarins," as they call them, whom they "serve." In these instances, they do about the same work as the full professors.

Sometimes more than 50 students attended practical classes, meant to be small work sections, which were intended to give them a more practical—as opposed to theoretical—instruction in the use of their subject matter. The sizes of the classes and the burden of the work often led to friction between the assistant and the professor. The assistants have to work twice as many hours as the full professors.

However, some of the assistants did not possess the qualifications required for their work. In some instances, students believed that the professors would have been more competent, but the latter were either unwilling or unable to take charge of the smaller sections. Thus, this shared dissatisfaction led to a similarity of interests between students and assistants against the professors.

This alienation on the part of the students and assistants is quite justified. On the one hand, the professor, conscious of his prestige and knowledge, refused to increase his contacts with the ever more numerous student body; he preferred to devote that time to his research. On the other hand, the assistant had to establish relations with a much too numerous group of students and do so without any assistance from the professor. However, if the professors guarded their academic advantages, most of them remained liberal, tolerant, and open to new ideas. What was involved was a conservatism linked to the privileges of the profession and not a social conservatism.

In fact, the crisis of May 1968 was as much a rebellion of assistants as of students, especially when one recalls the role of the *Syndicat National de l'Enseignement Supérieur* in the crisis. The assistants played out their revolt within a union organization different from that of the full professors. In so doing, they showed themselves to be closer to the leftist movements. Touraine has quite rightly remarked that "the appearance of the assistants as a particular category, defending their own interest, but also representing a strategically central element in the life of (university) departments will almost certainly be one of the most difficult results to abolish from the movement of May."

## THE DECLINE OF STUDENT UNIONISM

We would have an incomplete idea of the university crisis and of its consequences if we did not analyze briefly the phenomenon of student unionism. Since the Algerian War, the *Union Nationale des Etudiants de France* (U.N.E.F.), the principal organization of the student union movement, has witnessed an almost daily decline in its adherents. This situation is the consequence of a series of political stands it took during the war, which caused the government to terminate its State subsidies. In effect, U.N.E.F., which before the war was a basically apolitical union recognized by the government, committed itself politically against the war. Consequently, the government stepped in and cut off the financial aid which it had given the union until that time. A rival apolitical organization was created, the *Fédération Nationale des Etudiants de France* (F.N.E.F.). This new union, set up by outside pressure from the government, could only favor the explosion and division of U.N.E.F., which then passed into the camp of the opposition.

The U.N.E.F. has become a closed field of combat where political groups have replaced unionist tendencies and confront one another in open debate. The groups include the *Jeunesse Communiste Révolutionnaire* (Trotzkyist), the *Fédération des Etudiants Révolutionnaires* (also Trotzkyist), the socialist students, communists, and more diverse, ephemeral varieties of anarchists and "situationists." The National Office has had more and more difficulty controlling the situation. Deprived of all financial support, it has vainly multiplied its appeals to members for unionist discipline and payment of dues. Incapable of gaining a strong foothold in increasingly overcrowded schools and departments before May, U.N.E.F. had to content itself with running a few services and representing the students in a formal manner in negotiations with the authorities. These few services rendered to the students were not sufficient to mobilize the masses. Moreover, U.N.E.F. had no influence over the organization of university education (unlike in the United States), because it had no institutional means of making its power felt after its split with the government; thus, it found itself losing contact with the student mass, who showed indifference to its activities. Having no grasp of the realities of contemporary university affairs, U.N.E.F. lost more and more of its identity as a unionist organization and ended up by combining with other organizations which temporarily assumed control over it.

On the eve of the May crisis, U.N.E.F. was skeletal. Its National Office already knew that it was controlled by extremists. This tendency was reinforced by the results of the last student elections preceding the May upheaval. The mass of apathetic students abstained; the extremists voted. U.N.E.F. was at their mercy. Since it was then led by a militant minority, the union came to play an important role in the student revolt. Many students, who had been indifferent until then, identified with the radical minority. For most of them, it was the first time they had found a means of making themselves heard. Strikes and demonstrations exploded. To a certain extent, the mass of students awoke. U.N.E.F. and S.N.E.S. became the two institutional frameworks of the student revolt in May 1968.

In 1969, though the mass of students was no longer indifferent, it had been disoriented by the multiplicity of small, well-organized groups which, though united during the revolt, now became enemies. These small groups play an important role, however, for they are very active and violent and would like to be able to reassemble the student troops.

## THE POLITICIZATION OF THE STUDENT BODY BY THE ALGERIAN WAR

Parallel to the decline of student unionism has been the drop in the influence of the traditional political parties—and notably the Communist Party—among the young.

Immediately after World War II, French political parties found themselves at odds with the youth movement, which refused their tutelage. As early as 1945, the Socialist Party was virtually compelled to accord a certain autonomy to its youth organizations, and especially its student organization. In 1947, the Socialist Party "beheaded" the youth movement at the Congress of Lyon. Even the Communist Party was forced to "reorganize" the *Union des Etudiants Communistes* (U.E.C.), which had been taking clear and therefore potentially dangerous and embarrassing stands. Such animosity between party organizations and youth prevailed virtually up to the outbreak of the Algerian War. When the war broke out, the parties had no impact on the student population. Isolated and unappreciated by public opinion, rejected by the government and the parties, the young moved to the Left and their political positions became increasingly more radical. Seeing their friends drafted and sent to Algeria, and directly concerned themselves, they violently opposed the Algerian War as colonialist. There is a certain similarity between the reactions of French students to the Algerian problem and those of American students today with regard to Vietnam.

Since May 1968, the university has become politicized. In effect, a minority of resolute students has placed the knowledge taught by higher education on trial. They have called into question that knowledge, which, according to them, "is the slave of capitalism." If they so wish, these student groups can prevent courses from being offered. In his book, *La Révolution Introuvable,* Raymond Aron expresses his concern over the politicization of the university. The various schools in the university have become a "political instrument" in the hands of a minority, whose goal is to challenge the established power and not to prepare students for a later profession. In refusing to prepare students to fill socially useful functions, according to Aron, "the university fails to fulfill its duty and launches into life tens of thousands of graduates who are in danger of finding themselves unemployed."

Will good or harm come from this politicization of studies? The future will judge. As always, whatever the outcome, the crisis itself can be explained sociologically.

## THE MACROCEPHALISM OF PARIS

The French university crisis is original in the sense that it grew out of the university. From a crisis of education it grew into a crisis of the Gaullist regime. The student concentration in certain large cities, whether in France or elsewhere, has a very large impact on the types of demands and the forms of protest.

For the study of the strategy of urban guerilla movements, which have spread throughout the world during the last few years, it is important to make a distinction between the various countries affected. Countries may be divided according to whether they are,

a) macrocephalic (France, Japan, Argentina, Mexico);

b) pluricephalic (West Germany, Italy, Belgium, Spain); or

c) Anglo-Saxon (the United States, England).

The first category is characterized by a capital which dominates the entire country and has a large concentration of students. The second category groups countries whose large cities each have a major university center. The third possesses the peculiarity of having most of its universities outside major cities.

It is obvious that 30,000 students demonstrating in Berkeley, Madison, or Ithaca cannot create the same echo as an equal number of students demonstrating in the heart of Paris, Tokyo, Buenos Aires, Mexico or Berlin. It is not therefore by chance that the American students prefer to go to Washington for spectacular demonstrations. Moreover, such demonstrations disconcert police forces, which accounts in part for the difference between student demonstrations and those of masses of workers. In effect, while workers, directed by their union representatives, remain true to their original intentions, the audacity and imagination of students defy the police to predict their reactions in a given situation. The element of surprise which they employ is also fearsome, especially when they are concentrated in a capital city.

Thus, several thousand Parisian students can occupy a ministry or a vital government center and paralyze the entire capital, its normal activity, and the lives of millions of its inhabitants for hours or days.

However numerous they may be, students who demonstrate on campuses far from important cities can hope at most that their action will be carried by network television. Nonetheless, the student militants are proportionally as numerous in America as in France or in other European countries. If their action is more spectacular on the eastern side of the Atlantic, it is primarily because of the concentration of European students in major cities. (The crisis at Columbia University, in the spring of 1968, is an exception to this tentative typology, and is due in part to the very different topographies of New York and Paris.)

## THE ENDEMIC REVOLUTIONARY TRADITION AMONG PARISIAN INTELLECTUALS

As we have indicated above, the French student movement failed to receive support from the traditional political parties. However, it did create an echo among Parisian intellectuals. The appeal was answered for two reasons:

a) the revolutionary tradition is deeply imbedded in Paris, where several currents of thought test one another continually;

b) the Sorbonne, unlike campuses situated outside of large cities, is located in the center of Paris in one of the largest and most active intellectual, artistic, and literary communities in the world. Obviously, there is a certain osmosis between this community and the university. Moreover, Paris is an old city in which the revolutions of the past are inscribed in different quarters, most notably, the Latin Quarter. Students find themselves immersed in a fertile environment for nonconformist and revolutionary ideas, and any student agitation finds support in other circles (literary, artistic, theatrical, etc.). This Parisian intellectual ambience considerably amplified the university crisis of May 1968.

In his essay, *"Mai 1968: premières réflexions sur les évènements,"* Edgar Morin shows "that there was a dimension of a permanent game, which gave this youthful commune its originality." According to Morin, the students mimicked the barricades of French history and the guerrillas of "Che" Guevara. At the Sorbonne were concentrated "the most virulent and the most significant (traits) of the student commune." Lecture halls became the places where minds liberated themselves day and night in search of a dialogue. "The Sorbonne hummed with meetings, seminars, and commissions like a bee-hive." During the new phase, which began with the occupation of buildings, the Sorbonne was an immense theatre. Posters and grafitti on the walls constituted the decor. Writers and philosophers, such as Jean-Paul Sartre, came to offer their support to the students. Musicians were invited to play their works. Even lawyers came to present their problems. Space soon became insufficient, so the artists and students occupied the Odeon, the national theater near the Sorbonne, to pursue their round-the-clock debate. Never, during these seminars, was violence used. Everything was expressed in words and gestures. It was a verbal, histrionic revolution, a festival that was only possible in a center like Paris, reputed for its artists, musicians, writers, painters and philosophers. But not everyone succeeds at such callings: out of 16 painters, 10 or 15 live in poverty; for one celebrated writer, 50 or a hundred do not find publishers; for one famous musician, there are perhaps hundreds who die unknown. In the movement unleashed by the students, these frustrated individuals found a means of expressing their own dissatisfaction.

## INCIDENTAL FACTORS AS CATALYSTS

Attempting to explain the university crisis of May, whatever the profound causes and origins, one can always point to incidental factors, which serve as catalysts, as immediate motives. Under this heading, one could list a great number of elements, extending from the Vietnam War to the activities of the so-called Student Internationale. We will limit ourselves to four points:

a) In 1966, the Ministry of National Education, aware of the abstract nature of education in the university, decided to modify the system. The goal of Fouchet reform (so named because of the minister, Christian Fouchet) was to make university education more specialized, especially those studies in the schools of letters. It instituted a progressive cycle of studies and eliminated the annual certificates. Under the plan, the student was virtually unable to escape from a certain field of concentration once he had chosen it. The equivalent credits from programs of previous years were confusing and poorly defined. Introduced suddenly, the reform created a great deal of confusion in the university. What would the equivalent academic credits be between the old and the new systems? How would the academic year be organized? The confusion in the administration and in the organization of studies and exams provoked the students and provided them with a concrete target for their dissatisfaction. The Fouchet reform was one of the sources for the student protest two years later.

b) The very nature of student outbursts presupposes good weather. It was not simply by chance that the revolt erupted in the spring. It is more difficult to raise barricades in the cold and rain than it is when the sun is shining. The weather in May 1968 was particularly fine in Paris.

c) The presence of a large number of revolutionaries in the department of sociology at Nanterre could be viewed as the detonator of the revolt. It is possible that without the presence of a leader like Cohn-Bendit, the agitation would have occurred in a different form.

d) A certain clumsiness on the part of the government and the university authorities certainly played a role in precipitating the revolt. As an example, there was "the Antony incident." Antony is a university dormitory complex on the outskirts of Paris, which is composed of two parts, one for boys and one for girls. Until the eve of the events of May, regulations forbade girls and boys from visiting one another's rooms. The violations were undoubtedly numerous. Fed up with the situation and the irksome regulations, the students requested that the parietal rules be abolished. The Ministry of Education replied with indignation. To a certain extent, the minister was acting in *loco parentis* to guarantee the girls' virginity. In this light, the students' indignation is understandable. Over 21 for the most part, they saw the minister's reaction as a new form of parental authority and "moral order."

This particular example of government clumsiness, added to many others, encouraged the development of the already latent dissatisfaction among the students.

SUMMARY

Naturally the diverse aspects that we have analyzed separately for reasons of clarity are not independent. Their effect was cumulative. The set of them forms a "gestalt," a whole. In effect, the demographic explosion explains nothing by itself. Its effect added to the increase in the number of young people actually attending the university, which stemmed from the desire, widespread among people of all social levels, to see their children continue their studies.

Education became a phenomenon of numbers. The administrative organization of the university, inherited from Napoleon, no longer corresponded to mass education. Formerly valid, the university structure was outmoded 150 years later because in the interim the number of students had increased a thousand times and perhaps more. Centralization simply did not fulfill the needs of a university encompassing more than a quarter of French youth between the ages of 20 and 24.

Nor was the former system of university recruitment valid any longer. Nor is the abstract nature of university education comprehensible if one does not consider it in relation to the privileges of many professors. The professors' "conservatism" was also understandable in the light of the rise in the number of assistants, who were anxious to "take over." The unemployment of university graduates is in a sense the consequence of the abstract style of education.

These various factors, taken together, suggest an explanation of the collapse of the French university in May 1968.

There is no real educational planning in France, despite the warnings by such sociologists as Alfred Sauvy and others whose works have for years foretold of "the rise of the young" and its consequences. In retrospect, it is easy to predict the student revolt of May 1968.*

---

* This chapter was translated by Allen T. Rozelle.

For the sources cited in the text, and other selected works, *see* the following: Raymond Aron, *La Révolution introuvable* (Paris, 1968); Noëlle Bisseret, *La carrière scolaire d'une cohorte d'étudiants* (Paris, 1968); Pierre Bourdieu and Jean Claude Passeron, *Les Héritiers—les étudiants et la culture* (Paris, 1964); Pierre Bourdieu, Viviane Isambert-Jamati and Alain Girard (eds.), "Sociologie de l'éducation," *Revue Française de Sociologie,* numero spécial 1967-1968; Alain Girard, "Population et Enseignement," *Etudes Sociologiques* 1967-1968; Institut Français d'Opinion Publique, Jacques Duquesne (ed.), *Les 16-24 ans* (Paris, 1963); Henri Lefebvre, *L'irruption de Nanterre au sommet* (Paris, 1968); Le Thanh Khoi, *L'industrie de l'enseignement* (Paris, 1967); Roger Masters, "Les racines biologiques d'une révolte," *Preuves* (February-March, 1969), pp. 74-81; Ministère de la Jeunesse et des Sports, *Jeunes d'aujourd'hui* (Paris, 1967); Edgar Morin, Claude Lefort and Jean-Marc Coudray, *Mai 1968: la brèche* (Paris, 1968); Alfred Sauvy, *La montée des jeunes* (Paris, 1959); Alain Touraine, *Le mouvement de Mai ou le Communisme utopique* (Paris, 1968).

The best bibliographical commentary on the May 1968 crisis in France is: Philippe Bénéton et Jean Touchard, "Les interprétations de la crise de Mai-Juin 1968," *Revue Française de Science Politique* (June, 1970), pp. 503-544.

# THE ITALIAN STUDENT MOVEMENT

## From Reform to Adventure*

### Federico Mancini

Rebellion in the Italian universities was already detectable in 1966. The crucible of the student movement, however, was the month-long occupation of the Turin campus in November 1967. From Turin the rebellion spread throughout the country, making a clean sweep of the old party-controlled organizations.[1] Soon its unique traits began to take shape.

First of all, there is a flat refusal to participate in university decision-making. While the German S.D.S. has sometimes laid claim to *Drittelparität* arrangements and some S.D.S. people sit on student-faculty committees, though with the purpose that Lenin assigned to Communists in bourgeois parliaments,[2] the Italian students oppose codetermination. They "don't want to run the pigsty" with the professors, lest they be co-opted and corrupted. One reason they fight the government-sponsored university reform bill is that it aims to "cage" them by student participation in university governing bodies.

Besides, running the pigsty together implies the election of representatives, and disavowal of the principle of representation is a second trait of the Italian student movement. Nowhere has "direct democracy" been so uncompromisingly espoused as in Italy, though its original purism now seems in decline. Student assemblies are still held and lip service is paid to the sovereign author-

---

* An earlier version of this essay was delivered at a conference on "The Task of Universities in a Changing World," at Bellagio, Italy, June 26, 1969. Permission to reprint the present version was granted by the editor of *Dissent* magazine, where it appeared in the September-October 1969 issue.

[1] Prior to the 1967-68 academic year the Italian campuses were dominated by four associations: U.G.I. (predominantly Communist), I.N.T.E.S.A. (Christian Democratic), A.G.I. (Liberal), F.U.A.N. (neo-Fascist). They all entered lists of candidates for the election of student representative bodies whose main functions were to carry out cultural, recreational, and welfare activities. On this system, see my piece "Student Power in Italy," in "Student Power in University Affairs—A Symposium," *American Journal of Comparative Law*, XVII (1969), 371.

The current movement, *movimento studentesco,* is referred to throughout the article as the (Italian) student movement.

[2] Arnold Beichman, "Letter from Columbia," *Encounter,* May 1969, p. 15.

ity of the direct voice of the people, but such assemblies have proved time-consuming and unwieldy. Hence, more and more emphasis is laid on a new form of organization, the "grass-roots committees" (*comitati di base*), which are small and geared to specific problems and obviously more effective. An even more significant departure from the careless spontaneity of old is the progressive transformation of an open and constantly changing leadership into a semipermanent steering committee. This self-appointed Jacobin elite already shows all the symptoms of bureaucratic degeneration.

The third distinctive feature of the Italian student movement has been its remarkable ability to map out and implement a common strategy for the major campuses. Of course, this has been made easier by the highly centralized nature of the Italian university system: the rector of Palermo will respond to student challenge in much the same fashion as his colleague of Milan, because both are responding to the same ministerial circular. But, granted that the student movement has been lucky in not having to deal with a Hayakawa here and a Perkins there, the primary reason for its success in co-ordinating activities at various universities has been its own internal cohesion. The hard core of the movement is composed of Communists who find themselves at the extreme left of their party, anarchists, Trotskyites, Maoists of various persuasions,[3] and members of *Potere operaio* (Worker Power), a group with aspirations resembling those of the old revolutionary syndicalists. These sects have always expended considerable energy in internecine wrangles but, until a few months ago, have also managed to patch up their differences and rally dissenters to the general line. The moral tension of the militants, rather than their adhesion to the Leninist doctrine of "democratic centralism," and especially the undiscriminating character of police busts have contributed to this extraordinary achievement.

The strategy of the Italian student movement has varied with circumstances. In broad outline, its development falls into three phases: the last months of 1967, spring and autumn of 1968, and the winter of 1969.

(1) The first phase was characterized by a harsh critique of the university as an authoritarian "class" institution, but also by a determination to make

---

[3] In Italy there are at least five groups of Maoist inspiration: the League of the Marxist-Leninists, the Revolutionary Marxist-Leninist party of Italy, two Communist parties of Italy (Marxist-Leninist), and the Union of the Italian Communists (Marxist-Leninist). By far the most vital among them is the Union, which is slightly less sectarian and more loosely organized. On May Day, the Unionists were able to bring out at least 10,000 people to parade in all the major cities.

The Trotskyites are divided into two movements, respectively affiliated to the Posadas and the Maitan Fourth International. In the Italian student movement, however, the Trotskyites have played a minor role; at any rate, a far less important one than in France.

use of it. Future economic exploitation is anticipated in the university which is, indeed, often compared to a factory (a graffito at the Liberal Arts Faculty in Rome reads: *"FIAT is our university, the university is our FIAT"*). But the men and the facilities of the university can be turned to account with a view to producing new values, to laying the cultural foundations of the coming revolution. To achieve this goal, the student movement demanded a "restructuring" of courses: no more lectures delivered *ex cathedra* or teacher-dominated seminars but egalitarian "study groups" where professors, now called "experts," would co-operate with the students in approaching the subject matter (any subject matter) from more "relevant" angles and, above all, in debunking the myth of the neutrality of science (any science).

The study groups were conceived as models of a nongovernmental university and, for their most daring advocates, a nongovernmental society.[4] These notions, which resemble the schemes of a pragmatic anarchist like Paul Goodman, were often expressed in Che Guevara's phrase: "Society as a whole will have to be a gigantic school." Less loftily, the study groups were also supposed to provide activists with an opportunity to influence the inchoate mass. "Campus" and "college life" are meaningless terms in Italian universities where, except for a usually squalid cafeteria, students have no place to get together. Students meet "on the job," in the classrooms. Classrooms being the only places where new proselytes could be made, it was imperative for the militants to change the conditions of classroom work in order to insert the preaching of their gospel and legitimatize it.

Those were the days. . . . How many are the professors who look back in anger to the "study-groups period"? Surely not those—a huge majority—who turned down the students' offer (at that time offers were not always accompanied by threats and it was easy to show some backbone), nor the very few who agreed to participate in the experiment. Actually, the excitement of the latter—mostly liberals—was boundless. In Italy one becomes a tenured professor (a "baron") through cooptation by one's peers. To wield academic (baronial) power one must enjoy their confidence. But is there a more exalting experience for a liberal liege lord than seeing his power recognized, nay legitimized *also* from below? Indeed, the above-below relation remained by and large untouched. Being referred to as an "expert" was for the leftist professor not unlike the pleasure Count Honoré Riqueti de Mirabeau must have experienced when addressed as *citoyen:* in the study group it was he who did most

---

[4] The "study groups" were first theorized in the *Carta rivendicativa di Torino*, a document produced during the occupation of Turin University, which has for the Italian student movement much the same value as the Port Huron Statement for the American S.D.S. The charter is now republished in *Documenti della rivolta studentesca* (Bari, Laterza, 1968), pp. 253 ff.

of the talking and the replies of the radical students were still very much within the rules of the old game.

Besides, many a progressive member of the faculty felt that by agreeing to join the study groups he was contributing to a self-regeneration of the university, of whose wretched conditions he was agonizingly aware. The student-movement leaders did not conceal their revolutionary intentions; but the liberal professors hoped that, while theory remained revolutionary, practice could be steered along reformist lines. In time, they thought, the dross (the inordinate politicizing, the lack of interest in cool research) would be jettisoned; the substance (more vivid seminars and fewer drab lecture courses, more contact between teachers and students) would stick. Such delusions were soon exposed, but for once it is not the students who should be blamed for the liberals' defeat.

(2) The blame lay on Academe as a whole. The university might have taken up the student challenge by working to reform itself. It would have required patience, political skill, and some knowledge of adolescent psychology; at that stage, when only a few student chieftains really knew their own mind, efforts might have yielded fruit. Or the university might have counterattacked. Against the portrait that the radicals drew—a center entrusted by the capitalist system with the task of training its future slaves—it might have put forward a different image: a center of free inquiry and criticism, whose aims should be realized in a climate of political neutrality. But in Italy we had practically none of this; we had none of the soul-searching of the French professors after May or of American professors after Columbia. Cynical shrugs, condescending conversation, or vindictive indignation at "those cranks" were the reactions of most Italian faculty members.

Which, in turn, had a number of consequences. It radicalized many students who still hesitated at all-out confrontation. It persuaded the student leadership that the university could be neither relied on nor exploited. It brought grist to the mill of the fringe (left-Maoists and *operaisti*) who had been contending that the movement's only chance of survival was in an alliance with the revolutionary agents *par excellence:* the industrial workers in the north, the landless peasants in the south. In the history of the student movement, this was a major turning point. Until then most militants had thought that in revolutionizing the universities they were touching the jugular vein of the system; from that moment on, they knew this was not true. In order to revolutionize the universities, they had to get out of them—and, in the words of Rudi Dutschke, embark on "a long march through the institutions."

The study groups were given up. They were no longer useful; they entangled energies needed elsewhere: in winning over the high-school children (high schools were an obvious first choice among the "outside" institutions to be attacked); in helping the workers on picket lines; in organizing the slum dwellers of the large cities, and so forth. But what was to be done with the universities? Surely, they could not be left alone, for there the movement found its strength, its "masses" (not an ironical expression: Italian students number about 600,000). Nor could they be captured. The student movement understood in practice Lenin's critique of Blanquism. Besides, its leaders were not yet certain about their ability to mobilize a large enough number of recruits, or about the measure of the authorities' tolerance.

Therefore, a proposal was made by Vittorio Rieser—possibly the movement's cleverest strategist—to break the universities in two parts.[5] On the one side, a section should be left to the academic authorities for routine activities (courses, examinations, etc.); on the other, an "autonomous space" should be created to be controlled by the students for such initiatives as political meetings, workshops, and "anti-courses." Rieser's scheme obviously echoed foreign experiences: *e.g.,* the American free universities, the German *kritische Universität*. But it also served a practical purpose. The professors' university would play the role of a *Gegenvolk;* it would be the tangible incarnation of Evil. Its inbred authoritarianism and irrelevance would continuously beget frustration and dissent. The "autonomous space" would ensure the presence of the movement in the university and enable it to reap what the enemy had sown: in other words, it would be the movement's sanctuary.

The battle for "autonomous space" took place during the Easter holidays and ended in May after a number of "stiff" occupations. In June, having secured their rear, the students of Turin, Milan, Trento, Padua, Bologna, Pisa, and Rome were ready to start their long-planned "operation working class."

(3) The summer of 1968 was spent in analyses of the French May, in attempts at establishing contacts with fellow movements abroad (especially the German, whom the Italian students admire for their superiority in matters of theory) and, above all, in the search for ways to form a student-worker alliance. But this period of relative inactivity did not last long: a new tumultuous phase was beginning in Italy. First the chemical industry near Venice, later the tire industry in Turin and Milan, and the sugar refineries of Ferrara were upset by a powerful wave of strikes, often of the wildcat variety. The workers' decisions often bypassed or ran counter to union policy. Reminiscent of the factory councils (*consigli di fabbrica*) the young Gramsci had advocated in 1920, these workers' meetings invented or rediscovered tough forms of struggle—slowdowns, sit-ins, "staggered" walkouts, short and repeated (or "hiccup") stoppages. When they put forward a claim, they made it clear that it was nonnegotiable.

In November and December the crisis became acute. Hundreds of thou-

---

[5] Rieser's proposal was outlined in an article, "Strategia del potere studentesco," published in the Left-liberal weekly *L'Astrolabio,* March 31 and April 7, 1968.

sands of high-school students supported demands for freedom of assembly in the schools. Two Sicilian farmhands were killed by the police during a labor dispute and the emotions aroused in the public were violent. Normally sedate social groups, such as white-collar employees, higher government officials, school teachers, resident physicians in hospitals, began to display an unprecedented aggressiveness in their demands for better working conditions. Not even the courtrooms, where left-wing and right-wing judges engaged in incredible brawls, escaped the contagion of *contestazione*. The whole country seemed to be in a frenzy; the government seemed at a loss for solutions, and the Communist party—the Great Sphinx of Italian politics—was about to hold a congress that everybody expected to be crucial.

It must have been at this point that the leaders of the student movement decided to cross the Rubicon. This "objectively prerevolutionary situation" could be helped to blow up through a few "voluntarist pushes," in their words, through some *lotta leggera urbana* (light urban struggle). As Gramsci would have said, Italian society had grown "gelatinous" enough for a resolute vanguard to storm it.[6] If it could be brought home to the Communist bureaucrats that power was within reach, even *they* might awaken from their 25-year long sleep.

All this, however, was bound to take time. The student movement needed bases in which its commandos could prepare their expeditions into the cities and seek shelter afterwards: it needed its Sierra Maestra or—an even more alluring reference—its Yenan. For this, the "autonomous space" conquered in May was no longer sufficient. The universities had to be seized and kept under absolute control; in other words, they had to be destroyed as centers of teaching and research. It was a dramatic decision, even for people much toughened by a year of conflict and hard bargaining. New slogans appeared. The old graffiti were turgid, bombastic, at times sophomoric, but one could smile while reading them—or feel sympathetic. In January 1969 they acquired a sinister, anti-intellectual, even fascistic dimension: "When class warfare becomes acute, culture is of no use"; "To be a spectator means to be a traitor"; "Rape your

---

[6] Here is Gramsci's famous—and, in the days I am referring to, widely quoted-passage: "Ilici [Lenin, in Gramsci's prison vocabulary], it seems to me, realized that the war of movement victoriously conducted in the East in 1917 did not suit the conditions of the West, where only a war of attrition was possible. . . . In the East the state was everything and the civil society was primordial and gelatinous; in the West there was a balanced relation between state and civil society and when the state trembled, the robust structure of the civil society immediately emerged. The state was merely a frontline dugout behind which there spread a solid network of strongholds and pillboxes" (*Note sul Machiavelli,* Turin, Einaudi, 1949, p. 68).

The implication in extremist quarters, of course, was that the time of the "war of attrition" had come to an end in the whole West and especially in Italy.

Alma Mater"; etc. A brilliant scholar, who counts himself a fellow traveler of the movement and had just finished a thousand-page book on the use of analogy in philosophy and science, told me without flinching that the burning of the Alexandrian library by Amr Ibn al-As was the first example of a successful cultural revolution.

The new tactics consisted in keeping the universities occupied as long as possible and, during the brief lulls between occupations, in making demands which, if accepted by the faculties (and they often were), would make serious work impossible. Thus, the Bologna Faculty of Liberal Arts was requested to suppress the written test in Italian; most universities were forced to accept an arrangement under which students were entitled to refuse failing marks and take the same examination, month after month, until they passed.

It was bedlam, but the uproar remained largely confined to the campuses. One after the other, the delegates at the Bologna Communist Congress censured the "adventurism" of the student vanguards. The government finally moved. The truth at last dawned upon the student leaders: *there would be no revolution in Italy in the foreseeable future.* At the end of March the police broke into the occupied universities, with a tremendous deployment of men and weapons. In Rome they found five students asleep, no students in Bologna, and everywhere garbage, anti-Communist writings, broken furnishings and, oddly enough, a number of clogged toilets. Today, a rather lugubrious order reigns again in the groves of Italian Academe.

So far narrative, now interpretation.

In 1968 it already seemed clear that, despite Marxist jargon, the Italian student movement had little in common with socialism. At least in its Italian version, I wrote, the New Left might be the legatee not of the Old Left, but of the *Older* Left, the *philosophes* and particularly Rousseau.[7] Today, this seems even more evident. The student movement—or, more precisely, the non-Communist part of it, is *a characteristically bourgeois movement.* First, in the obvious sense that its militants are of bourgeois extraction (only 13 per cent of the Italian students have a lower-class background and these are very scantily represented in the rank and file of the movement, let alone its leadership). But also in the far more important sense, despite the movement's self-image, its traits fall into a familiar bourgeois pattern. This is not to deny the radical character of its protest; the contrary is true. Indeed, must all revolutionary critiques of the capitalist system be Marxist-inspired and Marxist-orientated?

One should not attach an excessive importance to words, even when they sound convincing. Any project can be adorned with suitable quotations from

---

[7] See Federico Mancini, "The Italian Student Movement," *AAUP Bulletin,* December 1968, pp. 431f.

Marx, Lenin, or the most recent patron saint of the movement, Rosa Luxemburg. It is equally easy to coin slogans with a Guevarist or a palaeo-Bolshevist ring, and to write articles explaining why and how one should love Chairman Mao, particularly when the authors operate in a cultural context (the Italian intelligentsia) which has been imbued with Marxist ideology for half a century.

Nor should one overrate the students' insistence on the leading role of the working class and their almost obsessive wooing of the working man. Bourgeois movements, too, have tried to involve the working class in their own enterprises. Italy has a long tradition of such movements. Obvious cases in point are Mazzini, Arturo Labriola, Gaetano Salvemini and, more recently, Carlo Rosselli and Piero Gobetti, Gramsci's liberal friend who saw in the automobile workers of Turin the emerging aristocracy of modern Italy.[8]

Let us forget the words and consider the deeds; let us go back to the trajectory of the movement and try to break through the screen of its own rationalizations. The university appears to the student both as a Leviathan and a Juggernaut: a huge, clumsy and crushing monster which *represses* him, *atomizes* him, stuffs him with an enormous amount of *irrelevant* information and eventually flings him—a badly-packaged marketable product—into the world of business, the civil service, or the professions.[9] His first reaction is a critique of the university in strictly liberal terms. Against the alienation he suffers, the student advances such characteristic "bourgeois" values as the right to resist indoctrination (why should we law students be taught that legal science must be insulated against the intrusion of value judgments and social facts? What kind of lawyers do they want us to become?); the right to inquire beyond the unreasonably stiff limits of the studies program (why should we students of government be offered but one course in Afro-Asian institutions, and none on Latin America? And why should the subject of this course be confined to the legal systems of a few "safe" Afro-Asian countries?); freedom of speech (why are questions in class frowned upon by most professors?); free-

---

[8] On Piero Gobetti, whose writings are unfortunately little known outside of Italy, see Giuseppe Mammarella, *Italy after Fascism. A Political History* (Montreal, Casalini, 1964), pp. 49 f.

[9] This description may appear to be a caricature: it is, actually, exceedingly sober. May I refer the reader to the so-called Brooks Report on the state of scientific research in Italy, published in 1967 under the auspices of O.E.C.D., and to *L'Università come impresa,* by G. Martinoli (Bologna, Zanichelli,1968). A good point made by Dr. Martinoli—whom the student movement's militants describe as a despicable reformist —is that Italian universities survive only because less than one-third of the registered students attend classes (though, theoretically, they are obliged to attend). If all students went to class, their very weight would cause the staircases and the floors of our universities to collapse.

dom of assembly and association (why are our requests for classrooms for political meetings usually rejected?).

Hence, the proposal to set up "study groups": these, despite the many catchwords in which they were couched, basically amounted to a new, *nonauthoritarian* way of studying *together* things *more relevant*. But this attempt, naïve or impractical though it might have been, ran into a wall, which allowed no room for future student initiative. On the other side, students found opposition—not of ideas—but of ossified structures (the universities) and of other institutions more violent (the police) or obtuse (the judiciary). Grievances that at the outset had been fundamentally cultural became political. The students embarked on an anti-institutional struggle (Dutschke's "long march") that manifested itself first as a refusal of, later as an all-out assault on, the institutions, above all the university.

But even this struggle, for all its harshness and the anger it revealed, is not founded on a "class" analysis of the university and the system that supports it. The university may be hell, it may stifle the students, deprive them of their power of self-determination and emancipation. *But it does not technically exploit them, it does not extract from them any surplus value.* In spite of the Roman graffito, the university will never be the students' FIAT; students *qua* students will never be part of the working class, and their protest is bound to be superstructural, that is, at bottom, vain or inadequate.[10] This appraisal, of course, will not be shared by people like Herbert Read, who wrote that, since institutions in the modern world "legalize tyranny and spread its invisible tentacles into every cell of life," it is at their breakdown that one should primarily aim.[11] But Sir Herbert was an avowed anarchist: namely, as any Marxist would tell you, a petty-bourgeois, radical day-dreamer.

A number of marginal elements confirm the irredeemably nonsocialist nature of the student movement. First of all, the "style" of its protest, which is impulsive, nervous, some say epileptic; at any rate, very different from that, as a rule patient and robust, of worker actions, when they are carried out under the leadership of the Communist party or the Communist-orientated trade unions.[12] Second, the character of its literature, which is basically socio-

---

[10] This is precisely the conclusion reached in an essay on the student movement by one of the most perspicacious Marxist scholars in Italy, the literary critic Alberto Asor Rosa. See his "Dalla rivoluzione culturale alla lotta di classe," *Contropiano,* I, 3, (1968), 480 ff. Professor Asor Rosa, however, admits that the movement might be or become a "problematic ally" of the working class.

[11] Herbert Read, "Pragmatic Anarchism," *Encounter,* January 1968, p. 61.

[12] See Giorgio Amendola, "La crisi della società italiana e il Partito comunista," *Critica marxista,* VII, 2 (1969), 46. Among the Communist leaders, the rightist Amendola is by far the least sympathetic toward the student movement, and whatever he writes about it has to be accepted with reservation. On this score, however, he is undoubtedly right.

logical (sociology, the bourgeois science!) and clearly eschews historic-economic analyses in the Marxist tradition. Third, its reaction to the developments in the Iron Curtain countries. The Italian revolutionary students have no sympathy whatever for the Yugoslav experiment. They took no interest in the Prague spring. When the Russians invaded Czechoslovakia, they accepted without turning a hair the Chinese view that the whole incident amounted to a rift between two revisionist cliques. When Jan Palach burned himself, they remained unperturbed. As a matter of fact, on the front of the Commercio Hotel in Milan, which the students occupied last November and still keep under control,[13] a huge inscription appeared: *"Down with Palach!"*

At first glance, this attitude seems outrageous and contradictory. In reality, it simply proves that the student radicals don't care about socialism. To say, as they do, that socialism has nothing in common with the systems of Eastern Europe and to point to their models of the just society by rhythmically chanting, *Cina-Cuba-Corea-Vietnam,*[14] may be amusing but is also shallow. By hook or crook, "socialism" is there too: between the Elbe and the Ussuri. It is a tangle of contradictions, failures and successes; it has brought emancipation to some, slavery to others. Probably, on balance, the liabilities outweigh the assets. Yet those who do not feel—no, not sympathetic to that mess, that toilsome and bloody human venture but just—involved in it, have no right to count themselves socialists. I hazard the guess that the students and the metalworkers of Prague would agree.

The above interpretation suggests that the Italian student movement is bound not to attain its long-range goal. In other words, no revolution is in sight, no "new-left"-inspired mass movement is likely to take root.

The reason is clear enough. The causes of the nation's present malaise and recurrent crises have been pointed out a thousand times: a parliament apparently unable to legislate, an inept central and local bureaucracy, a judiciary still thinking of Italy as a basically agrarian society, the most expensive and

---

[13] The hotel had been closed for two years; it belongs to the city of Milan whose urban development plan provided for its demolition. It was occupied on November 28, 1968, by students lodged in the university dormitories with the argument that the latter were inadequate (an unquestionable truth) and, at any rate, amounted to "cultural and sexual ghettoes" (a half truth). Presently, the hotel accommodates about 100 people, half of whom are students and the rest an assortment of working men and foreigners, especially Arabs. On April 11 the hotel was assailed by a fascist squad equipped with Molotov cocktails, but the attack was repulsed.

[14] It was probably with reference to these "models" that the new deputy secretary general of the P.C.I., Enrico Berlinguer, asked at the Bologna Congress the following rhetorical question: "What profit can be found in discussing Republics and Principalities which have never been seen or known to exist in reality?"

Very much in the style of Gramsci and Togliatti, the question was a quotation from Machiavelli: and, as usually, a felicitous one.

least efficient social security system in the Common Market area, a shameful health and welfare system, a wretched school system—in brief, a decrepit social structure that does not allow a more equitable distribution of the benefits accruing from the tremendous economic and technical progress of the last decade. The Italian problem, therefore, is to create efficient institutions, not to deny them. The Communist party, for one, knows all this perfectly well. Thus, while it demands "structural" or "strategic" reforms—reforms not assimilable by the system and hence potentially subversive—it concretely goads the government into taking such measures as would help streamline the system.

Why this is happening is not a question to be discussed here. For this analysis, two facts matter: (*a*) during the last few years the issues which the P.C.I. has most agitated have been decentralization of the legislative power, pension reform, hospital reform, town planning, high-school reform; (*b*) their remarkable electoral gains in May 1968 prove that in doing so the Communists have correctly interpreted the character and the direction of the protest spreading in Italian society.

It is precisely these facts—the interest of the P.C.I. in the rationalization of the system and its ability to represent the dissatisfied segment of the electorate —that make the position of the student movement hopeless. The movement actually had but one real chance: to force upon the P.C.I. a process of revolutionary hardening, that is, to stir up such unrest among the masses as to convince the Communist leaders that, by pursuing their previous strategy, they would have lost a considerable slice of their following. Considering the experience and the organizational strength of the two movements, the possibilities of the student movement were infinitesimal; in fact, they did not materialize.

The reverse took place: it was the Communists who turned the student revolt to advantage by beating the young radicals at their own game. Whereas the French C. P. was compelled by circumstances to commit itself right away on the issue of student extremism, the Italian C. P. was so lucky as to have time to reflect. Its leaders realized that the campus war and the spontaneous stepping up of class struggle in the nation at large were a gift of providence in two respects.

First, these events would force the parties in power (Christian Democrats, Socialists, Republicans) to draft far-reaching measures, and especially a university reform bill—that is, to tackle a number of burning problems which were bound to make mischief among them and inside each of them. The Communists, of course, would be able to profit from such differences by playing one faction against another, or taking up the cause of underprivileged groups (*e.g.,* the junior faculty in their conflict with the tenured professors), so as to weaken the government coalition.

Second, the P.C.I. felt that it might capitalize on the creeping chaos, the *chienlit rampant* which the students were spreading throughout the country. Not that the Italian Communists have any fondness for *chienlit:* like their French comrades or, for that matter, General de Gaulle, they hate the sight of it. But a little *chienlit* would enable the party, if it managed to have it stopped at the right time, to present itself as the guarantor of social peace, thus enhancing its prestige.

Consequently, the Communists beat their breasts in self-criticism for not having immediately understood the "deep roots" of the student revolt and stated that the latter had opened "a new front in class warfare" (which wasn't quite the same thing as saying that students were part of the working class, but came pretty close to it). In the autumn of 1968 they vigorously supported the high-school insurrection and in January 1969 they harshly attacked the police for shooting at the students who—in what should probably be regarded as their most futile action—had thrown tomatoes at the customers of a plush nightclub in that Italian Miami Beach, Viareggio. Having realized, however, that a frenzy of adult backlash was building up, particularly in the lower class, the C. P. drastically reversed its course. It did not approve of the February-March wave of occupations and, when the police broke into the campuses, its protests were mild and mixed with reproaches about student "vandalism."

At the outset Communists and extremists managed to coexist in the student movement, though with some difficulty. The charismatic leaders were all self-styled Maoists, but the Communists made up the bulk of the intermediate echelons and were no less belligerent than the others. In folklore (attire, hair style, rhetoric, songs etc.),[15] the two groups were so similar as to make it impossible for an outsider to tell them apart. Then, toward the beginning of this year, the Communist "university sections," which had always been regarded as part and parcel of the movement, appeared to seek the status of autonomous units. Conflicts broke out on policy, which were less furious but far more serious than the mostly theoretic wrangles of old. During the sit-ins of the late winter, the two factions clearly pursued diverging policies; today, on many campuses, they have proceeded to a formal rupture.

A couple of weeks ago, I saw in Bologna a *dazibao* (Italianized Chinese for "handwritten poster") calling a meeting of the "red-line comrades" for the next morning. It was an ominous sign. In the jargon of the revolutionary sects, the notion of "red line" implies that of "black line," where "black" stands for ugly, devious, nocturnal; and the black-line fellows are no longer comrades but renegades.

The strength and the prestige of the Italian student movement appear to

---

[15] The first lines of the most popular song were: "Johnson boia, Johnson boia, giù le mani dal Vietnam" (Johnson, you hangman, hands off Vietnam). Oddly enough, the tune was that of the refrain of "John Brown's Body."

be, at this moment, at an all-time low. The price the movement is paying for the blunder of the winter of 1968-1969 is very high. Apparently, its strategists had mistaken nationwide disturbances for an imminent revolution and had concluded that the advent of the revolution might be speeded up by turning the nation's major universities into "red bases." Now, many militants are in jail, others—the Communists—are hastily abandoning ship, and most rank-and-file students no longer respond to the old slogans. The government reform bill, a far-from-daring piece of legislation which grants the students a *Drittelparität* in the university decision-making bodies, has been drafted and laid before the Senate. The movement's last fortress, the Commercio Hotel in Milan, still holds out, but its days appear numbered. The occupiers have already been ordered by the bailiff to leave, and the bailiff is usually soon followed by the police.

Of course, there is no assurance that the present calm will last. The crucial question is whether and how the reform bill is enacted. In time, if the government manages to promulgate it, the situation will not greatly differ from that of France after the coming into force of the Faure *loi d'orientation*. The Communists will lay aside their largely verbal bias against co-determination, form some front organization and enter lists of candidates for the new mixed student-faculty committees. The left-radicals of the student movement will boycott the election of student delegates and stir up riots wherever they can, but they will suffer a definite retrenchment. In other words, they will be reduced to the status of a small and not particularly fascinating extra-parliamentary opposition, whose main function will be to train the leaders of the future Italian United Revolutionary party, if indeed the *groupuscules* of the extreme Left ever coalesce to form such a party.

But if the reform bill is not enacted or undergoes a further emasculation, a very different development is to be expected. The moderate or reform-minded groups which are beginning to fill the present power vacuum in the student body would collapse and the student movement could easily capitalize on the students' rage. Moreover, under such circumstances, the movement would certainly regain the support, though itself tactical, of the Communist party; and past events have shown how explosive this mixture can be.

The universities, which have practically not functioned for two years, would become impossible places to live and work in. The despondency of the younger professors would reach a climax and support already strong inclinations to seek shelter in private research centers and foreign seats of learning. The contention of the radicals that the role assigned to Italy in the international division of labor is to import patents and export brains would be confirmed. It would be a disgrace and, in the long run, a tragedy. Do the men who in government and the opposition command the allegiance of the Italians realize what is at stake?

# HIGHER EDUCATION
# IN TRANSITION
## The Case of the Universities
## in the Federal Republic of Germany

### Rudolf Wildenmann

## THE PROBLEMS

Ten years ago higher education in the Federal Republic of Germany seemed well established along traditional lines. The gymnasium, mainly oriented toward classical studies and recognized as the steppingstone to the university, was still largely the preserve of the middle class, with only about 4 to 5 per cent of the working-class youth enrolled in such schools.

Then there were the old and famous universities, though less than 10 per cent of each generation attended them. The old university fraternities had reasserted their influence in finding jobs for university graduates. Almost all attempts to create new student associations had been a failure. The political enthusiasm of the immediate postwar generation of students had dissipated, and student political organizations played only minor roles. The desire to secure a well-paid job as soon as possible was paramount. Only a very few were uneasy about the failure of attempts in the late 1940's and early 1950's to change the traditional structure of the German university and to broaden the opportunities for higher education.

Now, however, the universities are in a state of deep unrest. In many cases the structure has been almost revolutionized. At all universities assistants[1] and

---

[1] Assistants having their doctorate but not their "habilitation" have till now been considered "teachers" at the university. They were part-time members of the public service on a two-year basis which could be extended up to six to eight years. Because of the shortage of personnel, assistants without Ph.D.'s who had received their diplomas or passed the so-called state examination (for the most part, law and high-school teachers) might also be appointed. They were then on a part-time contract as public employees. Assistants in the general sense are the "Akademische Raete" (academic counselors) or "Wissenschaftliche Angestellte" (academic clerks). The important point is that all assistants were allocated to the universities according to individual contracts between the state government and the full professors. This arrangement made the assistants very dependent on the professor to whom they were assigned.

Since the restructuring of the universities, the assistants have been more or less freed

students are participating in the administration on every level. Four former young assistants have been elected university presidents at Berlin (the Free and Technical universities), Hamburg and Bremen. The parliament has been the scene of numerous debates about higher education, student protests, mass rallies and the use of force. In the last 10 years high school attendance has increased from 6 to 8 per cent to 15 to 20 per cent, and almost the same number of each generation is going to the universities. In Konstanz, Ulm, Mannheim, Bochum, Dortmund, Bielefeld, Trier, Kaiserslautern, Bremen, Augsburg, Regensburg and other places new universities have been founded or are in the process of being founded. State budgets for higher education have increased substantially. Almost all the teachers' colleges (*Paedagogische Hochschulen*) and a number of engineering schools (*Ingenieurschulen*) have been elevated to university status, while the number of professors has increased by one-third and is now near the 15,000 level. The number of assistants has risen to 40,000, an increase of almost 50 per cent, while the number of students has increased to about 250,000, or almost 100 per cent.

The "Wissenschaftsrat" (a body nominated by the president of the Federal Republic of Germany from lists submitted by central university associations) has published a series of papers dealing with various aspects of higher education. The German Research Association (an inter-university self-governing organization) has added new programs, *e.g.,* the so-called "Special Research Areas," and is supporting research with substantial sums of money. Under the leadership of the Social Democrats the federal government has made higher education one of its major concerns. Vigorous debates rage in newspapers, on television and within the universities themselves on how higher education should be carried on, what the tasks of the university are in modern society and so on. What is more, Marxist-socialist thought has been expressed ever more frequently in this political debate.

In sum, German higher education has become politicized within a very short span of time. When the newly elected president of Bremen University, a man in his early 30's, wrote an article in a prominent weekly newspaper on the subject of how to transform the university into a "political party," he was praised throughout the mass media. Despite all this, the German university remains a place for the education of the middle class, and as the enrollment of working-class youth increases—an event expected momentarily—the university's problems, especially the financial ones, will likewise increase.

To understand this rapid transformation one must pause to identify the winds of change that buffet higher education in West Germany today. They include: (1) the basis for student recruitment; (2) the effects of high school

---

from personal ties to particular full professors. A new category, the assistant professor (very similar to the American one), has also been introduced.

education on higher education; (3) the need for investment in terms of personal expenditures and facilities; (4) the relationship between universities and other institutions of higher education; (5) the structure of the university; (6) the sociopolitical role of the university in a changing society; (7) the task of central university organizations like the W.R.K. (West German Rectors' Conference) or the B.A.K. (*Bundes Assistenten Konferenz*—Federal Assistants' Conference); (8) the federal structure for policy making in educational affairs[2]; (9) changing attitudes of the university population, and (10) the effects of ideologizing political life.

I shall consider some of these problems in this paper.

## SOCIAL CHANGE AND CHANGE OF ATTITUDES IN THE UNIVERSITIES

In January, 1967, the Rectors' Conference of West Germany met in Frankfurt. On the agenda was a report by the rector of the Free University of Berlin, the sociologist Hans Joachim Lieber, regarding the student movement within his institution. His warnings that protesting students would soon become a familiar sight at other universities and that a vigorous political movement was being born were greeted skeptically by his colleagues. This particular meeting developed as before into more of a "handshaking" social event than an assembly of policy makers.

By May, 1968, when the same conference convened at Saarbruecken, the social side of the meetings had been all but abolished. The group passed a few defensive resolutions regarding the minimum requirements of university structure and education, but most significantly, the majority of rectors—a rather demoralized group— voiced their fear of what lay ahead (a few days later the most violent of several clashes occurred between police and students at Heidelberg University).

During the January, 1967-May, 1968 period the state visit of the Shah of Iran in June triggered widespread demonstrations and violence. In the spring of 1968 the state of Baden-Wuerttemberg—soon to be followed by all the other states—passed a law demanding that elected assemblies, comprising professors, assistants and students alike, produce radical changes in university structures within one year. In the period between December, 1967 and January, 1968, a group of rectors presented a paper dealing with structure and partici-

---

[2] In Germany, as in the United States, the states of the federation are responsible in matters of culture and education (*Kulturhoheit der Laender*). Recently, however, the federal ministry of education has been probing its constitutional rights to introduce federal legislation (*Hochschulrahmengesetz*) to impose certain minimum requirements on university structures, allow direct federal funding of universities, etc.

pation.[3] It was unanimously adopted by the rectors' conference (W.R.K.), despite the fears of some individuals that their professorial constituencies would vigorously oppose the proposed changes. In retrospect, this paper proved to be one of the major steps in reformulating the principles of university structure.

In the Bundestag, the scene of debates on higher education for the first time since it was founded, there was a deep undertone of resentment that German professors were not able to reform the university on their own. Student bodies, on the other hand, were ready to follow the leadership of the German Federation of Socialist Students, S.D.S. (*Sozialistischer Deutscher Studentenbund*) in policy matters and on questions of university education.

More than 300 articles and booklets have been published about this one brief period between 1967 and 1968. Most of them stress that radicalism has arisen from minorities like the S.D.S., and from the sectarian attitude of a few students. But even if it is true that the S.D.S. provided the violent leadership, the question still arises why the students were so ready to be mobilized.

Empirical analysis demonstrates that a remarkable change of attitudes has taken place among students. This change has created a basic conflict in society.[4] Students of today—as distinct from other youth of the same age and from the population in general—have a clear and rational understanding of the functions of democracy which they want to see realized in society. They reject radical conservatism (about 15 per cent of the population), are barely tolerant of the paternalistic conservatism (another 15 per cent) of traditional German society, and are rather worried about the lackadaisical participation in politics and the "output" orientation that characterize the majority of the population. They demand a change in patterns of political recruitment, and by this they mean no less than a change in the whole structure of political parties. Student bitterness, which focuses on the parties' oligarchical organization, and their small, elite leadership, closely resembles the frustration Robert Michels felt toward the socialist movement of his day.

---

[3] This group consisted of the rectors of Goettingen, Frankfurt, Konstanz, Freiburg and Mannheim universities. It produced a detailed program to reform university structures that covered administration, participation of the various groups in the university, rules and procedures, etc. It furthermore tried to define the role of the university in present society.

[4] See, *e.g.*, Rudolf Wildenmann and Max Kaase, "Die Unruhige Generation," paper, Institut fuer Sozialwissenschaften, Mannheim 1969; Max Kaase, "Youth and Politics," IPSA paper, 1970; and "Demokratische Einstellungen in der Bundesrepublik," in: *Sozialwissenschaftliches Jahrbuch fuer Politik,* Vol. 2, Munchen, 1970. Further: Rudolf Wildenmann, "Germany 1930-1970, the Empirical Findings," IPSA paper, 1970, also published in S.J.F.P., 1970.

Student rejection of the "establishment" was intensified by the fact that the 1966 Bonn government, the "great" coalition, effectively blocked any meaningful opposition in Parliament. There was room only for an extraparliamentary type of opposition led, for the most part, by students (and exploited by left-wing radicals). Since nearly 70 per cent of the students are inclined to vote Left-liberal (in the German sense), the Social Democratic Party (S.P.D.), the Free Democratic Party (F.D.P.), and even the Christian Democratic Union (C.D.U.) are forced to meet their demands. There is no question but that the crucial domestic issues with which the Bundestag is confronted today—namely, higher education and Eastern foreign policy—were brought to public attention by the student movement. In a way, only one comparison is possible: It was also a student movement which waged (unsuccessfully) the democratic revolution of 1848. But in the 1960's political change was possible; and the two-party coalition system of the Federal Republic of Germany is very sensitive to innovation.

This change of attitudes is to be found among all student strata. In many cases it is almost impossible to determine whether divisions within the student body are due to differences in attitudes (*e.g.,* between students of technology on the one hand and students of philosophy on the other) or to probability errors in measurement.

Compared with other attitudinal studies of top elites,[5] the attitudes of the students resemble those of elites in general, especially in the mass media, trade unions and party politics (including part of the C.D.U. leadership) and to a lesser degree the attitudes of elites in administration, industry and the lower echelons of social organizations. One of the most striking features of German society today is the similarity between present and "future" elites and their liberal, anti-taboo attitudes, and their susceptibility to and eagerness for social change. Almost every conflict in society is mirrored in this basic conflict between elites and the general population. And present domestic political struggles can be understood, in general, as struggles for influence between various middle-class elitist groups.

In such an attitudinal environment radical groups seemed to stand a good chance for support from within the university. And this probability of success was further strengthened by articles and comments in mass media. About half of the top mass media editors are dropouts from the university, a fact which has contributed to the sharp criticism of university structure found in newspapers and on television. Many structural reforms were overdue for several years. Educational investment had been comparatively low, and other interest groups had

---

5 "Elites in the F.R.G.," a preliminary report by Rudolf Wildenmann *et al.,* published in Mannheim, spring 1969. The study covered 800 individuals among some 1,500 top position-holders.

been much more successful in participating in the increasing national product.

As a result of this situation, the university was simply unable to cope with the increasing numbers of high school graduates. The educational policy of the early 1960's had opened the gates to a greater number of "new" and "old" middle-class youth, but this wave of new students could not be channelled or guided properly. The universities were and still are overcrowded.

Most of all, the very structure of German universities and the perceptions of academia made for an institution which would give almost unlimited scope to political debate and action. There was a close interaction between debates outside and actions inside the universities. Academic freedom, it seemed, was the very basis for political freedom. In Berlin and elsewhere, protesting students found asylum in the universities after clashes with the police; like the churches of the Middle Ages the universities were considered exempt from prosecution.

Various factors have to be analyzed in order to explain this change of attitudes. The structure of universities and the "great" coalition provided only the media and framework in which change was possible. It is obvious that one must be very careful not to explain this development only within the German context. But it is also true that special characteristics of the development have to be understood against that background of social change that occurred in German society.

At present there is less than 1 per cent unemployment, but about 800,000 jobs are open and the work force includes two million workers from other European countries and Turkey. This is a fairly good indication of the rapid and intensified industrialization of the Federal Republic of Germany (F.R.G.) which has taken place within the last 20 years. Even backward rural districts along the country's western and eastern borders have either been industrialized or become vacation resorts. The population's social mobility is very high, and public traffic facilities have been greatly improved. The tendency of people to measure political efficiency mainly in economic terms has become a dominant feature of public life. At the same time interest in higher education has increased. Since 1965 this latter issue has been second only to interest in future income. All middle-class attitudes, especially those of the urban middle classes, make this clear.

Simultaneously, public life is being perceived as more complex and diffuse. In spite of an affluent society—or better, because of it—citizens feel incapable of understanding the complex interactions of political and social life (70 per cent of the population).[6] Even politicians sometimes act like circus artists on the high wire—balancing, but making few moves in any one direction. In reality, students need not worry about their future lives, but in overcrowded

---

[6] This fact has been very well established by a number of empirical studies. For instance, *see:* Rudolf Wildenmann, "Germany 1930-1970," *op. cit.*

lecture rooms and under the constant pressure of contradictory propaganda, students find it hard not to develop an escapism that engenders an overall criticism of the social structure.

There is every evidence that this situation brought about the present strong influence of phenomenology on political thought. "Criticism of ideologies"—which has come to mean criticism of "capitalistic-fascist" ideologies—has become the prevailing intellectual orientation, with Berlin, Frankfurt, Heidelberg and Munich taking the lead. This, in turn, has stimulated new organizational patterns among the various Marxist-Leninist-Maoist groups. Violent attacks have been launched against representatives of the liberal school of phenomenology (e.g., Theodore Adorno of Frankfurt was attacked in a most cruel and deliberate manner by the S.D.S. shortly before he died).

It is fair to say that those very attitudes which first induced student bodies to follow the S.D.S. and Marxist leadership would turn to indifference and alienation toward these groups—if not to organized opposition—when the issues changed. Prior to the election of 1969 it was evident that a change of government would, in the short run, diminish the wave of protest—and this is what happened. But from another viewpoint it is likewise plain that more unrest will develop if federal and state governments and the universities are unable to solve some of the crucial problems. There is also the danger that the new Bonn government may serve as a shield for organized leftwing activities in the universities. (Threatening letters to professors have become quite "normal" without action being taken either by university administrations or the government.) Inside the universities, the reformist activity leading to new structures has also diminished the possibility of the radical Left being able to mobilize the student bodies. But these issues are far from being solved.

### THE ISSUE OF THE UNIVERSITY STRUCTURE

After the war there were many attempts to reshape the university structure and fit it into a new and broader context of higher education. Nearly all these attempts were—except for minor matters—in vain.[7] In the summer of 1968 a committee of the Ministry of Culture of Baden-Wuerttemberg, led by Ralph Dahrendorf, published its report on a "comprehensive university" (*Gesamthochschulplan*). The report incorporated many aspects of higher education into the university structure, and the university, in turn, was to be restructured in important respects. Dahrendorf supported Max Weber's criticism of the

---

[7] These were the so-called "blue" papers issued by the Rectors' Conference of 1948-49, and the resolutions of the "Hinterzarten" Conference, both of which can be read as if they were written today.

"Honoratioren"—*i.e.,* he advocated electing permanent presidents rather than a "revolving" kind of leadership. He also sought abolition of the traditional "faculties" (in the European sense) by combinations of interacting disciplines in research and teaching. The report envisaged new and more quickly completed curricula so that better education could be provided for a greater number of undergraduate and a smaller number of graduate students (somewhat like the Anglo-American system). It also proposed combining former universities and professional institutions into "units." None of its proposals, taken alone, was unique; many of them had been tried before at the newer universities like Konstanz and Mannheim. Its comprehensive view, however, was stimulating, to say the least.

What is remarkable is that the Baden-Wuerttemberg Ministry of Culture produced another university proposal at the very same time. This second draft had been prepared by a different committee, consisting mainly of professors of law. In almost every respect it followed traditional lines. Thus the ministry—like other ministries—showed two faces. At the first public hearing in the State Parliament of Baden-Wuerttemberg, called to learn the universities' attitudes,[8] charges and counter-charges filled the air, and Ralph Dahrendorf publicly resigned and joined the F.D.P., then the opposition party.[9]

The issues grew more and more confused. And a few weeks after the student, Benno Ohnesorge, was killed by Berlin police during the anti-Shah riots, this confusion helped swell the wave of violent unrest. But for the first time in Germany solutions to some of the major problems of university structure were being earnestly sought. During the Parliamentary debates the bill underwent considerable change, but once it was passed, the universities of Baden-Wuerttemberg were required to produce new statutes within one year.

The new regulations covered the administrative structure; the question of participation in the administration by all members of the university, including assistants, students and employees; the disciplinary rules of the university; changes in curricula and examinations; definitions of the status of academic personnel; the relationship of "autonomous" universities to the government (all German universities are state universities), etc.

The university bill stipulated that constitutional assemblies of professors, assistants and students be elected, a procedure that in itself was completely new. The assemblies, in turn, were authorized to frame new statutes within the given law. The new bill did not (and could not) regulate the status of assistants— and this proved to be of grave consequence. Since university personnel are regarded as "public officials," their status must be regulated by a federal bill which is still pending (fall, 1970). But in almost every other respect the bill touched

---

8 The author participated at that hearing.

9 He is now one of the European Commissioners at Brussels.

on the problems which are still either being debated in the Federal Republic of Germany or are part of the laws of other universities.

The traditional German university—like other universities—was governed by the faculty; the right of decision was reserved to full professors only. Actually, only a few professors, through exerting their personal influence, participated in the governance of most universities, while their colleagues, as is often the case, felt responsible only for their own—sometimes very specialized—disciplines. The practice of changing the rector and deans every year resulted in discontinuity of administration and wasted both money and personnel. More than that, the system of allocating funds only to full professors left their younger colleagues, such as the assistants, often totally insecure about their academic future. It is no wonder that the negative aspects of this structure became the focus of critical attention, and that the question of who was to be responsible for the institution and its tasks emerged as one of the crucial issues of the day.

There have been various attempts to solve this problem. In general, a representative administration, incorporating students, assistants and professors at each level, has been the goal. Differences, however, arise with respect to the quota for each "population," since the basic assumption is that different "interests" require representation by students or assistants rather than by professors. In the regulations of many universities the question of participation is determined by the so-called "one-third parity." This means that the decision-making bodies derive one-third of their membership from each "group." In most cases a quota has also been set for the representation of university employees, and this number has been added to the total number of elected representatives.

In effect, this structure has achieved an emotional and political solidarity between students and assistants, e.g., in Berlin or Hamburg. It has placed heavy pressure on professors, reduced their teaching and research capacity considerably, and produced an atmosphere of fear. Changing the structure so that more positive results can be obtained has been almost impossible. On the other hand, the growing ineffectiveness of the one-third parity rule has increased governmental influence. The search for solutions appropriate to the various aspects of university life has not been fruitful.

In only a few cases have different procedures in decision making been introduced. In many instances, students now participate in drawing up the curriculum (between 30 and 50 per cent of the respective committees set up for these purposes). Rectors are no longer elected for a one-year term, but for three-, four- or even five-year terms. In many cases presidents, appointed jointly by the university senates and the cultural ministries (as in America), have replaced rectors. All decision-making bodies—councils of departments, councils of faculties, councils of universities—are composed of representatives of professors, assistants, students and university employees. Financial allocations, including money for research, are now, to a great extent, being determined by the councils instead of by individual professors. Overall, the structure of German universities has been totally altered, with the result that "groups" other than professors exert much influence—even, sometimes, a decisive influence—in arriving at decisions.

No other country in the West has gone so far as West Germany in restructuring the universities. But the expectations of students to run the universities —seriously debated in public—outstrip the present reality. As the current leader of the assistants' organization phrased it in an interview with the weekly magazine *Der Spiegel*: "We must destroy the old university in order to rebuild a new one." And by "new" he meant a structure along the lines of student and assistant syndicalism. It is difficult to avoid the judgment that such concepts closely resemble notions prevalent in the eighteenth century; now, as then, there is the danger of a new "Staendestaat" on the horizon.

As might be expected, students and assistants in many cases could not produce enough candidates to fill the openings for representatives. A few of them did exactly that which they had formerly criticized so strongly. The one-third parity rule became a tool for replacing the professorial elite (or what was regarded as such) by the younger elite of students and assistants. This process is a significant indication of the distrust that pervades the academic community.

Moreover, it does not solve the central question of academic responsibility. It can be readily foreseen that the combination of political forces, student activism and inability of professors to act as political decision makers in their own affairs will result in a protracted conflict. Many critics of the university structure —rather famous, and, formerly at least, liberal professors—have just recently organized an association called "Association for Academic Freedom." The organization has been branded "reactionary," not only by leftwing student groups, but also by influential mass media. The question of "participation" in university matters is merely one segment of a strong and organized movement for greater participation in public life. As a minister of the S.P.D. phrased it: "Equality as much as possible, freedom as much as necessary." The university is simply the first institution to be confronted with demands for equal participation.

POLICY-MAKING AND UNIVERSITY FINANCES

In policy matters it is well to regard budgets and budgetary procedures as the financial expression of policy formulas. Financing of all higher education and of universities, in particular, serves as a good indicator of the prevailing state of affairs.

The German university is still, without exception, primarily financed by state budgets which total about $1.2 billion per year. Proposals to erect private universities have been made, but none have been realized. Federal money, along with state money, is provided mainly for construction and for "state" scholarships for students (so-called *Honnefer Modell*). The Bonn government also partially supports the German Research Association, D.F.G. (*Deutsche Forschungsgemeinschaft*), which provides for research grants, and the Max-Planck Society, an organization of research institutes not connected with the universities except by way of dual personal appointments.

Private donations are collected by a special central organization of the German Federation of Industry, and these are then given as a lump sum to the D.F.G. and the Max-Planck Society. The D.F.G. spends about $100 million annually for research; 45 per cent comes from federal and state funds, 10 per cent from private sources. Very few private foundations support research, and only the Volkswagen Foundation is strong enough to make substantial contributions to such study, especially in the new fields of liberal arts and social sciences. With $3 billion, private German foundations have a capital about one-seventh that of American foundations, and they spend about $40 million a year, considerably less, ratio-wise.[10]

This general structure of financing has several important features. The budget of each university is incorporated in the budget of the cultural ministries. Inside the ministries, therefore, there is strong competition for funds between universities and other branches of education. Public pressure, especially in the 1950's and early 1960's, has brought about a considerable increase in school funding, since the necessity for "better" schools was very strongly felt by the general population. The universities, however, were somewhat remote from the masses and from the special-interest organizations exercising pressure on parliaments. As a result, the investment in university education was very low, and there is almost no research money in the university budgets, even though some of the budget items are expressly labeled "for research and teaching." Available state money has to be spent for personnel, libraries and all sorts of equipment (except large equipment like computers, which is provided for by the D.F.G.). At universities having medical schools the practice of incorporating hospitals into university budgets has resulted in further heavy demands for money. There is always the saying: "The sick demand it."

This situation had many grave effects. First, there has not been sufficient teaching personnel. A teacher-student ratio of 1:30 is regarded as very favorable; many disciplines have a ratio of 1:50 or even 1:100 or more. With the exception of the natural sciences, technology and medicine, research has suffered, since the D.F.G. has been unable to provide the necessary funding. Only in the last three years was the budget for the D.F.G. raised from 200 million D.M. to 400 million D.M. No single institution in the F.R.G. knows exactly

---

[10] See Carl Timm, "Forschungsfinanzierung," in *Mitteilungen der Gesellschaft der Freunde der Universitaet Mannheim,* summer 1970. Carl Timm is general manager of the chemical trust B.A.S.F.

what money is being spent for what purpose. Thus, not only has research money been scarce; it has also been expended uneconomically. Generally, it has been left to the individual scientist to bargain for money, a situation which has resulted in further waste and inequitable distribution. If there was to be money available or not depended on the bargaining ability of professors, and the universities have not been in a position to produce even modest plans for development.

Furthermore, since money, in general, has been appropriated by state parliaments, a strong competition has developed among the cultural ministries and other interest groups represented there, with the latter carrying the greater weight. This infighting among parliamentarians at the state level also worked against schemes to invest more in universities. Any rise in university budgets was more accidental than planned. It was surely a distinct blemish on the shield of the F.R.G.'s so-called "economic miracle" that education ranked so low in public financial priorities. Universities, as well as high schools, developed an attitude of "let us share the poverty." The only policy possible was one of muddling through.

All these shortcomings left the universities defenseless when the number of students began to rise. (In 1975 enrollment will be, according to cautious estimates, twice as high as it was in 1968—around 500,000 university students.) The students, therefore, have become greatly concerned about better teaching. It does not require unusual astuteness to see the facts as they have been—and still are. There has also been an undue waste of talent. Talented young people do not consider academic careers rewarding. Thus, today, despite a sharp rise in the budgets for 1969 and 1970, not enough young, trained scholars are available. Standards have had to be lowered just to keep pace with the demands for teachers. Furthermore, in many disciplines a talent drain to foreign countries has been occurring, and it has been impossible to test new ideas and approaches. If professors made one mistake or political error more grievous than any other, it was their inability to draw public attention to their plight. It is true, too, that the established ruling group of professors in many universities did not feel the plight quite so keenly as their "poorer" colleagues in other disciplines. A deep cleavage developed between the scholars' perceived role and reality.

It is to the credit of the student movement that public opinion became aware of the situation. Parliaments, as a result, have been forced to spend more money on education, and faculties have been encouraged to restructure the procedures of budget allocation. "Unit" financing, whether these units are "Fakultaeten" in the old sense, or combined disciplines, has become a major feature. Professors now negotiate only personal contracts with their respective ministries. All other fund distribution has to be determined by the proper university councils, within the framework of their developmental plans. Long-term financing for research units with new approaches (*Sonderforschungsbereiche*) has considerably increased (financed by the D.F.G., it is now 60 million D.M.; by 1972 there will be 200 million D.M. available for such programs). Last but not least, the federal ministry has learned that the power of the federal government to invest in education is much greater now than was even dreamed of five years ago. One must wait to see if this awareness really leads to an improved situation in all disciplines, or if the notion that the economy of the F.R.G. must gird itself to meet the challenge of the Japanese economy (as expressed by Chancellor Willy Brandt) will lead only to another large-scale technological investment.

It must be emphasized that the universities (or the schools) themselves were unable, by their very structure, to improve their financial situation, not only because they did not make the appropriate decisions, but because they did not develop a sense of responsibility for education as such, unless it was concerned with their own discipline. Above all, there has been a lack of responsible leadership, and this gap has not been filled adequately by the central university organizations.

Prior to the period of intensive restructuring, three major organizations represented the university and its membership at the federal level: the West German Conference of Rectors, W.R.K. (*Westdeutsche Rektorenkonferenz*), the Association of German Students, V.D.S. (*Verband Deutscher Studentenschaften*) and the University Association (*Hochschulverband*), an association of professors representing their professional interests. In the meantime, a Conference of Federal University Assistants, B.A.K., has been founded, and the three earlier organizations have been changed considerably.

The W.R.K. consists of the rectors of the West German universities and Berlin. It operates according to the ideological assumption that it must represent the universities and all their members. The W.R.K. has the right to nominate candidates for the presiding offices of the D.F.G. or the members of the "Wissenschaftsrat," the council for the Federal Government appointed by the president of the F.R.G. It tries to co-ordinate the public activities of the universities and to channel their interests at the federal level, while its suborganizations at the state level try to do the same with respect to the cultural ministries. A general secretary's office is responsible for the transaction of business. But as a matter of fact, due to the very individualistic position of each university, the W.R.K. was, and still is, unable to formulate general policies. Each rector has had to be extremely conscious of his constituency, the academic senate of professors. Resolutions of the W.R.K. have been rare. It was only under pressure that this body became more effective in terms of formulating policy. But it is still not regarded as a major policy-making organization. It is mainly an organization for disseminating information. For example, the proposals for reforming the universities and setting standard curriculum requirements failed, without exception, to influence the policy of any university, discipline or ministry.

The V.D.S., the student organization founded in 1949, served for many years as a rather effective interest group. It participated in such important decisions as the introduction of a federal bill for the scholarships which about 40 per cent of all students receive today. On the other hand, the organization was very vulnerable to changes among its representative personnel. It quickly fell victim to the S.D.S. once the latter set out to conquer it. But the S.D.S. sought this victory only to destroy the old organization. Today no representative organization of students exists and it will probably take many years to rebuild one. Thus it is that the students lack any organization to carry out the tasks of co-ordination. It is a glaring deficiency.

The only truly effective organization has been the new federal association of assistants, B.A.K. Young scholars with a genuine interest in their university careers, frustrated by the old faculty structure, appear to have been just the right group to get things moving. The federal law regulating their status had forced them to be very dependent, not for their own academic achievements, but in their personal relationships with their professors. In effect, the system had led, at least partially, to exploitation and waste of talents; on the credit side of the ledger, it had been instrumental in developing long-lasting and strong personal ties among scholars.

The assistants, therefore, developed a feeling of academic avant-gardism and played a carefully calculated kind of pressure-group politics. In a sense, they became the "motor" for the students in their fight against professors and the general public. There are many indications that the assistants have contributed a great deal to new thinking in university life,[11] both in teaching and research, but it is also true that the old errors of former faculties are being repeated by their younger cohorts. Anyhow, there is no doubt that political leadership is exercised by this group more than by any other group in higher education, including university senates, and that the change in the structure of German universities will be a long-range development, and not just an "accidental" event.

If one may draw some cautious conclusions from these developments, it becomes clear that one of the major problems of higher education, and especially of the universities, is the lack of efficient organizations to represent the "interests" of academia. This idea must sound strange when set against the old notion of academic life, the "ivory tower" concept. But if we see the university as the center of a highly developed and specialized set of institutions of higher education in mass society, then it follows that it must participate in political processes, not only to gain its own ends but also to inform and to clarify all the problems

---

[11] The B.A.K. only recently published a new plan for the Federal Republic, the so-called "Bergneustaedter model," in which 63 university units were proposed. These units included the existing universities and various former "Fachschulen," semi-university institutions. The plan also asked for the establishment of a number of new universities.

349

involved. If the universities do not use their freedom to play the role of the "philosopher" against the "king"—as actors in socio-political power plays—who else will?

## REALITIES AND IDEOLOGIES

Humboldt's university, as perceived in the early nineteenth century, no longer exists, even though style, principles, traditional forms and ideologies prevail as if it did. Scholars are no longer the privileged members of wealthy families. The state is not the protector of academic freedom, but rather the governing agency for higher education. Universality of knowledge as an academic goal cannot be achieved by individuals as in former times; specialization is extensive today. Well-grounded knowledge in many disciplines has come to be a thing of the past.

It is not only the development of the sciences but also the question of education *per se* with which the university is confronted. Past curricula provided (and often still do provide) for studies as if each student was expected to become a scholar, not simply an educated person able to participate in social and professional life with a good chance of success and accomplishment. Modern society has developed a great demand for specialists able to learn new approaches rapidly. Above all, the high prestige connected with a small number of educated people possessing university degrees cannot be bestowed on immense numbers of students who are extrinsically motivated and seek more of a vocational education from the university. Titles and formalized careers have grown more and more obsolete.

In recent years, many concepts have been developed in order to solve these problems. First, there is the functional approach. It calls for a transformation of the universities into purely educational institutions. Some of the governmental plans, like the aforementioned "Gesamthochschulplan" of the state of Baden-Wuerttemberg, did not even mention research; mention was made only after the rectors protested. This path seems to be the one most often followed by parliaments and ministries. It must, however, inevitably lead to serious defects in the development of the disciplines if their "value" is to be judged solely according to the number of students they attract. What is more, certain disciplines like sociology, political science and psychology are seen as being unwanted.[12] This is just one more proof that this kind of functionalism is founded on hidden anxieties and motivations. Above all, however, these moderate plans for education are based on estimated demands of society for certain skills, and these, in turn, are derived from very rough "impressions" rather than rational calculations.

---

[12] There are many statements to that effect in all parliaments.

In this context it is important that we consider the specific ways in which tele-education is to be carried out. A central television organization as it is now being implemented, broadcasting "homogenized" subject matter, is nothing more than a kind of "bread and butter" functionalism.

On the other hand, the functional approach strengthens the tendencies among students to make the university a place for "free" study. Rejection of all vocational training, all examinations, all study regulations, utopian as such ideas may be, are very common demands. Needless to say, it is impossible to expect a high intrinsic motivation from every student. Only a few will meet such requirements. Liberal and Left groups in academia are much in favor of such concepts, which correspond to the old traditions of German universities.

As a result of these divergent interests, the university system is moving in different directions at the same time. In certain disciplines, like medicine and dentistry, the number of students is severely restricted. A central agency computerizes the admission procedures, and the high school grades are taken as basic criteria on the assumption that there is a high correlation between these grades and success in the university. There is, however, a great demand for medical doctors and dentists which cannot be met; and the population has become very sensitive to the question of medical care. It is an issue that arouses strong emotions. The same applies to psychology, where the regulations hold down the pool of trained people (who might be working in schools, for example).

The number of teachers is already too small to meet the rising demands for high school education. Moreover, teacher remuneration is still too low in comparison to positions in industry. Since opportunities for study in the various disciplines in order to become a teacher have been insufficient and are now formally restricted, there is almost no hope to overcome this malaise. Students in business management and economics have increased considerably. Having been trained, however, to handle high-level econometrics, the graduates now see themselves in a situation where they are almost unable to meet ordinary professional requirements. A change in these studies is only now beginning to be introduced. These are only a few examples.

The situation has been worsened by the fact that some of the universities, like Berlin and Bremen, have been transformed into centers of leftwing political activities—intentionally, it must be added, in order "to destroy the system." The danger of a semieducated, dissatisfied "revolutionary" intelligentsia is great, indeed. And in other places, like Marburg, some departments are already run by organized Communist cells.

The most basic problem today arises from the former policy of creating new opportunities for higher education without giving the university the necessary means to handle the influx. It was certainly necessary to raise the level of education generally and to open new opportunities. It could not be expected that an

351

industrialized society like the Federal Republic would be satisfied with a situation in which only very small numbers of middle-class youth had the chance for higher education, whereas almost 90 per cent had to be satisfied with very limited social roles. The movement to broaden educational opportunities, therefore, was nothing but reasonable, even though it became transformed into an ideological pressure.

On the other hand, the same parliaments which moved so forcefully into school education, to a great extent neglected to enlarge and broaden the economic basis of the universities. Appeals to change this policy failed, even though more money could have been available in the early 1960's. When the economic situation became critical, universities were drawn into debates about questions of status and procedures. In the winter of 1967-68, when the first wave of the new influx of students reached the universities, the rate of support was not increased, but reduced. The rather uninteresting ideological question of autonomy of the university seemed to be more important to politicians than the question of educational investment. On the other hand, with their house already on fire, professors were still greatly concerned about their personal privileges.

The most hopeful development today is the higher rate of educational investment that has been introduced and the realistic plans for extensive changes in curricula and examinations. There is hope now that the growing numbers of students can obtain an education "according to their abilities," that high-level academic education will be the focus of an extensive system of correlated curricula, and that scholars, too, will have a place inside, not outside, the universities.

# SPANISH EDUCATIONAL REFORM
# — THREE VIEWS

Ramón Bela

## INTRODUCTION

What has happened to youth today? What is going on in the world that makes youth riot, occupy universities, proclaim their rights so aggressively, and lash out at police authorities? Clearly a change is taking place.

In Spain the change, according to Professor P. Laín Entralgo,[1] is a dramatic one, and is in part due to the sense of unease which for thirteen years has prevailed in the Spanish university. The entire Spanish educational system needs revision. The problems of education have become major, nation-wide concerns; they are discussed on the front pages and in the editorial columns of our newspapers. Inside and outside educational circles, the theme of reform is constantly discussed. In 1968, as a result of this national preoccupation, a new team of recognized specialists in the Ministry of Education began an ambitious analysis and evaluation of the entire Spanish educational system. In February 1969, there emerged from their labors a White Book, presenting a complete study and analysis of the educational system. The Ministry of Education, in the introduction to the White Book,[2] indicated that the government's intentions are ambitious and will require time. I am going to deal with these ambitions and problems in later pages, abstaining from any attempt to cover all levels of education.

I am going to discuss first the organization of the Spanish educational system and then pass quickly to the social aspects of the Spanish university. Some areas of study and research which I will consider are the following: the problems of youth, the relationship of the Spanish university to the cultural institutions of other countries, and lastly—I shall pose the question— what importance does the Spanish university have in the larger national picture. Some university problems concern the private universities or, as we call them in Spain, free universities.[3] Other problems include the selecting of adequate teachers and the determination of the nature of the university pro-

---

[1] Pedro Laín Entralgo, *El problema de la universidad* (Madrid, 1968).

[2] *La educación en España: bases para una política educativa* (Madrid, 1969).

[3] Eduardo García de Enterría, "Sobre las universidades libres," *Cuadernos para el Diálogo*, V (extraordinario), mayo 1967, 79 ff.

fessor's dedication. Then, we have the problem of the recently founded twin universities in Madrid and Barcelona, the so-called autonomous universities. Finally, there are such problems as the disparate levels of cultural discrimination caused by disproportion of population and provincial topographical barriers, modernization and the methods of teaching, the centralization of educational administration, and finally, of primary importance, the sometimes unrealistic motives that influence students in the choosing of their prospective careers.

The educational system in Spain is based on the patterns established centuries ago and which once prevailed throughout Western Europe. The basic (1857) law of higher education, known as the *Ley Moyano,* regulates the Spanish educational system. Except for several minor reforms, the most important that of 1943, the system has remained that of the past century.

Until recently the state has maintained only 12 universities. There are four universities in Spain which are not run by the state: the Opus Dei University in Pamplona, the Jesuit University of Deusto in Bilbao, the Pontifical University of Salamanca which has lay liberal arts and pedagogy schools, and the Pontifical University of Comillas with lay branches in Madrid. In Spain the private university is not operated by the state; it is funded by the church in accordance with the general educational laws established by the Spanish State. These universities based their legal existence on the state's concordat with the Vatican.

Recently twin universities, or autonomous state universities, were established in Barcelona and Madrid. And a new university was created in Bilbao. Other new centers of higher learning are rising in large cities.

The Spanish university follows the French system. The individual components or schools are self-governing and relatively isolated from the other divisions or schools of the university. The primary concern of the Spanish university is not the old medieval Latin "convivium," or community of scholars, but the granting of degrees. The first concern of the student corresponds to the primary concern of the university, for a student's basic motivation is to obtain a university degree, which in turn is the key to a remunerative career. This is why during the university demonstrations in 1969, when the announcements for examinations were posted, student riots ceased.

Much of the structural trouble of the Spanish university reflects problems in the educational system at lower levels. During the Spanish Civil War a modification of the system was attempted, first with the law concerning secondary education in 1938, and then with the University Reform Law of 1943. These laws were in accord with educational concepts which were prevalent in Europe during the war.

Since 1956 the Spanish university has been in a state of political and educational crisis. The political questions which touched the university involved the political structure of Spain. The educational problem derived from two sources. One was the failure of education to adapt to the conditions of modern society, while a second was the failure of education to develop new and relevant teaching methods.

In recent times instability within the university has been a matter of gravest concern to Spanish educational authorities. We Spaniards are conscious of the fact that the society which education serves, is "retarded."[4] It is clear that all modifications made in the educational system will affect society. And at the same time, society determines the actions and functions of the university. If society is ill-organized or seems disorganized, the university will merely reflect this instability.[5]

Society influences the educational system in that it determines modes of teaching that respond to the different spheres of society, while at the same time the university serves as a great support to modern society, using the vehicle of teaching to better the social structure and thus in turn to create a more balanced and just society.[6]

Since 1959, Spain has undoubtedly undergone great changes as a result of the stabilization plan and the first economic and social development plan. One consequence of the improvement of the overall economic situation has been the overwhelming increase in the student population at all levels. Since 1933 the enrollment in primary education has increased 168 per cent. The high schools and vocational schools have had increases of 800 per cent and 445 per cent, respectively. Teacher training schools have increased 319 per cent, and the universities of Spain have boosted their student enrollment by 389 per cent. This physical growth of higher education has in itself produced turmoil and contributed to a sense of uneasiness and tension. For these and other reasons a series of intensive studies of the educational system have been undertaken. In the Ministry of Education's White Book, *Basis for a Policy on Education,* the specialists discussed proposals for a variety of educational reforms. In the introduction the minister of education began with a discourse given by the Head of State, which ended with this paragraph: "The challenge of our times is educational training and teaching, in which we are summoned with strong hope to obtain the most evident results."

The White Book offers a most ambitious educational reform program, and its full implementation will have to be gradual.[7] In the "Introduction" the minister observes that people tend to overlook that the university ills commanding public attention originate in the primary and secondary school sys-

---

[4] Angel LaTorre, "Universidad y Estado," *ibid.,* p. 15.

[5] Manuel Jiménez de Parga, "Nuestra universidad y nuestra sociedad," *ibid.,* p. 13.

[6] Carlos Iglesias Selgas, *Factores Estructurales y Educación* (Madrid, Boletín Centro Documentación No. 29, Comisaría para el SEU).

[7] *Bases para una política educativa* (Madrid, 1969).

tems. One serious failing in Spain's educational structure is that the high school emphasizes the traditional classicist curriculum, reinforced by a dogmatic teaching method which fosters an attitude of intellectual passivity in the student. The pupil is dedicated to the objective of obtaining a passing grade by memorizing his professor's lectures. This defect of the high school and its corresponding defect at the university level cannot be solved solely in the university itself.[8] It must be solved earlier and at a much lower level. This example suggests that all Spain's educational troubles at the university level are connected with the reform of the entire system. The government's reform plan is very ambitious, aiming above all at the preparation of youth to exercise the responsibilities of liberty and freedom, which in turn will foster social integration, a sense of national identity, and a broad-based and fluid society. This summarizes the general proposals which the government is contemplating for the near future. But there are also goals which encompass the next 30 years. In reality, all these projects involve very long-range planning.

One of Spain's principal educational weaknesses is the discontinuity of the different education levels and the lack of comprehensive, system-wide planning. For the professors themselves, as a consequence, one level of teaching is not correlated to another. The students suffer from the abrupt shifts that mark their passage from one system to another, since they cannot perceive relationships between the different school levels or the study plans and classes at the different levels. Although the three basic levels are disconnected, the advanced levels, nevertheless, tend to repeat endlessly the academic patterns of the lower levels.

Another problem facing Spanish higher education is the venerable system of pre-university examinations. This system was reformed in the years 1957, 1959, and 1963—and the frequency of the reforms indicates the extent of dissatisfaction with the effectiveness of the examinations.[9] The criticism of the examination system and of its reforms continues; and even among those successful in the examinations there are a great many who are simply not up to university standards, for the problem actually stems from the unsatisfactory education given in secondary schools. This explanation provides small consolation for the student who fails the examinations and who may be left with the feeling of having wasted his own time and his family's money. This is one of the causes of tension among the youth of Spain. The student is frustrated when he discovers that he cannot move to a level of higher learning.

Another problem is the rigid structure of the educational system. The Spanish university curriculum takes many years to complete, for there are a great

---

[8] *Ibid.,* p. 9.
[9] *Ibid.,* p. 18, No. 7.

number of required courses for graduation. Courses of study are both rigid and detailed. It is virtually impossible for a student to change his field of specialty, which means that if a student is uncertain about his vocation—and vacillations are very common during youth—his hesitation will harm both him and society. Nor is it easy to re-enter the university after once leaving to find work. Further, professional training and techniques are not up-to-date. Rigidity and the examination system combine to produce a form of strangulation. The White Book cites data to the effect that out of 100 students who entered elementary school in 1951, only 50 completed the course of studies. Of this number 18 went on to pass the fourth year of secondary instruction and received the basic high-school certificate. And of these students only five passed the university entrance examinations, with a mere three of the original 100 completing their university studies in 1967.[10]

The Spanish system notably lacks flexibility, both in its examination system and in its educational and professional orientation. The White Book, recognizing the need of a general re-evaluation of the educational output and the importance of improving the work of education, has proposed extensive changes. The intention of the proposals is that the student receive the full and proper education to which he is entitled. If the number of failed students is high (and it does seem to be excessively high), then research must be undertaken to ascertain the causes, and presumably there will follow an increase in the number of the successful, as well as a rise in their quality. We suffer from a lack of emphasis on deductive methodology. A restructuring of the system and its teaching would enable us to select fewer and better qualified students, while at the same time offering greater opportunity to all. Many problems and difficulties could probably be avoided, if the student was able to secure counsel and advice in critical moments of his life. The establishment of counseling services and in-service training for the teaching staff will yield a greater and more efficient productivity and allow better utilization of human resources; this, in turn, will contribute to the betterment of the individual by assisting him in the choice of his professional career.

There are many social dilemmas affecting the university. Some affect the student, others affect the teachers within the university social structure. And this structure is itself determined by the overall social system of the country. In Spain all the changes experienced by the country in recent years are visible in the university.

Our national goal is to create an open society with full social mobility and equal opportunity and with open access of any person to the posts and functions of the social community. We also seek to provide the individual with

---

[10] *Ibid.,* p. 24.

the possibility of developing and perfecting his personality through learning and knowledge. And we want to furnish equal opportunity to all, not only to attend the university but also to obtain their chosen degrees.[11]

Some statistics are available, but it is not easy to relate them to the problems of education. The statistics that do exist are few, confusing and incomplete. Professor Don Salustiano del Campo of the University of Madrid has dealt with this topic[12] in a two-part work, the first of which analyzes the social origins of Spanish university students. The second part describes and analyzes certain functions and malfunctions in the Spanish educational system and Spanish society.

The results are interesting. For example, the sons of unskilled workers in Spain represent 2.75 per cent of the total of university students. In the largest university districts of Madrid and Barcelona, where 65 per cent of all Spanish university students are centered, the percentage of students from families of unskilled workers is even lower—2.44 per cent in Madrid and 1.44 per cent in Barcelona. This percentage is lower still in the schools of engineering. In Madrid 1.95 per cent of the male students are sons of unskilled workers and in Barcelona the figure is even worse, 0.88 per cent.

The highest percentage of university students in Spain come from the middle and professional class, which gives the Spanish university a mesocratic character. This statement must be viewed against the context of the entire Spanish society, where the upper class is from 0.12 to 1 per cent, the middle class from 34 to 38 per cent, and the lower class, 62 to 66 per cent of the population. It would be extremely interesting if data were available on other aspects of the class origins of Spanish university students. For example, what career do most workers' sons pursue? What percentage of lower class children fail their university studies compared with the failure percentage of the average student population? In what proportion are scholarships granted to students who come from each economic category? It is worth nothing that last year in Spain an experiment was initiated to provide scholarships for lower-class students that would include salaries for the recipients and their families.

Another item of interest is the geographic origin of the students. In six Spanish provinces the student population corresponded with the local social population. Thus, these six provinces are ones that have higher per capita income.

The second matter which Professor del Campo discussed is the serious problem of social stratification, and the need to reform it. He insisted that

[11] Luis Buceta Facorro, *La democratización de la enseñanza* (Madrid, Comisaría para el SEU).

[12] Salustiano del Campo, "Procedencia social de los universitarios," *Cuadernos para el Diálogo*, V (extraordinario), mayo 1967, 42.

the criteria of merit in judging, selecting and rewarding students replace the old criteria of class, family, or social considerations. But as yet we have no means of determining the relationship of the educational system to the social structure. It may be that recent educational reforms will help to dissolve our social stratification, but the alternative cannot be excluded. So far, Professor del Campo stated, the reforms have strengthened the prevailing social structure. The White Book agreed with this statement, indicating that the educational system only partially fulfills the twin objectives of making education an instrument of social mobility and of providing open access for all students to higher education through scholarship and merit rather than family position or wealth.

Professor del Campo and the White Book agree about the necessity for developing a social conscience, facing the problems of the present and finding a rapid solution for them. Their concern is not so much to extend the educational system as to democratize it. Per capita income is growing and will enlarge our educational resources, but education is not yet available to everyone nor is the per capita income equally distributed. In Point 14 of the White Book it is accepted as a basic principle that all Spaniards will have equal access to education. It is recognized that in all industrial societies there exists an extensive system of public education which makes equal education available for all levels. While Spanish intellectuals have offered a variety of opinions on this topic, all have insisted on the need of change. In this awareness they are at one with the Spanish people.

Professor Jiménez de Parga argues that the Spanish university is class-enhancing or a class institution, since Spanish society is a class affair itself.[13] Professor Elías Díaz, agreeing, contends that the incorporation of the working class within the university system will dissolve the class fabric of the university. This incorporation should be brought about and it should be a genuine incorporation.[14] The present so-called labor universities, a form of trade school, do little more than to perpetuate the class system, and are not real centers of higher learning, with the single exception of the University of Córdoba which opened a center of higher education in the fall of 1969. These labor universities benefit working-class children only and are supported by the Spanish Workers Guild, which is similar to a trade union. A stumbling-block to resolving this problem has been the fact that there has been no participation by the Spanish people.

Everyone is aware of the problem and knows that means must be sought to bring about a change. Today the two government bureaus with the largest

---

[13] Manuel Jiménez de Parga, *op. cit.*

[14] Elías Díaz, "Diez puntos para la reforma universitaria," *Cuadernos para el Diálogo,* V (extraordinario), mayo 1967, 68.

budgets are the Department of Public Works and the Department of Education. Latest figures show a proposed budget of 41.665 million pesetas for the latter in the year 1970, higher than that of any other ministry. Despite this, the state must spend even more money. In proportion to the national income, the nation is now spending only 2.65 per cent of its revenue on education, far less than the other countries in Western Europe. The annual cost for each student in Spain was once $146. Along with recent changes in society this figure has been increased, and now $297 per year is budgeted per student in the technical schools and $235 in the university. These expenditures are determined for one year at a time.

Professor Prados Arrarte has stated that under the tax system of Spain 60 per cent of the educational budget is paid by the lower classes. But these funds benefit a higher-class group comprising 95 per cent of those educated, and the higher classes pay only 40 per cent of the total tax income.[15]

There is no standard system for admission of students to the Spanish university. Professional orientation and advisory and counseling services, which prepare the student to utilize the university, simply do not exist in Spain. The White Book suggests that the present entrance examinations are more of a barrier to university admission than a means of selecting students.[16] Before educational reform can be set in motion, research is necessary to ascertain if the numbers and distribution of students respond to demographic characteristics of the country and to the economic and social needs of Spain. An equally urgent problem is the need to alter the basic nature of the university population in such a way as to develop a more serious and conscientious student body rather than a merely numerous one. The growth in student number has been spectacular in recent years, but we must now turn our attention to student quality, student dedication and student commitment.

Not a great deal of data exists regarding the training of the Spanish people in proportion to the existing work opportunities, nor are structured data available regarding the production of professionals in proportion to professional job opportunities. The relative proportion of semiskilled or nonskilled workers to the total work population still remains high. In relative terms there has been a great change in the intermediate professional categories, and some changes in a few of the higher categories. The managerial and executive classes have remained relatively stable.

In sum, the changes noted above have been moderate and transitional, but they are nevertheless of considerable importance. Since the Civil War, the total Spanish population has increased almost 26 per cent, that is, a change

---

15 Jesús Prados Arrarte, "Los gastos de la educación superior en España," *ibid.,* p. 29.
16 *La educación en España: bases para una política educativa. Análisis del sistema* (Madrid, 1969), p. 81.

from 26 million people in 1940 to nearly 33 million presently. The White Book indicates that the future educational needs in Spain do not stem merely from the growth of the population, but from shifts in the original distribution. This redistribution arises from a new internal mobility which is the result of technical and industrial changes, and anticipated improvements in the economy.

The birth rate of the Spanish population will increase in the future but not with such speed. Since 1920 the birth rate has dropped from 30/1,000 to 21/1,000, and the death rate has dropped from 24/1,000 to 8.5/1,000.

Regarding the possibilities of employment, the White Book recognizes the need for future development of occupational and professional resources. Actual employment opportunities and training for employment have seemed, in the past, to be wholly unrelated, because the social patterns of Spain have grown and diversified but the growth and diversification have not been reflected in the educational system. The evolution of professional and occupational training, both qualitative and quantitative, has been slower than the demand. As a consequence, scientific and technical advances have produced great changes in the occupational structure. Spain is now undergoing the same tensions and growing pains that have afflicted other nations with a growing economy and accompanying change in society. The World Bank has observed that with the expansion of the Spanish economy, there would be a strong demand for high-level personnel such as engineers, researchers, scientists and technicians graduated from universities and special schools.[17] The Development Plan of 1963 responded to this report and identified those schools and divisions of the universities which would have to increase their production to meet the new demands.

To maintain the same rate of development as the other countries of the O.E.C.D., Spain will have to double the number of its university students. Studies show that during the next five years Spain will experience a significant 10 per cent decrease in the agricultural population, a 20 per cent increase in the industrial workers' population and a 20 per cent increase in the number engaged in general services. There will also be an increase in numbers of the middle and upper classes of society. The White Book summarized this point by saying that for 1971 the demands of the higher professions will require that the universities train 23,700 professionals, and to staff the ranks of the higher technicians Spain will need to train approximately 27,000. At the somewhat lower level of machinists, practical engineers and skilled technicians, Spain will need 52,000 trained personnel. But since the actual production of graduates does not approach these figures, we shall find ourselves hardpressed to obtain these increases. The most difficult category to fill will be that

---

[17] *World Bank Report of Spanish Economy*, pp. 551-552.

of technicians. In other levels of education, such as the vocational schools, the problem is even more crucial.

## THE RESEARCHER

Research is not a new problem in Spain. There has always been a certain amount of resistance to the idea of research within the university proper. This resistance has existed since the time when the first task of the university was conceived as the transmission of culture. In Spain at the beginning of the century research was considered an appropriate activity of the university and was centered in the *Institución Libre de Enseñanza.* Yet the old controversy persists: Should the university professor devote himself entirely to education and teaching or should he invest his time in research as well? Clearly not everyone should devote himself to research at the university, but possibly all professors should at least do some research. Research and teaching are not necessarily mutually exclusive but can coexist. A reasonable solution of the problem is to have the necessary flexibility that will allow the existence of both teaching and pure research. In any case, our need to increase the number of scientific investigators beyond the present level is urgent. This training of scientific investigators should begin in the earliest stages of the educational process and culminate in the university.[18] The university cannot fulfill its function if it is not strengthened by scientific research.

But in Spain there has always been a scarcity of funds for research. As the needs have always been great, long-term research projects have invariably been sacrificed for short-term ones. In the past petitions have frequently urged that the state concentrate its strength in the field of investigation. After a study to determine which type of research would produce the best results, the decision was reached that basic research should be carried out in the university, though not to the exclusion of other research centers.[19] This became a subject of much discussion at the end of the Civil War, when the *Consejo Superior de Investigaciones Científicas* was established for the purpose of carrying out research. Since 1939, nevertheless, research has been carried out in the university. But now there is a growing tendency to make it independent. Some areas of research located in the university have become famous, such as histology, in the School of Ramón y Cajal, with Achucarro, Río Ortega, and others. But it has been in the humanities where research centers have achieved more brilliant results, as, for example, in the history of Spanish law with Professor Altamira Crevea, the history of Spain with Professors Sánchez Albornoz

---

[18] *La educación en España: bases para una política educativa,* p. 102.

[19] Carlos Sánchez del Río, "La investigación científica y su repercusión económica," *Atlántida,* XIV (1965), 181 ff.

and Américo Castro, and the history of the Spanish language with Menéndez Pidal.

Ortega y Gasset believed that the university was for the education of intellectuals, but he also believed that the university should prepare future researchers. Many people believe this today. Professor Burillo thinks that the university cannot be considered a center of learning if it is not at least partially dedicated to scientific research. Professor D'Ors believed that centers outside the university itself must be utilized in order to unite and co-ordinate the various fields of scientific investigation. And Professor Sánchez Agesta said that one of the essential functions of the university is to be a center of investigation for the making and training of scientists and the training of professionals, and that every university must also train investigators who enrich the university itself.[20] Thus teaching and research are seen as activities which are different but which have essential mutual relationships. The *Consejo de Investigaciones Científicas* at its inception centered its activities on developing and maintaining the institutions which already existed. The investigative function has become a professional activity. In recent years a significant number of former investigators have become full-time professors at the university. In 1962 the Ministry of Education established a national commission for the furthering of research. Nevertheless, according to the O.E.C.D., the proportion of the gross national product dedicated to the funding of scientific education yields the following picture: In Great Britain 2.3 per cent was invested, whereas in Spain the figure is 0.2 per cent. In Spain there are nine researchers for every 100,000 inhabitants compared with a ratio of 30 to every 100,000 inhabitants in the more developed countries. Another problem, and a very serious one, is the lack of co-ordination between research and the instruments of economic production. And thus we have the paradox that Spain exports researchers and imports foreign inventors through the use of patents. In 1958 the government created the Advisory Committee of Scientific and Technical Research.

In summary, according to the White Book, the problems of scientific research in Spain are the following: (1) the lack of a clear relationship between scientific research and the Spanish university; (2) lack of co-ordination between research and the needs of society; (3) disproportionate funding that favors the scientific disciplines at the expense of the social and humanistic disciplines; (4) the scarcity of money; (5) and last, the lack of long-term policies. The government proposes in the White Book that the training and development of researchers be done in the university, and the higher technical centers and institutions, as well as in the *Consejo de Investigaciones Cientí-*

---

[20] Luis Sánchez Agesta, "La investigación y los fines de la universidad," *Arbor*, febrero 1950, pp. 191 ff.

*ficas.* The government will try to extend both applied and basic research, but it will also try to give research an academic character, thus linking it with teaching.

Ideally, the university schools or divisions will be primarily centers of administration and instruction serving the needs of students, apart from other possibilities offered by its highly specialized departments and institutes. Although each faculty has many of these specialized departments or institutes, they are to be devoted to the objectives of both teaching and research. The departments and institutes should join the teaching and research activities in such a way that the departments may dedicate themselves exclusively to teaching. The final integration and melding of research and teaching would be carried out in the later years of the student's training and would be effected by the professor himself in co-operation with the graduate student pursuing a master's or a doctor's degree. Under these circumstances the student would develop those vital qualities of a researcher like initiative, technique, methodology and the critical spirit which even his primary education would have begun to develop. This training would culminate in study for the doctorate, or perhaps beyond, as would the development of applied research in the universities and centers of higher learning. Some professors would dedicate themselves exclusively to research.

We hope that in the next legal reform of the Spanish educational system the following bodies can be established: an integrated committee representing the different levels at which research is carried out, including the university, the polytechnic institutes, the regional centers of scientific investigation, and the industrial research laboratories; a committee of coordination on a national scale, which would be composed of the rectors and presidents of the institutes and centers, the *Consejo de Investigaciones Científicas,* and other research centers both public and private; a national service of scientific and technical information for Spain and other countries. These centers would be established along modern lines with the aid of other foreign research centers. Commenting on these developmental plans, the Commission of the Spanish University Syndicate says that all true research must be parallel to and interdependent with the university departments, and that it would be desirable to integrate the research centers of the *Consejo de Investigaciones Científicas* with the universities to avoid isolating research from the instructional program, and to prevent the separation of teaching and study from the critical and creative spirit of research. I might also suggest that university degree programs emphasize training for research as well as the traditional theoretical training.

Our teams of researchers must be flexible and they must have mobility. The research centers may be different, but the mobility of the scholars between the centers should be the same. It is important that these scholars not work in isolation. As quickly as possible, the researchers should establish ties with the

Spanish National Programs of Research and the programs of other European countries. They should develop an effective system of exchanges of data and research personnel. We do have some institutes of scientific research dedicated to applied research in Spain, for example, the Nuclear Energy Commission and the National Institute of Aeronautic Technology. In these fields Spanish co-operation with the United States Space Research Laboratories of Maspalomas in the Canary Islands and the Robledo de Chavella near Madrid is well known. Other institutes include the Institute of Construction and Cement which does research on building and construction materials.

### THE STUDENT

The problem of the student attitude towards the university is very complex.[21] I have spoken of the social structure of the Spanish university, and now I will deal with the student and the social class to which he belongs. When Professor Jiménez de Parga called the Spanish university progressive, he was not describing the complete entity; his meaning is that it is progressive when contrasted with a Spanish society which persists in maintaining outdated modes and social structures that have long since been abandoned in more developed countries. Professor Jiménez de Parga said that the university student can only be explained in one of two ways: either he does not clearly understand his environment or he does not care to enter into social dialogue with his environment. Since the Spanish Civil War, Parga stated, there have been three different periods of student attitude. Between 1940 and 1945 the university encouraged a simplistic attitude. Between 1945 and 1956 the university encouraged the student to think that things were not as simple as they seem and that the world was filled with contradictions and complexities. From 1957 on the student has lived in the full complexity of the university.[22] I remember that the university never intervened in the political life of the country when I was a student. I feel that the old university has changed enormously. But more recent students contend that the university does not respond to present social needs. Their feeling has greater depth than my words suggest.

What is the university in the eyes of the Spanish student? Does the university exist as an institution in Spain? For many students the official university is a mere instrument or mechanism whose sole function is to prepare him for a professional career. Student activities and social life do not exist in the Spanish university as they do in American institutions. Spanish youth is

---

[21] *See* "Los movimientos estudiantiles," *Revista de Occidente,* No. 68, nov. 1968. Directed by Manuel García Pelayo, with answers by Pedro Laín Entralgo, Antonio Tovar, Ángel LaTorre, Alejandro Nieto Salustiano de Campo, Paulino Garagorri.

[22] Manuel Jiménez de Parga, *op. cit.,* 13 ff.

critical of the university's educational system and society, especially of the unjust system of admissions. Professor Altares says the Spanish university is a modern institution which serves to conserve the nineteenth century social structure.[23] With all its anachronisms, the university appears frivolous in the eyes of the rural town, whose population has the feeling of not being invited to a party for which they have helped to pay. The university has been a mainstay of the middle class on the one hand, and on the other, a great vehicle of communication that captures and transmits progressive ideology. The modern and progressive Spanish workers' movements were developed far from the hallowed halls of the university, yet it has been the universities which have transmitted their existence and principles to a larger audience. In Spain the university is caught between the fears and distrusts of the people and society. Crowding in the university has produced a barrier between the professor and the student. Another problem is the question whether the university is turning out true and fully qualified professionals. And problems have arisen because of the distance between student and professor. I shall limit myself to the most controversial points brought out in the White Book and to those student problems that have grown most pronounced in recent years. For example, they would include the right of everyone to an education, the policies and means used in granting scholarships; in both areas students regard our efforts as inadequate. And there are other areas of deep concern such as antiquated teaching methods, the need for modernization of the curriculum, and the many gaps in the curriculum.

Another issue to which the White Book addresses itself is the relative lack of student participation in university government. Greater numbers of students should participate and serve on joint commissions and committees with professors. These commissions would resolve problems within the university.

For the betterment of the university they must understand that the university's democratization must include one or all of the three following ideas: access of all to education; the participation of students in university government; freedom of speech. The right to education should be considered as basic and within the realm of other human rights. The government proposes that democratization of education must be so executed that the lower and working classes have the same educational advantages as the more privileged. The present system of scholarships has not been effective to date. Scholarships granted for university study numbered 3,936 last year and scholarships to the Schools of Engineering numbered 1,670. This number is very low in proportion to the Spanish population. The total number of university students regis-

---

[23] Pedro Altares, "En torno a universidad y pueblo," *Cuadernos para el Diálogo,* V (extraordinario), mayo 1967, 17 ff.

tered in 1957-58 was roughly 64,000, with another 5,000 in the technical schools. In 1966-67 the total number of registered students had grown to 106,000 in the university and 36,000 in the technical schools. This total of 142,000 students is exactly double the enrollment of 1957-58. The enlargement and crowding of the university and the consequent problems will grow in the future, and therefore we must move quickly to revise our system of student selection. University admissions will have to be made by committees designated by the rector. The object of this new plan is to limit student enrollments at each center according to its physical limitations. This limitation is sure to run head-on into the traditional Spanish system of admitting to the university all those who have completed the necessary secondary education.

To sum up this matter, we have pointed out a series of problems and the solutions which have been developed, excepting, of course, the political problems. The basic interests of youth have changed in recent times. Professor López Ibor has written that youth today is less interested in intellectual life.[24] This does not mean that young people study less or are less intelligent but it means that they have limited interests. They are interested in acquiring the practical knowledge to earn a livelihood, not necessarily as negative a goal as it sounds, for, after all, they are concerned with the essential aspects of life. And their chances of success are greater since these young people enjoy an authentic liberty. Parental control and respect for authority have been on the wane since the young were given greater opportunities for personal independence. López Ibor continues by saying that the task of training youth is therefore more difficult than it has been in the past. The young must now be taught with agile and subtle wisdom. The pedagogical tradition must be changed, and the knowledge which we impart to them must be more meaningful and deeper. Youth have to be persuaded that willingness to learn is a vital necessity in life, and that their learning must be based on ethical foundations.

## THE ECONOMICS OF THE SITUATION

One of the problems that the state and the Ministry of Education must face is the growing expense of the university and the problem of financing the increased expenditures. The White Book cites some resolutions for the near future. The expenses of the Ministry of National Education increased from 7.83 per cent of the national budget in 1950 to 10.30 per cent in 1968. This latter figure is divided into 6.70 per cent for current expenditures and 3.6 per cent for investments. In Spain the total amount of public funds spent per

---

24 Juan José López Ibor, *Discurso a los universitarios españoles* (Madrid, 1964). 4th edition, revised (Biblioteca del Pensamiento Actual, 85).

student is very low, considerably lower than in other European countries. In 1962 Spain spent $23 per student in primary education, $41 in secondary and $71 in higher. According to the secretary-general of education, the 1968 educational expenditures per student were as follows: primary level, $57; secondary, $127; teaching or normal schools, $203; the university, $235; and engineering schools, $297. Since 1968, educational expenditures have been divided between capital outlay and operating expenses with 74.9 per cent of the 1968 budget being spent on operating expenses. In recent years the capital outlay has increased due to the rise in construction costs. We anticipate for the future large capital expenditures on physical resources such as laboratories, libraries and plant construction. The operating expenditures for high school education are low in relation to other costs. One must understand the importance of Spanish high schools, 80 per cent of them private—the highest percentage in Europe. Another matter of concern is the insufficient attention we have given primary education. This is one of the most notable failings of our educational system. The outlay for primary education in proportion to the national income is uncertain because of lack of data. According to the scale made up by the White Book it is estimated that for the year 1966 $57 million, or 3.982.000.000 pesetas, were spent on primary education, which represents 3.7 per cent of the country's national income. It is expected that society's demand for teachers will continue to be pressing during the next few years. We also hope for improvement of the professional aspects of the teaching career.

We also need to devote attention to the problems of educational administration as well as to the teaching staff. The nature and structure of Spanish educational administration needs a massive revamping. According to the White Book, the state will try to effect a total reform of our system of educational administration so that it can more efficiently serve the new educational trends.

And at the highest level, the Ministry of Education itself should be reorganized; the Ministry will be divided into two main sections, administration and technology; it will be decentralized, with delegations or bureaus in each of the Spanish provinces. And we look forward to the training of highly specialized personnel in educational development, evaluation, educational and professional orientation, and to studying special educational problems such as university relationships and co-ordination with other institutions.

Because both our governmental and educational administration is highly centralized, our financial commitments to the many Spanish and foreign universities within our sphere of interest are made through the Spanish government. The organism that maintains our international cultural relationships with other countries is the Foreign Ministry through its director of cultural relations, and cultural relationships with the Americas and the Philippines are maintained through the *Instituto de Cultura Hispánica*. Other governmental units maintain relationships in specific fields with related foreign institutions, as for example, the *Consejo Superior de Investigaciones Científicas*, the Ministry of Education, etc.

Some Spanish universities have initiated agreements on their own with twin universities, as for example, the University of Madrid and the University of Bordeaux in France. These agreements are based on friendship and good will, and do not necessarily involve any extensive co-operative effort.

International relationships are becoming more and more important every day and these relationships have become steadily more easy to enter into. Spain maintains certain cultural institutions abroad, justified by the statistics that 3,000,000 Spaniards live outside of Spain: one million in Europe and two million in the Americas. In Europe and Morocco Spain has three high schools, and 176 primary schools. In Morocco there is a polytechnic university in Tangiers with a center in Casablanca. Programs in other fields are also maintained abroad, for example, our center in Canada. The Ministry of Education proposes to formulate a policy to assist these Spaniards outside of Spain and to develop links with other Spanish-speaking countries. We also have under consideration a series of cultural agreements for the exchange of teachers and recognition or reciprocity of degrees.[25]

---

[25] Extensive use was made in this paper of the White Book (*La educación en España: bases para una política educativa* (Madrid, 1969). Other books employed included: Jesús Burillo (ed.), *Antología de la universidad actual en crisis* (Madrid, 1968). Pedro Laín Entralgo, *La universidad en la vida española* (Cartagena, 1958). *La universidad* (Madrid, 1969).

# THE STATE AND MAJOR
# CONTEMPORARY PROBLEMS OF
# HIGHER EDUCATION IN
# YUGOSLAVIA

Ivan Maksimovic

Higher education in Yugoslavia is presently passing through a phase which some term a "crisis" while others see it as "the moment prior to crucial decisions and decisive structural changes." To be sure, Yugoslavian higher education is meeting those same challenges which the technical revolution, and the accompanying social upheavals, have forced on all universities.

Yet, certain aspects of the problems and difficulties are peculiar to Yugoslavia and are inseparable from the nation's postwar development. Since 1945, Yugoslavia has undergone an exceptional economic expansion, which has, in turn, led to the expansion of university education. As a result, problems have been created with which universities have been, or will be confronted. At the same time, one must keep in mind the noticeable differences in culture, economic level and specific features of various areas, since these have caused each Yugoslav university center to differ somewhat from its counterparts so far as local, regional and cultural-historical aspects are concerned.

Yugoslav society has as its goal the development of a special type of co-operation between social relations and institutions, which it calls the self-management system. This system seeks to develop, on the basis of socialist property, the interests of every individual to the greatest possible extent, whether that individual is a professor, a student or a laboratory aide. This obviously adds its special dimension to the university's problems. For reasons such as these, this report can promise no more than to describe the state's fundamental alignment, the problems of Yugoslav universities, and their complex causes. The impossibility of obtaining a definitive answer is reflected in the fact that even Yugoslav experts in this sphere differ substantially.

Every economic expansion depends upon the development of skilled personnel. The country as a whole and Yugoslav universities in particular are excellent empirical demonstrations of this statement. Along with the economic boom, postwar Yugoslavia has witnessed a "university" boom. For a country which in the 1920-44 period trained only 31,556 highly educated personnel in three university centers (or about 1,262 annually), it is remarkable that from 1945-63 some 120,268 experts in the economic and social services (or more than 6,330 per year) were graduated from the universities. In 1968 the total number reached 250,589 and the average between 1960 and 1966 rose to 16,000 per annum.[1]

Obviously, only an increase in the network of higher education institutions could have rendered this possible. The number of university centers has risen to seven, the number of faculties and high schools to 127, and higher education facilities may now be found in 22 cities in Yugoslavia. It goes without saying that these institutions have become the vehicles of economic and cultural dynamism in Yugoslavia.

In the same period the issue of educational costs at universities has attracted the attention of Yugoslav authorities and of others responsible for higher education institutions for various reasons. First, because the total outlay for education, compared to Yugoslavia's national income, has hitherto been relatively small, but according to the latest plan an increase is expected in the next few years. For instance, in 1956 the total outlay for education accounted for 2.6 per cent (in 1966, 4.3 per cent) of the national income.[2] The planned increase for 1970, to 5.4 per cent, would place Yugoslavia among countries which in the past decade have achieved outstanding results in the field of university education and which allocate the same percentage of their national income for this purpose (Sweden, Holland, U.S.A.). However, absolute differences must be borne in mind.

Second, the increase in the number of students and intensification of the teaching process call for substantially larger commitments than those allocated today. Data on specific Yugoslav universities show all indices of educational costs to be rising rapidly, as well as the absolute figures. For instance, personal expenditures increased during 1968 by 15.6 per cent; material expenditures by 20.9 per cent, and amortization by 48.6 per cent. Total outlays for university education increased in the same period from $134 to $156 million.

Third, the cost of a four-year education per student varies greatly from one university to another. In the Socialist Republic of Serbia the cost is about $10.000 per student in the Faculty of Veterinary Sciences in Belgrade; at the Faculty of Law and Economy in Nish it is approximately $1.300. This is due to significant differences in investment rate per student.

---

[1] All statistical data in this paper have been taken from statistical yearbooks of S.F.R.J. (edited by the Federal Institute for Statistics, Belgrade), as well as from the Yugoslav Survey, published by Secretariat of Information of the Federal Executive Council, Belgrade.

[2] In the total, higher education's share (universities and higher schools) has been less than 1 per cent of the national income.

However, it should be stated that the ratio between personal and material costs, including investment, is very unfavorable. For example, in the Socialist Republic of Serbia this ratio is 8:2, while in some developed countries this ratio is 4:6 in favor of investment costs.

High school education, which is more and more directed toward training in those technical and exact sciences so vital to Yugoslavia's economic development, has been considerably altered in structure and orientation. As might be expected, these changes have also affected the orientation of students. In the 1959-60 school year 25.1 per cent of all freshmen were enrolled in technical science courses. Six years later, in 1965-66, this percentage had increased to 31.8 per cent. In the same period enrollment in humanistic and social science courses declined from 44.1 to 41 per cent.

World-wide, the same sudden rise in enrollments at faculties of basic natural sciences (mathematics, physics, chemistry and biology) can be perceived. And, within the framework of the social sciences, there is evidence of greater interest in economic branches of knowledge. More than 16 per cent of all Yugoslav students are studying in this area, a figure which constitutes more than 37 per cent of the total number in social science faculties.

The expansion of university centers and in particular, the broadened network of faculties, which may now be found even in minor political and economic centers, have effected a great increase in part-time studies in Yugoslavia. Workers who would never previously have thought of studying at universities have been encouraged by the constitution to exercise extensive rights to the highest possible education. This situation has been exploited most of all by workers and employees in the undeveloped republics of Yugoslavia—Bosnia-Herzegovina and Macedonia. In these areas the number of part-time students was exceptionally high in 1966. In Macedonia such students constituted 29.7 per cent of all students, and in Bosnia, 26.6 per cent.

By and large, since 1966 this category of students has tended to concentrate on studies in the faculties of social sciences. As a matter of fact, three-fourths of all part-time students are studying the social sciences, while only one-fourth are in technical and basic natural sciences.

As we have noted, the result of this extraordinary expansion of the university network has been the production of a great number of experts who possess a higher education. This phenomenon has changed the entire "qualification" structure of the Yugoslav economy. In 1967 the percentage of experts with high school and higher education was 7.1 per cent (29.8 per cent of skilled and highly skilled workers) of the total number of employed persons in Yugoslavia. It is entirely correct to assume that this investment in human brainpower has brought about a profound change in those factors which are increasing the Yugoslav social product, and, moreover, that this productivity is assuming ever greater importance.

In the same way, the enormous increase—by Yugoslav standards—in the number of highly skilled personnel, plus technological improvements and rationalization of the economic system and methods of business operations, have made it possible for Yugoslavia to increase the national per capita income fivefold in comparison to the pre-war situation. In 1968 the average per capita income was about $600, and the goal of the seven-year plan (1964-70) is to raise this to $800. If achieved, it will set Yugoslavia on its way to becoming an industrially developed country—on a modest scale—one which will be able to participate in the international industrial community on a sound economic basis, even while maintaining and further developing its specifically national brand of political independence. And this is, in fact, the long-range goal of the socio-economic reform which is being cultivated so intensively in Yugoslavia today.

While it followed the economic expansion in time, the "explosion" in the dynamism of university education was the factor that made the economic expansion possible, and it led—as with the economic development—to a "crisis in the development of the universities." It is a crisis which, on the one hand, is analogous to that which has occurred in the economic sphere. It involves an increase in numbers, a rise in quality standards, in rate and unevenness of development, and also in lack of quality and in unsatisfied social needs for people of a particular type. This holds true in spite of the enormous and extensive increase in the number of persons with university education.

Yet, this is only one aspect of the problems which confront those responsible for higher education in Yugoslavia today. We might note once more that it is directly connected with the current economic development of the nation. Other subtler and more intricate dilemmas affect the Yugoslav self-management system, and these are social as well as economic in nature. They are inseparably linked to various external factors, or rather, to the ideological, technological and scientific ferment which prevails in today's world and in Yugoslav universities as well. Even though these "causes" and "consequences" are so closely joined that it is difficult to separate them, their careful analysis is useful to gain a clearer perception of all dimensions of the problems which await settlement in the future.

Yugoslavia's economic reform since 1966 has caused the development of two central goals, in both of which universities are directly implicated. One of these concerns the quality of personnel needed for the intensified methods of production and the rationalization of economic and social organization. The second, which stems from the first, concerns the more intensive development of science, especially those branches which relate to technological expansion and scientific organization of work. At this juncture, it would seem that a thorough reform of the university must precede any attempt to respond adequately to either of these goals.

The university is surely in sorry shape today. For political and social reasons, it operates to produce a certain type of expert, seeking to accomplish this end in faculties lacking both in continuity and in clearly defined economic and social goals. As a result, the cadres the university is forming are of inferior quality. Day by day, it becomes clearer that in its scope and structure the university is out of step with the nation's need for intensification and rationalization of the economy. Externally, this incompatibility is manifested by the university's lack of trained personnel and by the fact that the existing personnel are not being utilized.

It is obvious that personnel are being produced in the wrong proportions and that there is an insufficient number of professionals to train them. Almost half the total number of recent graduates came from social and humanitarian faculties while the number graduating from faculties of basic natural sciences and from the agricultural-forestry-veterinary faculties has declined. The three-phase instruction concept, with the first phase of two years aimed at rapid production of so-called medium-expert personnel for economy and service, can only be judged as a grievous error of social policy.

The economy has rejected this type of expert, and universities, moreover, have encountered trouble in reorganizing the relatively few instructors available and orienting them toward the important new curricular questions. As a matter of fact, the majority of the personnel formed in this way continued their studies. Practically speaking, it meant that studies were prolonged a third longer than normal—by 1.8 years in the 1959-64 period. It is only recently that the duration of the study period has been reduced. This example clearly indicates that even the positive experiences of developed economic communities cannot be mechanically applied.

The quality of instruction cannot be essentially altered for two reasons. At first, the territorial expansion of faculties, even down to the level of individual economic branches, and the separation of instruction and studies in the new faculties into sections, groups and departments appeared to be extremely effective and reasonable. But with the needs for narrow specialization soon fulfilled, the purely negative effects remained: an over-developed network of universities; an unreasonable exploitation of the teaching staff, laboratory equipment, and instructional aids; and the high costs of specialization for the individual student.

Thus we come to the even more complex question of the hazy status of scientific[3] studies in Yugoslav universities. To date, the ideology prevailing has led to a policy of separating scientific from educational work, and to a conviction that scientific work will be more efficient and will develop better

---

[3] The author uses "scientific" in the sense of "scholarly" or "scholarly research" (Ed. note).

in independent extramural institutes and economic laboratories. This profoundly negative outlook has, in various ways, affected the overall capability of the university as the vehicle of scientific progress and as an institution for the formation of top quality personnel.

Above all, it has harmed the university's master's and doctoral programs. At this stage of instruction, where it is imperative that the course offerings fit in with the instructors' scientific work, and where the teachers' direct contact with students is so essential, no policy has been established regarding either organization, financial support or personnel. From the standpoint of organization, postgraduate instruction is carried on in less than 50 per cent of the faculties, and broad differences exist among the various educational plans, programs and instructional criteria. Materially speaking, the community at large does not support such work but leaves it to interested economic institutions and individuals. There is also the tradition of instructors giving individual courses in the postgraduate area. So far as personnel are concerned, the comparatively small number of instructors at this level evolves from the instructors' commitments to research work outside the universities and from the fact that their work is subordinated to institutional scientific programs and not to the university. The result is that very few master's or doctor's degrees have been earned at Yugoslav universities during the past ten years.

The great gap between scientific work and teaching at universities might be less damaging to the quality of teaching and to the knowledge and ability of graduates, if the work load of the professors were carefully apportioned according to their backgrounds, and if they were permitted, at least temporarily, to devote themselves exclusively to scientific work. However, while the teaching staff employed at the university on a permanent basis almost doubled in eight years, and while the ratio between students and teaching staff does not seem inappropriate (about 20 to 1), the pattern is, in fact, unbalanced and on the whole prohibits continued, long-range specialization by teachers.

Moreover, the university is still overburdened with so-called "lecturers" (in the 1965-66 term they accounted for one-sixth of the teaching staff). Lecturers are not required to obtain a doctor's degree in order to teach at this level, and in our opinion, despite some outstanding exceptions, they tend to lower the quality-level of the teaching. The number of assistant lecturers and junior teaching staff is likewise inappropriate when compared to the number of associate and full professors. This may be explained by the poor material attractions the university can offer its best students. The low salaries offered and the little hope of doing scientific research, coupled with the university's limited financial resources, serve to discourage potential assistant lecturers. We should note here the overall unsatisfactory compensation system of the university when compared to other professions demanding a similar or even inferior educational background and experience. This issue has been thoroughly discussed in Yugoslavia in recent years, and has led to recognition by the public of the crying need to improve the material position of university teachers. Some positive trends, especially with regard to the personal incomes of teachers at red-brick universities and faculties, can be perceived. However, increases to date are still insufficient to insure that teachers will be able to devote their full time to duties at the university. Apparently, the present system of budgeting is unable to solve this problem, and the financial status of universities and their teaching staffs remains one of the major roadblocks to university reform.

All of the above issues, which cast light on the problems of financing, personnel, and teachers' working conditions experienced by the universities, also reflect problem areas between the universities and society in general. These involve the concept of self-management at universities and the place and role of the teaching staff and students, respectively. These are issues of extraordinary complexity, with several unusual aspects that must be considered.

So-called "university legislation" based on the constitution of the Socialist Federative Republic of Yugoslavia grants far-reaching rights to universities. Faculties and high schools are, in fact, institutions managed by the teaching staff (boards), together with representatives of the social community (councils). When special problems pertaining to administrative procedures, teaching and schedules are dealt with, the councils and boards are aided by representatives of the office staff and the students. At the same time, vertical decentralization of management was introduced. Universities in Yugoslavia are not unitary and obligatory institutions, but are voluntary unions of faculties. The decisions of these unions are not enforceable but serve as guidelines to faculties in their activities. As for financial needs and resources, the universities are financed by the national economy, social institutions, and a "community of education," an organization which through the national budget provides resources for the faculties' fundamental activities.

The kind of self-management adopted by Yugoslav universities is founded on the thesis that the actions and commitments of each individual and of the whole institution should be independent. It is a doctrine that encounters many problems in practice.

If the process of self-management and the autonomy of the university are considered to be based on the actions and interactions of interest-structures (the goals and interests of individual faculties or groups of faculties), and also as means for the technical co-ordination and organization of these interests, then, in both directions, many deficiencies become apparent.

The basic self-managerial theory, i.e., the principle of decentralization of interests, has revealed many anomalies in practice. Some of these have already been touched upon. The disintegration and rapid expansion of faculties occurred simultaneously, followed by the appearance of significant structural deficiencies with respect to the level of teaching, the irrational dispersion of faculties, the inequitable criteria for the hiring of professors and assistant lecturers and the unfair material rewards given.

At the faculties other problems pertaining to spheres of interests and technicalities grew more serious. In the matter of the sphere of interests, assistant lecturers, students and office staff joined in expressing their dissatisfaction with the degree of their participation in, and influence on self-managerial decision-making. Only on a few decision-making bodies were they even represented. At the faculty level in the technical domain, large numbers of self-managerial institutions (boards of classes, faculty councils, commissions and boards of the council, conferences of the whole faculty staff) dealt with the same issues and made controversial decisions. Similarly, they opted for goals that were unattainable because of the limitations imposed by the faculty in the framework of the self-management system.

With respect to the vertical co-ordination of self-managerial decision-making, the university, in its role as the union of faculties, also faces tremendous problems. Previously, we emphasized that the university is prohibited from exercising authority over its faculties. This restriction upsets the integration of staff and available assets which, from the standpoint of scientific and teaching values, could well be applied within the framework of the same or similar disciplines to the advantage of the whole university. Also, the overall objectives of universities are often only partially realized, since representatives to the university council feel more responsible to the faculties they work for than to the university's overall objectives. Thus, the function of the rector as the university's executive has become a merely formal one.

The inevitable consequence of this situation has been that the authority and influence of the university as a self-managerial entity have been on the wane while the influence of certain faculties, depending on the current interests of specific economic and social units, has been increasing.

Since the concept of an educational system that could be embraced by all Yugoslav nations is lacking, and since there is an inadequate grasp of the needs for and demands on highly qualified staff members, a definite widening of the gap between global and regional social and economic development has been the result.

During 1968 and also 1969 the relevance of students' involvement increased considerably at Yugoslav universities. Taking their cue from worldwide dissatisfaction with the "establishment," and because of specific problems in Yugoslav social development, students expressed their criticism of the existing situation by means of mass demonstrations and have otherwise voiced demands for many reforms in university life. Their criticism has hit hard at several points, such as the low degree of student participation in self-managerial decision-making in the university, the relatively few student delegates to these management organs, the poor material status of students (fellowships, campuses), and the low quality and inadequate organization of teaching (curriculum, quality and organization). Simultaneously, students raised objections to the status of universities in society, and they criticized the conditions affecting faculty graduates and teachers (the problems of placement, trends in economic policy, and the material standing of universities). Although the students' criticisms were somewhat radical and oversimplified, their very brashness brought fresh air to Yugoslav university society and caused authorities and institutions to ponder their problems and undertake a series of concrete measures to solve them during 1968 and 1969. As a result, a law on Compulsory Admittance of Graduated Apprentices in Industrial and Other Organizations was passed; and the material position of students has been substantially improved by fellowships and improved campuses.

Student involvement has, above all, been instrumental in making people see that the radical, long overdue reform of the university is the most important single political task. This awareness is shared by the country's supreme representative bodies and basic political powers, as was evident at the IXth Congress of the Yugoslav League of Communists and the forums of the Yugoslav Trade Unions.

Although some of the clamor for university reform merely echoes the differences in tradition, degree of development and national characteristics of the people, it can be safely said that, in general, Yugoslav universities consider reform necessary in the areas listed below. We must add that some of these areas have already been studied, and in a few cases, thanks to alert legislatures, the reforms have been instituted.

(1). *Reform of the Mechanism of Self-Management at the University.* This heading covers problems pertaining to the integration of what may be called university "sub-interests" (individuals, departments, and faculties). Operating within the framework of certain interest structures (boards, faculty councils and university councils), their petitions must be taken into account, and direct decision-making should follow whenever possible.

There must also be a more comprehensive determination of criteria for judging priorities in clashes between interests. This proposal presupposes that the Yugoslav university, as a whole, will be defined by its functional goals and that all sub-goals will be made subject to these. Implementation of these goals, insofar as they fulfill the major interests of all members of the university community, will depend on a more efficacious technical co-ordination. The aim will be to develop procedures which will facilitate execution of the faculties' main activities—scientific work and teaching. In terms of the self-management concept, the equality of technical co-ordination to other functions must be emphasized.

In our opinion, this matter of assigning precedence constitutes the central issue in the whole question of reform. Since every decision reached by universities has both technical and interest aspects, making a judgment between these aspects and then co-ordinating them can be seen to be a very complex process. Similarly complex is the integration of interest structures at the university (i.e., groups of teachers teaching the same subject, or groups of students on a certain faculty council). No less important is the process of technical co-ordination, since it poses problems of one kind for scientific work and of another kind for teaching.

(2). *Self-Managerial Rights of Students.* This aspect of reform includes many new features: the claim of students for broader and more direct participation in decision-making at the faculty level, their insistence on the election and re-election of teachers and executive officers (deans, rectors, members of the council), their involvement in the forms and methods of teaching, the financing of the university, and so on.

(3). *Universities and the General Social Policy.* It is readily understandable that the reform of the university cannot be achieved without more teachers and scientists participating in the representative bodies of republics and communes. There, they may exert more influence on an overall social policy and on a university policy as well.

(4). *Reform of Curricula and Programs.* Many analysts correlate the ineffectiveness of certain programs (from the standpoint of their quality, duration, etc.) with their total collapse. Thus, a re-evaluation of the curricula and programs is needed, and this re-evaluation must be founded on two premises: first, a scientific knowledge of the changes in the quantity and quality of professions in specific stages of social development, and second, a systematic review of these changes and consequent modification of existing curricula at the earliest possible time.

(5). *Complementarity Between Scientific Work and Teaching.* The close and essential connection that must exist between scientific work and teaching is recognized as one of the leading topics in the whole reform movement. Adequate facilities and a staff equipped to introduce modern scientific and teaching methods are both lacking, as are the desired new kinds of graduates. Universities must establish an organization having the authority to carry on this task efficiently and expediently.

(6). *Network and Staff.* The absence of long-range projections about the number of graduates, and the dearth of studies on changing skills resulted in the hodge-podge of high schools and faculties that now exists. Thus, under the present system, the most qualified staff, the richest resources, and the best facilities for teaching have been scattered inefficiently.

The twin aspects of the projected reform are interrelated: making sense of the existing network of high schools and colleges and merging of similar institutions and departments. Co-operation between faculties and other schools obviously presupposes knowledge about the backgrounds, numbers and specializations of the staff required for the future.

(7). *Financial Problems Involved in Reform.* It is obvious from the introduction that Yugoslavia's resources are limited from the standpoints both of teaching and training activities and also of scientific study at the universities. Moreover, the prospect is neither attractive nor encouraging for the best young teachers. A true reform demands that a strict correlation be followed between the national income and the rate of contributions to universities, as well as an increased portion for university education.

A great deal of attention is centered on the proposal for establishing two new yardsticks. The first, "the price of education," is supposed to solve the economic aspects of the relationship between university as "producer," and the economy and society as "consumers." The "price of education" idea is analogous to the supply and demand doctrine and would fix the responsibility for the costs of reproduction and income at the university level (personal expenditures and funds). By employing this concept, the material status of teachers could be improved and resources provided for scientific work at the university.

Another proposed reform embodies the idea of the "student as the dominant factor in the allocation of resources for education." The idea here is that the community (social organizations, economy, funds) would allocate the resources available to each student, in accordance with the duration and subject of the studies, the costs of the faculties involved, and board and lodging fees.

Such resources would enable the student to choose the faculty, the teachers and teaching aids, according to his interests in a particular faculty and a particular teacher.

It is believed that both of the proposed methods for financing (and in particular, the "price of education" idea) would represent a radical break with the present system of university budgeting, and would result in happier economic relations and a basic improvement, overall, in the material status of the university.

# PART FIVE

# AFRICAN UNIVERSITIES AND
# THE PROCESS OF CHANGE
# IN MIDDLE AFRICA

### F. X. Sutton

## TYPES OF AFRICAN UNIVERSITIES AND THEIR ORIGINS

Twenty-five years ago there were no universities in tropical Africa. Educated Africans there were, but most of them had been to universities outside Africa or to a very few institutions in Africa that offered post-secondary education in some form. My distinguished fellow-speaker, Ambassador Nicol, will be rightly offended if I do not mention the venerable institution he has headed. Fourah Bay College in Sierra Leone is nearly 20 years older than the university where we meet, with a history stretching back to 1827. Though it nearly foundered during World War II, it survived to become, under Ambassador Nicol's leadership, the University College of Sierra Leone. There had also been beginnings of post-secondary education in Ghana and Nigeria, and teachers' colleges were training many of the men who would play great roles in the independence movements of the next decade. But a full-fledged university—even a full-fledged college in the American sense—did not yet exist. Nowadays we can easily count as many as 34 institutions of higher education in tropical Africa; 12 to 14 of them would deserve the label "universities" in American terms, and another 10 would certainly qualify as "colleges" in our sense. This remarkable development began in the late 1940's, accelerated moderately in the early 1950's, and came into a great burst of development as the colonial territories became independent African nations in the years around 1960.

New universities in new nations must draw heavily on models and resources from abroad. The African universities have been shaped and developed under influences from two external sources: the colonial powers, and a largely post-independence input from American, United Nations and other sources. The colonial powers made their imprint first, with the result that most of the tropical African universities still are recognizably based on British, French, or Belgian models.[1] Later influences from America and elsewhere, as well as

---

[1] There are universities in Angola and Mozambique, but I am not acquainted with them and will have to leave them out of this discussion.

deliberate efforts of the independent African countries toward a genuine academic autonomy, have modified the character of many of these universities. But only five or six can yet be said to fall outside the colonial models. Among these few, I would list Haile Selassie I University in Ethiopia, the dormant University of Nigeria at Nsukka, Njala in Sierra Leone, Kisangani in the Congo, a Canadian-aided effort in Ruanda, and, of course, the University of Liberia and Cuttington College in Liberia. To understand the nature and variety of present-day African universities, it is thus convenient to look first at colonial origins and then consider other influences, adaptation and autonomous efforts.

The differences of British, French and Belgian higher education are complex, subtle and important to Europeans. But from a transatlantic perspective —or indeed the contemporary perspectives of Africa—they have had a great deal in common and, when extended into Africa, displayed similar patterns. All began in an appreciation that there should be some Africans with higher education and a conviction that they could be better trained in Africa than overseas; all tried to provide an education of assured academic standards to relatively small numbers; and all found the natural way to do this in linking the new universities in Africa with particular universities and the system of higher education in the metropolitan country.

a) *The Asquith and COCAST Colleges of the British.* The development of higher education in the African territories controlled by Great Britain had its beginnings in a commission that was appointed in 1943 under the chairmanship of Mr. Justice Asquith. This commission issued a report in 1945 that became the basis of policy throughout the Empire. Britain had by 1945 come to conceive its Empire as a trusteeship in which the colonies should be prepared, with deliberate speed, first for self-government and then in some distant future for independence. Universities were, the Asquith Commission said, "an inescapable corollary of any policy which aims at the achievement of colonial self-government." The future leadership of dependent territories should be educated at home so that the universities could be a "focus for intellectual self-expression of the people," and Britain ought to give financial aid in building these institutions.

In 1964, Sir Eric Ashby, the Master of Clare College in Cambridge, came to the other Cambridge to describe *African Universities and Western Tradition*[2] in a series of Godkin lectures. He had some sharp criticisms of the "Asquith

---

[2] Cambridge, Mass., 1964. Ashby has made the problem of reconciling national and local adaptations of universities with international quality the central theme of his *Universities: British, Indian, African* (Cambridge, Mass., 1966). Cf. pp. 211-223 on the Asquith Commission.

doctrine," which he clearly thought had come to be too reverentially regarded and deserved to be seen in its British narrowness and its limited perception of the needs of the escaping Empire, particularly in Africa. There was, he said, no attempt to seek out other models than British ones for the universities that were to be established in Africa, and there was a derogation of the applied sciences and technologies that was harmful to the course of African development. There were old lions in Britain in those days, and one of them who had served on the Asquith Commission, Sir Alexander Carr-Saunders, issued forth with a fierce and learned rebuttal in the pages of the *University Quarterly*.[3] It could not, he said, have been otherwise that Britain should have sought to build universities on the only models it really knew, and that the people who had to teach in them knew.

Such are the central issues that must concern any observer of this history. Whatever the imperfections of the Asquith model, it can certainly be said that it was rapidly put into effect. An active secretary of state for the colonies saw to it that a commission on West Africa was appointed simultaneously with the Asquith Commission and, despite a split in the Commission, university colleges at Ibadan and Accra were soon established, and in East Africa, Makerere College shaped to the new model. In accordance with the Asquith doctrine, these colleges emphasized a form of higher education that was selective, rigorous in intellectual quality, and rather conservative in range. But it was recognized at the same time that there were many forms of post-secondary education that did not fit comfortably into the central pattern of degree work in universities, and the idea of a group of colleges of arts, sciences and technology evolved to complement the university colleges in the Asquith pattern. These colleges came to be known under the acronym of their co-ordinating body in Britain as the COCAST colleges, and they had their principal African representatives at Kumasi in Ghana, in three locations in Nigeria, and in what was then called the Royal Technical College in Nairobi. Both these types of institutions, the Asquith colleges as the spawning ground of the future leadership of self-governing colonies, and the more technical and practically-oriented diploma-granting COCAST colleges, were to be residential institutions for rather limited numbers of students. Both turned out to be quite expensive, with annual costs approximating 1000 British pounds per student per annum. Britain undertook, through the Colonial Development and Welfare Acts, to provide much of the capital necessary for building these colleges, but imposed upon the local revenues of the dependencies to supply their recurrent costs.

The so-called COCAST colleges did not have happy careers. They were a conception which was a good diagnosis of African need but a bad diagnosis

---

3 June 1965, Vol. 19, pp. 227-39.

of African aspiration (and indeed of the aspirations of the British who initially staffed them). Too many Americans have failed to see that these colleges corresponded in their way to the American idea of junior colleges which was later so often confidently recommended for Africa. It was probably their timing, not their conception, that was wrong. In a situation where there was a great lack of Africans with university degrees, settling for something that seemed only marginally short of a degree was hard to tolerate and an inflation of academic ambitions became irresistible. The fate of the former COCAST colleges has been their evolution into full-fledged universities or university colleges on a footing at least ostensibly equal with the Asquith colleges. Nkrumah made Kumasi into the Kwami Nkrumah University of Science and Technology; the Nigerian establishments became Ahmadu Bello University, and parts of the University of Nigeria and the University of Ife; the Royal Technical College in Nairobi became, simply and more prestigiously, the University College, Nairobi.

All of these colleges were initially headed by British principals, staffed by British academics, and linked to British degrees through the device of a special relationship with the University of London. They were not, as hostile critics, African and otherwise, have often alleged, indifferent to the African situation in which they were established. Many examination topics appropriate to African conditions were accepted. A substantial effort to build the knowledge necessary for teaching in Africa was undertaken in research institutes, and it is easy to recall circumstances in which the colleges were regarded as dangerous hotbeds of nationalistic sentiment by the colonial governments. They were nevertheless still strongly British in character at the time of independence and, like other institutions overtaken in the sudden rush of political change, faced unexpectedly early demands for radical change. It is important to realize that their being British was not, at least in their early years, a characteristic that was ill-regarded by Africans. Sir Christopher Cox, one of the principal architects of the Asquith colleges and long-time educational advisor to the Colonial Office, once described three stages in the evolution of colonial attitudes towards education. First, there was the struggle with indifference and hostility; secondly, a period of adaptation to colonial conditions; and thirdly, a response to demands that there be no discrimination between education in the metropolitan country and in the colonies.[4] When the Asquith colleges were established, most African countries were firmly into the third stage, and it was unquestionably well accepted that the degrees granted in Ghana, Nigeria, or Uganda should be "London degrees."

This concordance between African and British ideals made possible impressive achievements. Observers like myself who visited these colleges in their

---

[4] Address before British Association for the Advancement of Science, *The Advancement of Science*, No. 50, September 1956.

early flourishing were impressed with the seriousness and industry of staff and students. There was remarkably little cynicism and unmistakable evidence that education of good quality was both possible and actually occurring.

b) *Universities on the French Model.* The universities set up in French African territories were more French than the Asquith colleges were British. That they have been so was in part a general consequence of the character of French colonialism and, more particularly, a consequence of the uniform, centralized and hierarchical character that education has had in France. There was in French colonialism a strong tincture of the universal ideas which France gave to the world in the Enlightenment and the Revolution. If the French carry France with them everywhere, they do so with a kind of non-discriminatory hospitality to those who can acquire their language and ways. Africans in the old British territories used to remark with some envy and some bitterness that it was possible for their neighbors in the French terri-tories to become accepted as Frenchmen, whereas they could never become fully British. But this hospitality has been at the price of an exclusive position for French culture (whereas the stiff and reserved British sense of racial and cultural distinctiveness has made easier place for a recognition of African identity and African culture).

When universities came to be established in French-speaking Africa after World War II, they were placed on top of an educational system that used French as the language of instruction from the earliest years, and in the logical application of nondiscriminatory principles became more strictly equivalent to education in France during the postwar years. Sentiments which demanded the obliteration of special African certificates and programs operated in the French territories as they did in the British. It was, therefore, not a matter of controversy that the University of Dakar should be established in 1953 un-der the same statutes that governed universities in metropolitan France and that it was decreed in 1957 to be the 18th university of France. The standards of admission, examinations and degrees were the same as in France, and the structure of faculties kept the familiar organization. The professors were al-most entirely drawn from the cadres of French university staff, and their members were assured of a place in the universities at home after a tour of duty at Dakar.[5] When other centers of higher education came to be established

---

[5] This emphasis on the University of Dakar being a French university responded not only to African aspirations of the time, but also to needs of the French in Africa. Like the universities in the Belgian Congo, the University of Dakar served the colonial population of West Africa. Unlike most of the British foundations in tropical Africa— the only significant exception being the University College of Rhodesia and Nyasaland —Dakar was a racially-integrated university with many French students interspersed among the Africans.

(at Abidjan [1959], Brazzaville [1959], and Yaoundé [1961]), they followed similar patterns.

The importation of French higher education into Africa was expensive, as it was in the British territories, and the French assumed a heavy commitment to its support: The capital costs of Dakar *and* its recurrent costs were for many years fully borne by the French government. The French tradition of free higher education had to be preserved, and it was necessary to provide considerably more for impecunious African students than was traditional in metropolitan France. The French had encountered the same difficulties as the British had in nonresidential secondary schools and were prepared for the need to establish *cités universitaires* at Dakar and at the other universities, so that the greater part of the African student body could be residential. (This feature was particularly needed at Dakar since that university, in its original conception, was a university for all of French black Africa and a great part of the student body came from places other than Senegal.) While at least one study has been made of the costs of the French and British universities in Africa,[6] I do not know of any satisfying precise comparison. It was my impression during some years of observation of the build-up of these universities that the growth of staff was slower in the French than in corresponding institutions in the English-speaking territories and, hence, that the recurrent costs per pupil were probably less. There were, nevertheless, high costs, and the problems of independent African governments in assuming them have been formidable after the initial period of French generosity. As on the British side, there has been much consciousness and some controversy among the French about the problems of adaptation of their African institutions to African conditions and needs, and it would be gross caricature to depict these institutions simply as inflexible and insensitive to their settings. Careful assessments of manpower needs antedated similar efforts in the English-speaking countries; the various faculties at Dakar and the great *Institut Français d'Afrique Noire* have strong African research records; and notable adaptations of curriculum and styles of instruction have been made. But, as I have suggested, they started from beginnings that were even more emphatically French than the Asquith colleges were British in character, and the problems of their ultimate Africanization are probably more difficult.

c) *The Belgian Establishments.* What the Belgians did in university education in Africa displays many apparent differences from what the English and French did, but there are underlying commonalities and I shall confine myself

---

[6] Jan Tinbergen, H. C. Bos, and W. Klyt, "The Financing of Higher Education in Africa," pp. 155-212, in *The Development of Higher Education in Africa*, report of the Tananarive Conference, September 3-12, 1962, UNESCO, 1963.

to a very brief description. The leading Belgian establishment was Lovanium University near Leopoldville (now Kinshasa). This university, as its name suggests, was linked to Louvain in a pattern not unlike that by which Ibadan was linked to London or Dakar to Paris and Bordeaux. It was staffed by professors who mostly came from Louvain. It educated young Belgians who were living in the Congo, as well as Africans, in the patterns and standards accepted at home in Belgium. It was residential and costly, and its capital and recurrent costs were a charge on the Congolese Government until independence. Belgium being the complex and divided country that it is, a single university linked to the Catholic University in Louvain would not do. Consequently, a state university was established at Elizabethville (now Lubumbashi) which was less firmly established at the time of independence but has survived the vicissitudes of the Katanga experience to continue another form of Belgian higher education in Africa.

Two general features of Belgian policy in higher education in the Congo deserve noting. One is the lateness of development of any higher education, with its well-known fateful consequences. The other is the relative openness which the divisions of language and religious affiliation gave to the system. In contrast to the French territories, the Congo had displayed some receptivity to English and the university traditions of other countries before independence; academic eclecticism promised to be easier and in fact has gone as far as permitting the establishment of an American style university at Kisangani.

d) *The U.S., the U.N., and Others.* In the decade of the 1950's the influences on African higher education were overwhelmingly from the colonial powers. There was, of course, as in other things, an American flavor in Liberia at the struggling University of Liberia (which typically had an American Negro head in those years) and at Cuttington College up-country, which reproduced the confessional American college in an African setting. Even Ethiopia had a kind of muted derivative of the British university college run by Canadian Jesuits in mufti. The vast changes that came over Africa in the 1960's brought 32 newly independent countries to add to the mere 10 that existed at the beginning of the decade. This new decade brought an independence from colonial influences in higher education too, but not in the sense that foreign imports were abandoned in favor of indigenous ideas and practices. The higher academic independence meant in effect the possibility of being eclectic, of reaching out to many countries for models and resources and seeking to blend them in some distinctive adaptation to local needs.

The principal new inputs came from the United States and the United Nations. These were the major new sources because they responded to the new thrust in African values and they had the means to do so. The thrust of African independence necessarily brought a deep questioning of the old colonial ascendancy. Africans who had meekly accepted the old prestige and authority of the colonials now turned to reject their values and the symbols that went with them. They questioned the style and standards of the old colonial education and they found ready allies in Americans and others who came with enthusiasm for African independence and no great liking for the types of education the colonial powers had brought. Many Americans who came to Africa in the heady years around 1960 found it easier to confront the educational systems they found than to work within them. The conflict was sharpest in the former British territories. There never was any real penetration in the ex-French territories. In the Belgian Congo it may perhaps be said that the American invasion was on the one hand adroitly absorbed (at Lovanium), or deflected onto new objectives at Stanleyville (Kisangani) and a new Ecole Nationale de Droit et d'Administration (E.N.D.A.) at Kinshasa. In the English-speaking territories we Americans felt much better equipped to bring a major new input in conditions we thought we understood and where it seemed evident that our inputs were needed. It was part of the new African assertiveness at the time of independence to begin to question the desirability of systems of education rigorously equivalent to those of the former colonial power. There was also a new concern for education that would more promptly and manifestly meet the needs of the country. The roots of these new emphases are no doubt subtle and varied. Education had spread sufficiently widely that it was beginning to be appreciated that it did not automatically produce valuable and productive citizens—the primary school dropout problem was already familiar at independence. The leveling spirit of independence also produced a general reaction against the severe emphases on selection and quality which characterized the sharply peaked educational pyramids of the colonial regimes. Into this situation American ideals of educational institutions of a widely democratic sort, dedicated to service to the surrounding society and operating on standards that seemed to offer a pragmatic alternative to British practice, had a strong appeal.

The general thrusts of American influence were the encouragement of expansion, emphasis on applied fields and the professions, greater autonomy from external standards, lower entrance levels and more rapid Africanization. Some of these effects occurred because Americans, like others, knew little about educational systems other than their own and tended to export what they knew. Other effects, like the emphasis on engineering and applied fields, occurred because it was United States Agency for International Development (A.I.D.) that had most of the money that could be used, and it was thought that it had to concentrate on applied and professional fields to serve its developmental purposes. The University of Nigeria at Nsukka in Eastern Nigeria was a new establishment that gave a chance for the American land-grant college model to be applied in Africa with large A.I.D. resources marshalled by

Michigan State University. But in general the new American inputs did not go to the establishment of new universities but rather towards reshaping the character and growth of existing ones. A great effort was made by some broadly tolerant and flexible individuals from both sides of the Atlantic to bring American and British efforts into effective co-operation. Men like Eric Ashby, Andrew Cohen, and John Lockwood on the British side used their influence and prestige to convince their colleagues that the Americans had not simply come to destroy standards and upset the accomplishments of the Asquith colleges. After some fumbling and quarreling, a pattern of co-operation was worked out that became particularly notable in the forming of the University of East Africa and in the establishment of the universities in Zambia and Malawi, all of which shared British and American representatives in their founding councils.

This American input into African higher education, while it has had a profound effect on the evolution of most of the universities that had been British, did not succeed in producing many recognizably American institutions. The University of Nigeria at Nsukka, which has been quite completely disrupted by the civil war, and Njala in Sierra Leone are possible exceptions. Perhaps the university in tropical Africa that now bears the strongest and most evident impress of American models is Haile Selassie I University in Addis Ababa. This university, like some others in Africa, was put together from a variety of previously existing schools, mostly of a professional character. A wide array of foreign talent and resources had gone into them with American, Swedish and German inputs predominating. Partly because of the sheer weight of the American inputs and also because its Ethiopian leadership has been largely trained in American universities, this university is easily familiar to one who knows our institutions. This is not to say that it is as close a replica of American universities as the British, French and Belgian universities in Africa were of their models. It has indeed many distinctive characteristics, but insofar as it betrays any identifiable foreign character, this is— as irritated nationalists and rebellious students sometimes assert—an American character.

The other major input in the independence and post-independence years came from the United Nations. This has come in a way that was initially somewhat oblique, and competitive with existing institutions. The Special Fund of the United Nations was originally established in the expectation that it would devote itself to surveys and pre-investment studies. In Africa, however, its emissaries quickly perceived that more trained manpower was necessary to industrial and other economic growth. Africa would not have the manpower it needed without more and better secondary education, and this implied the need for well-trained African secondary school teachers who were grievously lacking in the years surrounding 1960. (Shortly before independence in Nigeria, for example, 70 per cent of the teachers in secondary schools did not themselves have a full secondary education.) Self-government and independence in fact produced a serious drain on the meager supply of African secondary school teachers which already existed, since many of them found their way into more exciting, honorific and lucrative government positions. It has been one of the more serious deficiencies of the universities in Africa that they have not fixed with sufficient clarity and determination on the fact that the largest group of people in African countries who ought to have a university education are the secondary school teachers, and it is to the credit of the United Nations that it did not fail to identify the dearth of secondary school teachers as a crucial problem in Africa. The situation seemed clearly to call for a crash program. There was beginning to be a supply of people who were not attaining university admission, but who had completed the first level of secondary education—the ordinary school certificate in British educational jargon, or the *premier cycle* of the *baccalaureat* in French practice. Responding to this opportunity, the Special Fund of the United Nations provided large sums (that had to be complemented by funds from the aided countries) for so-called advanced teacher training colleges which typically have provided a three-year course on top of a secondary education. Institutions of this sort were established in the Sudan, in Nigeria, in Ivory Coast and elsewhere. It was quickly seen that these institutions provoked invidious distinctions between their graduates and the graduates of other institutions of higher learning, and policy shifted before long to bring this secondary teacher training into closer relationship with established universities, beginning in such places as Salisbury and Nairobi.

There has not as yet been, to my knowledge, any serious public assessment of this important input into the current pattern of African higher education. It has certainly been important and valuable in the emphasis that it brought to secondary teacher training in Africa, although it has had doubtful effects in encouraging the view that secondary teaching is a lesser career than the civil service and can be embarked upon with lesser qualifications. The graduates of African universities have typically preferred civil service positions to secondary teaching, and only as opportunities have become more restricted in the civil services have they been more receptive to opportunities in secondary teaching. But the fact that many of the positions in the schools have been filled through crash programs by people with lesser qualifications than ordinary university degrees has meant that opportunities in this field have been less abundant and attractive than they otherwise would have been.

It would require a closer knowledge than I possess of these institutions, assisted and stimulated by the United Nations, to judge confidently the nature of their educational inputs. My impression is that they have not been notably distinctive, since language limitations and the availability of staff tended to restrict the personnel supplied through the United Nations to familiar sources—the French staffing the institutions in the French-speaking countries and people from the Commonwealth staffing those in the English-speaking territories. In these latter, a reach beyond Great Britain, and in particular to India, brought somewhat different influences than was characteristic in the Asquith colleges, but my impression is that the differences were of second order importance. One also had the impression that the international character of the staff sometimes inhibited the development of a firmly-marked educational character in these institutions.

### ACHIEVEMENTS AND PROBLEMS IN THE SCALE AND CHARACTER OF HIGHER EDUCATION

The account that I have given of the types of higher education the colonial powers introduced into Africa suggests that they had a clear conception of the functions of university education in African society. The ruling idea seems to have been that an increasing share for Africans in the management of their own affairs required a small number of men educated to a level that Europeans themselves felt to be necessary to the modern management of such societies. Given the emphasis on selection by merit and talent, which was to an admirable degree carried out, one may perhaps justifiably speak of an effort to produce an African meritocracy. Had there been long years of gradual extension of self-government, this might not have been an unrealistic conception of higher education for African social change. Colonial societies were, after all, societies with a very small top. An elite exercised wide authority and it was easy and natural to assume that a self-governing African society would follow the same pattern. The close link of African higher education to the colonials' bases in Europe fitted a conception of continuing "special relationships" through a Commonwealth or a *Communauté*. Neither a radical change in the structure of independent African societies nor a radical cultural independence was envisaged—a failure of imagination that is hardly surprising or reprehensible.

These basic presumptions were of course largely implicit in the thinking that shaped educational planning in the 1950's in Africa. Year-to-year decisions tended to focus on available funds, supplies of secondary graduates, and admission standards. Definite conceptions of the proper scale for university education were not very clearly shaped until manpower considerations came to be fashionable in the late 1950's. By that time, as we all know, a great process of political and social change was already in train which made the conception of a slow progress through self-government to independence quite obsolete. This gale of change did not arise in the universities, but their existence helped hurry it on. In its fundamental character the social revolution that brought

African independence was a deeply democratic, indeed a populist movement. It asserted the fundamental worth of all Africans, whatever their status, and it had its proper expression in mass movements guided by popular leaders who were not necessarily themselves men of much education. The idea that self-government and independence would come when peoples were "ready" for it yielded progressively to the moral principle that any continued subjection to a colonial power was wrong. In the early stages of this decline of the moral basis of colonialism, it was, however, very important both for Africans and colonials to be able to argue that there was a sufficient supply of competent Africans in being or in prospect to manage a modern state. This argument could hardly be sustained unless there were available university-trained men and more on the way, and it was obviously greatly reinforced if there was a university in the country moving toward independence. In this sense, the mere existence of a university accelerated the independence movement. And of course the rapidity of political evolution in turn stimulated the development and expansion of universities in all sorts of ways. In the university world as elsewhere in these societies, what had begun as a rather deliberate and orderly process became a complex and scurrying riot of movement.

Two features of the great independence movement gave especially strong stimuli to the expansion and evolution of African higher education. There was in the first place the acceleration of what manpower planners call the *replacement problem.* The first step in African independence was to put Africans at the top of government. Even in West Africa this occurred when most of the positions in the society that required a university education were still held by expatriates. In granting a hurried independence to countries little experienced in self-government and ill-equipped with educated and experienced Africans, the colonial powers typically comforted themselves with the expectation that their nationals would long be needed and wanted. But it proved to be one of the more remarkable weaknesses of foresight among the departing colonial powers that they simply did not see the urgency with which Africans would demand the replacement of white civil servants, managers, professional men and even university staff. Africanization has everywhere gone more quickly than the colonials anticipated, and the pace has typically left African impatience unsatisfied. There has consequently been a strong sense of the immediate need for more Africans with higher education and, as a result, a strongly expansionist view of higher education.

A related source of expansionist pressure was what Tocqueville called "the restless striving that equality begets." The ideology of African independence declared Africans competent to manage their own countries, and the events of this great era have catapulted many Africans from lowly statuses into the highest positions in their lands. It became proper for young Africans to nourish the highest ambitions, and they have had the spectacle of exciting example before them. A sharp escalation of educational ambition quickly came about. It has often been a perturbation of educational planners in Africa in the last years that young Africans have been reluctant to regard any form of education short of a university degree as terminal. Many apparently sensible schemes for technical and specialized education have proven ineffective because the young men completing the courses sought further education on top of these courses rather than a career in the specialty for which they had been trained. This high aspiration was, of course, stimulated by the fact that government employment—overwhelmingly the largest locus of opportunities —was much more promising and lucrative for a man entering with a university degree than otherwise. Parents understood this pattern of opportunity as their offspring did and very remarkable levels of ambition quickly appeared among humble peasants. The situation has been a very interesting one to a sociological eye, because of the rapidity with which a new set of expectations appeared for large numbers of Africans; it is hardly surprising that they should have become "open" expectations of a high and vague sort.

In these circumstances it is certainly obvious that there was great appeal of new ideas in higher education such as Americans and others brought to Africa. In the early 1960's the external agencies that came to advise and assist African education put particular emphasis on the growth of secondary and higher education. They did so in part because they saw the new African nations engulfed in a populist demand for expansion of primary education. This expansion needed to be balanced by expansion at the higher levels of education, and of course this was the area in which it seemed easiest for external agencies to help. The most notable expressions of this doctrine were probably the Ashby Commission on Post-Secondary Education in Nigeria (1961), and the UNESCO conference at Addis Ababa in May 1961 and a second conference specifically on higher education at Tananarive in September 1962. The doctrine of the time called for expansion, Africanization, and practical adaptation of university education to development need, particularly through emphasis on the sciences. This doctrine has had great influence in the past decade with results in expansion and change of African higher education that I have already briefly noted. The achievements are in many ways remarkable. But there have been concomitant problems, and we must note both achievements and difficulties together.

The success of African higher education in meeting the replacement problem in a great many fields has been impressive. There remain troublesome difficulties in many occupations based upon scientific education, but in general the rapid departure of expatriates has not left enormous gaps that had to be filled by men with nonuniversity qualifications. There are, of course, difficulties attendant on rapid Africanization. Many governments now have the senior positions filled by relatively young men who, even if their experience

395

and competences are adequate to the positions, will block the advancement of latecomers for many years ahead. The difficulties of this sort play back into the mood and character of the universities as students become increasingly uncertain about their career prospects.

The policy of vigorous university expansion in recent years has undoubtedly been right. But we must not ignore the difficulty in setting the scale of African universities so that they can rapidly meet the demand for replacement of expatriates and yet not produce graduates at a continuing rate that will be greater than the growth of the economy can promise to use in worthwhile employment. India, Egypt and other countries have made starkly evident the possibility that higher education may reach a scale that is quite beyond that of employment opportunities. The men who have thought about African higher education have been aware of this danger, but they faced a peculiarly difficult problem, given the urgency of short-run demand. During the last few years, it has become evident that once an African country has replaced Europeans in existing higher-level occupations, the growth of new employment and the normal process of replacement of those retiring and dying does not call for a very high annual output of university graduates. There is consequently a serious danger that university enrollments may be expanded during the period of expatriate replacement to a level which may be excessive for the prospects of future employment.

I may illustrate the situation with the case of Tanzania, which happens to have had exceptionally good planning of its educational development in relation to manpower requirements. Tanzania, though it is approaching a decade of independence and has the normal pressures for advancement of its own people, still is far from having its citizens filling all the positions that require university education. A 1969 manpower survey counted 4,076 people employed in such positions (plus some 613 vacancies).[7] Only 1,403 of these people were citizens, and 2,673 were noncitizens. A careful projection of university-based employment over the next five years shows an increase at about 5 per cent per annum. The total of new university graduates Tanzania would acquire in this five-year period is estimated at about 2,700. This number is clearly insufficient to provide for replacement of all the expatriates by the end of the current five-year-plan period, while meeting the vacancies and the anticipated growth in employment. Tanzania has, therefore, realistically set a target of 40 per cent replacement in this period and aims to have full replacement by 1980. This looks to be an achievable target with approximately the rate of output of university graduates that will be achieved during the next five years. But consider the situation after 1980. Assuming a continuation of

---

[7] Second Five-Year Plan, v.IV: Survey of the High and Middle Level Manpower Requirements and Resources, pp. v + 18 (Dar es Salaam, Government printers, 1969).

the 5 per cent per annum increase in university-type employment, there would be 6,500 such jobs in 1980 (at 4 per cent this would be about 5,900, or at 3 per cent about 5,400). Five hundred graduates per annum would be 7.7 per cent of the first figure, or 8.5 and 9.3 per cent of the latter figures. Unless one assumes normal replacement rates at around 3 per cent or higher, even the very prudent Tanzania expansion threatens to produce some excess. That the hazard is real is confirmed by other African countries, some of which already have unemployed university graduates.

The scale of these figures is remarkably small. That a country now approaching a population of 13 millions should be able to meet its needs for university-educated people with an out-turn of only approximately 500 a year (or 1,000 if they remember to provide cultivated spouses) seems extraordinary from American perspectives. I find it almost embarrassing to recall that the state of Indiana, with less than half the population of Tanzania, has one university with roughly 50,000 students, and a state as tiny as Vermont, with only 400,000 people, has a university with as many as 6,300 students. The trouble, of course, is that African countries are distressingly poor and the employment opportunities they can offer to their people just as poor. If the manpower planners are right—and there seems to me no reason to think them grossly wrong—the colonial educational strategists were not unrealistic in their restrictive caution nor African nationalists unjustified in their refusal to accept such meager prospects.

The case for avoiding overshooting manpower needs and employment opportunities is a particularly compelling one as long as expensive standards of university education are maintained in poor countries. When university education costs 1,000 pounds per student per annum, as it has in many places, it costs ten to thirty times the annual per capita income in these countries. It costs us roughly one per capita income to maintain one student in a university for a year in the United States nowadays. If an American student fritters away his time or never effectively uses his university education, the loss to the United States is no doubt regrettable; but, proportionately, it is far less serious than the waste of a student year in a poorer country. It is no wonder that we find even a courageous educational expansionist like Sir Eric Ashby sternly advising that "not only the numbers going into higher education, but the content of curricula in higher education, need to be austerely adjusted to manpower needs."[8]

Even if everyone can agree that it is important not to be wasteful at the expense of very poor people who must pay the taxes to keep a favored few in the universities, it is very hard for people to be persuaded that small numbers are the right numbers. African leaders, pressed by demands for educa-

---

8 Sir Eric Ashby, *op. cit.,* pp. 274-75.

tional opportunity from their own people and imbued with a faith that education is the great way to removing the disabilities and hindrances to progress, have typically found any low ceilings to educational need oppressive. Manpower planners have been popular as long as they could conclude that expansion was sorely needed; when they point to the threat of surpluses, even at the highest educational levels, they are doubted or scoffed at; one recalls instances in which their patiently compiled tables have been publicly denounced. Outsiders have been reluctant to be unco-operatively conservative, and have frequently shared a democratic optimism about the ultimate good of a spread of education at all levels, regardless of what is hopefully called the "short-run" outlook for employment. The lines of effort have been directed towards: (1) Reducing the costs of higher education; and (2) trying to relate it more closely to development needs. As I have suggested in the brief sketch of newer developments in African higher education, the American, U.N., and other inputs have commonly been directed to these ends.

Time will, unfortunately, permit only a cursory discussion of the promise of these efforts here. One can readily agree that the pattern of higher education set by the colonial powers is very expensive for poor countries without seeing clearly how costs can be sharply reduced without damage to the quality of education. The obvious measures are to eliminate residential facilities, to sharply increase student-staff ratios, and perhaps to reduce the salaries of teaching staff. The first of these measures runs into the difficulty of surrounding poverty. If one depends upon students living at home or in "digs," either conditions for study are grossly unsatisfactory or opportunities are denied to poor students in favor of the few from better-off families. Possibilities of increasing student-staff ratio are certainly important in many places. They conflict with the tendency to expect research from university staff and with trends towards reduced teaching hours in universities around the world, but they are probably necessary. The possibilities of reducing the costs of university staff are significant, but, if pushed too far, they lead into the pattern of part-time and multiple employment which has grievously afflicted university development elsewhere. One of the great merits of university education in present-day Africa is that it is a full-time occupation for its staff, and there are evident losses if it should cease to be so.

The emphasis on professional and specialized education may in the longer run produce increased rates of economic growth, but in the short run it tends to increase the costs of university education per student. The most expensive faculties in African universities are the agriculture and medical faculties. The emphasis on increasing the numbers of students in agriculture faculties which has marked recent university development seems clearly related to development need in countries that are overwhelmingly agricultural. But it has thus far shown itself to be one of the most expensive kinds of educational investment and very slow to attract good students. Medical education is also quite as dismayingly expensive relative to other forms of education as it is in the richer countries, and engineering, while not so troublesomely expensive, still is more exigent than arts, pure science, or law.

The natural and proper response to these frustrating observations is to query the standards of professional education. Have they not been set too high? Will not more modest and less costly standards better serve the needs of fledgling countries? These are not new questions, and they have shaped some of the efforts in African education that I have sketchily described above. Possible solutions must accommodate the fact that there persists a strong resistance among Africans to any manifest differentiation in quality between education in Africa and education in Europe or America. The insistence on uniformity that marked the final years of the colonial era has yielded to differentiation in character and substance, but there is understandable reluctance to concede that African standards should be more modest. It should not be impossible to find models of professional training that are cheaper but quite as good as those practiced elsewhere, but it can hardly be said that they are at hand at the moment, and one of the most urgent tasks of African higher education lies in finding them.

The impetus to lowering university admission levels which the American and U.N. influences brought to Africa deserves notice in this connection. It does not, unfortunately, assure lessened costs. Building a three-year university course on top of a secondary education that extended through the sixth form has meant that more school years are passed at cheaper cost than in the American system of four years of undergraduate education with fewer years of preparation in secondary school. There are thus economic arguments on the side of the old practices and they have been influential in places like East Africa. If it were possible to gain popular support for higher education of various durations, there would be many educational and economic advantages in lower admission requirements. But inflationary pressures like those I have described earlier as operating on the colleges of arts, science and technology that the British established are still strong. It would indeed be remarkable if Africa could avoid the general tendency one sees throughout the world for courses and programs to rise to university degree level, and this is not a tendency that makes for reduced educational costs.

I hope that this mixed account of achievements and problems makes clear that there is no straight and obvious path toward the right kind of higher education in Africa. What the colonial powers started has often been denounced as narrow and elitist. So in many respects it was, and the complement of more buoyantly expansionist and democratic conceptions has certainly been needed. But the grim difficulty remains that African countries are very poor and the resources necessary to produce university-educated people almost inevitably mean that less can have it than want it, and the favored minority are some sort of elite. Difficulties over the proper style, level and content of higher education seem in fact a special form of the difficulties these countries face generally in the distribution of income, facilities and rewards. It is not an easy thing to be a poor country living in a rich world, educationally or otherwise, and adaptations to this fact always involve hard choices which can properly only be made by a people for themselves. The Africanization of higher education in Africa is as essential as it is inevitable.[9]

## THE AFRICANIZATION OF AFRICAN UNIVERSITIES

The rapidity of political change in Africa brought strong pressures on the universities in Africa to assume a more distinctly national and African character than has come easily to them. The intimacy of ties of the colonial establishments to the metropolitan countries had certain practical advantages. There was a sense of responsibility and pride in possession which meant that many people who understood universities worked hard to make these African establishments good ones and to see that they were properly staffed. It was possible for a considerable period for able young academics from European countries to spend a period in an African university as part of a career which they could continue in their own systems. Once it became apparent that self-government would pass rapidly into independence and a university overseas could no longer be seen as an extension of the metropolitan system, this responsibility and opportunity sharply declined and a correspondingly urgent need for Africanization appeared.

I mean Africanization here in the wide and comprehensive sense that includes governance, staffing and academic substance. The shift to African governance and staffing has gone most quickly in the former British territories, fairly quickly in the Congo, and rather slowly in the French universities. It is hardly surprising that the French universities should have been the laggards in this process, because of their dependence upon France for financial support, their close integration with the French system, the very small numbers of educated Africans who might quickly become university staff and the high qualifications which the French standards for university teaching imposed upon them. Even in universities with very small numbers of African faculty, an important role quickly has emerged for this African staff. It has had an authority in the councils of the university out of proportion to numbers, the diffidence of expatriate staff being prudent and understandable. There are

---

[9] I have discussed these general questions elsewhere. Cf. "Tolerable Rates of Economic Development and Social Change," in *African Social Research*, Dec. 2, 1966, pp. 99-116.

subtle differences among countries—Ethiopia, for example, now tolerates a measure of expatriate participation in governance that it apparently welcomes but might be questioned elsewhere. In any situation a great deal of tactful co-operation is required, and one of the most heartening observations of recent years has been the constructiveness and good will that both Africans and expatriates have displayed in these situations. But the need for a prompt and sure assumption of leadership by African academics has been evident to all.

The Africanization of staff has been pressed with good effect both by African leadership and by a series of programs supported by outside agencies. For example, the colleges in East Africa that had almost no African staff at the beginning of the past decade now have approximately 30 per cent of their staffs localized. The importance of sound judgment in this process can hardly be exaggerated. The young men now assuming teaching positions in African universities will be there during the first formative generation of these universities as African institutions. The task of choosing them is at least as delicate and difficult as in universities elsewhere. Unlike their expatriate predecessors, they will not go away or be sent away when they become disaffected or inert. But brilliant or mediocre, they are providing an indispensable element of indigenous responsibility and continuity in universities otherwise gravely beset by quick turnover in expatriate staff. Once African universities ceased to offer life-long careers for non-Africans, they have become dependent upon short-run assignments of men who, through idealism, desire for a change, or sheer need of a job, could come to them for a time. The numbers of such people needed have been very large, as a thorough study for the 1962 Tananarive conference anticipated. Particularly in the sciences, it will be a good many years before Africa can cease to depend upon a supply of expatriate university staff. The present arrangements for getting it from the United States and elsewhere are regrettably unsystematic and threaten further to deteriorate—a subject to which I want to return briefly at the end of this discourse. It would perhaps be a fair summary to say that we are now in midstream in this process of Africanization; the African universities remain heavily dependent upon expatriate staff whose influence over the course of university policy is now reduced but still strong.

The most important aspects of the Africanization of African universities are perhaps the most difficult to grasp. They have to do with the purposes and character of these institutions as educational and intellectual centers. During the early years of their establishment, most of these universities were quiet, industrious places in which students worked determinedly toward the great prize that a degree has been. Except at Khartoum and Dakar, they were not overtly very political institutions. Similarity to the mood of American students in the postwar and the Eisenhower years may only be superficial, but it seemed marked. Men and women were going to the university to work at their studies and prepare themselves for careers that looked promising. In the British establishments there was some of the traditional concern for the development of character and personality. One often heard regrets about the students' lack of reading that was not directly related to courses or other worries about the diffuse effects of the university experience. There was occasionally the perception that an internal student world existed that was hard to reach from the expatriate professor's podium, and that this milieu would have a great influence on the future lives of these young men and women. But it was not a milieu that often erupted in troubles, and there is at least abundant anecdote that it was a satisfied world in which students felt themselves destined to high things in their already or soon-to-be independent countries. They were nationalistic but not in particular application to their studies. The curriculum was basically accepted and there were no rebellious assaults on the fairness and appropriateness of examinations or degree requirements. As I have already indicated, similar good feeling existed among the staff. In effect, an English, or French, or Belgian education with light modifications to African conditions was accepted because students and staff knew little else and were satisfied in the rewards of pursuing it.

Nowadays there is a different objective situation and outlook for everyone concerned, and fundamentals must be reconsidered. I trust that I have already said enough about the hard problems of adaptation to tightening employment opportunities, economic constraints, and more sharply perceived development needs. These problems alone provide a formidable agenda, but one must add to them some others of great educational importance. There is, first of all, the basic fact that university education is overwhelmingly in English or French, languages which are mother tongues to hardly any of the Africans who are studying or teaching in them. The practical difficulties of maintaining university education in a European language on top of a school system in which, even if these languages have a major place, they are not taught by native speakers, are formidable. One already hears complaints in many places that the standards of English achievement by entering students are not good enough to permit proper levels of university education; indeed, I was told not long ago that the best thing the Ford Foundation could do for university education in a West African country was to improve the teaching of English in the sixth forms from which the university students came. Even in the days when African university students came from secondary schools that had largely European teachers, they had reading speeds in English that were little better than half that of American university students.

This matter of linguistic competence is so fundamental to the quality and effectiveness of higher education that no satisfactory results can be expected without solutions to it. I discuss this question in the general context of Africanization because I do not think it can be resolved by outsiders, although we can contribute much in the way of co-operation and technical assistance. The indispensable base of a solution lies in African commitment. Whatever the balance particular African countries may achieve in the use of their own languages and world languages, they must come to a confident and determined stance in these matters. The burden will lie principally on the generations of men now taking responsibility as students, faculty members, and administrators of African universities.

There are, of course, many other matters in the Africanization of the content of curricula and the encouragement of distinctively African intellectual and cultural efforts which must occupy the African universities in the next years. All of these must be shaped within a general sense of the character an African university ought to take in a modern African setting. The people who devised the Asquith colleges and the French universities and Lovanium had by comparison a much easier task. The men who will shape the future of genuinely African universities will have to try to understand how much they can be independent centers of critical intellectual thought, how much they must bend to national purposes, how hard they ought to try to meet international competition, and how they can balance the inevitable opportunities and seduction of the cosmopolitan intellectual world against the need for local identity and service.

It would be easy to leave this formidable agenda as a simple peroration. But I would be uncomfortable in doing so. We are learning in the advanced countries that too much can be expected of universities, and there is danger in imposing weighty expectations on struggling new ones in social environments where they have yet no settled place. The UNESCO Tananarive Conference on the Development of Higher Education in Africa declared that "African institutions of higher education are at once the main instrument of national progress, the chief guardian of the people's heritage and the voice of the people in the international councils of technology and scholarship."[10] I fear that this could be a dangerously inflated conception of the role of African universities. African countries are still in a fateful process of building unity, identity, and the institutions that will sustain them in the fundamentals of nationhood. Great popular processes must continue in which the roles of political leadership, mass movements and government must be fundamental. The role of universities in providing intellectual quality, critical judgment, and professional competence is an indispensable one, but we should not expect the universities to be prime movers or to escape a local coloration that will not always be becoming. Adaptation to African conditions may sometimes require more sympathetic understanding than satisfied contemplation.

---

[10] Report of the Conference, p. 13.

WHAT OUTSIDERS CAN AND OUGHT TO DO

I hope that I have given an account of the present state and outlook of African universities which suggests that they are only beginning the great process of adaptation toward becoming authentic African universities serving the needs of their countries and continent. The task of building a system of higher education is certainly among the more exciting and difficult cultural achievements. African countries began with narrow models but now have been exposed to widened ranges of choice. The possibilities have often been set before them in narrow and prejudiced ways, and sometimes Africans have simply been reacting vexatiously against what they know in embracing the offerings of others. Both in what has been brought to Africa and what Africans have acquired by going overseas for higher education, the materials for a creative synthesis should be at hand. But the task of achieving this synthesis is both an onerous and a delicate one. The years ahead will be ones in which African material resources will be painfully deficient for the experiments and constructions that should be undertaken. They will also be for a long time unevenly and imperfectly supplied with the professional competences needed for teaching and research. Both of these needs call for continuing co-operation of the richer countries in aid to higher education. I have particularly stressed the need for help in staffing and the inadequacy of our present arrangements. Particularly for the English-speaking universities, it seems little short of a national scandal that we do not have in this country a well-ordered system for bringing the talents and capacities that we could supply to meet the needs of these universities. One has only to see the stagnation and decay that occurs when a department or field is without leadership for a few years to appreciate the urgency of this form of technical co-operation. In the broad problems of Africanization that I have just discussed the need for co-operation may be less immediately evident, but it is nonetheless of great importance. Given the great weight of Western intellectual influences, it is simply inevitable that African higher education will be linked to our world in some essential and indissoluble way. The problem is not to break away from old colonial influences in a radical sense. It is rather for Africans to find a distinctiveness and sense of autonomy while participating in this wider intellectual world. Much will be done in hostile reaction and some things in undue passivity. But it will be far better for Africans and for ourselves if Africans can come to define their intellectual Africanness and the institutions that nurture it through a warm and continuing process of intellectual exchange. We must not fail to sustain that exchange.

# AFRICAN UNIVERSITIES AND THE STATE

## Academic Freedom and Social Responsibility

### Davidson Nicol

For many years, African universities were divided into categories defined by the different systems of their former colonial masters. African universities have, however, been moving more closely together, despite their diverse origins, as was evidenced by the founding of the Association of African Universities in Rabat in 1967. This Assocation has been attempting to overcome the differences derived from the colonial heritage and to formulate a common African pattern. But it is still possible to delineate marked foreign influences in the structure of African universities. This is hardly surprising, as the German influence, for example, on American universities still remains, and the Scottish influence on New Zealand universities is still obvious, even though the United States of America cannot by any means be called a satellite of Germany, or, New Zealand one of Scotland.

The continent can, broadly speaking, be divided into North Africa, Middle and Central Africa, and South Africa.

The majority of North African universities have been very much influenced by the French pattern. Morocco appears to be breaking away from this. Egypt, also, has for some years been reshaping its modern universities on a basis of Arabic culture, as demonstrated by its building of new universities in addition to that of Cairo, and by its improvement and expansion of faculties at ancient institutions like Al Ahzar, which for centuries had only faculties of law and theology.

The middle belt, including most of tropical and central Africa, has the most fascinating variety of universities. The earliest was Fourah Bay College in Sierra Leone, which was closely linked with Durham (a nineteenth-century British university) for many years before it became independent; the most recent variety has been that resulting from the Lockwood concept of bringing under the university umbrella many post-secondary institutions and modifying the high entrance requirements set by British universities. In between these two, other universities were modeled on London University in Britain, on the French university system, and on the Belgian Catholic Louvain University system. The American model, in most cases based on the land-grant concept, has been used at Njala (Sierra Leone), Nsukka (Nigeria) and also with some modifications in the Ethiopian and Liberian university systems.

The third region is that of Southern Africa with white minority governments, where the University in Rhodesia has links with London and Birmingham in Britain (in the latter case in Medicine), relationships which have been recently broken because of the Rhodesian rebellion. The Portuguese model is used in Mozambique, where an active rector has been trying to forge links with the University of Malawi; this represents an attempt at regional co-operation, arising from the Malawian quest for a rapprochement with white Africa. The South African university system, which stemmed from the purely examining institution of the University of South Africa, gradually produced independent colleges and universities. The University of South Africa still remains an examining institution for students of all races by correspondence, and for the Bantu colleges in particular. The latter arose from the decision of the South African government to pursue its well-known and controversial policy of separate racial development. The South African university system now consists of white universities and separate university institutions for other groups as blacks, mixed-blood or colored, and East Indians. With the black and the white groups, there are further differentiations into what may be described as tribal groups—the Afrikaner and the English tribes among the whites, and the separation of the black group into three institutions aimed at different language groups; for example, the well-known black institution Fort Hare College now has a majority of Xhosas particularly among its students.

Thus, the variety of African universities is great, considering that the total number of students cannot be much larger than the total of university students in California and New York together. The languages of instruction are about half-a-dozen and mainly European in origin and may be quite different from the mother-tongue of the students.

Academic freedom includes in its many definitions the freedom of the university to select its teachers and students, to set the contents and standards of its curriculum and research, and to provide a favorable atmosphere where professors and students are free to be involved in creative processes leading to the discovery of new truths and the confirmation of old ones. A university must have some measure of certainty of financial support to make this possible; when it has obtained this, it should have considerable, if not entire, control over the disbursements of its income. Academic freedom cannot be regarded as implying exemption from the laws of the land as far as libel, slander, keeping of the peace and sedition are concerned. But a wise government will overlook the apparent transgressions of scholars if it is obvious that their intent is objectively critical and not maliciously subversive—a distinction sometimes difficult to recognize by dictatorships, one-party states or military governments.

Academic freedom and university autonomy are interrelated. They may coexist, but this is not always so. Within a state, it is possible for university autonomy to be granted by the major financial supporter, the government. University autonomy is often interpreted to mean only autonomy from the government, but this may not be the only case. There may also be the Church or some other controlling religious body involved. True autonomy implies a governing body in which the financing authorities are present, but not predominant, and in which the head of the university and the representatives of the faculty, alumni, professional and other groups, including students, have a powerful voice in the running of the university. Academic freedom is best guarded by the influence which a governing body of this type can exert as a protection from interference by the financial authorities and the state. In a more positive way, on the other hand, the governing body, buttressed by the strong foundation of its academic freedom, can act as an interpreter to the university of its social responsibilities to the community.

The greatest infringement of academic freedom on the continent has been in Southern Africa, where, by the law of the land, the government has interfered on racial grounds in the universities' choice of students and staff. It has also limited the range of subjects available to non-white students, and has consciously kept them away from fields like scientific agriculture, engineering and mining, which would make them compete with, and certainly if only on numerical grounds later supersede a sizable proportion of whites. The so-called open universities of Capetown and Witwatersrand in South Africa have had their attempts at multiracial education virtually crushed, even though their proportion of African students was always very small. From a distance, it would appear that many of the staff of these universities, although sincere, were often half-hearted in their fight for racial equality. Their attitude is best exemplified by the following private communication from a don in Johannesburg in 1957. "For those overseas it is important to remember that virtually all white South Africans subscribe to the necessity of some form of segregation, while the general standards of education and civilization of the non-European remain low. The quarrel with the extreme nationalists is that they seem to deny the future national development of the non-European."

The white students at these "open universities" have shown greater dedication to the principles of racial equality by their peaceful demonstrations, protests, and by examples as that of the action of the Student Union at Capetown University which publicly, though unsuccessfully, invited a black African academic leader from outside South Africa to follow the late Robert Kennedy in giving one of their major annual public lectures.

There have been varying degrees of infringement of academic freedom in black African countries. The more spectacular ones have been those involving the activities of white foreign teachers when they make statements against black African governments. Although the agitation over these is justifiable, yet it has put a wrong racial emphasis on the question of academic oppression, as local academic staff of universities have suffered far more from the infringements of academic freedom by their own governments. The foreign tutor may suffer deportation and temporary loss of livelihood. As a rule he soon receives invitations from elsewhere and is compensated by the sympathy of the world press and occasionally by financial compensation from the college. The African academic who is in trouble faces long and lonely months in prison with his case unknown abroad while within his country there is unwillingness by others to intervene for fear of government reprisals.

The teaching staff in the higher echelons at most of these universities is largely composed of foreigners who are apt to maintain an independent and sometimes critical view of local government, as in fact they would do in their own countries. The strength of university advice or protest in national affairs in Africa is always muted by this fact of the predominance of white foreigners in key positions in the administrative and academic framework. Since these foreign staff are usually nationals of the former colonial power, or Americans suspected of C.I.A. activities, it is often easy for extremist local groups of resentful citizens to attack the university, not always without reason, as being bastions of reaction and neocolonialism. This is damaging to both sides, particularly when the criticism leveled is sometimes constructive, well-meant and justified. But in recent years, clamor at the university has been due more to local students protesting against the foreign and domestic policies of their own governments than protesting against discrimination by their foreign staff, as was more often the case in earlier days. This dramatic change in emphasis towards criticism by students of their own governments is not often admitted by politicians, who, as a rule, ascribe student unrest to the secret and subtle influence of their foreign teachers. It would be nearer the truth if the behavior of African students were ascribed more to familiarity with the effects of student demonstration in other countries obtained from the news media coupled with a feeling of exasperation at the corruption of their politicians and leaders whom they know better through friends and relatives than would any foreign member of the staff at the university. There is also the influence on students of activist African members of the senior staff who are sometimes frustrated by their exclusion from decision-making roles at the highest level in their own country, when they feel rightly or wrongly that they possess a greater competence to fill these than politicians in power.

The appointment of an African to the headship (principalship, vice-chancellorship, presidency or rectorate) of the university or college is by no means a complete answer to these problems. It may in fact be interpreted by the radical young as a means of slowing down Africanization and staving off the promotion of other Africans by erecting the facade of an African vice-chancellor. Expansion of the university, for example, resulting in the employment of more staff, usually brings in more foreign and white personnel, thus confirming the suspicion of extremists. On the other hand, an African university head may well prove to be a bulwark and defender of academic freedom, interpreting the ideals of the university to the government and people in a way in which the most dedicated foreigner could not possibly succeed in doing. He can also interpret the legitimate desires of the state to the university by translating them into academic suggestions and directing them towards activities which give reality to those pragmatic functions of a university relevant to the improvement of the community.

To uphold the powerful position which the university should have in a modern African state, it is important that there should be a predominance of Africans on the board of trustees and on the academic and governing boards of the institution. It is not difficult to achieve this in the board of trustees or university council, since by now there are sufficiently able African professionals, politicians and businessmen in each community for this to be done. It is not easy, however, to obtain this in the internal academic government of the university, since Africans in quantity are latecomers to the academic world. The situation is better in West Africa, where the unsuitability of the climate for white settlement in the nineteenth and early twentieth century forced religious bodies and governments to educate a cadre of Africans for key positions in the maintenance and, in some cases, expansion of European settlements and furtherance of Western education. It should also be noted in this connection that the ideals and far-sighted vision of a few Europeans and Americans in both missionary bodies and government, as well as in commerce, were strong reinforcements in the laying of these foundations.

There had been, for example, acting principals and senior tutors and lecturers from many parts of Africa at Fourah Bay College in Sierra Leone in both the nineteenth and twentieth centuries. Although their numbers were small, their seminal influence in their society was great, and prepared the ground for more rapid Africanization of staff and for the acceptance of the concepts of academic freedom among politicians and leading members of the community, many of whom had been their old students.

The situation in East and Central Africa and some of the French-speaking and Belgian territories was different. Because of the suitability of the climate for white settlement, opportunities for Africans were fewer and kept at a minimum. Institutions for higher education were for a long time nonexistent, as white settlers sent their children to Europe or in some cases to South Africa for their education. Thus, until the eve of independence, African graduates were few in these territories. Africanization of the academic and administrative staff and a predominance of informed Africans on governing boards and in the community has thus been initially limited. The effects of this have been noted by Professor Chagula, a distinguished former head of an East African university college. The impetus of development in these territories is, however, very great, and there is evidence that in another decade or two, they may well be in a position to reach or surpass those in West Africa, aided by their use of modern techniques and their openness to new ideas.

A major consideration in the upholding of academic freedom inherent in the background which we have outlined, is the great speed with which African governments and people wish to see their nations develop. They are inclined to view the university as existing chiefly as a source of supply for the manpower needs of their country in skilled occupations, and thus tend to regard every other activity as being either irrelevant or unresponsive to their urgent national needs. This view can be best understood by those who have visited or worked in these territories, and have witnessed the terrible shortage of skilled personnel in every field. Yet, persistence of this viewpoint in its concentrated form overstresses the functional nature of higher education, and soon suffocates its creative and idealistic aspects. These latter are not always as remote from reality as may at first sight appear; they should be interpreted to politicians and men of business as that part of university life which ensures that the functional segment shows steady improvement and adaptation to changing circumstances, through its drawing upon fundamental truths for improvement, making new discoveries possible for the immediate present and the fast-approaching future. Expressed in this way, academic freedom is more likely to be accepted among men who have no immediate or endearing memories of the predominantly Western world culture on which African universities are based, and whose familiarity with it may have been largely through racial discrimination, arrogance, and an implied form of inferiority of their own origins, as compared with those of European and Asian civilizations. This is one of the reasons, incidentally, why black studies and African culture should be incorporated as rapidly as possible into every situation which involves the black intelligentsia and those in contact with them, to ensure the upholding of academic freedom and of university autonomy as universal truths.

Academic freedom is not a commodity for bargaining; it carries with it a fulfillment of its own principles. Respect for it ensures that students are produced who will carry through to the next generation the torch of learning and the flame of truth. It bears with it the understanding that research carried out without pressure over a period will result in fundamental discoveries, or at least results which will benefit the community. It is understandable that in new countries where familiarity with a university system has not been present, much of this has to be taken as an article of faith by governments which finance universities. As a reciprocal gesture, the lack of development and skilled personnel in a developing country should call forth in the university a greater awareness to the necessity of being more immediately useful to the community.

This awareness of social responsibilities has steadily increased in African universities. Active and self-generated changes have taken place in adapting the curriculum or better still, developing one with depth and scholarship, which includes subjects relevant and useful to the community, and to many other aspects of African development. Welcome signs have been shown of co-operation among universities on this matter, and it was one of the main points of discussion at the UNESCO Conference on Higher Education in Africa held in Tananarive in 1963, and many others held since then.

The availability of undiscovered local material for research has often been a great attraction to scholars working in Africa. The results of their research in this and in almost every field will certainly prove useful in the immediate or distant schemes of planning for their respective countries, since the presence of valid data and information for nation-building is frequently absent or incomplete in most parts of Africa.

The contribution which the university can make may depend sometimes on the willingness of the staff to become involved with the local intelligentsia and citizenry; this is greater when there is a large number of local staff, and, when, in the case of foreign staff, some sensitivity to the local atmosphere is shown by them and there is some sympathy with national aspirations.

A considerable part of the intellectual reserve of an African nation is often situated at the university. The ready access to world scholarship and international organizations possessed by universities gives them a greater opportunity for transmitting and interpreting other cultures and the progress and achievements of other societies to their government and people. Universities should in addition act as patrons to local talent in performing plays by local writers, in sponsoring exhibitions of painting and sculpture by its own departments and by local artists, in organizing displays of folk dancing, in publishing books by local writers and journals for research workers in the territory, and by the dissemination of literary and objective information relating to the social scene. The university should maintain a professional responsibility to other levels of the educational system of the country. This is often best met through an institute and department of education at the university, and by encouraging individual members of the university staff to show interest in bodies and councils connected with school examinations. The organization of seminars and refresher courses for groups of teachers from infant, primary and particularly secondary schools is another aspect which should be developed. This interest in non-university areas of the national educational system is essential and rewarding, since, apart from the evident advantages to all concerned, it feeds back into the university better trained and abler pupils for its degree and diploma courses.

Until professional societies can be developed and become numerous, the university remains one of the few places in many African nations where a high standard of performance in research and practice can be upheld, and where adaptation to local conditions and maintenance of professional ethics can be discussed and initiated in a vigorous and objective manner. In many African countries the shortage of trained personnel cuts down heavily on the time available for reading, revision, reflection and research among professional men and women in the non-university sectors of society. These are activities which are essential to all professional people, but in many cases these opportunities are only available to those at the university.

Thus, the university in an African nation should not only direct its activities to its own staff and students but also to the intellectual and physical welfare and betterment of all sections of the population in a measure far surpassing that which is expected or indeed can be achieved by universities in more developed countries.

In circumstances where African universities and their home governments are at variance with each other, the heavy financial dependence of the former on the latter is an instrument of control, which can be subtly or overtly used. This heavy financial dependence on the state was present in the nineteenth-century German university, but as Sir Eric Ashby, a leading authority on world universities, has pointed out, this was not incompatible with academic freedom. In British universities and in the state universities of the U.S.A., there are dangers of erosion of freedom under these circumstances. In Africa, there has been much variation. A complicated system of financial control for the University of East Africa has not been able to satisfy fully the wishes of the national governments of the constituent colleges in Kampala (Uganda), Nairobi (Kenya) and Dar es Salaam (Tanzania), and some unilateral action has been taken in the introduction of new facilities and in restrictive awards of scholarships. These may be, however, conscious and deliberate steps towards splitting the federal university, in the immediate future, into full-fledged national universities,* a process inevitable in the long run and envisaged as a natural process of growth by some of us from its inception.

In some parts of West Africa, universities have sometimes complained of financial strangulation by the government, but where for some years commissions for national universities have been established, as in Nigeria, an effective shield has been thereby produced. The trustees or lay governing bodies of the university, when they maintain good relations with the academic governing boards, and when they contain leading politicians and men of weight and substance in the community, can also prove, as pointed out earlier, powerful intermediaries in maintaining the academic freedom of the university. They may prevent hasty and extreme actions of governments in withdrawing or

---

* This has already taken place. November 1970.

restricting their financial support of the university because members of the university hold differing views from them on political matters.

Finally, two important points must be made. Universities in developing countries must cease to show automatically contempt towards their national political leaders; there is occasionally a touch of arrogance in the pronouncements of universities to the chosen leaders of the people. Political leaders work under very trying circumstances, sometimes in fluid situations, and do not invariably enter politics solely for illegal financial enrichment. Secondly, on their side, governments in African countries should realize that the social responsibility inherent in the academic freedom of universities includes also elements of political responsibility, which may sometimes produce comments on the performance of their government which will not always be flattering or favorable.

Academic freedom carries with it a greater degree of social and political responsibility in developing countries than elsewhere. This should be made apparent with courtesy and respect to their governments. Combined with the traditional respect for learning usually present in these countries, this should lead to greater latitude being given to its existence and manifestation at their universities. Its scope may thus indeed become greater and of deeper significance than what, at present, exists in more developed countries.

# THE LATIN AMERICAN UNIVERSITY
## Present Problems Viewed Through the Recent Past

John P. Harrison

The need to readjust itself to the society it serves has been, for the Latin American university, a continuing, well-publicized and often violent process throughout the twentieth century. As Latin American society and the economy on which it depended had a combination of characteristics that set it apart from other major world areas at the beginning of the century, so its institutions of higher learning were faced with a different set of problems in meeting its needs. The differences within the area as a whole offered great national variations as to the level of economic prosperity and ethnic composition. The institutional structure of the university was remarkably uniform throughout the area but the pressures for reform varied with the political organization, social composition and level of economic development of the several countries.

The time-scale of any serious reform efforts quite naturally differed greatly throughout Latin America, depending on basic, long-term variations such as the proportion of European immigrants within the total population (Rio de la Plata), or a temporary manifestation of underlying conditions such as the presence of a particularly repressive head of state (Machado in Cuba). The similarity of structure, however, made it possible for the reforms delineated in the years 1915-20 by a loosely knit group of Argentine students, socialist ideologues and Ibero-American visionaries to be accepted in their totality throughout the area, as that which was necessary to reform the university. Thus sanctified as the *Reforma Universitaria,* this movement became the earliest effort at Latin American integration, even though its motor, perhaps, was more spiritual than educational in any institutional sense. The temporal dislocation in the application of reform can be indicated by the fact that while the University of San Carlos in Guatemala in the 1940's, certain other Central American national universities in the late 1950's and that of the Dominican Republic after Trujillo were implementing many of the reforms enunciated in Argentina in 1918-20, the author of the dramatic Córdoba Manifesto that served as the call-to-arms for Latin American university students, Deodoro Roca, wrote in 1936 that the reforms had not changed the Argentine university since 1918; that the university had, in fact, become "even more toxic"; that the professor was "still the same fossil. Except that now he is younger. And knowing more, his knowledge is of even less use than before." The disenchantment of Roca with the failure of the *Reforma Universitaria* to alter the system of higher education in any meaningful way found a wide acceptance among his reform-oriented contemporaries a quarter century after the movement had been formally launched. This group of intellectuals came to the conclusion that the "pure" university member was a monstrous thing and that to be effective one had to go outside of the university, for without social reform there could not be any real university reform. This interpretation of the function of university reform found a receptive audience in all parts of Latin America that had been touched by the *Reforma* and by the end of World War II became the predominant concern of student activists throughout Latin America.

The structural characteristic of the Spanish American university that first came under forceful attack by large numbers of students during the initial two decades of the twentieth century was more the creation of mid-nineteenth century Creole society than it was of the Spanish colonial administration—there were no universities in colonial Portuguese America or in Brazil until the 1920's. The ecclesiastical and literary nature of education that had dominated the colonial university was replaced during the second half of the nineteenth century by a university whose function, as perceived by the governing class that created it, was to prepare the professionals needed to serve society and to operate government. It is in the sense of professional as licensed practitioner that the Spanish American universities at the turn of the century and later in Brazil have been characterized as Napoleonic professional universities.

The universities were—and typically still are—organized into faculties and into schools within faculties. Each faculty represented a profession for which an officially recognized license to practice that profession was granted by the national government upon graduation. The most powerful governing unit was the superior council, usually composed of the rector, the secretary general, the deans of the several faculties and members appointed directly by the state. The rector, the chief executive officer, was either appointed by the state or elected for a specific term by the professors who held the chairs (*cátedras*) for those courses that had to be passed by the student to gain his professional license. The essential operating unit was the faculty, each of which had a council and a dean who were elected by the chair-holders of the faculty. Administratively, each faculty was thus a miniature of the university. Indeed, faculties operated as separate entities and their autonomy within the university was greater than the autonomy of the university as a whole within the state.

The basic unit of this system of higher education was the chair from which the required courses were taught. Once a professor gained occupation of a chair by election, appointment or public competition, his position was inviolable to an extent that he owned the chair for life. The subject taught was quite literally the fief of the proprietary professor. This characteristic of the professional university was well suited to use in Latin America as an institutional support for the social status quo. Its staying power is illustrated by the fact that in a traditional nineteenth-century faculty such as medicine where, after World War II, research activities first developed within the university, it was strongly argued in a major national university, as recently as 1969, that all research facilities should be directly dependent on and administered by the chair to which it was most closely related. In Spanish America this proprietary relationship of research to chair did not pertain to work in such newer faculties as economics or in the social science disciplines generally. In Brazil, however, when the universities were organized in the 1920's, the concept of the proprietary chair was put into effect in all faculties. The need to change the proprietary nature of professorships was later considered to be of first priority by those who were concerned with using the university as a mechanism to facilitate social change.

The conquest of higher education by the professional university did not, of course, totally erase the colonial past. One official aspect of the colonial university, the special privileges or *fueros* that belonged to all attached to the university, did not survive the political transfer from monarchy to republic. In practice, however, what had been specific legal immunities granted by the Spanish Crown to particular educational corporations informally gained in strength, because while the colonial university provided an inferior social cachet in comparison to its peninsular counterparts, the late nineteenth-century university became the fundamental—in the sense of minimal—institutional standard of measurement for elite membership. The relatively stable social and political structure that replaced the *caudillo*-dominated governments which had flourished in the vacuum created by the independence struggle was a university-based society to the extent that the ruling class which emerged unevenly throughout Spanish America found it an admirable instrument for maintaining a closed society. Thus it was in Chile, where the political structure was earliest freed of the uncertainties of regional and national *caudillos*, that the University of Chile was the first Latin American university to become an effective part of national society despite the fact that its predecessor was at best a second-level colonial institution. It was an attack on this function of the professional university as protector of the social system that initiated the twentieth-century effort to change the university by forceful means.

The Spanish American university of 1900 was a universe of professors rather than a universe of students, despite the fact that its line of inheritance stemmed from the student-organized University of Bologna in Italy, by way of Salamanca in Spain, rather than from the master-dominated corporation of the University of Paris. The colonial inheritance it maintained as an informal expression of special privilege for its members was as much the result of their representing solely the dominant and, in a certain sense, aristocratic sector of society as it was from any continuity of custom. As a master-dominated university, this characteristic was enhanced by the fact that the professors were all part-time in the university and devoted most of their energies to practicing their profession within society or serving as government officials. The professional university satisfied to an exceptional degree the needs of the existing social structure, was thoroughly integrated into it and, indeed, institutionally served as the guardian of the gates.

As the class served by the universities was small in size, so also was the student population. It was markedly concentrated in the national universities of the capital cities, so that the numbers attending these universities represented from 80 to 100 per cent of the national student population in Spanish America from Peru south. This was the area in which the professional university was most highly developed, where it was most thoroughly integrated within the traditional landed oligarchy and the growing commercial upper class, and where the effort originated to break this interrelationship between the university and the society it served. The largest and fastest-growing university in absolute numbers was the University of Buenos Aires, which had 1,942 students in 1906 and 7,530 in 1918. Other South American universities with more than a thousand students in 1918 were the University of Chile, 4,228; the University of the Republic in Montevideo, 1,651; the University of San Marcos in Lima, 1,471; the University of Córdoba, 1,104; and the National University of Colombia (one faculty of which was in Medellín), 1,035.[1] The faculties, typically, were physically separate from one another rather than occupying a single campus. The faculties of law and medicine attracted by far the largest number of students, e.g., 88 per cent at the University of Buenos Aires in 1900 and 83 per cent in 1918, although during this period there was a marked shift from law to medicine as the children of immigrant families apparently felt that medicine served them better than law as a means of gaining at least partial access to traditional society.[2] Teaching was done from

---

[1] All of the above student populations are from official contemporary sources with the exception of the figure for the University of Chile. The latter was taken from a thesis, and in this case the author arrived at his figure by adding the totals of the separate faculties as given in archival sources not immediately available. Judging from registration totals for the University of Chile in later years, it appears high to this writer.

[2] The student population of the Faculty of Medicine of the University of Buenos Aires in 1918 (4,562) was greater than the total number of students in the next three largest South American universities, omitting the University of Chile.

standard, approved texts by practicing professionals who taught part-time, and research was not in any way a university function.

Given the long-standing impression prevalent outside of Latin America that its culture is predominantly oriented to literature and philosophy, it should be noted that faculties of arts and letters were totally absent from some universities and only at San Marcos did one attract any substantial percentage of student enrollment in 1918 (16 per cent). The social sciences, as they are understood today, did not exist. The lack of students in these two subject fields is pointed out, in part, to indicate that, despite the quantitative data accumulated in the last decade showing a strong positive correlation between students of liberal arts-social science faculties and student activists, the *Reforma Universitaria* which increasingly sought to use the university as a motor for social change during the 1920's was fueled almost entirely by students from the traditional faculties of law and medicine. The indication is that something other than university education is the determining factor in orientation towards forced social change.

The first serious student revolt against this university was not essentially against its structure but rather against the way its directing councils used it to exclude certain elements of the population from its benefits. There was no objection to the function of this university: to turn out licensed practitioners of the professions most influential in society and government. As the only available door through which meaningful members could gain access to the full benefits of the existing society, the purpose of the revolt was to broaden the university portals. The original student uprising came, then, from those who wanted to participate more fully in the privileges of the existing Creole society rather than from those who wanted to transform it.

This event took place in Argentina, the one Spanish American country where economic opportunities were sufficient to have attracted a massive European immigration. The place where the ambitious element of this group clashed with the dominant class was the university, and within it, the faculty of law, the traditional profession for making one's way in either politics or business. The nature of the students' dissatisfaction was with the curriculum and the system of entrance examinations—previously, possession of a secondary school credential had been all that was required to enter the university. The party that expressed the political position of the immigrant population was the Radical Party and it should be noted that the students were essentially asking for government intervention in the examining process of the law school. As Congress did not provide a solution, the law students of the University of Buenos Aires took violent action in 1903 against both university autonomy and the conservative element that controlled the Law Faculty by physically occupying the building and declaring a strike that lasted throughout the academic year of 1904. The threat this strike posed to traditional society was forthrightly stated by one of the foremost members of this society in a newspaper article early in 1904, when he wrote of the "invasion" of the university by "heterogeneous elements," children of immigrants who did not have the benefit of a common culture in the home. This university phenomenon, he remarked, would obviously be more strongly felt when these same students later invaded society as professionals. The dispossessed had begun their revolt against the dominant sector of society through the institution of the university, and the economically least disadvantaged sector predictably made the first move.

The proprietary professors who represented the social values of the traditional ruling class in Argentina did not readily yield their positions, as can be seen by their being fully in control of the University of Córdoba a decade after the student strike of 1918 set off the *Reforma Universitaria* as a continental movement. By this time many of the first wave of reform-oriented students had entered professional life and abandoned their earlier commitment. Two lines of development can be discerned among those who continued to work in and—much more often—through the university for social and political reform. One may be characterized as a humanistically oriented group whose major concern was an attempted definition and support of what they considered to be the unique personality of Ibero-America. The model for this group among the *reformistas* of the 1930's was Victor Raúl Haya de la Torre, whom they considered to have produced the only visibly creative results of the reform movement: a partially realized vision of Andean integration plus the establishment in Peru during the 1920's of "popular universities." The goal of this group was what might be described as a Latin American cultural and political common market completely free of the United States.

The second element was more ideologically oriented and became increasingly more polarized in its opposition to the existing social structure, the top strata of which it identified as being the only sector of the population which benefited economically from the colonial relationship between Latin America and the highly industrialized nations.

The first group, while also anti-imperialist, was more influenced by the collapse of European civilization into the abyss of World War II, while the second force—which ultimately took over the field of university political activists—was influenced more strongly by the economic collapse of the early 1930's and the socialist response to the cyclical movements of a capitalist economy that so devastated its Latin American fringe. I have refrained from calling them a "group" because many ideological positions, often strongly opposed to each other, were represented. Their common goals were their opposition to industrial capitalism and the conviction that only with the violent overthrow of existing society could the changes they felt necessary be made. The university could be "reformed" only if this process took place first in the larger society. From this position any effective reforms, internal to the university, served only to bolster the traditional society and were, therefore, counterproductive by definition. World War II can be used as a convenient watershed dividing the mainstream of university reform into two periods: the earlier being an attempt to reform the university internally so that it could be an effective motor for social change; the second characterized, at least insofar as the political activists among the university community are concerned, by efforts to use the university as an instrument for either the rapid transformation or the destruction of the existing social order. Before examining the post-1945 university reform, the earlier specific proposals for internal institutional change should be summarized.

The cluster of proposals for the reform of higher education that comprised the original *Reforma Universitaria* were never anywhere implemented in their entirety. They included the notion of *co-gobierno,* or the democratization of the university through the participation of students in its governance; the concept of open or parallel professorships (*cátedra libre*); the selection of professors through open competition and the provision for periodic review of professional competence; the right of students to be graded solely on examination results; the establishment of popular or workers' universities to accommodate the lower economic strata; and provision for extension and summer courses by which students could take culture to the masses (the elitism even among revolutionary students made it impossible for them to bridge this class gap effectively). In synthesis, all of these were designed to make the university responsive to society as a whole rather than to service one particular privileged sector. Notable for its absence was any emphasis on university autonomy, possibly because the 1918 reformers at Córdoba expected—and got—government intervention for the immediate resolution of their problems with the traditional professors. Also absent were concern for pedagogical reform and the function of research, and even any seriously expressed doubts as to the structure or purpose of the university as essentially a professional licensing agency. Taken as a whole, the reforms did not bring about any meaningful change in the university as an institution nor did they substantially alter its role in society. They did succeed in setting in motion an ongoing public trial of the social system and the identification of youth with the necessity for thorough social reform on a continental basis. The concept of *co-gobierno* as the mechanism for democratizing the university and making it more responsive to society gained acceptance in principle throughout Latin America although during the quarter century after Córdoba it was put into effect in only a few national universities. Students as reformers were more effective working through their own federations than from a position of responsibility within the university; this becomes increasingly so, the more radical or revolutionary the political stance of the students.

The traditional structure of the Latin American university was only slightly affected by the years of reform efforts before World War II. The capacity of students to disrupt the operation of a university had been proven, as had the ability of forces external as well as internal to the university to use student federations to put pressure on national governments, and even to use these federations as organizational centers for public demonstrations to bring about the overthrow of governments obnoxious to them, like that of Machado in Cuba. In the postwar years students served as the street "shock troops" most in evidence immediately prior to the downfall of Perón in Argentina, Rojas Pinilla in Colombia and Pérez Jiménez in Venezuela. In each of these instances co-government did not exist, although student federations were in full operation, either openly or clandestinely. The colonial heritage of special privileges for members of the university community gradually acquired an extra-legal position sufficiently approved by society at large to enable students to carry out illegal activities with relative impunity, knowing that the law would be applied to them more leniently, if at all, than to others carrying out comparable actions, *e.g.,* labor groups. The simple fact of belonging to the university conferred elite status on its members.

The extra-legal assumption of special privilege through *de facto* personal immunities was essential to university activists taking the position that their primary function was to alter the existing social structure through forceful means if necessary. The concept of individual immunity stemming from membership, as student or professor, in the university corporation was gradually extended to the fiction that the physical grounds occupied by the university were territorially immune from invasion by agents of the state without the specific invitation of the university itself. This meant that anyone, whether belonging to the university or not, could find sanctuary on university property. As the emphasis of reform shifted from the university to society at large, the extension of autonomy from administrative to territorial independence became the primary issue for student reformers and their allies—and sometimes masters—in those national political parties opposed to the government. By the 1960's territorial immunity was sufficiently a part of the understanding of the term "university autonomy" that some rectors of major national and private universities publicly espoused it; university plebiscites proclaimed it; and harassed chiefs of democratic governments had to go out of their way to explain that (1) it did not exist and (2) public acceptance of this extra-legal interpretation of autonomy providing for a state within a state was against the national interest.[3] Heads of nondemocratic governments declared that not only

---

[3] The extent to which governments can be concerned about public reaction to standard, yet uninvited, law enforcement on university grounds is well illustrated by the means former Colombian President León Valencia used to rescue Carlos Lleras Restrepo.

territorial immunity but university autonomy in any form was counterproductive to an integrated state. While thus set temporarily to rest under present governments in countries such as Cuba, Argentina, Brazil and Peru, the viability of this extension of ancient custom is nowhere completely dead: even in Cuba where the social revolution has been most complete.

A definition of autonomy that will permit students, professors and invited speakers to openly criticize government policy and actions without interference and also allow the government to enforce the existing law without concern for the territory of the university is an issue that will not readily be resolved as long as there are political groups desirous of violently altering a social structure which a government wants either (1) to maintain, or (2) to change by evolutionary means, however rapidly.

A major theme in Spanish American literature published in the period immediately preceding Córdoba was the frustration and failure of individuals who wanted to realize national as well as personal ambitions. The *Reforma Universitaria* added to this altruistic nationalism a concern for the commonality of Latin America as a whole. The effort to design positive institutional university reforms capable of bringing this about failed. For revolutionary oriented students and for the majority of moderate students working towards a more rapid rate of social change through evolutionary measures, the failure was most satisfactorily explained by the dependent position of Latin American economies on those of the more industrialized nations. These agricultural and mining export economies had been short-changed by the industrial revolution and the langniappe that did remain in the area had been pocketed by the traditional oligarchy. The growing economic hegemony of the United States in Latin America was particularly marked in the years following World War II, so that the visible enemy that held them in thrall was the most pervasive presence of industrial capitalism in the area: the United States. This vision of neocolonialism has been, of course, constantly magnified by the propaganda of other world powers in competition with the United States.

It is difficult to give charisma to a process like university reform or industrialization. The *Reforma Universitaria* was effective in rallying the student population against the traditional past but it did not succeed in coming up with other than a temporarily successful local or national "god." It had, however, found a devil which might be more effective for the maintenance of a

---

As the Liberal Party candidate for the presidency, Lleras Restrepo was held prisoner by students on the National University campus. Fearful of public reaction and further demonstrations if police or the military "invaded" the campus, Valencia sent the soldiers that made up the presidential guard to free Lleras on the fiction that they were not the army but rather an extension of his legal personality as president of the republic.

collective movement than a deity, particularly when the anticapitalist socialist or corporate-state solutions were so varied a fare. Negative values are accentuated where tradition is as firmly established as it has been in Latin America. Hence the most revolutionary students, while maintaining representation in student federations, have effectively left the university to concentrate on terroristic urban guerilla activities which they view as the only practicable way of rooting out the accepted devil—domestic as well as foreign. The less activist radical students and professors remain within the university structure, where their efforts are usually directed towards the support of their national political party's platform—Communist, Socialist or Christian Democrat as in Chile— or simply for the overthrow of the existing government as in Brazil, Argentina and perhaps Mexico. The disruptive conditions of high politicization of reform efforts, particularly in the large national universities, continue to make it exceedingly difficult for universities to carry out meaningful internal reforms, or for reform-oriented, democratic governments to obtain from the universities the output of human resources and specialized research most urgently required for their national development efforts.

This high level of politicization reflects both the variety of solutions for social and political problems set forth at the national level and the strength of conviction among active students and professors that their particular ideology offers the only viable solutions. There is a high correlation between the extent to which a university is politicized and the degree of territorial autonomy it can enforce either through the interpretation of the law or by *de facto* public acceptance of the concept. The belief is widely held that there is not only a strong positive correlation between co-government and active university politicization but that a direct causal relationship also exists. The available evidence does not entirely support this assumption. Universities where students have no vote, or only an insignificant representation on governing councils, but where active student federations exist, are disrupted as often as those with a broad franchise for the election of university administrators. The former group probably is more active in taking to the street over national issues, particularly when prodded by an outside political organization.

The major student disruptions in Mexico of 1966 and 1968; the direct student participation in the overthrow of national governments in Cuba, Venezuela, Colombia and Argentina; and the continuing, if irregular university strikes in Brazil and Colombia, and in Chile before 1968 are examples of this. Perhaps the most persistently recurring example of a politically disruptive university in Latin America during the decade 1958-68 was the Universidad Central in Caracas. There, students actively participated in university government but the most distinguishing characteristic was that the legal and *de facto* strength of territorial immunity was the strongest in Latin America. The national universities in Uruguay, in Argentina between Perón and Onganía, and in Peru before 1968, had a continuous series of political disruptions along with the student vote. The author does not know of any proven method of isolating student participation in government in order to compare political disruption in universities with and without effective co-government. For example, it has proven impracticable, if not impossible, to accumulate statistics on so seemingly simple a matter as the number of days universities, or a part of them, have been closed because of student strikes. It is clearly of more significance in the larger universities, whether national or private, that draw from a broad national constituency, since these are the only ones that have immediate political significance. It also appears that active student federations are more significant than direct student participation in university governance. It seems axiomatic that the more widely democratic procedures are spread through the various levels of administration, the more time-consuming is the decision-making process; yet the recent (1969) Chilean experience, where there was the broadest electoral participation ever in any Latin American university—55,600 eligible voters including every member of the University of Chile community from janitor to dean[4]—indicates that a rector so elected has more personal power than his predecessors, who were chosen by vote of full professors (catedráticos) only. Among other factors, a rector so elected is free from his predecessors' allegiance to and dependence on a coalition of academic barons. This particular rector's power may, of course, be due largely to his personal political skill, but it is notable that no previous rector has ever been referred to by his opposition as capataz (plantation or hacienda overseer). In terms of broad available evidence, co-government does not appear to be a decisive factor in the politicization that has impeded the effective integration of the university into the national and regional development process.

Following World War II, particularly beginning in the early 1950's, efforts were made in many Latin American countries to "modernize" (the very word has since taken on a pejorative connotation for the active Left) their universities in order to produce technicians and scientists necessary for the functioning of a reasonably independent national infrastructure. New provincial and private universities and certain faculties of the larger national universities made, and continue to make, efforts at: introducing curricular changes, such as a program of common basic science and language instruction; introducing a general studies program for the first two years of the university; introducing graduate training and improved research opportunities adapted to the local economic

---

[4] The pattern for so broad a franchise was introduced a year earlier at the Catholic University of Chile. Opposition to the rector elected there has since arisen, but from the student federation rather than the student representatives. In mid-1970 both universities appear to have agreed that the franchise should be weighted as follows: professors, 65%; students, 25%; and non-academics, 10%.

and social reality; breaking down faculty isolation by working towards a departmental structure and establishing problem-oriented research centers; introducing absent disciplines believed necessary for national development, particularly in the social sciences and administration;[5] increasing the number of full-time, adequately paid professors; organizing professionally operated libraries and a unified library system; creating degree programs in technical and subprofessional fields, etc.

Each of these changes in the system of higher education listed above, plus many other similar ones, are extraordinarily difficult to implement. They find opposition from the entrenched, academically conservative members of the university community—whatever their political views—who feel their professional competence questioned and their personal power position within the existing structure threatened. The larger and older the university, the more prestigious and many-faceted is this type of opposition. For this basic reason, when many of the younger, highly trained professionals who had taken postgraduate work abroad returned to their universities in the decade 1945-55, the ponderous weight of institutional tradition frustrated their attempts to make university education within their country more responsive to the scientific and technical demands of a contemporary world society. The response was to establish new private or regional universities where this opposition either

---

[5] The social sciences have proven to be a singularly difficult problem in the reform of Latin American higher education. Their subject matter is the most sensitive academic area for a developing economy undergoing structural changes administered largely by planning-prone central governments. The ideological orientation, combined with varying theoretical models for the several disciplines, make them more responsive to politicization than other fields of study. The high visibility of the United States through its graduate training centers and the large numbers of North American researchers and consultants spread across the landscape have accentuated a natural sensitivity that becomes more acute as the angle of vision moves to the Left. Industrialists and businessmen in the private sector who have supported university development tend to become hostile as soon as these newly introduced disciplines concern themselves with problems of overall social structure or national economies rather than focusing on the specific problems of a particular industry or the applied aspects of farm management, rural sociology or business administration. With the exception of economics, which, in its modern form, developed from accounting or commercial schools within the university, the social sciences have been housed traditionally within faculties of Philosophy and Education (the specific title varies from university to university), where the professional degree granted is that of secondary school professor. This has thoroughly inhibited the professional development of disciplines such as sociology, psychology and anthropology. Further, it offers no encouragement whatsoever for original research or the level of methodological training needed for the empirical application of the discipline to other fields such as medicine or agriculture. Political science has been the fief of faculties of law and, except for the degree granted, the above-described conditions pertain to this discipline also.

would be absent or less marked; to organize a new faculty within a large national university; or to isolate themselves in a laboratory or new research institute which they could control at least for a time.[6] Each of these responses posed a series of major problems such as adequate financing, securing accreditation, staffing, efficient administration, relations with the local and national community and, where the reform was part of a larger established university, relations with student and national politics as well as the entrenched bureaucracy. Each reform effort aimed at modernization had its own specific set or combination of problems. Some idea of their nature and complexity can be gained from a partial description of one such reform: the attempt to establish a Faculty of General Studies at the University of San Marcos during 1964-66.

A program of general studies for the first two years at the university was designed: to equalize the highly varied quality and substance of secondary education, a problem which had become increasingly troublesome with the rapid rise in the university population; to provide the technical background and the intellectual orientation needed to develop those skills most in demand by governments beset by the problems of economic development; and to give students the time and information needed for a better selection of a career and thus, hopefully, to make better use of human resources by reducing the alarmingly high drop-out rate. The opposition came from a variety of sources. The conservative press opposed it because it would alter the traditional educational structure that supported the status quo, and because several of the professors who were on the committee that drafted the formal proposal subscribed to a more radical political philosophy than any previous Peruvian government had espoused. The chairman of the committee was a member of the *Partido Social Progresista,* a small, mainly urban-oriented socialist party dedicated to substantial social change, and, along with his better known brother, he had the name of being an anti-establishment intellectual. The Maoist-oriented Marxists who controlled the student federation of San Marcos and the official Communist Party both opposed general studies as an example of North American

---

6 Examples of new private universities thus founded are the University of the Andes in Bogotá and the Institute of Technology and Higher Studies, Monterrey, Mexico; of new provincial universities, the Universidad del Valle in Cali, Colombia, the Universidad del Oriente (several campuses) in Venezuela, and the University of Huamanga in Ayacucho, Peru; of older provincial universities that attempted an overall restructuring, the University of Antioquia in Medellín, Colombia, and the University of Concepción in Chile. Examples of new faculties or departments of large national universities are those of sociology in the University of Buenos Aires and the National University of Colombia, the Faculty of Sciences in the University of Chile and the Faculty of Economics of the Catholic University of Chile (a national university in constituency and impact). Newly-founded laboratories and research institutes are so varied that specific examples would be misleading.

intellectual imperialism. (The 1964 estimate of the cost of setting up this proposed Faculty was about $910,000, of which one-third was to be paid by San Marcos and two-thirds by the Ford Foundation. The Foundation had also provided U.S. consultants and covered the travel expenses of Peruvian observers in the United States and Central America.) Students who had been inclined to judge the general studies program on its substantive merits when the concept was first seriously broached in 1962, by 1966—when the plan was unveiled in all its detail—were in favor of total change and were ideologically opposed to reform through modernization. The dominant political party in the national legislature, *APRA,* opposed it because the president of the Senate, a prolific essayist and ex-rector of the University, was a candidate (and a successful one) to replace the then presiding rector. *APRA* wanted its own version of a general studies program, if one were to be adopted, and most certainly did not want a powerful new faculty controlled by anti-Apristas.

Support for general studies came from the university administration and from a group of intellectual-professionals who wanted substantial change in university training from either of two points of view: (1) the restructuring of society within a democratic framework; or (2) the adequate preparation of youth needed to make a national revolution effective within a modern world. The fact that the average age of this group was 35 to 40 provided another undercurrent of opposition within the university in the sense that it was the creation of a well-defined generational group and was thus at least resented, if not actively opposed, by the preceding "intellectual generation" within the *Facultad de Filosofía y Letras,* most of whom were ideologically and economically attached to *APRA.* The relative power of the opposing forces prevented the Faculty of General Studies from being established at San Marcos in 1966. However, the 1969 Organic Law for all Peruvian universities as set forth by the present revolutionary military government provides for the inclusion of the equivalent of general studies. Where the only standard of measurement is political and where radicalization of the student climate is an accomplished fact, it seems probable that within a "popular" university such as San Marcos, the only way to gain acceptance of the curricular and structural reform that will produce the scientific and managerial skills required for relative national independence in the contemporary world is for a reform government to have such total support at the national level that political opposition to the implementation of its educational program is either undesirable or impractical.

One element common to every postwar attempt at effecting a structural or curricular change in Latin American higher education that would better serve national economic and social needs and also bring them into a working relationship with the world of science and technology, has been the presence of a committed and educationally visionary individual or small, integrated group that initiated the effort and took the responsibility of leadership during the first years of the new institution's existence. A large proportion of such men had taken graduate training or advanced studies in their specialty in the United States and not infrequently looked to their North American colleagues for curricular and planning assistance and to United States philanthropic organizations for professional and financial support.[7] Thus the models applied were frequently derived from United States experience. Added to this is the fact that several of these newer universities, if not the faculties within the national universities, were oriented toward maintaining in power—through measured change—the existing dominant sector of society; thus it is clear why the politicized student federations of large national universities during the 1960's instinctively opposed every effort at improving the quality of higher education as an expression of that United States cultural imperialism that was robbing them of the opportunity to find their own educational solution. The extent to which this syndrome could pervert any effort at reform not directed towards immediate social upheaval is well illustrated by the attitude of the national student organization in Brazil towards the University of Brasilia.

The University of Brasilia was legally established in 1961 after several years of planning within the *Instituto Nacional de Estudos Pedagógicos* (I.N.E.P.) headed by Anisio Teixeira, perhaps the most inventive mind in the area of adapting educational structures to social reality in twentieth-century Latin America. The co-ordinator of the Center within I.N.E.P. having direct responsibility for the new university's structure was Darcy Ribeiro, later Brasilia's

---

[7] Conclusive data on foreign support of Latin American universities in terms of percentage of annual total university expenditures are not available to me if, indeed, they are available at all. The general lines of support from the United States for higher education are, however, clear. The two largest sources of outright grants in Colombia during the 1960's were the Rockefeller and Ford foundations. During the years 1960-65 the combined Rockefeller ($6,782,000) and Ford ($4,501,000) grants to Colombian universities totaled $11,283,000. Their fellowship grants for advanced staff training amounted to approximately another million dollars. The two next largest sources of funds were the Inter-American Development Bank ($2,600,000) and the United Nations Special Fund ($2,333,000) which, in effect, were totals available for "soft" loans. No other international or United States source provided over $300,000 during these years. Of the Rockefeller and Ford grants, over 99 per cent went to three of the 25 Colombian universities—Valle, los Andes and Antioquia, in that order. These were the universities demonstrably concerned with those structural and curricular improvements that could increase the industrial and technical capacity of the nation in terms of production and improved social services. In other countries such as Chile, where in contrast to Colombia the Ford contribution has been much the greater of the two foundations since 1960, a similar if not quite as spectacular a demonstration could be made, but in terms of subject-matter rather than institutional support: the grants have been made predominantly in agriculture and veterinary medicine; biology, physics and mathematics; economics and business administration; population problems and urban planning; and curriculum development.

first rector. A socialist-oriented intellectual, he and Teixeira were part of every group of any size that worked on the plans for the university. From the beginning Brasilia was marked by its leftist and, even more strongly, its nationalistic tone. The several planning commissions included many if not most of the best qualified, left-of-center Brazilian professionals with an interest in education. The people of I.N.E.P. believed that education should be for the "technological and industrial civilization of tomorrow." Brasilia was to be a corrective to that burgeoning type of higher education that gave little thought to cost, quality or function other than to use the new facilities as the old had been used, as a passageway from one social class to another. It incorporated the many educational reforms attempted singly or in combination by the Spanish American universities. It was a thoroughly nationalistic institution specifically designed to meet Brazil's desire for greater independence within the contemporary world. It was staffed by the best young scholars in the country and their participation was unanimously enthusiastic.

The University of Brasilia was, after three years of increasing success, effectively destroyed by the military government following the April Revolution of 1964. It had been closely associated in the public mind with the previous administration and was widely referred to as the "red" or "subversive" university.[8] With all of these attributes it is notable that the University of Brasilia was consistently attacked by the politically radical, government-supported national student federation on the grounds that because of its high standards it was "elitist" and thus "undemocratic." Although the University of Brasilia was clearly designed, according to its founding rector, to provide the human resources needed to lead in restructuring Brazilian society within a framework of national economic growth, the revolutionary Left opted against it on the familiar grounds that only after the social revolution could the training provided by Brasilia properly serve the national interest. In addition, its structure had been overly influenced by North American imperialist models.

It is difficult to imagine any Latin American national university achieving better solutions to curricular, structural, staffing and financial problems than the University of Brasilia did during its first three years. These solutions were designed to adapt higher education to the technological and scientific demands required to compete successfully in contemporary world society, while preserving an independent, nationalistic image at the same time. It was consistently attacked by the revolutionary Left and was destroyed by the conservative Right. The political naivete of its personally ambitious young rector, plus the lack of support from any established power base within Brazilian society, were negative factors not entirely peculiar to this effort. The evidence from this im-

---

[8] The author has used the unpublished work of a former graduate student, Charles O'Neil, for much of the above information on the University of Brasilia.

pressive example shows that even highly nationalistic, technically excellent solutions to higher educational problems are not likely to suffice in Latin America unless a political solution has first been reached—one that enjoys massive public support long enough to enable a development-oriented government to establish an unassailable authority.

All Latin American countries in recent years have encountered an explosive increase in the demand for a university degree if not for a university education.[9] The statistics on the high attrition rate at all levels of the educational system have been featured in national planning surveys and the many international organization studies published since 1960. Despite this, the absolute numbers of students completing a secondary education that is designed almost entirely to prepare graduates for entry into the university have increased at a faster rate than existing institutions of high learning can absorb them.

The large national universities have been traditionally the institutions that absorbed the increase in number of students. This was accomplished until the mid-1950's—with varying degrees of success in different countries—by creating new faculties with relatively low academic requirements and expanding existing ones where the requirements were least specialized and the facilities economical to operate and readily expandable. This process continues, but at a greatly reduced rate of growth. The high degree of politicization in the national universities, coupled with the lowering of standards in many faculties, resulted in the establishment in the 1940's of such private universities as the Tecnológico in Monterrey and los Andes in Bogotá. This type of institution took care of some of the specialized and quality-training needs but did nothing for the problem of mass. The expansion of existing Catholic universities and the founding of new ones during the 1950's and more especially in the 1960's relieved some of the pressure of numbers and established a few specialized teaching and research facilities of importance for national development. But, with the notable exception of the Catholic University of Chile, this role has been minimal. Some of the older provincial universities in major urban centers such as Rosario, Monterrey, São Paulo and Medellín expanded sufficiently to absorb an increasing percentage of the regional secondary school graduates and in several instances contributed substantially to providing specialized training for local needs within the framework of national development.

---

[9] The inherent conflict between education and certification has been emphasized as an important factor in determining the function of colleges and universities in the United States. This conflict becomes considerably more basic to understanding the dominant function of higher education when, as is the case in Latin America, certification is extended to a formal licensing monopoly for the practice of professions and eligibility for government employment, the fastest-growing sector of the economy offering employment to university graduates. No university has long existed in Latin America without the imprimatur of the state giving the holders of its degree legal parity with the graduates of any other university.

All the developments described above failed to solve the problem of creating sufficient space for those secondary school graduates who wanted a university education. The temporarily effective response was the founding in the 1960's of (1) second and third federal universities in capital cities, and (2) universities in provincial capitals that previously had been without higher education facilities. As an indication of the recent institutional birth rate, Argentina, Chile and Peru had a total of 16 universities in 1949, 27 in 1959 and 75 in 1969.[10] These new universities were usually of a low academic level, poorly staffed and without adequate physical facilities, all factors that tend to encourage political activities by staff and students.

The emphasis reform-oriented governments have put on primary and secondary education during the last decade, particularly in creating schools in rural areas and in the suburban concentrations that ring most large cities, makes it certain that short of major policy changes that would be politically difficult to implement the university population will expand much more rapidly than the population as a whole. The problem of mass will continue to haunt every aspect of university development in Latin America. Poor or unavailable higher educational facilities exacerbate the existing high degree of politicization that so effectively slows down or negates attempts at technical solutions. This, in turn, makes it difficult for a government to determine how to finance the high cost of training staff and carry on the scientific and technological research required by industrialization and economic development. There is even a question whether the smaller and medium-sized countries of Latin America can bear the cost of building an infrastructure adequate to support an independent development effort (in the sense of being a sufficiently contributing part of the international community that it does not have to rely totally on patents owned in other countries or on their graduate schools for the training of technical and scientific personnel) without resort to a common market or regionally operated structure for specialized higher education. The success to date of attempts at regional integration in higher education has been minimal, and there is no indication whatsoever that the concept has sufficiently broad political appeal for any government to support a major effort towards its realization.

The frustrations felt by democratic, development-oriented reform governments at the effects on essential research and advanced training by politically-motivated, university-wide disruptions are such that the research involved is increasingly being handled through para-university institutes or directly within government agencies. This development has had the effect of draining the universities of staff at the level required to develop graduate training, while no adequate substitute in the way of preparation of trained staff has been devised.

---

[10] This last total counts the 10 campuses (*sedes*) of the University of Chile, each in a different city, as separate universities. The system has a single rector as the University of California has a single president.

One way of summarizing the present situation of universities within Latin American society is to note that after more than half a century of intermittently violent reform efforts, the basic condition of dependence on the more industrialized nations of the world has not been resolved. The persistent and growing public association of the social and economic ills of the area with capitalistic exploitation and the hegemony of the United States makes any educational reforms that can be associated with the United States generally suspect and, to the revolutionary Left, unacceptable. This reaction, understandable in terms of past experience, can be self-defeating if relative national and regional independence is indeed the goal. Whatever social and political structure Latin America adopts, it will remain dependent or "colonial" unless it resolves the problem of internal control of the science and technology required for contemporary economic development. In this process the university has a decisive role, and if a society, either national or regional in scope, is going to determine its own future, no political panacea can replace the need for highly trained specialists and an institutional structure in which they can work productively.

# UNIVERSITY PROBLEMS IN JAPAN

Michio Nagai

I

According to a May 29, 1969, report of the Asahi Press, roughly 65 Japanese universities and colleges were suffering from disturbances of one form or another. The same number of disturbances were reported in 1968, while there were 38 in 1967, 25 in 1966 and 49 in 1965. These disturbances include several types: the occupation of an entire campus by students, the occupation of part of the campus, the student strike, and the closing of school by university authority.

These are high figures by any standard. If one knows anything about the numbers of universities and students in Japan, he will not be surprised to find that the situation is very critical at the moment. There are over a thousand universities and colleges in Japan, 473 of them junior colleges and 554, four-year colleges and universities.* Because university disturbances usually take place on the campuses of the four-year institutions, nearly one-sixth of these have been in a state of confusion during the last two years. Moreover, the disturbances were concentrated on the campuses of leading schools. Government-supported universities, which number 75, are, on the whole, regarded as the better schools in Japan. More than half of these have been hit by disturbances. Among private universities, the more important ones like Waseda, Keio, and Jochi, have been the scenes of similar events.

It is true that universities all over the world, both East and West, are experiencing common problems. Student power is a familiar term in many countries. However, in Japan there is at least one unique characteristic: the long duration of the disturbances. The University of Tokyo, Japan's leading institution, had difficulties in holding classes for 17 months. The Tokyo University of Education, another important institution, was closed for nearly nine months. Disruptions which lasted six months were not at all unusual on campuses of many universities. Similarly, some universities in Mexico were strikebound between August and December, 1968. So far as duration is concerned, the Mexican strike, which seems to be the closest to Japan in the West, was far shorter than most Japanese disruptions.

---

\* For the growth of universities and colleges in Japan, 1965-1969, see Tables 1 and 2 on pp. 442 and 443.

Under such circumstances, one can hypothesize that the reasons behind the disturbances in Japan are universal as well as uniquely Japanese. ( 1 ) As in other countries, students in Japan also strike for political reasons. ( 2 ) Like students in industrialized societies, Japanese students also complain about the problem of human alienation in contemporary society. ( 3 ) On the other hand, the old-fashioned policy and structure of the university seems most critical in the Japanese case. Consequently, the combination of these three factors—outdated university policy and structure, the political reasons behind student movements, and the feelings of alienation and anxiety among students —forms a unique Japanese type. In other countries such as the United States, political reasons and the feeling of alienation may be more crucial than poor university policy and structure in contributing to today's chaos.

## II

Japanese universities are clearly lagging behind the rapid changes in society. The most serious problems, however, are to be found in the present condition of private universities.

In most countries private universities began to receive public subsidies soon after the completion of the industrial revolution. This is understandable in view of the fact that in such areas of learning as engineering, medicine, science, agriculture and business management, where much money was needed, rapid development was essential in a new industrial society. Moreover, the expanded universities that followed in the wake of the industrial revolution had to open their doors to the general population, and it was obvious that not much tuition could be expected. The land-grant colleges proposed by Senator Morrill of the United States were the first of their kind in a new industrial society.

In Japan the first industrial revolution ended about 1906. The need for university expansion and development in the areas mentioned above was evident by 1910. At that time the Japanese government began to contemplate the possibility of university reform for a new age. In 1918 the University Ordinance was issued by the government. Unlike the Morrill Act, however, radical reform was not introduced. Instead of seeking sudden increases in subsidies for universities, the government decided to rely on private universities to carry the burden of the increase in student population and, to a certain degree, to develop the new areas of learning.

It is true that the number of public-supported universities and colleges was increased considerably as a result of the University Ordinance. However, this increase was small in proportion to the demand of this new society. Since that time, even to the present private Japanese universities have been suffering financial problems. Of course, there is a rather important reason for such a weakness in university policy. A hundred years ago in Japan one of the most important objectives of the state was to achieve economic independence within the shortest time possible. The state policy was to import ideas from advanced nations and to introduce them to the entire nation through education. The government decided to put more emphasis on primary and secondary education to effect the diffusion of these new ideas. By the same token, the government did not expect Japanese universities to create new ideas. Consequently, while education in the lower grades was strengthened, that of the upper grades, on the whole, grew weaker.

The completion of the industrial revolution demanded a radical transformation in this educational pattern. However, the inertia was much stronger than the social needs. And the government never ventured to change its outdated university policy.

Details of the development of universities in Japan between 1918 and the post-World War II period will not be dealt with here. It is only necessary and important to point out that resistance to higher educational reform existed even in the postwar period. Then in the 1950's and 1960's Japan surprised the world by achieving technological advances and, consequently, rapid economic growth. This new society required an even greater expansion in size and development of the newer areas of learning in universities. And once again, the government expected the private institutions, to a great degree, to take care of these needs.

Of the 1.6 million students in Japan at present, 75 per cent are enrolled in private institutions. Because government subsidies have consistently remained less than 5 per cent of private universities' revenue during the last ten years, the increase of tuition has been the only means of keeping expenditures in balance. Thus, we have one important reason for student strikes in private universities. In order to avoid strikes, private universities abandoned the sudden increases in tuition at the beginning of the 1960's. Instead, they decided to increase the amount of the matriculation fees at the time of entrance, when the students were less likely to complain. According to a report by the Ministry of Education in 1967, the average matriculation fee for private universities was 200,000 yen ($600). The average for the colleges of medicine and pharmacy was over 600,000 yen ($1,700). In 1969 a private medical college asked for 3,500,000 yen (a little less than $10,000) from every student at the time of entrance. Occasionally, some private universities receive large amounts of money from applicants' parents in the form of donations.

Even the increase in matriculation fees has not been sufficient to keep the budgets of private universities balanced. To recover their financial health, they have made attempts to keep the salaries of their employees low. For the same reason, they have tried to avoid increasing the number of full-time professors. In 1969 the proportion of part-time professors to all professors in private universities in Japan was 45 per cent. They received only 700 to 800 yen for one lecture (about two dollars). Therefore, it is not surprising that part-time professors cancel their lectures whenever there is an opportunity for better income elsewhere.

The aforementioned report of the Ministry of Education stated that 29 per cent of the revenue of private universities in 1966 consisted of all types of loans they had contracted and that 20 per cent of their expenditures were spent on paying and servicing these debts. In other words, many private universities in Japan have actually been bankrupt for some years but the government has not done anything about this situation. Thus, it is only to be expected that the content and quality of research and education in private universities today are much poorer than that required by society.

III

The government has undoubtedly been responsible for the deterioration of the quality of private institutions. Not only in the case of private institutions but in the case of public ones, too, both the government and right- and left-wing political parties have neglected university reform. Contrary to the rapid growth of business sectors of the country during the last two decades, the financial resources of universities have increased very slowly.

In 1968 the government defined the meaning of "the middle-range income group" for the purpose of taxation. According to this definition, those who belong to this group received 1.5 million to 4 million yen (a little less than $5,000 to $11,000) in 1968. Among college professors in both public and private institutions, only 28 per cent belonged to this group. In other words, most college professors were members of a lower-income strata than the so-called "middle-income range."

In spite of these facts, Japanese have been spending a large amount of money for education. Presently the proportion of educational investment to per capita income is as high as that of most advanced nations. But in Japan this is only true of elementary and secondary education. In higher education the proportion of educational investment to per capita income is only one-half of that of most advanced nations. Consequently, public-supported universities are poorly financed.

There are additional difficulties in the case of public universities, the most important of which is old-fashioned management. In such nations as the U.S.A. and U.S.S.R., where the quality and quantity of universities have changed greatly, university management has also experienced a great number of changes. The most important of these has been the delegation of the power of the faculty to other university-related groups. Professional management has developed especially in the United States. The ministry of education in the

U.S.S.R. and the boards of trustees in countries like the United States and the United Kingdom have become increasingly responsible for decision-making in vital matters.

Such changes have not taken place in Japan. Faculty autonomy remains powerful in matters that include the selection of personnel and the evaluation of their achievements, budgeting and planning of research and education, the improvement of the welfare of the students and the like.

It is nearly impossible, however, for large faculty meetings in today's large universities to deal with these matters. As a result, there is an absence of planning. It is also difficult for a large faculty to be responsible for the evaluation of colleagues without the help of outsiders. Again the result has been the absence of fair evaluation and the defense of the vested interests of faculty members.

Because of the dense population in Japan's urban areas, it has become incumbent for many universities to move to the suburbs. Yet there is no other body but the faculty meeting to deal with this problem of university relocation and amalgamation. At many universities endless discussions on this subject at faculty meetings reached no conclusions. The period of words was followed by the period of student disturbances.

Because professors were not evaluated, the contents of research and education did not show much improvement and students began to complain about the slow pace. At the University of Tokyo, medical students demanded the improvement of financial conditions for medical training and went on strike, but 17 months after the strike broke out the faculty still had not responded to this demand.

## IV

Although most of these problems have become exposed because of university uprisings, no solution has been reached for any of them. Until the end of 1968 there was hardly any comprehensive university policy proposed by any political party, the government, or any association formed by the university community. Because of the strong pressures exerted by radical student movements, the government, political parties, and universities have become suddenly busy formulating reform plans. Thus far, however, neither an agreement nor a compromise has been reached among these different groups. Instead, the government and the Conservative party try to bring outside elements into the university management while the universities try to maintain exclusive autonomy. This latter policy has been highly encouraged by opposition political parties.

There is no question that the changes in universities are largely the result of radical transformations in the larger society, especially in business. Accord-

437

ing to an estimate by Professor Misao Sekiguchi, the business sector invested roughly one thousand billion yen ($2,750 million) for in-service training and research in 1968. Businessmen now wish to build universities oriented to their own goals. The universities are, naturally, opposed to ideas of reorganization for immediately practicable goals.

Instead of coming to some practical compromise, the different groups seem to be politicizing their conflicts more and more each day. Such a trend is accelerated by the difficult international position in which Japan is placed. Korea and Japan are the only two nations in the world that are surrounded by the three giants of today, the U.S.A., the U.S.S.R. and the People's Republic of China. In addition, rapid economic growth has caused an imbalance of wealth among different sectors within the nation, adding another potential source of sharp political conflict. The student movements in Japan have reflected these international and internal conflicts during the last 20 years. The Communist student body (*Minsei,* meaning the Democratic Youth) has always been an important power both on and off the campus. Since the split began between the U.S.S.R. and the People's Republic of China, young Communists have been searching for a proper position in international relations. During the last few years, it has come closer to the position of the U.S.S.R., maintaining at the same time the integrity and independence of the Communist party in Japan. Since the latter part of the 1950's, noncommunist leftist groups have considerably increased their membership and have gained more power, mainly among the student population. Though there are differences in the position among groups belonging to this category, they share a common criticism of the Communist party: It has become another "establishment" and, like the conservative parties, has lost its vigor for reform. Since 1964 when the U.S. military engagement began to escalate in Vietnam, the noncommunist leftist groups have become more active and violent both on and off the campus. They have supported such political leaders as Ho Chi-Minh, Mao Tse-Tung, and Che Guevara. Both the Communist and the noncommunist student groups are sharply opposed to U.S. policies in Asia and to the policies of the Japanese government, which are, on the whole, in support of them. They claimed that the Security Pact between Japan and the United States should have been abandoned in 1970.

However, there is also a sharp conflict between these two groups. The Communist group is much more gradual in its approach, especially in internal politics. It is now suggesting that total political transformation is possible without breaking down the parliamentary method. Although it is asking for more student participation in university management, it regards the university community as a progressive element in society. In contrast to this position, noncommunist groups refuse to negotiate with the university authorities, maintaining that the universities themselves are a part of the corrupt establishment. Thus they claim that the existing universities should be destroyed.

On the basis of this argument, they occupy the entire campus or some buildings on campus, cancel classes and torture faculty members through the pressure of prolonged group discussions which sometimes last over a hundred hours. It is not at all surprising in this context that Communist and noncommunist groups fight each other, sometimes quite bitterly. On many of the campuses physical confrontations between the two groups have been waged since the middle of 1968, resulting in heavy injuries to students, although the number of deaths has been about ten, including both students and policemen.

Undoubtedly, political tensions among student groups complicate today's university problems. The Conservative party and the government try to suppress radical student movements. Faculty members are caught between pressures both from the government and the students—the results being that some support the government, others support various student groups, and still others try to maintain their independence. The majority of students attempt to maintain their neutrality, though the proportion of the students supporting the Communists and the noncommunists and those maintaining neutrality seems to be changing as the political situation and climate change.

V

In contrast to the United States, feelings of human alienation and loss of ideals are not as predominant among students in Japan. At times one finds the Japanese version of hippies in large cities like Tokyo and Osaka. However, in Japan the number of drug addicts is one of the smallest of any industrialized society. Changes in sexual conduct also seem to be much slower in Japan than they are in the United States and in Western Europe. Although there is increasingly more exposure of sexual conduct in various types of entertainment, Japanese youth seems to be more rigid in maintaining the traditional sexual morality than their counterparts in the West.

What is common between Japan and the West is the sharp generational conflict. Because social changes in the 1960's have been so rapid in Japan, communication between youth and adult has become increasingly difficult.

(1) The intensification of competition has been an important aspect of social changes. At the present time 20 per cent of those of college age are enrolled in universities and colleges. Roughly 72 per cent of all youth finish 12 years of schooling and nearly all complete the nine years of compulsory education. Competition to enter the better universities is bound to be intensified in such a situation. Ambitious parents and teachers try to prepare children—even at the primary school level—for later entrance to first-rate universities. Instead of a well-balanced education, there is a one-sided emphasis on prepara-

tory education at all levels of schooling throughout the country. The personality of children tends to become compartmentalized. The result being that only the part directed toward the entrance examination is strengthened. Upon entrance to universities, the student suddenly seeks to recover his total personality. This attempt seems seldom to be fully understood by adults, including both professors and parents.

(2) To use the expression of David Riesman, Japanese youth has become increasingly and suddenly "other-directed." Over 90 per cent of Japanese households own at least one television set, and a large number own two or three sets. In cities like Tokyo and Osaka, there are six or seven television channels. To say that Japanese children are brought up on television, which constantly presents to them rapid changes in culture and society both within and without the country, is no exaggeration. Children are quick in sensing changes and in adjusting themselves to any new situations. But the stability of their personalities cannot be easily established at the same time.

(3) It is also difficult for children today to transform themselves into adults in the traditionally established manner. Maturity comes quite early these days mainly because of the stimuli from commercial entertainment. Teenagers become politically conscious as a result of all sorts of teaching and agitation. On the other hand, it is not easy for young people to establish economic independence even after graduation from universities. Housing difficulties often delay marriage. Because of these difficulties, there is not a clearly defined transition from childhood to adulthood. Pent-up frustrations are frequently created by this lack of a distinct transition.

(4) Japan has been characterized by a loss of confidence on the part of parents whose tradition was discredited after the nation's defeat in World War II. Added to this has been the great importance on individuality and self-esteem resulting from sudden democratization. The so-called American "soft education" has also played its role. It is thus only natural that a strong individualistic quality has been lacking among children of the postwar period. Yet despite this cultural background, children and students today are exposed to the difficulties of rapid social changes where strong individualism is required. These are only a few examples of new aspects of the youth in a postwar period, and especially in the 1960's. Anxiety and uncertainty pervade the minds of students today, and they seem to have difficulty in expressing their problems adequately to their professors and parents. When engaged in discussions with adults on campus and at home, they grope for proper expression of their problems.

VI

At the initial stage of Japanese campus disruptions, students of both private- and public-supported universities criticized and attacked the outdated university policy and management. In the case of private universities, students complained about the rapid increase of tuition and matriculation fees more than anything else. Students of public-supported universities, on the other hand, criticized the outdated and poor management which was not able to reform such matters as boring lectures in general education, the apprentice-type training for medical students, poor living conditions in dormitories and the like.

However, as the political situation grew tense in 1968 and 1969, and as the reversion of Okinawa became a crucial international political issue in 1969, both the Communist and noncommunist student activists began to focus their strategies on political issues which were not clearly related to problems of university policy and management. This has been especially true since April 28, 1969—termed Okinawa Day—when representatives from Okinawa and progressive forces on the Japanese island were united in their claim for reversion of the island. In addition, some of the student activists, especially those belonging to the noncommunist Left, became more violent on the campuses and on the streets.

These changes in the situation gave the government an ideal opportunity and reason to draft a new bill which would suppress the spread of influences arising from student activism. In early August, the Conservative party in power proposed and passed a new bill in the Diet over the opposition of all the other parties. This bill, which may be translated as the Temporary Emergency Law for University Disturbances, in essence legalized both the permanent or temporary closing of any university which had not recovered from large-scale disturbances within a certain period of time. The law specified that the state of difficulties of a university was to be judged and determined by a mediation committee composed of people not directly related to the government.

There is no doubt that the effect of this law has been far-reaching. Universities, both private and public, began without hesitation to call police onto the campus to arrest student activists and to deal with any violence. It is reasonable to suspect that those universities which have long been troubled, were afraid that their institutions would either be permanently or temporarily closed.

Since August the disrupted universities suddenly quieted down. At the end of 1969 only a few universities in Japan were either closed or occupied by students. The Conservative party claimed that their overwhelming victory in the general election in December was due, in part, to the successful effect of the bill passed by the Diet in August.

On the surface, therefore, Japanese universities seemed quiet and normalized in the beginning of 1970. However, inherent problems in university policy and management have not yet been solved, even to the slightest degree. The Central Commission on Education of the Ministry of Education is aware of this situation. The Commission had been working on the question of university reform quite seriously throughout the period of the disturbances.

On January 12, 1970, this group's interim report on the reform of higher education was made public. It was still tentative, abstract, and brief. However, there were salient points in the report which had never been stated before, but which should have been said about Japanese universities a long time ago by a responsible group.

To point out a few: the Commission suggests that long-range planning in terms of content and financial support will be needed for the reconstruction of universities and colleges in Japan, and that there must be a responsible body in the government to deal with this task. It states also that the old-fashioned state-supported university should become more autonomous in its management and finance, and that the possibility of establishing a university somewhat like the public corporation, which may at least in theory, be more

TABLE 1.—Number of Universities and Colleges in Japan

1965

|  | National | Prefectural Municipal | Private | Total |
|---|---|---|---|---|
| Graduate School | 43 | 17 | 71 | 131 |
| Four-Year College | 73 | 35 | 209 | 317 |
| Junior College | 28 | 40 | 301 | 369 |

1967

|  | National | Prefectural Municipal | Private | Total |
|---|---|---|---|---|
| Graduate School | 53 | 19 | 90 | 162 |
| Four-Year College | 74 | 39 | 256 | 369 |
| Junior College | 23 | 41 | 387 | 451 |

1969

|  | National | Prefectural Municipal | Private | Total |
|---|---|---|---|---|
| Graduate School | 58 | 17 | 100 | 175 |
| Four-Year College | 75 | 34 | 270 | 379 |
| Junior College | 22 | 43 | 408 | 473 |

TABLE 2.—Number of Students

1965

| Male | | | Female | | |
|---|---|---|---|---|---|
| 822,612 | | (75.8%) | 262,457 | | (24.2%) |
| Four-Year | 785,437 | (72.4%) | Four-Year | 152,119 | (14.1%) |
| Junior | 37,175 | ( 3.4%) | Junior | 110,338 | (10.1%) |

1967

| Male | | | Female | | |
|---|---|---|---|---|---|
| 1,001,158 | | (71.8%) | 394,014 | | (28.2%) |
| Four-Year | 957,204 | (68.7%) | Four-Year | 203,220 | (14.6%) |
| Junior | 43,954 | ( 3.1%) | Junior | 190,794 | (13.6%) |

1969

| Male | | | Female | | |
|---|---|---|---|---|---|
| 1,105,618 | | (71.1%) | 449,482 | | (28.9%) |
| Four-Year | 1,059,705 | (68.1%) | Four-Year | 236,066 | (15.2%) |
| Junior | 45,913 | ( 3.0%) | Junior | 213,416 | (13.7%) |

independent from the government than the existing national universities, should be investigated. It also suggests that there be more government subsidies for private institutions and that institutions of higher learning in Japan be diversified in education and research.

As I have mentioned earlier, however, these ideas were still very abstract and tentative. Moreover, little has been said with regard to the role and status of students, the international exchange of scholars, possible modifications of the existing rigid, influential hierarchy of universities and colleges, and the encouragement of greater access of professors and students to formerly exclusive and cliquish institutions in Japan.

Universities and colleges, too, are gradually proposing modifications to the present structure. There will be more discussions of these proposals for some months to come. And it will take even more time before the changes are actually made.

In addition, political difficulties within and without the country will remain for some years hence. A more balanced economic structure within the country must be established as soon as possible. As long as the political situation in the Far East remains unstable, political tension will persist in Japan, especially among sensitive intellectuals and youths in universities and colleges. As the society achieves industrialization to a greater degree, newer problems will undoubtedly arise in social and cultural relations. No one can predict with any accuracy when and in what form Japan will build a post-industrial society. The combination of political difficulties and social-cultural changes will continuously bring more and newer problems to campus life. One can only hope that in the future the reformed Japanese universities will be more capable of dealing with these problems.

# HIGHER EDUCATION IN
# THAILAND

Nai Sukich Nimmanheminda

It is considered a good policy, when investigating or making a study of any subject to dig so deeply that all the possible situations may be readily and easily understood. In other words, we look back in order to look forward. In line with this belief, an attempt at a brief historical sketch of higher education in Thailand is justified.

## A HISTORICAL NOTE

*The Beginning of a University.* King Chulalongkorn, known in later days as King Rama V, reigned over Thailand from 1868-1910. During this long period of paternalistic rule, countless social changes and reforms were introduced into the country, including abolition of slavery, construction of the first railroad, introduction of modern public administration, building of the first school, and sending the king's own sons and a number of Thai students to study in European countries in order to build up a nucleus of trained personnel for future development of the country. The king himself set an example—long before any other Eastern monarch came to realize the true function of a ruler—by making several long visits and observation tours to Europe, following similar visits to most of the neighboring countries of Thailand, or Siam, as it was known in those days. Many ancient court customs, and traditions in general were modified or abolished. Quite a number of foreign words began to creep into the Thai language, and new ideas began to make headway in the everyday life of the erstwhile Oriental "land of the free."

Against this background of rapid social changes such as had never occurred before—a move towards modernization—the first medical school in Thailand was established in 1889.

In 1897, the first law school was founded within the Ministry of Justice, under the directorship of Prince Rabi of Rajburi, an outstanding son of King Chulalongkorn.

Towards the end of his reign, in 1902, King Chulalongkorn established the "Royal Pages School" within the Grand Palace, with an aim of training officials for government service. Graduates of this school were placed on a probationary training program for a certain prescribed period before being assigned to various offices of the government.

445

Thus when King Chulalongkorn died in 1910, a medical school, a law school, and a public administration school of sorts already existed, all aimed at producing the personnel needed most urgently to pave the way towards modernization and national security. However, all these institutions were under separate administrations, and it should be noted at once that all these professional schools trained their students for the sole purpose of serving in various departments of the government.

At the commencement of his reign, the new king, King Vajiravudh, better known as Rama VI, changed the name, "Royal Pages School," to "The Civil Servants School," emphasizing still more the fact that the graduates were expected to serve in the civil service branch of the administration; and at that time it was planned that this school should offer courses for prospective civil servants in the fields of education, medicine, agriculture, jurisprudence, commerce, foreign relations and public administration.

Nevertheless, by 1913, only the engineering school had been established, in addition to the Civil Servants School.

Then in 1916 by royal command, the Civil Servants School was elevated to the status of a university and was named "Chulalongkorn University" in memory of Chulalongkorn the Great. The medical school and the engineering school were simultaneously incorporated into this newly established university. Consequently, during its initial period, Chulalongkorn University consisted of four faculties or colleges, namely: The Faculty of Arts and Science, The Faculty of Medicine, The Faculty of Engineering, and The Faculty of Political Science, each offering a three-year program leading to a certificate. Thus, after an incubation period of 27 years, a university was born in Thailand, and higher education on the professional level began to assume a definite role.

Some years later, the law school of the Ministry of Justice was transferred to become an integral part of the Faculty of Political Science of Chulalongkorn University; on June 24, 1932, Thailand was forcibly ushered into a new revolutionary period of social changes, and this same Faculty of Law was once more detached from Chulalongkorn University, and, curiously enough, became a monocollegiate university by itself, known as "University of Moral and Political Science."

This brings us to the dawn of a new era, in politics as well as in higher education. However, it is advisable to stress the fact that the chief motive for the establishment of the first university in Thailand was to *train civil servants* to serve in the numerous branches of the government of a country which was emerging from a feudal past into the new era as a modern state, and concurrently fighting extremely hard to survive and keep intact her age-long independence. Politically, the period just covered was the time during which colonial powers were truculently active in Southeast Asia. In other words, the university established at that time was meant to provide the manpower required to run a sovereign country, fully determined to maintain the independence of its people, who had never been under alien tutelage.

*The Peculiar Emergence of Other Institutions of Higher Learning.* On June 24, 1932, a coup d'état was staged in Thailand, bringing to an end the absolute monarchical form of government and ushering in democracy of a sort to the country for the first time in its long history. The change was somewhat unexpected, and had a far-reaching effect on the life of the country and the people. Following the coup, a democratic rule in the form of constitutional monarchy was established; and from that very moment onward, the country plunged headlong into a series of changes and counterchanges in the political, military, economic, and sociopsychological spheres of life.

As a symptom of this wind of change, "The University of Moral and Political Science," concentrating heavily and solely in the field of law and jurisprudence, hastily prepared for new openings in legal and administrative fields in order to fulfill the aspirations caused by a new sense of political resurgence.

Significantly, it must be pointed out that the idea of a monocollegiate university came into fashion in Thailand following the establishment of this new university, led by a politically minded rector under the auspices of the Ministry of Education!

As a result, in 1942 the Faculty of Medicine was detached from Chulalongkorn University and became known as "The University of Medical Science," under the jurisdiction of the Ministry of Public Health. The reason given was that the separation would facilitate health and medical services to be rendered by the Ministry of Public Health. In 1943, the Kasetsart, literally "Agricultural Science University," came into being under the blessing of the Ministry of Agriculture, with the ostensible objective of improving the profession or field of agriculture. In the same year, The "Silpakorn" (or Fine Arts) University was instituted, also within the Ministry of Education, charged with the responsibility of engaging in the study and preservation of Thai art and archaeology.

Twelve years later, in 1954, when the teaching profession became more widely known and understood, "The College of Education" was established within the Ministry of Education. It is the first degree-granting college in Thailand, independent of a university, and organized on a much more modern basis. Its curriculum consisted of a strong liberal arts program, which branched out into both the academic and the professional-education areas in the upper years. The college was mainly concerned with the teaching profession, but it also gave prominence to educational research and educational administration for the first time in the history of education of Thailand.

Chulalongkorn University, which by this time was offering a four-year program in many professions, together with the other one-profession universities, pushed forward the best they could for a long time, performing what was expected of them until 1959, when another great change took place.

In 1958 another coup d'état occurred in Thailand. As a result of this important change, the first five-year plan for economic and social development of the country was inaugurated. As a consequence, all the five universities with the exception of the College of Education were transferred to the direct control and jurisdiction of the prime minister's office, ostensibly for better co-ordination and greater financial support. During this period, a kind of academic awakening took place. The universities adopted a new outlook as regards their offerings. They all agreed that they wanted to train youth in as many professions as they could in line with the requirements stipulated in the five-year plan. The programs for many professions tended to include liberal arts courses, especially in the earlier years, in order to establish a broad and strong basis for future specialization and professional work.

The year 1960 saw the attempt of the government to accelerate the manpower production, which resulted in a plan to establish four more institutions of higher learning for the country, mostly to be located in the provinces outside of the capital city of Bangkok. They are: Chiengmai University in the north; Khon Kaen University in the northeast; The Prince of Songkla University in the south, and The National Institute for Development Administration, a graduate school, in Bangkok.

All these new universities were organized on a modern basis.

We have now traced the development of higher education in Thailand from the beginning to the present day. It would be good to stress the fact that without exception all existing universities and degree-granting colleges in Thailand today are governmental organizations; and all the members of the teaching staff are, lock, stock and barrel, government officials, that is, civil servants.

As we already emphasized, when higher education first began, the aim was to train officials for the civil service. However, at the present moment, though the idea still holds true, the emphasis has been shifted to meeting the high-level manpower requirements in all sectors of economic and social life, and not necessarily to satisfy the demands of the civil service alone.

### THE PRESENT STATUS AND THE STRUGGLE TO GROW

*Current Situation.*   Thailand is now in the midst of its second five-year plan for economic and social development. As far as this plan is concerned, the universities and colleges are expected to play an important role. Characteristic of a developing country, the lack of trained personnel on all levels is a very serious problem. In Thailand there is a dire shortage of doctors, engineers, teachers, agricultural workers, economists, planners and people in certain areas of social sciences. To cope with this situation, institutions of higher learning are called upon to train more and more professional workers in those fields.

To do a better job in producing graduates who will measure up to the requirements in national development, each university is presently paying great attention to reorganizing its curricular offerings. Instead of being a one-profession institution, a host of programs in various professional areas is now offered. Furthermore, many curricula have added courses in science and humanities to provide for a strong base of general education before specialized work is done in the professional field. It is the expressed aim of all institutions to expand systematically, both in quality and quantity, so as to graduate a sufficient number of professional men as specified in the five-year plan.

In terms of quantity, the enrollment as classified by fields of study in the 1968 academic year is as follows:

| Fields of Study | Bachelor's Degree Level | Specialized Certificate Level | Master's Degree Level | Doctor's Degree Level | Total |
|---|---|---|---|---|---|
| Humanities | 2,468 | 32 | 69 | — | 2,569 |
| Education | 1,584 | 30 | 140 | — | 1,754 |
| Fine Arts | 867 | — | — | — | 867 |
| Social Sciences | 10,696 | 55 | 1,639 | 1 | 12,391 |
| Law | 3,386 | — | 36 | — | 3,422 |
| Natural Science | 1,776 | 4 | 155 | — | 1,935 |
| Engineering | 2,845 | 22 | 208 | — | 3,075 |
| Medical Science | 5,229 | 249 | 74 | — | 5,552 |
| Agriculture | 2,681 | — | — | — | 2,681 |
| Total | 31,532 | 392 | 2,321 | 1 | 34,246 |

At the present moment, the total population of the country is estimated at 33 million. Consequently, the university enrollment is just 0.1 per cent of the population. Of the university age-group (19-22 years old) of about 2.43 million, the enrollment constitutes only 1.42 per cent. This, of course, points out very bluntly that we still have a long way to go. According to the five-year plan, the universities and colleges, if they are to meet fully the requirements for the high-level manpower, must produce the following numbers of graduates:

Manpower Requirements of Trained Personnel
During the Five-Year Plan (1967-1971)

| Fields of training | Manpower Requirements for the 5-year period |
|---|---|
| Agriculture and animal husbandry | 2,200 |
| Forestry and fisheries | 900 |
| Medical science | 2,250 |
| Nursing | 6,000 |
| Engineering | 2,200 |
| Teaching | 49,000 |
| Science | 3,300 |

Obviously, the target figures are relatively high for a developing country like Thailand. But every one understands that the requirements have to be met somehow; and it is a great source of satisfaction that all the universities and colleges are quite conscious of the importance of their role in this rapidly changing society and are determined to forge ahead and achieve their objectives. Furthermore, it is the declared intention of these institutions to improve their training programs as well as to engage in the necessary research and extension-work activities, which are the three major functions of an institution of higher learning today. However, at the present moment, the training function dominates the scene. This is true for the simple reasons that the facilities and the needed personnel are extremely limited, and that many universities are still in their infancy. With the passage of time, we hope to accomplish what we have set out to do.

Again, as is expected of any enterprise, we are encountering some very serious problems. First and foremost, there is the shortage of teaching staff at the new universities. Particularly if they are located in the provinces outside the metropolitan area, this lack is acutely felt. This fact undoubtedly hampers increment in enrollment, and adversely affects research and other related activities. We are viewing this situation with grave concern. Next, there is the shortage of funds. In spite of the earnestness on the part of the government and the universities and colleges themselves to achieve the targets, on many occasions we are obliged to slacken our speed because of financial limitations. It has been found that only 3.17 per cent of the gross domestic product of the country is spent on education on all levels. It is our desire to increase it to 4 or 5 per cent if feasible.

Another problem, which is becoming greater and greater each year, is the fact that there is a great clamoring on the part of high school graduates to go to college, and that we do not have sufficient facilities to admit all of them, or all of those who are college material. Last June, about 20,000 students applied for admission to all the universities and colleges. Only about 9,000 were admitted. The rest would have to bide their time somehow, somewhere.

All these shortcomings and many more are presenting us with several hard nuts to crack; and whether we like it or not we have to exert ourselves to the utmost.

*An Attempt to Remedy: "The University Development Program."* In 1964 many agencies came to realize that careful and systematic planning in higher education was a necessary first step towards solution of the problems, already enumerated. After a series of studies carried out by Thai as well as overseas educators, one major recommendation was stressed, and that is, that in order to improve their educational standards and achieve expansion in enrollment, all universities and colleges should pool their resources and develop

450

strong graduate programs in certain specific areas in accordance with the man-power needs of the country, especially in connection with the national economic and social development plan. In 1967 a University Development Commission was established, and entrusted with the responsibilities of finding ways and means to carry out this recommendation. Immediately, a project was drawn up by the Commission, aiming primarily at producing a number of qualified teaching personnel for the various universities themselves, as the shortage of instructors has been very acute. The project was to be implemented through establishment of truly high-quality graduate programs.

In view of limited resources, it was decided that graduate work in the following areas would be offered *during the initial period,* namely: English, mathematics, physics, chemistry, biology, and economics. There are several reasons as to why these fields have been chosen. First, the basic sciences as well as mathematics are most fundamental for engineering, medicine, and agriculture, in which areas the manpower need is acutely felt; and expansion in these needed fields would not be possible without teachers in the basic sciences. Again, success in national economic planning and development depends to a great extent upon well-trained men in the field of economics. Furthermore, in view of the fact that a world language such as English is essential as a tool for advanced studies and research as well as international scholarly communication, an intensive program in the English language becomes a necessity for graduate students.

In connection with these graduate projects, a series of surveys and studies will be made to identify the potentialities and deficiencies in each institution. In addition, specific recommendations regarding the nature of the graduate courses to be offered as well as cost estimates and other necessary steps will also be made. For both surveys, and the implementation of the recommendations that will follow, universities in Thailand will need assistance from abroad. It is the intention of the University Development Commission to seek financial assistance and technical cooperation from overseas funding sources.

Once the shortage of teaching staff and research personnel in the universities and colleges is adequately dealt with, higher education in Thailand will have made a great stride forward. Institutions of higher learning will then be in a position to contribute fully towards meeting the manpower need and other needs of the country through their regular training programs, research work and extension work.

Thus the attempt to solve the problems faced by the universities of Thailand today will be made, as may be readily seen, through the so-called "manpower approach," on the premise that once the necessary trained personnel are obtained, other problems will, as a consequence, be solved through the efforts of these men.

At the present moment, the English language program is well underway.

Distinguished teachers of English, both Thai and others, have been recruited from all universities and colleges to conduct a very intensive course in the English language for promising young university teachers, who will teach, or are now teaching, mathematics, chemistry, physics, biology, and in some areas of the social sciences. As soon as they have attained the required proficiency in English, they will engage in graduate work in the various professional fields that are in great need, as well as in those basic sciences themselves. This, of course, indicates that strengthening of graduate studies in those professional areas will also have to be initiated soon, and not merely the English program.

Undoubtedly, to accomplish what has just been mentioned will take considerable time, and also assistance and cooperation from international friends, governments, foundations and agencies. The universities and colleges will try their best to perform their duties. They are determined to succeed in their struggle to expand and serve their country's interest.

## FUTURE TRENDS

Having seen how higher education in Thailand started, what problems it is now confronting, and what actions have been taken or proposed to be taken, it should be possible to predict what is in store for Thai universities and colleges in the near future.

It is evident that higher education has become very popular. Each year a great number of high school graduates apply for the entrance examination or equivalent matriculation, but only a small number can be admitted for want of space, facilities and teaching staff. Optimistically, this may be taken as a good sign, as it is a reminder that immediate action has to be taken, and taken carefully, considering all the ramifications of the problem. With limited financial and personnel resources on the part of the government, careful planning becomes most essential. Thus, in the near future, it should be no surprise for anyone to find that the role of educational planning is gaining in momentum at all levels.

Furthermore, all institutions of higher learning in Thailand are state-owned, and all staff members are government officials. The government, with its ever-increasing financial burdens and responsibilities, is not in a position to give all the necessary monetary support or "to go it alone" all the time, and thus it has become very apparent that popular public support is not only desirable but most imperative.

In fact, a legislative act has just been passed, permitting private-owned degree-granting colleges to be established for the first time in the history of Thailand. This March 6, 1969, law sets the stage for a new day in Thai higher education. It is hoped that private agencies will be sufficiently attracted to cooperate with the government in an attempt to produce more doctors, engineers, agriculturists and economists as required for national development. It is also hoped that privately-owned institutions, once established, will not become commercialized and profit-making enterprises.

While it is believed that privately-owned colleges may assist in promoting higher education in Thailand to a certain extent, another significant source of help is recognized, namely, international or regional cooperation. Currently, in Southeast Asia there is one promising agency operating on a regional basis, which plays a significant role in promoting the advancement of higher education in this part of the world. It is the so-called "South-East Asian Ministers of Education Organization," which has a council and a secretariat. This organization effectively enhances progress in higher education by establishing a number of training centers, each located in the country where it is felt a particular field of study will thrive, obtain the highest support, and achieve the greatest result. Scholars, university instructors, and advanced students are sent from the region to these centers for advanced training and research projects. Some of these training centers are the English Language Center in Singapore, the Center for Science and Mathematics in Malaysia, the Center for Agriculture in the Philippines, the Center for Tropical Biology in Indonesia, the Center for Innovation and Technology in Education in Vietnam, and the Center for Tropical Medicine in Thailand.

It is felt that, qualitatively, these centers will do much to contribute to research and higher learning in this part of the world.

Therefore, insofar as Thailand is concerned, the trend towards regionalism or international cooperation will have to be further strengthened. No small country in the present-day world can manage to survive by remaining aloof, turning deaf and blind to all that is going on in the fields of higher education in the rest of the world.

Again, as the course of action has been more or less set in terms of requirements for the nation's economic and social development, higher education, among other things, will continue to give emphasis to ways and means to satisfy the manpower needs in the field of medicine, engineering, agriculture, public administration, education, and some other areas of social sciences deemed necessary for national development. This would also mean that implementation of the "University Development Program," earlier described, is absolutely vital; and as this program would involve a great deal of investigating, planning and funding, universities and colleges will continue to seek cooperation from friends and allies.

Most certainly, as these institutions keep on growing and expanding, their research and extension programs will be strengthened. Until such time as research and extension work have produced fruitful results, and until graduates are serving in the various communities of the nation in a much greater number, it cannot be said that higher education in Thailand has served its purpose.

However, as a conclusion for this essay, it is interesting to note that higher education in Thailand since its inception has been directly associated with some phases of national development. When it came into existence back in the days of King Chulalongkorn (Rama V) and King Vajiravudh (Rama VI), higher education was meant to produce men to serve in the civil service of an emerging nation. Today, in the era of economic and social development, it has been called upon to play a more essential role in producing, among other things, professional men in various fields of study to satisfy the manpower requirements as stated in the National Plan for Economic and Social Development. Hence, it is no exaggeration to say that higher education in Thailand has always performed a well-defined duty in the rapidly changing society of the country, and will continue to do so for a long time to come.

# SOME ASPECTS OF HIGHER EDUCATION IN THE PHILIPPINES*

### Bernard J. Kohlbrenner

## INTRODUCTION

The Philippine archipelago consists of more than 7,000 islands located some 500 miles off the southeast coast of mainland Asia. Many of the islands are small and uninhabited and less than 2,500 of them are important enough to have been named. The two largest islands are Luzon in the north and Mindanao in the south and these two contain some 70 per cent of the land area of the country. The population is estimated at about 3 million and has one of the fastest growing population rates in the world. Magellan landed in what is now Cebu City in 1521 and thus discovered the area for the Western world and opened it up for colonization by the Spanish. But Magellan was killed by a native chieftain, Lapu-Lapu, who today is regarded as a native hero. Before the coming of Spanish influence the islands had had Chinese, Indian, and Arabic traders and settlers and influences from these peoples can be found in one or another part of the archipelago even today. When Legaspi came in 1565 to begin Spanish colonial rule he found that Manila was under the rule of a Muslim leader. With the military leaders came numbers of Catholic missionaries of whom many had a tradition of devotion to educational enterprises, such as the Franciscans, the Jesuits and the Dominicans. With the Christianization of the natives in the lowlands, the Muslims moved into the interior of the islands, especially those in the south. Today the Muslims (sometimes called the Moros) constitute a large and vigorous group and, because of a long history of troubles with the Christians, are usually referred to as a cultural minority that is frequently in conflict with the government. The Muslims regard the government as foreign to its culture and a constant source of irritation.

Although linguistic scholars are still not in agreement on the number of vernacular languages, the government recognizes eight distinct cultural-lin-

---

* The views expressed in this paper are those of the writer and are not to be attributed to the Ford Foundation or any of its field offices.

guistic groups, but Tagalog, the native language of Manila and central Luzon, has been made the basis for a national language which is designated as Pilipino or Philipino. This has been made a required subject in the schools and in programs for the preparation of teachers. English, however, is introduced as the medium of instruction in Grade III of the elementary schools and continues thereafter in all the grades. It is also the language of business and the professions.

The political history of the country can be divided into the following periods: (a) the Spanish rule, 1565-1898; (b) the Filipino Revolution, 1896-1902; (c) the American regime, 1898-1946; (d) the war with Japan, 1941-1945; and (e) the Republic of the Philippines, 1946 to the present.[1]

Foreigners visit chiefly metropolitan Manila and judge from such experience that the population of the country is highly dense and that many of the people engage in industry or government service. Such conclusions would be inaccurate because the great majority of the population are farmers and live in barrios or settlements of usually not over 2,500 persons. A barrio is a geographical unit and may remain on a map even though it may not have any population. There are a number of efforts being made now to balance agriculture with industry, as well as a great amount of discussion of how to attract tourists to the country to bring in more revenue. A recent study may be quoted here to indicate some of the serious economic problems arising from the type of agriculture that is prevalent:

> One of the biggest problems facing the economic development of the country is that agricultural productivity is low, a situation perpetuated by widespread absentee landlordism, inadequate agricultural credit facilities for the peasant, and tenant farming by about 50 per cent of the agricultural population. Land ownership is heavily concentrated—about five landowners on an average owning more than 30 per cent of the total farming area—while at the same time, farms are generally small.[2]

The extended, as contrasted with the nuclear, family is basic to the social and economic life of the Philippines.[3] Women share equality with men, they

---

[1] A good brief account of the items mentioned above, and several others, may be found in Arthur L. Carson, *Higher Education in the Philippines* (Washington, D.C., U.S. Department of Health, Education, and Welfare, Office of Education, Bulletin 1961), No. 29, Chaps. I and II. The author was president of Silliman University, Dumaguete City, for many years and a leader in Philippine higher education.

[2] *Higher Education and Development in South-East Asia,* Vol. 2, "Country Profiles" (Paris, UNESCO and the International Association of Universities, 1967), p. 544.

[3] An excellent brief summary of the family and general social structure is found in Fred Eggan, "Philippine Social Structure," pp. 1-49 in George M. Guthrie (ed.), *Six Perspectives on the Philippines* (Manila, Bookmark, 1968).

usually control the family's finances, and they prepare for and engage in all the professions as well as in occupations more traditionally for women. Women are far more numerous than men as teachers in the elementary and secondary schools.[4] They constitute more than 50 per cent of the enrollment in higher education and more than 65 per cent of the small graduate enrollment, making the Philippines unique in both respects.[5]

## BEGINNINGS OF HIGHER EDUCATION

Although the University of San Carlos, in Cebu City, can trace its origin back to 1595, the oldest continuing institution of higher learning is the University of Santo Tomas, in Manila. This goes back to 1611 and was raised to university rank by a papal order in 1645; it became a royal university in 1785 and was named a pontifical university in 1902.[6] The head of this institution is still called "Rector Magnificus of the Royal and Pontifical University of Santo Tomas." The Jesuits began educational work in Manila early in the seventeenth century, but they were forced to leave the country in 1768 to return in 1859 and begin what came to be called the Ateneo de Manila. Later they opened other institutions.[7] Higher education was reserved to male members of Spanish families but girls had opportunities in convent schools.[8] Later political periods were characterized by other educational undertakings but the current system is based on the present Constitution and subsequent Congressional acts and administrative and executive orders.

## THE PRESENT SYSTEM

The Constitution provides, in Article XIV, Section 5, that:

All educational institutions shall be under the supervision of, and subject to, regulation by the State. The government shall establish and maintain a complete and adequate system of public education, and shall provide at least free public primary instruction and citizenship training to adult citizens. All schools shall aim to develop moral character, personal discipline, civic conscience, and vocational efficiency, and to teach the duties of citizenship. Optional religious instruction shall be maintained in the public schools as now authorized by law. Universities established by the State shall enjoy academic freedom. The State shall create scholarships in arts, science, and letters for especially gifted citizens.[9]

---

[4] *Higher Education and Development in South-East Asia, op. cit.,* p. 545.

[5] *Ibid.,* pp. 563-564.

[6] Carson, *op. cit.,* pp. 31-32.

[7] *Ibid.,* p. 33.

[8] *Ibid.,* p. 30.

[9] *Constitution of the Philippines,* Article XIV, Section 5.

The system of schools developed to achieve the objectives stated above consists of a six-year elementary school divided into four years of primary grades and two of intermediate, a four-year secondary school, and a four-year program for the first degree in arts or science. There are programs lasting two years for associate diplomas and there are other special diplomas earned in one to three years. Medicine ordinarily requires four years beyond a premedical program, engineering degrees may be obtained in five years, and law requires four years beyond the first bachelor's degree. There are some instances of seven-year elementary schools which were a requirement in 1953, but the law has not been put into effect generally. Also, the increase in enrollments in the elementary schools has led to the practice of double sessions. Thus, the Philippines has a ten-year pre-university program rather than the twelve-year program common in many other countries.

The highly centralized administration of the school system is headed by a secretary of education in charge of the Department of Education, and there is a Board of National Education consisting of 16 members. All public and private schools are supervised by the Department of Education but state institutions which have their own boards of regents or trustees enjoy some independence. Otherwise, the state exercises control over practically all detailed items of school operation. The supervision and control is operative through three bureaus: public schools, private schools, and vocational education. In recent years the private colleges and universities have begun voluntary co-operative efforts to improve their institutions through such organizations as the Philippine Association of Colleges and Universities (P.A.C.U.), and the Philippine Accrediting Association of Schools, Colleges and Universities (P.A.A.S.C.U.). The National Science Development Board (N.S.D.B.) was established in 1958 to advance science and science education and has broad powers and receives and distributes monies in accord with its interests and responsibilities.

The magnitude of higher education in the country is indicated by a few items of statistical data. In 1965-66 there were 5,551,310 pupils reported enrolled in public elementary schools; 348,816 enrolled in public general secondary schools, as of May, 1966; and at the same time, 8,899 enrolled at the third level of public education (collegiate or normal). By grades in public schools these are broken down as follows: Grade I—1,344,381; Grade II—1,130,802; Grade III—1,014,991; Grade IV—860,751; Grade V—668,480; Grade VI—530,662, and Grade VII—1,243.

The dramatic drop in enrollment in Grades IV and V and the failure to restore Grade VII in most schools are evident from the above statistics. The percentage of pupils two years or more above the normal age for each grade is given as follows: Grade I, 15.98 per cent; Grade II, 19.42; Grade III, 22.7;

Grade IV, 23.51; Grade V, 20.24 per cent. The national government expenditures by departments, in 1966, indicate that 28.60 per cent of total expenditures was for the Department of Education which was, by far, the largest single item for all departments and for individual public educational institutions.[10] The breakdown of the total Department of Education operating expenses for 1966 indicates that 94.03 per cent were attributable to the Bureau of Public Schools, 0.24 to the Bureau of Private Schools; and 5.22 per cent to the Bureau of Vocational Education.[11] On the other hand, data released by the Bureau of Private Schools—although many schools did not submit their data—indicate the following for 1966-67:[12] Total elementary private schools enrollment—280,069; total secondary private schools enrollment—784,587; total collegiate enrollment—492,652; enrollment in 27 private universities—340,414, master's applicants—9,061, and doctoral applicants—223.

Thus, it is evident that the government schools are carrying the burden for the greater part of elementary education but the reverse is true on the secondary and higher levels. This makes the educational picture in the Philippines unique not only in Southeast Asia but anywhere else in the world. The statistical data available, however, come from various sources and are not entirely complete or dependable. Thus, it is said that in 1964-65 the total enrollment in state institutions on the tertiary level, including universities, and agricultural and vocational schools, was 59,960, while that in the private sector (universities, colleges, and vocational and agricultural schools) was 412,028.[13] For approval as a university, an institution must have a four-year undergraduate college of arts and sciences and an approved graduate program leading to the master's degree in arts and sciences or education. Also, approved universities must have at least three professional colleges, at least one of which must be in technology, agriculture or medicine, and must have a library of at least 10,000 bound volumes of collegiate books. The qualifications of administrators, faculty and the financial structure of the institutions are scrutinized before recognition is given to universities. Although the Department of Education has declared it does not aim to make all institutions conform to a set

---

10 *1966 Statistical Bulletin,* Research, Evaluation and Guidance Division, Bureau of Public Schools (Manila, August, 1968), pp. 2, 3, 8, and 81.

11 *Ibid.,* p. 55.

12 *Statistical Bulletin, 1966-1967,* Division of Evaluation, Research and Statistics, Bureau of Private Schools, Manila, pp. 2, 4, 5, 50-51.

13 Brother Andrew Gonzalez, "Private Institutions of Higher Learning and Manpower Development in the Philippines," Association of Southeast Asian Institutions of Higher Learning, *Goals for Southeast Asian Universities: A Seminar Report,* ASAIHL Report 1/1968 (Bangkok, Thailand), p. 46.

pattern, there is frequent friction between the private institutions and the Department.[14] But a detailed and careful supervision of many of the private institutions is necessary because so many of them are proprietary institutions, often conducted by families, as stock corporations for profit. The size of this sector in higher education can probably be found in no other country in the world.

## HIGHER EDUCATION AND MANPOWER NEEDS

As Hunter points out, the economy and society of the Philippines are quite unlike those of other Southeast Asian countries, both in content and especially in atmosphere and attitudes. Despite large governmental expenditures in education and social welfare, the economy is essentially capitalist. There is neither a planned nor a socialist atmosphere, thus having many characteristics comparable to pre-war United States. And yet, despite huge capitalist enterprises, the population is largely agricultural with many families and individuals living constantly near the starvation level.[15]

With much of higher education in the hands of entrepreneurs who conduct numerous educational institutions as business enterprises, there is an extremely high enrollment in courses and programs that have high prestige value but which many of their students will never enter, or enter for a relatively short time, or enter when they become emigrants to a foreign country. This latter phenomenon is particularly present in the brain drain of Filipino physicians and nurses to the United States, Canada, Germany, and other countries.

Even among those of the population who remain in the country, there is a high degree of unemployment and underemployment, especially in agriculture. "Full employment" was defined by the First Management-Educators' Conference in 1959 as follows:

> *Qualitatively,* it is that state of the economy whereby all persons desiring to work are able to find employment within a reasonable time at prevailing working hours, rates of payment, working conditions and in positions reasonably in line with their aptitudes, abilities and occupational interests.
>
> *Quantitatively,* it is that state of the economy whereby 96 or 97 per cent of the labor force is employed at prevailing rates of pay, hours of work and working conditions and at positions reasonably in line with their aptitudes, abilities and occupational interests.[16]

---

[14] *Higher Education and Development in South-East Asia, op. cit.,* pp. 553-554; 571-577.

[15] Guy Hunter, *Higher Education and Development in South-East Asia,* Vol. III, Part I, *High-Level Manpower, op. cit.,* p. 171.

[16] Quoted by Eleuterio Adevoso in *Philippine Education: A Forward Look,* Proceedings, General Resolutions, and Working Papers of the First National Conference on Education (Manila, 1965), pp. 117-118.

At the conference mentioned, Adevoso indicated that, in order to attain the concept of full employment, unemployment and underemployment would have to be reduced by five per cent.[17] It should be noted that in statistical data on employment and unemployment in the Philippines the beginning age used is that of 10 years, which corresponds quite exactly to the age at which a large number of pupils leave school forever.

At the same time, it must be said that it would be difficult to find another country in which the prestige value of a college or university degree or diploma is higher than in the Philippines. Individuals and their families with little income spend extraordinary amounts of money to obtain the highly valued symbols of advanced education. The products of the professional schools who must take external examinations frequently fail the examinations (even though they often enroll in special review courses to prepare for them), but if they pass there is a very high value attached to being called "engineer," "architect," "attorney," or "doctor." It has been observed, to take but one illustration, that in 1962, less than six per cent of the 4,600 graduates of law passed the bar examination that would admit them to practice their profession.[18] Such miseducation must lead to great personal frustration and, nationally, to enormous educational wastage. Similarly, when many students who have "gone through" an engineering program locate in less than professional careers, they may become ill-prepared technicians or, worse still, not even prepared as technicians. It is also common knowledge that good science teaching is seldom found in the secondary schools or in the third-level institutions. Some efforts to ameliorate this situation, such as the establishment of the N.S.D.B. have already been mentioned, but much more is necessary before the healing arts and the industrial development of the nation can have a sound scientific base. Of course, sociological factors are also involved: it is difficult to attract a scientist or physician to an isolated rural location where he would not find a milieu conducive to his vocational practice and his personal fulfillment. It is said that at least 60 per cent of the Filipinos never see a physician, nor will they until the economic, social and cultural levels of the nonurban areas of the country are raised. Also, the programs for the development of professional workers must include provision for the specifics required in the nation. An example of failure to do this is found in the absence of study of earthquakes and the necessary consequential technological adjustments in training engineers in a country that periodically suffers from earthquake phenomena.

A large increase of institutions somewhat comparable to the "land grant" colleges in the United States and also of junior colleges which would be

---

[17] *Ibid.*, p. 119.
[18] Hunter, *op. cit.*, p. 176.

especially intended to develop lower level technical skilled manpower, but not omitting the cultural and humane values necessary for all men in contemporary society, would seem to be highly desirable in the Philippines now and in the foreseeable future. A source previously quoted pointed out that the higher institutions of the country are producing too many teachers and too many graduates in business, liberal arts, and law but not enough in agriculture and engineering:

> Thus, there is an over-supply of college graduates aiming for high-level positions as top administrators, managers, technologists and professionals, and a serious lack of manpower for lower-level positions as accountants, senior clerks, small businessmen, supervisors of industrial plants.

> Actually, by process of elimination, graduates with Bachelor's degrees but talents, unable to qualify for high-level-positions, end up taking jobs on lower scales of the manpower hierarchy, even as junior clerks, and cashiers, but rarely as craftsmen.[19]

### HIGHER EDUCATION AND RESEARCH

Statistics given previously indicate only a small number of students engaged in graduate as compared with undergraduate work. This fact, in turn, would indicate that much, if not most or all, of the time of faculty members is consumed by teaching activities. In the situation in which the Philippines finds itself today, the colleges and universities are hard-pressed even to find enough faculty members to teach the large enrollments in undergraduate programs. Even to solve this problem, persons are often accepted as faculty members who do not fully satisfy the requirements for their positions. Practically all the institutions of higher education are dependent upon either government grants or student fees and neither category is sufficient to allow the universities to carry on all the activities they might wish. Research generally lags for lack of both resources and sufficiently qualified faculty persons on the one side, and lack of sufficient preparation and motivation on the part of the students. There seems to be inherent in the circle of Philippine higher education very high loads of teaching by the faculty and study by the students. Much of the graduate work is done on a part-time basis, either in evening classes or summer courses, or a combination of both.

Despite all these difficulties, Philippine universities struggle to make some provision for basic and applied research. Some is done by releasing faculty members to do their advanced work abroad, either in Europe or the United

---

[19] Gonzalez, *op. cit.*, p. 48.

States, and some of it has been made possible by outside support from, for example, American philanthropic foundations and grants from some European countries, especially Germany. Thus, the most spectacular research undertaking is found in the International Rice Institute funded mainly by American foundations and associated with the University of the Philippines. Below the level of this huge undertaking, there are innumerable small research projects being done in many institutions. Some of these are not in full-fledged universities but, for example, language research as found in the Philippine Normal College. Similar research undertakings are found in smaller agricultural and engineering projects. But, in addition to research related to more immediate use in the practical order, there is a good amount of research going on that springs from even more immediate sources, rather than merely a desire to know. Thus, considerable study has been made on Filipino family structure, Filipino value systems, and similar anthropological and sociological investigations. What would be called a type of "action research" in teaching is specifically named in Congressional legislation as a field of investigation quite proper in Philippine universities.[20] There are some instances where faculty persons are appointed as only research professors, but such are rare. And foreseeable future enrollments at undergraduate levels would seem to indicate that perhaps less, rather than more, research will characterize the work of the universities.

There are at least two viable, and perhaps necessary, steps that may be taken by colleges and universities in their responsibilities toward scholarly research. First, these institutions that have not yet done so should carefully scrutinize themselves, their situations, resources, untapped sources of faculty members and support, and then determine specifically their objectives. In such a process, these institutions may well exclude some of their present programs and activities. But what they decide to do should become much more clear and specific.

Secondly, just as has been done in a number of instances in the United States, several institutions may be able to establish one or another kind of consortium that will make it possible for institutions to avoid the attempt to offer too many programs but will, at the same time, permit cross-registration of students in two or more institutions to enable them to obtain the course work they desire but which may not be available in their college of original registration. This kind of co-operation is already available on a small scale, involving a small number of institutions, but it has possibilities of wider acceptance.

There appears to be rather common agreement among persons in higher education that both good teaching and good research should be found in col-

---

[20] Republic Act No. 4670.

leges and universities. Scarcity of trained and dedicated manpower and a dearth of sufficient funds to provide for both have impeded their implementation in many institutions. Many faculty persons who have gone abroad for their highest degrees have either never returned to their home country or, if they have returned, have left the universities and gone into more remunerative occupations. There is no one easy solution to this problem because of the dearth of full doctoral programs within the country and the general poverty of the nation, poverty that makes it difficult to keep open all the public elementary schools and retain their pupils sufficiently long enough. On the level of higher education, in which there is so much private enterprise, the profit-making institutions must pay a 10 per cent income tax, a donations tax, and heavy duties on imported educational equipment and materials.[21] Scarcely any leader in Philippine higher education would today argue that the universities have no responsibility for research, as did Cardinal Newman in nineteenth-century England, but the essential resources, the proper balance between teaching and research, and the most necessary research in the country today are all questions that do not receive a common answer.

### STUDENT ACTIVITY AND ATTITUDES

Most students of the Filipine people agree that the typical Filipino is polite, courteous, and friendly. This seems to be true for the students as well as the general population. But higher education in this country has had a share of the international dissatisfaction and disaffection of students. In the Philippines it was more prevalent in the Manila area than elsewhere but some appeared in other locations also. In late 1968 and early 1969 there were student demonstrations, sit-ins, strikes, and occasionally destruction of property of the institutions of higher learning. The demands of student groups were very similar to those in other parts of the world but, in the case of the Philippines, because of the prevalence of educational institutions run for profit, there was often a strong emphasis on what the students called high fees for tuition and other expenses. Most student confrontations with the administrators and faculty likewise included demands for better teaching and student involvement in decision making in the formulation of degree requirements, and in administration of student discipline. The prestige colleges and universities tend to be concentrated in the Manila area but they and most of the other institutions either offer scholarship aid to deserving students or have programs by which students can work off part of their financial obligations to the institutions. At the present time bills have been introduced into Congress providing for loans

---

[21] "Country Profiles," *op. cit.,* p. 572.

for poor but deserving students that will be paid off by the students when they begin to work.

In the midst of the student demonstrations, President Ferdinand Marcos issued an executive order that outlined student rights and responsibilities. The order is long and covers practically all the items that prompted student protests. Among the rights specified for students are the following: the right of admission to any college or university if the student meets the academic requirements and reasonable regulations adopted by the institution with the approval of the Department of Education; the right to be informed before admission of the policies, rules, and regulations of the institutions and fees connected with university activities; the right to be heard or to propose school policies; the right to due process; the right to organize a free student government; the use of campus facilities for student organizations; the right to hear speakers chosen by student organizations; the right to publish in campus organs without prior administrative or faculty censorship, provided that the publication expenses come from student funds; and the right to competent instruction. There are correlative responsibilities of students spelled out in the executive order.[22] In the Senate of the Congress a bill has been introduced—though not yet passed—that provides for a "Magna Carta for Students." This contains essentially the same rights and responsibilities for students as already are in effect through the promulgation of the executive order of the President.

## FINANCIAL NEEDS OF UNIVERSITIES

As pointed out earlier in this paper, the national government is spending, comparatively, a very large part of its total expenditure upon public education. But the needs for education and educational expansion on the levels of elementary and secondary schools are so great that there is little earmarked for higher education. Even in the University of the Philippines, the oldest and most prestigious of the state institutions of higher learning, a beginning liberal arts student would pay in tuition and fees approximately 199.00 pesos. (A peso is worth approximately 25 cents in United States money at the present rate of exchange.)[23] A comparable student in the most expensive private university in the country would be charged approximately 512.00 pesos. Faculty salaries are generally so low that it is a common practice for a faculty person to teach in more than one institution in the same year or to have teaching as one occupation and some other position as a second source of income. Many of the professional schools have faculties composed largely of

---

[22] Executive Order No. 170, "Promulgating the Manual of Student Rights and Responsibilities," February 15, 1969.

[23] University of San Carlos, *University Bulletin,* February 21, 1969.

part-time teachers. Although some contact with one's profession should be continued by teachers in that field, it may be questioned that the best professional education is possible when a majority of the faculty members are not full-time teachers. Mention should also be made of the very common practice in the Philippines of both husband and wife working, often in professional careers. Thus, there are many married women teaching in Philippine colleges and universities, their husbands often also teaching in the same institution or in another nearby, or engaging in a different occupation. Not only are faculty salaries low, but there is also, as is common in developing nations, little revenue available to colleges and universities to develop adequate libraries or to purchase expensive equipment for the laboratories. Even with some equipment being available, it is often not usable for long periods of time because of such handicaps as water shortage, low or interrupted electrical voltage, or breakdown of equipment which cannot be repaired in the country because of lack of skilled technicians. To offset these disadvantages, many universities have done remarkably well in having faculty members and students invent and make their own equipment for laboratory exercises. Such equipment may not be as sophisticated in design or structure as would be found in some other countries but it may be just as useful from the scientific point of view and even more valuable because the making of it has been a true educative experience. Nonetheless, this last statement should not be taken to mean that the colleges and universities in the Philippines are not in need of library books and laboratory facilities and equipment. In this regard the various foundations are giving substantial assistance but more is needed, provided the faculty will have the expertise to use equipment properly.

An illustration of costs for faculty is found in the case of Mindanao State University, the second full-fledged national university, which was opened in 1961. Since the university is located in an isolated area that has few cultural advantages, the University has endeavored to make its salaries and fringe benefits as attractive as possible, and the national government seems to be willing to support the institution rather generously. The university administration has based its salary scale on that obtaining in the University of the Philippines. In 1967 the salary levels in the two universities were as follows:

|  | Instructor | Asst. Prof. I | Asso. Prof. II | Prof. III |
|---|---|---|---|---|
| M.S.U. pesos | 3,432 | 4,632 | 6,540 | 9,300 |
| U.P. pesos | 5,880 | 8,400 | 11,580 | 15,660[24] |

The statement was made at the time of this study that the University of the

---

[24] Charles W. Hagen, Jr., "Faculty Development at Mindanao State University" (mimeographed), a study done for Educational Projects, Inc., Nov. 4, 1967, p. 32.

Philippines planned to increase its salaries by 10 per cent each year.[25] And the salary scale for Mindanao State University has been said to have ranged in 1968 from 4,623 pesos for the lowest grade instructor to 18,000 pesos for a research professor and 20,000 for a university professor.[26] A projection of student enrollment and consequent faculty needs for 1969-74 was made by the university in 1969 but this did not include projected salary ranges.[27] An example of faculty salaries taken from a private university that does not have the resources of the two state universities mentioned indicates a salary plan based on the number of teaching hours per week of the faculty members. Here the range is from 4.20 pesos to 9.00 pesos per hour of teaching, from first level of instructor to full professor.[28] Most faculty members would have a teaching schedule of approximately 18 hours, on the average.

Many of the Philippine colleges and universities have large numbers of faculty members who are of other nationalities than Filipino, such as members of Catholic religious orders who are numerous in the only Asiatic country that is largely Catholic in population, Fulbright-Hayes scholars, United States Peace Corps members, British Volunteers, and similar teachers of foreign origin and, usually, educated in foreign countries. These teachers from foreign countries constitute a substantial contribution to a developing nation. Even native Filipinos often receive their advanced training in either the United States or in Europe because advanced graduate programs are in their infancy in their own country. It will be a long time before the colleges and universities in the Philippines will be able to staff their institutions with teachers trained in their own country. There are, of course, many problems connected with so much dependence upon foreign preparation. Many who go abroad for their advanced education never return home, many are educated away from the traditional mores and value systems of their own country, and, in any event, it is a very costly program. Most Philippine colleges and universities will be happy to settle for a number of years to come with the majority of their faculties having the master's degree and only a few with the doctorate.

### CULTURAL RELATIONSHIPS

Inasmuch as so many of the teaching faculties in Philippine universities have had much of their higher education in other countries, there has arisen

---

[25] *Ibid.*

[26] Antonio Isidro, *Muslim-Christian Integration at the Mindanao State University,* University Research Center, Mindanao State University, Marawi City, 1968, p. 224.

[27] "Faculty Development Plan of the Mindanao State University: 1969-1974" (mimeographed), Marawi City, Philippines, March 3, 1969.

[28] University of San Carlos, *University Bulletin,* February 21, 1969.

a whole series of contacts and association with other nations and other cultures. After centuries of Spanish domination of the country, there still remain some strong ties with Spain among a small but influential group of Filipinos. And Spanish still remains as a required subject in the colleges and universities. The Chinese influence came early, as was mentioned previously in this paper; and the Chinese remain strong in mercantile establishments and there are a number of Chinese schools. The American occupation brought English as a language for government, business, and culture, as well as notions of a democratically organized government. The continuation of American military bases until the present time creates some ambivalent attitudes among Filipinos; they are keenly desirous of political independence but the Vietnam War is not far away and the government has eschewed war as a method of solving international problems. The sad and bitter memory of the Japanese occupation lingers among many of the older generation. The Muslims in the southern provinces often regard the government as foreign to their way of life and Mindanao State University was established primarily as a way of bringing this cultural minority into the mainstream of Philippine life. Native arts such as singing and the dance have been rediscovered and developed, and some dance groups have gone abroad and have been very well received. Crafts have been encouraged by the development by the government of what are referred to as the "cottage industries." The Philippines is a member of SEATO and there is today a strong tendency to look toward the other Asian countries. But the relations, political, economic, social, and cultural, are still strong with both the United States and Europe. The Philippines has the largest number of institutional members in the Association of Southeast Asian Institutions of Higher Learning, but then there are more such institutions in the Philippines than in any other country.

In a book published in 1963 by the American Universities Field Staff, entitled *Expectant Peoples: Nationalism and Development,*[29] the chapter devoted to the Philippines is headed "The Spoils of Nationalism: The Philippines." This was written by Albert Ravenholt, who had been correspondent in the Philippines and other parts of Asia for many years. It is his observation that if Rizal, a Filipino martyr among the first of the great modern nationalists, were to return to his country at the present time, he would disown much of what is being done in the name of the cause that he championed, because he would see that the struggle that he led with such dedication and disregard of personal sacrifice is being distorted to serve the narrow purposes of privileged individuals and special interests.

---

[29] American Universities Field Staff, *Expectant Peoples: Nationalism and Development* (New York, 1963).

CONCLUSION

In a paper read by Dr. Carlos P. Romulo, then president of the University of the Philippines, now president emeritus of the University and secretary for foreign affairs, at the First National Conference on Education in December 1964, he called for a "New Challenge and Orientation" in Philippine education. He, of course, concerned himself with the entire range of education, from the primary grades to the most advanced work in the universities. He pointed out that the Philippine system of education was failing both quantitatively and qualitatively. He made an urgent plea for rededication to the tasks of education and especially for national planning for education, particularly since: (1) The current system is failing both to reach a large enough segment of the potential supply of students and to give those who are enrolled a high enough quality of education, and (2) a great increase in enrollments is pending on all levels of education because of the rate of population growth. Regarding the situation of many of the poorly supported schools, including universities, in the private sector, Romulo expressed belief that the national government would have to grant some financial assistance "on a selective basis." As for the ideology motivating his proposed strengthening of Philippine education, he argued for:

> the urgent need to re-focus the minds and hearts of the Filipino youths to the riches and the achievements of their Filipino and their Asian forebears, a change which I have vigorously promoted in the State University and called 'Our New Asian Orientation.' This I feel is absolutely essential if we are to redress the imbalance of centuries in the socialization, the cultural conditioning of the Filipino. There is in this, no intention to turn our backs to world civilization, but instead sharpen our sense of participation in it by reinforcing our claim to a portion as our very own.[30]

Probably any university leader and most political leaders in the Philippines today would agree with these statements. And in no country are educational policies and decisions more dependent upon political processes than in the Philippines.

---

[30] Carlos P. Romulo, "New Challenge and Orientation," in *Philippine Education: A Forward Look, op. cit.,* p. 155.

# TASKS OF UNIVERSITIES IN INDIA

M. V. Mathur

Indian universities occupy today a nodal position in the effort at nation building and social and economic development. On them substantially rests the responsibility for promoting the acquisition of new knowledge and skills for development of physical and human resources, of transforming traditional values and attitudes to build a new society informed by equality and social justice, and of developing a climate for creative thinking and growth of individuality. For a proper appreciation of the role of the universities in the context of contemporary environmental change in India, it is necessary to view the problem from the historical perspective of their overall development.

Modern university education in India began in 1857 when the universities of Calcutta, Bombay and Madras were founded by the British. A fourth university —that of Allahabad—was set up in 1887. Prior to that, higher education in India was organized along traditional lines and covered mostly subjects like theology, indigenous medicine, Sanskrit and Arabic literature, astronomy, mathematics, grammar, rhetorics, law and the like. There was very little teaching of modern science and, therefore, the establishment of these universities, broadly speaking, started the modern education movement. It will be of interest to note that the first three universities established in India were patterned largely after the earlier model of London University. Paradoxically, by that time London University was itself abandoning that model.

The pioneering universities were primarily regulating and examining bodies, and it was much later that they took postgraduate students directly within their orbit. The typical institution of higher learning which thus emerged in India was the university which included a number of affiliated colleges under its wings. The colleges were live educational institutions and increased in number rapidly; they prepared students for degrees from the university with which they were affiliated. The representatives of the affiliated colleges came to the university and discussed the contents of curriculum, the way in which the scripts would be evaluated and, finally, the requirements for the award of degrees. It was only in the beginning of the present century that some thought was devoted to adding teaching to the functions of the universities. A start was made with teaching universities in the 1920's. The new universities provided opportunities for teachers and students to come in closer touch with one another, and they soon became important places for advancement of learning. The development of universities in other countries of South Asia has followed, in the main, a similar pattern.

As the years have gone by, the complexion of universities has changed. India has 76 universities. Of these, 24 are of the teaching type; and 52 are primarily of the affiliating kind, with a modicum of teaching wings. The affiliating functions in most cases overshadow the teaching role. It deserves to be emphasized that the predominantly affiliating character of Indian universities is normally not found in many other parts of the world. Even today, most teachers do not participate in the formulation of curricula. Nor are most of them involved in setting the examinations for their students. This has given rise to several difficult and complex problems.

Unfortunately, it is not uncommon in India to ascribe all the ills of the country to the British rule. It needs to be recognized that British rule in India brought in its wake several distinct advantages also. The country was knit into one entity through the development of communications and transport. One language, *i.e.,* English, became the generally accepted language of the intelligentsia, though even today it is understood by less than 1.5 per cent of the people. It has opened to them the doors to knowledge of modern science and art, and provided an important means of promoting unity of outlook among members of diverse religious and ethnic groups. Another significant contribution made by the British was the creation and consolidation of an organized civil service. It was partly to prepare Indians for the civil services that the universities were originally organized. If one were to look into the records, it would be found that the officers of the East India Company felt at first that the teaching should be done in the Indian languages, but some of the Indians themselves thought otherwise. They said "no," because by learning through their own language they did not expect to become recognized members of the new intellectual elite which was emerging. Today, however, it is generally accepted that the Indian languages should become the media of higher instruction. There is a strong movement for the changeover, which is obviously essential to accelerate the process of growth and fulfillment of the various sections of Indian society. But the needs of the people in the second half of the last century were different.

Later, the British also thought that they should develop a class of people who would understand English and thereby be able to assist them in carrying on the administration of the country. The Indian Civil Service was an elite service, very well organized, and well equipped to maintain law and order and other traditional functions of administration, and over the period the proportion of Indians in this service increased. The existing members of the I.C.S. and of its successor, the Indian Administrative Service (I.A.S.), have, in addition, been involved progressively in developmental administration. The British also built up a network of junior and middle level services. The civil service system bequeathed by the British has in several respects stood the test of time, and has lent stability and continuity to administration of the country.

The environmental context in which the Indian society operates today is much different from what it was during the 90 years (1857-1947) of rule by the British Crown, which witnessed the establishment of 19 universities in all. On the side of political organization, the country accepted the parliamentary form of democracy, a form of government which took even England, its birthplace, a few centuries to establish fully with adult franchise. Notwithstanding experiments during the British rule with limited franchise, a measure of local self-government and the association of the people's representatives in administration of subjects like education, health and labor, India's adoption of adult franchise in 1950 on a country-wide basis and its institution of the parliamentary form of democratic government were big leaps forward. I regard parliamentary democracy as the best form of democracy; at the same time, I regard it as the most difficult form of democracy. We accepted something which was really good, but very difficult to practice. I think that India's acceptance of Great Britain's model of parliamentary government is a great tribute to Britain on the part of Indians.

Simultaneously, we had to do something on the economic front since we had, in effect, missed the fruits of the first industrial revolution. Around the year 1700 India could not be classed among the underdeveloped countries of the world, but by the year 1800 it had become so, because the industrial revolution had taken place. It is an open question as to what might have happened if India had been a free country at the time of industrial revolution. Maybe we would have moved with the times as was the case in France, Germany and the United States. At any rate, that opportunity was missed. Perhaps the best commentary on it was the report of the Industrial Commission appointed by the British government in 1916 during World War I. It said that the British administration in India had neglected the development of industries. It recommended that a measure of self-reliance in industry was essential for defense purposes as well as economic prosperity. Such a realization led to a policy of protection and aid for indigenous industries, and though some progress was made, particularly during World War II, it was hardly commensurate with the needs of the country and its rapidly growing population. Thus, the second important challenge was how to compress the economic progress, which the rest of the world had achieved in about 150 years or so, within the compass of a few decades. We had also to promote education on a large scale. Traditional social values and attitudes also needed to be reoriented to help facilitate economic growth. We therefore thought of and adopted planning as the chief instrument of economic and social development. But Indians are, by and large, individualists and they could not conceive of exterminating the private sector. Therefore, we adopted a system of mixed economy in which the private sector would be given adequate opportunities to develop to the maximum possible extent.

## II

After 1947, people said, "Now it is our own government, everything has got to be done by the government"; and therefore the increase in facilities for higher education which has come about since then has predominantly been with governmental support. Again, one of the best vote-catching devices on the part of any politician is to promise to the people of his constituency that there will be a degree college in that area. Moreover, with the spread of political awakening, the demand among the people for better education has mounted. This double process has brought about a significant increase in the number of universities in the last two decades. There were 19 universities in 1947 on the eve of independence, the nineteenth being the one with which I have been associated for many years in various capacities—as a teacher, head of the department of economics and public administration, and later as its vice-chancellor (*i.e.*, President). The number of universities rose to 38 in 1957 and reached 76 in the beginning of 1969.[1] Several of the new universities have both affiliating and teaching functions. But interestingly enough, even today neither Calcutta nor Bombay nor Madras has any undergraduate students directly under its own faculty. They have postgraduate and research students but no undergraduates; the undergraduates belonging to these universities are all in affiliated colleges.

In addition, there are 10[2] institutions of higher learning which are deemed to be universities. These include Jamia Millia Islamia which is a nationalist university. Its founder was the late Dr. Zakir Hussain, who subsequently became the President of India. Similarly, we also have Kashi Vidapith which was founded in 1921 at Banaras, and Gujarat Vidyapith which was set up by Mahatma Gandhi at Ahmedabad. The latter two were organized during the time of the Indian nationalist movement when the leaders urged the boycott of the official universities and sought to train their followers and educate the people through new institutions. These, however, did not grow or develop to any significant measure. But they are good for certain branches of learning. There are also some other institutions like the Indian Institute of Science (Bangalore); Indian Agricultural Research Institute (New Delhi); Tata In-

---

[1] It has since risen and is presently 82 (in November 1970).

[2] This number is now nine; the Indian School of International Studies has become a part of the Jawaharlal Nehru University, New Delhi (1970).

stitute of Social Sciences (Bombay); Birla Institute of Technology and Science (Pilani) and the like.

Besides the universities and "Deemed Universities," there are five Indian institutes of technology at Kharagpur, Bombay, Madras, Kanpur and New Delhi, and two all-India institutes of medical sciences at New Delhi and Ghandigarh which form a part of the university system in India. Apart from the proliferation in the number of universities, there has also been a tremendous growth in the number of colleges and students. Today, India has about 3,000 colleges, compared to about 700 in 1950-51. The enrollment of students in universities and colleges rose from about 200,000 in 1947 to over 2,400,000 in 1968-69. The number of teaching staff has increased to 110,000. The phenomenal increase in educational facilities has created several problems and tensions. India has, today, the third largest university system in the world, next only to the U.S.A. and the U.S.S.R. But if we also take into account primary and secondary education, then we have in our educational pipeline more than 70 million students, the largest among UNESCO-member nations. It also deserves to be noted that the per capita income in India is virtually one of the lowest in the world. We have created ever-increasing aspirations in the minds of our people. Our constitution-makers expected us to provide free and compulsory education up to the age of 14 by 1960; however, we have not been able to achieve this as yet. In the Education Commission, where we were required to answer this problem, we felt that we would have to go slow. We might be able to attain this goal by 1985. Thus, if everything goes well, we would be about one generation behind. But if everything does not go well, it may be delayed further.

At the level of higher education today, a difficult situation has arisen—the number of entrants is now equal to what prior to independence was the total number of students in higher education. Every year we are adding over 200,000 students to our colleges and universities, as is shown in the following table:

Higher Education: Student Enrollment 1964-65 to 1968-69

| Year | Total[3] enrollment | Increase over preceding year | Percentage Increase |
|---|---|---|---|
| 1964-65 | 1,528,227 | 143,530 | 10.4 |
| 1965-66 | 1,728,773 | 200,546 | 13.1 |
| 1966-67 | 1,949,012 | 220,239 | 12.7 |
| 1967-68 | 2,218,927 | 269,960 | 13.9 |
| 1968-69 | 2,473,264 | 254,292 | 11.5 |

---

[3] Inclusive of the enrollment in intermediate classes under the Boards of Intermediate Education. The enrollment in 1968-69 in the university departments and colleges main-

This large increase in number, unsupported by a commensurate increase in resources, has tended to reduce the quality of education and has intensified the problem of educational unemployment. Is this true higher education? Does our higher education system prepare the students to eke out a living? Does it enrich their minds to be useful members of the society? Do we have adequate resources in men and materials to make the system really tick? These are the questions which one must ask. I shall try to discuss these issues a bit later.

III

In the changed environmental context since independence, the nature and scale of problems of university education have altered considerably. There is growing discontent in the student community, stemming from several causes. The explosion of numbers has placed a great burden on the facilities even though these are much larger than before. In the case of science colleges, colleges of technology and so forth, the people have accepted a ceiling on admissions because they see a visible connection between the resources and equipment that are necessary for the teaching of these subjects and the number of students admitted. But there is no such obvious limit on admission to arts and commerce subjects. As a result, we have colleges which do not even have sufficient books in their libraries. The student is too poor to afford books for himself. But still he is keen to get a university degree, because without it he sees very little prospects for himself.

In England, we have been told that once a person is admitted to the university, everything is virtually paid for by the state. This is usually not the case in India. There are only a limited number of freeships and scholarships. A large number of university and college students find it difficult to afford the minimum desirable facilities for boarding and lodging. One can readily visualize the hardship that they must undergo and the strenuous effort they must exert.

In a popular democracy you cannot deny the people their reasonable demands. All the same, you cannot allow people to go in for college education on a massive scale without ensuring that it will equip them well to earn a livelihood. Of the 2,400,000 students today, about 2,250,000 are engaged in undergraduate studies and about 150,000 are postgraduate students and research scholars. It is the former class which is largely responsible for student unrest.

The challenge of relating education to employment opportunities is a for-

---

tained directly by universities was 278,030. About 86.7% of the total enrollment was in the affiliated colleges.

´Source: *Education in Universities in India,* Ministry of Education and Youth Services, and *University Development in India—Basic facts and figures,* U.G.C., 1970.

midable one and delay cannot be brooked. What should a university degree-holder do, who, after knocking about here and there for a job, is unable to get employment? I know an old classmate of mine whose son has obtained a degree in engineering. Though he took the degree in March or April, 1968, he has been unable to get employment till now. Since he is my personal friend, he has written to me about it from time to time but I do not know what I can do for him. There are thousands of young people of that kind. They have started to challenge the very basis of the society we created in 1947. As I said earlier, we have set for ourselves most difficult goals on all sides—political, economic and social. But we have devoted little attention to modifying our systems and procedures to meet the requirements of these ambitious goals. Employment in government in our country carries great prestige. Most of our clerks, stenographers and typists are males, and these, in most cases, I think, are either third- or second-class graduates; quite a few of them are in science. While we have spent money to train them as science graduates, the only thing they are doing is typing. We can even find a number of persons with M.Sc. degrees in zoology or botany doing no more than writing notes on files. In India, difficulties also arise from the social values attached to intellectual types of work. An educated person generally looks down upon manual labor and would not be inclined to undertake it. In this type of situation, planning for a career is very essential. In a country where jobs are plentiful people can manage even without formal planning, but not in a country like ours.

The fact remains that unless we change the present system suitably, we are bound to face serious problems in the future. Students are graduating in large numbers with bachelor's and even master's degrees, but they are not getting suitable employment. As of today, 32,000 of our qualified engineers are unemployed. Whatever be the reasons for it, the country is not able to find jobs for them. Some of our students find attractive openings outside India. Is it really "brain drain" or does it symbolize a basic malaise in our system?

People like me (I could be classified as radical from that angle) have been suggesting that one of the most significant reforms would be to waive the requirement of a university degree for entry to the prestigious public services. We must detach the prospect of securing a good job in the civil service from the motivation of aspiring to a bachelor's or higher degree. Somewhat on the lines of the cadet system in the army, we should catch the prospective members of the higher civil services at a younger age and at the level of higher secondary school qualifications, thereby obviating the need for a bachelor's degree and preventing the rush to the colleges and universities. Those who are so selected as "probationers" for the civil service can then be put through a course of university education, equivalent to the honors degree level. Thousands of graduates and postgraduates seek good government jobs. They continue their search for such jobs until they pass the age limit of 25 (the maximum permissible for normal initial entry into government service) and then feel disappointed. Very many of these people later on accept clerical jobs. They remain a discontented class throughout their lives because they had aspired and equipped themselves for a much higher career. As it is, our present system first raises the level of their aspirations, then brings them down to earth, and finally keeps them dissatisfied all their lives. No wonder the number of demonstrations and strikes is rising among public employees.

While we should scrap the requirement of a university degree for initial entry to governmental service, we should not in any way discourage people from receiving higher education through all possible means. This would imply that there should be a large increase in the number of evening colleges and correspondence courses. Today, virtually the only method of receiving higher education in India is full-time day education. I think, if you compare the proportion of full-time university students in India with that of other countries having large university systems, India would possibly be at the top, because in the two other countries which have much larger enrollments—the U.S.A. and the U.S.S.R.—the number of part-time students is very high. We have just made a start with the system of evening and correspondence courses. Under this system, the cost per pupil could be considerably lower without loss of efficiency.

Another important consideration which we have to keep in mind in India is that there are vast sections of the Indian community which for various reasons have been denied opportunities of receiving higher education in the past. Whether it was on account of the social system or for political considerations, the fact of life is that these people did not develop and grow. Yet our constitution guarantees to them free higher education. These are the people belonging to what we call "Scheduled Castes" and "Scheduled Tribes." When they go to colleges, they are entitled to full scholarships covering tuition, boarding, lodging and incidental expenses. Reservations are also made for them in the public services. With the extension of these special facilities, many more members of these backward communities are now seeking higher education. Therefore, when we say "Don't open more colleges," this segment complains that the social 'haves' are denying these opportunities to the 'have-nots.' Therefore, we have to remove this feeling from their minds, by enabling them to enter even prestigious governmental employment soon after higher secondary examination.

IV

The affiliated colleges in India, numbering about 3,000, are almost entirely dependent upon the respective universities for their academic structure. It is the university which determines the syllabi and conducts the examinations; only a very small proportion of teachers of the colleges have a hand in these matters.

When the students talk to their teachers about the deficiencies of the syllabi, etc., the teacher says, "What can I do with the syllabus? Somebody else sets it. I cannot change it. I am prepared to give you something else, but I don't know whether this will help you in achieving a passing grade in the examination." Accordingly, it is a very strange type of relationship which exists between most teachers and students in India.

In the university where I have worked as a professor and of which I have also had the privilege of being the vice-chancellor (president), we have about 95 affiliated colleges. In an academic committee of this university—let us say, for economics—there are usually in all about seven persons. Two of these will come from other universities and five from within the university and its affiliated colleges. Thus, most of the teachers responsible for imparting instruction in the subject have very little to say about developing the courses and syllabi. There may be a brilliant teacher in an affiliated college who wants to do something in his own way. Maybe he can achieve it in spite of the system but not within its framework. Even the university teaching department finds it difficult to upgrade its syllabi. The university department head may be keen to go ahead, but others will say, "Look here, we have not provided the needed teaching facilities in other colleges. Therefore, if you do all this, what would happen to other students, because the same common system would have to apply to all." We have, therefore, to find some ways to overcome these difficulties. For example, in economics, unless people know something about mathematical methods, econometrics, etc., they will not have a bright future. But we cannot provide for teaching in these subjects on a compulsory basis everywhere; the necessary facilities for imparting instruction do not exist in every college. Therefore, what we do is to put them under alternate or optional papers. Some of the students in the university teaching departments offer these subjects and these students do extremely well in later life.

There are several difficulties in bringing about basic reforms in regard to the involvement of teachers in academic matters currently handled at the university level. Educational leadership in our country is still not strong enough to wrestle with the vested interests which do not want change. The university and college teachers themselves, for example, do not want a change in the existing system of evaluation, for that would take away their additional earnings accruing from evaluation of scripts. In my university about 15,000 candidates appear in a particular subject in the B.A. examination. Who evaluates the scripts? We have a system whereby for each subject there is a head examiner, an additional head examiner and a number of co-examiners. We remunerate these people for evaluating the answer books. This payment, in terms of American dollars, is a small sum, but in terms of what the individual teachers are able to add to their incomes, it is something which they look forward to. If we decide to have autonomous colleges, this income is likely to disappear. During the past 10 to 15 years, the salaries of teachers have increased as a result of the financial assistance given by the University Grants Commission, which is the central co-ordinating institution for developmental grants to universities. But the increases in salaries have never been linked to any reforms. I would very much prefer to have autonomous colleges with higher salaries for their teachers but without the present supplementary income for evaluation of scripts.

The Education Commission of 1964-66, presided over by Dr. D. S. Kothari, which reported comprehensively on the Indian educational system, recommended *inter alia* that an experiment should be initiated with the granting of autonomy to about 40 to 50 colleges. They should be given complete freedom in setting academic standards, selecting course contents and evaluating performance, the role of the university being confined to the award of degrees only. But as yet not a single autonomous college of this type has emerged.

Broadly speaking, there is hardly any student strife in India unless there are some teachers associated with it directly or indirectly. Therefore, we cannot think of reorienting university administration or management without providing for the participation in the academic matters of the younger teachers who form a vast majority of the total number of the teachers. It is, however, possible to achieve this objective to some extent in an informal fashion. I can say with the pardonable pride that I tried to do so, with some good success, during the past quarter of a century in my own department at my university. As a result, I have come to enjoy the love and affection of my colleagues. My colleagues have not moved to other universities even when chances for internal promotion were lacking, because they feel that they have much better working conditions in our department. During the days of my membership on the Education Commission, one of my colleagues from the Commission, Professor Roger Revelle came out with me to my university. He talked to our students and teachers and said: "You have done a wonderful thing, Professor Mathur. What better could we recommend in the Education Commission?" I replied, "This is something that an individual has been able to do in a small way. It is completely attached to the individual and has yet to be institutionalized and spread more widely."

We require every year about 3,000 university and college lecturers in various subjects. The competition for talent from business and government is quite keen. The private sector in India was perhaps never so prosperous as today. Of course, they always grumble against the government, but they are doing very well. The business world is today attracting many of our bright students by offering them lucrative careers. The government needs very many more educated and talented people today than it has heretofore required. The civil service today is a noble profession, marked by high prestige, even though the salary and allowances for senior positions are lower than the comparable emoluments in the private sector. The opportunities for obtaining higher positions, as well as more lucrative salaries, though limited in the civil service as compared to industry, are still better than those available in university education. We must, therefore, compete against the better opportunities which exist elsewhere for our prospective university teachers.

The tone of teaching in colleges and universities is usually set by the "marginal teacher," who is generally weak in his intellectual equipment. Therefore, something must be done to improve the marginal teacher. A point has already been made that the teacher today must not only reorient and sharpen his knowledge and teaching skill; he must also learn to love his students. Otherwise, there is going to be a great deal of student unrest.

But what are the causes of these difficulties? It is finance which we require to provide them with better libraries, and to improve facilities. If we want better teachers, we find it difficult to attract them because of the stiff competition for talent. Therefore, what I would like to do is to sit with them and ask, "Please tell me what is it that we should do in these circumstances?" If this kind of a dialogue could be started with the students, and also if we spare no effort to do all that we can within our own limitations, the students would try to understand our difficulties and be co-operative. They are not altogether unreasonable people. But this dialogue does not happen very often. Therefore, we should try to create conditions wherein the students and the teachers—younger teachers as well as older—could discuss matters of common concern. I assign great importance to the younger teacher because he is much nearer the students.

Some significant brain drain happens in India because the conditions in our universities are not good for bright young teachers. Many of even those who are not money-minded and who would like to stay in India ultimately decide to go abroad. This is happening because we do not provide good working conditions.

I have been to several countries in the world and I can say with confidence that the good students in India can compare favorably with good students anywhere. That is why when good Indian students go abroad to study at foreign universities, their performance is generally found to be satisfactory. They go abroad because we are not able to provide them with good facilities for specialized higher education. This challenge has got to be met by consciously promoting the development at least of a number of centers of excellence. Accordingly, increasing efforts have been made in India by the University Grants Commission during the past 10 years to develop centers of advanced studies. About 30 of them have already been developed, in natural and social sciences and humanities. These are at the postgraduate and research levels. We also have five institutes of technology, one of them supported by Great Britain, another by West Germany, a third by the U.S.S.R., and a fourth by the U.S.A. The fifth one was originally organized with the aid of UNESCO. These have done a far better job than many other institutions. In the field of medicine, we have two All-India institutes of higher medical education and research.

The centers of advanced studies have also played a useful role in helping to improve the quality of college and university teachers and giving them opportunities for creative work. I believe we also need about a dozen conglomerations of centers of advanced learning. We should, with the support of our own state and central governments, as well as with the help and co-operation of as many friends outside India as possible, concentrate on the development of such outstanding clusters of higher education. If this could be done, it would make a big difference.

V

There is no denying the fact that we need in India a number of reforms and changes in the system of university education and administration to gear it to the needs of the changing environment. In order to improve and expand university education to suit the present and future requirements of the country, two important enquiries at the national level have been made in India since independence. The first enquiry in 1948-49 was restricted to university education. The second enquiry, on which I also served as a member, was made during 1964-66 with a wider perspective, covering general principles and policies for development of education at all stages and in all aspects.

The latter enquiry was made by an Education Commission comprising 16 members. It was presided over by Professor D. S. Kothari and included the following five members from abroad: Professor H. L. Elvin, Director of the Institute of Education, London; Professor Sadatoshi Ihara of Waseda University, Tokyo; Professor Roger Revelle of Harvard University, U.S.A.; Professor M. A. Shumovsky, Director in the Ministry of Higher and Special Secondary Education, R.S.F.S.R., U.S.S.R.; and Mr. Jean Thomas, Inspector General of Education in France and formerly Assistant Director General of UNESCO. The Education Commission made a number of important recommendations and most of them have been accepted by the government of India, and incorporated in the shape of a policy resolution.

In our country, decision making in university education, however, is not centralized at the level of the government of India. If you want to bring about a particular reform at the university level, 17 state governments and 76 autonomous universities must also concur, individually, in the proposal. This does not happen easily.

The amount of money per capita spent in India on education is very small compared to that in the educationally advanced countries. The annual cost of college and university education in India for each student is about Rs. 500/- ($67). But if we take all types of education—primary, secondary and higher—

the annual expenditure per capita is around Rs. 15 ($2). (The corresponding figure for the U.S.A. is $300.) In order to promote the educational effort commensurate with the expanding needs of the country, the Education Commission has recommended a raise in the proportion of G.N.P. allocation from 2.9 per cent in 1965-66 to 6 per cent in 1985-86. This would mean an increase in per capita expenditure on education of all types to about Rs. 52 by 1985. The government of India has in principle agreed to move in this direction.

A substantial improvement in university administration in India can come about only through an enhancement of the capability of the educational administrators. They need to have better orientation not only in administrative and financial management but also in the art of getting the best from their staff and colleagues and in dealing more sympathetically—but still firmly—with the student community. They must also appreciate more the need for participative management in matters both academic and administrative. It is, therefore, of the utmost importance to arrange suitable training and orientation programs for college principals, university registrars and deans and, maybe, even for potential vice-chancellors. In my view, the need for such training is acute given the conditions of India today, and unless we do that, we may not be able to deliver the goods. The institution to which I belong at present, namely, the Asian Institute of Educational Planning and Administration, tries to train first- and second-level educational planners and administrators from various countries of Asia. It is run with UNESCO support. Efforts are being made to build up a similar institution for India—a staff college for educational administrators—and this may serve the needs of university administrators also.

## VI

The future role of universities must also be considered in relation to the broader environmental setting in which they are going to operate. I have already touched upon the need for a basic reorientation in our present practices of linking the entry to the higher civil service to a university degree. The entire policy of university education needs to be related adequately to the challenges which are likely to be posed by rapid growth of population, development of agriculture and industry and other environmental changes.

India today has about 540 million people, and this number is estimated to increase at the rate of around 2.5 per cent during 1970-74. This rate of growth may decline thereafter to about 1.7 per cent in 1980-81. We are experiencing a very large yearly increase in population. The population problem is most difficult—difficult in the sense that it is not just the birth rate which has intensified it. In fact, the birth rate has, of late, tended to decline somewhat. What has happened is that due to the measures that have been taken for improvement of public health etc., the longevity has increased and the death rate has gone down. If we were to intensify family planning measures, it might be possible to reduce the birth rate from 39 per thousand, as of today, to 25 per thousand during the next 10 to 12 years. Education, particularly university education, has a significant role to play in inculcating appropriate values and attitudes among the youth about family planning.

Education can also contribute significantly to accelerating agricultural and industrial development, which holds the key to the solution of the problem of increasing unemployment. Unless we are able to revolutionize our agriculture, we shall not be able to make much headway. At present, many of the university graduates in agriculture do not come from families which own agricultural lands, nor are they willing to go to villages to work on farms. Most of them become officers in the departments of agriculture. Several of them have gone into agricultural extension and community development schemes.

As as result of the use of high-yielding varieties of wheat and maize and increased use of fertilizers, food production has increased substantially in more recent years and we are in the throes of what has been called a "green revolution."

The green revolution is changing the complexion of social and economic power in the rural areas. It is largely the big farmers who can take full advantage of new methods and techniques. The small farmer has little capacity to invest funds in the larger amounts of fertilizers and other physical inputs which are required for high-yielding varieties. It is not easy for him to get loans at cheap rates. Being illiterate, he finds it extremely difficult to understand the procedures and fill in the prescribed forms. As a result, the rich farmer is becoming richer and the poor farmer is staying where he was; the gap between the two is increasing. This is going to cause tremendous social tensions in the countryside where over 80 per cent of the people live. It highlights the need for a rapid extension of primary education in the rural areas so that the poor farmers are able to complete the procedural formalities, understand what the extension worker tells them and read the pamphlets he brings to them. The agriculture extension workers do go to the illiterate farmers and try to help them. But real success will come only when the farmers themselves are functionally literate and trained enough to keep themselves in the vanguard of agricultural progress.

As of today, only about 30 per cent of our population is literate. Thus, you can well imagine what the number would be when everybody comes to school. In the age group of six to eleven—for which we have the statistics—about 75 per cent of the children are going to school. And in certain states or union territories, Delhi for example, this proportion is about 90 per cent. In Kerala, it is over 85 per cent for the age group of 11 to 14 years.

Though about two-thirds of the people in India today may be illiterate, I would hesitate to call them altogether uneducated. Many of them are educated in the true sense of the term—educated in the process of absorbing the cultural and moral traditions of the country. They would be far more afraid of doing a wrong thing than would a university graduate. They would not file a wrong tax return. They like to treat their guests well. Many of the good things which one would wish to impart through education are already present there. Therefore, to say that they are all uneducated would be wrong. But they are certainly illiterate. In order to make them fully literate, they will have to be put through schools and colleges. And when they would then read about world events and come closer to the world community through the mass media, it is likely that their aspirations would rise and that they would seek a change in their vocations. That might create a difficult situation. What then is the solution to the vicious circle of problems in which we are caught today in my country? The new generation which is coming up, is able to look at things more closely and, perhaps, a little more rationally than the older generation. The reason for this is that the older people take certain things for granted. The young people are challenging the old notions and ways. It is, therefore, high time to attune the system of education to the aspirations of the young.

Nobody, obviously, would blame India for choosing in 1950, when our constitution was framed, the kind of political, economic and social goals that it did. They embody the aspirations and desires of our nation. These are, no doubt, most difficult goals and we find ourselves in many difficulties when we set about to achieve them. Since the third general election of 1967, coalition governments, generally weak, have emerged in several states, and they are changing fast. We have perhaps entered an era of political instability. This may have its impact on universities. The chancellor of a university is the governor of the state in which the university is located and it is he who appoints its vice-chancellor. By and large, he is guided in this regard by the advice of the state government, *i.e.,* by the minister of education. Normally, the state government does not come into the picture in determination of the academic curricula. However, the impact of the state government is felt by the universities in the field of finance. Finance is a serious problem in all universities. Virtually all the finances of the universities, apart from tuition fees, come from the government. There are, of course, some other sources of finance such as donations, but these are very limited and are primarily given for capital expenditure and not for operating expenses. Thus, the state government has its say in the running of the universities through the control it exercises on their purses.

Our country is today faced with several formidable challenges, and I strongly feel that the university community should provide leadership to society in meeting them adequately. The university should not only serve the society but also mold it for a richer life for all. By analyzing contemporary problems objectively and impartially, by stimulating broader vision and fresh insights, and by creating a public debate on controversial issues, it can give a new shape and content to national and international thinking. On the formulation of national and world policies it can bring to bear long-range perspectives, which are likely to be forgotten by political leadership engrossed with considerations of a transient character. I am afraid that the universities in India have not performed the latter function to any significant extent. How to make the university community the leader of the society is a really challenging problem and deserves some serious thought in my country as well as in others.

# PART SIX

PART SIX.

# CLOSING REMARKS
## Reflections of a President

## Theodore M. Hesburgh, C.S.C.

In the 25 years that I have been associated with the university, as faculty member and administrator, I can think of no period more difficult than the present. Never before has the university taken on more tasks—and been asked to undertake many more—while the sources of support, both public and private, both moral and financial, seem to be drying up.

In the 314 years from the founding of Harvard until 1950, we grew in the United States to a total capacity of 3 million students in higher education. From 1950 to 1970, that number and capacity more than doubled to over 7 million students. Maybe our traditional ways of governance have not kept pace with our enlarged size and the new mentalities of both faculty and students. Maybe both we in the universities and the world beyond really expected too much of our university operation. We live in a university world of idea and imagination. But these alone will not insure peace, social justice, an end to racism and poverty.

Maybe our growth was too uneven, with the physical sciences getting the lion's share and all the other disciplines emulating the physical sciences' methodology to qualify for a larger share. This was doomed to failure for however attractive the humanities and the social sciences are, they become singularly unattractive once quantified, mathematicized, and unattentive to values. Having sold their birthright, these disciplines found in large measure that the mess of pottage was not forthcoming.

Maybe our problems relate more deeply than we suspect to the parlous state of the world around us—to its basic malaise, to its anomie, to its frustration and rootlessness. I suspect that we are, in the Western world and even beyond its boundaries, passing through an historical watershed which we little understand and which may be ultimately of more importance than the Renaissance, the Reformation, or the Industrial Revolution.

I doubt that anyone would be able to label our age, although it might be called the age of frustrated expectations, the age of protest against almost everything, the age of unlimited possibilities and disappointing results. It is an age that can put men on the moon yet create an impossible traffic tangle in every metropolitan center. It is an age of unbelievable wealth and widespread poverty. It is an age of sensitivity to human dignity and human progress, yet one in which there is relatively little of either, despite the available resources. It is finally an age where the hopes, the expectations and the promises of humanity have been more rhetorical than real. Because the university lives largely by rhetoric, although not by rhetoric alone, it has come to be blamed for much of the frustration. In a very real sense, the university has been oversold as the key to all human progress. There is a wide gulf between the blueprint and the reality, the word and the deed.

Given the actual state of the world around us, we in the university are little comprehended in that all of the world's anxieties are focused strongly in the university where there exists an explosive combination of young, searching minds that are invited daily to view all problems and every variety of response to them and a faculty that is problem-oriented and given to play to the generosity and idealism of youth. Also an administration that is only able to survive by responding positively and emphatically to the aspirations and hopes of faculty and students, however impossible they are of immediate accomplishment.

Into this explosive mix comes a strong cry for "law and order" from the so-called silent majority who are not anxious to face new approaches to human equality or social justice if these threaten their hard-earned gains. When the university responds negatively to this demand for law and order, which it rightly construes as "status quo," and continues to insist on stronger priorities for the nation, new initiatives for peace, for equality, for social justice, whatever the shock to the "status quo," then we have a super-explosive situation. The university is judged to be subversive, it is certainly not understood and it loses more and more of the public and private support that is needed to sustain it.

It is simply an historic fact that any group, and particularly a university community, does not understand not being understood. What is more serious, young people in the university do not realize how much the university depends upon the support of the larger surrounding society. Even less do they understand that when their frustrations about the problems of the larger community lead them to act in anger and, at times, with violence, there is only one normal response from that larger community, namely counter-violence and repressive action. Japanese university students practically closed the principal universities in Japan for a year or so until the Diet passed a law envisioning the permanent closing of some universities, especially Tokyo, the largest. Then suddenly the message was manifest and the violence dropped off.

One might speculate what would happen if some American universities which suffer constant disruption were suddenly closed down for a year or two. It might be healthy and it might be disastrous, but it could happen and it may.

It would have been incomprehensible to mention such a possibility, even speculatively, a decade ago. But it does demonstrate the present state of affairs that it is being mentioned today.

Some have tried to describe the present situation as the politicization of the university. It certainly is true that faculties, even at Harvard and Princeton, have taken rather unanimous positions on the Vietnam War that would have been unthinkable a few years ago. University presidents have also spoken out to an extent that has brought them condemnation from the highest levels of government and from a broad spectrum of alumni and benefactors. Students who were termed apathetic a few years ago are now deeply involved in political lobbying, electioneering for favored candidates, and protesting the actions of other political figures with whom they disagree.

There is some merit in all of this, but some thoughtful university observers call it the politicization of the university and the end of that objective, otherworldly, balanced and impassionate activity that has long characterized the university. Some see in all of this the end of academic freedom and a call for repressive action.

The fact is that almost every state in the Union has considered in its legislature some punitive legislation against faculty and students—about half of which has been enacted into law. Trustees and governors have practically forced the resignation of a number of presidents, for instance in Texas, Oklahoma and California. Feeling is running high against many highly visible universities and the witch-hunters are out and at work. Both federal and state programs of support for higher education have been reduced or tied to impossible conditions. Many private universities find themselves hard put to hold fast to the support they now have, much less to augment it. Disaffection with universities, their presidents, their faculties and their students is simply a growing fact of life that will probably get worse.

The great majority of the best university presidents that I have known, respected and worked with over the past years are simply resigning to escape what has become an impossible task: to keep peace inside and outside the university, when trustees cry "law and order" and students condemn this concept as another form of "status quo" in a very imperfect world. Alumni think the whole enterprise is coming apart at the seams, while faculty call for even greater changes than those now taking place. Benefactors lose confidence in the whole unruly endeavor when they are attacked by students or faculty because they are accused of giving money gained through what is proclaimed to be an unholy military-industrial alliance. Parents expect a control over their children which they themselves have never been able to maintain, while the students in turn want absolute freedom and certainly no one acting in the place of their parents, however ineffective these may have been. At this point, the president, who is believed to be in charge although his authority has been monumentally reduced, begins to see that he simply cannot succeed unless the academic community is a real community—something becoming ever more rare in university circles.

Many of the new experimental forms of university governance are aimed at building a stronger university community. Whether or not they will achieve this is simply conjecture at this point. In general, the trustee system has served American universities well, when faculties were allowed to decide academic matters and when students were given a reasonable voice in the arranging of their affairs. One might fault some university boards of trustees by noting that they have generally not represented the broad spectrum of the public they were supposed to represent. There have been all too few women, or blacks, or middle class, or younger people on most boards. Most of them, at least at the great private universities, resembled too much an exclusive club for W.A.S.P.s (White Anglo-Saxon Protestants). But this is changing as it should, and faculties and students are having an ever larger voice in those decisions that mainly affect them and their lives. Reform of governance alone is certainly not the total answer to the problems that face us.

So far, I have been mainly engaged in an analysis of the present situation facing universities in a changing world. The view, as I have thus far presented it, is admittedly pessimistic. As a committed optimist, I believe that at this time I should attempt to find a few positive aspects of the total picture.

To begin with, student and faculty unrest in our day—a world-wide phenomenon—is in large measure a manifestation of their moral concern for the priorities or the values of present-day society. One would find it difficult to fault them for those things they oppose: war, violence, racism, poverty, pollution, human degradation on a large scale.

It has been a quality and inclination of most young people, since the time that Aristotle accused them of being too vehement about everything, to see the world in absolute terms of good and evil, to be inspired by great idealism, generosity and enthusiasm, and often to give their all, to man the barricades for causes of justice and equality. Life, problems and solutions somehow seem simpler to the young who are yet unscarred by the acid of cruel experience. This is not all bad. Maybe the weary and cynical world today, more than ever before, needs this kind of youthful conscience to find its way out of the lassitude and ambiguity that attend so much of modern human life. Maybe the university is the only place on earth where we can bridge the generation gap by common moral concern on the part of young and old, faculty and students. Granting that students are often naive in their concern for instant solutions to very complicated problems, granting their addiction to absolute black-and-white judgments in matters that are often very gray, granting their lack of a sense of history, their rupture with tradition, and their inability to appreciate experience and competence, they still are concerned and are unafflicted by the anomie that is the cancer of so many of their elders.

Perhaps this calls for a greater dedication to teaching on our part, for great teaching can manifest competence without preaching it, transmit a sense of history without seeming to be antiquarian, show how much patience is to be valued just by being patient. Good teaching, nay, great teaching, may yet be the salvation of the university and of society in our day. It has been rather obvious that our professors have in large measure sought distinction through research rather than great teaching, through adherence to their discipline far beyond loyalty to their particular institution. The theory was that research would enrich teaching, but for all too many professors, it has largely replaced teaching. This has not gone unnoticed by the students who flock to the chosen few who still can profess and teach.

I do not believe that the university has by any means come to the end of its road, but I am willing to concede that it faces a fork in the road and must make some real decisions as to where it is going. Generally speaking, I would conclude that the university can and must remain politically neutral *as an institution,* although its faculty, students and administrators are free to take their own political stance, indeed must do so when faced with national and international crises with deep moral undertones. It is difficult for a president to do this as an individual, but he must always try to make this clear to the public. I am personally against faculties taking political stances as a particular university body academic, unless the matter is of supreme moral, national or international importance. Students are somewhat freer in all of this because they do not have such permanent attachment to the university. Alumni less so. Avoiding politicization in highly emotional and deeply polarized times is not going to be easy. The threatening loss of academic freedom or academic objectivity is reason enough to keep trying in every way one can.

Balancing the development of research in the physical sciences, the social sciences and the humanities may be somewhat easier now that the golden age for research support in the physical sciences seems to be passing. Since teaching needs all the importance, respect and reward that we can accord it, giving it some measure of priority may be at the heart of the solution.

The service relationship of the university to the communities that surround it—local, state, national and international—is something that needs great clarification for the survival of the university. In some cases, the university has become too much of a service station expected to solve problems by its actual operation rather than seek solutions theoretically and pilot-test them in a more microcosmic fashion. The university cannot become the Red Cross immediately attending to all manner of social emergencies. It is not an overseas development corporation or a foreign or domestic Peace Corps. It may well have strong intellectual and educational ties to these and other service organizations, but it should never confuse its university identity or task with theirs.

Universities should be ready to experiment with new forms of governance, but I see no great value, in fact great loss, in confusing the specific tasks of trustees, faculty, administrators or students. Maybe we should proclaim more often that the prime function of the faculty is to teach, that of the students to

493

learn and that of the administration to make the conditions for teaching and learning more fruitful. Trustees can be enormously effective to the whole operation if they appoint and protect good officers of the university, help keep the institution financially viable, and support against any power inside or outside the institution the integrity of the whole operation and its best priorities as they emerge from the total community, including the alumni. Every community needs, especially in troubled times, some final authority, some strong protector. Trustees have fulfilled this role for the better universities that have emerged in America.

One is often reminded of Charles Dickens' opening statement in *The Tale of Two Cities:* "It was the worst of times; it was the best of times." I think this can well be said of the state of the university in the rapidly changing world of our day. We can survive the worst if we achieve the better or, hopefully, the best.

# NOTES ABOUT THE CONTRIBUTORS

RAMÓN BELA heads the United States, Canada and Europe Department of the Instituto de Cultura Hispánica in Madrid. Besides serving on the Institute's board of directors, Professor Bela is also Executive Director of the Fulbright Commission in Spain. He has taught public law at the University of Madrid and worked on the Spanish commission for co-operation with UNESCO. Professor Bela has participated in many international conferences, and, among other organizations, he is a member of the *Asociación Internacional de Estudios Coloniales de Madrid.*

GEORGE Z. F. BEREDAY is Professor of Comparative Education at Teachers College and in the School of International Affairs at Columbia University. He is also Director of the Center for Education in Industrial Nations. A Carnegie Fellow in Law and Political Science at Harvard Law School in 1963-64 and 1964-65, Dr. Bereday was Fulbright Professor at Tokyo University in 1962, and Exchange Professor at Moscow University in 1961. He is the author of *Comparative Method in Education* and co-editor, among others, of *The Changing Soviet School, Politics of Soviet Education, Public Education in America,* and *Essays on World Education.* His *American Education Through Japanese Eyes* and *Innovations in Higher Education in Western Europe and Mass Education Countries* are in press.

THOMAS P. BERGIN, Dean of Continuing Education at the University of Notre Dame, was educated at Notre Dame, the University of Vermont and the Maxwell Graduate School of Citizenship at Syracuse University. A member of the Notre Dame faculty since 1947, Dr. Bergin has headed the Department of Business Administration and served as a consultant to the U.S. Department of Commerce. In the summers of 1960 and 1961 he worked in Washington, D.C., in the Area Redevelopment Administration. Dr. Bergin is the author of many articles in his special field of interest, economic growth and development.

LORD BOWDEN, Principal of the University of Manchester Institute of Science and Technology, is a graduate of Cambridge. Among Lord Bowden's achievements have been his wartime work in perfecting the radar system for identifying friendly aircraft, and the distinction of being the first man ever to sell commercial digital computers in the world market. His book, *Faster Than Thought* (published in 1953 and still in print), and his numerous papers, have all focused on the problems and development of education and the history and development of computers.

JOHN BRADEMAS, Congressman from Indiana's Third District since 1959, graduated from Harvard University, magna cum laude, in 1949 and from Oxford University, where he was a Rhodes Scholar, with a Ph.D. in social studies in 1954. Prior to his election to Congress, Mr. Brademas taught political science at Saint Mary's College, Notre Dame, Indiana. A member of the House Committee on Education and Labor and chairman of its Select Education Subcommittee, where he has played a leading role, he has helped to write most of the major federal legislation concerning elementary and secondary education, vocational and higher education, drug abuse education and the National Arts and Humanities foundation. Congressman Brademas is also author of the International Education Act of 1966 and the Environmental Education Act of 1970. He is a member of the Central Committee of the World Council of Churches and of the Board of Overseers of Harvard and is a Fellow of the American Academy of Arts and Sciences.

ROBERT F. BYRNES, Distinguished Professor of History at Indiana University, was the first director of that institution's International Affairs Center. A specialist in Russian and East European history, Dr. Byrnes has traveled extensively within the Soviet Union and throughout Eastern Europe. On one such occasion, in 1962-63, he was a participant in the exchange of scholars between the Soviet Academy of Sciences and The American Council of Learned Societies. Dr. Byrnes, who received his undergraduate and graduate education at Amherst and Harvard, has written several books including *Pobedonostsev: His Life and Thought*, a biography of one of Russia's most prominent churchmen and statesmen. He was also general editor of a seven-volume study of *East Central Europe Under the Communists*. In 1955 he helped found the Inter-University Committee on Travel Grants, and he headed this 56-university consortium from 1960 through 1969.

OLIVER J. CALDWELL, Professor of Higher Education and Assistant to the President Emeritus of Southern Illinois University, was born in China of American parents and is a graduate of Oberlin College. A teacher both in China and the United States, Professor Caldwell served with the Office of Strategic Services in the Far East during World War II. He later joined the Bureau of International Educational and Cultural Affairs in the Department of State, transferring after several years to the U.S. Office of Education as Assistant Commissioner for International Education. Professor Caldwell is the author of approximately 100 publications.

MATTEI DOGAN is Director of Research at France's National Center of Scientific Research, to which he has belonged since 1953. Currently a member of the French National Committee for Scientific Research, he has also served on the executive board of the Center of Sociological Studies in Paris. He is chairman of the research committee on political elites of the International Political Science Association and a member of the standing committee on Social Science Data Archives and of other international committees. Among his publications are *Les Françaises Face à la Politique, Partiti Politici e Strut-*

*ture Sociali in Italia,* and *Quantitative Ecological Analysis in the Social Sciences.* He has contributed chapters to 15 books and published more than 40 articles in scholarly journals.

F. G. DREYFUS, Director of L'Institut d'Etudes Politiques in the Faculty of Letters of the University of Strasbourg, received his Doctor of Letters degree from the Sorbonne. Named a *Lauréat* of the French Academy in 1967 and winner of the Strasbourg Prize in 1969, Professor Dreyfus has published several books besides being responsible for the direction of the *Revue d'Allemagne.* Titles of his books include: *Documents d'Histoire Contemporaine, Les Forces Religieuses dans la Société Française, Sociétés et Mentalités à Mayence au XVIIIe siècle, Le Syndicalisme Allemand Contemporain, Le Temps de Révolutions, La Vie Politique de l'Alsace de 1919 à 1939,* and *Histoires des Allemagnes.*

M. A. FITZSIMONS is Professor of History at the University of Notre Dame, where he also edits *The Review of Politics.* He studied at Columbia and Oxford universities; his doctorate is from Chicago (1947). His publications include *The Foreign Policy of the British Labour Government, 1945-1951* and *Empire by Treaty.* Dr. Fitzsimons has edited *What America Stands For, Diplomacy in a Changing World, The Catholic Church Today: Western Europe, The Development of Historiography,* and *The Image of Man.*

LAWRENCE H. FUCHS is Professor of American Civilization and Politics at Brandeis University, where he has also served as Dean of Faculty, Chairman of the Politics Department and Chairman of the Educational Policy Committee. Holder of a Harvard Ph.D., Dr. Fuchs was—from 1961 to 1963—the first Director of the Peace Corps in the Philippines. Besides many articles, books authored by Dr. Fuchs include *The Political Behavior of American Jews, Hawaii Pono: A Social History, John F. Kennedy and American Catholicism, "Those Peculiar Americans": The Peace Corps and the American National Character,* and *American Ethnic Politics.*

WILLIAM HABER has been a professor at the University of Michigan since 1936, serving for a time as Chairman of the Department of Economics and, between 1963 and 1968, as Dean of the College of Literature, Science and the Arts. Since 1968 he has been an advisor to the president and the executive officers of the University. Dr. Haber has had a long association with both the federal and state governments, particularly in the areas of manpower, Social Security and labor relations. Both as dean and in his present advisory position, Dr. Haber has enjoyed a unique vantage-point for observing the problems of the university as it accommodates to the changes in society. His books include: *Industrial Relations in the Building Industry, The Michigan Economy, Unemployment Insurance in the American Economy, Michigan in the 1970's, Social Security Programs, Problems and Policies,* and *Labor Relations and Productivity in the Building Trades.*

JOHN P. HARRISON is Director of the Institute of Inter-American Studies, and Professor of History at the University of Miami, Florida. After completing his graduate studies in history at the University of California, Berkeley, Dr. Harrison became the Latin American specialist for the National Archives of the United States. In 1955 he joined the Rockefeller Foundation, filling posts as Assistant and Associate Director for the Humanities with special responsibility for programs in Latin America. From 1962-1967 Professor Harrison was Director of the Institute of Latin American Studies at the University of Texas. In July 1967 he rejoined the Rockefeller Foundation as an Associate Director for the Humanities and Social Sciences and served as the Foundation's representative in Chile, from 1968 through 1970. His publications on Latin American universities include *The University versus National Development in Spanish America.*

REV. THEODORE M. HESBURGH, C.S.C., President of the University of Notre Dame, studied at Notre Dame, and received degrees from the Gregorian University in Rome, Holy Cross College, and The Catholic University of America in Washington, D.C. He has been President of the University since 1952, and has served on many national and international boards and committees. At present, he is Chairman of the U. S. Commission on Civil Rights; Chairman of the Academic Council for the Ecumenical Institute for Advanced Theological Studies in Jerusalem; a member of the Carnegie Commission on the Future of Higher Education, the Board of Trustees of the Rockefeller Foundation, the Board of Directors of the American Council on Education, and several other foundations and institutes. He is the author of several books on theology and on education, among them, *God and the World of Man, Patterns for Educational Growth,* and *Thoughts for Our Times.* Among the many honors Father Hesburgh has received are the Meiklejohn Award of the American Association of University Professors and the Charles Evans Hughes Award of the National Conference of Christians and Jews.

PATRICK HORSBRUGH is an architect of British birth who now directs the graduate program in Environic Studies at the University of Notre Dame. On two occasions he was responsible for large-scale plans for the redevelopment of London, one known as High Paddington and the other New Barbican. Professor Horsbrugh's special interest in university design developed while he was recommending a site for the proposed federal capital of Pakistan. In the course of this work he concluded—and so advised—that the new federal capital must contain a university for the Moslem people as a whole. His writings have continually emphasized the need for environmental beauty, both in the world in general, and in educational institutions in particular.

HERBERT JACOB is Professor of Political Science at Northwestern University. After receiving his Ph.D. degree from Yale in 1960, Dr. Jacob taught at Tulane and the University of Wisconsin before moving to Northwestern. He has held a National Science Foundation Science Faculty Fellowship and has published several books, among them *German Administration Since Bismarck, Studies in Judicial Politics* (with Kenneth Vines), *Politics in the American States* (co-editor and contributor), *Justice in America, Law, Politics and the Federal Courts* (editor), *Debtors in Court,* and *Elementary Political Analysis* (with Robert Weissberg).

STEPHEN D. KERTESZ, editor of this volume, is Director of the Institute for International Studies at the University of Notre Dame. After receiving his doctorate at the University of Budapest, he studied in Paris, Geneva, at Yale, Oxford and The Hague. He was *privat-dozent* at his alma mater and served in his country's Foreign Ministry. Secretary-General of the Hungarian Peace Delegation in 1946, Professor Kertesz resigned from the foreign service in 1947 while Minister to Italy. He became Professor of Political Science at Notre Dame in 1950 after two years as a visiting lecturer in the Yale Law School. Dr. Kertesz is the author of *The International Responsibility of the State, Diplomacy in a Whirlpool: Hungary Between Nazi Germany and the Soviet Union,* and *The Quest for Peace Through Diplomacy.* He has edited seven volumes and contributed to numerous other books and periodicals.

BERNARD J. KOHLBRENNER, Professor Emeritus in Graduate Studies in Education at the University of Notre Dame, spent 1968-1969 as a Ford Foundation Project Specialist working with three universities in the Philippines. After receiving his doctorate in the History of Education at Harvard, Professor Kohlbrenner taught at Syracuse and St. Louis universities before coming to Notre Dame. Formerly a consulting editor for the McGraw-Hill Book Co., he edited a series of eight volumes on education for this firm. He is also a joint author of the standard *History of Catholic Education in the United States.*

IVAN M. MAKSIMOVIC is Professor of Political Economy in the Law Faculty of the University of Belgrade and was formerly Vice-President of the Yugoslav Association of Economists and a member of his country's Economic Council. Professor Maksimovic has studied and lectured in some of the world's leading institutions, including the London School of Economics, Harvard, Berkeley and the Brookings Institution in the United States, the Prague Academy of Science, the Economic Faculty in Budapest and Moscow University. In addition to directing the Center for Economic Investigation at the Institute of Social Science and editing *Economic Thought,* a Yugoslav scholarly journal, Professor Maksimovic is the author of *Political Economy of Socialism and the Post-classical and Present Theory in the West, Present Trends in Contemporary Economic Thought,* several other books and many articles dealing with socialist economic thought and university problems.

FEDERICO MANCINI is a chair-holding professor at the University of Bologna, Italy, where he also received his *Libera Docenza* degree in the Faculty of Law. Since 1957 he has been Professor of Politics at The Johns Hopkins Bologna Center of Advanced International Studies. Most of Professor Mancini's writings (three books and numerous articles) have been about Italian law and labor relations. He has, however, also contributed political essays to many journals and edited a book in Italian on the Franklin D. Roosevelt era. He was active in the drafting of Italy's equivalent of the American National Labor Relations Act, and most recently conducted a seminar at Harvard on the Italian labor movement.

M. V. MATHUR has been Director of the Asian Institute of Educational Planning and Administration in New Delhi, India, since July 1968. During a long and distinguished career since his formal education at the University of Allahabad and Harvard, Professor Mathur has acted as the Chief of Staff Regulations and Policies Division of the United Nations Secretariat, and was professor, Dean, and later Vice-Chancellor (1966-68) of the University of Rajasthan, Jaipur. He has also been president of the Indian Economic Association. With his training and experience in both the teaching and planning functions, Professor Mathur has been called to serve on many advisory and policy-setting bodies including the Third Finance Commission and the Education Commission in India. He is co-author of *Planning, Panchayati Raj and Democracy, Panchayati Raj in Rajasthan,* and others.

PHILIP E. MOSELY is Director of the European Institute of Columbia University, as well as Professor of International Relations and Associate Dean of the Faculty of International Affairs. After receiving his doctorate at Harvard, Professor Mosely taught at Union College and Princeton and Cornell universities before going to Columbia. He has visited and studied in Russia and the Balkan countries for protracted periods on several occasions. As an officer of the Department of State during World War II and immediately thereafter, Professor Mosely served as advisor to Secretaries of State Cordell Hull and James F. Byrnes at inter-Allied conferences. From 1955 to 1963 he was Director of Studies at the Council on Foreign Relations in New York City. Dr. Mosely is the author of *Russian Diplomacy and the Opening of the Eastern Question in 1838 and 1839* and of a collection of historical and policy studies of Russia and the Balkans entitled *The Kremlin and World Politics.* He is also the editor of *The Soviet Union, 1922-1962: A Foreign Affairs Reader.*

MICHIO NAGAI, a native of Japan, received his Ph.D. in Educational Sociology at Ohio State University. Besides teaching in Kyoto University and Tokyo Institute of Technology, Professor Nagai has been a visiting lecturer at Columbia, Hong Kong and Stanford universities and at El Colegio de Mexico. Among his books and articles written in Japanese are *Higher Education in Japan, Possibilities of the University,* and *Modernization and Education.* Professor Nagai is presently a member of the Editorial Board of the Asahi Shimbun Press.

DAVIDSON S.H.W. NICOL has been Sierra Leone's Permanent Representative to the United Nations since December 1968. He served on the U.N. Economic and Social Council in 1969 and on the Security Council in 1970-1971. Educated in West Africa and at Cambridge, England, Dr. Nicol was Principal of the University College of Sierra Leone for eight years before becoming Vice-Chancellor of the University from 1966 to 1968. Besides being consulting pathologist to the government of Sierra Leone, Dr. Nicol is an Honorary Fellow of the Ghana Academy of Sciences and a Fellow of the Royal College of Pathologists in London. He has also been active in professional educational organizations such as the Association of African Universities, the Conference of West African Universities and the Executive Council of the Association of Commonwealth Universities in London.

NAI SUKICH NIMMANHEMINDA, Thailand's Minister of Education, was trained in British schools as well as in those of his own country. In addition to holding teaching and administrative positions at Chulalongkorn University, Minister Nimmanheminda has served his nation in prominent political and diplomatic posts. From 1963 to 1967 he was ambassador to the United States, and just prior to assuming the leadership of the Ministry of Education, he was Director of the Southeast Asian Ministers of Education Secretariat.

TORGNY T. SEGERSTEDT has been Rector of Uppsala University in Sweden since 1955. After receiving his doctorate at the University of Lund, Professor Segerstedt taught sociology and moral philosophy at both Lund and Uppsala. Chairman of Sweden's Social Science Research Council since 1959 and of a similar group sponsored by the Bank of Sweden since 1965, Dr. Segerstedt has also written many articles for the daily press on contemporary educational topics. In book form he has authored *Value and Reality in Bradley's Philosophy, The Problem of Knowledge in Scottish Philosophy, Social Control,* and *The Nature of Social Reality.*

GEORGE N. SHUSTER, born in Lancaster, Wisconsin, was educated at the University of Notre Dame, the Université de Poitiers, and Columbia University (Ph.D.). The major positions he has held are Managing Editor of *Commonweal* (1925-1937); Fellow of the Social Science Research Council (1937-1939); President, Hunter College, New York (1939-1960), then President Emeritus; and Assistant to the President, University of Notre Dame (1961-——). He has had extensive periods of U.S. Government service. His many books include three concerned in whole or in part with cultural affairs: *Education and Moral Wisdom, The Ground I Walked On,* and *UNESCO: Assessment and Promise.*

FRANCIS X. SUTTON, Deputy Vice President of the International Division of the Ford Foundation since 1968, is the author of *The American Business Creed* and many articles on educational and developmental subjects. He served for five years as an assistant professor of sociology and general education at Harvard, where he received his Ph.D. in 1950. While he has also taught and lectured at such universities as M.I.T. and U.C.L.A., his principal responsibilities have been concerned with the Ford Foundation's programs in Africa, in the behavioral sciences, and in project planning and evaluation. From 1961 to 1963 Dr. Sutton was a member of the Board of Foreign Scholarships of the Council on Foreign Relations.

KENNETH W. THOMPSON, Vice-President of The Rockefeller Foundation, prior to 1955 taught political science at Northwestern University and the University of Chicago. A Fellow of the American Academy of Arts and Sciences and a member of the Council on Foreign Relations, Dr. Thompson belongs to numerous professional societies, serves on the Board of Directors of the Union Theological Seminary and is active in various allied fields. Author of four books, *The Moral Issue in Statecraft, American Diplomacy and Emergent Patterns, Political Realism and the Crisis of World Politics,* and *Christian Ethics and the Dilemmas of Foreign Policy,* Dr. Thompson has co-authored four other volumes and contributed to more than 20 books and to many professional journals.

BERT M. TOLLEFSON, JR., has been Assistant Administrator for Legislative and Public Affairs at the Agency for International Development since May 1969. A native of South Dakota, Mr. Tollefson first went to Washington during the Eisenhower years, and participated in the establishment of the Food for Peace Program. He has traveled extensively throughout the world in furthering international co-operation, and has represented the United States at world meetings of the Food and Agriculture Organization and International Bank for Reconstruction and Development. Mr. Tollefson has helped to initiate innovations in world feeding programs, including the distribution to some 100 nations of the new low-cost, high-protein food, CSM (corn, soya, milk).

DOUGLAS V. VERNEY is a Professor of Political Science at York University, Toronto. Previously he taught at the University of Liverpool, England. He has been visiting professor at the University of Florida and Columbia University. Professor Verney's books include *Parliamentary Reform in Sweden 1866-1921, Public Enterprise in Sweden, The Analysis of Political Systems, British Government and Politics,* and *Political Patterns in Today's World* (with D. W. Brogan). He was president of the *Canadian Political Science Association* 1969-1970, and since 1970 he has been editor of *Canadian Public Administration.*

HERMAN B WELLS, President of Indiana University from 1937 to 1962 and University Chancellor since 1962, was successively a student, faculty member and Dean of the School of Business Administration at Indiana University before his accession to the presidency. He has held leadership posts in state, regional, national and international organizations of higher education and has served on numerous boards in the fields of education, finance, research, social welfare and philanthropy. Dr. Wells has also been a member of several U.S. delegations and presidential commissions and has written extensively on education and on finance.

RUDOLPH WILDENMANN is Professor of Political Science at the University of Mannheim (Germany) and a visiting professor at the State University of New York at Stony Brook. After receiving his Ph.D. from Heidelberg in 1952, Dr. Wildenmann worked as a journalist until 1956, when he entered the Ministry of Domestic Affairs in the Federal Republic of Germany. He began to teach at the University of Cologne in 1959 where he received his 'habilitation' in 1962. His publications include: *Macht und Konsens als Problem der Innen- und Aussenpolitik, Zur Soziologie der Wahl,* and *Politik und Waehler.* Apart from his activities as a teacher and scholar, Dr. Wildenmann has also served in a number of administrative and political functions, *e.g.,* as rector of the University of Mannheim and as a consultant to the Bonn Chancellery.